The First Verm
in the Civ

The First Vermont Cavalry in the Civil War

A History

JOSEPH D. COLLEA, JR.

McFarland & Company, Inc., Publishers

Jefferson, North Carolina, and London

LIBRARY OF CONGRESS CATALOGUING-IN-PUBLICATION DATA

Collea, Joseph D., Jr., 1947–
The First Vermont Cavalry in the Civil War : a history / Joseph D.
Collea, Jr.
p.   cm.
Includes bibliographical references and index.

ISBN 978-0-7864-3383-4
softcover : 50# alkaline paper ∞

1. United States. Army. Vermont Cavalry Regiment, 1st (1861–1865)
2. Vermont — History — Civil War, 1861–1865 — Regimental histories.
3. United States — History — Civil War, 1861–1865 — Regimental histories.
4. Virginia — History — Civil War, 1861–1865 — Campaigns.
5. United States — History — Civil War, 1861–1865 — Campaigns.
6. Vermont — History — Civil War, 1861–1865 — Registers.
7. United States — History — Civil War, 1861–1865 — Registers.
8. Soldiers — Vermont — Registers.   I. Title.
E533.61st.C655   2010   973.7'443 — dc22   2009043824

British Library cataloguing data are available

Front cover: *Battle of Cedar Creek*, October 19, 1864, an 1890 artwork
from Kurz & Allison Art Publishers (Library of Congress)

Manufactured in the United States of America

McFarland & Company, Inc., Publishers
Box 611, Jefferson, North Carolina 28640
www.mcfarlandpub.com

For Mom and Dad,
whose support was as unwavering
as their love was unconditional

Acknowledgments

To fashion a history book, it is the author, often in a state of solitary confinement, who ultimately must craft the finished product. However, any success is dependent upon a number of other people who assist him in accessing the materials stored in an assortment of repositories. Were it not for the dedicated, knowledgeable individuals who manned the desks and searched the stacks at various locations, my ability to draw upon available resources would have been severely diminished. In the end result, the fullness of my story would have lacked the richness with which I was able to infuse it. I therefore owe sincere thanks to folks at the following locations: the Bailey-Howe Library at the University of Vermont, Burlington, Vermont; the Fairbanks Museum and Planetarium at St. Johnsbury, Vermont; the Gettysburg National Military Park Library at Gettysburg, Pennsylvania; the National Archives in Washington, D.C.; the Library of Congress, Washington, D.C.; the National Military Library at Carlisle, Pennsylvania; the Rauner Library at Dartmouth College, Hanover, New Hampshire; the Vermont Historical Society in Barre, Vermont; the Vermont State Library in Montpelier, Vermont; and the Virginia State Library in Richmond, Virginia.

In addition to those who worked at the various institutions above, there were individuals—acquaintances and relatives—who also provided invaluable assistance. First, there was Mrs. Annie Boutin, a colleague at Hartford High School. All I had to do was explain to Annie how I wanted the outcome to appear, and she was able to engage the right electronic process. Beyond just sharing expertise, Annie is a charitable soul who derives satisfaction from being able to help people.

Next was my wife, Barbara, a business teacher by calling, who brought her finely honed attention to detail to bear on proofreading several chapters, helping to instill an element of quality control to the finished product. My son, Joe D., and daughter-in-law, Laurena, lent their computer talents, providing valuable technical assistance to get some important pictures properly scanned and calibrated.

Then there was my son Bob, forever "Bobby" to me. Though a scientist/mathematician by nature and a college student in a rigorous engineering program, he generously offered his valuable time and his own wizardry with a computer to produce maps that were so essential to the proper telling of the 1st Vermont's story. His willingness to tweak here and tweak there again and again to satisfy his fussy father is very much appreciated. Without his assistance, any maps I may have fashioned would have been crude and amateurish by comparison, if in fact they ever came to be.

Francis Guber was most generous in permitting the use of pictures from his fine collection, not to mention taking the time to reformat them for me to meet the requisite publishing standards.

Mike Hathorn is another gifted teacher; he has developed an expertise with computers which he was graciously willing to share in any moment of my need.

Finally, I would like to acknowledge a debt of thanks and gratitude owed to Miss Racheal Gage, who assisted me in the capacity of a volunteer researcher for several years. During this time, Miss Gage painstakingly reviewed materials and took copious notes from microfilmed newspapers, the *Official Records*, and other primary source documents. The information she collected was maintained in a well-organized format and provided the author with a rich trove of research data that helped flesh out the book and give it some of its finest detail.

Table of Contents

List of Maps

Preface

Given the volumes already written about the American Civil War, it is hard to imagine that unplowed ground still exists. Yet, worthy topics do remain. The saga of the 1st Vermont Cavalry is one. Novices, like most of their blue-coated brethren, these Vermonters early on took their lumps from the Confederacy's best. Schooled by Turner Ashby and John Mosby in the art of mounted warfare, their prowess steadily increased until the regiment held its own. Though they were initially short on military acumen, no one ever questioned the mettle of these hardy New Englanders, many descended from the fabled Green Mountain Boys.

With time, the entire Union Army came of age. Riding the crest of its success was the cavalry corps. Led by charismatic personalities like George Custer and Phil Sheridan, it prospered. By 1864, the long transition from being inept patsies to vital cogs in a magnificent fighting machine was complete for Federal troopers in the Eastern Theater.

By association, let alone by their own competence, the 1st Vermont's place in history would seem secure. Why, then, is the regiment not enshrined more notably in the pantheon of storied Civil War regiments? The exploits of the 20th Maine and the 54th Massachusetts are deservedly among the war's many well-chronicled units. But for these Vermonters, obscurity has been their fate. Still this oversight did not come as any real surprise. In a postwar speech before a 1st Vermont reunion, former commander Colonel Charles Tompkins prophetically lamented, "Comrades! I have attempted no history of the regiment. Alas, I fear that one will never be written."

Exactly how the colonel's prognostication has been true until now has plausible explanations. While here and there were educated men, the bulk of the regiment had limited formal schooling; they were veterans whose stories were enthralling but whose ability to write a lengthy book lay beyond their grasp. Then there was the humble, taciturn nature of Vermonters, who would never say more when less would suffice. Personifying this trait, Sergeant Mark Rogers of Company B wrote to his folks in a letter dated "July, 1863": "We fought at a place called Gettysburg, but you don't want to hear about that."

Oh, but to have sat at the feet of Sergeant Rogers, my great-great uncle, for an hour or to have walked down a country lane with his brother trooper, Sergeant William Rogers, my great-great-grandfather. "Yes, dear sirs, I beg to differ with you. We do want to hear *all* about it." As Alvin Kiernan, author of the splendid World War II memoir *Crossing the Line*, wrote about his Civil War progenitor:

> Grandfather served in the Georgia infantry.... [I have] often longed for his version of personal memories ... [but he] left no such record. I often wondered what William Peters, aged sixteen years old at the time, ever found again in the seventy-five years of his long and prosperous

1

life on an isolated Georgia farm to match the experience of that day [at Gettysburg]. Still it must have remained, locked up inside of him.

I, too, have entertained similar wistful thoughts, not only about my great-great-grandfather, but about the whole 1st Vermont. Would they have agreed with Kiernan's assessment that "war has remained the defining experience of my life"? For many members of the Vermont Cavalry, a significant number of whom were impressionable youth like Kiernan's grandfather and the Rogers brothers, the Civil War was a crucible which shaped their thinking for however long they lived after the guns fell silent. Their unfailing support of veterans' organizations, participation in patriotic ceremonies, attendance at reunions, publication of memoirs, and even the purchase of portions of former battlefields are illustrative of their quest to keep proud memories alive and the exploits of their respective regiments preserved for posterity.

This book represents but one small contribution toward fulfilling that quest. My intent is for you to learn of the ultimate sacrifices of men like John Chase, Oliver Cushman, and Addison Preston; of the regiment's unwavering courage at Greenwich, Gettysburg, and Stony Creek Station; and of the poignant words of Perley Cheney, Charles Chapin, and William Wells. Then, together, by having heightened our awareness, we will have successfully accomplished all that they who fought so long and hard ever really asked of those for whom they helped preserve the Union — and that is to be remembered as patriotic men who did their duty.

In a letter to the *Montpelier Green Mountain Freeman*, dated December 20, 1862, a trooper of the 1st Vermont called upon readers to do just this: "Whether we have been faithful in the discharge of our arduous duties, in this time, it does not now become us to speak. Let the future history of our country answer." His request echoes across almost a century and a half to you. How often does history whisper in your ear and ask for an appraisal? How often are the living afforded an opportunity to repay a debt to their forebears?

1

Recruitment
The Birth of a Regiment

Like so many answering the call, enlistees in the 1st Vermont came for varied reasons. To end the rebellion, escape the farm, or experience an adventure were common motivators. The typical recruit was a Vermont native, in his late teens, slightly built, five-foot six-inches tall, and weighing 135 pounds. Most who came were men of the soil, a hardy lot inured to the outdoors and the caprices of nature.

Ironically, their beloved regiment almost never existed. But for the persistence of Lemuel Platt, Vermont might not have fielded a troop of cavalry. Assuredly, fine infantry units were produced, none writing a prouder history than those of the famed "Vermont Brigade." Some men, however, yearned to ride to war. Such feelings were not new, for cavalry has always had a romantic allure. But the War Department had the final say. Unfortunately, the prevailing opinion there was that mounted units were too costly to outfit and too time-consuming to train, particularly for a war expected to be short-lived.

Undeterred, Platt approached Governor Erastus Fairbanks, but Vermont's chief executive held to strict construction, believing that existing militia laws did not permit outfitting cavalry units. But Platt, a tall, dignified Colchester farmer, was not easily dissuaded. Intending to use his political clout, Platt traveled to Washington. If his home state was not going to grant a commission, perhaps a direct appeal to Federal authorities would bear fruit. Once in the nation's capital, Platt's connections opened doors, allowing him access to Secretary of War Simon Cameron. Accompanying him to the momentous meeting were two distinguished Vermonters: the venerable Solomon Foot, United States senator, and the ambitious Thomas Canfield, assistant manager of Washington's military railroads. As hoped, their collective persuasiveness proved successful. A pleased Canfield wrote his wife on September 4, 1861: "Mr. Platt goes from here to raise a regt. of Cavalry from Vt. Senator Foote [*sic*] and myself got the Sec. of War to accept it and appoint Mr. Platt Col. of the Regiment."[1]

Colonel Platt had forty days to raise ten companies. From the outset, he offered no delusions about his military expertise, openly sharing the history of his limited experience: "I have been to general training three times," he said, "and under guard twice."[2] If soldiering was not his forte, what then were Platt's capabilities? The *Manchester Journal* framed the essence of the man in its observation that "no better appointment could have been made. Col. Platt's energy, tact, and business talent, and extended acquaintance throughout the State, combined with his personal popularity, commend him to the position."[3] With the clock ticking, Colonel Platt began the enlistment process. First, he

RECRUIT S WANTED!

TO FILL UP THE

Vermont Cavalry Reg't,

For the purpose of keeping full the ranks of

The Celebrated Vermont Cavalry Regiment!

Now, Noble-hearted Men and Boys, call at

THE RECRUITING OFFICE,

No. 10 State Street, Montpelier,

Under Sign of the

Old United States Flag,

which shall never be trodden under foot by rebels, while Patriots of Old Vermont " come to the rescue" with willing hands, and share in the glorious cause.

Pay $20 per Month, with Rations,

$25 Bounty at time of Mustering into U. S. Service, and the remaining $75 Bounty at the expiration of the term of service. $4 premium paid to each Recruit.

TRUSSELL & HATHORN,

Recruiting Officers of Vt. Cavalry.

A mid-war announcement to attract replacement troopers, this recruiting poster not only appealed to patriotic motives but also included additional pecuniary incentives that became necessary inducements as the early war fervor started to wane (Francis C. Guber Collection).

appointed recruiting officers to staff a network of stations around the state. Selecting the correct individuals was critical, for they could do much through the power of their personality and standing in the community to draw recruits. Living up to his expectations, Platt's agents easily filled the regiment's ranks, exceeding the recruitment window by just two days. November 19, 1861, saw the 1st Vermont Cavalry mustered into Federal service.

Inducing 1000 volunteers to share the life of a cavalryman was simple when compared to the Herculean task of whipping them into fighting shape. Molding green recruits brought many challenges. Precious few had any previous military experience. Even more disconcerting was the resistance to authority so deeply ingrained in their collective psyches. The regiment's chief surgeon, Ptolemy Edson, offered his analysis of this phenomenon: "These officers they [enlisted men] recognized and obeyed by a tacit compact, springing from the same good nature that elected them, and from recognition of the necessity of organization and subordination. But in so doing they by no means surrendered their right of independent judgment and the consequent expression of their opinions."[4]

Though the Vermonters' insouciance toward authority was often aggravating, their commitment was unquestionable. They threw themselves into training with a zeal that overcame their woeful lack of preparedness. Early on, a dearth of equipment, arms, and horses was inhibiting. One of the regiment's defining moments came with the distribution of their uniforms. Eagerly the troopers donned the dark blue jackets trimmed with yellow braid, brass scales adorning their shoulders, the trousers of light blue, and the wide-brimmed hats of black felt turned smartly up on one side. Tall black leather boots completed the outerwear.

Slowly Camp Ethan Allen took on a military appearance. Tents were pitched, picket lines for horses strung, and guard posts manned. Drills, by company in the morning and battalion in the afternoon, taught large-group maneuvers. For the first three weeks, expectations and exertions were light. All drills were conducted dismounted. This steady diet of marching was loathed by everyone, all men whose romanticized visions of war saw themselves charging about on horses rather than stomping around on foot. Their flagging enthusiasm received a much-needed boost when sabers were finally issued. As weapons of destruction, the gleaming steel blades were vastly overrated. But as morale builders, the boys-inside-the-men liked waving them about, imparting a martial air to their otherwise mundane training. Curiously, the swinging of swords was about the only weapons training they would ever receive, for Civil War armies wasted little ammunition on target practice.

As the novices practiced, the process of acquiring mounts was played out daily in the regimental corrals in the forefront of the encampment. So important was this responsibility that no less a personage than Colonel Platt led the three-man procurement team. These inspectors did not lack choices, for competition was keen to supply horses. Prompt payment at a fair price awaited those who could sell their string to the government. Since profiteers were plentiful, caution was always imperative to insure that transactions were scrupulously conducted. While distributions of uniforms and arms were milestones, the most anticipated day of all was the one that brought the assignment of horses. The method chosen was simple, leaving the pairings to chance. Mounts for a given company were lined up along a picket rope. Next the men fell in opposite the waiting horses. Then, it was only a matter of walking forward, the first man and animal in the facing lines becoming a match and so on down the file until the hundredth trooper and the last horse were introduced. The distribution method proved efficient, but another aspect of the plan was soon jettisoned. While presorting the horses by color for each company was aesthetically pleasing, the arduous campaign in the summer of 1862 had precipitously depleted equine numbers. Waiting for the right color horses to match the needs of a given company's dismounted personnel was a luxury that war would not permit.

Memorable to the troops, the distribution process was equally significant to the people of the state. Pride ran deep in Vermont. Though a small state, its mighty contributions to the war effort were highly disproportionate to its size. In addition to the brave men sent south, considerable satisfaction was taken in the magnificent Morgan horses the Vermonters rode. Throughout the war, efforts were made to maintain a steady flow of replacements, thereby sustaining the superiority these horses gave the regiment. Slightly shorter than government regulations specified, these hardy steeds were the envy of other regiments in the army. What they lacked in height was more than compensated for in strength, endurance, and speed.

Despite the fact that most recruits were farm boys, proficiency in equestrianship was not a universal talent. Walking behind a plow horse did not require the same skills as riding a cavalry mount. Not surprisingly, mastering the requirements of close-order mounted drills and regimental-scale maneuvering made for interesting moments. A saber drill became a whole new experience on the back of a horse that was no more familiar with the procedure than was his master. For some, riding was a challenge all by itself, let alone trying to perform a maneuver in unison with other equally unschooled comrades. The resulting bumps and bruises were growing pains never mentioned by recruiters.

With the onset of cold weather, health concerns surfaced. In spite of adequate supplies and shelter, sickness visited the camp. Having so many men bunched together offered fertile ground for the spread of contagions. Measles and mumps were prevalent, making the first losses in the regiment the result of microbes and not bullets. Long before shots were fired in anger, life-and-death struggles were fought in the hospital tents of Burlington. Between the muster on November 19 and departure on December 14, three troopers died in camp. The unwanted distinction of being the first belonged to Private William Martin. The exact cause of his demise has been lost in time, but it fell within the time frame when measles hit the camp. Drawing scant attention, Martin's passing was quick and quiet.

Next to succumb was Austin Harris. A soldier of but four weeks, his death on December 1 was attributed to congestion of the lungs, a pulmonary complication consistent with measles cases. The next day Harris' remains were taken for shipment to his grieving family in Brattleboro. With eight troopers as pallbearers, the regiment stood at the depot, heads bowed as chaplain John Woodard offered appropriate prayers. In many a mind there no doubt lingered the thought that there would be others yet to mourn in the days ahead. But since Harris died in relative calm, his passing did not quite carry with it the same stunning impact as would later violent battle deaths.

The outbreak occurred just as excitement started to build toward the long-awaited day of departure. What a cruel twist of fate to have willing volunteers, anxious to do their part, struck down on the eve of leaving for the seat of war. Among this star-crossed lot was Private Jonathan Smith, who caught the measles. When the regiment left, he remained behind. Further exacerbating his problem, Smith also contracted diphtheria. The seriousness of the boy's condition prompted John Fiske, a hospital steward, to write an urgent letter on the 18th to Smith's father, Cyrus, telling him that his son was gravely ill. The elder Smith's heart must have sunk when he read Fiske's admonition: "You had better come immediately after receiving this as we may expect an unfortunate termination of the disease at any time."[5] Two days later, the commander of the hospital guards wrote Cyrus Smith that his son was "dangerously sick" and suggested that the boy would find it gratifying "if you sir or any of his friends could come to see him."[6] Though the lieutenant appealed to Jon's father, it fell upon his mother's shoulders to make the painful journey. Arriving at noon on the 21st, Mrs. Smith hurried to the hospital where her beloved offspring greeted her. "O mother," said the dying youth, "I'm glad you've come. They told me you'd come today."[7]

Mrs. Smith now commenced a lonely three-day vigil. She tried to remain optimistic, but by mid-afternoon on the 23rd she had accepted the ominous conclusion that all was lost. After rallying briefly, Private Smith drifted slowly away until his soul left this earth on the day before Christmas 1861. Ever after, the holiday season would not be the same for the Smith family. Though time would dull the pain, the memory of a life cut short and a child whose promise went unfilled would never fade away. Balanced against the numbing grief was the comforting assurance that the family was at least privy to all there was to know about their loved one's passing. By contrast, not all despairing families had such closure, for many never received conclusive evidence of their missing soldier's ultimate fate, let alone the particulars of his death.

Though his mother was present in his hour of passing, Private Smith's comrades were far away, riding toward winter quarters at Annapolis. In time, the sad news caught up with the column. Captain Addison Preston, commander of Company D, felt obligated to extend his sympathies. Over his abbreviated career, Preston would pen many letters to the families of fallen soldiers, but his missive to the Smiths represented his first such effort. Choosing his words carefully, he composed a simple note of condolence, intended to bring a measure of comfort to the grieving parents. "It would have been perhaps more glorious and sufferable to him to have fallen on the field of battle," wrote the kind captain, "but even then he would but be serving his country and obeying orders as he was doing at the time of his death."[8]

About this time, deployment rumors started, predicting all sorts of destinations. Such conjecturing was not the sole domain of the soldiers, for others, highly placed in Vermont and Washington, also took a keen interest in the 1st Vermont's future. One key individual who kept an ear to the ground regarding the regiment's destination was Thomas Hawley Canfield. Positioned in the War Department, Canfield learned that there were to be "3 rendezvous sites for cavalry in the winter of '61-'62 — Annapolis, Harrisburg, and Elmira."[9] A fourth option, holding the regiment in Burlington, particularly interested Canfield because, no matter how demanding his wartime job, the enterprising mind of Thomas Canfield never drifted far from matters of economics. He knew that all forage, horse, and cattle contracts were negotiated through Washington. Furnishing the military with its copious needs would be lucrative. Knowing this, Canfield worked industriously to funnel war-generated business to Vermont interests. If in fulfilling the army's needs, he and his friends were beneficiaries of windfall profits, so much the better.

Whatever Canfield envisioned, his thoughts were very much in keeping with the tenor of the times. It was undeniable that the War Department in 1861 fostered a climate wherein dishonesty was rampant. One of the worst culprits was none other than Canfield's boss, secretary of war Simon Cameron. So pervasive were the secretary's misdeeds that

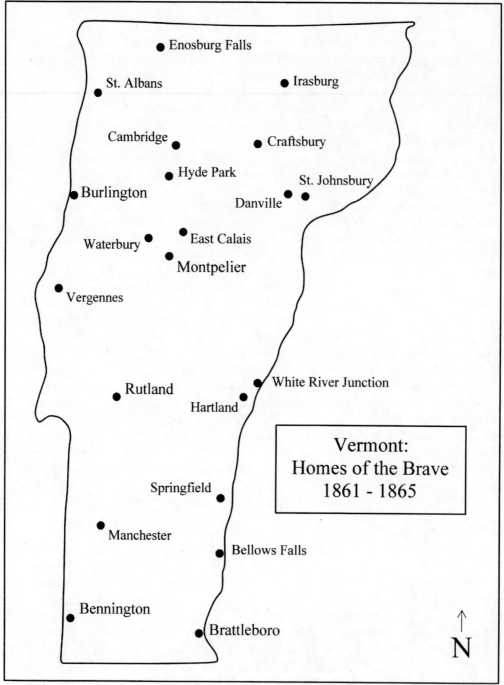

Enosburg Falls

St. Albans

Irasburg

Cambridge

Craftsbury

Hyde Park

St. Johnsbury

Burlington

Danville

East Calais

Waterbury

Montpelier

Vergennes

Rutland

White River Junction

Hartland

Vermont:
Homes of the Brave
1861 - 1865

Springfield

Manchester

Bellows Falls

Bennington

Brattleboro

N

Drawn by Bob Collea

the president was ultimately compelled to ease his appointee out of office. Before resigning, the Pennsylvania politico left Lincoln with an embarrassing trail of mismanagement. However, though Canfield worked under Cameron, there is no indication that he was in league with the scheming secretary. Unlike Cameron, Canfield had no intentions of trying to defraud the federal government. He only attempted to use his positioning to supply a need and in the process turn a personal profit. By the standards of today, this appears a questionable practice, but, within the context of the times, such insider trading was quite common and acceptable.

But the cavalry's status did not remain in limbo for long. Much to Canfield's disappointment, the matter was expedited around him. Endeavoring to terminate the stalemate, Colonel Platt sought the assistance of his old friend Abraham Foot. Wielding his influence, Senator Foot ended the bottleneck on behalf of his pet troops. "It is of ... importance that the regiment should leave the State for the South ... before cold weather sets in," the Senator urged, "[for] men and horses would both suffer in camp here after that time."[10] In short order, confirmation came from the War Department. The regiment was bound for Annapolis. Thomas Canfield regretfully acknowledged that holding the 1st Vermont in Burlington for the winter was now a lost opportunity: "Senator Foot has written to General Thomas to order the regiment here and the telegram has gone to the Governor — this ends the matter."[11]

The news set off a round of speeches, parades, and balls. December 12 was earmarked as the grandest day of all. The Rutland & Burlington Railroad put on an extra run and charged passengers only for a one-way fare. The governor would make an appearance, taking full advantage of the opportunity to address the troops. Since newly elected Frederick Holbrook had been ill when he took office, his inaugural speech had been presented on paper rather than delivered in person. Therefore his excellency's opportunity to speak at this significant event was his first public oration of consequence since taking office. He rose to the occasion, sharing with the troops his heartfelt pride in their commitment. "Although we can not entirely shut out sober reflections at the thought of so many young men, the flower of our people, going out from us to the stern realities of war," Holbrook said, "yet we rejoice that when our *Country* calls, we are able to respond with so complete an offering. No compulsion, but each soldier cheerfully volunteering his services."[12] Following Holbrook's remarks, regimental battle flags were presented. These important pieces of military identification were "a State flag of heavy blue, richly embroidered (not painted) with the coat of arms of the State; a United States flag of silk, and four guidons of red and white silk."[13] The state flag was also emblazoned with Vermont's motto, and the national colors were inscribed with the name of the regiment.

As the final days passed, many realized that their time at Camp Ethan Allen had been a unique experience. Not only did it afford the men of the 1st Vermont a chance to establish bonds of trust and friendship amongst themselves, so also did an affinity develop for their host community. So well were they treated by the good citizens of Burlington that the hospitality made a lasting impression. In 1865, when the time came for the regiment to be mustered out, a fervent request was made that they disband at Burlington. For those whose fortune it would be to survive and return, a brief ceremony marked the end of almost three-and-a-half momentous years, not only in their lives but also in their country's history. In the process, boys would grow to be men, and a nation would be poised to become a world power. Their personal characters and the national character would be concurrently forged and tempered by an experience that would leave neither the same for having endured it. Both the troopers and their homeland would have maturity thrust quickly upon them. From Burlington to Appomattox and back, the wheel was destined to go full circle for these mounted sons of Vermont. But at the stroke of midnight on December 13, 1861, the journey of a lifetime still awaited its first step.

2

Training Days
You're in the Army Now, Boys!

Located on the eastern shore of Lake Champlain, Burlington in 1861 boasted a population of approximately 7,700. A thousand temporary residents were introduced into the scene on October 16, 1861, when the 1st Vermont Cavalry assembled. As companies arrived, each was assigned an alphabetical designation. Thus the contingent from Chittenden County became the much-coveted "Company A," while the last to detrain from Addison County became "Company K." For the next two months, the regiment became a focal point of interest to the community. Curiosity was high about the 1st Cavalry, destined to be Vermont's only mounted regiment. From its inception, the regiment was the darling of the people.

Room for this human influx was found on the flat upland to the northeast of the town. "In the early 1860's, the corner of North Avenue and North Street presented a view of a vast unbroken space with a few trees on the hillside of the ravine holding the sod. The Chittendon County Agricultural Society used the area on North Ave bounded by Manhattan Drive and Pitkin Street as fairgrounds, erecting a building called the Floral and Mechanics Hall."[1] Christened "Camp Ethan Allen," the grounds gradually evolved into a military cantonment. One particularly nettlesome problem from the start was obtaining equipment. Captain Gardner S. Blodgett, assistant quartermaster for the army, had been detailed to help Platt. Dispatched to Washington to work directly with the War Department and manufacturers' representatives, even this experienced officer ran into difficulties due to short supplies. This logjam was explained by a Burlington daily: "[E]very arm of the service is pressing for supplies, and every branch of the manufacture is pushed to the utmost to meet the demands on it for war purposes.— When thousands upon thousands of wants are crowded together, some must wait."[2] The 1st Vermont was fortunate, though, in having the indefatigable Thomas Hawley Canfield in the War Department. Using his contacts to press for Vermont interests, he provided help when bureaucratic paperwork threatened to slow processing down. In one instance, Canfield saved Captain Blodgett a three-week wait for the Treasury secretary to sign a requisition. Canfield accomplished this feat by ignoring the secretary's edict that all paperwork was to be processed in the order received. "I played messenger in the face of this order and put this [requisition] through 5 offices in one day, jumped it over all others and got the warrant made out and ready for the Sec. of Treasury to sign within 4 hours after it came from General Mieg's office."[3] According to Canfield, Blodgett left Washington October 4 "with everything fixed up about tents, blankets, etc, but it will take a little time to transport them to Burlington."[4]

The lack of tents was temporarily overcome by using the buildings of the agricultural society. In short order, wooden barracks accommodating 800 men were constructed. Eventually, the fruits of Captain Blodgett's tireless efforts materialized. Camp equipage began pouring in from the factories. Blinn reported on October 13, 1861, that the "Sibley tents had arrived."[5] These were set three to a row with two rows allotted to each company, sixteen enlisted men to a shelter. Since the grounds were too limited for the proper spacing and order, "the ends of the rows formed the arc of a circle."[6] Much to the chagrin of purists, it would not be until winter quarters were established at Annapolis that a regulation campground could be laid out. Until then, the large rectangle with wide streets and appropriately aligned and measured distances between tents had to be eschewed. But, in spite of the delays and inconveniences, visitors to the camp on October 16 noticed "the good order which seemed to exist through the encampment. Despite the wet and cold weather they have been exposed to, the men appear well contented and cheerful."[7]

With its equipment, uniforms, and horses starting to give a visual identity to the regiment, the challenge now belonged to the officer corps to infuse a military presence, bearing, and precision in their charges. The governor commissioned the upper strata of leaders, selecting an impressive group of solid citizens. One Burlington paper characterized them as being "men of the right stamp."[8] With the exception of the youthful Dr. Ptolemy Edson, they were established individuals who had built reputations over time in careers and the communities from whence they came. Fifty-year-old Lemuel Platt had a commanding presence, organizational skills, and business sense. George Kellogg, a forty-five-year-old attorney, "like his immediate superior officer is unfamiliar with the duties of a soldier or officer" but was considered "strong and indomitable in whatever he

Left: **Dr. George Gale.** *Right:* **Dr. Ptolemy Edson. The 1st Vermont was doubly blessed to go to war with two highly regarded surgeons on its staff, kindly men whose ministrations were deeply appreciated (Francis C. Guber Collection).**

undertakes."[9] In the transplanted forty-five-year-old Englishman William Collins, the regiment boasted its only high-ranking officer with prior training in the art of war, for he had studied at the Woolwich Military School and later commanded a British artillery battery. Surgeon George Gale, also fifty, was a "truly scientific and thorough surgeon" who possessed an admirable bedside manner as manifested in his "kind and genial temperament."[10] Adjutant Edgar Pitkin was deemed to be "a valuable man" who came to know the officers and was thus able to provide his superiors with much information "regarding their respective antecedents, characters, attainments, etc. his judgment was excellent."[11] Gray-bearded Quartermaster Archibald Dewey was considered a good and competent man of "high character."[12] High acclaim was also bestowed upon Ptolemy Edson, who in time came to be widely admired by the regiment, his ministrations bearing out the predictions about him that "all who have friends in the regiment may rest assured that they will have if they need it, the kindest and best medical care."[13]

Though not a part of the command hierarchy, another providential appointment was that of the Rev. John H. Woodward, a Congregational minister from Westford, as the regimental chaplain. The impetus for his selection came from the favorable results of an informal ballot among the company captains; the ballots were then forwarded to the colonel. "A pastor of long and high standing and high influence, a man of decided ability, and genial sympathies and companionable qualities, he will gain the confidence of the soldiers and be a true friend and kind advisor to all" was the ringing endorsement that the *Burlington Daily Free Press* gave to this appointment.[14] A natural leader to whom people gravitated, the Reverend Woodward resigned his seat in the Vermont senate to become the cavalry's chaplain.

In choosing higher-echelon officers, the role of the rank and file was limited to ratifying nominations. As for captains, lieutenants, and second lieutenants, the enlisted men filled these positions through elections. Reasons were many as to how a given individual merited his command. Some were viewed as instinctive leaders. Others had been active recruiters, largely if not solely responsible for a company's quota being met and then, in a sense of fair play, being duly rewarded by the enlistees for their efforts. Some were plainly popular with their troops from a perspective of personality and conviviality. But as Stephan Starr pointed out, experientially "there was little to choose among lieutenants, captains, majors, and colonels. With few exceptions, all were equally ignorant."[15]

Qualifications notwithstanding, time would prove that the men had in fact exercised their freedom of choice judiciously. While occasional ne'er-do-wells were selected, many excellent candidates were picked, warriors who by any measuring stick proved themselves in the heat of battle. Though some resigned after relatively brief service, others stayed for the duration. Among this original group, there were men whose destiny it would be to wind up prisoners, incur wounds, and perish in battle. In some instances, cowardice would rear its ugly head, but exemplary courage was by far a more common virtue.

In time, the presence of inept officers worked itself out. For various reasons, these individuals gradually left, and in their places deserving men from the ranks were promoted. But as of October 16, 1861, be they good, bad, or indifferent, the men charged to train and lead the regiment for at least the next four-and-a-half months were in place. When the regiment faced the enemy for the first time on April 17, 1862, the combined efforts and leadership skills of the existing officer corps would be about 80 percent responsible for the fine showing the 1st Cavalry would make. The kudos for the other 20 percent of its success were owed to Colonel Jonas Holiday who, though leading the regiment for a mere five weeks, did so with diligence and intensity when it came to exposing his men to rigorous discipline.

After pitching their tents, the troopers' introduction to military regimentation came via "General Order No. 1," issued by Colonel Platt on November 8, 1861. This edict promulgated the routine that would guide the soldiers through their day. Beginning with reveille at 6:00 A.M., it specified the time and order of activities. Stable calls, guard duty, messing, lights out, and taps established a set routine. The intent of a tightly planned schedule was of course to instill discipline, part of the grand design to create a viable fighting force. Stable duty amounted to the care and feeding of horses, the soldiers' most important responsibility next to maintaining their weapons. Guard mounting was an exercise to learn the correct practices and procedures for protecting the camp. The newly elected leaders had a support role to play in this important duty, acting on a rotating basis as "officer of the day." As officer of the day, Wells led a twenty-five-man detail. He was expected to regularly ride a circuit of the guard posts to check on them over a period of twenty-four hours between 8:00 A.M. and 8:00 A.M. In a tightly laid out camp on friendly turf, the assignment was a piece of cake; however, checking outposts in a war zone could encompass risky travel in all kinds of weather.

As the regiment rounded into shape, dress parades evolved as important events, providing entertainment for the public as well as practice for the troopers. Like novices trying to ride bicycles, initial attempts at parading were awkward. At one of the regiment's first public appearances in early November, not everyone wore a complete uniform. No one sported a weapon. Understandably, the whole entourage proceeded at a comparatively slow pace, feeling its way along unsteadily. Too soon in the training process to be thought of as a parade, one generous reporter nevertheless called it "a fine show, as they came prancing down Main Street, four abreast."[16] Mounted troops often had that kind of mesmerizing effect. The sheer size of a man and animal together made for an impressive visual encounter. The jingling of metal, creaking of leather, clopping of hooves, whinnying of horses, and shouting of commands added an auditory element that heightened the whole experience of watching a column of cavalry. Most onlookers probably concurred with the prophetic Burlington journalist that "the regiment shows good material, and will prove itself one of the most efficient in the service."[17] A week later, Burlingtonites were treated to their first full-scale dress parade. On Saturday afternoon, November 9, the procession wound its way through the city. According to an eyewitness report, "[T]he ranks numbered about 600, and the lines, four abreast, extended nearly *half a mile,* and made a truly imposing appearance."[18]

But the real coming-out party for the regiment was scheduled for Wednesday the 13th. To do right by this auspicious occasion, Colonel Platt had invited the legislature to observe the results of his efforts. In a show of support, the Vermont Central Railroad provided free transportation for these dignitaries. Not to be outdone, the Rutland & Burlington Railroad made its own charitable proposal, offering to "carry passengers to Burlington and back on Wednesday for fare one way from Rutland to all stations north to witness the parade of the Cavalry Regiment."[19] Over 1000 excited spectators thronged into the city. Upon the legislators' arrival, an honor guard of forty troopers escorted them to camp. After reviewing the troops, the governor expressed himself "highly pleased by the superior quality of the material of the regiment, both men and horses."[20] To insure the continued availability of homegrown manpower, Governor Holbrook issued a curious proclamation that had a decided state's rights bent to it. In this edict, he prohibited "any and every person, not having authority from this State or the United States, [from] enlisting, recruiting, or employing, or attempting to enlist, recruit, or employ, any person in this State, for military service without this State."[21] As the war dragged on, this proclamation helped to keep the ranks of Vermont's regiments filled with sons of the Green Mountain State.

By mid–November, the 1st Cavalry had reached the halfway mark in its posting at Burlington. The warm, picturesque fall days that had accompanied their enlistment and matched their buoyant moods with its breathtaking beauty slowly gave way to gray, dreary times that brought bone-chilling cold, a harbinger of winter snows, and matched the dull monotony of repetitive drills. But during this four-week interval, much had been accomplished: a command structure was installed; the routines of soldiering were introduced; and the process of training for war was begun. While daily drills continued until the regiment left, the remaining two fortnights would bear witness to some of the pomp and circumstance that were also very much a part of military life, helping to bolster the men's spirits and imbue a sense of purpose to their mission. So, too, did inevitable and difficult good-byes have to be said to family and friends. The end of the beginning was rapidly approaching.

3

Departure
Look Out, Johnny Reb —
Here Comes the 1st Cavalry!

After much delay, the departure date was established: Saturday, December 14, 1861. The regiment's impending movement by rail represented a unique logistical undertaking, for it was the first time in Vermont's history that cavalry had gone off to war. Without a blueprint, a plan had to be devised from scratch. Ultimately, the resources of three railroads were harnessed. Starting on the Rutland and Burlington road, the trains would diverge for the leg south of Rutland toward Troy, New York, to the tracks of both the Rutland and Washington and the Western Vermont railroads. These two lines paralleled each other, varying between twenty to thirty miles apart on a north/south axis, until joining east of North Bennington.

Five troop trains, totaling 143 cars, were marshaled to haul the regiment. Averaging twenty-eight units per train, the format for starting the 1st Vermont on its 550 mile journey to the war zone was beautiful in its simplicity. First, the ten companies were reconfigured into five squadrons. Then one squadron was assigned per train. Eight horses were placed in a freight or cattle car, four at each end facing toward the middle. The open center provided space for forage, saddles, accouterments, and four men. The remaining four troopers to whom the other two pairs of horses belonged rode in passenger cars. The idea was that the four riders in the freight car and the four in the passenger car would at intervals switch locations, so the task of caring for the animals could be shared.

The first departure was set for eight o'clock, with succeeding trains leaving on the hour. To meet this timetable, the horses were fed and watered at 3:00 A.M., tents struck at four, and breakfast taken at five. The first companies marched to the depot at seven. So well did the entire process go there was but a single mishap. This occurred when "a private ... was severely kicked by his horse in putting him aboard the cars, but who departed with his regiment, was obliged to be left at Middlebury for surgical treatment."[1] With unerring accuracy, ol' Dobbin gave the poor soldier a shot in the groin. Nothing like being "wounded" before the train even left the station!

Throughout the loading, interested spectators thronged around the depot on Water Street. The citizenry had become quite attached to the cavalry, feelings that Sergeant Ide reported were mutual: "The people of Burlington turned out in considerable number to see us off and as a general thing we were well satisfied with our treatment by them."[2] Also among the crowd were many who had more than just a passing interest in the regiment,

15

these being loved ones who lived close enough that they were able to watch their own special boy in blue depart. Lieutenant Henry Wheeler, recalling these poignant moments, wrote how "we bade our friends a last good-bye, and clung to outstretched hands til the moving train broke our grasp; as we kept our lingering gaze upon the dear ones until they were entirely out of view, and still looked fondly in the direction of those whom we left, and then settled down on our blankets and our saddles with our horses, we began to realize the significance of the separation which had just taken place."[3]

Hearty cheers from the crowd marked the departure of each train. Lieutenant Wheeler was surely not the only soldier lost in his thoughts with mixed emotions. Memories of home and family were in the forefront of many minds, just as were trepidations about the war and impending battle. Leaving the safety of Vermont for the uncertainty of a camp somewhere near the front made the whole "you're-in-the-army-now" scenario much more real. For these young recruits, every mile down the track was part of a great unknown.

As exciting as the sojourn was, it saw tragedy. James Hogan, a private in Company E, was missing when his train reached New York City. Desertion was suspected, but a dispatch received a short time later solved the mystery. It contained the grisly news that Hogan's body had been found near Sunderland, Vermont, lying on the railroad track, cut to pieces. A local laborer made the gruesome discovery when he saw "what he thought was a bundle of rags but which upon inquiry proved to be the body of a man."[4] In a letter to his father, Eli Hawley Canfield related what a friend had graphically told him about the discovery of poor Hogan's remains: "His head was found in one place crushed to atoms, his legs and arms in another, his liver in another ... in fact he was literally torn into small pieces."[5] Were it not for a belt found nearby marked "James Hogan, Company E, Springfield, Vt." and the distinguishing characteristics of a cavalry uniform, even circumstantial identification of the body may not have been possible.[6] After help was summoned, all responders could do was help pick up the scattered remains and place them in a box.

The discovery of Hogan's mangled corpse prompted an investigation. Affidavits were taken from soldiers on the train, serving to establish that Hogan was alive in the early evening of December 14. Further statements were gathered to the effect "he was not under the influence of ardent spirits but appeared to be quite sober."[7] That someone could fall off a moving train was entirely plausible. While the evidence was quite incontrovertible that Private Hogan had been run over, there were just enough unanswered questions to take what was in all probability nothing more than a horrible accident and shroud it with a touch of uncertainty. The military wanted to tie up as many loose ends as possible, but the war, time, distance, and lack of witnesses precluded conducting much more than a cursory investigation.

While not gloriously, Trooper Hogan still died while in the service of his country, becoming the regiment's third fatality. Friends would miss him. Sadder still, he had a young family in Charleston, New Hampshire, who would feel the loss even more. His wife, Abby, of but two years and his little daughter were now without the family breadwinner. But Mrs. Hogan was to have even more misery to bear. Her baby, Alice, whose first birthday fell on the day her father's body was found, passed away only a little more than three months later. This blow was followed in June by the bittersweet birth of another child, a son whom his father would never see. Such is the hidden cost of war. No, the war didn't stop for James Hogan and just barely took note of his passing, but without doubt there were Vermont troopers who paused to think of how fleeting life could be and to wonder when and how their own hour of death might come.

As the trains crossed into the Empire State, the moment marked for some soldiers the last time they would ever see the vistas of home. Passing through Troy, New York, and then on down the storied Hudson Valley was the trip of a lifetime. Much more awaited the awestruck soldiers when they arrived in New York City, even then a magnificent setting dwarfing any of the communities from whence the troopers hailed. While Monday the 7th would see their journey resumed, for all practical purposes Sunday was an R & R day for the men to do whatever struck their fancies. According to Lieutenant Wheeler, not too many of the boys elected to spend the Sabbath Day making their hometown ministers proud, for as he later stated, "[I]t is safe to venture the statement that the congregations in the churches were not perceptively increased by the presence in the city of the First Vermont Cavalry."[8] Rather than sleep, many passed the hours until early in the morning walking the streets, taking in the strange and wonderful sounds, smells, and sights that captivated their senses at every turn.

When it came time to leave, the 1st Vermont departed in grandiose style. Astride their fine Morgans, the regiment paraded down Fifth Avenue, onto Fourteenth Street, and then over to and down Broadway until reaching the Battery. Since it was early in the war, military formations passing through the city were still a novelty. As a result, the procession attracted large crowds. Further heightening the interest was the fact that this contingent represented "the first complete regiment of cavalry that has passed through the streets of New York since the present war began."[9] The folks who turned out that morning were not disappointed. They were greeted with a splendid cavalcade! As it turned out, the day was memorable not only for those who watched but also for those who rode. Somewhere amidst the horse soldiers, Mark Rogers also observed the grand spectacle. He was awed by the rousing send-off as "along the whole route of march vast crowds manifested their curiosity and approbation, and at many points huge national flags, with patriotic mottoes, were displayed, and fair hands waved greetings and farewell to the Green Mountain Boys."[10]

In retrospect, it is a wonder that the regiment was able to present as impressive an image as it did. Charles Blinn had some insights to offer which, while not surprising since the Vermonters had roamed the city unfettered on the 15th, nevertheless give one cause to marvel at how the parade was ever effected with any degree of decorum. First, Blinn asserted, "many of the boys went away last eve and have not yet returned."[11] If nothing else, their absence created gaps in the ranks. Second, he noted, "many who returned are too drunk to sit on their horses."[12] But regardless of some comrades either being under the weather or AWOL, the regiment somehow pulled off its highly visible march, making it to the docks in two hours with only minor mishaps and no embarrassment. Boarding ferries, the regiment crossed into New Jersey. After a brief march, they took a boat ride to Jersey City where they again boarded waiting trains. This next-to-the-last leg of their journey saw them pass through Harrisburg and Baltimore before detraining in Washington. In spite of minor difficulties, the overall experience had been exhilarating for the regiment. According to Josiah Grout, "[O]ur journey from Burlington to Washington was one continuous ovation" as "the ladies lunched, the gentlemen cheered, and the school children waved us on our way to the front."[13]

Thankfully spirits were high upon reaching their destination, for the next twenty-four hours would be extremely deflating. First, both men and animals had to go for a day without sustenance. As if the lack of vittles wasn't sufficiently aggravating, the accommodations provided proved to be downright disconcerting. Benedict described them in jarring detail when he wrote that "the regiment was piloted to an abandoned cemetery on Capitol Hill, where, jaded, hungry and nearly frozen, they stumbled into graves recently emptied of their former occupants, and camped without straw, wood, or rations."[14] The campsite took even Lemuel Platt aback, though his sense of humor helped him accept the situation. "We were quartered in a very picturesque place viz — an exhumed burying ground the holes all open. Once and a while a stone or monument left."[15] It was not much of a stretch for a young soldier to get a trifle spooked at the thought of sleeping in such surroundings, knowing full well that it was only a matter of time before he would be in harm's way and a candidate for a pine box himself. Hindsight being 20/20, another less ghoulish spot would have made for a more sensitive choice for recruits going off to war. This inglorious site came to be referenced by the men as "Camp Potter's Field."

Yet, as bad as the men had it, the unprotected animals had it worse. The much-respected Captain Henry Flint offered his assessment of their plight in a letter to the *Orleans Independent Standard*: "Our short stay in Washington proved conclusively that it was folly to think of picketing our horses there through the winter months; so long as it is dry weather they will do well, but three hours rain will soften the ground where they stand, so they will have a mud hole half a foot deep under them, filled with clay and water, making an excellent plaster for some objects but not for horses."[16] Wet feet over a prolonged period of time were breeding grounds for crippling and potentially life-threatening diseases.

Since the regiment's stay in Washington had presented hardships, the news of its imminent departure to its permanent camp was enthusiastically welcomed, the report being that "the announcement was received with three cheers and a tiger, and the camp was ringing with joyful shouts when I left it."[17] This odd-sounding display of excitement and approbation was a decidedly quaint nineteenth century affectation used for special occasions. It consisted of three rapid shouts of "Hurrah! Hurrah! Hurrah!" followed by a low, bestial "Grrr ... Grrr."[18] Undoubtedly, it had a more impressive impact coming out of the throats of a thousand men than it does being read from a printed page. So it was, on the war's first Christmas Day, that history would record that the Vermont Cavalry was on the road by 6:30 A.M. Its destination was the capital of Maryland, located approximately forty miles to the east over uneven terrain.

Passing through areas that had not seen much of a military presence up to that time, the 1st Vermont presented an odd spectacle to the locals. Frank Wheeler, then a corporal, gave a candid description of what the Marylanders witnessed: "Our appearance on that march must have been picturesque. Every man was supplied with an outfit for housekeeping.... In addition to our regular equipments of saber, pistol, haversack, canteen, lariat ropes and pin, feed bag and blanket, we had knives, cups, forks, plates, frying pans, coffee pots, shawls, mattresses, pillows, valises, satchels, brushes for horses, hair and boots, and other things too numerous to mention here, and all these things were in some unaccountable way attached to horses and ourselves, so that we had when mounted — and a position gained only by the dexterity and agility — formidable breastworks in our front, and towering bulwarks in our rear. We were in appearance a caravan. With our horses unused to marching, our riders unused to driving, and our officers unused to everything in the service, we went much of the way at a pace little short of a charge."[19]

It required two days to reach Annapolis, the intervening night's bivouac being made in a pine grove at Marboro. The chosen site was christened "Camp Wood." Since the supply wagons had not kept pace, supper that night consisted of bread. With fires available, "skillygaree," a favorite make-the-best-of-it dish, became the "special of the day" on many improvised menus. One trooper who actually looked forward to this plebian meal was young Henry Holt from Hartland. He had written his parents about this prevalent form of army chow, telling them how much he actually preferred hardtack to soft bread. Knowing that these distinctive-looking army crackers were unfamiliar to civilians, he described them as being "made of flour and water and baked in square pieces about five inches square, hard as the deuce, and it is good to put in some water and let it soak and then fry it in some grease, and they taste like donuts."[20] Hunger pangs that night spared no one, regardless of rank. Even Colonel Platt felt the same tightening in his stomach, in the process chiding his friend Zadock Canfield that even "your beans would have helped in the emergency."[21] Since tents were not available, the men improvised. Some built lean-tos out of tree boughs, cushioning the ground with a mattress of leaves. Others were content to "form a circle around a blazing fire with our saddles, and lay down upon a damp, chilling Maryland soil for rest and sleep."[22]

Once in camp, before drifting off to sleep, many reminisced about this special day, while others kept silently to themselves with forlorn thoughts of home. As one of the boys conveyed the reflective mood of that evening, "[W]e passed Christmas Eve in a wood. Our conversation was turned upon Christmas geese and turkeys, and friends that were far away. Probably it was the first time that many of us had spent a Christmas away from our homes."[23] Trooper Wheeler concurred with this feeling: "[T]his was not to us a merry Christmas, and through all of the experiences of our subsequent army life there were few marches that seemed more severe than the first march."[24]

They were all dressed as soldiers, yes, but human still inside. They were about the work of men, true, but many yet boys too young to vote. They were encamped with a thousand others, but alone with their memories. Though unrecorded for posterity, that tears slipped down more than a few cheeks that night would not be a surprising. Being less than two weeks removed from their beloved Vermont, only the toughest could have conceivably avoided homesickness on this special night. The situation was especially difficult for young Mark Rogers. In addition to being far from home and hearth for the first Christmas in his life, his brother William's sickness in Burlington weighed heavily on his mind. Though the elder Rogers would soon recover and rejoin his brother at Annapolis, it was only by focusing on the hope of this eventuality that Mark Rogers could eventually fall asleep.

The regiment awoke Thursday morning, "refreshed and strengthened for the march of another day, which was cheerfully performed."[25] Their upbeat attitude even surprised Colonel Platt. "I have heard but little complaint," he later noted of the two-day ride.[26] The horses were fed oats from the supply that each trooper carried with him, hay being unavailable as the supply wagons never came up. Any meager morsel a man may still have had in his haversack constituted his breakfast. This segment of the ride took them through a portion of Maryland, which was viewed as being quite prosperous. Unlike the warm receptions accorded their passing time and again en route from Burlington to Washington, they were greeted only by silent stares on the part of the white populace they passed.

The regiment covered the remaining twenty miles of the journey in approximately the same amount of time as the first score, arriving at their destination just after dark.

Unfortunately for them, the day's march ended in a field two miles outside of Annapolis. Since the supply wagons again failed to materialize, the men endured another night sleeping tentless and hungry. However, the hospitality extended to them by neighboring campers proved to be very timely and much appreciated. The 5th New York Cavalry gave shelter to all of the sick among the Vermonters, providing them with whatever they could to make the ailing newcomers comfortable. The relationship begun that night would become fast and firm, its bonds further forged and strengthened on numerous occasions during the war as the two regiments fought side by side.

While there was some grumbling about the ineptness of any planning which twice left them without supper, the exhausted men soon dozed off under a canopy of stars. At daybreak, the smell of freshly brewed coffee greeted them, supplied by their new friends from the Empire State. Invigorated, they rose to face a new day and the challenges that awaited them in "Camp of Instruction" as they continued their evolution from raw recruits to well-trained troopers.

4

Annapolis
The Molding of a Regiment

For boys who had grown up inland, life at the seashore proved pleasurable, adding more memories to those of the long train ride, the wonders of New York City, and the sights of Washington. The encampment was on a slight rise of ground with a trough in front that went straight down to the water. The ocean's proximity afforded questioning minds a chance to explore an environment totally foreign to that in which most had grown up. It was during this time that many were introduced to the delicacies readily available from King Neptune's larder. William Wells could be counted among those Vermonters who developed a predilection for one particular type of seafood, revealing that it was "easy to get oysters" while admitting also that he had eaten "a great many," as he had grown "very fond of them."[1]

As beckoning as the ocean was, there was plenty to do in camp. Their tents had arrived by noon the first day. These were quickly erected, so the men had some protection. However, the process of winterizing their cover, providing suitable shelter for their horses, and then adding creature comforts for themselves required considerably more work. Two basic ingredients for every camp, they already had. The first was an honorary name: "Camp Harris." While not of their own choosing, the appellation was nevertheless kept, as the camp's initial occupants, the 5th New York, had selected it in recognition of their benefactor, Senator Ira Harris. The second item that they possessed was the Sibley tent. Conical, its canvas form was eighteen feet in circumference at the base and twelve feet tall at its peak. It was held up by means of a center pole, which stood on a three-legged cast iron tripod, and was anchored around its bottom edge by stakes. A metal ring was sewn into the canvas near the top and suspended by chains from the pole, giving an extra measure of support and stability. Entrance was gained through a generous eight-foot, six-inch opening. A five-foot opening in the upper rear section of the canvas further enhanced ventilation. A cap was available to put over the top if the weather grew inclement. Under field conditions, it was expected to house a dozen men. In long-term situations, the tents could be modified to accommodate up to twenty.

To adapt this all-weather tent for use in a cold climate as well as provide added headroom, a system of perpendicular boards were used to lift the canvas off the ground. Called "stockading," the tent bottom was fastened onto the top ends of wooden slabs that were set into the ground in a circle the size of the tent's base and projected above the ground about 3 feet. The wooden slabs were placed in a circular trench that had been dug out prior to imbedding them. An earthen embankment was then piled up firmly around the outside of the wall. The benefits afforded by stockading were two-fold: it increased the interior vertical space, making the tent more commodious, which allowed the construction of bunks; and it afforded greater warmth by putting the main living space below ground. The construction project was usually finished off with a plank floor. There were those around with the requisite skills needed to hang wooden entrance doors. With so much available talent, the process of putting up suitable quarters progressed rapidly.

After erecting their tents, the men turned to protecting their horses. Since leaving Burlington, the long train ride and then exposure at the Washington camp had taken a heavy toll. As one sympathetic soldier noted, "They have not seen the inside of a barn since they left Vermont."[2] Along the way, some had died, others had become sick, and many had lost their tone. Construction of stables began in early January. In appearance, these buildings had the look of extended lean-tos, with a longer roof slanting down on the backside and a short slanted one on the opposite, or company street side, in saltbox fashion. Some indication of their beneficial effect on the animals' health may be gleaned from a letter penned by Captain Henry Flint, dated February 8, in which he comments that "our horses are looking as plump and fat as they did before they left Burlington."[3]

For the soldiers' families, one of the most important events that winter was the introduction of the "allotment system." The state law was intended for the aid of Vermont volunteers in transmitting portions of their pay to designated beneficiaries. Sign-ups for participation in the allotment plan commenced with the regiment falling out on the parade ground. One of the state-appointed commissioners opened the proceedings by discussing the system's safeguards. Next the roll was read by company, starting with its captain and so on down through the ranks. Each man's allotment was duly recorded on the commissioners' rolls. Like so many aspects of military life, success in obtaining soldiers' pledges was directly proportional to the leadership's modeling an appropriate example. To be sure, there were misgivings and misunderstandings about the plan's operation. Yet, in spite of their concerns, the troopers of the 1st Vermont took their responsibilities seriously, authorizing $14,026.00 in allotments. This amount was $3,500 more than that of any other Vermont regiment.

To try to save the men from themselves and curtail frivolous spending, one of the main thrusts of the commissioners' pitch was the soldiers' duty and obligation to look out for their dependents at home. The parallel concern was that any failure of the troops to do so could lead to a drain on the ability of public and private charities to fill the void. Trooper Hannibal Jenne exemplified individuals who did not let the distance from Maryland to Vermont cause them to lose sight of those dependents left behind him, for in the case of his parents "they received from their son ... out of his pay in the army all of the money he received excepting the sum of five ($5) dollars per month."[4] But perhaps it was young Lieutenant Oliver Cushman of Company E who best summed up the compelling duty that so many of his comrades felt. In a touching postscript, he let his heart speak in a letter from Camp Harris dated February 7, 1862: "I wish mother wouldn't talk of 'repaying' money that I send home — really it hurts me that she should. As if I will in a life repay all I have received from my parents."[5]

Lest the idea be imparted that Camp-Harris-by-the-sea was a precursor to Club Med, it should be duly noted that the facility was also referenced as "Camp Instruction." Even though situated on beachfront property, its mission was far more purposeful than the locale might imply. What Colonel Platt lacked in his knowledge of training soldiers, the brigade's commander, General John Hatch, possessed. A West Pointer, Mexican War veteran, and regular army captain, the diminutive general brought a commanding presence to his fledgling brigade far exceeding his 5′ 4″ stature. What the men could expect from General Hatch was an adherence to the manual. A by-the-book kind of guy, his philosophy of dealing with troops was spelled "d-i-s-c-i-p-l-i-n-e." An appraisal which is highly illustrative of this characteristic was penned by an observant Vermont soldier: "Our general ... is not verbose; his orders are brief — given but once — and he requires obedience to the letter. If stables are to be built 300 feet long — 299 feet will not satisfy him — nor will he suffer them to be 301 feet in length."[6]

By the time housekeeping arrangements had been completed, the end of winter was in sight. With the approach of spring, a heightened sense of urgency and purpose pervaded the camp. The pace of training picked up noticeably. Of all of the instruction that the cavalrymen received, drills geared toward developing proficiency with their sabers were a consistent thread since Burlington. In fact, one trooper even called the daily sword exercises as being "the most pleasant part of our duty!"[7] Though some concern was expressed over their quality, one of the enduring side effects of so much time spent drilling with sabers was a disproportionate reliance on them as the cavalry's weapon of choice. Without doubt, being on the receiving end of a thunderous, sword-waving attack must have been an unnerving experience. Given this context, it is not surprising that procuring firearms was not a priority. In fact, it was not until the first week of February that the men finally received their allotment. James Esdon excitedly shared this most important benchmark with his parents, telling them "we have just received our revolvers. They are six shooters and we have ten carbines to each company."[8] The carbines, manufactured by Sharps, lived up to, if not surpassed, expectations. The pistols, on the other hand, were produced by the Savage Company and never met with the same level of satisfaction. But for the time being, once these weapons were placed in the soldiers' hands, their transition from citizens to warriors was complete. The Sharps carbine became legendary in the annals of history, its breechloading capability and resulting rapid rate of fire making it a great leveler of odds when a cavalry unit was pitted against superior numbers.

The Savage pistol, though, presented a different story. Henry Flint's first impression of this sidearm was understandably neutral, commenting that he was "unable to say whether they are good revolvers or not. They seem to be a strong and destructive firearm."[9] In time much room for improvement in the .36 weapons was duly noted. As Horace Ide dourly commented, "[These] revolvers were rightly named, as they were cocked by pulling the trigger and I have no doubt but that more of our own men were shot by them accidentally than were Rebels."[10] Looking at a Savage revolver, one's first impression is that the weapon appears unwieldy, particularly when compared to the sleek and solid lines of a Colt or Remington .44. The use of a double-trigger arrangement housed within the trigger guard, one a large ring that set the hammer and rotated the cylinder when pulled and the other serving to fire the weapon, was more than likely a contributing factor in the realization of Ide's fear of an accidental discharge. Eventually, as the availability of improved weapons increased and the fallibility of others was demonstrated, the cavalry's sidearms were upgraded significantly as men came into possession of either the very popular Colt or the high-quality Remington pistols. By war's end, only something over 14,000 Savage revolvers were produced, as compared to over 129,000 army-issue Colts and 124,000 of Remington's comparable model.[11]

As departure grew imminent, a bit of regimental housecleaning was conducted by purging the ranks of the unfit. Henry Flint had forecast this likelihood, writing home that "[If] this, with other cavalry regiments, is to pass an inspection, and we shall probably lose some men. None but perfect men, physically, are to be retained."[12] The author's great-great grandfather William Rogers commented on this winnowing process when he told his parents that "we are again to have an inspection here in a few days and discharge all that ain't fit for the cavelry [sic]. I heard that they had thrown out thirty-one of one company in the New York Cavelry [sic]. I think that is picking around pretty close."[13] Private Delinus Melvin of Company C was an example of a soldier who found himself in precisely this situation. Joining in the fall of 1861, he was mustered out on March 9, 1862, his unfitness resulting from a fracture to a bone of the left arm that made it evident he would have to ride one-handed. While it would not be surprising that a cavalryman with a bad limb would be deemed a liability, what is astonishing is that Melvin ever got into the service at all, for his disability was a "united fracture of the ulna of 3 years standing, producing an inability to guide his horse properly and causing pain from drilling."[14] In other words, he was already damaged goods when he joined the cavalry!

Passing an enlistee with a preexisting physical shortcoming was not an unusual oversight. More often than not, though, a discharge was predicated upon an injury incurred while on active duty. One such individual was Flavil Woodward. A private in Company E who joined the cavalry as a hale and hearty factory worker in 1861, Woodward "contracted a double inguinal hernia from his horse falling on him in February of 1862."[15] The severe blow caused him much pain. As a result, surgeon Gale signed a discharge certificate for Private Woodward on March 8, 1862. Another soldier whose military career similarly wound up curtailed was G Company's Private Patrick Malone, a hardy Irish immigrant-laborer. He lay incapacitated in the camp hospital on March 9, due to the lingering aftereffects of a horse's kick. Apparently one of those from the Emerald Isle short on luck, he received the injury just one day after the regiment was mustered! Prior to his discharge on March 12, 1862, he had been deemed unfit to perform his military duties for the previous sixty days. As the 1st Cavalry rode off to the front, poor Patrick was on a train with his lame knee headed for Vermont.

There was another parting of the ways in late February that had nothing to do with injury but much to do with common sense. In tendering his resignation, Colonel Platt graciously bowed to the obvious. Possessing no previous military training, he was clearly unsuited to lead a combat command. That he resigned came as no surprise to his men. As Sergeant Ide recalled, "Colonel Platt used to come around and talk with us, saying that he could feed and clothe us as well as anyone, but he did not think that he would make much of a warrior to lead us in action."[16] There was no disputing that he had labored hard to field the regiment. For this, he was owed a debt a gratitude. But he entertained no fool's desire to have on his inexperienced shoulders the responsibility of leading troops into battle, much less carry the burden on his conscience of perpetrating a bloody disaster. Of all of the soldiers from Vermont who gained varying degrees of fame in the Civil War, Lemuel Platt was just as much a hero as the next man. Though most gained their accolades with sword or pistol in hand, Platt's honor is due him because he had sense enough to lay his weapons down.

Platt's departure, however, stirred controversy. The dissonance revolved around the naming of his successor. The 1st Vermont's own Lt. Colonel George Kellogg coveted the appointment. To his credit, Platt's frequent absence from a visible command posture had put Kellogg in charge of the regiment on a day-to-day basis. Working on Kellogg's behalf, friends circulated a petition but, as William Wells noted, "only 3 Captains have signed it," and though he had the opportunity, he did not sign it.[17] As Wells defined the issue, Platt and Kellogg were "at swords points with each other" because Platt was bound and determined that Kellogg was not going to succeed him.[18] The contentiousness ended when General Hatch gave Captain Jonas Holiday the colonelcy of the regiment. The choice was almost preordained. Holiday was an old friend of Hatch's; in fact, both men hailed from the western part of New York State. In addition, Holiday had not only his superior's backing but also West Point training and field experience with the 2nd United States Cavalry. In character and temperament, it is also not surprising that Holiday would appeal to Hatch, as Ide described the new colonel as being "rather grave in his demeanor."[19] Benedict's similar observation that Holiday was "grave, a thorough disciplinarian" could easily have applied to Hatch, making them soul brothers of a sort.[20] By contrast, Kellogg lacked these intangibles.

With the advent of spring, the rumor mill began to generate possible scenarios as to the cavalry's final destination. One foresaw it going to Texas. Another version had them being sent into the Western Theater to join the Army of the Cumberland. In the end, neither of these materialized, and the cavalry's ultimate destination remained a mystery right through to early March. Possibly among the first to learn the real skinny were the men of Company C, as related by Lieutenant Oliver Cushman in a letter home dated March 7, 1862: "But I haven't told you what is the news—Our captain came down the Co. street tonight just after 'Retreat' while we were at supper and called the Co. out to hear the news—'Boys, we have marching orders—we are required to be ready to start tomorrow or next day at the furthest.' Oh! You ought to have heard the shout that went up–'Three times and a tiger'—We are going to Poolesville, Md."[21]

Even as they exited Annapolis, some of the men already sensed that it had been a special experience, one not apt to be repeated. The romantic in Charles Blinn conveyed this feeling when he wrote that "here we spent undoubtedly the happiest part of our soldiering."[22] It is not hard to fathom why thoughts of the first winter that the regiment spent together quickly assumed a nostalgic aura. Up through the Camp Harris experience, though a war raged, the 1st Vermont was not yet a part of it. The death and destruction that the conflict would soon visit upon them were then only matters for speculation, as yet realities not a part of their experiences. No favorite horse had been downed by enemy fire, no dear tent mate wounded by a cannon's blast, and no beloved leader silenced by volley of rifle fire. A degree of guilelessness still existed in the regiment as its tents were struck on March 8, an innocence that slowly dissipated with each passing mile marched down the road away from the peaceful campsite and toward the maelstrom of war.

5

Moving Up
Don't Let the War End Without Us!

A confident 1st Vermont left Camp Harris. "I have faith that the Green Mountain Boys will fight like brave heroes," wrote Trooper George Spofford, "should they be brought to the test, the time of which may not be far distant."[1] Much of the esprit de corps displayed by the men was attributable to their new commander, thirty-four-year-old Colonel Jonas Holiday, who had joined the regiment on February 22nd. While the men had respected Lemuel Platt, Holiday was seen as the key to ultimate success. "We know that in Col. H. we have a man fully competent for the station, and one whose only aim and desire is to place us among the best drilled in the field," revealed Private Augustus Sampson.[2] To Henry Holt, the changing of the guard was just the medicine that the regiment needed: "Our old Col. has resigned and we have got one from the Regular Army. He is tough ... he is finally hard on us Volunteers just like any damn regular."[3]

Over the previous two weeks, the colonel was a whirling dervish about the camp, inspiring the troops with his visibility and attention to details. Blinn observed him "in the saddle morning to eve, attending to the drilling and wants of the regiment."[4] Another trooper was impressed with how "he also takes care to inspect the men, their arms, clothing and quarters, and the result is already apparent in the clean faces of the men, and the improved state of the blackening on their boots. If any laxity or looseness prevailed in our camp previous to his arrival, it is now done away with."[5] Tall, full-bearded, bushy-haired, ramrod-straight, and serious-minded, in a very short time Holiday won the support of his men.

It was well that his impact was quickly felt because on Friday, March 7, 1862, the long-anticipated order came: "Forward march to Poolesville, was the watchword that rang through the camp last night, and cheer after cheer arose from the company streets, as the cheering news passed down the lines," recalled Private Sampson.[6] Departure was set for Sunday, March 9. Dawn saw the final preparations. Rations were drawn, canteens filled, horses saddled. At 8:00 A.M., the regiment moved out. It was a glorious morning for a ride as winter was ending in eastern Maryland. "The weather has undergone a decided improvement since I last wrote, and the sun that only occasionally peeped through a cloud of tears, is now a daily visitor, and the sweet notes of the robin reminds us that spring is nigh" expressed feelings shared by many.[7] As the regiment departed, they were given a much-appreciated salute. Expressing genuine camaraderie as well as good luck, the 5th New York formed ranks alongside the roadway and gave the Vermonters three hearty cheers. The gesture was touching in simplicity and priceless in meaning. While they could not have known it then, these two regiments were to team up in numerous engagements, creating deep feelings of mutual respect.

The initial leg to Washington took a day-and-a-half. The first day they traveled in the sun and the second through a drizzle. But rain or shine, it felt good to be free of winter quarters and finally going forth to do battle. In the upbeat perception of Private Jeffrey Hart, "We had a pleasant march from Annapolis."[8] Reaching the capital at 2:00 P.M., the muddy streets greeting them were a dubious reminder of the previous discomfort when they had last encamped there. This time, however, the accommodations were much more palatable. Instead of tents in a cemetery, they got barracks on East Capitol Hill. Even the horses had the good fortune to be housed in covered stables.

On March 13, 1862, the regiment journeyed to Poolesville. Colonel Holiday invested its stay there wisely in drills. That "the colonel stops every night in camp and looks after the men" was common knowledge.[9] Evidence that he continued to endear himself to his men was demonstrated when they christened the Poolesville site "Camp Holiday." After two weeks, news of the regiment's final destination came. During their hiatus at Poolesville, the high command in Washington had engineered a major organizational change, the upshot being a revised assignment for the Vermonters. Transferred from McClellan's to Banks' authority, their objective was now the Shenandoah Valley instead of the Peninsula. Under Banks in the Valley, there would be opportunities for mounted forces to be employed more meaningfully.

But this was all history as yet unwritten on the historic evening of March 27, 1862, when at the stroke of midnight the long-awaited directive sending them to the front came. "Those who were asleep were soon awakened by the continuous noise and cheering, and rest was suspended for the remainder of the night."[10] Appetites were whetted to get to the seat of war as quickly as possible. In the words of one soldier, "the First Vermont stands a fair chance for acting its part in the drama."[11] One who sadly could not share in the good news was William Livingston. Private Livingston had taken ill during the encampment. His health steadily deteriorated, forcing him to stay behind. Much to his comrades' dismay, Company F learned the next day that the young soldier had died. All of twenty-one, Livingston became the fifth member of the 1st Vermont to die in uniform but not in battle. As a sad postscript to the tragedy of someone passing in the flower of his youth, a baby daughter was born to Mary Livingston and her late husband on April 12, 1862. What should have been a happy event occurred with the shadow of her father's death hanging heavily over the poor child's family. Even worse for the infant, named Nellie Elmira, the unexpected passing of her mother in November of 1864 left the toddler an orphan, compounding further the loss of a father she never knew.[12]

On the 29th, the regiment reached Harpers Ferry. The 1st Vermont's arrival triggered an array of personal thoughts in reaction to the scene that lay before them. Initially, there arose a visceral response to the devastation visited upon a breathtaking vista. Blinn saw before him "a truly desolate though vividly romantic spot. Here the Shenandoah and Potomac rush through the mountains and the little village hidden away among the hills is one of God's delightful dwelling places — what a pity that the cruel hand of war should commit such ravages as here to be witnessed."[13] The first sight observed was the jumbled mass of iron bridge girders, locomotives, and cars that had been toppled into the river. Entering the village, scenes of further destruction awaited. Governmental property was in ruins. Regardless of how wasteful, some justification was understandable for leveling military objectives, but damage was unfortunately not limited to these sites.

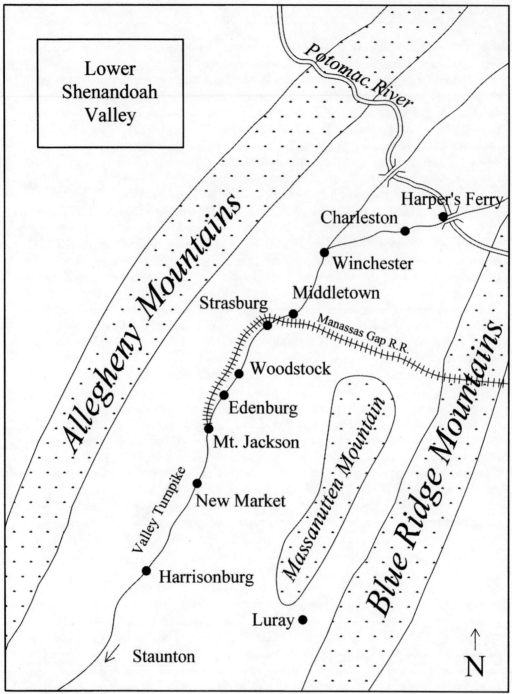

Lower Shenandoah Valley

Potomac River

Harper's Ferry

Charleston

Winchester

Middletown

Strasburg

Manassas Gap R.R.

Woodstock

Edenburg

Mt. Jackson

Massanutten Mountain

Valley Turnpike

New Market

Allegheny Mountains

Blue Ridge Mountains

Harrisonburg

Luray

Staunton

N

Drawn By Bob Collea

Caught in the path of war, "the beautiful dwelling houses are smashed and torn to pieces."[14]

The interlude at Harpers Ferry was brief, for the regiment was ordered south on March 31. As they rode, discarded equipment, horse carcasses, and missing fence rails served notice of soldiers having recently passed. Moving deeper into enemy territory south of Winchester, the 1st Vermont made the acquaintance of the most important man-made contribution to the Shenandoah region: the Valley Turnpike. First used in 1840, it was built employing a technique relatively unusual for its time. "Macadamized," the road was "constructed of gravel layers set in a cement bed, with limestone shoulders."[15] Connecting Winchester to Staunton, this highway provided an even, weather-resistant surface for eighty miles. While intended to expedite commerce, the thoroughfare proved a boon to military operations during the war.

Anticipation, rising with each passing mile, was abruptly squelched by an untimely death on the morning of Saturday, April 5, 1862. The regiment broke camp that morning and started for Woodstock at eight o'clock. They had progressed but a mile when the news of "a most sad and deplorable accident" wound through the column.[16] Private Henry Smith was among the first to learn the bad tidings: "After we had gotten 2 miles, a sgt. rode up to Major Collins, who was a few feet from me, and said: 'Major, your colonel is shot.'"[17] The inconclusive wording of the sergeant's statement fostered hope that the injury might not be fatal. However, the truth was that the wound was mortal from the moment the bullet entered the colonel's skull. In his final moments, the body "was taken onto the bank and laid upon a blanket. The heart still beat, and fluttered but in a moment the last sign of life vanished without a struggle or a groan."[18]

In the days that followed, it became easier to piece together what had happened than it would ever be to ascertain why. This much was known. He had been with the regiment all morning, lending his steadying influence to getting the men up and moving. After the lead elements of the regiment had gained the turnpike, Colonel Holiday rode back into Strasburg to meet with the provost marshal. Completing his business, the colonel returned toward the moving column, accompanied by a bugler and an orderly. The threesome in a short time came to a stone bridge over a small tributary to the Shenandoah. Here they halted. The bugler was ordered to bring Adjutant Edgar Pitkin back. A few minutes later, Holiday dispatched the orderly to hurry the adjutant along. Having freed himself of any possible interference with his intentions, Holiday "was seen by a soldier some distance in the rear to wheel his horse suddenly down the bank to the left, take a bye road down and across the brook to the east bank of the Shenandoah."[19] As Pitkin rode up, he saw Colonel Holiday making his way on foot through the bushes along the riverbank. He shouted to the colonel but received no response. "The adjutant heard a pistol report and ran down to the river and found the Colonel lying partly in the water, his Savage revolver beside him."[20] Adjutant Pitkin and the orderly rushed to the fallen soldier, and together they prevented the body from floating off with the current. Shortly after the mortally wounded man was placed on the ground, Dr. George Gale arrived. But Colonel Holiday was beyond any lifesaving ministrations

At this point, a wagon was brought up, and the body was taken to Strasburg. Early on the Sabbath, April 6, 1862, preparations were made to return the colonel's earthly remains to Burns, New York. In a simple, dignified ceremony, "the regiment was drawn up in a line ... then all filed up and took a last look."[21] Chaplain Woodward offered a prayer and some appropriate remarks. A detachment then escorted the body to Winchester. From there, the coffin made its way by road and rail to southwestern New York, where the deceased was delivered to his family. Interment followed in a small rural cemetery. The simple seven-foot cenotaph marking the officer's final resting place tastefully notes only that the colonel had "died at Strasburg, VA." Predeceased by his father, the sorrowful task of burying her beloved son was left to a distraught mother. Perhaps being buried alone, at home, brought to Jonas Holiday the only peace he had known of late. Not since that day over two decades before, when he had left the tranquil beauty of the Finger Lakes to embark on a military career, had the weight of expectation and command been lifted from his shoulders. Though not a gallant death, Holiday's was certainly an outcome of the conflict. Another casualty of war, he deserved as much thanks for his contributions as he did pity for his passing. For a man who was not a Vermonter, their leader for scarcely a month and an enforcer of stern discipline, the outpouring of sentiment over Colonel Holiday's passing was in some ways as unexpected as it was widespread throughout the regiment. "So short a time connected with the 1st Vermont Cavalry, he had gained a firm hold upon the hearts of officers and soldiers, and was held in the universal regard and respect of the whole regiment, who mourn the loss of a man whose place they fear will not be easily filled," was the fitting eulogy from one soldier.[22]

Eventually, one individual surfaced who possessed insight into Holiday's personal torment. Dr. George Gale at the court of inquiry provided evidence substantiating his colonel's distressed condition. The surgeon commented that Holiday "had not been well during his time with the regiment."[23] He had been nervous and excitable, "to wit as a calming agent the doctor had given Holliday [sic] a bottle of chloroform to use in small doses to steady himself" but which was soon taken back by Gale as "he [Holiday] was using too much."[24] One of the debilitating problems which Colonel Holiday not surprisingly experienced was excessive sleep deprivation, averaging no more than two hours per night since the first week of March.

After brief deliberation, the court of inquiry handed down its verdict: "That the deceased, J.P. Holliday [sic], late Colonel of the First Vermont Cavalry, came to his death from a bullet wound, made by some person or persons unknown, but from the evidence adduced the court is of opinion the act was committed by his own hand."[25] The official book on the case was now closed, only one day after the shooting. The war would go on, but the men would always wonder the why of it all. Amidst much speculation, the prevailing explanation seemed tied to his mental instability, with "the act having been committed during a temporary fit of despondency."[26] His angst was grounded in the fact that Holiday inherited his new command just as the unit was being moved to the battlefront. As a man to whom every detail was important and each decision laden with implications, Holiday very likely became overwhelmed with his perception of so much to do and so little time left in which to accomplish the tasks. Regardless of the faith others had in him, Jonas Holiday proved his own worst critic.

Then, as if the shock and sorrow existing in the wake of Holiday's death were not enough, the 1st Vermont was buffeted by another unexpected blow. On Monday, April 7, the honor guard, returning from Winchester, stopped in Strasburg to rest. During this break, twenty-five-year-old Private Thomas McCullough bent over to strike a match to light his pipe. He was lounging next to a cast-iron stove at the Virginia Hotel when the unthinkable happened. "While stooping his pistol fell from the holster and exploded [after the hammer struck the stove] the ball entering his breast and killing him instantly."[27] The bullet pierced not only McCullough's heart but also the regiment's, for the young man was considered "a model soldier, loved by all who knew him."[28] Upon learning of the accident, Lemuel Platt telegraphed headquarters that he would pay for McCullough's remains to be sent home to Burlington. Soon an escort headed back to Winchester on a second mournful journey, bearing the body of another fallen comrade. From there, McCullough's remains made their way home, arriving on the evening of the 14th, where the deceased would eventually be interred with full military honors. In one forty-eight hour span, Horace Ide's grim diary entry had been substantiated. His first impression of the Savage pistol had seen it as being potentially more harmful to its owner than the enemy. That two Vermont cavalrymen lay dead from its bullets while no rebels had so much as been wounded proved unerringly prophetic.

The passing of Colonel Holiday left a void in the hearts of the Vermont Cavalry, for they had come to view him as a special officer to whom their destiny was firmly tied. The moment that they became leaderless, military orphans of a sort, the regiment was "cast into a deep gloom ... for fear that ... they may not find another who will fill the place of the one they have lost."[29] On the night of the colonel's passing, a group of officers sat vacillating between being crestfallen about the suicide and pessimistic concerning the regiment's future. Surgeon Gale felt motivated to give them a verbal slap in the face, hoping in the process to shake them to their senses. "Gentlemen, our duty is with the living and not the dead. There is material enough in this regiment to save it."[30]

Of paramount concern was the selection of a new commander. Lieutenant Colonel Kellogg was again on the scene, ready to take over, but his popularity remained spotty. Two months elapsed before a successor was named. The chosen one would be Captain Charles H. Tompkins, formerly an officer with the 5th United States Cavalry. His father had been a general and a quartermaster, and his grandfather was a former governor of New York. But beyond whatever clout his lineage may have given him, Charles Tompkins had already gained a measure of personal acclaim when, as a lieutenant, he led a "gallant dash at the enemy at Fairfax Court House, last summer, with a squad of cavalry."[31] This skirmish not only went into the books as the first engagement of the war in Virginia but also served to produce a Medal of Honor for young Tompkins. The 1st Vermont was getting a bona fide hero as its commander.

However, Tompkins was not in the picture on Saturday, April 6, 1862. During the interim, Lieutenant-Colonel Kellogg willingly took charge. There was much for him to oversee. In addition to picketing, patrolling, and protecting supply trains, Kellogg knew rail and telegraph lines needed to be guarded. Almost as if to underscore the dark mood of the hour, an unseasonable snowstorm hit. But at least the men were now positioned to make substantive contributions, thereby giving themselves a sense of regimental purpose as well as a focus to take their minds off the recent tragedies. The cavalry was assigned to "guard duty four nights in five, but they do not complain, and are ready to go at all times.... [A]ll I have to say is 'Come' and I have all the men I need for the work."[32]

Almost lost amid the unexpected events in that first week of April were two important changes in the command structure of the larger force in which the 1st Vermont was a member. First, on April 4, Nathaniel Banks was authorized to act independently. His area of operations was called the Department of the Shenandoah and comprised "that portion of Virginia and Maryland lying between the Mountain Department and the Blue Ridge."[33] While coordination would be essential between the two commanders, Banks was no longer McClellan's subordinate. These changes came just the men's spirits got a needed lift: John Hatch arrived to command a newly formed cavalry brigade, consisting of regiments from Michigan, Maine, Vermont, and New York.

One of the ironies of the Vermont Cavalry's impending appearance in battle was that much of the strategic planning which brought them to the scene of action in mid–April occurred outside of their commander's control. Decisions made by Lincoln, McClellan, Lee, and Jackson — and long ago by Mother Nature — would dictate Banks' responses. In

Following the war, pastoral tranquility would return to the war-ravaged lands, but for the duration of the conflict, Massanautten Mountain would maintain a formidable presence southeast
of Strasburg and southwest of Front Royal, watching over all martial traffic passing along the
Valley Turnpike within its shadow (Library of Congress).

the president's case, his ever-present concern for the safety of Washington consistently
restricted the Army of the Shenandoah's latitude to maneuver. The specter of Banks'
being outfought always made Lincoln fearful of a rebel thrust from the west. In turn,
decisions made by General McClellan in the Peninsular Campaign affected the war in the
Valley. Successes by the Army of the Potomac against Richmond would make Lincoln
breathe easier about his own capital and lessen pressure against Banks. Conversely, any
delay or failure by McClellan would proportionally raise the president's anxieties about
Banks' status, for Lee might divert forces west to tip the balance against him.

But it would be "Stonewall" Jackson, working in concert with nature, who had the
most profound effect upon the fortunes of Nathaniel Banks. Jackson had planted the first
seeds of concern at Kernstown. With his smaller force, he had attacked Union troops on
March 23 near Winchester. Though he lost that engagement, Jackson's defeat was coun-
terbalanced by the increased cautiousness his bold stroke put into the already hesitant
steps of Banks' advance, the heightened paranoia roiling in Lincoln's mind, and the disrupting effect on the delicately balanced execution of McClellan's plans. The Confederate leader's gamble at Kernstown paid dividends not often accruing to the losing

commander. As Jackson began his slow withdrawal up the Shenandoah Valley, General Banks seemed satisfied with letting him set the tempo. Much to the consternation of Lincoln and McClellan, Banks advanced at a snail's pace. He had at least some justification: his long lines of logistics, stretching back to Washington, were not yet operating smoothly and reliably. Factor in the vagaries of the weather, which ranged from sunny and warm one day to snow or hail the next, and it could be argued that conditions were not optimal for an aggressive push by anyone, let alone the cautious Banks.

But there was yet another profoundly inhibiting factor weighing heavily against any advance. Unlike inclement weather or an interrupted supply line, this one was not going to go away. Tens of thousands of years ago, when the forces of nature shaped the topography of western Virginia, they fashioned a most useful ally for the Confederacy known as Massanutten Mountain. A massive stone range extending southwestward for fifty miles from Strasburg almost to Harrisonburg, the outcropping could be crossed at only one point, a road running through a gap that connected New Market in the Valley proper with Luray fifteen miles to the east. This breach lay thirty miles below Strasburg and twenty above Harrisonburg. The importance assumed by the imposing Massanutten was that it ran parallel to the Allegheny range in the west and the Blue Ridge Mountains to the east, thereby creating two valleys. Through the larger valley between the Alleghenies to the west and the Massanutten ran the North Fork of the Shenandoah, while to the east the Shenandoah's South Fork flowed between the Blue Ridge and the Massanutten, forming the smaller Luray Valley. Any movement from Strasburg to Harrisonburg up the Shenandoah Valley by Banks meant having the Massanutten Range towering to his left. Of significance to Banks, who would advance via the Valley Pike, was not so much the unfortifiable and uncrossable Massanutten but rather intrigues being plotted out of sight in the valley beyond.

That the mountain could shield clandestine activity was entirely possible, since the road connecting Luray west to the Valley Pike at New Market through Massanutten Gap also accessed a road to the north along the eastern side of the Massanutten range. Utilizing this alternate route, an army could eventually rejoin the main turnpike at Strasburg. In effect, Massanutten Mountain acted as a huge screen, capable of shielding Banks' worst nightmare: a rebel force moving north through the Luray Valley while his own moved south in the Shenandoah. If a circumlocution was ever completed, an enemy force once in his front could eventually reappear behind him, sitting comfortably astride his lines of communication and supply, not to mention his avenue of retreat.

But if Banks ever fully committed his men to action, he would have other strategic concerns, again compliments of the topography. Eighty miles southwest of Strasburg, Staunton was a worthy objective, for the capture of this upper valley town would sever a vital railroad line to Richmond. However, any Union advance that deep into the Valley added another byway of which to be wary in the same manner as the New Market-Luray road through Massanutten. This second route to the east skirted the southern end of the Massanutten, connecting Harrisonburg with Conrad's Store. From this crossroads, an army could travel north to Luray and from there access the available tactical options. Even if an enemy force had no designs on effecting an end-around with Luray as its pivot point, the position at Conrad's Store, like Luray, offered an immediate proximity to any adversary passing across its front on the Valley Pike. This situation would present tantalizing possibilities for an opportunistic commander to mount a flank attack.

It was into this broad panorama that the Vermont Cavalry moved on March 31.

Banks was genuinely pleased to see them come, for he had been badgering Secretary Stanton for additional mounted men. His existing allotment was badly worn down by the many demands placed upon them. New arrivals were pressed into immediate service. While protecting supply lines, serving as videttes, exchanging occasional potshots with the enemy, and capturing a few prisoners finally provided active participation in the war, the troopers of the 1st Vermont longed for sustained action. Some of the men still harbored a fear that they might be denied a chance to get in a few good licks. Sergeant Ide was among this number, noting in mid–April that "it was generally thought that the war would soon end and it would be doubtful if we should get a chance to help crush the Rebellion."[34] Josiah Grout later remembered these days as being a time when "we amused ourselves as best we could by gazing at the south bound tracks of Jackson's army, calculating the probable number of days before McClellan would enter Richmond, and wondering whether we would have a chance to do any actual fighting before the war closed."[35] But for the first two weeks of April, firefights with Ashby's command provided about the only significant action. However, the status quo was about to change.

On the 15th of April, Banks finally committed to an advance. Much to the men's satisfaction, the cavalry assumed the lead. Edenburg would be the jumping off point for the big push against Jackson. The immediate objective was New Market and its vital location at the crossroads of the Valley Turnpike and the Luray Valley road. So swiftly was the decision made and orders given to the 1st Vermont that "the tents were left standing with the sick, camp guard, and deadbeats; in all 100 men or more."[36] That night the men camped by the side of the road, "standing to horse" in the event that any sudden movement was required. They were off at four in the morning on Wednesday the 16th. The unusual hour, building excitement, and gathering momentum created an occasion indelibly etched in the minds of many Vermonters. One trooper recalled the setting vividly: "We all felt like heroes, when we all started out. It was bright moonlight; and as we came out of the woods, the band of the Second Massachusetts was playing splendidly; and the music and the moonlight and the long lines of bright bayonets, made a fine scene for one to grow romantic over."[37] By evening, lead elements were at Edenburg, seven miles from Mt. Jackson, where a key bridge over the North Fork of the Shenandoah was located.

The setting sun that spring day witnessed a continuing Union buildup. All of the assembled troops remained in a constant state of readiness, prepared to move out instantly. For the cavalry, this meant that horses stayed saddled. The ground would be the soldiers' bed. Sentries were on full alert. The cool night air was alive with tension and anticipation. "Some tried to snatch a little sleep, but our thoughts were too busy with the probable events of the morrow to permit rest."[38] With midnight approaching, glory awaited just a matter of hours and a few miles down the pike.

6

Mt. Jackson
A Reputation Is Born

The day of reckoning began a few minutes past midnight on Thursday, April 17, 1862. Muted orders were given. Preparations to move out were quickly made. By moonlight, the Vermonters gathered up their gear and checked their horses' fittings. In the lead of 15,000 men, the regiment's spirits were high. At long last, they were going into action! George Benedict aptly described how "the column moved forward ... under whispered commands, though the tramp of hoofs and rumble of artillery must have announced to all around that a heavy force was in motion."[1] While maintaining secrecy was desirable, the missteps of inexperienced men, their fumblings in the darkness, and the size of their force conspired to render any element of surprise wishful thinking.

General Banks had finally cast away all abandon! They were advancing against Jackson's troops dug in on the hills ahead. A few forward troops were stationed at Mt. Jackson, six miles southwest down the Valley Turnpike. Closing this gap would not take long over the gently undulating and frequently curving roadway from Edenburg to Mt. Jackson. As for Mt. Jackson, topography defined the hamlet's location. Mill Creek, on its southwestern border, emptied into the larger North Fork of the Shenandoah River. Yearly, the small tributary's waters were deepened by the spring thaw, though not enough to pose an obstacle. The broader Shenandoah flowed along the eastern side of the town. Across the river towered the massive Massanautten. To the west, the land rose upward to Little North Mountain and then on to the Alleghenies. Populated by several hundred souls at the war's outbreak, the picturesque little community had been named in honor of President Andrew Jackson.

Astride the Valley Turnpike, Mt. Jackson was in the path of warring armies throughout the conflict. Its strategic importance came from being the southern terminus of the Manassas Gap Railroad, an abbreviated trunk of the Orange and Alexandria Railroad. Branching off at Manassas Junction, the secondary track ran slightly northwest to Strasburg and then southwest to Mt. Jackson for approximately eighty miles. From Mt. Jackson to Staunton there existed a forty-two mile gap until the tracks of the Virginia Central Railroad picked up service. While plans existed to join the two sections, by the outbreak of the conflict all that had been accomplished was to survey the proposed route and grade the portion between Mt. Jackson and Harrisonburg.

As Banks' army advanced southward in the spring of 1862, Confederate authorities strove to move engines and rolling stock ahead of the invaders, trying to save irreplaceable equipment. Over time, a significant accumulation of railroad property grew in the yards at Mt. Jackson. With the outnumbered Confederates slowly retreating, not only did Mt. Jackson appear likely to be captured but also its assemblage of valuable railroad materiel. Considering these possibilities, the decision was made to save as many of the train components as possible. Through tireless effort, several engines and freight cars were moved overland. However, by the predawn darkness of April 16, these rescue efforts were over. Belatedly, rebel forces tried to destroy what remained. Horace Ide saw the same phenomenon, noting that the "army had reached Edenburg and about daylight saw the smoke arise from the rolling stock of the Manassas Railroad that the rebels were burning at Mt. Jackson."[2]

Previously, Union forces had not advanced with any celerity. The snail's pace of Banks' advance was attributable in part to his overly cautious nature, but certainly the skilled delaying actions authored by Captain Turner Ashby contributed. A member of the rebel force, the Rev. James Avirett, observed how "Ashby had been engaged in an ongoing game of cat and mouse in retreating down the Valley as Jackson's rearguard," commenting further that Ashby's "mode of retreating from one position to another was as novel as it was perilous to the enemy."[3] Turner Ashby, one of the Confederacy's earliest heroes, was a gifted leader of cavalry. In resisting the Union advance, he seemed to intuitively know when and where to make a stand. When enemy pressure became too strong, he ordered a retreat until the next bend in the road, outcropping of rock, or hill afforded another suitable position from which to renew resistance. Should the enemy retreat, then Ashby's men would follow, ready to contest the same turf all over again.

A halt was called at 3:00 A.M. Trooper Blinn recalled sitting in silence, awaiting the next move in the unfolding drama. At the first light, officers reconnoitered the enemy's position. Smoke was seen curling up, revealing the rebels' efforts to destroy equipment and supplies. Confederate artillery located on the heights could be seen as well as heard. A Federal battery was sent forward to open up counterfire. Then the much-anticipated orders arrived. The air was electric with anticipation as word went down the line: have the cavalry prepare to charge!

At this epic moment in the history of the 1st Vermont, a memorable send-off was given to the regiment: "As we were filing past the column of infantry to advance at Mt. Jackson, having been ordered by General [James] Shields to charge and save the bridge over the Shenandoah, threatened by Ashby and his regiment, I remember hearing the men of an Indiana Regiment call out: 'Let the Green Mountain Boys go at them. They are all sons of Ethan Allen and will show the Michigan boys something new.'"[4] It was a source of spine-tingling pride for these untested, nervous troopers to have such words of encouragement echoing in their ears as they bravely moved forward to test their mettle in battle.

Cognizant of the lead role which they were about to play, young Frank Platt, the captain of Company A, was motivated to address his men with words that befit the import of the moment: "Boys, I want you to remember that no one is to leave this ground tonight, and, if any man leaves, I shall call him a coward as long as he lives."[5] Clear, pointed, and laconic, he cut straight to the heart of the matter. Pride and honor were put on the line. While individuals in his regiment had previously been under fire, it had been desultory and ineffective. But if the rebels up ahead resisted, the moment of destiny when the regiment would receive its baptism of fire was imminent. Five companies were set to make the foray. Hindsight being 20/20, the captain really need not have worried. The 1st Vermont Cavalry would establish for itself a reputation as being a stalwart, dependable, and

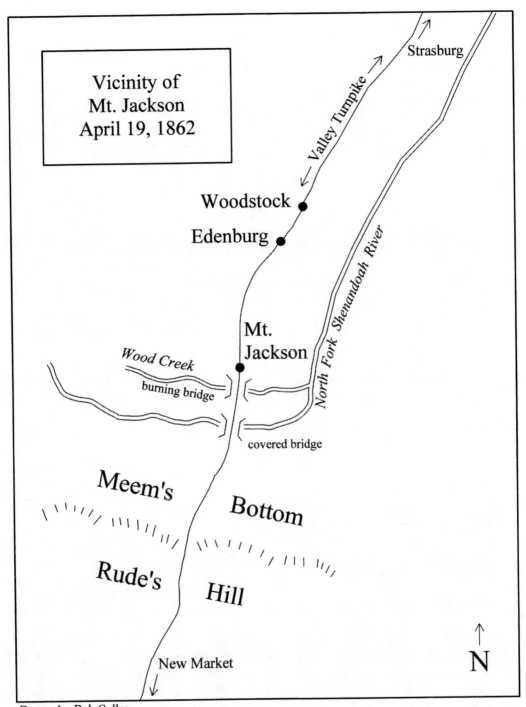

Vicinity of
Mt. Jackson
April 19, 1862

Strasburg

Valley Turnpike

Woodstock

Edenburg

North Fork Shenandoah River

Wood Creek

Mt.
Jackson

burning bridge

covered bridge

Meem's

Bottom

Rude's

Hill

New Market

N

Drawn by Bob Collea

brave regiment. The proof, of course, all lay in the future. But, in a matter of minutes, the cornerstone of their fame was about to be laid. Charles Blinn probably expressed the feelings of many of his brethren-in-arms when he entered the following thought in his diary: "Having never smelt powder before, we were somewhat timid for fear someone would get hurt."[6]

Then the long-awaited order rang out crisply and clearly: "Draw sabers!" Metal slid against metal as five hundred swords were unsheathed from scabbards. Adrenaline silently rushed through veins as 500 hearts beat faster. "Then the order was given ... to clear the road for the Vermont Cavalry," Private Henry Smith vividly remembered, "and away they went, led by Lt. Col. Kellogg, yelling so loud they could be heard for two miles."[7] The long blue line leaped forward, 125 horses in length from beginning to end. With the troopers riding in a column of fours, the advance was strung out for a quarter mile. At first they trotted. Then they galloped. Gathering momentum, the regiment's speed increased to a dead-run as they swiftly covered the mile-and-a-half into the town, all the while accompanied by much "cheering and screaming in the wildest excitement."[8]

This was the way they had always imagined it! This was why they had enlisted in the cavalry. It was a horse soldier's "Kodak moment" if there ever was one, imprinted indelibly in each participant's mind for the rest of his life. In the recollection of Private Lyman Wright, "We was ordered to make a charge thru the town when we got thare tha [they] began to fire in to ous [us] the bals come close to my hed [head]."[9] Being in the midst of the charge as Wright was, sight was not the only sense activated. The sound of pounding hoofs on the roadway, the gritty taste of dust in the air, the feel of a muscled mount beneath, and the smell of gunsmoke combined to fill his brain with a profuse sensory montage that was intermixed with loud gunshots, buzzing bullets, wild yelling, and parched throats. Though admittedly very early in a war that would come to witness many cavalry engagements on a much grander scale than this limited sortie, General Shields himself was nevertheless supposed to have described the event as "the finest cavalry charge he ever saw."[10]

As the juggernaut thundered into the village, burning trains of lumber could be seen off to the right. Shots rang out from a house as the troopers careened passed. On their left, they flew by a recently constructed hospital complex. Coming up on their right was the town's little Union Church. Directly ahead, rebel cavalry were beating a hasty retreat out the opposite end of town. At this point, Lt. Colonel Kellogg ordered a halt. Since General Shields' orders specified the cavalry's furthest advance to be the village proper, the objective had been achieved. But fate intervened. Whether it was due to the sight of their departing foe, the passion of the moment, or the momentum of the charge, not everyone reined in his horse. Some continued in hot pursuit of the rebels, who threw a few shots of discouragement at the oncoming Vermonters. Undeterred, troopers in Company A under Lieutenant Joel Earhardt, Company B commanded by Captain George Conger, and a portion of Company D led by Lieutenant William Cummings stayed on the enemy's heels.

Their energized chase took them quickly through the small burg. Barreling out of the south end of town, the Yankees passed John Koontz' sturdy two-story home. With the house on the cavalry's right as they rounded a downsloping curve that went slightly to the left and then swung back to the right, the Vermonters reached the banks of Mill Creek. According to an eyewitness, in the first portion of their charge to glory the Vermont troops "dashed wildly through a deep creek, whose bridge was on fire, and gained the surface of a plain half a mile in length. Here the race was for life, with the rebels having some forty yards start. Our horses were evidently the fleetest, and the scene was exciting to the highest degree."[11] It was at this juncture that the early morning's activities ratcheted up a notch. What had started as the rapid investment of a lightly defended town was about to broaden in scope. A direct clash loomed between Ashby's rearguard and the Federal spearhead. Finally, the Vermonters were afforded an opportunity to close with an elusive enemy!

The skirmish site was about a mile southwest of Mt. Jackson and 1200 yards past the Mill Creek crossing, with a level stretch of land and then a small hill visually separating the smaller stream from the substantially deeper river ahead. The focal point of the developing action was a yet unseen covered bridge, highly reminiscent of those found in abundance across New England. It was the very same kind of structure that Vermonters crossed innumerable times in the course of their civilian lives. But soon the friendly, bucolic feelings evoked from childhood by the sight of this traditional 19th century symbol were about to be intruded upon and supplanted by new associations: the uncertainty, tension, and fear that impending battle brings. There would be those who would never look at a covered bridge again without recalling Mt. Jackson. The turnpike ran straight and true from the northeastern, or Mt. Jackson, side through the southwestern portal and then crossed about a mile-and-a-half of bottomlands, until it went up a hill and on toward New Market. At a length of 125 feet, it was an impressive structure, spanning the turbulent waters of the North Fork of the Shenandoah River.

The bridge's vital importance was derived from the impassable barrier that the water would present if the wooden structure were destroyed. For the Confederates, eliminating the bridge created a defensive moat, while for the Union forces an intact span allowed continued pressure against Jackson's army. The strategy was therefore quite simple for Banks' army: to drive their enemy from the hill, they had to reach the hill; to get to the hill, they had to cross the river; and to cross the river, they had to take the bridge. Well aware of the strategic implications, Ashby was intent upon creating a schism. As a part of his tactics to slow down the Union advance, bridge destruction was a primary means of interdiction. In fact, he had been so successful at it that the North Fork Bridge was the only original structure still standing on the route south from Harpers Ferry to Mt. Jackson! The duty of carrying out such important assignments was often given to the most trusted individual around. In this case, Captain Ashby himself shouldered the responsibility, selecting as his means of destruction one of nature's oldest forces—fire.

The Vermont cavalrymen, rigorously pursuing the retreating rebels, came over the crest of the intervening hill and abruptly found themselves looking down on the North Fork Bridge. The distance was but a few hundred feet, all of it sloping downhill, the turnpike entering the span on a slight angle with no intervening flatland. Below them, a dozen or so Confederates prepared to fire the structure. A battery led by nineteen-year-old Captain Robert Chew protected the bridge-burners. In Chew, the Vermonters were facing one of the rising stars in the Confederate service. A former student of Jackson's at the Virginia Military Institute, Captain Chew had helped revive the concept of horse artillery. A highly mobile unit using lightweight guns, its cannoneers rode their battery's horses into battle. This technique increased the men's ability to arrive on the scene with their weapons while it decreased the time required to make the guns operational. The assignment at the bridge was tailor-made for their services. They could come up fast, lay down supporting fire, and then depart quickly.

The rebels saw the approaching Yankees. Combustibles were stacked against the wooden structure and awaited but the touch of a torch, which was instantly applied when the Federals hove into view. The rebel horse artillery opened fire. Sizing up the situation, Lieutenant Earhardt ordered a charge. Down the sloping pike they swept, riding pell-mell toward the bridge as smoke started to curl up from flames licking at the tinder. In an

One of the young and enthusiastic Vermonters in the Mt. Jackson charge, Sgt. Henry E. Smith would maintain his zeal for the cause, reenlist in '64, and serve for the duration (USAMHI).

instant the Vermonters clattered onto the bridge deck and collided full-force with the enemy. Yankee and Rebel horsemen exchanged gunfire in its dim confines. Confusion reigned supreme. Horses stumbled in the melee, throwing their riders.

It was this stage of the battle that Private Ralph Straw, known then as "Ralph W. Merrill," described in a letter home: "[W]e saved the first bridge that has been saved on the Shenandoah river. 8 of us went through and took a cannon that was in the other end and blazing away at us. It killed 2 horses and wounded 1 man.... I am sure I killed one man at Mt. Jackson and I will kill some more before I leave the state."[12] In testament to bureaucratic insensitivity, after eighteen-year-old Private Merrill/Straw was missing in action a month later during Banks' Retreat, his parents' application for a pension was denied because "Ralph Straw" was listed as a deserter in the fall of 1861 from the 4th New Hampshire Volunteers. The fact that he later enlisted, fought, and died as a member of Company D, 1st Vermont Cavalry, as "Ralph Merrill," however, carried no weight. It was overridden and negated by the fact that the Pension Bureau refused to "recognize the legality of this enlistment nor any claim for service rendered there under. The law views him as in continuous state of desertion during the whole period of this enlistment."[13] This must have all come as a further shock to his already grieving parents. Those poor folks had believed by virtue of their son's correspondence in early January that he had been "transferred" from the infantry to the cavalry, citing as one of his reasons that it was "better to drill on horseback than to be stuck on foot."[14] Unfortunately for them, young Ralph was prone to exaggeration and capable of outright prevarication. To wit, he wrote in a January letter of being "in a skirmish the other day where the balls flew as thick as hail around my head," his flight of fancy even going so far as to include the boast that "there is no lead or steel enough in the South to draw a drop of blood from me."[15] Contrary to Merrill's recollection or fantasies, no shots would be fired in anger at the 1st Vermont for another three-and-a-half months.

That he could have participated in the fighting at Mt. Jackson is plausible — all, that is, except for the capture of any artillery piece and the death of a rebel, but then Private Merrill just couldn't help himself. He had to embellish even when it was unnecessary! In the end, though, he did not have to gild the lily, for his death in battle needed no artificial accentuation. It stood on its own merit. But unfortunately for Ralph Merrill, who on his last day left this earth a hero, Ralph Straw's enigmatic life made it impossible for Merrill's sacrifice to be properly recognized. That he was guilty of desertion is technically correct. The government held firm to this position, though young Straw had viewed his unauthorized career change as simply an upgrade. For the seven dollar a month pension involved, his former employer chose to stand on principle rather than give in to compassion.

But Ralph Merrill's saga was just a future postscript amidst the more pressing issues then at hand. Unbeknownst to the Vermonters, the man before them wielding a torch was none other than Turner Ashby. In the face of a more rapid Union advance than anticipated, the dismounted guard accompanying Ashby scattered. Caught alone, the fabled leader appeared a goner as he faced the onrushing enemy. As the Reverend Avirett described the succeeding events, "[F]our troopers rode up to him, ordering his surrender. Firing, they missed him, but one ball went through his horse's lung. Just then a dismounted man shot the foremost assailant, then the second and the third were shot and the fourth rode away."[16]

His refusal to surrender and the hairbreadth nature of his escape added to the aura already surrounding Ashby. His heroics did regrettably cost him his powerful white charger, Tom Telegraph. Fatally wounded, the stouthearted animal nevertheless remained faithful to the end, carrying his master to safety before expiring. As lucky as Ashby was to escape, one of his subordinates was not as fortunate. Among the four rebels captured in the furious action about the bridge was a young lieutenant, initially thought to have been Ashby himself. But he turned out to be Ashby's adjutant. In spite of disappointment in not bagging a richer prize, the little vignette did produce one of the regiment's first heroes, Corporal John Chase. Braving the storm of fire in the bridge, Chase pursued two retreating rebels, rode them down, and took both prisoner at gunpoint.

This personal adventure by Corporal Chase was a sidebar in the larger action that saw Union troopers emerge from the covered bridge in hot pursuit of the Confederates, who were heading across a plain towards a hill about a mile away. The flatland between the bridge's southwesterly exit portal and the hill encompassed a "meadow ... a mile or so square, and in the spring of the year ... one of the grandest sights in America."[17] To the locals this beautiful spot was known as Meem's Bottoms, while the upland where Ashby and his men sought refuge from their pursuers was called Rude's Hill. Rising roughly 100 feet above the flats, it afforded a sweeping view from east to west across the Valley from the Massanautten to the Blue Ridge. From this prominence, artillery could rake the lowland. Any hostile force trying to take Rude's Hill would do so only under a hail of iron. As the Vermont cavalry traversed the flats, shells from enemy artillery rained down. Then off the hill came Ashby's cavalry, having reversed its direction and gained reinforcements. This action would constitute the second phase of the bridge engagement. The beautiful meadow at this moment had the unfortunate possibility of becoming a killing field. In the face of this barrage, the 1st Cavalry grudgingly retreated back to the Mt. Jackson side of the bridge. The rebels swarmed in and immediately picked up where they had left off, renewing efforts to burn the structure down.

The skirmish could have concluded right then and there. Certainly the bridge would have been destroyed and the Union advance stymied. Yet no one would have faulted the Vermonters for failing to prevent it, as they had already extended their efforts beyond the original order. But this was not to be the case. Displaying the doggedness that would become a hallmark, they were not yet ready to let the enemy have his way with the bridge. More heroics were still to come. Seeing that the enemy was again in control of the bridge, Chaplain Woodward turned back, seeking reinforcements. No ordinary "Messenger of God" was he. At fifty-two, Woodward was one of the regiment's elders. But this man of the cloth never looked at age as an impediment, for he was often found in the thick of action. Due to his combativeness this day as well as in future engagements, admirers in his regimental congregation labeled him their "fighting preacher." A journalist would later praise the good chaplain for the militaristic bent he displayed at Mt. Jackson, making the case that there was not much call for any preaching that day but plenty of need for fighting! Of this he wrote: "If you ever saw the Chaplain, reader, I will answer you that if you should you would know at a glance that the fiery energy of the man must have vented. He could not consent to do nothing."[18] In a later era, the constrictions of the Geneva Convention would have frowned upon men of the cloth actively trying to save souls clad in blue one moment while in the next just as passionately trying to take those dressed in gray. But such were the passions of the times that even a minister got caught up in the fray.

Chaplain Woodward's quest for support was rewarded when he found Major Collins with two companies. A detachment was ordered to accompany the minister back toward the North Fork Bridge. With all of the drama and sense of timing that would have made a Hollywood director proud, Lieutenant Joel Earhardt, rebel bullets whizzing past his head, yelled to these men, "Will you go with me and save that bridge?" to which they reportedly responded in rousing unison, "We will!"[19] In an instant, orders were given, sabers drawn, a bugle sounded, and a charge was off down the hill again toward the bridge. The final phase of the struggle had begun. Once again, the rebels dispersed rapidly in the face of a furious onslaught. Heedless of the fire and smoke, the Vermonters raced across the bridge and out onto the plain. They chased their departing foe until renewed fire from the hilltop batteries necessitated a withdrawal. "We went within 10 rods of thare canons," Private Wright later disclosed to his sisters, "one shell burst over my hed and a pese [piece] of it struck my hors on his neck but did not hurt him much."[20] This time, however, they withdrew only to the bridge, not back across it.

Having again wrested the span from the Confederates, they had no intentions of giving it back without a fight. For a few minutes, though, doubt existed about how much of the structure would actually be reclaimed, for flames were licking briskly about its weathered sides. Several quick-thinking troopers dismounted, grabbed their horses' nosebags, and ingeniously employed them as buckets to transport river water for dousing the conflagration. It was during this firefighting effort that George Fay of Company B received what amounted to the severest wound suffered among the Vermonters that day. According to his comrade George Austin, their company charged across the burning bridge, and, after reaching the opposite end, "was ordered to dismount and extinguish the fire."[21] "The enemy was shelling us very hard," he remembered, "and while [he was] engaged in extinguishing the fire a piece of shell or wood from the bridge struck ... George ... in the side of his head."[22] The object "struck the left side of his head, lacerating the scalp very extensively and producing a severe concussion of the brain."[23] Private Fay recovered and remained with the regiment, though sporting a five-inch scar to remind him of Mt. Jackson for the rest of his life.

At this point, the seesaw contest ended. Though rebel skirmishers kept up a long-range fire from the plain, once Union artillery was brought up, its ominous presence put to rest any thoughts Ashby entertained of a second counterattack. Still, the Confederates maintained a bellicose posture, throwing shells from Rude's Hill over the meadow toward the bridge. Whatever they possessed in zeal, unfortunately for their cause, turned out to be utterly lacking in effectiveness as their barrages were thwarted by what the Vermonters took to be defective shells. As reported by one eyewitness, a shell did in fact pass "directly through the bridge, and another exploded so near our dashing lieutenant as to bespatter him completely from head to foot without doing him any serious damage."[24] One projectile did detonate "in the bridge while six men were in it" but they miraculously suffered no injuries.[25] Among this lucky half-dozen shaken but unharmed troopers was Lyman Wright, who probably did nothing for his family's peace of mind when he shared with them his involvement in the incident: "[A] shell burst in the bridge whilst i was in it." He marveled that "it was one of the grate wonders in the world that some of us did not git kilt."[26] In fact, the overall paucity of casualties for the Vermont Cavalry that day was truly amazing. A few men who were banged around and bruised when their mounts fell appeared to account for most of them. As the war progressed, injuries suffered in mishaps involving horses occurred with a maddening frequency, rendering otherwise fit soldiers unable to fight. Wright confirmed two injuries of which he knew, these being when "Henry Patterson['s] hors fell and hurt him some and Oris Knight got hurt some."[27] The Regimental Day Book noted cryptically that "one horse and equipment [were] lost in a skirmish at Mt. Jackson."[28] For the Confederates, the tally amounted to several wounded, a half dozen captured, a few horses killed, the field lost, and of course a bridge surrendered.

By early afternoon, the day's fighting had concluded. In the saddle and on the move since midnight, most of the men had experienced twelve to fourteen hours of virtually nonstop attention to duty. For many there had been no pause to rest, let alone eat. Having saved the bridge proved to be both a blessing and a bane to weary cavalrymen. While its capture meant that the enemy could be aggressively pursued, it also meant that the best time to do this was immediately. Since the rebels were in retreat, the logical decision was to seize the moment and continue the chase immediately. Thus the Union advance pushed forward, halting for the night only three miles north of New Market. "In the afternoon, we tride to cut off the rebels but tha run to fast for ous" was how Lyman Wright remembered the day's activities for the 1st Vermont coming to a close.[29] As the men prepared their bivouac, Private Blinn observed that they did so "with the feeling of having done our duty nobly," noting with a degree of extra satisfaction that "the ground upon which we repose our weary limbs was occupied by the enemy last night."[30]

Before the men drifted off to sleep, many lingered over a last cup of coffee or a pipe of tobacco. In twos, threes, and small groups, they relived the day's stirring events. In the soft glow of campfires were shared observations and thoughts gathered from hundreds of different perspectives on the day's experiences. Tired as the soldiers were, the high that came with having survived their first combat generated a rush that did not subside easily. Consensus surely had it that there had been heroes aplenty. Lieutenant Joel Earhardt was one name on everyone's lips for leading two gallant charges against the bridge. Chaplain John Woodward deserved a share of recognition for bringing the reserves in the nick of time. Additionally, some had witnessed the good reverend's inspiring coolness under fire when, after his cape fell off in the retreat back to the bridge following its first capture, he calmly dismounted and retrieved his lost article of clothing, all in the face of the onrushing enemy. Trooper Elijah Page "received a gunshot wound in the right leg below the knee," the first of a remarkable four injuries that he would suffer in the first four months of combat![31] Corporal John Chase was surely extolled for single-handedly capturing two enemy soldiers. Captain Frank Platt and Lieutenant William Cummings were singled out for their courage in riding alongside Earhardt in the second charge. Those who saw him could not forget the reckless but brave Captain George Conger, who "crossed the bridge and was the craziest man you ever saw," it being all his men "could do to keep him from charging on the enemies batteries alone."[32] Captain Addison Preston was seen exhibiting personal bravery in the fight. Private Austin Freeman, after his horse had stumbled and thrown him to the ground at the bridge's entrance, was due laurels for running over to a rebel trying to light the kindling, grabbing the man by the throat, and taking him prisoner. Not to be forgotten, somewhere in all of this were the Rogers brothers. While singularly undistinguished, but at the very least as brave members of Company B, they had participated in the two glorious charges against the North Fork Bridge, forays that Ashby himself witnessed and is alleged to have referenced the second as being "a desperate charge."[33] Suffice it to say, by their courage alone, Mark and William did the family proud!

In addition to recounting deeds of daring, the Vermont boys would rehash among themselves the events of the skirmish as they either participated in them or witnessed them. Few would disagree that, yes indeed, it had been a very good day to be one of the cavalry boys. They had finally "seen the elephant," and to the last man had all lived to tell about it. It was best to savor the feelings of triumph and relief now, for there would be precious few days in the three years of war that lay ahead when an engagement would not result in losses of some kind. While certainly the hundreds of randomly fired pistol balls, rifle bullets, and artillery shells expended by the enemy at Mt. Jackson could have at any time mortally wounded members of the charging Vermonters, the gods of war were most kind to them this day. It was almost as if the cavalry was given the unique opportunity to experience the ordeal of battle, while at the same time being spared the pain and death that often accompanies it. Of course, the fight had been dangerous, and no one in his right mind would have predicted a bloodless triumph. But that, in the final accounting, was the welcome reality this day.

The entire engagement at Mt. Jackson probably lasted about an hour. What, then, are we to make of the day's events? Clearly, in terms of numbers engaged, time elapsed, and ground covered, it was but a skirmish. The events that April day did not significantly alter the outcome of the campaign in progress or the war overall. Granted, preserving the bridge did permit General Banks to press his pursuit of General Jackson. In the words of one proud trooper, "We ... saved a bridge over the North Branch of the Shenandoah, which has since been of incalculable importance to us in transporting our army stores."[34] It was in that sense an unequivocal tactical triumph. Against the panorama of the Civil War, it was a noteworthy but not notable event.

Yet, although this little contest may have lacked significance in terms of impact on the war, it was most assuredly a seminal event in the history of the 1st Vermont Cavalry. It represented their initial exposure to sustained gunfire and artillery shelling. Proof was in evidence that the months of hard drilling had paid off handsomely. The discipline instilled by Colonel Platt, General Hatch, and Colonel Holiday had brought immediate returns. The cornerstone of an enduring reputation was firmly laid. As one soldier proudly boasted to the homefolks, "This affair gave the Vt boys quite a name at once in the Division."[35] In spite of the unexpected loss of their leader, the misgivings of Banks, and their lack of combat experience, the men of the 1st Vermont had acquitted themselves superbly. Since the events of April 17 proved to be one of the high-water marks of an otherwise dismal campaign, their contribution became all the more significant. "To you and the forces under your command the Department returns thanks for the brilliant and successful operations of this day" were the words of praise telegraphed by secretary of war Edwin Stanton.[36] Few would dispute that the 1st Vermont Cavalry rightfully earned a fair share of those laurels. These descendants of the fabled Green Mountain Boys had demonstrated an admirable coolness under fire, a steadfast willingness to obey orders, and an unwavering courage in battle that were to become their trademarks throughout the conflict. In the hall of heroes at Valhalla, the conduct of the 1st Vermont Cavalry that April morning must surely have brought a proud smile to the face of Ethan Allen, the old patriot and patron saint of all soldiers from the small state of mighty warriors. Colonel Charles Tompkins would later christen them "fearless riders," and that they surely were, this day and all the days of warfare to follow, from the bridge at Mt. Jackson to the fields of Appomattox Court House.

7

Banks' Advance
The Valley Will Be Ours

By preserving the Mt. Jackson bridge, the 1st Vermont gave General Banks the means to pursue the enemy. With uncharacteristic swiftness, Banks followed the retreating Confederates. Soon his troops had swept on to New Market. In the face of Banks' pressure, Jackson moved his command out of the Valley and into one of the strategic east-west gaps in the mountains: Conrad's Store. Of the two combatants, Jackson faced the greatest urgency because his troops were sorely needed to help save the capital.

But a stalemate existed in the Valley. Banks could advance no further south without exposing his flank; yet Jackson's numerical inferiority prevented him from a head-on engagement. Following Mt. Jackson, mounted probes went out regularly as Banks sought the Confederates' whereabouts. Far from being glorious like the Mt. Jackson charges, these workaday missions were nevertheless dangerous. The morning of the 19th saw Company H reconnoiter in concert with several companies from the 69th Illinois Infantry in the direction of the Massanautten. Pursuing the enemy around the mountain's base, the Vermonters killed a picket, which served to whet the hounds' appetites. What followed was one of those running gun battles often characterizing cavalry engagements. The chase started when the Union's advanced guard came upon a wooden bridge and was fired on by an enemy force some 200 strong. These Confederates were surprised while preparing to torch the structure, thereby eliminating a potential crossing point for Banks. These rebels were a detachment dispatched by Jackson to burn three strategic bridges in the vicinity. Under the command of Jed Hotchkiss, their orders were to set Columbia, Red, and White bridges ablaze. When Lieutenant Frank Huntoon's troopers came unexpectedly upon them, the enemy's incendiary efforts were focused on Columbia Bridge.

A bend in the road had obscured the larger Confederate force from the approaching Vermonters. Suddenly confronted with unfavorable odds, the bold Huntoon surprised the rebels, and quite likely some of his own men, by charging. This aggressiveness interrupted Captain George Sheetz's command, which had "set to work putting hay in the mouth of the bridge and ... set fire to it."[1] Coming hard and fast, the Vermonters delivered a volley. "Some forty-four Federal cavalrymen under Lieutenants Franklin T. Huntoon and Charles A. Adams charged across Columbia Bridge and put out the fire that had already been kindled."[2] In a scene reminiscent of Mt. Jackson, the Yankees not only saved another bridge but also drove the enemy force drove back half a mile, until the rebels made a stand. On came the hard-charging men of Company H. As battle was about to be joined, the enemy fled. The chase resumed for another mile, until Huntoon called a halt. He realized that further pursuit was fraught with danger, as the wild chase had left their supporting infantry far behind. Deep into no-man's-land, the prevailing wisdom was to call it a day. This the company did — except for eleven zealots. Oblivious to orders, they kept going for another mile-and-a-half! Unknown to the Vermonters, the boldness they displayed in charging their foes may not have been the sole reason for their adversaries' hasty departures. While such aggressive tactics were disconcerting, Hotchkiss later confirmed that the rebels' resolve may have been diluted by another cause: too much applejack!

Of those who had ridden out, only one Vermont trooper came back a bit worse off for his experiences that day. This individual was Edward Gee. In the small detachment led by Sergeant Job Corey, Gee was among the supercharged fanatics who kept up the pursuit. For Private Gee, his foolhardiness was halted by an errant rebel bullet. "My horse was shot under me, [and] the horse reared and fell over backwards," Gee recalled, "catching me under him and then rolled over on me so that the pommel of the saddle took me in the left side, right in the region of the heart."[3] Carried to a nearby barn, Gee received immediate treatment from the regimental surgeon. Hospitalized and discharged, continued ill health necessitated convalescence at his brother's residence in Rutland. Tough and determined, Gee subsequently enlisted in the 14th Vermont Infantry and eventually served out the war in the 9th Vermont Infantry.

Without doubt, the mission was successful. Not even a drenching rain dampened spirits. At the highly tolerable cost of two wounded horses, the forty-two riders of 1st Vermont performed admirably. "In all, we captured twelve prisoners, fourteen horses, revolvers, carbines, shotguns, sabres, pitchforks ... in addition to wounding ... a good many of the scamps so that they had to be supported on the retreat" was Private Frank Baldwin's positive assessment.[4] Of equal, if perhaps not greater, importance to Trooper Baldwin was that the good name of the 1st Vermont remained unsullied. He proudly noted in a letter home how "not a man flinched or showed the white feather although they were face to face with the rebels."[5] Equally significant was the fact that no serious injuries were sustained.

For the men of the 1st Vermont, good fortune still persisted after almost a month of frontline duty. Spirits were high. Feelings of invincibility and immortality, often associated with people in the prime of youth, made many a young trooper impervious to danger. Frank Baldwin undoubtedly expressed the thoughts of many comrades when he wrote of the day's events: "We expect to have some more fun directly."[6] War was still an adventure to be embraced rather than feared. In their heart of hearts, they all knew their lives were not charmed. That the Angel of Death would visit them was inevitable. Empty saddles in battle and open spaces around campfires would occur — but these chilling thoughts were not for today. At the close of this Friday, April 19, 1862, the thought that war was still a lark remained for the 1st Vermont.

On the 24th, the regiment moved out under newly appointed chief of cavalry General John Hatch — destination Harrisonburg. As the regiment approached the town, Hatch ordered sabers drawn. "Out came the blades, and then the order came 'Forward, trot,' and we set out at a gallop down the hill towards the village of Harrisonburg (as we afterwards learned) lying about a half mile beneath us."[7] Anticipating another Mt. Jackson, the cavalry thundered into the little burg ready for battle. The rebels offered but token resistance. With the exception of "a few crying women and grinning negroes, the streets were as still as a Northern Sunday."[8] Prepared for battle as they were, the lack of opposition did not disappoint the men. As a member of Company A candidly wrote, "[O]ur brilliant charge was a very pleasant one, giving us all an opportunity to be brave, and no one a chance to be hurt."[9]

Then Saturday, April 27, 1862, dawned. Starting out slowly, the aftermath of its events would indelibly mark the 1st Vermont, finally introducing it to the harshest of all war's grim realities: the blood of a fallen hero. A morning scout went off to McGaheysville. Located ten-and-a-half miles east-northeast around the base of Massanautten Mountain from Harrisonburg, the sleepy hamlet lay near the South Fork of the Shenandoah. The mission's importance was highlighted by its leader's stature and size of his command. General Hatch took direct charge, heading a detachment of approximately 175 men. Companies A, D, and K of the 1st Vermont contributed the bulk of the manpower, along with two batteries and some troopers from a Michigan regiment. Extra muscle was added by two supporting infantry regiments; however, their absence at the rendezvous point caused General Hatch to move ahead without them, ordering that they were to follow post haste.

Contact with the enemy was soon established. The ensuing action escalated rapidly. In some ways, the opening moments were reminiscent of the experiences of Lieutenant Huntoon's patrol of the 21st. On its approach to McGaheysville, Captain Platt's vanguard easily brushed back several of the enemy pickets and entered the town at a gallop, driving rebel cavalry before it. A spirited chase ensued, until the rebels reached their main force. In an instant, the pursuers became the pursued when the rebels "swarmed out of the woods and soon turned the tables so that Company A was soon going the other way as fast as their horses could carry them."[10] Caught up in the original pursuit, Captain Platt had not notified the main body of his company's pell-mell chase, leaving the main column with no inkling of what was transpiring up ahead—until the thunder of hooves, a crackle of gunfire, and shouts of warning came suddenly barreling at them! "But General Hatch gave the order to charge and the men in the front of Company D remaining firm, and returning the fire in a minute the tables were turned again and away we went after them."[11] In an instant replay of the first contact, the rebels beat a hasty retreat back through McGaheysville with Union cavalry in hot pursuit. For the three members of the Baylor clan who rode with the 12th Virginia Cavalry, this counterattack almost ended catastrophically. First, the paterfamilias of the threesome was severely wounded, while son Richard's horse "became unmanageable, and, in plunging, broke the saddle-girth and landed him in the road."[12] As if this was not ignominy enough, Trooper Baylor chose to hide in a rather undignified spot. Scrambling through a house located off the road, he "ran out of the back door, jumped into a chicken-coop and got up on a roost."[13] Though Union troopers scoured the area, even peeking into the hen house, they did not discover his lofty perch.

Meantime, while Richard Baylor sought sanctuary among feathered friends, his retreating comrades had rallied on a steep hill beyond the town. From there, they fired upon their pursuers. Hatch's response to this stiffened resistance was to have his artillerists blast away, hoping to shake his adversaries' resolve. After a few rounds, Company K drew its sabers and advanced. In the regiment's third charge of the day, the pleasurable sight of the enemy taking flight again rewarded the Vermonters. After assessing the situation, General Hatch decided that it would be prudent to withdraw. He was particularly concerned that the lack of infantry support exposed his artillery to a risk that the cavalry could not sufficiently mitigate. Besides, the main objective of his reconnoitering had been accomplished: determining whether or not Confederate forces still held Swift Run Gap.

While the intelligence gathered was useful, the capture of only two prisoners and a solitary horse added no luster. Certainly valuable experience was gained, and the regiment's growing reputation for courage under fire was enhanced. But, in light of the price paid, some would argue that the cost was too high. Company A's loss of Private Stephen Morse, who became a POW when his horse was shot down, was unfortunate but rectifiable in time with his exchange. However, the fate befalling Corporal John Chase did not have a happy ending. Already a hero for his captures at Mt. Jackson, Corporal Chase duplicated this feat in the midst of the second charge at McGaheysville. What made this exploit more astounding than its precursor was that Chase performed this act after being mortally wounded. When the Vermonters rode through the village, someone fired into the passing horsemen. The errant bullet perchance struck John Chase.

For Corporal Chase, it was the course and not the source of the projectile that mattered. Striking him in the hip, the ball passed into his abdominal cavity by way of his bowels. Though he stayed in his saddle, he grew faint from loss of blood and eventually had to be helped down from his horse. As author Stewart Brooks observed in *Civil War Medicine*, "penetrating wounds of the stomach ... were about 90 per cent fatal. In the event the small intestine was involved, death was inevitable."[14] Along with the recognition that such a wound was terminal was the knowledge that considerable pain and suffering would accompany the victim's final hours.

But just as Trooper Chase had a fearless heart, so also did he possess a strong constitution. His toughness permitted him to remain alive for twenty-four hours, until the afternoon of the 27th. Though hearts went out to this popular trooper, all were helpless to do much except see to his comfort. Before passing away, he was visited by General Hatch who, according to Adjutant Edgar Pitkin, was very complimentary. "You noble sufferer, you have been an honor to your state," were the general's words.[15] Corporal Chase's final moments proved to be as inspiring as they were heartrending. In obvious pain but lucid, he managed to tell his company commander, Captain Addison Preston, that of which the dying soldier was inordinately proud: "I took my man, Captain. I took my man. Tell them I tried to do my duty. I believe that it is a just cause. I have tried to do my duty."[16]

When death finally released him from his sufferings, there never seemed to be any doubt that his mortal remains should go home. Members of his company respectfully chipped in towards the cost of the $150 needed to lay out Chase's body in a metallic coffin and have it transported to northeastern Vermont. According to Henry Ide, "We donated our ration money which had accumulated at Annapolis to the amount of $70 and a subscription had been taken in Co. D (to which I gave four gold dollars), and it was understood that Captain Preston had to pay the balance in a few days."[17]

It took until Thursday, May 8, for Chase's corpse to arrive in Danville, Vermont. Though far from his comrades-in-arms, he was surrounded by friends and family amidst the Green Mountains. Not that the deceased made his final ride home alone, for on his final journey he had been accompanied by his fellow trooper and brother, Loren. As preparations for the funeral services were being made, Chase's family took solace in their time of grief from caring words sent by those who had served with John. General Hatch wrote Governor Holbrook a published message, referencing Corporal Chase as being "a man of excellent character, respected by all who knew him."[18] But it was Addison Preston, writing the widowed Julia Chase, who perhaps best put into words what so many felt about the fallen hero: "It becomes my painful duty, to communicate to you, the death of your husband, who died yesterday, from a wound received in a gallant charge upon the enemy on the 27th. The loss to me is great, but to you it must be greater, and the affliction severe. He died a noble death, honored and applauded by the Generals and privates of the Division for his superior bravery and daring. His name is upon all tongues and his reward is in Heaven.... Would we were all as brave as he."[19]

A popular officer who led from the front, Colonel Addison Preston's proclivity for being where the action was would eventually cost him his life at Hawes' Shop, after only two weeks as the new commander of the regiment (Francis C. Guber Collection).

Once the body arrived, services were immediately held at the Methodist church in Danbury. The flag-draped coffin was placed at the head of the nave. On top of the flag "lay the trophies of his bravery and courage — the six-barreled rifle taken from the Lieut, and the sabre from the last rebel taken."[20] The service consisted of carefully selected prayers, appropriate scriptures, suitable dirges, and a heartfelt eulogy. The little church was filled with mourners. Some were there out of respect for a local war hero but most were present because John Chase was one of them. Before the war, he had been active in the congregation. In particular, he had served as the superintendent of the Sabbath School, walking two miles into town every Sunday to teach his students. His pastor saw John Chase as a kind and gentle soul, serving God well through his successful work with children. When this faithful member of his flock decided to enlist, the Reverend McMullen tried to dissuade him, arguing that his church and his family needed him more. But at thirty-seven, Chase was older than most of the 1st Vermont's recruits. Being a mature individual, he did not make decisions lightly, let alone one that carried with it such import. His response, almost predictable for such a devout Christian and loyal American, was that "he had thought over it, and prayed for direction, and the conclusion was, his country demanded his services, and, he would go, and fight for truth and freedom."[21]

From the church, the deceased was borne a half-mile to Greenwood Cemetery for interment with full military honors. An honor guard of soldiers and a band playing martial music led the funeral procession. After a brief graveside ceremony, a volley was fired, and then "the brave soldier was left alone to his glory."[22] The final resting place chosen for Corporal Chase is a beautiful spot. Located just off a country road, the site lies on a hillside in the eastern foothills of the Green Mountains, with a spectacular view across the Connecticut River lowlands to the distant White Mountains. While time has weathered the tall gray-white slab that is this soldier's simple gravestone, it has not diminished the timeless example set by one of Vermont's truest sons. As the mourners departed, they did not leave their beloved John alone. On his left, he had dear company for all eternity. Standing in mute testimony to the fact that this man's life, even before it had ended so abruptly, may not have been a bed of roses was another tombstone engraved with the name Chase. It marked the resting places of his first wife, Catherine, and his five-year-old daughter, Rachel, both of whom had passed away within two weeks of each other during the summer of 1857. A man of lesser faith than John Chase might not have survived these two difficult blows.

Among the last to take leave was Julia Chase, John's second wife of only four years. She must have been a gracious lady, permitting her husband to be laid to rest beside his late spouse. Adding to her stress, she had in tow two stepchildren, six-year old Jennie and eight-year old John, as well as the offspring of her union with John, two-and-a-half-year old Herbert. Like so many others across the land, their lives were forever altered by that briefest of moments when their husbands and fathers went from being living, breathing soldiers to dead and fallen heroes, surely a bittersweet memory of which to be duly proud yet deeply saddened. For John Chase, a man who sacrificed much for what he believed to be a greater good, his epitaph can be found on his tombstone. Only faintly legible now after almost a century-and-a-half of enduring the elements, the fitting inscription for a Christian and soldier reads:

> Servant of God, well done
> Thy glorious warfare is past,
> The battle is fought, the race is run
> And though art crowned at last.[23]

Beyond the shattering effect that Chase's death had upon his family, many in the ranks of the 1st Vermont were given reason to contemplate its implications, too. Certainly there was a brother along with tent mates, company friends, and acquaintances across the whole regiment who would miss this pious, unassuming, and brave man. Riding into battle with a man the likes of John Chase at one's side was always comforting. But more than the loss of this singularly good human being, there was the chilling realization that finally a Vermont trooper had lost his life in combat. As Edgar Pitkin described the eerie feeling, "He was the first one who has fallen from our number and the charm which he secured to surround us is broken."[24]

By the time Corporal Chase was laid to rest in the Green Mountains, much had changed in the Shenandoah Valley. On May 5, Banks decided to pull his command back to New Market. Instead of being only twenty-five miles from Staunton and thereby causing concern for its opponent, the Army of the Valley now sat forty-four miles away. Banks' force now went from being a potential attacker to the possible object of an attack. "Stonewall" Jackson, given an opening, was about to loose the dogs of war. Banks' worst nightmare was about to materialize. Worse yet, this retrograde movement did not even have to be made. From the skirmish at McGaheysville on the 26th until the retreat, there had been no disastrous incidents adversely affecting Banks' troops. The front had witnessed only a continuation of regular patrols and sporadic encounters.

While all may have appeared quiet, Banks' take on circumstances was to the contrary. The general had correctly concluded that his opponent was receiving reinforcements. He also began fretting that his lines of communication were too long. The result was a plan for his army's return to New Market to be put in motion. So quickly was this decision made and implemented that troopers, manning an all-night picket post on the Port Republic road, returned the next morning to find the camp struck and contingents of the army already moving north! Though unrecognized at the moment for what it represented, the apparent success of Banks' tactical withdrawal would in due time be converted into a strategic blunder by Jackson.

On May 11, Banks gave up the ghost of any hope of victory in the Valley. The retreat commenced. Cavalry acted as the rear guard, their mission to delay any pursuers while the slow-moving infantry and wagons gained safety. With mixed emotions, the 1st Vermont performed its duty. Protecting the army's vulnerable rear was an important assignment; however, to find themselves retreating over lands and objectives only recently won was a disheartening turn of events.

8

About Face, March to the Rear
Banks' Retreat Begins

Banks and Jackson shared similar causes for concern. The Confederate's apprehensions were based upon a worst-case scenario: Banks' command moving from the north and joining Fremont's corps heading east from Franklin toward Staunton. This union would give the Northerners a combined force of over 30,000 troops against the Southerners' aggregate of slightly under 20,000. From Banks' perspective, without Fremont's troops, he would be matched against Jackson with an insignificant numerical superiority. As the variables came into play, the big picture in the Shenandoah Valley crystallized. By the end of April, it became clear that the pendulum was now swinging in the rebels' favor. The reversal started once Jackson's army of 6,000 linked up with General Richard Ewell's 8,000 men from the east. Eventually, this force was joined by General Edward Johnson's 3,000 soldiers who had for a time been all that had stood between Fremont's host and defenseless Staunton. Once Jackson committed himself, Banks and Fremont had a brief window of opportunity that could have spared them from the onslaughts that would come, but only if they moved swiftly. A display of aggressive, coordinated troop movements by the Northern commanders could have crushed Jackson's army, driven its remnants from the Shenandoah, and rendered any assistance to the beleaguered Lee inconsequential.

Timing was everything. Jackson was most vulnerable from May 4 to May 7. These were the inclusive dates when his troops first entered Staunton until the eve of their attack against Fremont's advanced elements at McDowell. By sunset on the 8th, one-third of Jackson's mini-army had attacked a portion of Fremont's troops under General Robert Milroy, forcing them to retreat. Jackson then harassed his defeated foe all the way back to Franklin. Now Staunton lay 50 miles away. Any juncture with Banks was going to be down the road if it was going to materialize at all. Of course, a link-up could still occur, but only if Banks was going to be around to be joined.

Removing the potential threat posed by Fremont had necessitated chasing his lead elements back into the mountains. This caused a short-term trade-off. While as of May 12 the Union force was now situated far from Staunton, so also was a part of Jackson's army. Though not quite as golden a moment as the 4th through the 7th had been, an opportunity still beckoned Banks. In temporarily removing himself from the proximity of Staunton, Jackson had left Ewell there with about 11,000 men to oppose Banks' 19,000 troops. Should Banks decide to exploit the situation, Ewell could have found himself in dire straits.

However, as of May 5, Banks had determined that his work in the Shenandoah was done. He no longer gazed south. Instead he focused on points to the east beyond the Valley. Whether he saw joining Washington's defenses or assisting in McClellan's invasion as his eventual destination was moot. That he was preparing to leave was the operative factor. From the moment any thought of pushing his army ahead to Staunton was replaced by an about face, the safety of his men was jeopardized. Once Jackson had eliminated Fremont as a threat, Banks' fate was sealed. The only questions remaining to be answered were where and when the hammer blows would fall. As a part of the Army of the Valley, the 1st Vermont was soon to pay a price for Banks' failings. Until now, outside of Holiday's unexpected suicide and Chase's untimely death, the first month in the war zone had gone well for the regiment. They had acquitted themselves admirably, exhibiting early on that they had both courage and tenacity. The month of May would still bring them the action they craved, but the results would be more costly than they would have preferred.

The cavalry's change of base, though hurried, was conducted without any glitches. Twenty-three army conveyances plus several appropriated farm wagons were used to carry the Vermonters' equipment. The relocation was completed on Sunday, May 4, 1862. The next day, the troopers went into camp along the roadside. Once situated, cavalry life reverted to what had been its normal pattern since entering the Valley. Still, amidst the rounds of routine patrols and foraging expeditions, the events of some days stood out more vividly than others. One of these more noteworthy occasions was an engagement known either as Sommerville Heights or Columbia Bridge, the former being a small hamlet several miles beyond the bridge, while the latter was a covered span over the South Fork of the Shenandoah seven miles southeast of New Market. The fracas began innocently, like so many often did, though it escalated quickly from the level of a seesaw firefight into a heavy skirmish.

In an effort to secure the bridgehead, a brigade of Union infantry was ordered to take up fortified positions around the crossing. In support, Companies A, B, G, and H of the 1st Vermont were posted nearby at Honeyville. Hostile action commenced in the afternoon of May 7 when advancing Confederate forces drove in the Federal videttes posted east of the bridge. This aggressiveness triggered an immediate response by Union general Jeremiah Sullivan, commander of the bridge guard. He ordered a counterattack by six companies from the 13th Indiana Regiment, Colonel Robert Foster commanding. The infantry's push quickly established contact with the main rebel force that fell back in the face of superior numbers. Following the retreating enemy, the Yankees' hot pursuit carried them through Somerville. At this juncture in the running fight, Colonel Foster halted his troops. As a hedge against being caught in a trap somewhere up ahead, the colonel deployed five companies to the high ground off the road at Somerville. One infantry company continued on with the probe. Foster's scaled-down advance went another two-and-a-half miles before halting at a burned bridge. As the Indiana troops were lounging about taking a thirty-minute rest break, Company B of the 1st Vermont rode up to join them.

Foster told Captain George Conger that darkness precluded any further movement against the enemy. The Vermonters' role would now be that of a rear guard. Having communicated these intentions, Colonel Foster marched his Indianans back to Somerville, linked up with their comrades positioned in the heights, and then proceeded another mile back towards Columbia Bridge. They halted there to let the Vermonters close up. But no blue-clad riders materialized. Instead, two single couriers arrived in rapid succession, one from the west and one from the east. The first came from General Sullivan back at Columbia Bridge. Almost as a portent of the news that the second rider would bring, the general alerted Foster to be wary of an enemy ambush by keeping pursuit limited.

Unfortunately, the man who most needed to know what Sullivan had forewarned had already found out — the hard way. The second rider came from Conger. His dispatch was terse and to the point: "We are surrounded; come to our assistance."[1] While getting a relief force up and moving, Foster could be excused if he wondered what had happened. Acting as a rear guard, the cavalry should have followed the same route back that the Indiana infantry had just traversed without incident. From the messenger, Foster learned the disquieting news that "the captain of the cavalry, in direct violation of my orders, instead of following my rear, had gone some 4 miles up the river, and encountered the reserve of the enemy and was surrounded."[2] As intolerable as the disobedience of orders is in the military, this did not hinder for a moment the energy expended to extricate the besieged troopers. In addition to Foster's effort, back at the base camps wheels were turning also. General Sullivan immediately sent two more companies forward, while at Honeyville the Vermont Cavalry saddled up.

The 1st Vermont rode hard, not with any anticipation of arriving in the nick of time but rather as liberators. From the information filtering back, all of Company B had already fallen into the clutches of the enemy. Worse still, Chaplain Woodward was with them. His penchant for wanting to be with his flock had placed him in harm's way. Early in the course of the day's work, Woodward had captured two rebel cavalrymen who had tried to hide in the rooms of a local farmhouse, boldly demanding of one scared youth hiding behind a bedroom curtain, "Jonathan, come out! I want you!"[3] Small wonder that he received the sobriquet of "Fighting Preacher" and was held in such high esteem by his men! In glowing testimony to this unique man of the cloth, one soldier wrote, "We have a splendid chaplain. I consider him a man of sterling worth, of undaunted bravery, perfectly cool in trouble. The music of the balls does not excite him in the least. He will shoot his pistol at the rebels with as good an aim as any private. He encourages the boys with his presence and is just the man for the place."[4]

Thus, driven by a sense of urgency tinged by trepidation, two companies of the 1st Vermont hurried toward Somerville. Concurrent with these efforts, Foster got his men going down the road from whence they had just come. Taking all six companies with him, he again put the bulk of his force in the hills above Somerville, leaving a reserve down on the road. However, from this position, the Indiana troops were destined to advance no further. Rather than bringing any relief to the trapped Vermonters somewhere ahead, they found themselves fighting their own desperate battle with Confederate infantry and cavalry. When the rebels began a flanking movement that jeopardized his lines, Foster countered by pulling his men back. Slowly and grudgingly giving ground, the Union troops fought until darkness caused the warring parties to disengage.

While the relief efforts were getting underway, the 1st Vermont was trying to extricate itself from its predicament. Reducing their maneuverability were twelve infantrymen whom they had picked up along the road, Indianans cut off from Foster's force during his fighting withdrawal. As they moved closer to Foster's embattled men, "Conger found the enemy's infantry filling the road in front between the river on one hand and a precipitous bluff on the other."[5] Conger's immediate impulse was to unsheathe sabers and attack, but subordinates talked him out of this potentially disastrous decision. In the forefront of those advising restraint was Chaplain Woodward. Responding to Conger's expressed intent to order a charge, Woodward said, "If you do, every man will be lost; we must swim the river."⁶ When the captain threatened to shoot any man who opted to follow the chaplain's suggestion, the good reverend stood his ground and told his commander that no one would follow him if he elected to mount an assault. Fortunately, tempers ebbed, cooler heads prevailed, and the tense exchange passed. An escape route was eventually discovered. Though less glorious for all and somewhat undignified for some, it served its purpose. Scouts sent along the riverbank had turned up a spot suitable for crossing. The company then "fled to the river and swam their horses across, an infantryman holding on each horse's tail."⁷

Having made their escape from under the rebel's guns, the weary troopers soon found that their time of trial was not yet over. For when they had almost made it back to the safety of Union lines at Columbia Bridge, darkness descended. Pickets tended to get trigger-happy when they could hear but not clearly see oncoming riders. Even though the Reverend Woodward, who had gained the lines moments ahead of the main body, tried to assure them that the shadowy riders were comrades, friendly fire nevertheless whistled towards Company B. After the Vermonters had quickly retreated beyond range, their intrepid chaplain convinced the sentries of their error, rode out to the cavalry, and personally led them back. Their return set off two celebrations in the Honeyville camp that night. The first occurred when the companies that had joined the rescue mission welcomed the supposedly captured troopers back amidst "much rejoicing."⁸ Then, another round of jubilation was ignited when Major Collins' detachment returned. These men had made the trip back with heavy hearts because of their futile effort: "The force was returning ... sorrowful indeed. What? Captain Conger, his company, and Chaplain Woodward prisoners? No, no one would have it so; but so it must be, as for our assisting them — that was in vain."⁹ Much to their utter amazement and unabashed joy, upon entering the camp they saw Company B and their chaplain! Albeit rather oddly worded, nevertheless thankful and rousing cheers to the tune of "three times three were given to Captain Conger and his boys. Long may they wave!"¹⁰ Also to be found somewhere amidst the exultation were William and Mark Rogers of Company B, out of harm's way for at least another day.

Tuesday, May 13, witnessed the beginning of the last leg of Banks' northward retreat, one that took his army to Strasburg. The slow-moving infantry and baggage train left Haymarket first on Monday. The cavalry followed the next day, acting again as the rear guard. While the troopers' responsibility was to delay the pursuing Confederates as long as possible, it was a task capable of only limited success. Ashby's aggressive cavalry, like rushing floodwaters, lapped close to their departing adversaries and often reclaimed vacated territory before the sound of Yankee hoofbeats ceased to reverberate in the distance.

En route to Strasburg, the 1st Vermont's measured withdrawal saw them bivouac for two nights on a hill halfway between Edenburg and Woodstock. Familiar sites of recent glory greeted them in reverse order in their ride north. Down the slope off Rude's Hill, across Meem's Bottom, over the North Fork of the Shenandoah, and on through Mt. Jackson they marched over terrain and past landmarks still fresh in their minds. Could that April morning's glorious baptism of fire have occurred almost a month ago? For some, it was difficult to hand back territory uncontested whose possession had once been so fiercely wrested from the enemy's grasp. But, in a war that would prove to last far longer than anyone could have imagined, there would be opportunities to return. Though Southern sympathizers in the middle Shenandoah might rejoice at their deliverance for now and the Union cavalry bemoan its demeaning ride northward, it would be their destiny to meet again before the guns fell silent.

By the time Banks' force had reached Strasburg, the Valley Army's personal Rubicon had long since been crossed, the fateful die clearly cast. As their predicament stood on May 13, Nathaniel Banks was probably the one least responsible for the precarious situation in which his troops now found themselves. While the effective removal of Fremont's force from initiating any immediate joint action against the enemy was disconcerting, that in and of itself it did not signal a death knell for Banks' command. In the days immediately following the Battle of McDowell, Banks still had approximately 20,000 men under his command. Even in a worst-case scenario against Jackson and Ewell, the Union commander could still field a force roughly equal to that of his enemies. Even if the political general was doomed to defeat once horns were locked with the wily professor, any hopes that Banks might have entertained for victory in a fair fight among comparatively sized forces were dashed by his superiors. The meddling civilian leadership, looking over his shoulder from Washington, decided that 10,000 of his men would better serve the cause of freedom elsewhere. Should Jackson now elect to come at him with all available Confederate forces, Banks stood to be outnumbered by three to one. The best that he could do now, given the vulnerability of his seriously weakened army at Strasburg, was to assume good defensive positions and prepare to face whatever fate the enemy had in store for him. Unfortunately, his efforts would prove to be too narrowly concentrated, focusing on the expected enemy incursion down the Shenandoah Valley and in the process seriously neglecting the parallel route by way of the Luray Valley on the eastern side of the Massanutten range.

Meanwhile, Ashby's cavalry never let their Yankee counterparts forget that the war was but a brief ride down the road. Rebel detachments were known to charge out of the darkness at pickets, which brought everyone quickly to alert and frequently interrupted a sound repose. To keep the enemy on their toes, Union patrols often played a game of cat-and-mouse with Ashby's scouts, whom they tried to snare but found too elusive. Of course the crafty rebels sought to turn the tables whenever possible. In one such instance, they scored an unusual coup when "they captured two of our pickets, who were bathing in the brook; the nude pickets must have felt cheap, when they allowed themselves to be pounced upon by the redoubted guerillas."[11] One wonders which fate the two hapless soldiers dreaded more: the time that they would spend in the hands of the enemy or upon their parole the welcome they would receive from snickering comrades gleefully revisiting their embarrassing capture.

Since the layover at Strasburg was to be of an extended though albeit undetermined duration, military routine quickly placed its stamp upon camp life. Reveille was at 4:30 A.M. and taps at 9:30 P.M. Sited in a field bounded on two sides by stands of ash and pine, the regimental bivouac was in a prime spot. Even the ever-present specter of war could not hide the fact that it was spring in Virginia, with the buds and blossoms sprouting forth in profusion against a landscape growing greener with each passing day. Not that a trooper could take in any more of it than he could see from camp or while out on patrol, due to an order had been issued prohibiting anyone from leaving camp without a pass or being on duty outside of its perimeter. As the hapless nude bathers could easily affirm, enemy troops lurked in the shadows, waiting to grab the unwary man who had let his guard down.

In this vein, it should be pointed out that every night a camp guard was on duty, acting in the capacity of what now might be called "military police" to save the men from themselves by watching the inside of the grounds. Their presence was meant to dissuade any form of nocturnal departures from the camp, just as the pickets were posted to prevent unwanted enemy incursions into the camp. It was a great source of pride with the 1st Vermont that their regiment was "the only one in the Cavalry department, and in fact the whole command of Banks, which has no camp guard. This treating us with 'distinguished consideration,' Gen. Hatch knows well that we don't go out of camp, without leave, and saves us the trouble of posting a guard round the camp. Is there not another regiment in the U.S.A. who can boast as much?"[12]

In addition to the reunion of the 10 companies of the 1st Vermont, another significant event that took place during this interregnum was the arrival of the Vermonters' latest

commander. On May 15, Colonel Charles Tompkins finally arrived, having wrapped up his affairs in Annapolis. For the third time in less than three months, Lieutenant-Colonel Kellogg was required to step graciously back into his subordinate role. While it was a move that duty dictated that he must make, it was not done without wounded pride for a man who had entertained visions of himself as regimental commander.

For the time being, Banks had most of his 1800 cavalrymen deployed south of Strasburg. Believing that the enemy would come from that direction, a cavalry screen served as an early warning system. Continuing this line of thinking, it made perfect sense to garrison and fortify Strasburg with his remaining "4,476 infantrymen" and artillery consisting of "ten Parrot guns, and six smoothbore pieces."[13] Included under his command, but useless to the immediate defense of Strasburg, Banks had another two regiments, roughly 1000 infantry troops, whom he was ordered to send to Front Royal. From

The third regimental commander of the 1st Vermont, Colonel Charles Tompkins' cachet contained Regular Army experience and a Medal of Honor, both of which gave him instant credibility (Roger G. Hunt Collection/USAMHI).

this detached position, their function was to protect the Manassas Gap Railroad, particularly the large trestle near Buckton Station, about four miles from Strasburg. While dutifully complying with his superior's directive, he made sure that Stanton knew that "this will reduce my force greatly, which is already too small to defend Strasburg."[14] No longer formidable, the depleted army that Banks now led paled in comparison to the mighty legion which he had once led. With his offensive capabilities hamstrung, Banks could only wait for the rebels to come forward and join battle.

With this golden opportunity beckoning, "Stonewall" Jackson had every intention of obliging the Yankees. First, Ashby's cavalry would keep pressure on Banks' southern front. Its function was dual-purposed: to be a screen and a feint. Three companies were detailed to establish a highly visible presence before Banks. Positioned southwest of Strasburg, the major's men "dug earthworks and continuously marched around as though reinforcements were constantly coming."[15] However, the real but carefully shrouded strike was to come by way of the Luray Valley. The plan called for the combined forces of Jackson, Ewell, and Johnson to seize Front Royal and then move against Strasburg from the east, all the while with Banks' men looking south in anticipation of an attack from that direction. The much-feared end-around Massanutten Mountain was about to be exploited. The extent to which Jackson's clandestine posture succeeded can be witnessed in Banks' communication to Secretary Stanton the afternoon of Thursday, May 22, 1862: "From all of the information which I can gather — and I do not wish to excite alarm unnecessarily — I am compelled to believe that he meditates attack here. I regard it as certain that he will move north as far as New Market, a position which commands the mountain gap and the roads into the Department of the Rappahannock, and enables him to co-operate with General Ewell, who is still at Swift Run Gap. Once at New Market, they are within 25 miles of Strasburg.... We are compelled to defend two points, both equally accessible to the enemy — the Shenandoah Valley road, opening near the railroad bridges, and the turnpike."[16] In reality, Banks was far more accurate in his final pre-onslaught assessment than he could have imagined, prophetically concluding: "[T]he enemy is in our immediate neighborhood in very great superiority of numbers."[17] But as the lion slowly opened its mouth to engulf Banks' head and the beast's hot breath and cold shadow simultaneously fell upon the general, the intended victim remained oblivious to the imminency of his danger, continuing on as he did in his telegram to ask for more men and heavier artillery to beef up his defenses. Yet, even as his plea sped across the wires, it was already too late.

9

Banks' Retreat
See How They Run

It was regrettable that General Banks' mission ended so fruitlessly. Initially he had experienced slow but measured success. But, in the face of only limited resistance, Banks' innate deliberateness coupled with his superiors' overly cautious posture stifled all momentum. Now, immobilized at Strasburg, Banks could only wait, while his adversary secretly pushed his main force up the Luray Valley and then subdued the defenders of Front Royal. By the time Banks realized Jackson's gambit, it was almost too late.

Serving as a screen, the 1st Vermont was positioned south of Strasburg on the 23rd. Reconnoitering south through Woodstock, no hostile presence was encountered. Saturday morning, the fateful 24th of May, started in similar fashion, though the air was a bit more ominous. Rousted at 2:00 A.M., ordered to strike the tents, pack their baggage, and prepare to march, it appeared unlikely that Vermonters would be returning. But for the moment, another detachment was ordered back to the Woodstock vicinity. At approximately 5:00 A.M., Colonel Tompkins headed out with eight companies of the 1st Vermont. Banks had ordered another patrol because he believed that "Jackson is still in our front."[1] Tompkins halted within a half-mile of Woodstock, sending scouts out just beyond the town. However, the results remained unchanged: no enemy troops sighted. Most of his command returned to camp at 9:00 A.M. As a precaution, Tompkins left Captain Conger and Company B two miles north of Woodstock. Conger was to remain until four o'clock and then rejoin him. When they eventually returned, the men of Company B reported some enemy activity, though by then this intelligence was moot because the retreat to Winchester had begun.

Once Tompkins departed, Major Collins was left with the remainder of the regiment. At 10:00 A.M., "Companies F, C, and E, under command of Captain Hall ... were ordered to report to Major-General Banks for immediate service."[2] Two hours later, Major Collins with A and G Companies, along with detached elements from other regiments, were dispatched to scout a vital side road connecting Front Royal to Middletown. Though how this troop shuffling occurred is difficult to ascertain, Company E eventually wound up with Collins' ill-fated column instead of Hall's and Company C left Hall at some point to rejoin Tompkins. Having finally decided to move, Banks was now anxious about what lay in store along the way, thus the rationale for the probe led by Collins' to the east and Hall's initial foray north.

After waiting at the old campsite until 3:00 P.M., Colonel Tompkins was ordered to "bring up the rear of the army and destroy all public property after the army had advanced beyond Strasburg."[3] Before leaving, Bugler Ira Batchelder recalled that they "burned what stuff had been left by the teams which had already gone on towards Winchester."[4] This limited destruction turned out to be to all of the burning that the 1st Vermont would engage in that day. No sooner had Tompkins' column reached Strasburg than counter-manding orders arrived. Indicative of the fluidity of the situation at that time, Tomp-kins was now instructed to link up immediately with General Hatch.

Even for cavalry with the ability to move off-road, much was happening along the pike between the two commands. Had the worry been only over troops, the logistics of Banks' northward progress would have been a relatively straightforward task. But there was much encumbering the Union army. Its impedimenta were staggering: hundreds of wounded in ambulances, over 500 supply wagons, and numerous sutlers' conveyances. The train stretched over 7 miles. The baggage left first. The infantry followed. The cav-alry drew their customary rearguard slot. As the 1st Vermont abandoned Strasburg, the regiment's own train, consisting of nineteen wagons and two ambulances, waited up ahead. Commanded by Quartermaster Archibald Dewey, they had moved out earlier. Once over Cedar Creek, Dewey reported, "the teams were formed in line facing the road, so as to be able to proceed to the front or the rear, without the confusion likely to arise in making a full turn, as it was now certain that the enemy was in force on both sides of us, and it was uncertain which way we should find it necessary to proceed."[5]

As Tompkins moved his force northward, taking the same route towards Middle-town that the other Vermont detachments had already trod hours before, the stories of the three disparate commands ceased to have any degree of similarity. Certainly they all shared the anxieties, fears, and confusion into which most elements of Banks' army were eventually plummeted. But it was their relative locations — in the van, midpoint, or rear of the column — that dictated their experiences that Saturday. How each company ulti-mately fared in terms of casualties was a direct result of the assignment pulled. Of the four units of Vermont Cavalry operating on different parts of the field that day, Hiram Hall's troopers had the least difficulty. This assessment by no means denigrates their con-tribution, for men would wind up just as dead, just as wounded, and just as missing from Company F as they did from the others. But in terms of a relatively straightforward objec-tive, Hall's single company was able to perform their mission without serious interfer-ence. It appears that Banks employed this detachment to scout the turnpike ahead as his army made its way to Middletown and then on to Winchester. The infantry's baggage wagons followed in their wake with the marching companies of foot-soldiers close behind. It was this slow-moving, vulnerable column that the rapidly moving Confederate spear-head encountered at Middletown. "When we came in sight of the pike," wrote John Wor-sham of the 21st Virginia Infantry, "it was filled as far as we could see from one end to the other, with Yankees on their way to Winchester, and we had surprised them on the march."[6] Prior to the rebel attack, the Union column was swept by artillery fire. Jackson arrived on the scene at this moment to witness the deadly and unnerving effect that the shower of shells had upon Union troops, observing from the saddle that "the road was literally obstructed [with] the mingled and confused mass of struggling and dying horses and riders."[7] Then the Confederates boldly slammed into the infantry's baggage train. The exposed, defenseless Union column was quickly severed.

Advancing into the village, General Jackson was informed by townspeople that Banks' men had been streaming through Middletown since early morning. Correctly surmis-ing that the bulk of the retreating troops lay to the northeast, Jackson ordered troops to

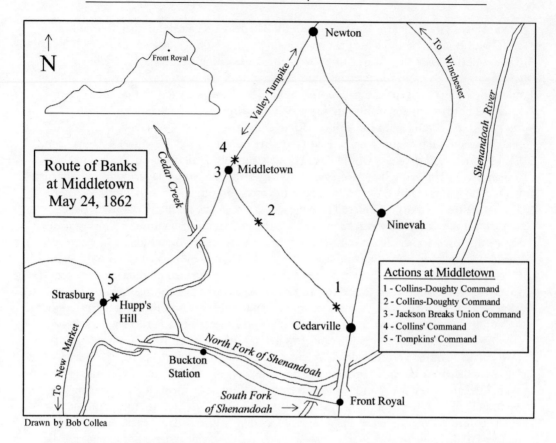

N

Front Royal

Route of Banks
at Middletown
May 24, 1862

Cedar Creek

Valley Turnpike

Newton

To Winchester

Shenandoah River

4
3 ● Middletown

2

● Ninevah

5
Strasburg ● ✳
Hupp's
Hill

1
✳

Cedarville ●

To New Market

North Fork of Shenandoah

Buckton
Station

South Fork
of Shenandoah →

● Front Royal

Actions at Middletown
1 - Collins-Doughty Command
2 - Collins-Doughty Command
3 - Jackson Breaks Union Command
4 - Collins' Command
5 - Tompkins' Command

Drawn by Bob Collea

take up pursuit in both directions. If there was a silver lining for the Federals amidst the chaos, it lay in the fact that the Confederates had struck their marching column when only their supply and baggage trains were passing through the village. While there was no denying that valuable materiel were lost, it also meant that the largest manpower component of Banks' army had already passed through ahead of its enemy. By contrast, for those who came next in line, the cavalry and their train, the retreat would become much more of an ordeal. But at least the mobility of the cavalrymen gave them a better chance of circumventing the rebels now blocking their way than if the infantry had been cut off.

The first troopers caught in the vortex of battle were those led by Major Collins. Called to Hatch's headquarters in the early morning, they were eventually combined with five companies of the 1st Maine, Lieutenant-Colonel Calvin Douty commanding. From Middletown, their mission was to probe east, seeking the enemy who had taken Front Royal the previous day. According to Major Collins, the plan was for them to ride out of Middletown "in an easterly direction, by the Chapel road, to the Front Royal and Winchester pike; to proceed up [i.e., south] toward Front Royal until the force which had been stationed at Front Royal should be found by us."[8] As they headed out into a veil of uncertainty, before their work was done, Collins' men would engage in the heaviest fighting that any Vermonters experienced that day. Dutifully, the column of seven companies rode east. Their first hostile contact came on the narrow road about one-and-a-half miles west of the turnoff from the Front Royal–Winchester turnpike. Advanced guards exchanged shots before the enemy broke off the skirmishing. Douty and Collins elected to fall back several miles to Providence Church.

Retreating to the chapel, the cavalrymen found themselves in a more tenable position. After an interval of perhaps a half hour, the rebels arrived and opened fire on the Maine and Vermont troops for a second time. Major Collins determined with his field glasses that a force of considerable size was bearing down on his command. "I can see Infantry, Cavalry, and Artillery coming this way," Private Charles Gardner of the 1st Maine heard him say, "and we will mount and fall back to Middletown. Take it cool, boys, and don't be afraid."[9] In an admirable display of courage under fire, the Federal column maintained an even pace, as rebel artillery crashed into surrounding treetops. Along with assessing the strength of the enemy force, Collins also saw putting up a delaying action as a part of their mission. Sergeant Frank Ray of Company G capsulized their efforts: "Our squadron Company A & G of our cavalry and two or three Companies of the Maine Cavalry were sent off toward Front Royal to find out the exact position of the enemy and hold them in check until our baggage got out of the way."[10] Up to this point, the Douty-Collins tandem had handled their men well and given a good accounting. However, once reaching Middletown at noon, Douty entertained thoughts of continuing on to Strasburg.

At approximately two o'clock, activity picked up again. Much to Douty's relief, General Hatch's column was reported riding towards Middletown from the south. Concurrently, rebel artillery shells began arching into town, announcing the arrival of the Confederate vanguard. These troops, marching west over the Cedarville road, had been the ones whose progress Douty and Collins' men had contested earlier. With their appearance, the situation in Middletown deteriorated quickly. The rebels dearly wanted to interdict the Valley Turnpike, thereby cutting off further Union retreat towards Winchester. The timing of their breakthrough occurred just when Banks' cavalry, along with its cumbersome baggage, was about to pass the critical road juncture in Middletown. Earlier in the day, Ashby's cavalry had been at this same vantage point but with numbers insufficient to do much more than sow temporary panic. In short order, Federal infantry had brushed them aside. Though some damage was inflicted and confusion caused, large portions of Banks' men and equipment nevertheless made it to safety.

But now the dynamics were radically different. Rather than just a detachment of cavalry, Hatch's troopers faced infantry and artillery elements with support moving up rapidly. Reacting immediately, General Hatch led the five companies immediately under his command out of town in a westerly direction. Taking a route parallel to the Valley Turnpike, he sought to regain the main thoroughfare and a reunion with the rest of Banks' army via various side roads. It wasn't until reaching Newtown that he met up with friendly troops. The clock registered 10:00 P.M. on the 24th before the sanctuary of Winchester was achieved.

When he swung his command out of Middletown, Hatch had expected Douty and Collins to follow suit. This, however, was not initially the case, mainly because no orders were issued. While Douty would eventually catch up with Hatch two miles beyond the village, Collins' men could not follow until fighting their way out. In the process, due to the severity of losses incurred, Major Collins and many a trooper would not be riding with them. Borne of the confusing swirl of events, Major Collins mistakenly headed off in the wrong direction. Douty blindly followed. Dust from the baggage wagons as well as Hatch's departing command filled the air, curtailing vision. Artillery shells exploded, frightened horses reared, wounded men moaned. A Vermont trooper described the bedlam in the streets: "The rebels ... opened fire upon us from their batteries. Many of the shells passed harmlessly over our heads, but it was anything but pleasant. I assure you, for us, unused as we were to the 'smell of powder,' to sit quietly on our horses to be banged away at without having the power to return fire."[11] The Confederate batteries responsible for the rain of discomforting fire were posted on a ridge about 400 yards south of Middletown. The bombardment lasted for thirty minutes, though for those defenseless men who endured the experience it must have seemed much longer. The effect was deadly. Jackson himself viewed the scene: "The turnpike, which had just before been teemed with life, presented a most appalling spectacle of carnage and destruction. The road was literally obstructed with the mingled and confused mass of struggling and dying horses and riders."[12]

With the exposed men sitting like fish in a barrel, injuries occurred. "It was here that poor Thomas Hall fell mortally wounded by a piece of shell. He was taken into a house and had his wound dressed by a surgeon, and there we were obliged to leave him, for we had no ambulance to carry him on, and I do not think he lived long after we left him."[13] Even though capture was imminent, Hall's brother Alexander steadfastly refused to leave him, remaining to comfort his dying sibling. Also during the course of this random shelling, after having two horses shot from under him, the resolute Lieutenant Alonzo Danforth of Company G was painfully wounded in the head by a fragment of metal: "When his horse fell they asked him if he was hurt, he said, 'they have shot me, but not bad, give me a horse, damn the cusses.'"[14] Covered in dirt and blood, Danforth was remounted but then had to be gently though firmly led away by his men as he prepared to charge the offending rebel batteries alone.

Thus it came to pass amidst the chaos that Major Collins had inadvertently struck off in the wrong direction. As Collins would report, "The dust from the pike began to rise and envelop us in such dense clouds as to shut out all objects from our vision at a distance, and so intense was it at times that our file-leaders were not distinguishable."[15] Writing to his father, the founder of the regiment, Captain Frank Platt of Company A corroborated the unusual nature of conditions, describing the roads as being "so dusty, we could not see what was ahead of us. I could not even see the man ahead of me. This accounts for not seeing where the General had gone with his command."[16] Though Collins would later come under some approbation for this miscalculation, in his defense the situation was at best confusing and certainly fluid. To have taken no action at all would quite likely have only invited disaster in some other way.

After a short wait, the order was given to charge. The direction blindly chosen was northeast out of Middletown. Over the course of the next forty-five minutes, this errant advance would result in three desperate charges as futile as they were valiant. Initially, the attacking unit consisted of the entire Douty-Collins force, though at no time would all be collectively engaged. The narrowness of the road and funneling nature of the terrain worked against coordination. After the detachments' first foray was repulsed, only Vermonters participated in the next two charges. Of the attacks, the first one could best be labeled as unplanned, while the second and third were calculated risks.

The initial advance commenced at a "brisk trot" but quickly accelerated into a fast-paced "gallop."[17] Henry Kyd Douglas of Jackson's staff witnessed this event from a defender's vantage point. "There was little hesitation," he noted, "for the commander decided promptly to go to Winchester in spite of the obstacles. 'Forward, trot!' and with gleaming sabres forward they came, boldly and well."[18] The troopers rode for a mile through a gauntlet of rifle and artillery fire. Private John Cummings, in the lead with Company A, remembered being "fired on from the flank by enemy infantry and artillery ... horses and men being mowed down in heap."[19] Their initially rapid progress up the road came to an abrupt halt when they ran into the "rear of the baggage train, which, being deserted by the drivers, was tumbling down the pike in wild confusion, impeding our passage and seriously checking" any further forward progress.[20] In the words of a correspondent, "The foremost were suddenly stopped, and those behind, unable to restrain their horses, fell upon one another, forming a large pile of men and horses, some of whom, pierced through with sabres of their own comrades, were killed, and many in the promiscuous heap were crushed, and died unable to extricate themselves."[21] According-ing to Lieutenant-Colonel Douty, riding to the head of the column, he "passed over the bodies of men and horses strewn along the road till I had come up to near the center of Company M [Maine troops], the third company from the rear, where I found the bod-ies of men and horses so piled up that it was impossible to proceed."[22] Sergeant Cor-nelius Morse of Company A described the horror of the scene from an attacker's perspective when he wrote that the rebels "shot down whole sections of fours at one time.... [S]oon the road became blocked with men and horses, lying in a confused and mangled mass, the dust preventing those in the rear from seeing what was before them, so that the horses that were not shot down tumbled over those that had already fallen, so that few got out without being dismounted."[23] Typical of a victim's experience in this melee was that of Company A's venerable John Bain, the forty-four-year-old Canadian warrior. His lot proved to be not unlike that which befell many of his comrades in this phase of the action. When his horse went down, it landed on Private Bain's left leg, frac-turing it just below the knee. Captain Platt, commander of Bain's company, then by chance witnessed the unfortunate trooper's predicament become worse: "At the same time, while he was down under his horse, his skull was fractured by the kick of another horse."[24] Tough as he was, Bain still suffered from headaches, vertigo, impaired hearing, and visual problems. He would experience lameness in his injured leg for the rest of his life. Since his recuperation took all summer, he was unable to return to active duty until the following September.

At the same time John Bain was injured, several other troopers in the immediate area were simultaneously put out of action. Herman Frost, Cornelius Ellis, and Charles Daniels experienced similar fates. Private Frost offered a simple postwar insight into what can impede a soldier's memory about the scope of events in which he is participating: "Now at the time of my wound, it is not probable that any person saw me receive it; for we had no time to wach [*sic*] one another, as we all had plenty to do in watching the enemy."[25] All three troopers, riding abreast in the numbers 1, 2, and 3 positions of a row, had their horses shot out from under them. In the process of being dehorsed, each man received a different type of wound. Frost took a piece of shell in the face, the jagged iron cutting a three-and-a-half inch gash across the bridge of his nose and up to his left eye. The falling Ellis was struck in the head by Frost's saber and then knocked senseless by the hooves of horses behind him. Daniels was rendered unconscious when tumbling from his collapsing horse. In retrospect, it is a wonder that any of the four men lived to tell their tale, for as Private Ellis later recalled, "[T]he enemy fired on us with grapes and canister and chain shots and mowed us down like stalks."[26] Similarly, Charles Adams went down hard and was knocked unconscious after his horse was shot. It is not surprising that somewhere in the midst of this confusion Private Adams received an abdominal injury. Private William Langshore witnessed Adams' ordeal as he "saw many horses pass over him, both with and without riders."[27] Taken prisoner in the aftermath of the engagement, Adams was fortunate enough to be paroled in a relatively short time.

Following this first attempt to extricate themselves from the killing zone, Douty and Collins' commands became separated. The split occurred just when the logjam of men and horses in the road had halted Douty's forward progress toward the head of column. In the next instant, the Maine officer was caught up in a stream of retreating troopers. "I fell back," he later wrote, "and reformed the remainder of my command in the street about the middle of town."[28] Again coming under rebel fire and deeming that "a second attempt to advance was useless," he proceeded to lead his men along the same general route taken by Tompkins.[29] By virtue of this expedient action, he certainly saved the lives of many soldiers entrusted to his command. Unfortunately, Collins was not following along with the 1st Vermont.

Realizing that his command now stood alone, Major Collins wasted little time prevaricating. Based upon the flawed assumption that the main body of Banks' army lay just ahead, he concluded that his command's best chance was to charge forward and cut through the enemy forces. Somewhere in the disarray, as if he didn't have enough problems, Major Collins was victimized by a freak injury, sustained when the "the fragment of a shell which exploded near me struck my left holster, cutting the brass tip from the end, and striking the end of a Savage pistol, glanced, wounded my left knee, and, passed, inflicting a severe wound on the right side of my horse."[30] Though in pain, Collins resolutely remained at the head of his troopers.

The order to charge was given once more. Past the rows of blazing rifles, through bursts of exploding shells, and into a hail of grapeshot the Vermonters rode. Again they traversed the obstacle course of "wagons broken down, overturned, some with their contents scattered, some sound and untouched, some with good teams, some horseless, sutlers' stores, officers' luggage, knapsacks, Bibles, cards, photographs, songbooks and cooking utensils—a general wreck of military matter."[31] While making headway, the results were still the same: no breakthrough and mounting casualties. Somewhere in the maelstrom of action, Private Henry O'Hayer was hit by a bullet that entered through his left lung and exited from his back. The ensuing incapacitation was further exacerbated by a second injury. Being unhorsed by the impact of the minie ball, O'Hayer fell to the ground, whereupon the following troopers' horses "went over him and injured his knee."[32]

One of the few in the initial muster not a native Vermonter, Private O'Hayer found his way into the cavalry as a blacksmith after immigrating to America from Ireland. Captured on the Middletown battlefield, he remained in rebel hands until paroled. Shortly after his release from prison, Private O'Hayer was granted a disability discharge in January of 1863. A company mate of O'Hayer's named Daniel Pattison, one of the regimental elders at forty-five years of age, suffered a similar sequence of fates. Wounded, captured, and exchanged, Pattison too received a disability discharge because he had "received severe internal injuries in a fall from and with his horse Middleton [sic], Va in a cavalry charge with his company.... When he was taken prisoner by the enemy and marched to Lynchburg, Va during severe weather without sufficient protection his injuries and exposure have served to affect his eyes to partial blindness being unable to perform his duties."[33]

As the enemy fire continued to pour in and losses mounted, the Vermonters' straits worsened. To remain where they were was to court destruction. To charge again was to afford the beleaguered troopers at least a fighting chance. In the previous two assaults, most of the obstacles to their forward progress had been the random wagons and assorted debris scattered haphazardly about the turnpike, necessitating that the columns slow down. In the third charge, the Confederates had purposely blocked the road with additional wagons. Four were strung tightly across the road, forming a barricade completely obstructing passage. To the right and left along the roadside leading up to the wagons were stone walls. Behind these, Southern infantry on the right and cavalry on the left enjoyed the benefit of well-chosen defensive positions, creating with the wagons a cul de sac. For the well-protected rebels, targets of opportunity would be everywhere. As Captain Platt remembered, "It was here that very many of the poor boys were killed. Many more were thrown from their horses, and killed by the horses running over them."[34] It was in this segment of the day's action that Platt experienced a one-on-one duel with a Confederate officer. Singling Platt out, a rebel cavalryman jumped the intervening wall astride his horse, seeking to bring the Vermont officer down with a well-placed carbine shot. However, Platt temporarily thwarted him by ducking behind a nearby wagon. In a rare depiction of personal combat, related in correspondence to his father, Frank Platt told how "I leaned forward on my horse, dropped my sabre, and snatched my pistol from my holster, cocked it, and raising myself suddenly, fired. The ball struck him in the breast. He dropped his carbine, threw up his hands exclaiming 'My God,' and rolled from his saddle. I rode around the wagon to assure myself that he was dead. I do not think he moved after he struck the ground."[35]

The experiences of others, like Private Daniel Russell, were indicative of the rough handling that the Vermonters received when trying to mount their escape from the shooting gallery in which they served as moving targets: "After the enemy sent a charge of grape that cut down the rear rank of Company A, Company G following after A had to leap the fallen bodies. Russell of Company G was thrown down. As his horse fell, the animal landed on the trooper's left leg. Then other men and horses came tumbling together.... His left shoulder was hurt by his horse stomping on it as were ribs broken by horses stepping on him."[36] In addition, Private Russell received "2 saber cuts on his left shoulder" from the blades of comrades tumbling about him.[37] Captured and later paroled, he was to be hospitalized for many months in Fairfax and Brattleboro, not returning to active duty until April of 1863. Married for fourteen years prior to his enlistment and a bit long in the tooth as recruits went, Russell nevertheless, like so many of his comrades, had gone off to war a "strapping and powerful man ... and to all appearances healthy."[38] But the lingering effects of his battle wounds and the rigors of captivity adversely impacted his once-robust constitution, so much so that he was unable to re-up with the regiment when his three-year enlistment expired in the fall of 1864.

While Russell's losses were of a personal nature, history suffered a blow when the faithful diarist Charles Blinn also went down. His friend, Private George Cobb, riding "in the next column of horses" immediately behind him, watched helplessly as Blinn "had his horse shot and fall heavily upon him crushing his head against a stirrup of another cavalryman who had a horse shot at the same time. The infantry firing was very heavy at the time and a ball may have hit him [the horse]."[39] Cobb further related how, after his horse too was shot, the Confederate General Jones "helped me to extricate Blinn from the dead horses," estimating that about twenty animals from his company had perished in the day's fighting thus far.[40] Like so many of his dismounted compatriots, Private Blinn was incarcerated in a rebel prison. Close to four months' confinement left him weak after bouts of scurvy, dyspepsia, and dysentery. Upon his release, fellow soldier James Shanion recalled Blinn's being "detailed as a clerk at the Brigade Commissary Department for several months."[41] This light duty allowed him to regain his strength before returning to the field.

Unlike Troopers Russell and Blinn, Bugler William Flowers, who was also of Company G, did not fare so well. A young artist from Great Britain, the transplanted Englishman suffered an "injury to his left shoulder ... by being thrown from his horse."[42] After enduring seven months of captivity, he was exchanged in December of 1862 and subsequently given a disability discharge. Trooper David Tubbs, identified by Lieutenant Joel Earhardt as the kind of soldier who "performed his duty faithfully," was struck down by a bullet that passed between two ribs and through his left lung before exiting from the side of his body.[43] This once robust farmer from Colchester had to leave the cavalry the following October due to this injury, one that would hamper him for the rest of his life as he tried to cope with the total paralysis of his left arm and hand.

During the three-charge sequence, the most significant wound was that incurred by Collins. Already impaired by the freak knee injury, the major was put out of action by a saber blow to his head that knocked him unconsciousness. When he awoke, it was as a prisoner. However, just prior to being rendered hors de combat, Major Collins made what may have been the most important command decision of his comparatively brief cavalry career. The tactical stratagem that Collins conjured up on the fly saved what was left of his hemmed-in companies attempting to break out of their turnpike deathtrap. As the thundering column approached the blockade of wagons, what was already a predicament had the potential to become worse. If the lead elements of the charging column were abruptly halted and turned back in confusion by the barricade, it would in all likelihood have caused another jam-up. With enemy fire raining down from three directions, any massing of troops presented targets too easy to miss. Up to this point, Collins had made mistakes. But riding forward, sword held high as he urged his men to advance, Major Collins observed a chink in the rebel defenses. On both sides of the line of wagons, he perceived slight gaps between the wooden blockade and the stone wall, creating openings just wide enough for a horse and rider to slip through to safety. The order was quickly given for the column to split and oblique, half going to the right and half to the left. Though Collins was denied the fruits of his quick thinking, many of his men owed their freedom to him. Still, a number of comrades ended up making a reluctant trip to Richmond. Collins, meanwhile, fared much better. Left at Front Royal because of his injury, the wounded officer had the good fortune to be liberated six days later by Rhode Island troopers who recaptured the town.

Some Vermonters escaped by squeezing past the wagons. Others improvised. Among those who creatively extricated themselves were Captain Platt and Lieutenant Edwards. In what must have been a dramatic sight, Edwards and nine Vermont troopers followed Platt, who well remembered the spectacular moment: "I then gave the order to take the stone wall to the left, turned my horse that way, and he took the wall without touching it."[44] Due to the helter-skelter, every-man-for-himself climax to the fight, it was very difficult initially to make any accurate accounting of losses. Platt and Edwards, for example, kept their little band to the woods and side roads, finally arriving in Winchester around nine that evening.

Company C, under the command of William Wells, had an eventful day too. By starting out as the third unit back in Collins' charge out of Middletown, they were spared participation in the calamity that befell their comrades. According to Captain Wells, "We charged the Pike, turned off into some woods half a mile distant, the rebels shelling us all the way and in the woods."[45] His company survived the gauntlet of fire without any casualties, in the process making their commander proud because "my boys behaved well, taking into consideration that they offered no defense."[46] Eventually, Wells' unit hooked up with General Hatch's command, and together they caught up with the infantry several miles south of Winchester. They were immediately turned around and became the rear guard for the main body. As pressure by the pursuing Confederates forced them closer to the troops they were screening, Wells' men had the unexpected and harrowing experience of being subjected to "friendly fire." Awakened by the sound of approaching hoofbeats, Massachusetts troops who had been sleeping by the side of the road jumped up and began shooting at supposed rebels, who proved to be Company C. Fortunately darkness, grogginess, and the swiftness of it all combined to confine the damage to the death of a few horses. It was not until midnight that Captain Wells and his men entered the relative safety of the Federal lines in front of Winchester, their work for the day finally done after almost eighteen hours in the saddle.

10

The Williamsport Crossing
To the Safety of the Far Shore

The day after the Middletown misadventure was dicey for Banks' command. In Preston's opinion, the situation was so tenuous that "in many respects it was Bull Run and if they had followed us the next day they could [have] succeed[ed]."[1] Self-preservation was the paramount concern on May 25. While Wells was making good his escape with Company C and the remnants of Companies A and G were extricating themselves, Lieutenant-Colonel Tompkins tried to preserve the rest of the regiment and its train. The most noticeable difference was his route. As the other contingents headed northward, circumstances forced Tompkins south toward Strasburg.

The timing of his arrival in Middletown could not have been worse. With no other Union soldiers still around, rebel attention could be showered upon Tompkins. For thirty minutes, his troopers and three cannon held the Southerners back. In Lieutenant Henry Flint's assessment, "The rebel infantry, except their skirmishers, remained under cover, and from their movements it became evident that they wanted to have us charge through the town, which, had we done so, would have left but few to tell the fate of the unfortunate."[2] From Quartermaster Archibald Dewey's viewpoint, "the firing was brisk for over half an hour, when the battery, being threatened by a flank movement of the enemy ... was forced to limber up and retire."[3] Quickly the 1st Vermont recrossed Cedar Creek and fell back toward Strasburg, regrouping on Hupp's Hill. Soon the 5th New York joined them. A hurried council of war was held to determine their next course of action.

In the meantime, the cavalry's wagoners and train guards played out their own intense drama. Having waited patiently on the Middletown side of Cedar Creek, these men heard the din of battle, but they held their ground. A buzz arose when word was received that the trains up ahead had been attacked, but Wagonmaster Clark Stone provided a calming influence. Even when battle was joined right in front of them, they held their posts. Once the tide of war finally washed over them late that afternoon, the drivers and guards acquitted themselves admirably. Moving slowly downhill towards the ford, they were under constant fire from skirmishers, "who swarmed around within pistol-range and shot down wagoners and horses."[4] When a horse was hit, the team's progress often halted, causing the driver to jump down, cut a mount from the traces, and ride off in an effort to save himself.

Private John Huse was one who took this unorthodox means of escape. Wounded in the hand, he leaped from his seat. Luther Wakefield, a guard who witnessed Huse's predicament, recalled that "his horses fell or at least the two wheel horses were down and the leaders were snaking them along. Huse was on top of the horses, those that were down."[5] Once the team made it to the bottom of the incline and "got to the crick I helped get a mule from a team that was tangled in the crick [and] helped him on to him."[6] Several wagons had actually traversed the creek before a fusillade of rebel bullets knocked down several of the animals still in the water. "When the passage through the water was obstructed by dead or disabled horses the order was given to the drivers to save themselves by cutting out each a horse for himself."[7] In this way, a fair number of teamsters avoided capture.

Though drivers usually labored in anonymity, at least one gained a measure of recognition for his conduct that day. This noteworthy soldier was fifty-eight-year-old Loren W. Young, "Father Young" to those who knew him. An ambulance driver, he had two sick men entrusted to his care. Amid the retreat, Young paid no heed to urgings of others to abandon his wagon, mount his favorite mule, Old Grey, and depart the scene. At great personal risk, the old teamster took his van off the road, wove through the woods, and avoided smashed and careening wagons until eventually able to regain the roadway. Ultimately he brought his charges to safety. In praise of his efforts, a correspondent wrote: "One such soldier is worth a dozen beardless youths, who, to a great extent, fill up the ranks of our army. Three cheers for 'Father Young and old Grey.'"[8]

However, endeavors to save the wagons went for naught. Rather than surrender their contents, a last-ditch attempt was made to burn them. But even those efforts were aborted. For the Confederacy's deprived troops, plundering the possessions of their well-supplied enemy proved to be Christmas in May. It was from the capture of these and other commodities that Confederates dubbed Nathaniel Banks with the mocking sobriquet "Commissary." Though millions of dollars' worth of goods were taken, this tactical success proved to be a strategic setback for Jackson. For his famished men, their immediate agenda became pillaging Yankee stores rather than killing Yankee soldiers. Distracted from the pursuit, they thwarted their leader's objective of destroying Banks' army. From the Vermonters' perspective, "every officer in the regiment lost all but what they had on their persons."[9] Personal items, of course, could be replaced. However, stored somewhere in one of the few wagons that went up in flames were not only irreplaceable regimental record books but also the 1st Cavalry's priceless flags. Why they were furled and stuck away in a wagon, no one remembered. Regardless of that puzzle, the loss of their colors was deeply troubling. The regiment's only solace was that the enemy had not taken them in battle.

As the volume of Confederate fire increased, the Hupp's Hill position became untenable. The feisty Tompkins contemplated crashing through enemy lines to rejoin Banks. But Tompkins had to ponder not only the fate of his own six companies but also several others who had joined the hilltop defense line. Considering the fate of Collins' breakout attempts, his chances for success were problematical. Yet, Tompkins readied two companies of cavalry on each side of Hampton's battery as the big guns blazed away at the approaching enemy infantry, pushing ever closer and beginning to envelop the Union flanks. Fortunately, before any charge was ordered, an alternative was advanced. Major Edward Sawyer suggested that side roads existed over which they could retreat. By skirting the rebels, the Federals might be able to rejoin the main force to the north. While Sawyer acknowledged that "they might fight their way through the enemy ... it would be at great sacrifice."[10]

Discretion prevailed. After a brief council of war, Tompkins agreed to lead his men eastward toward the uplands and then northwestward along routes roughly parallel to the Valley Turnpike. Riding deep into the night, his command covered over fifty miles, arriving at their destination around 1:00 A.M. on May 25. The ride was arduous, pushing everyone to the point of complete physical exhaustion. A soldier in Company K recalled his condition: "I was *played out*, so I lay down beside my horse on the wet ground, cold and hungry, and fell asleep almost instantly."[11] Riding amidst Tompkins' column that fateful evening was one trooper who was particularly relieved that the day's odyssey had finally ended. This individual was Mark Rogers. While Corporal Rogers participated in the day's action, he did so only with discomfort. It seems that on May 20 Rogers had incurred a painful wound when a sword, propped against a tree, accidentally fell and struck a pistol lying at its trunk. The saber landed on the firearm in just such a way as to discharge the weapon, sending a bullet smashing into Rogers' hand. "This ball took effect on the fingers of his left hand, causing the second finger of his left hand when the wound healed to double-up."[12] For a cavalryman, a hand injury was at least discomforting if not debilitating. Considering that at any time a weapon or the reins might have to be handled, a wound such as his certainly adversely affected the man's ability to perform his duties. While his value to the regiment might be suspect, there is no questioning Rogers' pluck, opting to be present for duty rather than invalided.

As the weary men bedded down, they took a few moments to review the day's fast-paced events. One question was on everyone's mind: who was missing? Many were the battle-hardened troopers who drifted off to sleep in Winchester with heavy hearts, concerned over lost friends. Soldiers had disappeared before, but those numbers were comparatively small compared to the staggering losses that some companies stood to absorb. Rumors made the rounds that Companies A and G had been captured in their entirety. Among those missing that first night of the retreat were Merrill Barrett, Daniel Wilson, and James (or John) Byron Holden. None would ever see the Green Mountains again. Only nineteen, Trooper Barrett fell into rebel hands on the 24th. He spent his days in captivity at Lynchburg, where he perished from scurvy during the summer. Private Wilson of Company K was killed outright during Tompkins' fighting retreat, leaving behind his poor mother and younger brother, who had counted on his allotted pay to sustain their meager existence. Though these two men, along with many others, would leave behind those who would mourn their loss, the death of James Byron Holden touched a special chord in Company H.

From all accounts, young Holden endeared himself to Company H by virtue of his friendly, sincere demeanor. As his captain, Dr. Selah Perkins, wrote home of the boy, "He was brave, quiet, and true.... [H]e had no enemy."[13] Somewhere during the retreat, possibly at Hupp's Hill, Private Holden was mortally wounded. He was taken to a home in Strasburg. By his side was Harley Peterson. Private Peterson had taken Holden's plight personally because the two had become fast friends. As he later wrote to Holden's grieving father, "We were both sick in the hospital at Annapolis, and since then to the day he was shot, we had bunked together."[14] Even as he lay suffering, the good soldier in Holden inquired, "How goes the battle?"[15] When he learned that Confederate forces were approaching, he implored his faithful friend to leave. "I was with him in Strasburg after he was wounded, but left him at his own request, to seek my safety," wrote Private Peterson, adding, "I did all I could to make him comfortable."[16]

Even so, Holden did not lack for medical attention in his final hours. Surgeons from the 1st Maine Cavalry remained behind, giving themselves up to care for the wounded.

Though the worst was feared, Holden's fate would not be known until the 1st Vermont returned on June 8. At this time, Trooper Peterson learned the painful truth in the village graveyard: "On the board placed at the head of the grave is inscribed: 'John B. Holden, Co. H, First Vt. Cavalry, died May 26, 1862.'"[17] While Holden had expressed the desire that his body should be returned home, the exigencies of war did not permit this humanitarian gesture. His widow, Elizabeth, would have to mourn without a chance to say a last farewell. She was in due time spared a lifetime of sorrow, however, when she joined her departed husband in death in December of 1864. As a sympathetic gesture, Holden's personal "effects [were] sent to his heirs at the time" in Clarendon, including his blanket that contained no less than eight bullet holes.[18] Peterson, who suffered from the young cavalryman's passing just as did the boy's family, offered them solace with the thought that "like a true soldier and lover of his country, his blood, like many others, was shed in the same righteous cause."[19]

Fourth in the sequence of regimental commanders, Colonel Edward Sawyer's most enduring contributions proved to be in recruiting others to do the fighting, which he participated in only sparingly himself (Francis C. Guber Collection).

Although not among the missing, Major Edward Sawyer experienced a crippling accident. Somewhere during the escape, his horse fell. In the process, Sawyer badly bruised an ankle. Sent home to recuperate, several months would pass before he was fit for duty. As Tompkins wrote in his after-action report, the accident was effective in "depriving me of the services of a valuable officer."[20] This feeling, however, was not universally shared in the officer corps of the 1st Vermont. Sawyer's prolonged absence, coupled with his return sporting colonel's eagles, generated much rancor. This promotion was especially irritating, since, on a visit home only a few months before, Sawyer had left as a captain and returned a major. This prompted an observation by the ever-acerbic Sergeant Ide that "it was found out that Vermont was quite as good a place to look for a promotion as on the 'Tented Field.'"[21]

While Ide confined his comments to his diary, Captain Joel Earhardt complained directly to Secretary of War Stanton. Pulling no punches, he pointed out that Sawyer's absence in Vermont "is believed by many—was occasioned not by a fall from his horse while in the service, or exigencies of recruiting service—but the sting and shame of venereal disease."[22] Captain William Merritt was ordered to investigate Earhardt's as well as other charges. He reported that "Sawyers [*sic*] lack of experience works greatly against his being regarded with favor, by officers of the regt, who served in the field while he was absent sick or recruiting—officers who claim with reason, a superior knowledge of military matters."[23] When the dust settled, Earhardt's resignation was duly accepted after a strong rebuke, costing the regiment a proven leader and brave soldier.

Though Sawyer remained, his questionable conduct would lead him to another day of reckoning in the coming fall. But for now, there were more pressing matters. With the dawn on Sunday, May 25, 1862, the worst was over. For the most part the Union army had won the race to Winchester, but their situation was still grave, as Jackson and Ewell were approaching. For the weary cavalrymen, renewed hostilities began all too soon on the 25th, when pickets on both sides opened up in earnest at approximately 4:00 A.M.

Heavier action commenced at first light when Confederate artillery began shelling the Union infantry camp southeast of Winchester. After several hours, superior numbers prevailed, and the Confederate infantry gained the upper hand. Union troops fell back through Winchester and out onto the turnpike in the wake of their departed wagons. Due to the simultaneous collapse of the Northern lines on both the southeastern and southwestern edges of town, the infantry's disengagement quickly turned disorderly. What a sharp contrast this hasty Federal departure made to that triumphant day only six weeks ago when they had "marched in with flags flying and bands playing 'Yankee Doodle,' 'Hail Columbia,' and 'Dixie.'"[24] While deserted streets had met the onset of Union occupation, the army's leave was taken amid a flurry of activity. Winchester's residents, nowhere to be seen when their conquerors came, now drifted into the streets, as if needing to visually verify that the hated enemy was in fact vacating the town. In the eyes of weary rebel soldiers, the sight of Yankee backs was heartening and the liberation of the town gratifying, but confiscated supplies were again the most highly prized rewards. To one Marylander, "the amount of plunder accumulated by the regiment was indescribable."[25]

To begin the day, the 1st Vermont spent most of the morning posted north of Winchester. There the men "waited on the side of the pike while the long wagon trains, followed by crowds of stragglers and camp followers, streamed by."[26] But this welcomed respite was not destined to last. Before long, they were ordered to the front. The advancing Vermonters encountered blue-clad infantry in full retreat, rebels nipping at their heels. Unable to be of any use holding the line, Colonel Tompkins led his command immediately out of town via a side street. This allowed them to avoid the main thoroughfare, "crowded with infantry who were throwing away knapsacks, bands their knapsacks, and so forth, and realizing that there was no room for us, we tore down the fence at the right side of the road and passed along in the fields."[27]

Safely out of the maelstrom, the regiment reformed. Then, "the 3rd squadron under Capt. Preston ... was ordered to cover the retreat, consequently they were last to leave the city."[28] Taking two batteries, the Vermonters doggedly stood, fought, withdrew, and then repeated the sequence all over again. As Lieutenant Josiah Grout remembered the action, "We were sorely crowded by the enemy all day Sunday, were obliged to make occasional stands to save the trains, participating [in] cavalry brushes, in which little affairs few were hurt."[29] Their valiant efforts were rewarded. After two hours, Jackson gave up his aggressive pursuit. The main column soon gained Martinsburg and then the Potomac twelve miles beyond. The cavalry halted at Martinsburg, while the rest of Banks' command crossed into Maryland through the night and on into the next day.

In performing this assignment, Preston's men were subjected to the unsettling experience of being "fired upon from windows of houses as we left."[30] Colonel George Gordon, commanding the 3rd Infantry Brigade, also observed this same treachery, as his "retreating column suffered serious loss in the streets of Winchester. Males and females vied with each other in increasing the number of victims, by firing from the houses, throwing hand grenades, hot water, and missiles of every description."[31] Even the locals noted this aberrant behavior by their neighbors. "The citizens in town have become demons almost," wrote Julia Chase, supporting this with her belief that "Louis Brant has ... shot down one or two of the Federal soldiers and one was shot at Mr. Reed's door."[32] Riding amidst the retreating 1st Vermont's troopers who came under such fire was James Esdon, providing him with an eyewitness account of how "one man was shot and another had his horse shot from under him while leaving the town, the very women fired pistols out of the windows of houses at us; some of them however suffered the [same] fate as that of some rebels which were shot down."[33]

Private Esdon was in all probability referencing a comrade in Company D. Ashbell Meacham was believed to have been a victim of a treacherous potshot. Private Meacham was mortally wounded when he took a bullet through his back and heart. One second he was riding down the road, and then in the next instant he reflexively threw up an arm, letting his saber fall to the ground. Before he pitched from his saddle, two comrades caught him. Realizing that he was incapable of riding, they gently placed him on the ground, where he would soon die by the side of the road. No one felt the passing of this young soldier more deeply than his aging father, Henry, back in Guildhall, Vermont. Ashbell had resided with his dad before the war, dutifully serving, as the elder Meacham later recalled, as "my sole dependence to carry on [the] farm and to support myself."[34] In the briefest of moments, the effect of this single deadly bullet could be said to have lasted a lifetime, for it cost an old man both his cherished son and only means of provision. While a very moving and highly personal loss, housed within the context of the great national tragedy that was the Civil War such vignettes were all too common.

Such perfidy did not sit well with the Vermonters, leaving them unfavorably disposed towards Winchester. Captain Henry Flint was quite vehement in his feelings, emphatically opining that "there is but one thing which will purify this place and *that is fire*."[35] In light of their festering distain, it was curious, when the 1st Vermont did eventually return in the early summer of 1862, that they engaged in no acts of reprisal. The only logical explanation for this was that time may have served to dissipate their anger and cooler heads realized that a communal population should not be held accountable for the acts of an irrational few. Being the last to leave Winchester meant that for the Vermonters their turn to cross the Potomac did not come until the morning of May 26. Upon their arrival at the riverbank the previous night at sundown, they had come upon a sea of humanity. In the word-painting of Nathaniel Banks, "A thousand camp-fires were burning on the hillside, a thousand carriages of every description were crowded upon the banks, and a broad river lay between the exhausted troops and their coveted rest."[36]

A combination of means moved the army safely to the far side. The valuable munitions trains got the preferential treatment afforded by the one ferryboat, while supply and baggage wagons had to use the ford. The infantry was treated to the novel experience of being taken across in boats requisitioned from the pontoon train, the current being too swift to employ them in their intended fashion. As for the cavalry, they too had to make their way over via the ford. At a depth of five feet, the river did not prove to be a barrier of any significance to them. Though a few horses, mules, and pieces of baggage were lost, all troopers in the main body were on the northern side by noon.

Over the course of the next several days, missing parties of different sizes came in without further incident. Their reception by battle-hardened troopers, who had agonized over lost comrades, was often touching, as on one occasion "cheer after cheer went up from our noble men as they met them with open arms and moist eyes."[37] The camp in which the regiment slowly reconstituted itself was in a pleasant wooded area about two miles from Williamsport. With the baggage train having been lost, none of the basics like tents or blankets were available. Yankee ingenuity, however, led the resourceful troopers to fashion themselves crude shelters of wood. Josiah Grout summed up the sentiments shared by many compatriots when he noted the following: "We felt a deep sense of relief when about noon on Monday we found ourselves north of the Potomac. It had been hurrying times since Friday, and we were a hungry, tired set of fellows."[38] According to Sergeant Ide's estimate, such fatigue should not have been surprising as the men had marched somewhere in the neighborhood of "at least 75 miles" since the retreat had begun.[39] For those who made the longer, more circuitous trek to safety with Colonel DeForest, the distance traversed was more like 120 miles!

For William Wells, however, being worn out was possibly not his most pressing problem when he discreetly acknowledged that the "saddle is a little sore," though his admittedly strategic application of "Trask's Magnetic Ointment" was an indication that the real seat of the irritation was more firmly attached to his own body than it was to his horse's![40] Made in Buffalo, New York, Trask's ointment was used as a "remedy for pain, nervous headache, inflammation of the bowels, burns, fever sores...."[41] Faith in its curative value was based upon the "magical powers of magnetism" to heal.[42] Before dismissing this idea as just one more quack concoction amidst an array of 19th century patent medicines that abounded in the land, it is worth noting that there are many today who swear by magnetic bracelets as a pain reliever. While Trask's has gone the way of so many of its contemporary elixirs, it has nonetheless managed to achieve an immortality of sorts through its bottles, which are highly sought after by collectors.

In the days that followed, while Wells suffered his indignity in silence, the preliminary projections of massive losses by the 1st Vermont, "300 Missing" according to one paper, were tempered gradually until what had seemed a terrible disaster became far less so, until the final accounting determined that approximately 60 men were actually lost.[43] As Wells wrote on May 29, "loss of the regt is decreasing every day as more men turn up."[44] Sometimes the return took the form of a large group, such as when "on the 27th of May about 150 of the regiment who had gone off over the mountains with Colonel DeForest came in by way of St. John's Run, so that our loss was not so much as supposed."[45] Other times, small parties found their way to safety. In one of these instances, John Huse took a slow, painful, and roundabout route to get to Williamsport. "Exposed for three days and two nights" to the hardships of nature while suffering from his hand wound, the going was slow due to a combination of blood poisoning and rheumatism.[46] After spending several days recuperating at the home of a Hancock surgeon, Private Huse was moved by canal boat to Williamsport. However, being unable to walk due to an injury to his back in the fall from his wagon, a concerned comrade, John W. Smith, was obliged to help him onto his horse and take him to the regimental hospital. From there, Trooper Huse was sent home to Vermont for a period of anticipated recuperation. However, by the fall, his mobility had still not returned sufficiently for him to be considered an able-bodied soldier, and he was discharged. Like so many of his brothers in arms, surviving the moments of actual combat was no guarantee that a given individual would continue to play a useful and productive part in the war.

In retrospect, it is surprising that deaths during the retreat were limited to but five men, especially when there were several instances of intense enemy fire directed at highly exposed troopers. This low mortality rate was partially attributable to the difficulty in hitting a moving target as well as the fact that there were many instances where Confederate artillery rounds were seen to explode prematurely. The truth was that the ranks were more severely thinned by the loss of approximately seventy POWs than by deadly fire. Though many eventually returned to the ranks, some had the misfortune to survive desperate fighting and then die as a prisoner. Zabina Landon was one such individual. Ejected from his saddle in one of the desperate charges by Collins' hemmed-in command, Private Landon, like many others, "was run over by horses and received an injury to his head."[47] Easily captured, he spent time hospitalized at Lynchburg, where he contracted the diarrhea that was to take his life in August after he had been sent on to incarceration at Richmond.

Others suffered grievous injuries that eventually led to medical discharges. David Tubbs took a bullet in his left breast during one of the charges that Company A made. Passing slightly downward through the upper trunk of his body and then his left arm, it exited just below his elbow. While the projectile penetrated a lung on its way through, it was the arm injury that led to a long-term problem, causing "total paralysis of the left hand and fingers."[48] For Trooper Tubbs, the litany read like so many others: fought, wounded, captured, exchanged, furloughed, and finally discharged in the fall of '62. A similar fate befell John Hogan, a young Irish immigrant who toppled from his wagon into Cedar Creek after taking a gunshot wound in the left thigh. As it turned out, the track of the ball was such that it "apparently severed cords that serve to extend and bring back the lower extremity of the leg."[49] When his mobility proved to be too severely limited, the military had no choice but to discharge Hogan, once he had returned from captivity and did not recover. Also mirroring the wounded/captured/discharged scenario that ended the military careers of Tubbs and Hogan was their company-mate Albert Hutchins, who was unlucky enough to have a "gunshot wound of the right knee, [his] right arm broken, and three ribs of [the] right side broken."[50] A rebel soldier inflicted the first wound, knocking Private Hutchins from his horse, which then fell on him to account for the broken arm. A shell fragment caused the rib damage.

For countless soldiers like Hogan, Hutchins, and Tubbs, the journey to war, having begun amidst hopes and dreams of adventure and glory, concluded abruptly and painfully. But what were the ramifications for the 1st Vermont of this ill-fated expedition into the Shenandoah Valley? The prevailing attitude of the rank and file was very upbeat. They did not seem to be in the least bit broken in spirit by the recent turn of events. Certainly the dramatic reversal of fortunes on the field of battle, coupled with the unexpected loss of so many comrades, had a sobering effect on the regimental psyche. But the irrepressibility of such a young and spirited group could not be denied for long. Two factors in particular worked in favor of the 1st Vermont's ability to shake off any post-retreat doldrums and bounce back ready to try again. One was that they did not wallow in any group responsibility for the debacle. Frank Platt observed that "our regiment lost everything but its good name, and that it will never leave."[51] Assuredly, the men of the 1st Vermont had gained the respect and admiration of their new colonel, who wrote glowingly of them in his after-action report that "the men ... bore their arduous duty with the courage and steadfastness of old and well-tried soldiers, and behaved through the day in a manner to surprise and excite the admiration of their commander."[52]

The other indicator of the regimental morale was their desire to return for a little payback. Captain Frank Platt espoused such bellicose sentiments in a letter home, stating that he would most likely be unable to get a leave and actually wouldn't want one "if we are going back soon, for I would like to go up the valley once more. I do not think the soldiers will leave a building standing."[53] Chaplain Woodward unleashed a good dose of fire and brimstone when he prophesied "we thirst for a day of reckoning with these saucy rebels, and to them, God willing, it will be terrible."[54] Other than just simply wanting to best their opponents in battle, there was a definite undercurrent of revenge driving the cavalry's motivation to get back across the Potomac. Their chance for retribution would come, but for the present they needed to get the regiment back into fighting trim.

11

The Aftermath
Putting the Pieces Back Together

For an army so recently humbled, the defeated Yankees' spirits were high. None possessed a better outlook than the 1st Vermont. In their heart of hearts, the men knew that, while they had been outmaneuvered, they had not been outfought. Having lost most of their belongings and equipment, refitting was needed. Foremost among their requirements was a stand of colors. From the perspective of morale, this constituted a critical matter. Upon hearing of this loss, the regiment's founding father, Colonel Lemuel Platt, started a subscription campaign to fund new banners. The patriotic citizens of Burlington responded magnificently. Sewn within a fortnight, the flags were rushed to the front. Granted that these replacements did not possess the historic lineage of those previously borne in combat, the second set at least restored the regiment's identity. It also more deeply cemented the existing bond between the troops and their adopted city. "The Cavalry Regiment is the pride of Vermont," voiced the *Burlington Times*, "and we rejoice to see that Burlingtonians claim the honor of furnishing the colors, by which we swear to live and die."[1]

While flags made for prouder soldiers, other commodities would produce better fighters. Among the incoming shipments were sabers, fashioned from high-quality steel. But the true prizes were improved firearms. First, there were the Remington-Beals revolvers. A light, sturdily crafted sidearm, in ease of handling and durability alone it was far superior to the Savage pistols. Though there were some skeptics like Wells who initially "was not sure how well they would work," the name Remington soon came to symbolize a superior handgun.[2] In addition to this fine sidearm, several hundred Sharps carbines were procured. Their compactness made this model ideal for mounted troops. Weighing only eight pounds and measuring 39 inches long, its rapid rate of firepower enhanced the tactical capabilities of the cavalry. The use of one-piece linen cartridges, loaded through the weapon's breech, allowed the carbineer to shoot his gun eight to ten times per minute. Companies D, E, K, and I were given these carbines and designated as "heavy cavalry," while the remaining six were "light cavalry" armed with sabers and revolvers.

While Banks' command regrouped, the war continued unabated. Jackson left the Valley and assisted Lee in driving McClellan from the gates of Richmond. Before the 1st Vermont rejoined the fighting in June, the Army of the Valley underwent major restructuring. Out of it came the three-corps Army of Virginia. John Pope was given overall command, with the resilient Nathaniel Banks becoming a subordinate. Much to the satisfaction of the Vermonters, General Hatch remained chief of cavalry.

As ordered, General Banks got elements of his command in motion. In a late-night wire on June 1, he informed the secretary of war that Union troops had occupied Martinsburg. On Monday, June 2, Banks' lead elements neared Winchester, where the enemy's return was awaited with dread. It seemed to be fairly common knowledge around town that civilians had fired shots at Banks' soldiers. As Private John Smith's letter of May 27 to his family indicated, at least one Vermont trooper harbored similar thoughts: "We may now look for a rapid re-occupation of the territory form which General Banks made so masterful a retreat, and, along with it, we hope to see the dastardly rebels who fired from windows upon our troops, and murderously assailed our sick and wounded soldiers, chastised as their savage conduct deserves."[3] Arrests were made, and random searches of homes became daily experiences somewhere in town. While certainly oppressive measures from the perspective of its citizenry, Winchester's reoccupation by Pope's command did not result in the much-feared reprisals.

Up until now, only four Vermont companies under DeForest's command had participated in reinvesting Virginia. Then, on June 13, 1862, the rest of the Vermont Cavalry moved up. Rested and reequipped, they were ready for action. Crossing the Potomac, they camped at Middletown. Shortly thereafter, General Pope assumed command. Three days later, the brigade moved eleven miles east to Cedarville. Then, on Sunday the 29th, its mission changed dramatically. Preparatory to Banks moving his corps east of the Blue Ridge, a reconnaissance-in-force was ordered to scout southwest to Luray Court House. Sources had reported Confederate cavalry at Luray. Pope needed to know whether these enemy horsemen represented merely a defense perimeter or the vanguard of an advance. Knowing that the wily Jackson had outflanked Banks via this route, Pope wanted to be sure that nothing was brewing again. The expedition was commanded by General Samuel Crawford, with Colonel Tompkins leading the cavalry.

Crawford's force covered about fifteen uneventful miles the first day, halting near Milford, Virginia, and leaving only nine miles to traverse on the morrow. On the road at 5:00 A.M., Captain Preston and Company D took the lead. Two pickets were encountered. Though both escaped capture, only the second one did so toward Luray. But his timely warning was enough. Loading up their wagons, the rebels evacuated the village. By the time Preston's vanguard arrived, their train was a distant vision. Trailing the wagons, the Federals noted four companies of Confederate cavalry. Ever game for action, Preston offered pursuit. Attempting to buy time, two companies of rebel cavalry "finally came to the right about and tried to charge us."[4] They encountered a blue-jacketed buzzsaw dashing toward them. On sighting the enemy "drawn up in line just outside of town upon the New Market or Gordonsville Road," the Union advance quickened its forward movement.[5] Preston had ordered his men "to the gallop march, and as soon as it was within charging distance, to charge."[6] Only a few Confederates actually charged, while the Union cavalrymen were strung out in accordance with whose horses were fastest. What Preston's attack lacked in precision was more than made up for in élan. In the estimation of an imbedded correspondent, "The charge led by Captain Preston, of Company D, First Vermont Regiment, was spirited, and was returned with spirit."[7] As often happened in cavalry clashes, "The meeting of the two forces was a desperate one, and for a few moments a hand-to-hand fight ensued."[8] Outnumbering the enemy permitted Captain Preston greater tactical latitude, which he skillfully exploited by calling up two companies for support. The pressure brought against the rebels eventually proved effective. Soon they broke and ran. Company L maintained a brief pursuit that was soon terminated, as the commander's orders had been to only reconnoiter to Luray. Heading back, they re-formed their column for the return to Front Royal. After a full day of marching, fighting, and marching, the weary expedition arrived in camp at 9:00 P.M.

The mission was judged successful, determining that the Confederate cavalry screen was unsupported. In a rare postmortem, Captain Preston shared with Lieutenant Grout his rationale for engaging the enemy outside of Luray. Considering that theirs was intended as a recon mission, attacking a retreating enemy could be viewed as unnecessary. If so, then why was the charge made? Exactly how the subject was broached, Grout never shared, but he was able to provide valuable insight into the thought processes of one of the cavalry's finest field commanders. "Preston's reason for precipitating the dash was that it would do the men good to practice the work of war," wrote Lieutenant Grout.[9] Furthermore, "his idea was that even good soldiers realized fear in first engagements, and that practice was the best agency for overcoming the dread of battle; that when accustomed to it, fighting was very much like other work."[10]

As military endeavors go, this expedition was flawless. Nevertheless, a dark cloud hovered over the Vermonters, nullifying any joy from a successful mission. The reason for grim countenances was the death of eighteen-year-old Private Joseph Gordon. During Preston's charge, Private Gordon "was shot ... when riding as was his custom in advance of his company, and had discharged all the shots of his revolver and carbine at the enemy."[11] The intrepid trooper was drawing his sword when a ball from a rebel pistol struck him squarely in the forehead and plowed completely through his skull. Toppling to the road, he lay motionless. Once the enemy departed, the mortally wounded hero was tenderly placed in a makeshift ambulance and "lived to be borne about four miles on the return when he died in a wagon captured at Luray."[12] Gordon was buried at Front Royal on July 1 with full military honors: "His favorite horse was led under arms behind his coffin, and the whole regiment followed in mournful silence."[13] Private Gordon became the eighth Vermont cavalryman to die in combat and the eleventh overall death in the regiment; but the close-knit nature of locally-raised companies exacerbated the impact of each and every loss. Tears flowed unabashedly that July morning as the popular boy-soldier was laid to rest.

But the most difficult task fell to Edgar Pitkin, for this sensitive, erudite regimental adjutant had to transmit the heartrending news of a beloved son's untimely passing. In his letter, the officer informed the grieving family that they could be proud of Joseph. "My sorrow at thus being compelled to communicate to you the saddest intelligence possible," wrote Pitkin, "is only relieved or lightened by the fact of his habitually soldierly bearing and conduct and his unblemished reputation as a man and his enviable bravery and coolness in the discharge of his duties when he nobly and unflinchingly fell."[14] He told the deceased's parents of a singular honor bestowed in memory of their son. When the regiment's campsite was relocated on July 1st, Colonel Tompkins ordered it christened "Camp Gordon." Yet Joseph Gordon's finest epitaph may have come from his former comrades in arms, appearing as a letter to the editor. By writing "if Newark has more like him let them come to the rescue of the nation," they sincerely showed the depths of their feelings for their fallen brother.[15] Walking away from the burial site, those who truly knew Joseph Gordon grieved over the passing of their friend. They knew that a soldier's soldier had been lost — not only the caliber of man everyone wanted riding next to them in combat but also the kind everyone hoped that he too would be when battle was joined. Joseph Gordon's memory would now join with that of John Chase, and together these two young heroes would still accompany their comrades, riding in spirit across three more years of sanguinary warfare.

It was at this time that General Pope asserted himself as commander of the Army of Virginia. Bringing together all of the fragments under his authority, he relocated them to the eastern side of the Blue Ridge, preparatory to moving into north-central Virginia. The recent expedition to Luray had been a precursor to Pope's intended change of base. With the side door now clear, the cavalry led the way toward Culpeper, forty-three miles south and to the east of Front Royal. Starting out on Sunday, July 6, they made but ten miles before bivouacking for the night. This advance into central Virginia brought the troopers into the rolling hills of the piedmont, closer to larger and more concentrated enemy forces. Conversely, the country offered ideal terrain upon which mounted troops could maneuver. Therefore a cavalry screen, moving slowly ahead of the infantry, could provide valuable service as an early warning system. In the process, Hatch was expected to secure two railroad bridges, one over the Rapidan River and one over Mountain Creek. These structures would be important to his supply lines once his whole army had shifted forward.

The next day the cavalry did not get moving until 4:00 P.M., in part due to brutally warm weather. By the evening's halt, progress was but another fourteen miles. This relatively unhurried pace belied the importance attached to investing Culpeper. Had Pope been more alert, a harbinger of Hatch's future performances was evidenced in this methodical advance. Pope had even gone so far as to inform Banks shortly after noon on the 7th that his subordinate should "send the whole of your cavalry and a battery of artillery, under General Hatch, to make a night march upon Culpeper Court-House and the crossing of the Rapidan," emphasizing once again the need to post "strong pickets to Orange Court-House and at least 20 miles in front of Culpeper toward Richmond."[16] Though two Vermont companies, led by Captain Conger, did conduct a quick reconnaissance into nearby Sperryville on the second night, no attempt was made to reach Culpeper.

On the third day out, the cavalry moved over near Amissville, remaining there for three days. Hatch's brigade had now advanced a grand total of thirty-six miles in six days! Granted some degree of caution was in order, especially when deep in hostile territory, but the snail's pace towards Culpeper should have concerned Pope. The results that he was getting from his spearhead were not at the level the situation required. While Pope was providing a stage upon which his mounted arm could perform, Hatch seemed incapable of seizing the opportunities afforded.

Hatch's cavalry finally reached Culpeper on Saturday, July 12, 1862. Along the way, shots had been exchanged with rebel pickets. Since the Vermonters were in the lead, they incurred losses. Among those wounded in the firefight was Sergeant Marvin Mason. A resident of Craftsbury, the twenty-two-year-old had a bullet pass through his upper arm, fracturing the humerus. According to Dr. Edson, though the bone did eventually heal, there was "so much shortening of tissue that the forearm cannot be extended" which made Trooper Mason unfit for duty.[17] Though awarded a disability discharge the following November, the patriotic Mason would not stay home. He eventually enlisted in the Invalid Corps, wherein he served until March of 1864. At that time, the plucky farmer reenlisted in the Vermont Cavalry, ultimately rising to the rank of 2nd Lieutenant before the war's end.

In a curious coincidence, the same skirmish that saw Private Mason injured also brought the wounding of Sergeant Eben Grant. Josiah Grout was with him when Grant was hit, noting how "the ball entered the upper side of the arm below the elbow and came out the elbow ... which wound shattered the bones of the arm."[18] If Marvin Mason's story was a lesson in perseverance, then Eben Grant's legacy was one of toughness. In hindsight, it was truly amazing that the man was still in Federal service at war's end, considering all of the trying experiences which tested Grant's mettle. The litany began in the fall of 1861 when the horse that he was astride reared so far back that both rider and mount fell over in a heap, leaving Grant with a hernia. Then the errant minie ball blew out his elbow at Culpeper in 1862. In 1863, the seeds for rheumatism were believed planted when the entire command was exposed to a "horrid storm and both horse and soldier suffered greatly from it."[19] Then on June 28, 1864, at Stoney Creek Station, a bursting artillery shell caused deafness in his right ear that would progressively worsen. The soldier's final misfortune occurred the next morning when he was taken prisoner. For a lesser man, captivity might have been the coup de grace to any spirit that the individual had left after three years of hardship. However, for the irrepressible Grant, it was just one more hurdle to be surmounted. After eight months in captivity, Grant capped his inspiring military adventures by escaping from the rebels' clutches. Taking leave of the prison compound at Charlotte, North Carolina, he made his way through the mountains to the safety of Union lines at Knoxville, Tennessee, a month later. After a well-deserved thirty-day furlough, he was back with the 1st Vermont in time to muster out with the regiment on June 29.

But an entire regiment the likes of Mason and Grant could not overcome poor leadership. Taking Culpeper had been the plan. Expending a week to move forty-three miles had not. As if the inexcusable time lag was not regrettable enough, Hatch's tardy arrival in Culpeper was accompanied by a major gaffe. It seems that "the party sent to burn a small railroad bridge by mistake of orders destroyed the Rapidan Bridge."[20] It was probably best for Hatch that Pope could only contact him by telegraph, after the "whoops, we burned the wrong bridge" news reached headquarters. While Civil War telegraphy could not convey emotion, it is likely that Pope's follow-up message was dictated through clenched teeth: "The object of your movement was to preserve the [rail]road, not destroy any portions of it."[21]

The needless delay in the Culpeper advance, coupled with torching a valuable span, should have given Pope an inkling of some serious leadership flaws in Hatch. The same hours squandered by the slow Northern advance were providential moments for Lee and Jackson. Having completed the last of the grueling Seven Days' battles on July 3, the Army of Northern Virginia needed a grace period. Every hour the Southerners were spared having to react to encroachments by Pope's army contributed to their rejuvenation. Once Pope's lead elements got to Culpeper, however, they posed a threat that had to be checked. Wherever they went next could cause real damage, especially if it was toward the rail lines at Gordonsville. Located twenty-nine miles south of Culpeper and eighty miles west of Richmond, Gordonsville gained its military significance as the juncture of the Virginia Central and Orange and Alexandria railroads.

In his own defense, John Pope did not deserve the fate about to befall the vanguard of his army. He tried mightily to impress upon Hatch the importance of interdicting the Virginia Central. The 13th of July was pivotal. The clock was ticking for both Hatch and Pope. On that fateful Sunday, Lee decided to dispatch Jackson to blunt Pope's spearhead. The scenario unfolding was irony at its piquant best: had Banks held Jackson's men in the Valley longer in May, McClellan conceivably would have had a better shot at defeating

Lee in June's Peninsula Campaign, while if McClellan had made a better showing in the Seven Days' battles of late June and early July then perhaps Jackson would not have been available to dash over in August and whip Banks again at Cedar Run.

The very next day, Pope communicated to Banks what should have been the perfect counter to Lee's scheme: "Keep your cavalry going. Push [a] strong force to Gordonsville, and if possible destroy the track east and west of that place."[22] This would entail a march of twenty-eight miles. There was added hope that General Hatch could even strike south another twenty-one miles to destroy the James River Canal. Comprehending the basic order was the easy part for Hatch. However, imbuing the raid with all of the "promptness and vigor, quick and long marches, boldness and skill" expected by Pope were not so transferable.[23] Even the prospect of a possible promotion did nothing to light a fire under the man. With his brigade a full day in advance of the main body, Hatch's normal proclivity towards timidity heightened. In Ide's estimation, on the nights of the 15th and 16th, "General Hatch was in rather a nervous state and every time the pickets were fired upon by bushwhackers we would have to saddle up and remain so all night."[24] As if his lack of aggressiveness wasn't hindrance enough, Hatch made matters worse by delaying his departure, contrary to Pope's admonition on the 14th that "no time should be lost."[25] Compounding his slow start, Hatch expanded what was intended to be a quick-hitting, mounted strike-force into a plodding column that included infantry, artillery, and a wagon train! The first day out, after leaving at 6:00 A.M. and progressing south but a few miles, the order was given to halt for the night. Soaked after marching in a driving rain, many were the troopers wondering the why of it all. Breaking camp at 2:00 A.M. the next morning, the raiders headed west toward Madison Court House, making the first day's movement toward Raccoon Ford a feint for the benefit of loyal citizens who were sure to inform the enemy of his column's direction. After covering about ten rain-soaked miles the next day, Thursday, the 17th of July, Hatch's command bivouacked on the north bank of the Robertson River's swollen waters. The next morning, four companies of the 1st Vermont were off on a reconnaissance-in-force toward Gordonsville. When they returned with the information that enemy troops lay about seven miles to the south between the Federal column and Gordonsville, Hatch made the unilateral decision to scrub the mission, returning to Culpeper on the 19th. What should have been the "Gordonsville Raid" was reduced to nothing more than the "Gordonsville Ride."

General Pope was incredulous when he learned of the abject failure of Hatch's mission, especially the knowledge that the rebels possessed Gordonsville with all trackage intact and operational. In Pope's exasperated words, "I never dreamed of such a thing. The whole movement ... was purely a cavalry operation, to be made rapidly and for a specific purpose."[26] When the race was over, the Confederate troops riding the iron horses beat the Union troops riding the cavalry horses to Gordonsville. While General Pope did get to see the initiative that he had sought, it was the wrong side displaying it.

For most of the 1st Vermont, the episode amounted to nothing more than a very wet inconvenience. For some, though, the experience was a personal disaster. Two of these luckless troopers were none other than the Vermont Cavalry's soldier-diarist Horace Ide and his companion Conceader Durlam. Serving as videttes for the column's movement towards Gordonsville on July 18, they became overzealous in the pursuit of two Confederates, riding right into the clutches of hidden rebel infantry. Ordered to surrender, the two troopers complied quickly rather than being blown out of their saddles. In the difficult times that followed, Corporal Ide proved to be the more fortunate of the two, as he served only two months of incarceration before his parole. But Private Durlam contracted diphtheria. Ide and other prisoners did the best that they could to care for their comrade, but, lacking medicine, nothing could be done to halt the ravages of the deadly disease. Mercifully, the end came quickly — Durlam expired after a week. His was body was tenderly washed by his friends, placed in a wooden coffin, and buried on the banks of the James River, a crude plank headboard marking his place of final rest.

For Mr. and Mrs. Frederick Durlam in Concord, Vermont, Private Durlam's tragic death had multiple ramifications that weighed heavily on their minds. Above all, the aging couple lost a beloved son, causing lifelong heartache. Then there was the seemingly incomplete destiny of someone dying young that eats at the minds of those left behind, wondering what the departed might have accomplished with a full life. For the Durlams, there was also the economic impact that accompanied a male offspring's untimely death: their old-age insurance policy got cancelled. While they certainly never thought of him in such crass terms, the hand-to-mouth existence that subsistence farmers lived meant financial difficulties in their twilight years. A "poor and needy" pair, "after his enlistment he (Conceader) regularly transmitted to his mother ... Betsy Durlam all of his pay while he was a soldier."[27] While the pension his mother was granted helped to fill the financial void, the government could do nothing to replace the empty chair at the Durlam's supper table.

Like so many events in war, Troopers Ide and Durlam were victims of circumstance; specifically, John Hatch's repeated failure to take objectives in timely fashion. Considering the incredibly lackluster performance by Hatch over the previous ten days, it is a wonder that Pope had any more faith left in his subordinate. Yet, no sooner did the Gordonsville fiasco end than Hatch was inexplicably entrusted to carry out still another raid. Pope, however, made it clear to Banks that Hatch had better not botch this one: "He lost an opportunity to distinguish himself greatly and to render immense service to his country" was Pope's stinging appraisal of Hatch's recent efforts that prefaced a new set of orders.[28] The next sentence was fraught with foreboding: "He still has the chance, and I trust for his own sake he will not lose it."[29] This time his cavalry was ordered farther to the southwest. The objectives were again rail and telegraph lines. Pope first wanted as much track as possible destroyed east of Charlottesville toward Gordonsville before Hatch was then to move to the western side of the town and damage the railroad heading to Lynchburg. The commanding general estimated that thirty-six hours would be required to accomplish this mission. To avoid any misunderstanding, he issued detailed orders: Hatch's troopers were to take two days' rations, keep stops to a minimum, use speed to their advantage, stay out of Gordonsville and Charlottesville, and avoid engaging enemy infantry and artillery. They were expected to live off the land and seize locals as guides. The only leeway allowed Hatch was to return by any route that suited him.

Though Pope had suggested that four or even five companies could handle the job, Hatch blithely disregarded his superior's advice. Instead, he assembled a formidable host of fifteen hundred riders! To his credit, the general moved out quickly this time. As ordered, Hatch saddled himself with neither slow-moving foot soldiers nor supply wagons, but to his undoing he remained overly cautious. Once scouts brought back word of enemy forces ahead, he immediately turned to the northwest, sidestepping through Swift Run Gap into the Luray Valley. Here his men were safe but so were the tracks of the Orange and Alexandria Railroad. By the time Hatch's men had completed their circuitous route back to Culpeper, they had covered 110 miles. Two prisoners constituted all the damage inflicted upon the enemy. As Josiah Grout recalled this unfulfilling odyssey, "[W]ith three days' rations, we made a five days' observation.... This was a fruitless movement. We saw nothing but country and found nothing but hunger."[30] In his dispatch of July 27 to Banks, Hatch alleged his failure was due to the "utter breaking up of his horses, the state of the roads, and the storms."[31] Pope had heard enough. The order removing Hatch from command arrived later that day. Unfortunately, while John Hatch's methodical approach matched that of Banks, it was not at all copasetic with Pope's desire to advance rapidly. Given multiple opportunities to shine, Hatch's star only dimmed with each botched mission. Hatch was relieved of his command on July 30. Though he remained popular with his men and stayed in the army, his affiliation with cavalry was over.

When the calendar turned to August, Pope was left to deal with a deteriorating situation. The genie in the form of "Stonewall" Jackson was out of the bottle. Confederate forces in growing numbers were massing in front of Pope and they were wanting very much to strike a blow. There is an anecdote about Jackson that sums up the prevailing Southern attitude where the invading Pope and his troops were concerned: "This new General claims your attention," someone remarked to Jackson as he set out. "And, please God, he shall have it," Jackson replied.[32]

12

More Hard Riding Under Pope
But With the Same Results

July's campaigning proved hard on the men and animals. Oddly enough, the regiment experienced little full-scale combat; but frequent movement, improper diet, and insufficient rest exacted a heavy toll. In one soldier's experience, "[L]iving almost all of the time in the saddle the opportunities for writing letters are limited.... [T]he past three or four weeks [the month of July] have been weeks of hard service for the Cavalry in this Department."[1] A comrade further detailed the grim situation, telling how "three days frequently pass without unsaddling the horses, and the backs of the poor emaciated brutes are first sore, then burst rotten; still they are kept at work."[2] While it would have no effect on the workload, it was at this point in time that John Hatch departed. In his place, John Buford assumed command of the Second Corps' cavalry. Though a solid leader, Buford's name was not yet a household word. In a cavalry career lasting only seventeen more months, Buford attained enviable status. He became the first of several legendary officers under whom the 1st Vermont would thrive.

Two days later, a reconnaissance-in-force to Orange Court House was ordered. Knowing Jackson's whereabouts was of paramount importance. To ascertain the disposition of any enemy troops before them, General Samuel Crawford took a mixed command out on Friday, August 1. Among the members of the mounted force Buford brought along were the 1st Vermont, 5th New York, and 1st Michigan, plus a squadron of the 1st [West] Virginia Cavalry. Thinned by the rigorous summer campaign, the force tallied only between 750 and 1000 horsemen. It seemed that each day's roll call revealed additional gaps in the ranks. By an almost four to one ratio over battle-related deaths, disease would be the greatest single killer. The regiment's most recent loss was George Lowell, who died on July 28. The trooper's troubles began when his horse stumbled, threw Lowell, and then landed on top of him, causing injury to his side and arm. Then, while recuperating, the luckless private contracted typhoid fever. On July 11, the soldier was furloughed home to East Calais, where he could receive the absolute best of care. En route, "He became sick in Baltimore and a doctor had to be called to give him some medicine."[3] Fortunately, Lowell had a traveling companion, one Calvin Stowe, "who had met him at the Hagerstown Hospital and stayed with him til [their] arrival at Montpelier."[4]

At the depot there, the Good Samaritan turned over his charge to a friend of Lowell's named Henry Sumner. But Lowell's health had deteriorated to the point that Sumner did not want to put him through any more distressing travel. Other than to make his final days comfortable, there wasn't much that the attending physician could do for the dying soldier. Finally, on the 20th of July, Lowell was taken the rest of the way home. Unlike so many in both armies, Lowell was spared the despair of dying far from home. For whatever solace it may have brought, he at least got to say good-bye to his family and be buried in a marked grave. With his wife, Luvia, now by his side, his earthly remains lie on a hillside facing the morning sun. From beneath the boughs of a maple, the plot looks to the horizon filled with the undulating peaks of the Green Mountains. Prominent across the bottom of a rectangular tombstone of white granite, in raised letters, are words obviously having significance to the departed trooper: "Member of Co. H 1st Vt. Cavalry." It seems that the association which resulted in Lowell's passing was borne no ill will by his family but rather instead was chosen to represent the measure of the man for the ages. One could hardly blame Luvia Lowell if she was less than enamored with the Federal government; however, it was the pension bureau with which she waged a war of her own. Since her husband had passed away at home, proving his death to the military's satisfaction was necessary. Aided by a sympathetic relative, Smilie Bancroft, a local justice of the peace, Mrs. Lowell corresponded with the War Department, requesting that her claim for a widow's pension please be processed. As Judge Bancroft wrote on March 19, 1863, "Her claim was made out and mailed to your office on the 22nd day of January last [1863] and as she has not received any reply from you she feels quite anxious about the same as she is in a very destitute situation."[5] She eventually got the pension. The family persevered, their lives went on — and so did the war. As the dirt was just beginning to settle over George Lowell's newly interred coffin, the 1st Vermont was mounting up for its mission to Orange Court House.

They were on the march by 4:00 A.M. the next morning. Fording the river and snaking along the Rapidan's south bank, the 1st Vermont closed on Orange Court House. Somewhere along the line of march, the initial casualty of the day occurred. In a fluke accident, Private John Smith, a blacksmith for Company C, got his "foot caught in a wagon wheel while on horseback, turning it outward."[6] Due to the excessive torque placed on the joint, it was violently wrenched. Smith henceforth had difficulty walking because of his bent foot. Within three months, he was discharged, depriving the cavalry of his services. But accidents happened, and, while Private Smith was being treated, the raiders continued on with their march. Progressing about six miles, the column approached a junction. Companies D and I of the 1st Vermont were ordered ahead as skirmishers. A squadron from the 5th New York followed immediately behind, ready to give support. In a matter of minutes, rebel pickets were encountered four miles from the village. Shots were exchanged, the enemy troops driven back. A running gun battle on into town ensued.

With the intention of giving the rebels' main force little time to steel itself, the hard-charging Vermonters shifted from pursuit mode into attack formation. Swinging to the right, five companies continued on into town while the 5th New York went to the left and then down other streets. Soon both forces were heavily engaged. Initially, the New Yorkers cleared the Confederates from their front. As rebel officers tried to regroup their men, Company H of the 5th New York hit them. This unit had completed a 180 degree arc from whence they had begun their charge, causing them to approach the confused enemy from behind. The timing and placement of their fortuitous attack inspired the rebels to rapidly depart. The best route open to them led back the way that they had just come. Thus, by virtue of the 5th "making a dash into the rear of the rebels, who doubtlessly thinking their time had come," caused them to wheel about and charge "down the main street upon the column of the 5th, which broke and fled in terrible confusion, breaking up one of the companies of the 1st Vermont which was borne down by the weight of numbers."[7]

At the same time that the New York troopers advanced on their left, the Vermonters were heavily engaged in another sector. Initial penetration into the village's tree-lined streets had been met with silence. "On the entrance not a soul could be seen," one soldier recalled, "an ominous sign."[8] The town soon proved to be anything but deserted. Instead it was crawling with rebel cavalry who opened up a heavy fire. Being forced to fight in village streets was not a cavalryman's preferred field of battle. As they moved up Main Street, the Vermonters were hit by a flank attack from the direction of the railroad depot. Just as this thrust gained momentum, the crush of the rebels fleeing the New Yorkers flowed hurriedly through the town and into their midst. Before long, "the main street of Orange Court House was packed with the contending horsemen, the choice spirits of both sides pushing into the thick of the fight, the timid withdrawing."[9] Confusion reigned as companies intermingled, and men became separated from their comrades. Individual engagements sprang up amidst the swirl of the larger battle. "Captain Earhardt of Co. A, with a half dozen of his men, was surrounded by twenty or thirty rebels" was how one trooper recalled one group's desperate straits.[10] Confronted by increasing pressure, the 1st Vermont gave ground. A correspondent described the regiment's being "attacked by the enemy, about 500 strong, surrounding our forces on every side."[11] The predicament in which the Green Mountain troopers found themselves was dire at best. Four companies of the 7th Virginia Cavalry comprised the spearhead. "After driving the enemy from the town," reported Colonel William Jones, their commander, "[they] found themselves confronted with such overwhelming odds as necessitated a retreat."[12]

The "overwhelming odds" to which Colonel Jones referred were created by Companies F and G joining the fray. At this precise moment, a half hour after hostilities had commenced at 1:00 P.M., these Vermont troopers got the rare opportunity to rescue their own. Adding special satisfaction, this deliverance was effected with swords. Gleaming brilliantly in the afternoon sun, the ominous-looking blades were held high as the men and horses thundered forward. The order to charge was accompanied by a bugle's shrill staccato and an enthusiastic shout. William Wells felt that attacking the enemy with an edged weapon was preferable to a firearm because the "rebs will stand and let you shoot at them all day but will not [stand before] the sabre."[13] A violent collision between the charging Yankees and the head of the fast-moving rebel column ensued. The timely arrival of the Union reserves blunted and then turned the Confederate advance. In the final analysis, this determined charge by the two gutsy, undermanned companies led by Lieutenants Wells and Hall saved the day. "We went in with a yell," wrote Homer Ruggles, "and the rebels broke and fled in every direction, and we after them, running them down and taking them prisoners."[14] Swords were swung viciously as the Vermonters pursued the retreating enemy. In one notable duel, a Confederate major boldly reined in his horse, wheeled, and stood his ground, ready to take on a trooper from Company F. For all his confidence in his swordsmanship, the officer wound up stretched out in the dusty road with a cut on his head and soon-to-be POW status to show for his effort. As William Wells later recorded the glory of the moment, "[O]ur forces started to fall back when F and G mounted a saber charge and drove the rebels like chaff before the wind."[15]

Strangely, few Vermont cavalrymen were hurt in this hotly contested action. One who did was Company K's Collis Ikey, suffering not one but two injuries. The first was caused by "a minie ball passing through his left arm, shattering the bone, and passing into his left side, striking a rib and passing around near to [his] backbone where it was [eventually] extracted."[16] As if a .69 caliber bullet pinballing through his body was not painful enough, Private Ikey then incurred "the rupture of both groins" when "thrown by his horse upon the pommel of his saddle."[17] Three months and several hospitals later, Ikey received his honorable discharge.

For some elements of the Vermont Cavalry, the skirmish at Orange Court House did not end when the rebels exited from town. Pumped by their success, adrenalin-charged Companies F and G kept going. In a spirited chase, they went through a barnyard, across a lane, over a hill, through a wood lot, in and out of underbrush, and ended only when the enemy was pinned ingloriously in a large ditch. During the pursuit, as rebel troopers were captured, Captain Wells sent them off under guard. Eventually, the frequency of sending men back caused Wells to wind up conducting the chase with but five men. Somewhere amidst the confusion, the Confederates realized that they outnumbered their pursuers. Turning, they surrounded their erstwhile captors. Rather than surrender, Wells commanded his men to run. The rebels ordered them to halt, and amidst a shower of Confederate lead the Vermonters raced "their horses back as fast as possible to keep themselves out of rebel hands."[18]

While Wells' band barely escaped, not all of their comrades were as lucky. Privates John McLaughlin and Alonzo Hoyt of Company C were captured during the mop-up stages of the operation. As they slowly returned to Orange after the steeplechase pursuit, the Vermonters were hailed by a group of unidentifiable troopers. Weary, their guard down, the two men responded to the waving group's beckoning. Innocently duped, they obligingly responded, only at the last instant realizing their error. For the unfortunate Private Hoyt, this detainment represented the second time that he fallen into rebel hands, the other instance being Banks' retreat. While incarcerated but briefly, it was the second go-around in enemy hands that adversely affected Hoyt's health. "Confined in Libby and Belle Island prisons for two months and that by reason of cruel treatment and starvation he contracted his problems."[19] "Problems" probably should have been capitalized because the poor man had a plethora: diarrhea, typhoid, pneumonia, and pleurisy. By the time his enlistment expired, Hoyt had experienced enough. He opted to go home in the fall of 1864 rather than sign up for another hitch. While he spent the rest of his life with impaired health, even moving to South Florida for its climatic benefits, the old soldier still survived until 1918 and the ripe old age of 80!

As for John McLaughlin, he remained in captivity just under two months—a brief confinement compared to what many later endured. Private McLaughlin nevertheless was exposed to adverse conditions long enough to aggravate two preexisting maladies— a heart ailment and rheumatism. Being fifty-two years old when he enlisted probably did not work to his advantage. What was termed "ill-treatment by the enemy" did not help either.[20] After his parole, McLaughlin spent time convalescing in hospitals. Eventually returning to duty, he was scheduled to be discharged in the fall of 1864 when his three-year hitch expired. Instead, infirmities not withstanding, McLaughlin gamely reenlisted as a Veteran Volunteer and stayed on through June of 1865.

In addition to the wounding of Ikey and three other troopers and the capture of Hoyt and McLaughlin, only one other Vermonter suffered any deprivation. This individual was Ellis Draper of Company B. Taken on August 2, Private Draper remained in rebel custody at Libby Prison until paroled on September 2, 1862. During his incarceration, he was a model prisoner, especially generous in providing humanitarian assistance to others sharing his fate. Upon his release, he was given an unusual letter of recommendation from one of his prison-mates: "This young man Draper has been some time imprisoned here and has been useful to the officers of the Army of V[irginia] who are in confinement. On this account, I should be very glad to hear that his application for fifteen days furlough is successful."[21] Once free, Private Draper wrote a letter of his own requesting the leave. "I have the honor to apply to you for a furlough of fifteen days," he stated, "for the purpose of transacting business for a number of officers of our army who are now in close confinement at Richmond and to whom I have been useful in various ways while myself in prison."[22] He went on to buttress his plea by noting that he had "been seventeen months in active service ... had no furlough during this time and ... [had] a wife, family, and friends who I am anxious to see once more."[23] Unfortunately the repatriated Draper never got his leave. Upon his return, he was promptly confined first to the post hospital at Fort Delaware and later at an institution in Washington, D.C. His condition was such that he was discharged in February of 1863. Draper's rather odd rationale for having sought a furlough in the first place may be in part explainable by the unusual nature of his illness. When he parted company with the army, Private Draper did so upon his release from a hospital for the insane where he had been treated for mental instability. Whether he entered the service with the illness or became disoriented by the privations of prison was not discernible from his records. But it may have been that Ellis Draper was a gentle soul whose psyche was just too fragile to cope with the hardships of war. There was, however, at least one silver lining to the tragedy. A tailor by calling, Private Draper was one of a few disabled veterans whose war-inflicted infirmities did not preclude a return to his prewar occupation.

The aftermath of the day's fighting left the cavalry with several mop-up tasks. Of immediate military significance, there were railroad tracks to be torn up and telegraph lines to be cut. Then there was the matter of burying the one New York soldier who had lost his life in the encounter. This was attended to in a simple service conducted on the outskirts of town amongst a grove of trees. "During the entire skirmish, 25 of the enemy were killed, 2 mortally and several severely wounded, and 52 prisoners taken," which meant that arrangements had to be made for securely transporting the POWs back to Union lines.[24] Temporarily, the county courthouse was pressed into service as a holding pen. As for tending to the enemy casualties, these were obligations left to their comrades who would reinvest the village once the Union forces departed. To some extent, the care of the wounded had already begun. During lulls in the fighting, citizens of Orange had scurried out into the streets and spirited the wounded as well as the dead back into their homes. As was the case on any battlefield, there was also the detritus of war left lying haphazardly about the streets: "Hats, caps, haversacks, and all kinds of arms were strewn around promiscuously."[25] Deceased rebels and horses were also scattered about the town. The upshot of the engagement was one with a very positive outcome for the Vermonters. More than a score of the enemy were killed and over two score and ten captured. Confederate rail and telegraph communications were disrupted. The expedition left the vicinity but continued on an extended reconnaissance.

For the remainder of Pope's summer campaign, the 1st Vermont performed vital service as an all-purpose unit. They did some scouting, a little rearguard duty, and tangled briefly on several occasions with rebel troops, most notably at Waterloo Bridge. By the time they went into winter quarters, they had virtually nothing left to give. The men and the animals were thoroughly spent.

13

Rebuilding the Regiment
The Winter at Fort Scott

For the winter of 1862–63, the 1st Vermont set up in "Camp Stoneman," on the lowlands before Fort Scott. An earthen bastion in the Arlington Defense Line, the fort was named for the old war hero Winfield Scott. Overlooking the Four Mile Run Valley, the fort provided immediate protection for the converted Aqueduct Bridge and the Long Bridges leading to Washington and the heights near Arlington.

To state that the Vermont Cavalry "rode" into this encampment needs qualification by the word "barely." However exhausted the men were from the summer's demands, their horses were equally played out. Among the priorities to be addressed, none was more pressing than acquiring replacement mounts, as the summer's campaigning had exacted a heavy toll. While flying lead brought down many horses, equine physiology was also susceptible to debilitating as well as fatal microbes. From the standpoint of ailments, it was not surprising that the state of health for even the sturdiest of horses was sorely tested by the rigors of cavalry life.

As their constitutions wore out, horses became increasingly disease prone. The two most common afflictions were "glanders" and "greasy heel." Greasy heel was a bacterial disease of the skin above a horse's hooves, identifiable by an oozing gray matter. Swelling was often present along with tenderness. The animal usually appeared lame. In a grisly, worst-case scenario, the hoof fell off. Contributing to the incubation of the disease were insufficient diet, constant exposure to dampness, and rough riding conditions. The other scourge of horseflesh was known as "glanders." Unlike greasy heel, glanders was communicable within the species. Infecting the mucous membranes and lymphatic system, its most noticeable manifestation was a pustular discharge emanating from the nostrils. Infected animals had to be destroyed.

However dreaded these diseases were, the most frequent and often fatal injury was the combat wound. With all of the whirling, rearing, and intermingling that comprised a cavalry engagement, it is not surprising that the horses incurred wounds. Factor in the comparative size of a horse, which dwarfs that of a human, and Captain Willard Glazier's observation is quite prescient: "In battle the horse is a larger mark than a man and hence more frequently victimized than the rider," the captain noted, "so that there is always a much larger proportion of casualties among horses than men of a cavalry command in every engagement."[1] Though unintended, the defenseless horse was often the exposed cavalryman's best protection.

As the 1st Vermont limped into camp on weary mounts, a demoralized air hovered over the men. They amounted to a cavalry unit in name only. From the first week of September when it had entered the Washington line until November 1, the regiment had seen its quotient of serviceable horses drop from 335 to a mere 14![2] Commenting on this nightmare was Private Albert Sawyer. He accurately deduced what the status quo was going to be when he wrote his aunt, telling her that "we do not know how long we are to stay in this place but we will not move many miles probably 'til we get our horses."[3] Then he shared a thought that was undoubtedly felt with equal compassion by many other comrades. "Perhaps we will not get our horses until spring," Private Sawyer wrote his aunt, "at least I hope not if we stay any where in this vicinity unless we have shelter for the poor things, the ones that are here have a hard life of it."[4]

The "dismounted blues" was a refrain picked up by even the newest recruits. Albert Greene was such an individual, having been in the cavalry only since September 29. The young bachelor from Highgate told his family how the regiment "had no horses yet but expect them within one week."[5] While his folks were probably relieved at his being temporarily afoot, it is unlikely that Private Greene shared their feelings. Young men did not enlist in the cavalry with expectations of being rendered horseless little more than a month into what was to be a career hallmarked by its mounted panache. Equally green but just as grounded was newcomer George Calkins. Private Calkins, also a late summer recruit, wrote of the same scenario, describing how "we had our horses inspected and we had one serviceable horse in the company."[6]

However, relief was coming. Lt. Colonel Addison Preston and Assistant Quartermaster Captain R.W. Clarke had been ordered home to procure more horses. Authorized to buy 900 animals, these officers were prepared to expend $100,000. Starting from Brattleboro on October 22, they traveled to St. Johnsbury on the 30th. This stop was followed by one at Barton on November 4 and 5 and then Derby Line on the 7th and 8th.[7] In support of their efforts, the boys at the front lobbied the homefolks. According to the well-chosen words of one officer, "We are anxiously awaiting the arrival of our horses so that we can join in the advance upon the rebels; it is by far better for a cavalry regiment to be in active service than laying around in comparative idleness, especially under the shadow of the capitol! I hope Vermont will send some good horses to us for one half the efficiency of a cavalry regiment depends upon the quality of its horses."[8]

How successful was the buying mission? After three days in St. Johnsbury, 100 horses had been acquired. Moving on to Barton, they added another 125 to their lot, which was started for Fort Scott by rail on November 19. Those who knew horses felt that the price range in which they were able to consummate their deals was very favorable to the government, with the lament being stated that in ordinary times a ceiling as high as $125 could have easily been reached. The editor of the *St. Johnsbury Caledonian*, in his paper's November 7, 1862 issue, called his readers' attention to an odd economic phenomenon: when military needs made horseflesh a highly desired commodity that prices would remain so low. This was followed by the *Caledonian*'s striking a proud posture in observing that "the supply which is constantly brought forward is but another evidence of the vast resources of the country."[9]

Altogether, the first batch sent tallied 225 animals. Benedict commented on the officers' efforts when he noted "the condition of the regiment improved somewhat during the closing months of the year," when "the dismounted men were remounted upon 500 horses from Vermont."[10] Horace Ide stated "purchases in Vermont and government issue brought the number of serviceable horses to 552 on January 1, 1863, and to 668 by the 24th."[11] Procurement efforts concluded in April, the success of which was evidenced by the fact that the 1st Vermont, as consolidated at Fairfax Court House on June 16, 1863, consisted of 879 men, mounted and ready for duty. As they began the summer's campaign, the Vermonters did so astride their trusted Morgan horses.

Considering all of the grueling marches, limited sleep, and short rations cavalry units endured, it is not surprising that an attachment borne out of shared experiences developed between horse and rider. In a conflict witnessing the sacrifice of so many human lives and the accompanying sadness inflicted upon friends and families, it may seem hard to believe that there could be any tears left to shed for animals. What started out as a match amounting to a blind date frequently grew into a marriage of sorts. So devoted did these relationships become that a man's horse grew to be a combination of old friend, faithful companion, and beloved pet. Together they shared hardships and dangers, inconveniences and sufferings, and trials and tribulations. The longer they served in tandem, the closer they became. In Captain Glazier's view, "a horse and rider have learned to love one another and the animal manifests affection and confidence quite as evidently as a human could," a feeling returned in kind by the fact that "some men would rather injure themselves than have their horses harmed."[12]

Lorento King espoused such feelings when he proudly wrote the homefolks that "I kept the same horse I had in Burlington. I guess she is a good fighting one.... If she lives, and I don't stop *breathing*, I reckon she will go to Vt. with me. I can show you a *war* horse, *which* is a horse."[13] King's letter is intriguing regarding this mount. It may well have been a much more special animal than he realized. Considering that he was writing in the spring of 1863, it meant that his horse represented two minorities: the first being that she was a mare, which cavalry horses generally were not; and the second, since Private King professed having ridden her since Burlington, his horse would have been one who had already survived much: the tortuous train ride to Washington; the spring advance up the Shenandoah Valley; Banks' Retreat at the end of May; Pope's demanding summer campaign; and the outbreaks of disease, all of which served to make this remarkable animal potentially one of the lucky fourteen who were present for duty on November 1, 1862. While Lorento King died from disease in March of 1865, the fate of his nameless warhorse has unfortunately been lost in time. Though she may have deserved a fitting memorial, it will have to suffice as her legacy that a duty was fulfilled to the utmost of her ability. Like thousands of other Morgans, she quietly and anonymously helped the 1st Vermont achieve honor and glory.

Replacement horses were not the only deficiency requiring attention. The men, too, were physically spent. Once the regiment entered camp, the process of resting the tired and weary, healing the sick and injured, discharging the infirm and disabled, and recruiting the hale and hardy began. Many must have functioned on sheer willpower. Once the regiment stood down, their bodies crashed. As one trooper described the phenomena, "[O]n our arrival here exhausted nature could hold out no longer and our sick list began to swell day to day until it reached the large number of one hundred and sixty."[14] For those disabled who wound up being released between September 6, 1862, and April 1, 1863, their cases generally fell into two categories: those who arrived at Fort Scott with a preexisting condition and those who contracted an ailment or injury at the winter encampment.

With respect to the soldiers who arrived already suffering, their infirmities were varied. "Banks' Retreat" caused many debilitating injuries. With all of the rapid movement associated with the army's sudden departure from Virginia, a variety of noncombat mishaps had occurred. Then, before some of these had a chance to properly heal, Pope pushed the cavalrymen up to and, for some, beyond the limits of endurance. This served to aggravate injuries. Fatigue too had a tendency to make men more error-prone. Those with battle wounds were understandably taken care of quickly, but many troopers with less obvious maladies gutted it out through the summer. Eventually, worn down by the rigor of cavalry service, these "walking wounded" finally gave in to their ills when the regiment was taken off-line.

Private Daniel McDixon was one who manfully bore his pain as long as he could. But in the end, unable to perform his duties, a disability discharge was the only viable option left open to him. On the 1st of May Private McDixon suffered an "injury to the spine causing partial loss of power in [his] lower extremities."[15] The accident triggering this problem was the result of his horse rearing back and then crushing him. What made the twenty-seven-year-old McDixon's condition all the more incapacitating was the vital nature of his work. A farrier for Company A, he helped keep the horses shod and in good health, acting as a combination blacksmith and veterinarian. McDixon's job was physically demanding, but due to his injury he could not perform even basic tasks. Since he had "not been on duty so as to be serviceable for many months" prior to his November 3 discharge, his loss had come at a most critical time for the cavalry, when its horses were in dire need of attention.[16]

Company G's Sergeant Avery Sibley was another trooper with a painful, horse-related malady. In his case, a "shell burst sent his horse to the ground" in one of the charges on May 24, injuring his left breast. Compounding the problem was his capture and subsequent confinement at Lynchburg, where he was alleged to have "received no medical treatment for his injuries."[17] Released in September, Sergeant Sibley made the circuit from the parole center at Annapolis to the convalescent facility at Alexandria before finally rejoining the regimen. But the sickly man who returned almost four months later was not the hardened soldier who mounted up at Middletown. Having contracted diarrhea, malaria, rheumatism, and defective eyesight, Sibley's current physical condition did not remotely approximate the prewar constitution of the former railroad section hand. Since in Surgeon Gale's estimation Sibley was "not able to do full duty any portion of the time," his prognosis in supporting a December 1862 discharge was that his patient's health troubles would "improve out of the army and finally he will recover of it altogether."[18]

Adding to the list of those discharges coming as a direct result of duty-related accidents, there was a spate of fluke mishaps that befell some men. Being in a noncombat mode for several months was no guarantee that individuals would not find ways to harm themselves. Charles Turner, a veteran of the 1st Vermont Infantry, did not have a lot of luck his second time around. First he was captured during the summer of '62. After his release, he spent time in Camp Parole, Maryland, where he believed that he had contracted rheumatism from sleeping on the cold ground. The coup de grace for Private Turner was a self-inflicted gunshot wound. "While cleaning his pistol ... [he] accidentally shot [his] left ankle."[19] This led to his disability discharge on February 2, 1863. Another soldier who placed his life in jeopardy was Andrew Hart of Company I. One of the original recruits, this unfortunate trooper damaged his upper respiratory system as a result of partially drowning. It seems that Private Hart and several companions were watering their horses in the Potomac. As his mount waded out into the shallows, it stepped into a hole, causing Hart to be pitched into the river and stunned by a blow to his head. In confirming the accident, Josiah Grout wrote how "Hart had remained under water some number of minutes and when taken out was supposed to be dead but by the aid of restoratives was resuscitated."[20] Though he survived, his lungs were permanently damaged. Never again able to do much physically, his inability to engage in the routine duties of a cavalryman, let alone the more rigorous expectations of combat, left doctors no other option than to send him home.

Once they were out of their saddles and able to rest, it was not unrealistic to expect the troopers' health to rebound. However, sanitary conditions in a military camp of the Civil War era offered no guarantee that healthy individuals would stay that way. Not surprisingly, those in an already weakened condition were much more susceptible to diseases. While camp life afforded a welcome refuge from rebel bullets, many men still wound up with a fight on their hands. In the case of Samuel Blair, his trials began and ended very quickly. Admitted to the regimental hospital on October 18, 1862, the private from Company B was diagnosed with typhoid fever. On October 26, 1862, the eighteen-year-old boy-soldier lay dead, having lived to serve only three weeks short of a year in the grandest adventure of his young life. For Thomas Rowlen, the ride to war was also woefully brief. Mustered in on August 25, Private Rowlen never got to hear a shot fired in anger. Shortly after his arrival at Fort Scott, he contracted a particularly severe case of diarrhea, which precipitated his death in an Alexandria hospital on November 29, 1862. Unlike young Blair, who had never married, Rowlen was a forty-four-year-old father of five. The last of these five was Brittania. Regrettably, she had lived but four months when Thomas passed away. All the poor girl would ever know of her father came from the memories of others.

During the course of the winter, many other Vermont soldiers joined Troopers Rowlen and Blair in needless deaths. In a later era, advances in medical science might have saved them. Private Curtis Field left this earth on September 22, dying in the camp hospital of typhoid fever. October 7 marked the passing of Squire Shedd, who expired in the regimental hospital from chronic diarrhea. On November 3, Henry Hall died in Alexandria from wounds received in combat. Sixteen days later, Private Sylvester Crumb became another victim of typhoid fever. The same disease took twenty-six-year-old Albert Lantz of Company M on February 16. A new recruit from western New York, Private Lantz had been with the regiment barely six weeks when he was taken ill. So quick was his demise, occurring but three days after he had entered the hospital, it is unlikely that his family even knew that he had taken a turn for the worse. Just as cruel, Lantz probably never learned that his wife had given birth to his second son, Willis, on the 12th. While the young boy would forever share a common day of celebration with the memory of our 16th president, such was his fate that he would pass all of his birthdays without his father's presence. The Lantz boys thus became two more children of their generation whose lives the Civil War inexorably altered. When a final count was taken, there were a score who succumbed to an assortment of ailments contracted while the Vermonters were stationed at Camp Stoneman.

While the vicinity of Fort Scott proved deadly for some men, the site was by no means a dangerous place during the fall and winter of 1862–1863. From the standpoint of whistling minie balls and flying shrapnel, no one died on the premises due to enemy action. In fact, from October 1, 1862, to April 1, 1863, there was not one single battle death in the regiment. Yet the ranks still precipitously thinned during the winter encampment. Slightly over 100 men were discharged. To make good these losses in addition to those having occurred during the summer's fighting, the regiment required an infusion of new blood. This replenishment would be effected via two means. The first was the addition of new recruits, and the other was the return of paroled POWs.

The largest influx came from enlistments. Approximately 230 new recruits were signed up to restock the existing companies. Among this pool was nineteen-year-old Charles Stone. After enlisting in August, he was told to come back on September 2 to begin his military career. From then until September 25, his daily routine would commence with "roll call, drill from 9½ to 11, dinner at 12, drill from ½ past 1 till 3 P.M., roll call at six."[21] When they weren't engaged in matters of instruction, the men had time to themselves. Like their soon-to-be-comrades at the front, Trooper Stone noted, "The remaining portion of the time is spent on writing letters to friends and lounging about the hotel."[22] John Frost tried to bolster his dad's spirits by admonishing him "to keep a stiff upper lip and forget that I have gone to war. I shall come home in the spring."[23] Upon their arrival in Washington on October 4, they had sufficient time to tour the city while awaiting orders to join the regiment. Eventually, an escort brought them to Camp Stoneman.

Stone and his companions were not initially assigned to a specific company. He found temporary quarters with D company, though feeling that he "did not find the old boys as glad to receive us as we expected to find them."[24] The cold shoulder sensed by Stone could have been derived from many sources, such as veterans just being leery of newcomers. Maybe the close knit bonds of relatives and neighbors already in the company did not allow them to take an immediate shine to a "stranger" in their midst, or possibly the man being replaced was a special fellow and anyone trying to fill his shoes had to prove his worthiness. But by the 10th of the month, the replacements had been disseminated among Companies A through K, with Stone finding a home with Company B. Unlike their predecessors recruited in the fall of '61, these new additions to the Vermont Cavalry would not have as much chance to drill before being thrust into active duty. One pessimistic soldier noted this lack of preparation, attributing it to the divided and spread out nature of the regiment's picket-postings through the winter so that "drill was altogether out of the question."[25] "Although we have received several hundred recruits and several hundred new horses," he went on to acknowledge, "I very much doubt if the Vermont Cavalry would do the fighting today that it would six months ago."[26]

Fortunately, his concerns, while not without merit, did not materialize. In part, this was due to the different style of warfare engaged in by the Vermonters from February through May. Small unit actions were more common during this time frame wherein fortitude was a more useful quality than the ability to perform a textbook drill. However, in the absence of the opportunity to hold sufficient training, there was luckily another source of readily available expertise into which the novice troops could tap. By being sprinkled in among veterans, these second generation recruits could soak up valuable knowledge from battle-tested troopers, and it behooved the veterans to get them up to speed tout de suite for the well-being of everyone in the company. The occasion could easily come when the survival of the latter depended upon the gun in the hands of the former.

In addition to the individual replacements, another 200 troopers were added to the ranks upon the arrival of Companies L and M. With a liberal dose of regional pride, the *Burlington Daily Free Press* passed along its observations that Company M contained "some of the best young men in town" and then went on to gush that Company L "is one of the very best that that has ever been raised."[27] Like their predecessors in the muster of '61, the new recruits went south in full uniform but without weaponry. Unlike the original ten companies, Companies L and M were not assigned mounts until they arrived in Alexandria.

Overseeing the recruiting process on behalf of Vermont Cavalry had been Captain John Woodward, the chaplain's son. To its credit, the Vermont press was very supportive of his efforts. "It is not likely that any additional companies will be raised for this regiment, or that any other cavalry regiment will be raised in Vermont," was the forewarning that appeared in one article which further advised that "to young men of vigor and good spirit, desirous of entering this reputable branch of the service, the present occasion is likely to be the only one available."[28] Paid ads ran in various newspapers trumpeting this "last opportunity for those preferring this arm of the service to enlist."[29] In these classifieds could be seen the subtle shift that had perforce entered the recruitment process only one short year after 1st Cavalry was formed. No longer able to count solely on patriotic fervor to bring out willing volunteers, monetary incentives were offered.

Next to the 400 plus recruits that joined the 1st Vermont in fall of 1862 and the winter of 1863, the regiment received the good news that an additional, much-needed boost in manpower would be coming soon from a different source. A correspondent reported the story: "Those of the First Vt Cavalry paroled on September 12th and delivered to Gen. Dix on the 13th, are exchanged, and all who are able will join the regiment as soon as they receive clothing, & c."[30] While amounting to only about three dozen men, any additional manpower was most welcome. Another dozen or so former POWs returned on the 15th of September, so that the regiment got back around fifty men via the parole process. Unfortunately, these former prisoners were in differing states of health, to the extent that all were not equally able to return to active duty. A few died shortly after their liberation, while several others had to be discharged due to chronic conditions that seriously impaired their functioning effectively. Regardless of their final destinations, all were reintroduced to free soil at Annapolis after a steamer ride up the coast from City Point. The Maryland location to which they were repatriated was in the process of evolution, fast becoming a hub of activity as one of the three centers that facilitated the reintegration of ex-POWs back into the Union army. A Boston reporter gave an estimate of "10,000 paroled prisoners there and new arrivals from 50 to 100 ... made daily."[31] Here, recently returned prisoners were given medical treatment and then released. Initially the buildings and grounds of the United States Naval Academy were sufficient to serve these purposes; however, as the volume of troops to be handled increased, so did the size and scope of Camp Parole's operation. Eventually, the facilities of St. John's College were appropriated. When more space was required, the army constructed barracks. From the original site that was known as "Camp Parole," once he was formally exchanged, a Union soldier might be furloughed, discharged, or sent back to his regiment. For some poor souls, the wretchedness of their condition upon return was irreversible, and as a result they never left. What is now the Annapolis National Cemetery became their final resting place.

The Vermonters who arrived at Annapolis in September of 1862 were mostly individuals captured during "Banks' Retreat." At the time, they had been among the healthy ones taken to Libby Prison and Belle Isle with a reasonable expectation of survival before quick exchanges. Those seriously wounded when captured were usually paroled on the spot. The other September returnees represented individuals taken in the summer of 1862. In one sense, their fate was kinder than that which awaited their brethren captured later in the war. This latter group, participants in raids that often penetrated deep behind enemy lines, was not customarily exchanged in a short time, if at all. Instead their accursed lot was to languish, and in far too many cases to die, in Southern prisons. With a system in place to process not only those returning through Camp Parole in Annapolis but also recuperating patients via the convalescent camp in Alexandria, transitioning had become more organized than in the past. Slowly the strength of the regiment grew as the time to mount a new campaign approached. Even though the Confederate success at Fredericksburg in December would dampen spirits that Antietam had lifted, there was still optimism in the ranks that winter. In the words of one confident Vermont cavalryman, "I think we will have Yankees enough here pretty soon to give the rebels what they need.... We will make them lay low for black ducks this spring."[32]

14

Ashby's Gap
A Blaze of Glory to End the Year

While their posting to Camp Stoneman was for a respite, the inescapable fact remained that certain duties still had to be performed. One of these necessities was manning the outer ring of videttes, intended to protect the army from surprise attacks. Across a wide arc stretching from Dranesville on Broad Run to the northwest of Washington south to Mt. Vernon on the Potomac, an alert presence was imperative. Though there was much about the uses to which cavalry were put that was being rethought, bearing the brunt of picket duty was not yet one of them. Their inherent mobility made mounted forces attractive for maintaining far-flung outposts. The downside was the overworking of horses as well as men. "Indeed, it was not until 1864 that Sheridan impressed upon Meade the wastefulness of thus rendering thousands of cavalry mounts unserviceable through unnecessary picket duty, which could be performed by infantry."[1]

Initially, the lack of numbers severely hampered the regiment's contributions to the picket rotation. The day after the Vermonters arrived in camp, Addison Preston verified his company's sad condition. "I have but 24 men fit for duty," he wrote. "The rest are worn out."[2] Until November, most of those who were available could not do much save lay about the camp. "The Vermont cavalry has for a time been laid upon the shelf for want of horses," was Josiah Grout's assessment of their immobility.[3] Over the next two months, the regiment contributed as best it could. As one man proudly observed in mid–December, "Not a scout or reconnaissance of any importance has been made for the past three months without a detachment of the 1st Vermont."[4] What he neglected to mention, however, was that there were some occasions in November when that "detachment" was no more than a token presence.

Over time, Camp Stoneman underwent a gradual metamorphosis. As the fatigued troops recovered their strength and serviceable mounts became available, the cantonment looked more like a staging area and less that of a convalescent camp. Prior to the horse situation going from bad to worse, the regiment got in a few last licks. The most notable opportunity began on Saturday, September 20, 1862. Intelligence had been received that a sizable wagon train, possibly as many as 900 conveyances, was moving north towards Martinsburg to resupply the Army of Northern Virginia. A quick mounted strike through Ashby's Gap was judged practicable.

Here was a golden opportunity for the Union cavalry. The chance to execute a daring stroke beckoned, though the enterprise was undeniably a long shot. Even if the enemy's location could be accurately estimated, it was still problematical Union troopers could intercept them. For the mission to succeed, distance and terrain had to be considered. The ride amounted to a one-way trek of 55 miles due west, most of it uphill on the outbound journey. Regardless of which troops drew the assignment, they would have to be drawn from regiments still in varying stages of recovery.

At this juncture in its history, the 1st Vermont had the misfortune to come under the command of a petty, jealous field officer who never appreciated this blue chip unit. Instead, Colonel R. Butler Price disingenuously expended effort minimizing its contributions. Since the Vermont Cavalry was now a part of the Department of Washington, General Buford had been replaced as its commander on October 12 by General Samuel Heintzlemann. While a brave soldier who bore the wounds of battle, Heintzlemann was also a stern, cautious individual. As a corps commander, he was out of his league. If he made mistakes in judgment, however, they were done out of incompetence, not malice. The same could not be said of one particular subordinate, the man who became the Vermonters' nemesis: Colonel Price. Originally with the 2nd Pennsylvania Cavalry, Price was given command of the 3rd Cavalry Brigade, which included the 1st Vermont, 1st Michigan, 2nd Pennsylvania, and 1st Virginia Regiments. Price would lead the expedition to Ashby's Gap, much to the eventual chagrin of the Green Mountain troopers. After one mission under him, the name "Price" would leave a bitter taste in the Vermonters' mouths.

Assembling a column of 750 troopers, he included some 260 men drawn from the 1st Vermont. Heading out at 4:00 P.M., Price led his command northwest toward Aldie. As the contingent entered the village, many sick and wounded Confederates were discovered. Offering no resistance, these men were immediately paroled. But valuable time was lost to the processing. With darkness setting in, the Federal troopers camped by the road. Being deep in unfriendly territory, pickets maintained their posts with extra vigilance. Horses remained saddled and bridled. The men slept on their arms.

The morning of September 23 saw the detachment move out early, Companies B, G, and H formed the advanced guard. The seven miles between Aldie and the next community, Middleburg, were traversed without delay. Moving rapidly, the Federals encountered a dozen rebel pickets. Approaching to within 10 rods, the Yankee cavalrymen fired. Though only a single return shot was fired, the rebel marksman's aim proved unerring, as the ball struck Private Henry Holt in the hip, precipitating the young soldier's unexpected death one month later. This shocking turn of events took his family completely by surprise, for in a cheery letter home dated October 6, he gave no inkling of the grief ahead: "Today my wound is getting along first-rate, The soreness is out of it pretty much now but I can not step on my foot yet, but shall get on crutches in a day or two.... We have got a very good doctor in our ward...."[5] Holt's wounding was regrettable but in no way deflected the Union cavalry from their goal. By weight of numbers and swiftness of movement, the Vermonters, led by the intrepid Lieutenant William Cummings, built up forward momentum, permitting them to easily drive the Confederate videttes out of Middleburg. Once Cummings had invested the little town, another group of 900 convalescing Confederates was captured. Their release was processed in the same manner as the Aldie prisoners, though not until later in the day.

But for now, pursuit of the retreating enemy was sustained in earnest. Out of Middleburg and through Upperville, an intermittent gun battle ensued. In Trooper Henry Smith's experience, "They would stop at every hill and fire at us and run."[6] From its onset outside of Aldie, Colonel Price reported "skirmishing was kept up from that point to a

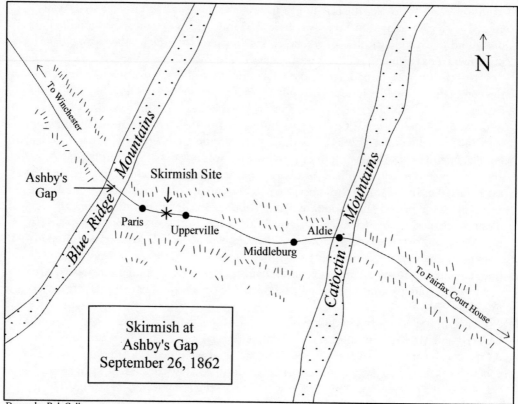

Skirmish at
Ashby's Gap
September 26, 1862

Drawn by Bob Collea

distance of ten to twelve miles."[7] The rebels' tactics presented more of a nuisance than
an impediment. The 1st Vermont continued to surge ahead. The chase abruptly ended
"about 5 miles beyond Upperville [when] the rebs made a stand, about one regiment of
them."[8] This opposition turned out to be the 6th Virginia Cavalry under Lieutenant-Colonel John Shackleford Green. The Confederate leader had chosen the spot well at which
to interdict his enemy's advance. Arranging his men across the Vermonters' intended
route, he stationed them between two stone walls running parallel to the road. If Yankee
horsemen wished to continue toward the Shenandoah Valley, they would first have to deal
with the foreboding presence arrayed before them. Estimated at anywhere from 150 to
400 men, the rebel force calmly sat with pistols drawn. Grim visaged, they awaited their
enemy's response.

With this ominous presence looming up ahead, the three advanced companies of
Vermonters were in a predicament. Their no-holds-barred pursuit had chewed up ground
quickly, causing them to far outdistance the remainder of the regiment, not to mention
the main body of the Union column more than a mile away at this dire moment. Tacti-
cally speaking, no support troops were readily available. What followed could best be
described as an "oh-oh moment"—that instant when a realization sets in that circumstances, as they are unfolding, are not exactly the most desirable. Such a critical situation requires an instantaneous decision, often with life-altering consequences. Not only
might a promising future lie in the balance but a good name could be on the line too.
These were the kind of stakes on the table for the 60-odd men of Preston's party that fall

afternoon outside of Upperville, Virginia. Whether it be by the low-ball figure of two-and-a-half to one or the high-end estimate of over six to one was irrelevant — Perkins' command was substantially outnumbered. Certainly the rebels were cognizant of this numerical disparity, providing them with good reason to believe that "they might capture or rout the little band that was so daringly advancing against them."[9]

For the moment, the two groups remained rooted in defiant postures, squared off across several hundred yards of roadway. Drama built as pulses quickened. Though the tension rose, nothing happened. The outnumbered Vermonters seemed to be somewhat "disconcerted by the firm front and absolute silence of the enemy."[10] Interminable seconds passed like minutes, yet neither side flinched nor displayed any inclination to cut and run. Finally, the Virginians moved to terminate the stalemate. "The rebel columns advanced to a position where they could fire upon us, and we could do nothing but go forward," wrote a Vermont trooper.[11] Such an advance by the Virginians was taken as a prelude to a charge. What transpired next was the stuff of which heroes are born, reputations made, and legends created: Preston ordered a charge. But it was the manner in which he did this that was so memorable. No less a warrior than George Custer would come to laud Addison Preston for his pronounced ability to lead men in combat, a soldiers' general praising a soldiers' colonel because he possessed the "right stuff."

While Custer was not at Ashby's Gap to see Preston in action, what the Vermont colonel proceeded to do was very much in keeping with the fearless leader whom Custer came to appreciate. The idea was an amalgam of pure genius, a flair for the dramatic, and the exigencies of the moment. Alone, Preston left the impasse on the road and circled out into the field beyond the stone wall. Then he pointed his charger at the barrier and urged him forward at full speed. Suddenly and surprisingly to the troops on the other side, horse and rider "leaped the stone fence into the road in front of his men, and, waving his saber and shouting to them to come on, dashed straight at the force in his front."[12] Briefly Colonel Preston, gesticulating with his sword toward the enemy as his horse twirled, sat by himself in no-man's-land. Many on both sides were undoubtedly in a state of temporary immobilization at the feat just witnessed. A bit theatrical? Perhaps. Rather risky? No doubt. But courageous and inspirational? Unquestionably! Captain Selah Perkins of Company G quickly joined his superior in front of the column, as did Captains Flint and Earhardt, along with Lieutenant Adams. Not a single Vermont trooper wavered as the gallant sixty raised their sabers in unison, let out a whoop, and followed their leaders at a gallop. In the eyes of their former commander, General James Hatch, participants in the charge "won immortal honor."[13]

The rebels' response was to sit "like statues on their horses, fixed, and immovable, until we were within a few rods of them."[14] The hard-charging Yankees had to know what was coming. The gap between attacker and defender shrank to less than twenty yards. Still the rebels sat. Then a loud explosion drowned out the thunder of hoofbeats. "At a very short pistol range," triggers were pulled in unison, and the enemy's firearms spat tongues of flame as the rebel cavalry unleashed a concentrated hail of lead at those who would do them harm.[15] The crashing sound of hundreds of gunshots reverberated across the hills, followed in quick succession by two more volleys. The immediate aftermath of the scene possessed a surreal quality. Somewhere between 450 and 900 bullets were fired in close proximity at sixty humans. Yet, through the wafting smoke, it could be seen that most in the three-score targeted men amazingly remained in a fighting posture. Perhaps all the more astounding, just as the heavy fusillade was unsuccessful in blunting the spirited charge, so also did it not kill a single Vermonter! In various eyewitness accounts, Vermont soldiers described an experience in which they rode through what should have been a lethal killing field. One participant referenced the rebels as "delivering a deadly fire into our rapidly advancing and heroic men."[16]

For the sakes of the men and their families, it was well that these bullets were errant. How this phenomenon occurred poses an interesting question, for it would seem that the Confederates had the Union troopers dead to rights. Yet miraculously, the after-action tally for the entire fight amounted to one killed and eight wounded among Preston's troopers. Of those, the solitary death and one of the woundings did not occur until the two sides were engaged in desperate hand-to-hand combat. This means that only seven soldiers incurred wounds in the opening attack. How could that be? Beyond the hand of fate, there were several contributing factors. First, the Confederates were firing slightly downhill and may have inadvertently aimed high. Attacking soldiers, hunched forward in their saddles as their mounts headed upgrade, may have presented difficult targets. Given the close proximity to the enemy from which the charge was launched, many of Green's men in their haste may have hurried their shots. Finally, there was the element of surprise, the rebels possibly caught off-guard by the sheer audacity of their outnumbered foes who so brazenly dared to advance instead of retreat.

For some of those Vermonters wounded at this juncture, active participation in the war promptly ended, their commitment to their country fulfilled in blood. The frontal locations of their wounds high on the body were consistent with being hit as they followed Preston forward. Though none proved fatal, seven of the injuries were incapacitating enough to result in disability discharges within six months. Company G's Barney Scully received the most gruesome of the wounds. A pistol ball crashed into his face to the lower right of his mouth. Records indicate that "the bullet knocked out three teeth and a portion of the jaw."[17] Private Scully spent the next six months in hospitals. In addition to living with disfigurement, he carried the bullet lodged in his jaw for the rest of his life. As he grew older, the aftereffects of the wound worsened, as it was wont to break open inside of his mouth. Amidst the pus-laden discharge was often found small pieces of bone. Yet, in spite of all the suffering, Scully was a tough old bird who survived the war, coped with his problems, and lived on into the 20th century.

Two of Scully's comrades in Company G, Abram Day and Sorel Tinkham, were also incapacitated in the charge. Private Day took a painful wound in the chest, the bullet passing just above his third rib on the right side of his body. Due to the permanent damage done by the missile penetrating his lung, Day's military career was over. Sadly, the wound's long-term effect precipitously shortened his life. He survived the end of the war by just eleven years, dying in the summer of 1876. Trooper Sorel Tinkham received a flesh wound in the calf, which proved more serious than first thought. The corporal from Shaftsbury had to leave the service in December because of the disabling condition that his injury caused.

The last trooper struck down in the charge was Frank Dragon. Hit fully in the chest, the severity of Private Dragon's wound was certified by Colonel Preston himself. He wrote that the soldier was injured by a "ball passing through his body [and] coming out at the back," barely missing his spine in the process.[18] As Dragon was believed to be mortally wounded, he was left in a hospital in Upperville. There he eventually "fell into the hands of the enemy," though much to Company B's surprise "he afterwards returned to the regiment [but] in disabled condition" on October 19, 1862.[19] Dragon was immediately admitted to the hospital. Since the bullet also damaged his right lung as it ploughed through his body, Dragon was deemed unfit for the rigors of military service. He was given a disability discharge in December. Unlike some wounded veterans whose lives were drastically altered, Frank Dragon's story does seem to have had somewhat of a happy ending medically. Despite the severity of his wounds, he was married six months later and was healthy enough that he was not only able to sire eight children but also live until 1920. His wife, however, undoubtedly would have debated just how wonderful the twilight years of his life had unfolded for her. Trying to make ends meet and provide for the Dragon brood, she took in boarders. For her crotchety, cantankerous, and often liquored-up husband, "the noise and confusion of children and boarders annoyed [him] which caused him to move to the Soldiers' Home" in 1906.[20] As if estranging himself from his wife and family wasn't bad enough, the old warhorse told everyone at the home that he was single and, in keeping with this sham, contributed nothing to the support of his wife. Private Frank Dragon proved to be a hero with feet of clay.

The lone officer injured but living to recover and remain in the service was Charles Adams. Lieutenant Adams was wounded very late in the advance, most likely as the opposing lines melded, for he "rushed into the thickest of the fight, declaring he would avenge the death of his captain."[21] This scenario was plausible because the demise of Captain Selah Perkins, did not happen until the gap that separated the opposing forces was traversed, placing Adams with him among the rebel troops. He may also have benefited from the immediate medical attention that he received. While in hindsight his presence at the battlefront seems risky, regimental surgeon Dr. Ptolemy Edson was at the wounded officer's side at almost the instant Adams left his horse. Dr. Edson later accounted for this when he wrote that "the part of the Regt. to which I was attached, acting as advance guard, was ordered to charge the rebels ... and in said charge Charles A. Adams ... received a gunshot wound in the right clavicle.... I was on the field and dressed the wound."[22] In spite of his wound being dressed on the field, Lieutenant Adams' complete recovery was slow. To help facilitate his recuperation, he was granted a thirty-day furlough. The pain and discomfort of having a bullet lodged in his clavicle persisted, the wound being aggravated by the cavalry's "extremely active service in the summer of '63."[23] Since the tissue damage did not heal completely, Adams was forced to go back under the knife and have the ball removed 10 months later. In spite of his delayed recovery, the durable Charles Adams returned and served with distinction until the end of war, achieving first the rank of Brevet Lt. Colonel for his meritorious service in the field.

Wounded at Ashby's Gap and later captured at Brandy Station, Major Charles Adams' leadership capabilities moved him steadily upward to the ultimate reward of brevet lieutenant-colonel at the end of the war (Mike King Collection/USAMHI).

Considering what they had just experienced, a handful of wounded men after such a charge were very light casualties indeed. Nor did their collective good fortune desert them. In the next phase of the skirmish, the tenacious little band continued to defy the odds after taking the fight to their enemy. While Companies B, G, and H remained the only Vermont troops in the roadway, they were no longer fighting alone. Another forty or so men from Companies A and I had weighed into the fray. "Company I deployed to the right as skirmishers and Company A to the left" was how Private Smith remembered their disposition.[24] For the boys on the road, their straits assumed a different look. Surviving the charge for them was akin to going from the frying pan into the fire. Only now, instead of attacking into the face of a superior enemy force, they were intermingled with it.

Once the lines blended, one distinct benefit that the Vermont troopers had was their beloved sabers. During the interval of the charge, with the Yankees' firearms holstered in favor of well-honed blades, the tactical advantage belonged to the rebels. The killing power of their revolvers extended far beyond the reach of Union cavalry's swords. But, once the bodies of the attackers and defenders were hopelessly commingled, the advantage shifted. Lieutenant-Colonel Green of the 6th Virginia was one Confederate soldier who could definitely have attested to the effectiveness of cavalry swords in close combat. He took no less than five saber cuts to the head, including a slash purported to have been delivered by Captain Perkins. These repeated blows left Green dazed with a bleeding and fractured skull.

The engagement at Ashby's Gap lasted maybe another ten to fifteen minutes once the hand-to-hand combat started. Most conspicuous and memorable for their gallant roles in this phase of the skirmish were Addison Preston and Selah Perkins. Lieutenant-Colonel Preston, after leading the charge, found himself in the rear of the enemy force. This odd turn of events came to pass because the momentum of the attack had carried him through his opponent's massed ranks and out the other side. Though unharmed, his position was precarious. No sooner had Preston gathered himself together to face his foes than he saw them turn towards him as they prepared to flee. It had all of the appearances of them now charging him! His situation as seen by one of his men instantly became "a struggle for life itself."[25] But Addison Preston was a man up to challenges. That he willingly put himself in harm's way happened because he led by example. Eventually his luck would run out on another battlefield later in the war, but, on this particular day, his boldness was not to be denied. When two rebel troopers came at him, their pistols at the ready, he quickly neutralized the one on his left when "he managed to knock up one of the revolvers and disabled its owner with a back-handed blow with the hilt of his saber."[26] Then he dealt a stunning though not fatal blow to the man on the right. The danger from the second assailant was the most threatening as the man had his revolver pressed against Preston's chest. With his adversary temporarily distracted from the saber blow, the Vermonter grabbed the pistol's barrel and tried to deflect its aim away from his body. At that instant, the weapon discharged; "its ball grazed the colonel's palm, went through his clothes, laying open a flesh wound upon his breast, and passed through his right arm, inflicting a painful but not dangerous wound."[27]

Preston's aggressive response temporarily saved him from doom, but he was immediately confronted with another threat. The surge of rebel cavalrymen funneling back down the road was carrying his horse along with them. Caught up in the crush, wounded and surrounded, his prospects of escaping alive did not appear good. But cool under pressure, Preston kept his wits. He jumped down off his horse and dodged among the retreating rebels, hoping that in the confusion of the moment they would be more intent on saving their own hides than taking his. Somehow he made it to the side of the road, where, totally drained from his ordeal, he calmly sat and waited for rescue. Gutsy to the end, "though faint from loss of blood, [he] retained command till Price came up with the main body."[28]

As for Selah Perkins, his bravery was just as evident as Preston's. The captain, however, was just not fortunate enough to survive the engagement and live to bask in the richly deserved acclaim that his heroism brought. Riding beside his colonel, Perkins hit the waiting rebels full force. Swinging his sword, he waded unfalteringly into the melee, ready to engage all comers in hand-to-hand combat. Being in the forefront of the attack and riding a white horse, Captain Perkins "made a conspicuous mark, and was one of the first to fall."[29] Before he was shot down, the Vermont officer had opened a severe wound in the head of Lieutenant-Colonel Green. In the instant that Perkins' sword was striking bone, the rebel officer held his pistol to Perkins' head and killed him instantly. Incredible though it may seem, given the intensity of the engagement, Captain Selah Perkins would be the only member of the 1st Vermont Cavalry to perish at Ashby's Gap.

Though but one man, this solitary loss was deeply felt by the regiment. Selah Perkins had been an individual blessed with many exemplary qualities, unflagging leadership and sterling character being two of the most conspicuous. By virtue of his education and culture, he was somewhat of an anomaly in a regiment heavily populated with subsistence farmers. The son of a doctor, Perkins had graduated from Union College in New York and the Castleton Medical School in Vermont. Following in his father's footsteps, he became a physician in Castleton, practicing there until the war intruded. A moving force in the recruitment of the Rutland Company, he was not surprisingly elected captain of Company H. His death at Ashby's Gap cast a pall over the regiment as the men mourned the passing of this exceptional individual. Officers were requested by Lieutenant-Colonel Preston to wear a black crepe mourning badge on their left arms for thirty days as a show of respect for their fallen brother. Heartfelt eulogies poured forth in the press as people sought to express their feelings via the written word. One such touching effort appeared in the *Rutland Daily Herald* on behalf of the regiment for the special benefit of Perkins' wife and three children: "We all beg to condole with you in this, our, as well as your great bereavement. You mourn for a kind and affectionate husband, and we for a brave and daring leader. He died, as the brave leaders always fall, at the head of his command, and his last soul-stirring cry of 'forward' will long be remembered by those who followed him. Again we offer you our heart-felt sympathies, trusting that 'He who doeth all things well,' will guide and comfort you in the dark hour of affliction."[30]

Selah Perkins had much for which to live. A growing family, a worthy career, and a promising future all awaited his return to Castleton. Nevertheless he had gone off willingly, seeing the war as "a struggle for the continuance of this country" in the words of one who knew him.[31] While he could just as easily have opted to be a member of the medical corps, where a doctor's skills were always in short supply, his nature would not let him function behind the scenes when he could be up front in a leader's role. Were he able to select the appointed time and place of his death, he might well have agreed with the assessment of one trooper who wrote of his departed captain that "no man can ask to die more valiantly or in a better cause."[32] Escorted by the wounded hero Charles Adams, Captain Perkins' remains were brought back home to the Green Mountains for burial. As he had fought and died defending these earthly spires, it was only fitting that they should provide an eternal vigil over his final resting place. His funeral services commenced at 4:00 P.M. on October 12, 1862, from the impressive Brick Church in Castleton. From there, his body was borne just west of town to its final resting place. The cortege crossed a small wooden bridge over the nascent waters of the Castleton River, proceeded up an incline, and came to halt on a large plateau, which was Hillside Cemetery. The burial ground was relatively new then and did not contain many remains as yet. When the captain's marker finally arrived, its two-foot by two-foot by three-and-a-half foot size was distinctive from the thin white slabs that were most commonly used. Resting on a pedestal base, his tombstone appeared as a massive, but simple, square of gray/black-flecked Vermont granite. The Captain's final three-line epitaph read: "Dr. Selah Gridley Perkins, Killed at Ashby's Gap, September 22, 1862, age 36 years."

He was the first of the Civil War generation of warriors laid to rest at Hillside. He would not be the last. Over the years, scores of others would join him. Some, like Lieutenant Luther French of the Second Vermont Infantry, suffered battle deaths too. Time eventually caught up with the others. It makes for a very stirring sight to stand at the gravesite of Captain Perkins and survey the burial ground. From this location, but a slight turn in either direction is required to see scores of flag-adorned plots. Resting in their black, gold-lettered GAR markers, these banners blanket the cemetery. A cross-section of Vermont's regiments is represented. Soldiers of the 2nd, 11th, and 14th infantries rest there along with one of Berdan's Sharpshooters and of course Captain Perkins of the 1st Vermont. The impressive forest of red, white, and blue pennants is indisputable evidence that many of Perkins' patriotic friends and neighbors in the Castleton area did not hesitate to answer their nation's call. For Selah Perkins, the good captain's last ride ironically brought him to Hillside almost a year to the day from when his military career had begun amid the panoply of his company's muster. So it was that the great Civil War had taken another man that his family, country, and regiment would dearly miss. Following World War I, much would be written of the "Lost Generation" of young men whose deaths had cost mankind millions of individuals in the prime of life, men who had much to give but whose potential for peacetime contributions untold was never fulfilled because they made the ultimate sacrifice. America experienced a similar loss in the 1860s, when over 600,000 of her sons died prematurely from war. While individually they may not have had enough earthly time to do all that they would have wished, collectively they helped settle issues once and for all that were rending the nation. In and of itself, their contribution of a single, united nation may have been the greatest gift that they could have ever given, no matter how long they lived. That is how sacrifices become legacies—and soldiers do not die in vain.

For relatives left behind, time tempered the grief but never erased the memory of their fallen soldier. Lieutenant Adams' comforting presence not only honored the sacrifice made by his captain but also permitted his loved ones to know exactly what had happened. Still, no words about inspired leadership and heroic action could dispel the awful truth that among the Vermonters only Captain Perkins had perished that day. If only he had not been so swift to join Preston, if only his horse had been a little faster, if only he had swung his sword at Colonel Green a trifle quicker, maybe he would have survived. While having no choice but to forge ahead with their lives without him, Perkins' family would be forever haunted by the what-might-have-beens.

While Vermont's gallant captain lay dying in the road, the little band of troopers whom his actions helped inspire quickly took the measure of their Confederate counterparts. Once the lines closed, the outcome of the engagement was never in doubt. It was over in minutes. The Union onslaught was brought home with such determination that the rebel force was unable to stem the tide. After token resistance, the 6th Virginia broke ranks and hurriedly departed the scene. Put in the vernacular of a common soldier, Private Henry Smith made the observation that the "rebs were completely routed and skedaddled out of sight."[33] Though the Southerners took off in all directions to escape the supercharged Vermonters, most of them went on up through the gap to safety. The Vermonters pursued them as far as the hamlet of Paris but could not catch up. The Union force reined in there, having learned that a superior enemy force guarded the pass. After a brief rest, the weary pursuers returned to the ambush site. The day's fighting was over: "Four men of the 6th Cavalry were killed, 13 wounded, and 14 captured, but only five wagons were taken."[34] From rebel captives, the Vermonters learned that their intelligence reports had been partially correct. "If we had there 24 hours sooner," lamented Henry Smith, "[we] could have taken 900 wagons."[35] Though the expedition had clearly fallen far short of its intended objective, ample satisfaction was still derived from the manner in which the enemy's blocking force had been manhandled.

In the end, though the spoils of war proved paltry and the death of Perkins staggering, the burgeoning reputation of the 1st Vermont glowed ever brighter after its shining performance at Ashby's Gap. Fortunately their actions spoke louder than Colonel Price's words, for the leader of the expedition seemed to do all that he could to minimize their contributions. His after-action report certainly made him suspect in this regard through its errors of omission and expansion. "In passing the village of Aldie, at Bull Run Gap," Price wrote, "we encountered the pickets of the enemy."[36] However, he was painting with too broad a brushstroke for in actuality his "we" was 1st Vermont alone. But his most egregious slight was in stating that "skirmishing was kept up from that point [outside of Aldie] to a distance often to twelve miles when the advance, aided by two companies of 1st Vermont, whilst closely following a party of about sixty, came suddenly upon the main body — of the 6th Virginia Cavalry..."[37] While he does reference the support given by "two companies of 1st Vermont," he makes no mention of the fact that the more salient group, the "party of sixty," were also Vermonters, who took the critical lead from Aldie right through the immortal charge that claimed the brave Perkins' life. Altogether, there only two instances that "1st Vermont" appeared in Price's report. While six of its officers were specifically lauded for their outstanding conduct in the course of the fight, never was their regimental affiliation ever stated or any unit praise directed at the Vermont Cavalry. The most that a reader could conclude from reading this document was that the 1st Vermont was merely one of many participants in the events at Ashby's Gap. But the exemplary degree to which they performed was not in evidence, much less the knowledge that "the entire loss of the expedition fell upon the Vt. Cavalry, it being in the advance and the only one engaged in the fight."[38] Rather than be rightfully given the star billing they so richly deserved, the regiment was relegated to the status of the supporting cast!

But for all that Colonel Price did which could have adversely affected the morale of the regiment, his efforts ultimately proved to be fruitless. Addison Preston knew what his men had accomplished and unabashedly told them so: "The Lieut. Colonel commanding, wishes to return thanks to the officers and men under his command during the late expedition to Ashby's Gap, for their promptness in obeying orders, and their courage and bravery while engaging a determined foe."[39] In those few simple but sincere words lay

While picket duty was often a lonely and dangerous assignment, there were moments when a vidette's alertness gave way to contemplation, though remaining mounted and facing the enemy was at all times mandatory, regardless of weather conditions (Library of Congress).

the difference between Price, the commander, and Preston, the leader. Every human being, soldiers included, likes to be told on occasion that he is doing a good job, all the more so when the speaker is a revered and respected officer like Addison Preston. While Preston's praise was deeply appreciated, the men of the 1st Vermont already knew in their hearts just how good a fighting unit that they had become. "Every man was proud of himself and prouder of the regiment" were the words of a trooper whose feelings reflected his comrades' durable self–esteem.[40] "When asked to what regiment we belonged, there was not one of us who did not straighten up a little bit in the saddle, as we answered, 'To the 1st Vermont Cavalry.'"[41]

Even after the humiliating disaster that was Bank's Valley Campaign, the brutal summer's service under Pope, and the gross misfortune of being included within Price's orbit, the men of Vermont still looked forward to the summer of 1863 with high spirits. However, before they trod the glory fields of Gettysburg where they would earn new laurels and deepened respect, the horse soldiers from the Green Mountain State first had to duel with a clever foe that waged war in a most unorthodox but undeniably effective manner. John Singleton Mosby, partisan warrior deluxe, was about to introduce the 1st Vermont to the hazards and frustrations of guerilla warfare.

15

Picketing and Patrolling
Someone Has to Do It

For Civil War cavalrymen, acting as a picket, or vidette, as mounted guards were called, meant being positioned ahead of the main line in no-man's-land. Regardless of where his post was sited, nocturnal picket duty was a lot like Halloween — only every night and much more dangerous. While the 31st of October had its ghosts and goblins to fray the nerves, guards standing the graveyard shift in the winter of 1862–1863 often had visits by denizens who were more real and far deadlier. As if the elements and sleeplessness were not discomforting enough, somewhere out there in the shadows lurked the enemy, intent upon capturing or killing unwary sentries. "Often these posts are in thick woods," a Northerner observed, "where the soldier stands alone, cut off from camp, cut off from his fellows, and subject only to the harassings of his imagination and sense of fear."[1] It was not by accident that pickets were ordered to "always remain in their saddles, their horses' heads in the direction of the enemy. Their instructions [were] to be vigilant, to keep their revolvers or carbines always in hand, prepared to fire instantly should it be required."[2] The end of the night "between dawn and daybreak, when all was still and dark and mysterious," was a time of tense moments when the slightest sound or movement was magnified a thousandfold.[3] Many were the owls, squirrels, and deer that failed to answer a jittery sentry's challenge, causing a gunshot to shatter the quiet, arouse the reserve, and bring help to quell a false alarm.

Yet, alert as a guard might be, a determined adversary could still succeed. Rebel scouts ferreted out the location of videttes before sundown and "then come stealthily in the night under cover of woods, and fire in that direction at random, if they can't see the sentries."[4] The Dranesville area was alive with clandestine enemy activity. One Vermont cavalryman recalled "there had been a [great] deal of shooting of pickets at Dranesville, supposed to be by the farmers who live by."[5] Private Charles Stone of the 1st Vermont's Company A, posted in the same picket chain, echoed this sentiment, lamenting how "pickets here are often fired on by guerrillas every night and standing picket here is very dangerous."[6]

When taking prisoners became the objective, the enemy often resorted to trickery. During the first week of February, Privates George Weber, Patrick Hogan, Daniel Dixon, and Edgar Wright of the 1st Vermont fell victims to a clever ruse while manning a post on the Leesburg Pike. As unsporting as it may seem, "They were surprised by some of White's cavalry who came towards their post, dressed in Union clothes and our jackets, and were thought to be some of our own men, of some other cavalry regiments. Our boys let them come close up and were immediately taken prisoner."[7] So effective was the disguise that the surprised pickets had no time to defend themselves. Even though war imparted a deadly seriousness to the scene, the whole episode had a puckish air due to the way the partisan rangers invested the position. They did not approach quickly nor employ any tree-to-tree surreptitiousness. Instead they brazenly rode up, and, according to George Duncan, who was a fall enlistee and friend of Weber's, "Part of them got off and went to the fire to warm there, they talked a few moments to the boys, then reached their hand under their overcoats and drew their revolvers and told them to surrender which they had to do."[8]

Embarrassing as this episode was for the Vermonters, this would not be the last time that Confederates disguised in the garb of their enemy would use such a stratagem. Cunning Confederates again made instant POWs of Vermont troopers during the night of February 15. Charles Stone and his fellow pickets were victimized because Eli Hibbard failed to give the alarm, causing the troopers to be overrun before they could react. By "dismounting and coming up on foot," Private Stone wrote, "they had each man by the collar with revolvers at our head before we had time to draw our own.... [W]e surrendered to superior numbers."[9] Hannibal Jenne lamented the sudden loss of his friend Charles, hoping that "our boys will be back soon for we miss Stone very much [as] he slept in the tent with me [and] is very well liked."[10] Within the week, Stone and his woebegone companions were in Richmond. The problem was getting so out of hand that immediate action was needed to ameliorate the situation. "Non-commissioned officers in charge of the picket posts, have written orders not to allow any of the men to leave the post or take off their arms or sleep while on duty," was the report out of Dranesville to the *Burlington Press*.[11] Circumstances eventually deteriorated to the point where, once night fell, sentries were ordered to no longer follow customary protocol. If approached, rather than issue a position-revealing challenge, the soldier on duty had license to fire!

While the guerrilla bands became quite proficient in capturing pickets, there were nevertheless occasions when even their best efforts failed them. One foiled attempt involved Vermonter Josiah Fobes. On December 27, 1862, Private Fobes had been dispatched to locate the officer of the day, Lieutenant William Cummings, and his party, as they made the rounds of picket posts. Fobes was to warn them of an approaching enemy force. After successfully delivering the message, the still-green trooper was headed back when he met up with another mounted party. "He rode up thinking they were our own men," wrote company-mate George Duncan, "when he found out that they were rebels."[12] Adding to the ignominy, Trooper Fobes' horse was taken from him in exchange for a mule! His captors started off briskly, still hopeful of bagging Cummings' party. In order to keep up, Fobes was obliged to put spurs to his reluctant beast of burden. Objecting to this unwonted abuse, the mule registered his displeasure, kicking up such a fuss that Private Fobes got off. When his captors seemed oblivious, he escaped into the woods. For all of Fobes' trouble, Cummings and several members of his party still wound up captured after "the rebs fired a volley which wounded the lieutenant and his horse."[13]

While not too well known, clandestine operations were occasionally conducted by selected Union troops, quite possibly through their efforts saving a picket or two from rebel clutches. In today's parlance, these would be identified as counterinsurgency forces. Their purpose could have been to gather intelligence or simply just carry the war to the enemy. Frank Ray described a man in his company, one Sergeant Calvin (nee Alvah) Haswell, who apparently became adept at such stealthy endeavors. "I send him out with three or four men every few days," Ray informed his sister, "and he has captured one rebel Capt., three Lieuts, and a dozen men with[in] a few weeks. He is a very brave soldier and not afraid of old Nick himself."[14] The officer clearly held the sergeant in high regard as he did others in his company, offering the opinion that "I have got 15 or 20 men in my comp. that are as brave as any that ever lived or ever faced a rebel."[15] Lieutenant Ray and Sergeant Haswell may have latched onto a good idea. Had someone been a bit more insistent and persuasive, the 1st Vermont had a nucleus that could have operated against Confederate forces in the style of Mosby's Rangers.

Once relieved from picket duty, men became available for patrols and scouts. Patrolling was potentially the less hazardous duty, as it basically entailed riding the picket line and checking local roads to make sure that they were free from enemy incursions. The assignment's duration was of a short-lived nature because patrols were not expected to venture far from the main base. Scouting, on the contrary, was inherently fraught with danger because it amounted to departing from the safety of one's defenses

Captain Alvah Haswell functioned at times as a commando who led stealthy sorties against enemy pickets during the winter of 1862–1863. The 1st Vermont lost the services of this valuable warrior when he was first captured at Miskel's Farm and then wounded September 13, 1863, at Brandy Station four-and-a-half months later (USAMHI).

and a penetration of some distance into and even beyond no-man's-land. The purpose of a scouting mission might be to look for enemy movement or reconnoiter his positions. Detachments sent out for such purposes could be gone overnight or for several days. Unlike patrols and pickets, if a scouting party ran into trouble, support was unlikely to be nearby. For the men involved, their experiences ran the gamut from the routine and monotonous to the difficult and dangerous. Still, regardless of the obstacles, it was for just such challenges that men joined the cavalry. John Frost of Company H reaffirmed one other good reason for making this decision when he wrote his parents in late January of 1863: "I am well and tough but no tougher than the day. I have been to Frying Pan on a patrol. The roads are very bad. I could not help thinking how much better I was off than the infantry soldiers that are in the field, passing through the mud on foot."[16]

While Private Frost's experiences were often uneventful, such was not always the case. An excellent example of how unexpectedly the situation could deteriorate occurred on Wednesday, February 18, 1863, when a relatively simple mission turned into a frightful ordeal. It began when Lieutenant Frank Ray was dispatched to Leesburg with fellow officers Cheney and Grout, "in command of a hundred men to search the town and make several arrests."[17] Due to heavy snowfall, the day was more conducive to sitting in a rocker beside a warm hearth than plodding down muddy Virginia byways. In addition, three creeks of varying sizes needed to be crossed. As if nature had not done enough to make the trek miserable, the temperature warmed enough for freezing rain to pelt them. In the words of one beleaguered participant, "It was with no enviable feeling that we set out on our weary march to Leesburg."[18] Starting late, the Federals did not reach the last obstacle, Goose Creek, until 10:00 P.M. With the nearest bridge burned, the only option open allowing forward progress was fording the water barrier. But this was no small undertaking. Intrepidly but perhaps foolishly, the detachment effected a night crossing, though not without a harbinger of things to come. Trooper Elisha Scott of Company C nearly drowned when he took a tumble from his horse into the turbulent waters.

Scott's near fatality should have been taken as an omen of worse still yet to come, for only two days had elapsed since tragedy had struck a returning column near the very same place. On Thursday, February 12, a mixed detachment, including elements of the 1st Vermont, was on a scouting mission toward Winchester. Out four days, the column was returning to Dranesville, when Private James Rush, who had only just joined the regiment in October with Company L, perished doing exactly that which Elisha Scott had tried to do. Attempting to cross the swollen waters of Goose Creek on February 16, his horse lost its battle with the swift current. Swept away by the roiling waters, he drowned. Adding to the misery born out of the accident was the fact that closure was never effected because the trooper's body remained unrecovered.

Even though some were shaken by Scott's brush with death, Cheney's party proceeded undeterred to Leesburg. Here the command rounded up eleven prisoners who were "suspected of being spies and smugglers in the employ of Jeff Davis & Co."[19] At this point in the early morning, the already demanding trek took on Odyssean proportions. First, the force was split into two units. Perley Cheney would lead one back and Josiah Grout the other. This may have been done to confuse any potential pursuers, for Grout "was in possession of information concerning the whereabouts and force of the enemy, by reason of which I considered it important to effect a return to camp with as little delay as possible..."[20]

Regardless of intent, the two commands faced the same deterrent: fast-moving water. But "while on this scout," as Josiah Grout later recalled, "it rained hard for about 22 hours, flooding and rendering all streams in this vicinity dangerous to cross unless bridged."[21] According to Frank Ray, "When we returned, the streams had risen more than four feet so that the streams were more than seven feet deep and running at a fearful rate."[22] The first to confront this problem was Cheney's group, entrusted with spiriting the prisoners into Maryland. The plan was to cross the Potomac at Point of Rocks; however, after slow going along muddy roads, they did not arrive at the ferry until 8:00 A.M. on the 19th. To their dismay, the conveyance was rendered inoperable by the swift waters. An immediate decision was made to recross the smaller and hopefully less swollen Goose Creek. The first two fords proved impassable. Then a second ferry was discovered. Uncertain as to whether this presented an option or a deathtrap, debate led to an impasse. Finally, a pair of brave volunteers stepped forward. As if the raging waters alone did not offer sufficient challenge, the danger was compounded by a falls downstream. Margin for error was slim. Unfazed, the soldiers-turned-sailors poled their craft halfway across the treacherous creek before losing headway. Then the current determined their destiny. Protecting their faces, the soldiers resigned themselves to a wild ride, as their wooden craft pitched and turned toward the falls. To the amazement of onlookers and passengers alike, the boat survived both the falls and the rapids below while remaining right side up.

Though having progressed farther downstream than intended, the good news was that the boat and its intrepid crew had gained the opposite shore. Of course, new problems existed, such as how to get the boat back in the event that others wished to risk their lives, too, and getting horses to the two men who had already crossed. It was decided to let a horse risk its life by swimming across the creek. After a touch-and-go struggle, the animal made it, but the effort was considered too dangerous to be repeated. The troopers' luck held out, though, as they procured another mount from a resident and made their way safely back to camp.

Meanwhile, the remainder of Cheney's party continued searching for a fordable spot. When this endeavor proved fruitless, the column detoured further inland and uphill until they hit the Little River Turnpike at Aldie. From there, they moved cautiously eastward, dodging rebel patrols sweeping the countryside. Thankfully for the weary Union cavalry, no confrontation materialized. Hungry and exhausted, Cheney's column arrived safely in camp at 4:00 P.M. on February 20. The round trip, which should have been twenty-eight miles as the crow flies, had taken two days and wound up being in excess of forty miles!

If Cheney's column had experienced a fair share of luck, then it fell to Grout's command to be ill-starred. Departing Leesburg after Cheney's force was on its way to the Potomac, the second group retraced their steps to the banks of Goose Creek. Stymied by the same raging waters, the detachment halted while options were pondered. At this juncture, Lieutenant Josiah Grout recalled how Private Rufus Bean "was one of two brave boys, from the command, who volunteered to try the crossing and ascertain its safety."[23] After a parting salute, the young troopers rode into the swift-flowing creek. To the horror of helpless onlookers, "They were both swept from their horses by the irresistible witness of the current in trying to cross over."[24] Bean drowned before any help could be extended, though his companion was saved. To the army's credit, some men kept searching for Bean's body. John Frost and Bean had been tent mates, with Frost remembering his departed comrade as a "good boy and soldier."[25] Since he was aware that "Rufus's horse came into camp but [with] no rider," by the tone of his letter Private Frost seemed to have come to grips with the reality of never seeing his friend alive again.

Even with the death of Bean, the day's tragedies were not over. Moving downstream, the Vermonters arrived at Broad Run into which Goose Creek flowed. What possessed anyone to think that the larger body of water might be the more passable is unknown, but Lieutenant Charles Pixley "volunteered to go over first, saying to his boys that if he got over safely they might follow."[26] In a chilling repetition of Rufus Bean's demise, "the Lieutenant was last seen going downstream in the boiling water."[27] Midway in his crossing, Pixley's struggling horse threw him into the river. An eyewitness reported that Pixley "came up once and held onto a stump of a tree for a moment, and his boys heard him say, 'O, Boys,' just as he went down for the last time."[28] Private Frost, who forever bore the memory of watching first Bean and then Pixley swept away, wrote how it was "pretty hard to see the boys drown and be unable to render any assistance."[29] But he had no choice, for as others attested, "it would have been sheer madness to attempt to save him [Pixley]."[30] Sadly, Charles Pixley had been a lieutenant only eighteen days, but, by engaging in a dangerous task which he could have ordered another to do, he clearly demonstrated superior leadership skills that would have augured well for a bright future as an officer.

Eventually Grout's detachment returned, bearing the sad tidings about Bean and Pixley. Being a private, Bean's circle of acquaintances was tighter than Pixley's. Though their deaths were just as distressing to their respective families, the lieutenant's touched more people across the regiment. In the wake of his passing, there seemed to be a genuine out-pouring of feeling. Though they left no record of the experience, the Rogers brothers knew him as their company commander. Most likely William and Mark would have concurred with the prevailing opinion that "Lieutenant Pixley was a brave officer, a gentleman, and a true soldier."[31] In writing to Eliza and Alfred Pixley, Colonel Sawyer pictured their beloved son as "a good and meritorious officer ... [who] lost his life while in the discharge of and in the line of duty."[32] Pixley's body was eventually located along the riverbank and was sent home to Enosburg Falls. All across the country, battlefield deaths indiscrim-inately affected countless lives. For Mrs. Pixley, the spring of 1863 was indelibly burned into her memory. Charles died in February, followed by her husband in May. Since her son had "given her all of his earnings except enough to cloth [*sic*] himself in an econom-ical way," she qualified for a military pension.[33] As if she needed any reminders, once a month a government check came for the rest of her life — and with it a rekindling of old memories.

February 1863 had been difficult for the Vermont Cavalry. Mother Nature had been most fickle, alternating pleasantly warm days with those of bitter cold. But gradually winter in Virginia relinquished its grip on the land and slowly gave way to spring. As if fighting the elements was not demanding enough, the harassment of pickets steadily intensified as the enemy became better organized and grew bolder with its hit-and-run tactics. Never during this time period did the 1st Vermont operate as a cohesive unit, let alone have an opportunity to drill together. Both esprit de corps and efficiency suffered. Through it all, though, the Vermonters persevered. They took their lumps, they learned, and most of all they never lost confidence in themselves. Uncomfortable as things had become, there were still darker days ahead. The situation was going to get worse before it got better — but it *would* get better.

16

Aldie Mill

Mr. Mosby Up Close and Personal

As the 1st Vermont Cavalry nestled in its winter quarters, an event occurred in the hills of Northern Virginia that would significantly impact the regiment. Drawing scant attention at the time, its footprint would loom large in the history of not only the 1st Vermont but the Civil War as well. On this hallowed occasion in Confederate history, ten men were detached from Jeb Stuart's 1st Virginia Cavalry to commence what would become twenty-eight months of guerrilla warfare. Commanded by the incomparable John Singleton Mosby, this nucleus grew to eight companies. Eventually known as the 43rd Ranger Battalion, this unit became masters of hit-and-run warfare. From their first encounter in the early spring of 1863 until the start of the Gettysburg Campaign, the 1st Vermont and Mosby's partisans clashed frequently. Initially these encounters did not go well for the Federals, who absorbed repeated hits from the rebels but were unable to retaliate with any meaningful blows. Frustration clearly underscored the feelings of one Vermont cavalryman when he wrote that "we are willing to meet the rebels in [a] fair open field fight anytime, but the guerrillas do us the most harm. They are constantly hovering around our camp, ready to pounce upon our soldiers whenever they can get an advantage. They steal up to our picket posts at night, surprise and overpower our men, and march them off before any reinforcements can be brought from camp. We have lost quite a number of men taken prisoners in this way."[1] However, it wasn't until Monday, March 3, 1863, at Aldie, Virginia, that an encounter of any sizable consequence took place between these adversaries. Aldie was a hamlet about thirty-four miles northwest of Washington, D.C., and thirteen miles from the large Union cavalry outpost at Dranesville. Situated in the piedmont, it was on a direct road running through Ashby's Gap to Front Royal. Though not a precipitous ascent, a patrol moving from Dranesville to Aldie still found the ride taxing because the route was gradually uphill. If it passed on through Aldie to Middleburg and Upperville, a detachment would encounter more of the same, as the incline continued to increase. Periodically resting the horses was advisable. One ideal stopping point was Aldie. Here a gristmill provided a convenient roadside facility with water and open grounds. Along with the big brick mill, the location featured three other support facilities: a granary for storage, a smaller country mill, and a residence for the miller.

The meeting of warring parties that March day was a chance encounter, though the rebels' suspected presence in the vicinity was definitely the catalyst that set two Union patrols in motion. The ill-fated affair that evolved at Aldie can be envisioned as having four distinct phases. In the opening stage, troopers of the 18th Pennsylvania and 5th New York cavalries were sweeping through the Middleburg area, hoping to bag Mosby. Phase II consisted of a chase during which Mosby unsuccessfully endeavored to catch these Federals. In Phase III, troopers of the 1st Vermont Cavalry appeared on a Mosby-hunting expedition of their own, only to have the tables turned. The final phase occurred in the weeks that followed and consisted of finger pointing, leading to the termination of two officers' careers.

The hunt commenced with high hopes. Major Joseph Gilmer with 200 troopers marched out of camp in the early morning hours of March 2. The expedition's destination was Middleburg, a small community about twenty-five miles away with strong pro-Southern sympathies. Gilmer believed that there he would find many men who rode with Mosby. By taking them into custody, he hoped that he would "do something about Mosby's unrelenting and successful attacks."[2]

But, as Mosby later confirmed, he had "never had been in the village except to pass through it."[3] Though the Federal troopers definitely caught the townsfolk unaware, the surprise was on them. Executing their orders to round up every male, all their efforts produced were "a lot of old men whom they had pulled out of bed."[4] At that point, seeing that he had no plume-hatted Mosby or wiry youths among the assembled graybeards, Gilmer could have called it a night and left the citizenry irritated but unmolested. One of the most compelling reasons for his intransigence may have been John Barleycorn, for Mosby later asserted that the major had been making liberal use of spirits on that cold March night.

Regardless of the inspiration's origin, Gilmer decided to haul the townsmen away as prisoners. Time was of the essence, for Mosby could appear at any moment, and, coincidentally, Mosby and his men were in fact out and about at the same hour. This concurrence had come to pass because "Mosby had ordered his men to meet at Rector's Crossroads, from which he planned to assail federal picket lines."[5] However, before setting out, word reached them of the Yankees' improprieties in Middleburg. Hurrying over to the beleaguered community, Mosby hoped to nip at the heels of the Union force. At the very least, a few unwary stragglers might fall into his grasp. Having only seventeen men, he could not realistically expect to do much more than harass his adversaries. Unfortunately, by the time the partisans reached Middleburg, the Yankees had departed. From the townspeople, Mosby was able to glean valuable intelligence regarding the size of the enemy contingent, their time of departure, and the route they took.

At this point, the curtain descended on Phase I. As if there wasn't enough cavalry activity around Middleburg that morning with Gilmer and Mosby traipsing about the neighborhood, onto the stage to open Phase II at sun-up rode another troupe of performers, its presence as unknown to the first two as theirs was to it or each other. This detachment of fifty troopers, from Companies H and M of the 1st Vermont Cavalry, was commanded by Captain Frank Huntoon.

Having left Annandale earlier that morning, the patrol reached Aldie by noon. Along the route of march, no hostile activity had been encountered. If the developing situation could have been viewed on a radar screen, three blips would have been evident, all moving along the same northwest/southeast plane. The middle blip, Gilmer's party, was moving slowly toward the southeast, just west of Aldie. A second blip, directly behind Gilmer, would have represented Mosby's band, currently between Middleburg and Aldie, heading in the same direction as the Union troops but moving at a faster clip and rapidly closing the gap. Approaching Aldie from the opposite direction and moving northwest would be Huntoon's patrol, the third blip. The developing scenario had all of the makings of a collision, as none of the three parties knew its exact location relative to the others. Gilmer was definitely hoping that rebels were not behind him, Mosby fervently wished that Yankees were ahead of him, and Huntoon had no idea that the other two were heading straight toward him.

As Huntoon's patrol closed within hailing distance of Aldie, Gilmer's vanguard was already through the village and had established visual contact with the 1st Vermont's lead riders east of the town. Here the confusion started. When the Vermonters formed a skirmish line, Gilmer's scouts broke off contact, returned to the main body, and reported incomplete findings: riders ahead. Major Gilmer, acting on sketchy intelligence, erroneously deduced that they must be Confederates. The fact that Gilmer had a sizable force and Mosby's bands tended to be small were variables never considered. As Lieutenant-Colonel Robert Johnson reported to the brigade's commander, "Major Gilmer, instead of throwing out a party to reconnoiter, turned off with nearly the whole of his command in the southerly direction of Groveton to gain Centreville."[6]

Of course, Gilmer's turn altered the dynamic between the forces of Huntoon and Mosby. For Mosby, he would still wind up confronting Yankees, the only downside being he would be accosting the wrong group. On the other hand, his job was now easier. Instead of chasing down an enemy who anticipated his arrival, he was about to engage opponents blissfully unaware of their impending fate. For Huntoon, who thought that the only force to his immediate northwest was friendly, the consequence was letting his guard down a bit too much. As for Gilmer's column, though saved from the deadly clutches of adversaries, it had unwittingly been confronted with another problem. By rerouting to a secondary road, the surface conditions over which Gilmer's overloaded party now had to travel were deplorable. Combating Virginia mud became his new challenge. It was a phenomenon which the Vermont Cavalry had found to be a major nuisance since its first arrival in the Old Dominion. William Wells wrote in the spring of 1862 that "You have no idea of the kind and quantity of mud in VA. There is no bottom to it."[7] Weighted down in many instances with a rider and a prisoner, the Yankees' horses soon began to find the going extremely difficult. Any headway made by his retreating detachment became measurable in feet rather than miles. Eventually so many horses were lost that the prisoners had to be released if the command was to save itself.

The third phase opened with Huntoon's patrol in Aldie, as Mosby cautiously approaching the northwest side of town. In accordance with established procedure, Huntoon planned to post pickets after halting. In this decision, "Captain Woodward assented and advised that they send out pickets at once, which was done; a corporal, and two men upon each of the roads."[8] At this point, the sequence of events starts to speed up. The pickets barely had time to gain an advanced position, when riders climbing the upgrade just west of Aldie approached them. Mosby later recalled that the meeting was a shocker to both sides: "Just as I rose to the top of the hill on the outskirts of the village, I suddenly came upon two Federal cavalrymen ascending from the opposite side. Neither party had been aware of the approach of the other, and our meeting was so unexpected that our horses' heads nearly butted together before we could stop."[9]

The rebels reacted quickly, taking the Yankees prisoner. In the meantime, two other cavalrymen were spotted further down the road. Having finally established contact, Mosby was still in the dark because he thought "he had come upon Gilmor's [*sic*] rearguard."[10]

But the rebel chieftain's only confusion was about what unit lay before him. When confronted by an enemy, there was never any indecision on Mosby's part as to what to do next: "A charge was immediately ordered."[11] For Huntoon's patrol, the stop at Aldie had afforded a nice respite. Some took the opportunity to recline about the grounds. Others went inside the mill to lie down, and a few wandered inquisitively among houses in the vicinity. For the most part, they had seen to or were attending to the needs of their horses, bringing them water from behind the mill and grain from the bins inside. A few of the animals had been led over to a nearby blacksmith's shop for shoe repairs. Many of the horses, unsaddled, were tied to a fence. Perhaps thirty minutes had elapsed since the halt began. A correspondent from the 1st Vermont pictured the tranquility of the afternoon as putting the soldiers in a totally unguarded state: "No more suspecting of danger were they than were the citizens of ancient Troy on the night of her downfall."[12]

Among the first to observe the hard-charging Confederates may have been Huntoon and Woodward, who sat perched upon the front steps of the mill. What they witnessed coming at them was a lone rider, then six men following closely behind. Probably unseen by the Northerners but closing fast were another dozen-and-a-half partisans plus ten or so citizens who had joined in along the way. While the identity of these rapidly approaching horsemen was not immediately certain, little doubt about their intentions was left after a rebel yell pierced the afternoon air, along with several pistol shots snapped off in the Vermonters' direction. Soon the shooting reached the level of a fusillade.

After a few seconds of disbelief that froze the Federal troops, the cavalrymen sprang into action, which is a generous way of stating that most of them ran in every direction. What they very clearly did not do was offer organized resistance. The mounted Confederates, leaving the Yankees few options, hemmed in those in the mill yard. Some Vermonters jumped upon their unbridled horses and tried to effect an escape toward Annandale. Others ran for the wooded slopes of Bull Run Mountain. A few even sought refuge in the wheat bins of the mill! Only a handful offered resistance. Since the Vermont Cavalry was not known to display cowardice, one would have to conclude that their uncharacteristic reactions were due largely to the swiftness with which the rebels set upon them. The subsequent scattering of their force did not contribute to the establishment of a centralized rallying point. Only Captain Woodward, who mounted his bridled horse while brandishing pistols, and a few others exchanged volleys with the Confederates. Several dismounted troopers fought in a rather unconventional manner, that being to swing hand-held bridles as flails. This unorthodox technique was credited with delivering severe blows to the noggins of several charging rebels as well as knocking the hat off Mosby!

From the Confederate perspective, the most worrisome time came in the skirmish's opening moments. Charging down the hill behind Mosby, the guerillas focused on two blue-coated riders they saw on the pike ahead. Intent on the capture of what seemed easy prey, the rebels failed to notice the danger on their right. Once the attackers were halfway down the slope, the mill clearing came into view. To the Southerners' astonishment, they beheld an unexpected sight: a squad of Union troopers reclining about the grounds. Even more fortuitous, the Vermonters seemed as yet oblivious to the intruders' presence. The need to assume any posture of defense had yet to register. Further compounding the partisans' initial surprise, they had to watch helplessly as their leader's horse failed to stop at the mill. Instead, the excited animal whizzed past at top speed. With his horse now in charge, Mosby was carried helplessly past the melee developing at the mill and borne off in the direction of a second body of Federal cavalry, this one mounted and on the opposite side of the Little River. As his high-spirited steed approached a small bridge, Mosby decided that the only expedient option open to him to avoid capture or injury was to part company with his horse, a choice successfully executed with a leap and tumble. He was afoot only briefly when a partisan gave him his horse. Adding to Mosby's good fortune, the Union force across the bridge abruptly headed off quickly down the pike. By choosing this response, they effectively removed themselves from any part in the skirmish. Almost as if to insure that they would not return, this particular Union retreat was shadowed by an unusual rebel presence, later confirmed by Mosby: "...with one man I rode down the pike to look for my horse. But I never got him — he chased the Yankees twenty-five miles to their camp."[13]

With the threat behind him removed, Mosby then turned his attention to the mill. By this time, resistance had largely been neutralized. Inside, the Confederates were pulling Union soldiers from their hiding places. Those rousted from the mill were easily identified, as they wore uniforms caked with white flour. Contrasting with the easy subjugation of his comrades, there was one bona fide hero that day dressed in blue. Though as surprised as his compatriots, Captain John Woodward gave a good account of himself. Dashing from the steps, he bridled and mounted his horse. Riding across the Little River bridge, he sought to rally the troops resting there. Mosby spotted him and correctly deduced Woodward's intent. To guard against any threat from that direction, Mosby ordered one of his men to watch for aggressive movement. Closer examination revealed that the captain was alone, so the rebels attacked him. According to an account in the *Vermont Journal*, Woodward was not easily subdued: "Having fired every shot in his revolver, he drew his sabre and was dashing among the rebels when his horse was shot dead upon the spot and falling, pinned the Captain to the ground. He was unable to extricate himself, but he would not surrender. He drew a pocket revolver from his coat which contained but two shots and blazed away at the rebels, mortally wounding one."[14] After wounding an enemy officer, Woodward did not capitulate until Mosby himself leveled a revolver at him. Then, out of bullets, injured, and pinned beneath his horse, the brave captain reluctantly surrendered, resigning himself to a few months in captivity over eternity in a pine box. For any soldier to have fought as Woodward did was highly commendable, but, for a young officer experiencing his first taste of combat, the captain from Chittendon County gave an exemplary accounting of himself.

In appearance, there was nothing fiercesome about the twenty-three-year-old Woodward. He was slightly built with small, rounded shoulders and had a long narrow face with a high forehead. His face was clean-shaven; his eyelids drooped slightly, giving him a sleepy look; his nose and ears were perhaps a bit too large for is head; and his straight, dark hair was worn neatly trimmed, parted on the left, and grown rather long in the back in ducktail length. But looks can be deceiving, for inside of the diminutive, 5'4" body of the minister's son beat the heart of a lion. Granted he won no medals that day, but Woodward's courage would not go unnoticed. After being moved to a local farmhouse, the young Vermonter received an unexpected visitor. On toward evening, the injured captain looked up to see none other than John Singleton Mosby standing by his bedside! Though Confederate policy forbade paroling officers, Mosby was so impressed with Woodward's heroism in the face of overwhelming odds that he had come to personally release him. In the process, the renowned guerrilla leader complimented both the injured officer and his defeated comrades. Mosby is said to have told Woodward that the young officer "was the bravest and best fighting man he ever saw."[15] In addition, Mosby acknowledged that he "had a very high regard for the Vermont Cavalry. He told Captain Wood-ward he would not have paroled him had he belonged to any regiment but the 1st Vermont."[16] What more worthy accolade could a soldier ever receive than praise from a respected adversary? Captain Woodward spent the night as a guest of an Aldie family, and the next day he was brought back to camp by a detail of the 5th New York.

As the curtain closed on Phase III, Mosby regretted only that five invaluable men were wounded, one mortally. On the other hand, both Federal forces had much to rue. Major Gilmer suffered the loss of his integrity. The 1st Vermont incurred the cost of seventeen men as POWs. One prisoner to whom the day's events proved especially unkind was John Kinehan. A recent enlistee, his experiences at Aldie left indelible marks on his mind and body. It seems, as Mosby's men prepared to leave, the prisoners were told to mount any available horse. The animal Trooper Kinehan appropriated had stirrups set for a much shorter man. Kinehan recalled how he had "attempted to lengthen them and while so doing was approached by one of Mosby's men who tried to strike him over his head with his saber. He dodged, causing the blow to fall upon his right shoulder which was somewhat protected by his shoulder scale which deadened the blow but it nevertheless resulted in breaking his collarbone."[17] While he had the good sense not to retaliate, Private Kinehan had no reservations about taking his case to Major Mosby. His Irish temper aroused, Kinehan proceeded to "remind him that having surrendered under promise of treatment as prisoners of war they were entitled thereto."[18] While his surprised comrades looked on, Kinehan took considerable satisfaction as "Mosby severely reprimanded the man who had struck him and spoke to and of him as a deserter for whom he had no respect," adding his personal endorsement that the "Vermont boys were brave men and should be treated as such."[19] After having his shoulder bandaged by a rebel surgeon, Trooper Kinehan made the trip by horse to Culpepper and then rail to Richmond, where he was incarcerated for three days. He was then paroled to Annapolis, eventually exchanged, and arrived back with the regiment in time to fight at Gettysburg.

The fourth and final phase, begun on the day of the skirmish, took months to play out. Only two individuals were spotlighted: Major Gilmer and Captain Huntoon. Huntoon was languishing in Libby Prison, so there was no urgency for a rush to justice. However, since Gilmer could still lead another ineffective wild-goose chase if preventative action was not taken, twenty-five days after he contributed to the debacle at Aldie he was brought before a military tribunal, on Friday, March 27, 1863. Two very serious charges were lodged against him, the first being Drunkenness and the second Cowardice. Though Gilmer pled not guilty, the findings of the court, handed down on July 23 pronounced him guilty of the charge of drunkenness but not guilty of cowardice. The result was still career ending. Major Joseph Gilmer was sentenced to be cashiered.

At the same time Gilmer was facing disciplinary action, a case was being prepared in absentia against Captain Huntoon. Once paroled and returned to Fort Scott, he was not permitted to rejoin his regiment. Instead, what awaited him was General Heintzelmann's conclusion that Huntoon's alleged misconduct at Aldie had rendered him unfit to be an officer. Since "such recommendations of the commanding officer of the regiment ... are generally approved without investigation," Huntoon's fate was sealed.[20] As extracted from Special Order 139 issued by the secretary of war on March 25, 1863, the jarring decision was formally promulgated: "By direction of the President the following officers [officer] are [is] hereby dismissed from the service of the Untied States, with loss of all pay and allowances now due or that may be due them [him] ... Captain F. Huntoon,

1st Vermont Cavalry, for disgraceful conduct in allowing his picket guard to be captured."[21]

Camp scuttlebutt had it that the captain was in trouble, as Blinn noted on the day of the incident: "much blame attached to Huntoon for failing to properly guard against surprise in the enemy's country — it is rumored that he will be dismissed."[22]

Huntoon had defenders, men who knew him personally and had ridden with him in battle. A former captain in the 1st Vermont publicly praised his former comrade: "A braver and nobler officer never drew sabre in the cause; a more prudent and careful one does not exist; one better informed cannot be found in the regiment unless one might except the Colonel, and it is as unfortunate for the service to lose such a man as it is unjustifiable and mean to assail him, when he lies a prisoner in Richmond."[23] In the end, the whole affair came down to simply another case of scapegoating. Only two officers were present at Aldie. One had clearly performed heroically. No matter what he had done, Huntoon's actions paled by comparison. Since the cavalry was made to look bad, a head had to roll. Huntoon's was available.

What was the truth? His military record was the best indication of Huntoon's mettle. First, he enlisted for ninety days in the 1st Vermont Infantry, serving until mustered out in mid–August. Then he joined the Vermont Cavalry. In the election of officers, Huntoon was chosen a 2nd lieutenant in Company H. While this method was no guarantee that those chosen were necessarily the best suited to hold rank, his selection does give some indication that the rank and file held the man in high regard. Standing six-feet two-inches tall and weighing in excess of 200 pounds, he certainly presented a commanding presence. As the following excerpt from a trooper's letter would seem to indicate, Frank Huntoon definitely cut a conspicuous figure among his men, even though they were then still drilling at Camp Harris and only in the early stages of their military careers: "The First Lieutenant in Co. H, Huntoon ... is gaining scores of friends every day, and ranks among the finest officers of the Regiment, and one who will prove himself true and gallant under any circumstances."[24]

Those who knew the man clearly expected much of Frank Huntoon the soldier. If these people were correct in their assessment, he must have been deeply mortified by the abyss into which his career had unexpectedly fallen. It is not the least bit surprising that he was not content to let his reputation be tainted with a dishonorable discharge. In a final act that was perhaps the most revealing of all about his true character, after his dismissal, he subsequently enlisted in the United States Navy. Signing up in Chicago, he commenced his service on July 26, 1864, shipping out first as an ordinary seaman on board the USS *Great Western*. A few months later he was transferred to the USS *Ouachita*, where he attained the rank of yeoman. He was honorably discharged from the navy on August 28, 1865.

That he might harbor ill will toward the military would be understandable. However, rather than wallow in bitterness, Huntoon jumped back into the fray. By so doing, he established a military record that was both very unusual and highly commendable. Not many could claim service in three branches in one war, making it very hard to imagine someone who fought on foot, on horseback, and at sea a coward. After his case was later reviewed, the War Department reached this same conclusion. As a result, on January 2, 1866, "by direction of the President ... the foregoing orders of March 25, 1863, from this Dept., as dismissed this officer was thereby revoked, and that he was honorably discharged from the service of the United States as of the date (March 25, 1863) of the aforesaid order."[24] Furthermore, this exoneration qualified him for a pension. A giver and not a taker, Huntoon waited until he was sixty-nine years old before finally seeking Federal assistance. When the wizened veteran finally applied, he wrote a brief but compelling letter to the Bureau of Pensions in 1919 in which he expressed feelings as well as his need:

> Gentlemen
>
>   I am returning application and evidence. I have always been opposed to a soldier receiving a pension and I never would accept one until old age and sickness compelled me — about 8 years since — Uncle Sam's red tape makes one feel like a criminal — I do hope you will send it when due — I need it — badly.
>
> Yours truly,
Franklin Huntoon[25]

Fifty-six years had elapsed since the disaster at Aldie. In one sense, Huntoon was probably owed much more than the fifty dollar allowance which he was receiving monthly at the time of his death in 1922. As a minor skirmish amidst the Virginia hills, Aldie represented but one among hundreds of similar fleeting encounters that occurred during the Civil War. Yet, though its big-picture impact was negligible, as an event in the lives of the citizens of two communities, two hundred and fifty Union soldiers, a few dozen partisans, a Confederate captain, two Federal captains, and a Yankee major, it was unforgettable, and to some life-altering. For John Mosby and his followers, it enhanced a fledgling but growing reputation for daring actions. For the 1st Vermont Cavalry, which had an established reputation for excellence in traditional combat, it marked a rude introduction to an unconventional style of warfare, one that would require considerable adjustment on their part before they could give back the punishment they took.

17

Herndon Station
Outfoxed by Mosby Again

For all the glory that came the way of a Civil War cavalryman, there were times when a horse soldier had to pay his dues. One of those occasions when dash gave way to drudgery was picket duty. Like medicine and vegetables, regardless of how important pickets were, it was an assignment universally loathed. Sometimes, though, the luck of the draw could yield an assignment that was downright tolerable. One such occasion was St. Patrick's Day, Tuesday, March 17, 1863, when a detachment of the 1st Vermont found itself at Herndon, Virginia. Twenty-five troopers strong, 2nd Lieutenant Alexander Watson's detail was posted twenty-three miles from Washington, D.C. Its task was to stand guard at a sawmill, located on Folly Lick Run, and a nearby train depot that now housed a store operated by a local entrepreneur, one Mayo Janney.

In addition to the pickets, there was coincidentally a second Federal presence in Herndon that morning. Major William Wells, Captain Robert Schofield, and Lieutenant Perley Cheney had ridden over from Dranesville. Leaving at 10:00 A.M., the officers were on an investigative assignment. In effect, "the trio of Vermonters formed a commission which dealt with civilian complaints against Union forces."[1] Specifically, Wells had been ordered to determine if there was any substance to allegations of theft from local farmers. Had he read a letter to the editor, dated February 15, 1863, in the March 24 issue of the *Burlington Free Press*, he would have noted that a trooper clearly validated the citizens' outcries when he wrote: "There has been a great deal of shooting of pickets at Dranesville, supposed to be by the farmers who live close by. Our men plunder and steal, and they take this way to have their revenge."[2] The investigators spent some time at the railroad station, looking about and speaking with the troopers. At approximately one o'clock, Wells' party had completed its business and was preparing to leave.

As the officers were about to depart, they received a gracious offer to dine at the Herndon home of known Union sympathizers. Faced with continuing on with empty stomachs, the invitation for a home-cooked meal was gratefully accepted. Thus, by one-thirty in the afternoon, the stage was set. Major Wells' party, plus 2nd Lieutenant Watson, were enjoying a fine repast, good conversation, and a welcome interlude from the war. The soldiers on guard duty, their horses tied to a picket fence, were also in a relaxed posture, some eating while others were "either lying around in the sun, reading some book, or otherwise engaged."[3] After being on duty for forty-eight hours, all were anxious to get back to the relative comfort of the main camp.

What these unassuming Yankees did not know was that Mosby's partisans were

The unpretentious little depot of Herndon Station was the scene of much embarrassment to the 1st Vermont, when Mosby and his men bagged the entire picket post plus four officers dining obliviously nearby in a private home (Library of Congress).

about to pounce. Since the videttes anticipated the approach of a friendly force, a column coming up the road from Dranesville signaled no alarm. The time of day, of course, added to the element of surprise. As Mosby later explained his unorthodox gambit, "I thought I would try my luck in the daytime ... as most of my attacks had been made at night, I knew they would not expect me in the day."[4] After crossing the railroad tracks about three miles northwest of Herndon Station, Mosby's band threaded its way on foot through the surrounding pine forests along a winding bridal path. Eventually they moved out onto the Dranesville-Herndon road in the rear of the picket post, effectively coming between the Vermonters and their base. By clothing some of his men in blue uniforms, approaching from a "friendly" direction, and timing the masquerade to coincide with the hour when relief was expected, it is easy to see how Mosby's ruse succeeded.

Reaching the road, the Confederates rode slowly toward their objective until coming upon an advanced picket position. Lulled into a sense of security by what he perceived to be comrades, the sentinel continued "reading a newspaper" and was "captured without difficulty."[5] Two hundred yards ahead they saw the sawmill and the troopers lounging about the grounds. "They were as unconscious of the presence of danger as if they had been at their own peaceful homes among the Green Mountains.... They saw us coming, but mistook us for friends," wrote Mosby.[6] Once the intervening gap had been halved, a saber charge was ordered. Mosby is purported to have emphatically shouted, "Surrender you d — d Yankee sons of b — — s," thereby giving his attack the distinction of being one of the first X-rated raids of the war![7] With no time to offer organized resistance, the pickets scattered into any available structure that could offer both immediate shelter and ultimately a defensive position. Some were captured right away; others made it into nearby houses. A fair number sought refuge in the sawmill. In these first few minutes of action, the Vermonters were barely able to snap off a few ineffective shots.

Once the momentum of the charge had passed, the Confederates were faced with the task of rooting the Union troopers out of their sanctuaries. Time was of the essence. At any moment, the road from Dranesville could bring the long-awaited relief troops. It was not in keeping with Mosby's modus operandi to become embroiled in a prolonged engagement with larger enemy forces. In this particular instance, it was entirely possible for his men to get caught between the fire of a mobile force attacking him from behind and those soldiers holed up in the nearby buildings.

Moving swiftly, the rebels subdued the troopers taking refuge in private residences. As Ranger Scott described this phase of the engagement, "an effective fire was soon opened up at the enemy through the thin weatherboarding with which the houses were encased. A speedy surrender was the consequence."[8] Once this source of resistance was overcome, Mosby's command turned its attention to the sawmill. A considerable number of Union cavalrymen defended its upper floor. With many possessing carbines, they might have held out until help arrived, inflicting unacceptable casualties upon the exposed Confederates in the process. Quick thinking and fast action were in order if Mosby was to achieve success. Fortunately, these were traits with which he was well endowed. As Mosby himself so succinctly phrased it, "the promptness with which the opportunity was seized is the reason that they were lost and we were saved."[9]

Mosby wrote that he and his men were effectively hard on the heels of those who disappeared into the sawmill. He claimed that that no sooner had the last Yankee cleared the doorway than he rode up, dismounted, and along with other partisans ran into the mill. Ever willing to try a gambit, Mosby started up the stairs to the second floor of the mill, but not before he shouted out an order to torch the building. This ploy had its desired effect. The trapped soldiers clearly heard his chilling command. Visions of an agonizing death flashed through their minds as the Vermonters looked around and saw themselves sitting amidst dry timbers and wood shavings. Mosby described the ensuing events: "As I reached the head of the stairway, I ordered a surrender. They all did so. They had the alternative of doing this or being roasted alive. In a minute more, those in the mill, in preference to cremation, chose to be prisoners."[10]

With the capitulation of the sawmill's defenders, the subjugation of the picket post was complete. The partisans suffered but a single wound. One Union casualty occurred in the fracas, as Private Blinn Atchinson of Company A, went down, suffering the ignominy of a pistol ball in the left buttock. For him, there was an upside to his painful wound. Since it looked severe, he was deemed too much of an encumbrance to move, so the Confederates left Atchinson behind. Another casualty of Mosby's raid did not show up in any official accounting, but the loss was one that Mosby found both laughable and worthy enough to mention in his memoirs. It seems that Mayo Janney, proprietor of the store in the Herndon Railroad Station, was drawing a jug of molasses for a customer when the attack commenced. Once the shooting started, Janney's focus shifted to the commotion outside. Forgetting about the flowing sweetener, he wasted no time in distancing himself from the scene of action. When he finally worked up the nerve to return hours later, much to the dismay of his mercenary heart, Janney found the barrel of molasses empty and the floor shoe-deep in the sticky substance.

Even though seven pickets had escaped, the partisan force still had a nice bag of prisoners, horses, and equipment to show for their efforts. The absence of serious casualties was a definite plus, and, as always, outwitting the Yankees had been fun. Also, more important to the "Cause" than to the man, the legend of Mosby's guile as a skilled guerrilla leader was burnished a little brighter. He was "gaining quite a notoriety capturing Yankees!" as Montpelier's paper expressed it.[11] Another Vermont publication, using a quaint colloquialism of the times, said that he was "getting to be 'some pumpkins'" and added the high accolade that "He is a second Ashby."[12] While grudging admiration was shown for Mosby's boldness, he was nevertheless still viewed by many as someone in "the bushwhacking business," a decidedly lowly enterprise, noting that "He and his party, like Captain Semmes of the 'Pirate Alabama,' are always Present to capture an inferior force unawares, but is nowhere when pursued by an equal force."[13]

But for the sharp eyes of Captain Mosby, the day's work would have concluded. However, as the victors were leaving town, Mosby noticed four horses tethered in front of a private residence. He was struck by their upgraded fittings, a dead giveaway that they belonged to officers. Ever opportunistic, he dispatched James "Big Yankee" Ames into the house with a squad of men, ordering them to search the premises. Upon entering the domicile, the rebels noticed that a meal was set out for more people than those seemingly present. The homeowners insisted that their guests had left. However, Wells, Schofield, Watson, and Cheney were in fact still present. As they had been sitting around their hosts' table enjoying food and hospitality, riders could be heard approaching at a rapid pace. At that point, "the Major got up went to the door, and saw quite a squad of Cavalry coming, when he turned he made the remark that the relief had come, and went back and sat down to the table."[14] No sooner had he reseated himself at the table then shots rang out, followed by shouts and a commotion outside. Looking from a window, the dinner party had a painfully clear view of the short fight. The rapidity with which the post fell left the four officers with few options. To make a run for their horses would have put them in plain sight of Mosby's men. They could have opened fire, but that would have meant engaging a force outnumbering them at least ten to one. The decision finally made, while admittedly not the manliest, was probably the sanest, given the circumstances: they chose to hide!

Having secured the lower floor, Ames' party, pistols at the ready, made its way warily up the stairs to the dimly lit second story. A quick look around produced no results. There was, however, still one spot unsearched. A small trapdoor connected the upper floor with a garret. Sergeant Ames had located his quarry. Somewhere jammed together in those close confines were the four Union officers. Leery about charging into the darkness, Ames opened the door and "called to the Yankees believed to be there to 'come forth and surrender.'"[15] No sound emanated from the pitch-black interior. At this juncture, a humorous outcome broke the tenseness of a situation which, within the context of war, had tragedy written all over it. Sergeant Ames decided to break the impasse by firing a shot into the darkness and did so. Muffled voices were briefly heard. After another surrender demand went unheeded, a second shot was fired. This one produced a most desirable though highly unintended effect: "There was a stir and crash, and instantly a human being was descending through the ceiling. He fell to the floor among the men. The flash of the pistol in his face had caused him to change his position, and in so doing he had stepped on the lathing and fallen through. His descent had been easy and without injury to his person. He was thickly covered with lime dust and mortar. After he was brushed off, we discovered that we had a major."[16]

In a rather undignified way to be captured, Major William Wells quite literally fell into the hands of Mosby's men. It probably did nothing to assuage the major's pride when several of the rebels burst out laughing at his grand entrance. With his dark beard and blue uniform turned gray/white by the plaster, Wells had looked all the part of an apparition. It was probably just as well that he could not see the reaction of his comrades still upstairs, who were noted as having "rather enjoyed the laugh we had on the major."[17] After the four officers were disarmed, the rebels prepared to rejoin their cohorts, waiting outside with the first batch of prisoners. Before exiting the house, though, they had one last piece of business to carry out. "Mosby's men then made their second charge of the day," partisan Scott recalled, "and attacked the dinner table, and soon dispatched it."[18] Suddenly, Lieutenant Cheney attempted to escape. As reported from eyewitness accounts, Lieutenant Cheney

While enjoying a convivial meal, Perley Cheney suffered the ignominy of being captured while hiding in a garret, with even his ensuing escape attempt being unceremoniously aborted (USAMHI).

"succeeded in mounting his horse, and had nearly made his escape from them ... but was hotly pursued by the enemy, firing upon him, which was returned, and he was only taken prisoner when his horse stumbled and fell."[19] On what was otherwise a most forgettable day for the Vermont Cavalry, Cheney's brave attempt to escape stands out as a singular high point.

Before departing, Mosby created three separate parties. One segment was comprised of the prisoners and their guards, who were placed under the command of the reliable John Underwood. This procession started off in advance of the others, heading for Fauquier County. The second group, the largest and led by Dick Moran, was ordered to follow along in the wake of the first detail. Mosby, commanding the third party of but twelve men, not surprisingly saved the most dangerous assignment for himself, which was acting as rear guard.

Finally, when the Confederates were the least vulnerable, the long-awaited Union relief party hove into view. Commanded by Lieutenant Edwin H. Higley and consisting of thirty troopers, the Vermonters knew that their mission had radically changed. From passively relieving a picket post, they were now aggressively attempting to rescue captured comrades. This necessity had been conveyed to Higley by one of the Herndon videttes. He had been away from his post, seeking a canteen of milk, when Mosby's band had swept in so unexpectedly. By the time the guard returned, he found the outpost overrun. Skedaddling down the pike towards Dranesville, the man eventually met Higley's oncoming party.

As he would be later vilified for doing, Lieutenant Higley approached Herndon cautiously. He led no spirited charge to rescue the prisoners. As Mosby's rear guard withdrew, a few ineffective shots were fired after them. Though the Union troopers doggedly pursued for approximately a mile-and-a-half, they were hampered by muddy roads, snow having blanketed the ground that morning. Though Mosby's men possessed the fresher horses, being encumbered with prisoners slowed their getaway. Their slight headstart was gradually overcome. In time, the Confederates passed over Horsepen Run, whose swollen waters made fording difficult.

As the last partisan cleared the creek, Higley's force appeared on the opposite bank and opened fire. A few Federal cavalrymen bravely attempted to follow. But Mosby turned back as if to attack, dampening their ardor. After watching the enemy pass over the crest of a hill, Higley headed back for Dranesville. While Higley's relief party was making its way toward Herndon, another much larger force had been dispatched from Dranesville to intercept the rebels. Post commander Major Charles Taggert of the 2nd Pennsylvania did this based upon intelligence that he had received of the Herndon disaster, most likely from the handful of videttes who had eluded capture. Within ten minutes, a 300-man force thundered out of camp. As Charles Blinn recalled, their efforts bore no fruit: "We hastened some twelve or fifteen miles, to a place called Gum Spring, where we found their tracks in the mud, but as the citizens informed us that they were two hours ahead of us and had most likely gone through Aldie and Middleburgh, the pursuit was abandoned."[20]

When the sun finally set on April 17, 1863, the embarrassing affair at Herndon Station was mercifully over. There were, however, to be serious ramifications. The most obvious impact was the fact that twenty-five Vermont cavalrymen and twenty-six Morgan horses were spending their first night in captivity, the horse-to-soldier differential of one being due to the fact that the severely wounded Private Atchinson had been left behind. Mosby caught up with the lead portion of his tripartite force in the friendly surroundings of Middleburgh, whereupon he paroled the twenty-one privates. The next morning they were released at Paris, Virginia, and set to walking the thirty-one miles back to Union lines by way of Harpers Ferry. Before leaving, the Confederates split up the booty acquired from the Herndon Yankees among themselves and the citizenry.

But it was the long-term impact of the Herndon fiasco that had the most profound effect. A tremendous furor arose in Vermont over the apparent ease with which Mosby toyed with the Union army. Representative of these feelings was the *Burlington Daily Free Press*, which conveyed its displeasure in these stinging sentences: "On this transaction, as well as two or three a good deal like it, which have happened lately, we have only to say that we count them disgraceful to our officers, and men so captured ... and if our Yankee officers and men cannot contrive sure ways to prevent being deceived, and to stop being surprised in such an easy way as they have been, they had better go home and have more wide-awake men put in their places."[21] The *Vermont Journal* echoed these sentiments by publishing a letter which opened with a biting comment that "Vermont cavalry stock used to be at a high premium; just now it seems to be a little below par. Surprise parties may be a good thing, in civil life, but they are pretty rough on our cavalry."[22]

In all probability, the timing of the Herndon incident, so close upon the heels of Mosby's celebrated abduction of Vermont General William Stoughton from his bed, served to exacerbate concerns. As often happens with debacles, an outcry arose, which led to an official investigation. In such a case, even with initially good intentions, too often the simplest solution was chosen: find a scapegoat. Careers often hung in the balance until a finding was made and the case closed. For the purposes of the Herndon "cover-up," every indication was that the finger of dereliction would point at Lieutenant Higley. When did the snowball commence rolling downhill at him? The starting point was Major Taggert's March 23 report on the "Affair at Herndon Station, Va." In this document, he concluded: "Every effort was made by me on receipt of the intelligence to capture the party, but with no avail. Had Second Lieut. Edwin H. Higley, Company K, First Vermont Cavalry, who had started with the relief for the post, consisting of 40 men, together with 10 of the old guard, who joined him, performed his duty, the whole party could and would have been taken."[23]

As an extra added piece of personal bacon-saver, Taggert concluded his report with a recommendation: "I cannot too strongly urge that orders may be given that all.... Outposts must remove behind the lines."[24] If military reports could have been copyrighted, Wells would have had Taggert dead to rights for plagarization, for he had already expressed in writing his concern about the vulnerability of the advanced positions. As Taggert well knew, "General Heintzelman, commander of Washington's defenses, had begun about this time to investigate the too frequent captures of positions of Taggert's command."[25]

The whole matter of the untenable nature of the picket posts had already been laid before Heintzelman in a communiqué written by Wells and signed by all of the officers of the regiment. In it, he stated the facts of the matter, particularly noting that there currently was no natural defensive line upon which to anchor and shield the pickets, identifying in the process the nearby Difficult Run as being able to provide the desired protection. However, the lockstep of military protocol and chain of command kicked in and overrode what common sense should have dictated was a good idea. As reported by Sergeant Ide, General Heintzelman sent the correspondence back with the following admonition: "Respectfully referred to Colonel R.B. Price commanding Cavalry Brigade. All communications should come through the regular channels. When General Heintzelman wants Major Wells' advice he will ask for it."[26]

Colonel Price referred the matter to Wells' commander, Major Taggert. Taggert was upset, especially since he was being cast in a bad light, and demanded an explanation from all signatories of the document. Wells stood his ground on both counts in question. First, the positioning of the picket screen did pose a problem everyone agreed was evident, and second, he was not being insubordinate in presenting the letter directly to General Heintzelman because at the time of its delivery Wells in fact commanded the regiment in its camp near Fort Scott. While in effect tabling the matter, Taggert clearly was displeased over the whole episode. It is entirely within the realm of possibility that he was at that point not favorably disposed toward officers of the 1st Vermont. The fact that Wells considered Taggert to be an excessive drinker would indicate that the feelings of disdain might have been mutual.

Since self-preservation is a basic instinct of the human species, it may well have contributed to the inclusion of the two most operative phrases in Taggert's whole after-action report: "Every effort was made by me," as in "don't blame," and "Had ... Higley ... performed his duty ... the whole party *would have* been taken," as in "blame him."[27] Perhaps the best defense of Higley's actions was offered by partisan Scott in his memoirs. Too bad for Higley, though, considering all of the mud that his name had been dragged through, the support did not become public until after the war. In his book, Scott wrote, "Mosby halted the rear guard with Moran's men at the crest of the lane, formed by two high fences which led up from the stream 100 yards to the top of the hill. The stream was deep and Mosby's plan was to sit until the pursuers had crossed it, and then charge. He felt that in this event, he would have captured or destroyed almost the entire party."[28]

Hindsight bears witness that Higley's decision not to force a crossing was indeed a prudent choice. Certainly it was a conservative decision, one that carried neither great reward nor excessive risk. But, with Mosby's command concealed in ambush, Vermont lives were assuredly saved by Higley's timeliness in breaking off contact. In the meantime, Edwin Higley had to endure his own personal hell on earth. Major Taggert placed him under arrest for cowardice and then "procured an order dismissing him from the service without trial or hearing."[29] Higley, true to his fighting spirit, refused to let the matter end in his disgrace. He appealed to the proper authorities, and got his case reopened and referred for review to a military commission. Higley based part of his defense on the fact that "he claimed that he had not so many men as Mosby and that, according to military rules, strictly speaking, he hade no right to go beyond the picket post as his was a picket and not a scouting party."[30] Perhaps most significantly of all, Higley could proudly point to his own war record, showing that he was promoted for bravery in the field from Orderly Sergeant to 2nd Lieutenant.

Through all of his tribulations, Higley maintained the support of his men. It was reported in the *Sentinel* that "the boys were all indignant — when these gallant officers [Frank Huntoon being the other] were dismissed."[31] His stock among them surely rose higher when he passionately made it known that if he was ultimately not reinstated as a 2nd Lieutenant in Company K then he "intended to enlist in his own Company as private, and prove to his enemies that he is, at least, not a coward."[32] When all was said and done, acceptable closure for Higley was brought to the case. As Benedict reported it, "Lieutenant Higley had no difficulty in establishing his character as a brave man, nor of relieving himself from the charge of inefficiency in pursuit of Mosby. The commission found no ground for the charges of cowardice and breach of duty."[33] Upon the commission's recommendation, secretary of war Stanton took appropriate action to reinstate the lieutenant. Edwin Higley was given back his proper rank, his command returned, and three months' back pay issued. There would of course by no compensation for the anguish and humiliation the man had to endure while striving to clear his name.

While Mosby had bested the Vermonters at Herndon, other meetings were still to come. Time would be required for traditionally trained troops to achieve parity in fighting guerrilla forces. Beyond the basic need to survive, there was yet another very powerful motivating force: pride. The acclaim, which the regiment had attained at Mt. Jackson, had been very satisfying. But fame can be enduring only when the original cornerstone is built upon over time by an increasing body of achievements. The stock of the Vermonters in the spring of 1863 was not what it had been six months previously. One of its own assessed their current status in a frank yet hopeful tone when he observed, "It is very unpleasant for me to write of such affairs as the present, having been accustomed to write only of the brilliant episodes of my regiment.... I hope I may not again be obliged to write of surprises or defeats, but only of those brilliant cavalry exploits which have characterized us hitherto, and have rendered this regiment the pride of the native state. We feel that these surprises have much injured our reputation. There is no doubt of this. Every man knows it, and I believe that every man, who has a spark of pride within him,

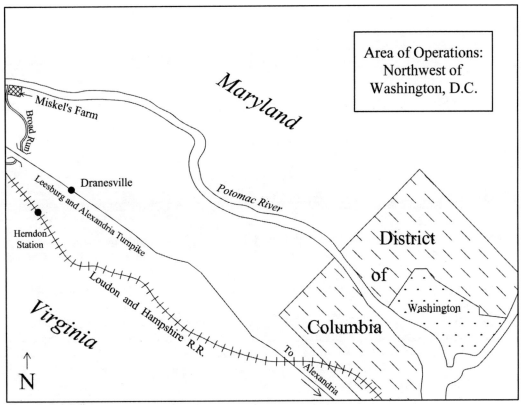

Area of Operations:
Northwest of
Washington, D.C.

Maryland

Miskel's Farm

Broad Run

Dranesville

Leesburg and Alexandria Turnpike

Herndon
Station

Potomac River

District

of

Columbia

Washington

Virginia

Loudon and Hampshire R.R.

To Alexandria

N

Drawn by Bob Collea

will swear by his saber to retrieve what is lost. Vermonters shall yet again be proud of their regiment."[34] In a matter of months, the war would provide opportunities for redemption. At Greenwich, Hanover, and Gettysburg, the 1st Vermont would quickly and permanently regain its lost status. Until then, they had to suffer the taunting sounds of a Civil War era folk song titled "Mosby" resounding in their heads:

> At Herndon station a few days ago,
> A Major was placing his pickets, when lo!
> Mosby came rushing up with a squad,
> And captured the Major and all of his guard.[35]

18

Miskel's Farm
Disaster Along Broad Run

For a soldier, a bugle sounding "To horse!" at 2:00 A.M. had an entirely different impact than that same instrument announcing "Reveille" at 6:00 A.M. As Charles Blinn told the *Free Press,* a shrill summons before dawn on April 1, 1863, was not to be scoffed at: "The sound of course — meant something and was promptly obeyed, and in ten minutes Company A was in line and headed by Lieut. Edwards was moving out to form in the column."[1] Several inches of wet snow and a north wind added to the men's discomfort, further exacerbating the harsh reality of venturing forth on empty stomachs. The assignment was not novel — apprehend John Mosby. A major difference on this sortie was the column's size, 150 riders. Every available Vermont trooper had saddled up.

A tip that Mosby was in Dranesville had triggered the hunt. Major Charles Taggert, post commander, ordered a detachment out. Led by Captain Henry Flint, the party was divided into two squads: one armed with pistols and the other with carbines. Among the men of Company B who left with sleep in their eyes that cold morning were Troopers Mark and William Rogers. Almost a year had passed since their first exposure to combat at Mt. Jackson. Little did they suspect that this would be their last ride together for some time.

Meanwhile, Mosby, too, had been out hunting. Finding only sutlers at Dranesville, he opted to stop for the night at a friendly farm eight miles down the Leesburg Pike and two miles back from the main road. Later he admitted being uncharacteristically careless: "I confess that on this occasion I had not taken sufficient precautions to guard against surprise. It was 10 at night when I reached the place where the fight came off on the succeeding day. We had ridden through snow and mud upward of 40 miles, and both men and horses were nearly broken down; besides, the enemy had fallen back a distance of about 18 miles."[2] In addition to fatigue, a second contributor to Mosby's lack of vigilance was his reluctance to order partisans to do guard duty. Citizen-soldiers served at their own pleasure and accepted subservience to a commander only to the extent that they so chose, placing any officer in charge of such forces in a tenuous leadership position.

Unaware of the partisans' altered plans, Captain Flint's column proceeded rapidly to Dranesville. Arriving before daylight, they made for the suspected safehouse, anticipating guerillas camped about the grounds. Nearing the site, Flint approached from a direction different from that which the enemy might have expected. Though a double envelopment was properly executed, Mosby's absence made all for naught.

With Plan A aborted, Captain Flint called an impromptu counsel of war. The decision was to continue the pursuit. Recently fallen snow made the tracks of Mosby's band quite discernible. Flint's detachment followed the trail for approximately three miles to the point where Broad Run led down to the Potomac. Leaving the turnpike, a column of twos was necessitated as "our cavalry boys passed through a considerable forest where their progress was retarded, and restricted to a bridle path, so that the captain's command trailed a long distance."[3]

The delay was no one's fault. But, as the 1st Vermont's approach was being impeded by forestation, partisan Dick Moran was bringing a warning of the nearby enemy force. He had spent the night at the home of a friend rather than bivouacking with his comrades. Flint's column had chanced to stop at that very house. Concealing himself until the Yankees left, Moran then rode furiously to warn Mosby. As Moran made his desperate dash, he undoubtedly replayed in his mind the last words Flint uttered as he exuberantly departed: "All right, boys, we will give Mosby an April Fool!"[4]

The loss of courageous leader Captain Henry Flint at Miskel's Farm cast a pallor of gloom over the Vermont Cavalry, as the good captain was its first officer to die in battle (Francis C. Guber Collection).

Moran's fortuitous placement occurred when Mosby halted at the Miskel property. Located north of the Leesburg Pike, the farm was situated on grounds sloping down to the Potomac. In spite of its positives as an overnight stop, highly questionable was the tenuous position that it put the Confederates in with respect to escape. Lieutenant Josiah Grout of the 1st Vermont noted this: "Mosby was cornered. To the north was the Potomac; to his west, Broad Run; and we occupied to his south."[5]

The impending battleground was multifaceted, each portion displaying a different degree of activity at dawn. The quietest area was soon to become ground zero: the farmhouse, barn, and enclosed yard. Here were the partisans and their horses. Some men had slept in the farmhouse. Others had sought refuge in the loft of the barn. Their horses were unsaddled and in many instances unbridled. With the final moments before the battle ticking away, most partisans were sleeping. Some here and there were stretching and yawning. A few had already partaken of a limited breakfast.

The second focal point was Flint's troopers. After having wound their way three-quarters of a mile through scrub growth, Flint's contingent "came to an open field which was fenced and on the further or river side of which were the Miskel farm buildings."[6] The farmhouse and barn loomed eighty rods ahead behind another gated fence. Lieutenant Grout recalled that since the first entrance "was so hung as to do its own shutting ... we fastened it open."[7] Without hesitating, Captain Flint ordered a charge. In a move that would prove disastrous, the gate was closed behind the last rider. Why Captain Flint felt the urgency to hasten forward will never be known. Lieutenant Grout advised him to wait for support. Perhaps Flint thought the rebels vulnerable because he held the element of surprise, an advantage delaying could compromise. However, by not halting, Flint denied himself two-thirds of his potential firepower, going in with just fifty men pitted against eighty.

At 7:00 A.M., Mosby was standing in the barnyard. The 1st Vermont was breaking into the outer field. Dick Moran was riding up "at breakneck speed, waving his hat, and shouting, 'Mount your horses! The Yankees are coming'!"[8] Seconds made all the difference. So it was that Mosby heard Dick Moran's shouts. He recalled that "by the time we got into the enclosure where our horses were, I saw the enemy coming through a gate just on the edge of a clump of woods about two hundred yards off."[9] Pounding through, the Union cavalry headed for the barnyard, an area "surrounded by a high fence and connect[ed] with the narrow enclosure which surround[ed] the house and it open[ed] through a plantation gate into the field of cultivated land."[10] The situation appeared grave for the rebels. In John Munson's estimation, "It looked as though the light and life of the Guerrillas must be swept from the face of the earth. Never before or again would federal troops have such a chance to secure Mosby and wipe out his men. They were three or more to his one, and they had him corralled in a perfect trap, as perfect as they could possibly have made it."[11]

Any modicum of surprise the 1st Vermont initially possessed had dissipated. Mosby watched them the whole time, his emergence from the house coinciding with the Northerners' gate-to-gate dash. Given those vital seconds, he warned his troops. They reacted quickly, a handful rallying to him in the open yard. Outside the inner fence, a portion of the Union cavalry had fanned out in a semicircle facing the gate. From this position, they began to exchange shots with the partisans. Lieutenant Grout witnessed a few men attempting to gain access to the barnyard by pulling down fence rails. A hail of fire drove them back, killing two troopers. One Vermonter so distinguished himself that a guerilla felt compelled to tell the captured Horace Ide his feelings, saying, as Ide recalled it, that "he saw one of our men, Sergeant Ferry of Company I, do the bravest thing he ever saw. That was that he rode up to the fence and tried some time to throw it down while there were twenty men on the other side firing their revolvers at him."[12] Miraculously, all six feet and two-and-half inches of Carlastan Ferry emerged unscathed.

At this point, Flint, Grout, and several troopers rushed the gate. Companies B and C sat poised, their sabers drawn, waiting for a breach. Flint shouted, "Forward! Company I, forward! with those carbines!"[13] The attackers, in a column of fours, headed for the narrow opening. A heavy concentration of fire fell on them. In the spearhead of the Union column were Lieutenant Grout and Privates John Reed, Ephraim Brewster, and Augustus Paddock. In the lead was Captain Flint, "swinging his saber and crying 'Come on'!" as he sought to inspire his men to follow his gallant example.[14] One officer described the ensuing action as follows: "The rebels held their fire until we got near, then delivered a murderous volley — the carbineers returned their fire but without effect, as carbines are not very effective when men are mounted on raw horses."[15] Quickly, the closed gateway clogged with rearing horses. A second rush faired no better. This time, perhaps spooked by the intensity of rebel fire spewing into their faces, many of the horses began to rear, wheel, and run from the scene. With their bodies shielded by the fencing and their pistols steadied on its rails, the rebels unleashed a deadly fusillade. Fired at pointblank range, the initial barrage knocked the daring Flint, Brewster, Paddock, and Reed from their saddles.

Private John Reed, one of the elders at forty-four, succumbed on the battlefield to a severe chest wound. Private Augustus Paddock, "Gust" to his family and friends, was shot clean through the shoulder, the ball entering his left breast, traversing his body just under the shoulder blade at an angle, and then exiting from his back.[16] Though the wound was painful, the thoracic cavity was fortuitously not penetrated. Eventually Private Paddock was carried to a nearby farmhouse, to which his cousin Ephraim Brewster had already been brought. Regrettably, Paddock was left behind. Brewster recalled how "we laid there, until three in the afternoon, when the surgeon came with an ambulance and examined us. Three of us, he thought might be carried to camp, ten miles from there, and over a very rough road. Cousin A. could not be moved. I was very sorry to be separated from him, but could not help myself."[17] However, oblivious to a triage status that did not give him much chance for survival, the sturdy young farmer struggled to his feet and walked a quarter mile to another farmhouse, whose inhabitants saw fit to nurse him for ten days. On April 11, he was transferred to the Armory Square Hospital in Washington, D.C. Upon his return to the regiment in July of 1863, the severity of his wound permitted only light hospital work elsewhere. His overall pulmonary weaknesses were such that they subsequently necessitated his transfer to the Veteran Reserve Corps in March of 1864, where he served until his final mustering out in the summer of 1865.

As for Private Brewster, he miraculously escaped injury in the initial blast of Confederate fire. Unscathed, he shortly found himself confronted by a partisan whom he engaged in a pistol duel. They fired several shots at each other until Brewster was hit twice. He recalled the encounter: "The first ball passing through my leg and as the second one passed through my groin I rolled off my horse without much exertion on my part, I can assure you."[18] After lying on the ground for a few moments, Private Brewster raised himself up on his hand to look around. Along with Reed and Paddock lying near him, he recognized the prostrate form of Henry Flint positioned face down in the dirt. The brave man's body was pierced by no fewer than five bullets or as many as twelve, depending upon which account is accepted. This riddling of his body was not surprising, for as Grout noted, "Captain Flint rode probably ten feet nearer the enemy than the rest of us."[19] He lived only briefly once he fell. Private Brewster recorded his beloved leader's dying moments: "I worked myself along to him and got there just as a rebel came up to take his arms and mine. I asked him to help me turn him over on his back, which he did. He did not speak after I got to him. I held his head while he breathed his last, then laid a rail under it."[20]

While these personal tragedies were being played out, the battle swirled above them. With Flint down, the men of Company I had the tables turned on them. Unable to continue due to the closed gate and high fence, their attack floundered. On the heels of the loss of Captain Flint, the demoralized Vermonters were about to be subjected to an enemy swarming at them like angry bees. Amidst his foes' mounting confusion, the always opportunistic Mosby seized the moment to do what he did best. Ordering the barnyard gate flung open, Captain Mosby led a charge—on foot! Twenty partisans joined him, with others following as they got their horses saddled and bridled. After one of the partisans gave up his horse to his chieftain, Mosby waded into the thickest of the fight. At this stage, the sides were fairly even. Furious hand-to-hand combat ensued. Brief in duration, it was decisive in outcome. The combination of rebel audacity and firepower proved to be too much.

Though the Vermonters tried to stem the tide, the swiftness with which the enemy was among them thwarted their efforts. While no Confederate account mentions it,

Ephraim Brewster referenced another possible factor contributing to his comrades' confusion: "...the rebels had on our uniform, so that it bothered us to tell which was friend and which was foe."[21] As the Southerners surged forward, the 1st Vermont gave ground, eventually retreating from the vicinity of the barnyard gate. The action now shifted to the first entranceway across the field. Self-preservation became paramount. Unfortunately, when the retreating troopers reached the exit, they found the gate not only shut but also obstructed with rails per Captain Flint's order. It was during this breakout phase of the battle by the Confederates that the 1st Vermont incurred a number of losses, particularly among its junior officer corps. Lieutenant Eli Holden was struck on the left side of his head by a saber, a blow forceful enough to have almost scalped him! So deep was the cut that Dr. Edson remembered "that the wound was unhealed for some weeks after his [Holden's] return to the regiment."[22] Lieutenant John Sawyer took a pistol ball in his shoulder, contributing to his seizure. But the most grievously wounded officer in this stage was Josiah Grout. It happened while he was at the outer gate, trying to simultaneously stem the rout, restore order, and prepare a counrcharge. In spurring his horse quickly away to avoid an assailant, Grout only succeeded in momentarily escaping injury. By helping his master dodge the initial confrontation, his horse inadvertently carried him into the enemy's midst. Alone against overwhelming numbers, the brave lieutenant fought gamely.

Partisans surrounded him, demanding that he dismount and surrender. Grout indicated that his wounds precluded compliance. Several of his men came to his aid and gently laid him under a nearby tree. Attesting to the severity of rebel fire, the lieutenant later noted that seven bullets had pierced his clothes and one lodged in his right hip. His sturdy mount took three hits. Though not fatally injured, Grout was in excruciating pain. Ephraim Brewster said, "I never saw anyone suffer as he did with his wound. The ball struck a nerve, and every time his heart beat, it felt as if melted iron was running down his leg, even to his toes."[23] When the first of the wounded were brought back to camp hours later, Lieutenant Grout was left behind to die. However, "he survived and was afterwards brought in by his brother, Lieutenant-Colonel Grout of the 15th Vermont, under a flag of truce."[24]

In the melee at the outer gate, the 1st Vermont suffered heavy casualties. The fence line effectively barred escape. Bunched against the rails, the Vermonters presented defenseless targets. For the Confederates, it was like shooting fish in a barrel. A witness described how "a crowd gathered helplessly as Mosby's men emptied their pistols into the mass."[25] It was in these confused moments that twenty-one-year-old Albert George of Company C went down, the result of taking two wounds to his body. One bullet lodged under the corporal's shoulder where it remained for the rest of his life, while the second pistol ball "fractured his femur," ultimately leaving him with a "stiff knee," a "leg two inches shorter" than the other, a stay in the hospital, and his discharge in 1864.[26] Orrin Putnam was also injured in the maelstrom. He had the grim misfortune to "receive a saber wound to the head on the left side near the temple."[27] Splitting his skull bone, the rebel's blade opened a three-inch gash and exposed Putnam's cerebellum. The severity of the cut required the placement of a silver plate over the opening to protect the brain tissue. After eight days as a POW in Richmond, Private Putnam was paroled. This good fortune joyously meant not only his freedom but also better care than would have been afforded a prisoner.

Mercifully, this phase of the action ended when the pressure of so many men and horses caused the gate to burst open, providing an avenue of relief from the slaughter pen. Nevertheless, they had been costly moments. In addition to the men cut down by gunfire, there had been "a much larger number, whose escape was prevented by a choke in the narrow gateway, and were captured."[28] Among those who later showed up on the MIA list was Sergeant Mark Rogers of Company B. Quite likely, he was taken prisoner either in the traffic jam at the gate or the pursuit that followed. For his brother William, a worrisome week lay ahead until word came that the prisoners taken at Miskel's Farm had been released and were on their way to Camp Parole.

Once through the gate, the remnants of Companies B, C, and I scattered. The rebels gave chase for several miles, though aggressive pursuit had its dangers too. Sam Chapman attested to this, noting how "capturing men in their retreat is no pastime."[29] Caught up in the excitement, Chapman boldly rode between two Vermonters, calling upon them to surrender. Instead of capitulating, they swung at him with their sabers. One of them stunned Chapman by smiting him severely on the head, thankfully with the flat side of his weapon. At this moment, a comrade of Chapman's came to his rescue, dehorsing one Yankee and capturing the other.

The grave wounds Josiah Grout received at Miskel's Farm deprived the 1st Vermont of an energetic, capable leader, but his eventual recovery and long life preserved his services for the state that he eventually served as governor (Francis C. Guber Collection).

The scene unfolding around Chapman was wild, pursuers and pursued firing shots at each other as their horses raced along the roadway. One participant in this helter-skelter chase was Horace Ide. Approaching Dranesville, he detected blue-coated riders behind him, so he slowed his horse's gait. Much to his surprise, one of the men shouted "Surrender you damned Yank."[30] With that, the rebel discharged his pistol. But to his amazement, not to mention Ide's, the partisan's horse dropped dead! Ide conjectured that as the Confederate brought his gun up to fire it across his body, his hand was jarred, in turn applying too much pressure to the revolver's trigger. The half-raised weapon then inadvertently sent its charge crashing into the head of the poor beast!

Later the subjects of much controversy, included in the rout were Companies D and G, commanded by Captain George Bean. Neither unit had participated in the fight. According to a critical fellow officer, "Captain Bean instead of charging attempted to stop the others from running, so instead of stopping the retreat he lost the day and the whole command ran."[31] Grout accords Bean the ignominious distinction of being the first to reach the Union camp, "bareheaded, shouting 'the rebels are upon us!'"[32]

Though there is little glory in being routed, Lieutenant Charles Woodbury qualified as another of the fallen heroes. While retreating, Woodbury halted frequently, imploring others to stand firm. After three miles, the determined young man "made a last effort to rally the few men left unhurt."[33] Sergeant Ide heard Woodbury shouting: "Turn round boys, for God's sake and stop them, there is only a few of them."[34] As Woodbury pivoted to face the onrushing enemy, a bullet to the brain felled him.

Woodbury was not alone among those who underwent a harrowing experience. Although not called upon to sacrifice their lives, the futures of William Belding and William Moncrief of Company G were nevertheless altered. Sergeant Belding was a soldier's soldier. A comrade, Frederick Cook, "always considered Belding one of the best soldiers, in his attention to duty and one of the most gutty in a fight, that there was in the company."[35] During the retreat, partisans caught Belding, and one delivered a saber cut to the top of his skull. Somehow he escaped back to camp at Difficult Creek, where Dr. Edson stabilized Belding's condition and sent him on to the regimental hospital. While in time the contusion healed, nothing could be done to reverse the adverse effect that the hard blow had on his hearing, which became impaired. Riding in the same mad dash as Sergeant Belding was William Moncrief. Like Belding, Private Moncrief and his tent mate Alvah Haswell were both wounded and captured. Before long, they found themselves in Libby Prison. Haswell's wound was slight. Moncrief's appeared ghastly though it was not life threatening. Described by Stephen Clapp, riding alongside Moncrief when he was hit, the bullet passed "in the back of his [Moncrief's] neck and came out in his face."[36] Committed as he was durable, Sergeant Moncrief took his parole eighteen days later, returned to active duty shortly thereafter, eventually reenlisted, and served throughout the remainder of the war. In the estimation of Private Haswell, "no better soldier or truer man ever faced the enemy or done more noble service for his country."[37]

At this point, Mosby left Miskel's with eighty-three prisoners and ninety-five horses in tow. Following a brief rest in Middleburgh, the retreating column pushed deeper into the safety of "Mosby's Confederacy," ultimately reaching Culpeper. From there the captives were entrained for Richmond. Unlike prisoners taken later in the war, they were paroled within a few days. Among those released on April 7, 1863, at City Point, were the Taft brothers, Levi and Milo of Company A. Both were in excellent health at the time of their capture and did not suffer the least bit from their incarceration of one week. The same could not be said for Private Thomas Owens, who had received a painful gunshot wound to the right elbow, costing him full use of the arm once the joint fused during the healing process. The trek to Richmond was for him a journey of agony.

As Mosby's men were escaping, the main Union cavalry encampment hurried to mount a relief party. Led by Major John Hall under a flag of truce, the detachment set up a field hospital on the Miskel's farm. Through the efforts of Hall's party, eighteen troopers were brought back. Among these men was Harley Sawyer, who took a painful, incapacitating wound to the chest: "It entered where the sternum met the clavicle, passed downwards and backwards, leaving the body ... [near] the scapula [on] the left side."[38] Along with tissue damage, the offending pistol ball caused injury to his left lung and inflicted what would become long-term impairment in his use of his left arm. Also saved were Privates Ephraim Brewster and Albert George, both heading for lengthy stays in an Alexandria hospital. The wounded John Frost was moved to the regimental hospital, but his case proved terminal. In addition to caring for the wounded, Hall's party also had the mournful duty to recover the bodies of Captain Flint and Lieutenant Woodbury. A correspondent summed up the regiment's feeling: "Well, all it has amounted to is this; we have lost some of the best officers in our regiment, those who were loved, and respected and mourned by all, and some 70 men, wounded, killed, and taken prisoners. It is a terrible blow to us, and one which it will take a long time to recover."[39]

For the Confederates, the "Battle at Miskel's Farm" would rank as one of the war's highlights. It was nothing short of astounding that the sixty-five partisans suffered but one killed and three wounded! That they went from being completely surprised to driving their enemy from the field made the engagement as complete a reversal of fortune as there ever was. To their credit, the partisans never panicked. Above all, they demonstrated complete faith and trust in their leader.

As fine as the day had been for the rebels, it could not have been much worse from a Union viewpoint. Foremost among the regrets was the loss of eight men. While family, tent mates, and company comrades would miss them one and all, the deaths of Henry Flint and Charles Woodbury were particularly crushing to the regiment. "A great gloom prevails in camp over the loss of two fine officers as ever entered the service of their country," lamented Charles Blinn.[40] Recalling a brief vignette that illustrates how both officers endeared themselves so deeply to their men, Blinn told how "only yesterday they joined us in a game of snowballs and tonight they lay stiff and dead."[41] As for Captain Flint, though he may have made some errant decisions, there was no disputing the man's courage. Tall for a cavalryman, he had a long, narrow head that had two distinguishing features. One was his beard and mustache that were kept closely trimmed except around his chin, at which point the whiskers reached almost to his chest in a rather wild, briar-patch manner. Perhaps as intended, this hirsute look made him appear much older than his twenty-four years. The other was his soft, blue eyes, conveying a warmth that was the very essence of the man. Josiah Grout, himself a revered member of the regiment, spoke for many when he eulogized his friend and commander: "Captain Flint patriotically, conscientiously, and fearlessly gave a generous, noble life to the cause. Few old soldiers rest more honorably among the green hills of Vermont."[42] Following Captain Selah Perkins, Captain Flint and then Lieutenant Woodbury were only the second and third officers to perish in combat from the 1st Vermont. After almost a year of fighting, three officers and nineteen men clearly are not staggering losses. But in a close-knit unit like the 1st Vermont—comprised of relatives, friends, and neighbors—each death was dearly felt.

On Friday the 4th, the officers' bodies were brought to Washington. An honor guard placed them on a train. Snow was falling hard in the northeast as trains carried them to Vermont, decorating the landscape with a beautiful yet fittingly somber mantle. It was a scene that Flint had viewed only a few weeks before on a furlough, affording him a special opportunity not given to every soldier: saying a last "good-bye" to family and friends.

On Sunday, April 12, 1863, mourners came together in Irasburg. It was reported that "appropriate services were held in the Congregational Church which filled to overflowing by the numerous friends of the deceased."[43] Afterwards, his mortal remains were taken to a little rural cemetery just outside of town. On a small hill in the shadow of Belvedere Mountain, Henry Flint was laid to rest. Home amidst the grandeur of north-central Vermont, a native son rests peacefully eleven hundred miles and one hundred and forty-five years removed from the violence of Miskel's Farm. A tall granite shaft—selected by his grieving parents to sustain the memory of their beloved son—marks his gravesite. On its western face, the Flints had inscribed two simple sentences, a fitting epitaph that echoes the strength of his cause, the depth of his sacrifice, and the measure of his heart: "He gave his life for his country. Greater love hath no man."

As Henry Flint was being eulogized in Irasburg, a similar service for Lieutenant Woodbury was held thirteen miles southward in Craftsbury. Charles Woodbury's gravesite is in a wayside cemetery just off the highway in Craftsbury Common. It is a quiet, dignified burial ground in a setting that time and history have long since left alone. Yet the violent event that brought Lieutenant Woodbury to this peaceful place is clearly etched in the white marble marker above his head: "Killed at Broad Run, Va, April 1, 1863." For all eternity, visitors are apprised that they stand in the presence of honored remains. Among the mourners that spring afternoon was Charles' wife, Nettie, who dearly knew the depth of her loss, and his twenty-month old daughter Mattie, who mercifully would not remember this sad day but in time would come to realize its impact. Learning of her husband's death hit Mrs. Woodbury (known to her friends as "Fanny") like a sledgehammer. Like so many with a loved one in the service, Fanny had likely lived every day with the ever-present worry about her dear Charlie compartmentalized in her brain. The demands of daily life would perhaps have allowed her to push the fear into the background, but concern for his safety was never far from consciousness. According to a neighbor, Miss Frankie Brown, "when the news reached her [Fanny Woodbury] she dropped almost senseless upon the floor."[44] Frankie described her friend's shock as being such that "she is almost raving crazy and has not shed a tear."[45] In a sad twist of war-related fate, Fanny, in her fifties by then, would thirty-five years later marry seventy-seven year old Amasa Randall, a former trooper in her husband's company. When the two announced plans their intentions, friends urged her to reconsider, as Randall was of questionable character. To her everlasting regret, Fanny Woodbury went ahead with the ceremony, one which forced her to give up rights to her first husband's pension. She soon learned the error of her decision when "Randall began to abuse and ill-treat her, and soon after deserted her, failed to support her, and left her sick and dependent on charity."[46] The contentment and companionship, which she had sought in her declining years, were not to be. A single bullet, fired far away on an April morning long ago, had an impact still felt over three decades later.

Miskel's Farm had proved tragic for both tiny Craftsbury and Company D. Charles Woodbury was dead, Augustus Paddock and Ephraim Brewster were wounded, and William Chamberlain and Eliab Smith were among those captured. For Frankie Brown, the emotional burden placed upon surviving family members by the war was already a personal experience, for she had recently lost a dear brother, Elijah, to the conflict. With his passing still very much in the forefront of her mind, Frankie found the events of April 1 quite distressing. She revealed her feelings to another sibling, sharing how "the late disaster has caused a great deal of excitement in this little town. I have never realized so much about this awful war as I have for the past two or three months. It has been brought so near home."[47]

The sense of loss was felt far beyond home. Demonstrative of heartfelt sympathy, a series of "Resolutions" were presented to the families of the two deceased officers by their former comrades in arms in which the men "deeply lamented" the passing of Flint and Woodbury, "whose courage, ability, and fidelity commanded the respect and confidence of the entire regiment, and whose high, manly character won the esteem of all of their associates, and whose earnest and self-sacrificing patriotism commends them to an honorable place in the remembrance of every citizen of their State and country."[48]

This was a very special tribute which the family undoubtedly appreciated and hopefully derived some solace from in their time of grief. Later, the heart and pen of Josiah Grout produced yet another beautiful memorial, a simple yet moving epitaph to his fallen comrades, fashioned in a prose imbued with all the charm, style, and sincerity of a bygone

era: "Flint and Woodbury were from Orleans County, and one sleeps in the quiet cemetery near Irasburg Common, and the other in the cemetery of Craftsbury Common. They
enlisted together, were mustered in together, endured the hardships of the service
together, breasted the dangers of battle together, and finally were mustered out, on that
beautiful April morning together. May love and peace hallow their slumbers until the last
old soldier of the Vermont cavalry has crossed the river."[49]

In their "Resolutions," the officers of the 1st Vermont paid homage to not only Flint
and Woodbury but also to the enlisted cavalrymen who perished along with them. The
six other empty saddles that day made the Battle of Miskel's Farm the worst tally of "killed
in action" which the regiment had incurred up to that point. By the standards of previous engagements, these casualties represented a significant loss. While there would deadlier days ahead, at that time eight deaths were tough to accept. Like the fallen officers,
each enlisted man had a story to be told and loved ones who were to mourn and miss
him for decades to come. Among them was John Reed, whose passing would make his
wife, Harriett, a childless widow, leaving her after twenty-five years of marriage with
nothing but his memory, her grief, and a pension. There was Private Abel Coburn of
Company B, a subsistence farmer who left a wife and four children, two of whom suffered with clubbed feet. Thirty-five years of age, he had been in the service barely six
months when he succumbed to pistol wounds. There was bachelor John Morton, also a
private, who endured a slow, agonizing death in a hospital from a mortal gunshot wound
that pierced his bowels, and left elderly parents to mourn for him. Horace Bradley, Company A, had served less than seven months when he was struck down, "shot through the
body, the ball entering his side and passed through him of which wound he died."[50] His
poor mother, Polly, suffered not only the loss of a beloved son but also her chief means
of support, as Horace's deadbeat dad, Eber, had deserted Mrs. Bradley and left her alone
in Richmond, Vermont, with nine children to clothe and feed. Horace, ever the good
son, had seen to it that his mother had received a monthly allotment from his pay.

Yet another tragic death was that of Private John Frost, made all the more heartrending by his youth and because his parents too relied so much upon his moral and financial support. Though having served but eight months in Company I before he died, he
had dutifully sent home over a hundred dollars to help his folks retire an outstanding
debt. He poignantly closed a letter to them with the encouragement "to keep a stiff upper
lip and forget that I have gone to war. I shall be home in the spring."[51] But the engagement at Miskel's Farm transpired before he got that much-anticipated furlough.

Private Frost almost missed his rendezvous with death because, up until March 1,
he had been sick with a cold and sore throat, caught, he believed, while on a scouting
patrol to Ashby's Gap in December. In a letter of "March 1st, 1863," which his parents
probably received only shortly before he perished, John wrote how "I came in last night
with two others from Dranesville. William came in with us. I rode in his ambulance and
drove the horses and he rode my horse. I was in the hospital at Dranesville two weeks. I
am in the company now but am exempt from all duty."[52] When the call came for volunteers to mount up in the early morning of April 1, 1863, Private Frost was barely back on
full duty. Given his weakened constitution, no one would have thought less of him if he
had opted out.

Receiving his March letter and then hearing of the disaster that befell the regiment,
his family may have breathed a sigh of relief, erroneously believing that he would not
have been a participant. But the young man who proudly and playfully signed his first

letter home "your soldier boy" would thereafter be coming home only in spirit, for his earthly remains would be interred in Virginia. For poor Mrs. Frost, John's passing was not to be her only heartache and sacrifice to the Union cause, as a second son was destined to die later in the conflict, a prisoner at Andersonville.

In addition to those whose very existence was ended forever by death, there were others for whom the battle was a profound, life-altering experience. Two men, in diametrically opposite ways, would find their post-battle careers to be radically different than either would have anticipated. Josiah Grout saw his star ascend brightly, while George Bean's flickered out ignominiously. For Lieutenant Grout, his wounds had made it touch-and-go for a while; however, he not only survived but also lived on into the twentieth century. In appearance, Josiah Grout, Jr., presented a look of intensity and resoluteness. He possessed an angular set about the jaw and chin, which, along with his high cheekbones, imparted a determined look to his face. Though he sported a dark mustache and a cleft of hair under his lower lip, neither in reality helped to harden his generally youthful countenance, he being all of twenty-two years old in 1863. Like so many of his comrades, he was comparatively small in stature and wiry in build, possessing an inner toughness that served him well through the hardships of war and a difficult period of convalescence.

In the short run, his military career was over. Though he later received a captain's commission for bravery in action and Colonel Addison Preston's endorsement, Grout failed back-to-back physicals. Having no choice, he was granted an honorable discharge two years from the day he enlisted. Though abbreviated, as Lieutenant Grout fondly recalled, "this two year period of service was the grandest section of my life. I would not exchange its experiences, hardships, dangers and sufferings for the joys, pleasures and triumphs of the balance of my allotment."[53] Grout's military career experienced a brief revival following the St. Alban's Raid. With the north country in an uproar over the possibility of further enemy depredations out of Canada, the governments of Vermont, New York, and Massachusetts banded together to form the 26th New York Cavalry. Comprised of companies from the sponsoring sovereignties, their purpose was to guard the border. His patriotic heart burning still, Grout tried for reinstatement to the 1st Vermont late in 1864. However, the incident at St. Alban's and subsequent local unrest gave him an excellent opportunity to help out closer to home. He therefore volunteered to serve in one of Vermont's two companies. Common knowledge of his bravery and leadership capabilities made him an obvious choice to be an officer, first with the rank of captain and then eventually major. By war's end, he was the commander of the "Frontier Cavalry" stationed at St. Alban's. In the postwar years, Grout continued to serve his beloved state with loyalty and dedication, eventually gaining election to the state legislature. The crowning glory of Grout's distinguished career was attaining the governorship of Vermont in 1896.

As bells rang in praise for Josiah Grout after Miskel's Farm, in grim contrast they only tolled for George Bean. To begin at the end, Captain George Bean was dismissed from the service for what was identified as his "cowardly" performance. While his decision-making that day was decidedly ineffective, the feelings on the part of others about his actions were mixed. Josiah Grout, whose opinion carried much weight, felt that "Captain Bean did not come out of the woods into the field and took no part in the fight. His part of the detail rendered no service. It was when Mosby saw that our supports were failing us that he swung out of the yard. Had we been supported the day might have been different."[54] Various publications added to the negative assessment and publicity surrounding Bean's effort with articles like the one that appeared in the *Rutland Daily Herald*, stating that "it is true that the reserve failed to give support ... [and] it would have been safer had Bean advanced to the support of Flint's attack instead of retreating."[55]

Not everyone, however, saw Bean's actions at Miskel's Farm as sufficient cause for dismissal. In Horace Ide's opinion, while "there was some talk about the 'reserve' not coming to the 'support,' but according to my observation, there was no 'reserve' and all came onto the field as fast as possible."[56] But the die was cast when General Julius Stahel submitted his report of the engagement in which he committed his subordinate Colonel Price to investigate the matter and recommend accordingly any officers whose performance warranted dismissal. Some would certainly have perceived a déjà vu element to this scenario, the twin embarrassments at first Aldie and then Herndon Station having also led to charges being brought against Lieutenants Huntoon and Higley respectively. In again trying to affix the blame for another disaster on someone, George Bean became the target of the probe. In Benedict's assessment, "Captain Bean was severely blamed for failing to support Flint with our rear squadron, and upon recommendation of General Stahel, who now defends the cavalry defenses of Washington and wanted to punish someone, was dismissed from the service."[57]

Even without the mixed reviews of his performance, Captain Bean had two strikes against him from the start of the investigation. First, his recent military record was suspect. This was not always true, for in the beginning his military future seemed promising. A blacksmith by trade, he joined the Vermont Cavalry's first recruiting class. Enlisting as a private, his leadership skills won him election to rank of second lieutenant in October and subsequent promotion to captain the following April. However, his performance during "Banks' Retreat" tarnished his record. Captured at Middletown on May 24, 1862, he was dishonorably discharged in October of the same year. Though he quickly won reinstatement, as of November 11, there were some for whom a cloud would henceforth be seen hanging over his head. Those individuals were not at all surprised when charges were brought against Bean in the wake of Miskel's Farm. His dismissal on April 28, 1862, for "cowardice" only confirmed what they had always believed. Unlike so many of his comrades, George Bean elected not to go home after the cessation of hostilities. In an interesting twist, he relocated to Alabama, where he resided for the remainder of his life. He may have decided that two charges of cowardice lodged against him in less than a year would render postwar life in Vermont uncomfortable. Untouched by bullets, Bean was yet another of the war's countless victims.

The second strike against Bean was totally beyond his control. Flint and Woodbury had died gallantly on the field of combat. Grout was severely wounded. Granted that Flint made some flawed command decisions, he nonetheless went down leading a charge into the barrels of the enemy's guns. When it became necessary for the higher-ups to find their requisite scapegoat, the three fallen heroes were above recrimination. But Captain Bean's past history and his lack of any apparent effort to aid his beleaguered comrades made him the leading, as well as the only, candidate who would be charged.

In addition to Captain Bean's ineffectual decision-making and the rendering of so many of their officers hors de combat, there were other factors contributing to the Federal defeat at Miskel's Farm. Though individually none may seem pivotal or crucial, it is when they are viewed collectively that their import becomes evident. One of these key elements was weariness. The Vermonters had ridden through most of the night, while the partisans slept. Similarly, the Southerners' horses had been fed, watered, and rested, but the Northerners' mounts were called upon to slog through the wet and cold without food. The presence of so many blue-uniformed Confederates was believed to have slowed and even withheld return fire from the 1st Vermont for fear of hitting a friend. Ide offered another intriguing possibility: the debilitating finger-numbness from hours of exposure that made handling weapons difficult. Adding some credence to this argument is the ineffectiveness of Federal marksmanship, with but one rebel killed and three wounded throughout the engagement.

When all was said and done, the Battle of Miskel's Farm was a disaster of significant proportions for the 1st Vermont. Tough lessons were learned, but at the cost of much grieving and suffering. While the regiment would return to fight another day, Miskel's Farm would always remain a dark experience in its collective memory. Mosby knew how extremely fortunate he had been. He recognized that his foe was a worthy opponent to be reckoned with, noting in his report of the engagement to General Stuart that the 1st Vermont was "one of their oldest and best regiments."[58] Had the regiment collapsed into a morass of self-pity and recriminations, then Miskel's Farm would surely have been seen as its undoing. However, the pluck, resiliency, and resoluteness that comprised the fiber of these men from the Green Mountains would never let that happen. As subsistence farmers, many of them understood from childhood that there would be lean times as well as times of plenty. Perseverance was a singular attribute that was shared by many. It wasn't hard to transpose the former outlook and the latter quality to military pursuits. As a regiment, they would endure, they would learn, and in the end they would survive. While bloodied at Miskel's Farm, they remained unbowed. Eventually, the time would come when their evolution as a regiment would reach maturity. When that day arrived, they would meet the enemy on the field of battle and emerge victorious. Then the bitter memory of Miskel's Farm, while not expunged, would at least be assuaged.

19

Greenwich

Last Chance to Even the Score with Mosby

With General Stuart's blessing, John Mosby decided to upgrade his harassment of the Federal supply line. Always thinking, the rebel chieftain conjured up an intriguing stratagem. "If you would let me have a mountain howitzer," Major Mosby wrote his superior officer, "I think I could use it with great effect, especially on railroad trains."[1] Eager to support his daring subordinate, Jeb Stuart sent the requested artillery piece post haste. The howitzer, or mountain rifle, that Mosby received was somewhat of a curiosity in the Eastern Theater of Operations, where terrain was not always advantageous to its deployment. But Stuart uttered no misgivings to his trusted subordinate. The mountain rifle sent to him had a "bronze barrel that was forty-two inches long, weighed 200 pounds, and had a two and one-fourth inch bore. Able to fire a twelve-pound projectile, the weapon seemed disproportionately constructed in that its wooden wheels and carriage appeared too large, dwarfing the barrel. Appearances notwithstanding, the mountain howitzer was a useful weapon of proven capabilities. In the right hands, it could be an effective tool of destruction.

As luck would have it, Mosby's ranks contained just the man who could skillfully apply the weapon to its intended purposes. His name was William Chapman, a former officer in the Dixie Artillery Battery. When the unit was disbanded in the fall of 1862, he returned to his old stomping grounds in Page County as a recruiting officer. While in the area, he did some freelancing with Mosby's men. Chapman came to like their style of fighting and decided to cast his lot with the guerrillas. When the new gun arrived, Chapman was the natural choice to instruct a volunteer crew. Little did these novices know that their training would be tested the very next day. They would probably have been just as surprised to learn that in less than twenty-four hours their howitzer would be in enemy hands. Acquired as a mobile offensive weapon, its last deployment would ironically see it utilized in a defensive posture. While the howitzer performed its intended function well, it ultimately proved to be an albatross for Mosby's guerrillas. Regardless of its compact size, being a wheeled contrivance limited the ground it could traverse. Roads and open fields would work, while fences, forests, and gullies presented obstacles. In turn, the partisans' customary practice of scattering to the four winds following a strike would have to be significantly altered, if the weapon was to be safely borne away after an attack.

But no such negativity clouded the horizon as Mosby and his command headed toward Greenwich on a warm spring day, camping for the night a few miles beyond in a

Near Catlett's Station, this north-central Virginia depot, Mosby derailed a train and then blasted a hole in its engine with a howitzer, leading up to his defeat and the weapon's loss at Greenwich (Library of Congress).

pine woods. Even in the face of constant Union patrols along the vital railroad line, armed guards on the trains, and cavalry camps strategically placed to provide immediate support, Mosby was undeterred from his mission to interrupt the flow of military supplies along the Orange & Alexandria. The location chosen to lay a trap was near Catlett's Station, seven miles southwest of Greenwich. On Saturday, May 30, 1863, Mosby and his men arose early. Unwittingly, Yankee buglers helped their enemies get an early start on their destructive plan. As Mosby later recalled, we were "awakened in the morning by the reveille in the Union camps, which were a mile distant on either side of us."[2] Moving cautiously through the pinewoods, the band of erstwhile train-wreckers was able to stay under the forest's cover until but one hundred yards from the track. Though his ploy was risky and the odds stacked against success, Mosby truly believed that the gamble was worth taking. From his perspective, "An attack, even by my small band, at such a critical time, might create an important diversion in favor of Gen. Lee. If this could be done, then the loss of a gun, and even of my whole command, would be as dust in the balance against the advantage of it."[3]

While such boldness is difficult to curb, its benefits were equally hard to deny. Though Stuart would hardly have viewed Mosby and his command as quite so expendable, he recognized that Mosby's high rate of achievement was borne out of his willingness to take chances. Were he to approach a mission with any less daring, he would not have been so likely to achieve the same level of achievement. For another to pick an ambush site in an area swarming with enemy patrols and situated amidst cavalry camps would have seemed like madness. But for the "Gray Ghost," it was very much in keeping with the way he had conducted his war within a war.

The spot chosen to execute the plan was two miles southwest of Catlett's Station. The strategy was simple. A rail was selected, and its anchoring spikes removed. Without close inspection, it appeared to be seated properly on the ties, though no longer securely in alignment with the adjoining rails. This severance alone would probably be enough to derail the engine, though it was also possible that the lead elements could have passed over it safely. Leaving nothing to chance, the rebels interjected an extra bit of deviousness. A long wire was run from the loosened rail across the open ground to the forest's edge. Debris was used to conceal the metal filament. Standing behind a tree would be a guerrilla, waiting to yank the wire. By tugging at the proper moment, he would cause the rail to move out of line and insure the derailment of the engine.

Up to this point, the only result would be halting the train and perhaps at best a temporary interruption in service along the line. Given time, Yankee engineers and mechanics would have the equipment back on the tracks and any minor damage swiftly repaired. This is why the howitzer was so important. Not only did Mosby want to halt the train, he also desired to ruin it. Once the missing rail stopped the locomotive, the howitzer would then deliver a coup de grace. With this fate in mind, Lieutenant Chapman estimated where he thought that the derailed engine would come to rest. Next he sighted and loaded the weapon and his five-man crew stood ready. Telegraph wires were cut. All save one took cover. That lone sentinel stood by the track, waiting to signal the arrival of a supply train. The trap was set.

Patience, luck, and audacity soon paid off. The time was 9:00 A.M. The Confederates had been concealed but briefly when a sentry indicated a quarry's approach. Chapman's crew were poised for action. If a Yankee patrol didn't happen along and the engineer failed to discover the tampered rail, the trap would be sprung. The sound of the locomotive grew louder. Comprised of twelve cars, its load consisted mostly of forage. To protect its consignment, the train carried two dozen guards. From Mosby's perspective, the plan unfolded perfectly. "The engineer, not suspecting danger, was driving at full speed," he observed, "when suddenly the locomotive glided from the track. The infantry guard fired a volley.... In an instant, a shell from Chapman's gun went crashing through the cars."[4] Eventually a second shell penetrated the boiler of the engine, not only rendering the iron horse effectively hors de combat but also adding the shriek of escaping steam to the commotion. While Mosby's men destroyed the engine, the train guards escaped into the woods. As much as they might have wanted to give chase, the rebels undertook none. Being deep in enemy-held territory meant that once the first shots were fired, Mosby's men were on borrowed time. Union cavalry could be expected momentarily. Once any pretense of opposition was gone, the work of destruction began in earnest. Cotton bales found among the freight were used to ignite a raging fire.

With tell-tale smoke rising into the late-morning sky, clearly demarking the scene for any would-be rescuers, the rebel force rode away. If the day's work had concluded here, it would have been pats on the back all around. Once again the wily "Gray Ghost" had tormented his foes! He had incurred no losses, while costing the enemy valuable forage and equipment. Short-term importance was definitely derived from the break in rail service, for, as Mosby espoused, "one of the most effective ways of impeding the march of an army is by cutting off its supplies."[5] Yes, Mosby would have been content to let May 30 be remembered for the morning's work. The "Catlett's Station Raid" could easily have been a nice addition to the growing legend in which Mosby always outsmarted the Yankees. But such was not to be the case. For bearing down on the site were detachments of Union cavalry, determined to exact retribution.

Knowledge that trouble was afoot became quickly evident. Colonel Robert Mann reported that "he heard from his camp artillery firing in the direction of Warrenton Junction. The train from Bealton had just passed up, and, believing it to have been attacked, he immediately went with a detachment of the 5th New York, under command of Capt. A.H. Hasbrouck, a detachment of the 1st Vermont, under the command of Lieutenant-Colonel Preston, and a small detachment of the 7th Michigan."[6] The rescue column had 250 riders. Angry as disturbed bees, Mann's troopers rode fast and hard. The 5th New York was sent cross-country to try to intercept the raiders. The remainder of the Union force swept along the tracks to the derailment site. Thirty minutes elapsed before they arrived. Once there, they picked up the rebels' trail. Initially, the Federals advanced warily, for they knew not the composition of the enemy's force. The sound of cannon could have been Stuart's horse artillery, and by then Stuart's reputation for showing up where least expected had preceded him. Since Mosby was not known to use a heavy gun, his hand in the fracas was not everyone's first supposition.

It was at this juncture in the fast moving events that the howitzer went from asset to liability. Having to drag this cumbersome weapon along forced the retreating partisans to favor established roadways. This in turn necessitated that the party stay together and not practice the tried-and-true method of scattering in different directions when pursuit got too hot. Abandoning the howitzer was not an option either, for the South could ill afford to trade fieldpieces for locomotives. After traveling only a mile, Mosby's men found the road ahead blocked by the 5th New York. While some Union horsemen were observed on the high ground in front of them, the large volume of dust in the air served notice that "the main body was in a depression out of sight beyond those on the hill."[7] Sam Chapman was ordered to toss a shell over the prominence and see what kind of reaction was elicited. Killing the horse of the detachment's second-in-command and unceremoniously unseating him was the extent of the explosion's damage but by no means the only outcome. For, even when inaccurate, artillery fire can still have an unnerving effect. No one knows whose name might be on the next round. Sufficiently motivated, the detachment's commander made his decision to vacate the roadway.

At this stage, there quickly developed a chase that bore a striking similarity to a fox-hunt, albeit with an ironic twist. In the eyes of Captain Glazier of the 5th New York, what now transpired was "an activity so near and dear to the hearts of many Virginians though with the roles decidedly reversed from their accustomed and preferred juxtaposition."[8] Over hill and dale they flew. With the Vermont and Michigan boys joining the New Yorkers, a sizable group now nipped at Mosby's heels. Though the partisan force had gained about a mile of separation, the reinforcements imbued the Federal troopers with the courage to come on strong again. Seeing the distance between the two forces shrinking, Mosby ordered Chapman to fire off another shell. This salvo caused the pursuers to drop back out of range; but once the howitzer was limbered up and moving again, so too were the Federals. Occasionally, a few rebels were stationed along the route to ambush the onrushing pursuers. Like the artillery fire, these actions momentarily checked the enemy's advance and allowed the retreating Confederates to put a little more distance between themselves and their pursuers.

But Mosby sensed that continued flight was futile. Having covered almost seven miles at top speed, the Confederates' horses were tiring. Soon his little band would be overtaken. With the odds against him almost five to one, the outcome of any engagement was likely be in his adversary's favor. Deciding to face the inevitable on his own terms, Mosby sent most of his force ahead to find an advantageous spot for making a stand. To buy time, he and four troopers acted as a rearguard. Bold, outrageous, it was Mosby at his inspirational best. His true leadership qualities were manifested at times like these, when he placed himself in harm's way because he would not ask of his men that which he would not do himself.

It was with no little surprise that the leading elements of the 5th New York, their vision up the road temporarily blocked by some woods, rounded a bend and abruptly discovered this determined blocking force. Momentum carried Lieutenant Elmer Barker and two of his troopers unintentionally into the rebel rear guard. Hasty but accurate shots were exchanged. Barker's companions and their horses received wounds. One partisan was wounded, another killed. With the odds two to one against him, the young lieutenant gamely fought for his life. "I fired all of the shots in my revolver," Barker later recalled, "and then drew my sabre, they trying to shoot me, crying 'Surrender, Yank,' and I trying to kill them."[9]

When he finally broke off the rear guard action and rejoined the rest of his troops, Mosby could readily see that the site for the last stand was well chosen. With an artillerist's trained eye, Lieutenant Chapman had selected a location that would allow him to utilize his howitzer to maximum effect. In the words of partisan John Scott, if the enemy wanted the howitzer, then "Mosby resolved to make the Yankees pay as dearly as possible for it."[10] Situated at the crest of knoll, the weapon was aimed down the roadway. Any direct approach by enemy troops would mean charging into the cannon's mouth. Increasing the defender's odds was the roadbed's erosion into a sunken lane with high banks on both sides, topped by fencing for several hundred feet. This served to create a funneling effect, channeling an advance into the cannon's field of fire while limiting how many could charge abreast to the width of a narrow defile. For the attackers, this meant that no more than four troopers could advance side by side. While the howitzer represented an imposing obstacle, not to be overlooked was the remainder of the partisan force drawn up in a battle line across the road and to the rear of the fieldpiece. With each Ranger having two revolvers at his disposal, there was every guarantee that a hail of lead would soon be whizzing down the sunken lane to accompany the cannon's shells.

What transpired on the little rise of ground in the middle of then "Fitzhugh's Lane," so named for the owners of Grapewood Farm, was in military parlance a "skirmish." But when bullets start flying, men start getting hit, and blood starts flowing, nomenclature becomes insignificant. Death as a possible outcome, a given individual's performance under fire, and which side prevails become the only realities that matter. Thus, whether it was labeled as a battle or a skirmish, be it called "Greenwich" or "Grapewood Farm," is a less consequential detail.

The endgame began when the Federal cavalry hove into view, riding down Fitzhugh's Lane. At a range of several hundred yards, Chapman ordered the howitzer fired. The ensuing explosion sent their antagonists scurrying into nearby woods. This afforded but a brief respite. The Union troops, having doggedly chased Mosby's men for several miles, were prepared by now for whatever it would take to terminate the matter. Thus commenced what brigade commander Robert Mann called "an extremely hot affair for a small one."[11] The honor of leading the opening charge was given to the 5th New York's Lieutenant Elmer Barker. "That gun must be captured," exclaimed Lieutenant Barker, "and who will volunteer to charge it with me?"[12] Then, with a detachment of twenty-five men, the brave officer rode off to slay the now much-despised howitzer and its crew. "The Federals came on in gallant style," observed Ranger Scott, "and, in column of fours, crowded into the lane."[13] The onrushing cavalrymen were met with a shell. Rather than waver or be deterred, Barker again spoke to his boys: "I think we can get that gun before they fire again," to which their game reply was "Let's go!"[14] They got close, within twenty feet, before another blast hit them. This one, consisting of grapeshot, tore brutally and indiscriminately into the flesh of both men and horses. Three men were killed instantly and seven wounded.

Among those hit was Lieutenant Barker, who could now personally attest to the terrible destructive power of grapeshot. Scattering with a shotgun-like spread, the heavy inch to inch-and-a-half iron balls cut a bloody swath in whatever stood before them. Fired in clusters ranging from nine to twenty-one separate projectiles, they proved to be a deadly antipersonnel device. In Barker's case, being at the head of the charging troopers caused him to be hit full force. By his own account, he received two balls in his "left thigh, one carrying off my stirrup and the sole of my shoe, and four or five entered my horse."[15] Only the unpredictability of the balls' flight path prevented him from fatal wounds, saving these instead for those who rode around and behind him. However, though outnumbered on the field, at the point of attack the rebels held the upper hand because Barker's charge had been unsupported. With the advance blunted, Mosby was able to lead a countercharge, driving the Federals back a half mile in disarray.

After "three furious charges had been beaten back, sorties in which the New York boys alone suffered," it became the 1st Vermont's turn to test their mettle against the enemy.[16] Preceded by a rousing cheer, Lieutenant John Hazelton led the Vermonters up Fitzhugh Lane. Parts of Companies C, H, and I, along with several determined New Yorkers, made up the attacking force. Estimates placed the number of riders at between fifty and seventy-five men. Their charge inspired Trooper Aaron Crane to wax eloquent as he shared his impression of the moment: "And they did charge ... [these Vermonters] who swept through the pass like the wind and with as little care for the wide mouthed monster that menaced them with instant death."[17] Four times the howitzer roared, but the blue-coated cavalrymen were no longer to be denied their prize. The final discharge was delivered from twenty feet. Then the 1st Cavalry swept in among the rebels, riding past the now silent howitzer and sabering the gunners. The little bronze artillery piece became the focal point of the rebels' last stand. Around it, the conflict raged. Mosby's men blazed away with their revolvers while the Vermonters swung their swords. It was in this part of the melee that Lieutenant Chapman was cut down. Here, too, Sergeant Job Corey of Company H became the only Vermont cavalryman to lose his life.

From all accounts, the twenty-two-year-old Corey was a trooper's trooper. Brave and stalwart, this patriot served his country well. Corey's company commander, Captain

Charles Adams, credited the young soldier with leading the charge that captured the howitzer. Sergeant Carlos Barrows witnessed his comrade's last act: "Sergeant Corey was riding at the head of the company and was shot dead. I was near him and saw him fall."[18] Both Job and his brother Stephan, a corporal, had been members of Company H, participated in the dash up the knoll, and arrived at the howitzer at about the same instant. As Job received his death wound beside the gun, his sibling gained a measure of retribution by firing a shot that "struck down the gunner as he applied the match one last time."[19] Their actions inspired Captain Charles Adams to say "two better soldiers no mother sent into the field than Hannah Corey."[20] In the aftermath, Sergeant Barrows had the honor of personally escorting his comrade's body back to Fairfax. Such was the high esteem in which the men of his company held Corey that they paid to have the hero's body embalmed and sent home to his grieving mother. Like the Vermont Cavalry's Loring Chase, who had lost his brother John earlier in the war, Stephen Corey remained in the army to serve out his three-year commitment. It took time for his arm, shattered by grapeshot, to heal, but he was back in the saddle by fall. After being wounded again and captured at Brandy Station on October 11, 1863, he was paroled in November. Having tempted fate enough for one lifetime, Corporal Corey decided not to reenlist, returning home in the spring of 1864.

The death of Job Corey occurred just after the Vermont Cavalry had gained the crest of the hill. Standing next to the prized artillery piece, Lieutenant Chapman swung its rammer as a weapon, until he was put out of action by a wound in his thigh. Two members of his crew, Privates Fount Beattie and Richard Montjoy, stood by him in a hopeless but gallant effort to save the cannon. At about this same juncture in the skirmish, Lieutenant-Colonel Addison Preston approached the flank with additional troops. Using the popular vernacular of the times to describe the enemy's hasty departure, Private Henry Smith wrote home how "our own regiment charged and sent them skedaddling."[21] Outnumbered and outgunned, Mosby's men reluctantly left not only the field of combat but also, most regrettably, their prized howitzer in enemy hands. Proud of his men, Addison Preston savored their spontaneous reaction to victory as "cheer upon cheer went up when the field was cleared."[22]

Absolved of the need to travel only on byways that could accommodate the cannon, the partisans were now free to scatter. With the woods and thickets their allies once again, they disappeared quickly. The Federal cavalry tried to offer pursuit. But as Colonel Mann reported the next day, "Our horses were completely blown when we had overtaken the enemy, so rapid had been our pursuit, and after thoroughly scattering them to all points, in that thick country I found it impossible to follow up with the hope of catching them."[23] Though no more prisoners were taken, some satisfaction was gleaned from retrieving many of the items stolen from the train, which, in their haste to lighten their loads, the harried rebels had discarded.

It was now early in the afternoon. The Union force had been on the go for some five hours. That men and animals were spent came as no surprise. Regardless of the engagement's size, there was the inevitable after-action tidying up for the troops to do. First, there were fifteen wounded men who required attention. The bodies of four deceased Union cavalry had to be prepared for transport. The fact that the enemy captured no one was good news. The destruction of eleven horses was an unfortunate outcome of such a brisk encounter. As for the Confederates' losses, it was known that they amounted to six killed and twenty wounded.

In the afterglow of a successful mission, well-deserved accolades were forthcoming. General Stahel duly rewarded their efforts when "he ordered double rations of whiskey to be issued to the company for their gallantry in taking Mosby's cannon."[24] In one newspaper account, the correspondent owed that he could not "close without expressing the idea that the Vermont Cavalry have wiped away a few bygone stains, and that Jeff Davis will be somewhat dissatisfied with Mosby's ordnance returns for this quarter."[25] But it was left to the regiment's own Lieutenant-Colonel Addison Preston to put the day's events in proper perspective. In simple but sincere language, the much-respected officer conveyed to Peter Washburn, adjutant and inspector general for the State of Vermont, his personal assessment of what his troops had accomplished: "Men could do no more. As a feat of daring it has not been exceeded during the war."[26]

Be it a skirmish or a battle, the affair that began in mid-morning near Catlett's Station and ended in the early afternoon on Grapewood Farm brought new laurels to both sides. Mosby won plaudits for his derring-do and an offer from General Stuart of another piece of ordnance. The often-beleaguered Northerners, run ragged by Mosby for almost six months, finally were rewarded with victory. The competing units that day would go on to other fields of glory in the war, but they would never be called upon again to test each other's mettle. In one sense, it was perhaps best that they parted ways at this point in time. Their jousts, while contested in deadly earnest, still for the most part were cloaked in an aura of civility. Most assuredly men had died, and that was sometimes unavoidable, particularly when they charged up a narrow road into the mouth of a cannon. But much of the contact between Mosby and the 1st Vermont had been quick, fleeting small-unit actions. More men wound up captured than killed. Prisoners were generally exchanged in a short span of time. But as of June 1863, the war would begin to take on a far more ominous countenance for mounted forces. The Union cavalry began to operate in much larger aggregations. Battle deaths rose. POWs would longer be so readily swapped, finding themselves instead sent respectively to Andersonville or Elmira for much longer durations, and, in far too many instances, for eternity. As frustrating as they had been, the days of playing cat-and-mouse with Turner Ashby and John Mosby were over for the 1st Vermont. The old infantryman's jab of "whoever saw a dead cavalryman" was soon to become as hollow as it was unwarranted.

20

Marching North
A Rendezvous with Destiny Awaits

For the Vermont Cavalry, the prelude to Gettysburg consisted of riding, much of it under oppressive conditions. Even the uncertainty of battle took second place in some minds to the weather. "I am hoping the fighting will soon be done," was the expressed desire of Trooper George Caulkins, "for we have to undergo so much in the dust and hot weather."[1] Scratchy wool uniforms, repetitive food, and inadequate sleep made the last week of June and the first two weeks of July a brutal experience. By William Wells' account, Vermont troops were "in the saddle night and day," called upon to fight "15 battles in 16 days" and engage both "infantry and cavalry."[2]

The pace of the campaign started out gradually. For the Vermonters, the last week of June amounted to a hopscotching ride from Northern Virginia through Maryland to Pennsylvania. Though directly about 85 miles, the regiment's zigzag route added extra distance to their overall trek. Over the course of the march, the 3rd Division started out behind the northbound infantry until orders leapfrogged it into the van. Fanning out in front of the army, the cavalry's mission was to serve as its antenna.

With Federal cavalry heading north, Stuart's troopers were also on the move. One portion remained attached to Lee's main body. Led by John Imboden, their assignment was to travel to the east of the northward-moving Army of Northern Virginia and seal off the mountain gaps from Yankee eyes. The remaining cavalry, 6000 strong under Jeb Stuart, swung in a wide arc up to the northeast. The 26th of June found them in Rockville, Maryland, working their way to the east of the Army of the Potomac. Here, Stuart crossed his Rubicon. As later written by Colonel Alexander Long, Lee's military secretary, "Either from a misapprehension of instruction or the love of the éclat of a bold raid, Stuart, instead of maintaining his position placed himself on the right flank of the enemy, where his communication with Lee was effectively severed."[3] The rebels' situation was further complicated by the celebrated capture of a 125-wagon supply train. What seemed like a lucky break would become an impediment of unforeseen magnitude. Slowed to the ponderous pace of their prizes, Stuart's troopers would not arrive at Gettysburg in timely fashion. The idea had been for the bold cavalier to ride halfway around the Union Army from the right, while Lee was to skirt past it on the left. While the prospects of the Confederate Army in all of its might and glory coming together in south-central Pennsylvania was disturbing, of more immediate importance to the Federal cavalry was that Stuart's position had his columns riding up from the left and behind the Federal cavalry. Facing to the north, Pleasonton's Corps were not expecting gray-clad troopers to materialize from the southeast.

155

Initially, Federal troopers were oblivious as to the whereabouts of their adversaries. Plodding along muddy roads, the 26th of June saw the 1st Vermont pass through several little villages. Typical of these enclaves, Adamstown rolled out the welcome mat for the passing troopers as waving citizens greeted their arrival. Such a warm reception had not been tendered to these cavalrymen in quite some time. For the past year, they had grown accustomed to scornful looks as they passed through the Old Dominion. Confirmation that the men appreciated such encouragement was shared by Albert Greene, commenting how "it seems like home to go through such places where they wave the stars and stripes as we pass and give cheers to us."[4] As exuberant as these lads may have been, a much-needed rest was in order. Camp was established three miles out of town on what Captain Glazier referenced as "a day of much interest among us, and of no little excitement — a day of changes and reorganization."[5] In rapid succession, a series of orders altered the command structure. Joe Hooker was out and George Meade in as the leader of the Army of the Potomac. Julius Stahel was relieved of his cavalry, and Judson Kilpatrick gained its use. Elon Farnsworth and George Custer were promoted to generalships in command of the 1st and 2nd brigades of the 3rd Cavalry Division. Such a sweeping reorganization on the eve of battle was as unprecedented as it was risky.

Still buzzing from the momentous events of Sunday, June 28, 1863, the reorganized cavalry set out early the next morning. The sun shone brightly on another humid day, making dehydration a serious concern. Sadly, the route of march became easy to follow by the trail of expired horses along the roadsides. When the long column crossed into

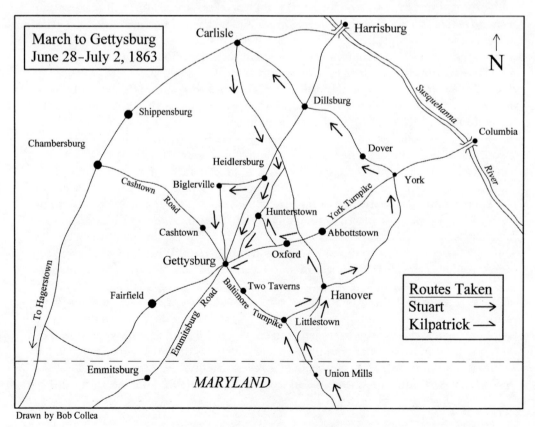

Drawn by Bob Collea

the Keystone State, a loud cheer rose up from the ranks of the 18th Pennsylvania, who were happy to be on home ground once again. Sergeant Ide remembered how "just at dusk we entered the little village of Littlestown and we began to see the differences between campaigning in an enemy's country or amongst friends."[6]

Renditions of the "Star Spangled Banner" and "The Red, White, and Blue," among other selections, filled the summer night and were met with cheers from the parched throats.[7] Tired as the men were, having come thirty miles, their spirits soared when they saw and heard a choir of young women assembled on the balcony of the Union Hotel to greet them. Caught up in the spirit of the patriotic sentiments expressed, the troops began to enthusiastically join in with the ladies. Quickly, the spontaneity of the moment rolled down the line as more and more men were impulsively moved to lift their voices in song. Eloquent in its simplicity, the impromptu hootenanny spoke volumes about how people in less-sophisticated times unabashedly revealed their innermost feelings.

The gratitude of the local populace at their salvation knew no limits.

While lacking the visual appeal of other generals and not universally beloved for aggressive tactics that cost lives, "Old Kil" was so respected by the 1st Vermont that the men rode en masse to his headquarters to bid him adieu upon General Judson Kilpatrick's transfer to another front (Francis C. Guber Collection).

Their thanks were extended to include forage and foodstuffs. Not the least bit dissuaded by the midnight hour, the townsfolk came with their bountiful gifts to the cavalry's camp. With the men having to be on the road at six, this much appreciated buffet created a very short night. Many were the troopers who had barely cared for their horses before falling asleep. Lost in a sound slumber, Kilpatrick's men had no inkling that Stuart's troopers were bedded down only a scant seven miles to the southeast.

One trooper especially thankful for the halt was Azro Hackett. A bugler in Company M, he arrived in an ambulance. His once-cherished instrument lay flat as a pancake, discarded back along the road. The accident that caused both the bugle's destruction and its owner's incapacitation appeared unavoidable. It seems that the regiment was nearing Littleton when it had to cross a small span over a creek. "As ... Hackett was riding in his proper place with the company, his horse stepped through a bridge made of small poles," related Lieutenant George Servais, "and in struggling to regain his feet threw off ... Hackett and fell on him, injuring his shoulder and side."[8] With the narrow bridge blocked, the column halted. The resulting commotion saw several concerned officers converge on the scene. Then Addison Preston arrived, assessed the situation, and said, "Captain, leave some men to get that man up and move on. You must not stop one minute!"[9] While this may have appeared callous, Preston's decision was grounded in the realities of the moment. The hour was late, and the enemy lurked out there somewhere. Military expediency dictated that the column remain moving and alert rather than at a standstill and distracted by the plight of a single horse and rider.

With the column proceeding forward, five men stayed behind to help the pinned trooper. First they worked Arzo free and laid him by the side of the road. Then they extracted Hackett's horse. However, it was not until the mount was brought over to Hackett that the full extent of his injuries was realized. "We helped Hackett up," Lieutenant Sevais later wrote, "but he was so badly hurt as to be unable to ride."[10] Not that anyone should have been surprised. A thousand-pound horse toppling unto a one hundred-and-fifty pound man was not ever going to produce an outcome favorable to the human. Fortuitously, the ambulance train happened by at this precise moment. The darkness and the need to get going precluded a thorough examination that night, but the next morning the extent of the trooper's injuries was in evidence. The incapacitated soldier "was very badly hurt all over.... [H]is right side and back was hurt very bad and he thought his right shoulder was broken and his right knee was badly swollen."[11] Arriving when it did, the ambulance was a godsend for Hackett. The next day, however, Arzo Hackett probably viewed the slow-moving conveyance differently, as it led to his capture during the engagement at Hanover. In keeping with his run of bad luck followed by good luck, Trooper Hackett was spared any time in a rebel prison by being given his parole virtually on the spot. Though he would remain enlisted for the duration, the innocent mishap on the way to Littlestown would effectively remove Arzo Hackett from active duty, causing him to spend the next eighteen months convalescing in eight different hospitals.

A body wracked with pain caused Trooper Hackett to awaken early the next morning. He was not alone in his wakefulness, for the troops were moving at daybreak on June 30. Few, if any, were fully rested. Most were riding on empty stomachs, as time for preparing breakfast was not allotted. But the impending ride to Hanover was expected to be an easy jaunt, only nine miles to the northeast over damp, but at least not dusty, roads. The terrain was gently rolling hills covered with ripening fields. The foremost elements of the Federal column reached Hanover at about 8:00 A.M. The Vermont Cavalry arrived at 9:00 A.M. Simultaneously, the rear guard was just leaving Littlestown. Meanwhile, Stuart's troops, in motion at first light also, were progressing along the Baltimore Pike. Their respective routes placed them on a collision course. However, until the Confederate cavalry arrived as spoilers, the Union horsemen experienced a most pleasant day.

Initially, the citizenry withheld their exuberance, unsure of who these approaching riders were. The Hanoverians' uneasiness was understandable, as rebel forces had passed through on the 27th. One large body of cavalry off in the distance appeared the same as the next. Anxious minutes passed. Then, once the dusty horde made its entrance into the town, its true identity was apparent. Pastor William Zieber of Hanover's First Emmanuel Church was in the crowd of onlookers and witnessed the crowd's collective reaction firsthand. "When the advance guard of these troops entered Frederick Street from the southwest," he recalled, "loud cheers of welcome were heard both from the men and women because we saw they wore uniforms of blue and carried an American flag."[12]

From the perspective of the marching troops, Albert Greene was duly impressed by the crowd's reaction: "We came here yesterday in the forenoon, such cheering as I never heard before as the people gave us as we arrived in the village.... I tell you it seemed like home the folks were so glad to see us come to keep the rebs away."[13]

Much to the delight of the famished soldiers, the citizens of Hanover did not come empty-handed. The middle of town became the focal point of an impromptu feast as "the ladies ... assembled at a market square in the center of the village and were distributing to the hungry soldiers edibles of every description."[14] Henry Ide remembered "how the good people brought out food of all kinds, such as pie, cake, coffee and so forth, and we were enjoying ourselves immensely."[15] Helping create a festive mood, "Flags waved everywhere. Bells were ringing. Hundreds of schoolchildren stood in the market square singing songs of welcome."[16] According to Private George Lewis of Company K, the Vermonters had "stopped, perhaps half an hour. Some dismounted and some did not."[17] For the tired, dusty troopers far from home, this brief interlude represented "a scene perhaps unsurpassed in all of the marches of the war."[18] Hard on the heels of the Vermonters, succeeding units in the 1st Brigade cycled triumphantly through Hanover. The troops rode in on Frederick Street, went through the main square, and then departed via Abbottstown Street. Each regiment got its chance to enjoy a short halt and avail themselves of the food and attention showered upon them.

The 5th New York had just concluded its respite, and the 18th Pennsylvania was slowly entering Hanover when the scene changed dramatically. While all knew that the pleasantries were only of limited duration, no one anticipated the abruptness with which they would be curtailed. At approximately 10:00 A.M., the placid morning was interrupted by a deep booming sound. Understandably, "The frightened young ladies inquired and were assured by the soldiers that undoubtedly the citizens were firing a salute in honor of our arrival."[19] "Just then a Shell burst," recalled Sergeant Ide, "and we came to the conclusion that people didn't generally fire Shells for a salute."[20] In an instant, confusion reigned supreme. Captain John Hammond of the 5th New York deserved credit for his concern about the plight of the cavalry's unselfish hosts. Picking his way through the frightened crowd, Hammond got to the central square where he loudly announced: "Citizens will please go to their homes and into their cellars. In a few moments there will be fighting in your streets."[21] What was happening? Other than the realization that an unknown number of enemy troops must be in the vicinity and firing on the village, uncertainty abounded. The simple truth, soon to become painfully obvious, was that Confederate cavalry forces had rolled up the rear guard and were descending upon Hanover.

The first to know of the enemy's presence had been the 18th Pennsylvania. A forty-man detachment anchored the extreme end of the marching column, which stretched for several miles ahead of the Pennsylvanians. In a bold charge, this detachment successfully fought its way past a slightly larger Confederate force that had accidentally gotten between it and the rest of the regiment. In a fluke occurrence, a scouting party of the 13th Virginia had come up obliquely from the southeast. Intersecting the Littlestown Road via the Westminster Road, the Southerners had in effect cut Henry Potter's band off from the main body. Sizing up the situation, Potter told his men to remain calm and ride slowly, acting as if nothing was amiss. Upon his command, the Pennsylvanians opened fire on the rebels and then charged through them. Once past the surprised Confederates, Captain Potter's men rode pell-mell for their comrades located at the edge of town. As the pursuers closed on the fleeing Yankees, they came under a withering crossfire from dismounted carbineers and the detachment that they had been chasing. This stopped the charge in its tracks and turned the enemy back on its heels. The inexperienced Pennsylvanians had acquitted themselves admirably in this their first taste of combat.

But before the Union troops could appraise the situation, the rebels were charging back at them. Only this time, they came from both the front and the flank, and they appeared in far greater numbers. The little scouting party had turned into regimental-sized forces. The thunder of approaching horses, whizzing of pistol balls, and yelling of determined foes all alarmed the Pennsylvanians. The situation was chaotic, with careening ambulances, frightened citizens, and surprised soldiers all clogging the streets. As the rebels bore down, organized resistance melted away. Lieutenant-Colonel John Phillips of the 18th Pennsylvania recalled how "for a moment all was confusion. The impetuous charge of the enemy brought some of their troops into the mist of our men, and hand-to-hand contests were had with the same."[22] The concurrent Confederate assaults had the disastrous effect of cutting the hapless 18th Pennsylvania in two. The contingent of troopers caught between the two enemy forces was able to extricate itself from the predicament by heading west out of town on side streets, the Confederates choosing not to pursue. The second segment of the severed Pennsylvania column headed out of the village by way of the Abbottstown road. Vermont troopers observed these results, Company M's Sergeant George Lewis recalling how "as we marched along we met the 18th Pennsylvania Cavalry, retreating on the run. We got out of their way onto a side street."[23]

In their enemy's wake, rebel horsemen swarmed all over Hanover. Organized resistance dissipated rapidly. Isolated pockets of men fought on as best they could. Side streets, alleys, and back lots became the scenes of small, hotly contested actions. Fighting was reduced to close-in combat with swords and pistols. Further adding to the confusion caused by enemy troops popping in and out of view was the unexpected presence of well-meaning civilians assisting the wounded.

In the decisive rout of the Pennsylvanians, Stuart's legions enjoyed their singular success in an otherwise forgettable day. Once the rebels' attack began to lose steam, momentum swung to the Union side. Unfortunately for the Confederate fortunes that day, their vanguard advanced unsupported. Immediately behind them was the infamous supply train, effectively blocking additional troopers from the fighting front. But the primary reason that Confederate designs were thwarted was the immediate reaction by the remainder of Kilpatrick's brigade. As the retreating Pennsylvanians ran into the rear of the 5th New York, the New Yorkers grudgingly gave ground, buying time until they could re-form. While these events were unfolding, the sound of gunfire alerted the foremost regiments in the column that the situation was amiss behind them. General Kilpatrick reacted immediately, turning back from the head of the column and racing to Hanover. Tossing abandon to the wind, he covered the mile with such speed that he rode his horse to death. Elon Farnsworth, about to see his first action as a brigade commander, also headed at breakneck speed to the sound of the guns. Before departing, he had the presence of mind to order the 1st West Virginia and the 1st Vermont to countermarch toward town as well.

Meanwhile, the New Yorkers, joined by remnants of the 18th Pennsylvania, successfully halted the rebel surge. Swords swinging, the Yankees waded into the enemy's ranks. Confederate resistance was heroic but brief. The determined 5th New York drove them until halted by fire from an enemy reserve force, advancing eagerly into the fray. A charge by these Virginians provided sufficient impetus to turn the attacking Federals around and harry them back into Hanover. At this tenuous moment for the beleaguered New Yorkers, the dynamic presence of General Farnsworth exploded upon the scene. So newly minted was their brigade commander that he wore a blue shirt borrowed from General Pleasonton, adorned with a single star on its collar. For those still harboring doubts about his rapid promotion, Farnsworth's quick thinking and personal bravery showed him ready for the challenge of the hour. Again the rebel cavalry was driven off and forced to seek shelter behind its artillery.

At this juncture in the rapidly escalating events, the West Virginia and Vermont troops arrived on the scene. The West Virginians were immediately dispatched through town and out in a southeasterly direction on Baltimore Street. The regiment eventually became embroiled in a vicious tussle with South Carolina troops. The Southerners had been advancing toward the left flank of the already engaged 5th New York and 18th Pennsylvania that were positioned to face the Confederate artillery and cavalry southwest of Hanover. As the sole uncommitted regiment in the brigade, the time now came for the 1st Vermont to contribute. The Vermonters were assigned two disparate duties. The less exposed assignment, protecting Samuel Elder's battery, was given to the 1st and 2nd battalions. They were also positioned as the reserve in the event of an enemy breakthrough. Nevertheless there were those who thought that this static role was not the best deployment of a comparatively fresh regiment. Only a portion of Major John Bennett's 3rd Battalion was sent forward. Company D, led by Captain William Cummings, and Company M, under Captain John Woodward, moved out on the Littlestown Road to shore up the Federal line. From this position on the Union left, Companies D and M eventually "assisted in repelling the enemy by a vigorous charge, capturing about 20 men."[24] The other half of the battalion, Companies A and H, were held in reserve on the public common.

In his after-action report, Lieutenant-Colonel Preston lauded Bennett's men for their steadfast conduct, commenting on how "this battalion, during the day, was warmly engaged, and succeeded in repelling several enemy attacks."[25] The 1st Vermont's losses were extremely light, with but a single man wounded and sixteen captured. This, of course, was nothing more than a reflection of the luck of the draw that placed the Vermont Cavalry at the head of the marching column. By the time Preston got them back to the scene of the action, the fighting in and around Hanover had peaked. Thomas McGuire and Allen Wright received the only two injuries of any significance suffered by Vermont troops. McGuire went down with a gunshot wound, while Wright suffered a fractured sternum when he hit the ground hard after his horse was shot. Since Private Wright's recovery was projected to be long-term and problematical with regard to its completeness, army doctors felt compelled to give him his medical discharge little more than a month later.

With respect to Private McGuire, he eventually rejoined his company, though neither the convalescent nor the cavalry profited from his return. For the twenty-two-year-old Irish immigrant, the transition from laborer to soldier had never gone smoothly. Possessing a truculent attitude, McGuire's demeanor did not easily mesh with military authority. Not surprisingly, McGuire found himself in an Alexandria jail for the first two months of 1863, followed by another arrest in April. This second detainment led to detached duty at the Second Brigade's headquarters until the end of June. His reinstatement to the ranks came just in time for him to participate in the Gettysburg Campaign.

After recuperating from the wound received at Hanover, he rejoined the regiment, where his attitude again got the best of him. McGuire was subsequently arrested for the third time on August 7, 1863, and scheduled for a court-martial. Two charges were levied against him: (1) Using contemptuous and disrespectful language to his commanding officer; and (2) Conduct to the prejudice of good order and military discipline. Being judged "guilty" on both charges called for McGuire "to be confined at hard labor on Government work for one year, to lose ten dollars of his monthly pay, each month during the same period, and to wear a 32 pound ball attached to his left ankle by a chain six feet in length."[26] As if these punishments were not stiff enough, the place designated for his incarceration was the dreaded Fort Jefferson in the Dry Tortugas. The fair-haired, fair-skinned Private McGuire was eventually spared what would have most likely been an agonizing experience in the Caribbean when Fort Delaware, on Pea Patch Island, Delaware, was redesignated as the place of his confinement. But this turmoil all lay in the future, for today McGuire was one of the wounded heroes of Hanover.

Around noon, the action waned. Only sporadic firing on the outskirts of town could be heard. Though its streets were now quiet, evidence of desperate fighting was everywhere. Dead and dying men lay in the dust along with scores of horses. The smell of black powder hung low over the village. During this interlude, there was still much activity in Hanover. Kilpatrick arrived and set up his headquarters in the Central Hotel. Companies D and M of the 1st Vermont were pulled back and rejoined the rest of the 3rd Battalion in reserve. Citizens and soldiers worked feverishly to barricade the streets with wheeled equipment, boxes, barrels, fence rails, and iron bars, their goal being to create obstacles that would impede enemy troopers. Perhaps the most important benefit from the sixty-minute respite was the opportunity to tend the wounded. Army doctors worked in impromptu concert with civilian physicians to bring relief to suffering men. The good citizens of Hanover again displayed their generous nature by willingly taking the wounded into their homes.

In addition to the humanitarian value of the temporary ceasefire, militarily it permitted time for more troops to be brought up. This proved to be no boon for Stuart, as his resources were limited. But for Kilpatrick, the window of opportunity not only allowed him to dress his lines but also gave fresh units time to converge on Hanover. The first of these was the intrepid Custer, bursting upon the scene with the 1st and 7th Michigan in tow. Like Farnsworth earlier in the day, this was the general's first chance to lead his new command in battle. Sporting a gold star on his shirt, a flamboyant velvet jacket, and a sombrero-styled hat, George Armstrong Custer was anxious to make the most of the opportunity before him. Sent by Judson Kilpatrick to protect the right of the New York–Pennsylvania line, Custer would not be content to mark time. That afternoon, Custer's dismounted troopers fought Fitz Lee's cavaliers to a standstill. The ensuing action took on a seesaw, back-and-forth nature. At dusk, firing gradually diminished. Exhausted soldiers were content to let themselves be enveloped by the security that darkness brought.

Although troopers on opposite sides of the line were equally thirsty, hungry, and weary, nightfall would not bring the same degree of succor to the Confederates as it did to their adversaries. Stuart had a decision to make: what to do next? Compounding the matter was the fact that time was a luxury he did not have. Every hour in delaying their departure put Stuart's men in greater jeopardy of being caught between the infantry behind him and the cavalry in his front. Reluctantly bowing to the constraints of the moment, the Confederate cavalry was ordered to commence what would become a gru-

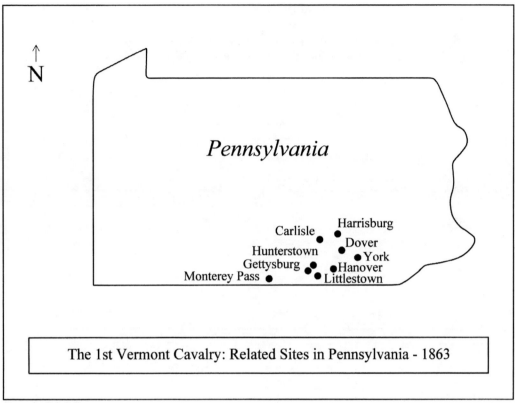

N

Pennsylvania

Carlisle •   Harrisburg •

Dover •

Hunterstown •   • York

Gettysburg • •   • Hanover

Monterey Pass •   • Littlestown

The 1st Vermont Cavalry: Related Sites in Pennsylvania - 1863

Drawn by Bob Collea

eling all-night march. Swinging wide to the right to avoid Hanover, the retreating Southerners headed for York.

While Stuart and his troops plodded wearily through the night, Kilpatrick's division was afforded several hours of well-earned rest. Roll calls would determine the absence of many Union troopers, somewhere in the vicinity of 150 all told. The approximate breakdown was 11 killed, 88 wounded, and 50 missing. For those taken prisoner, their presence was just one more burden that the Confederates did not need; therefore, when the opportunity presented itself, the retreating column was shortened by divesting itself of its POWs. While their comrades were being released twenty miles away, the remainder of the 1st Vermont was for the most part deep in slumber. Since no one knew what the next hour, let alone the following day, would bring, the soldiers slept on their arms. Unfortunately, the division's troopers had to catch whatever sleep they could on empty stomachs, for the supply wagons had not arrived with their loads of much-needed rations. However, a night of discomfort was more than rectified the next morning, as "the kind and ever-to-be-remembered ladies of Hanover cooked all night, and at day-break all men fed."[27]

As demoralizing as the occasion had been for the Southerners, the engagement at Hanover had been a banner day for the Northern troops. Farnsworth and Custer, the much scoffed-at boy generals promoted only days ago, had acquitted themselves superbly. Displaying the leadership and dash that Pleasonton had anticipated, they rewarded his faith in them many-fold. In the same fashion as their dynamic new commanders, the Union cavalry held its own against its vaunted adversaries, fighting Stuart and his all-star cast to a standstill, if not a strategic victory, as well. Once again, evidence was provided that parity between the two mounted arms may have finally been achieved.

For the 1st Vermont, the level of engagement at Hanover paled when compared with their involvement at Gettysburg, but conversely the regiment's degree of measurable success proved greater in the smaller of the two events. In the grand design of the war, the Battle of Hanover is due recognition for its indirect though important effect on the larger engagement's outcome. But it is in the story of the development of the Union Cavalry where Hanover's place is firm and undeniable, serving as one more confidence-builder in the two-year quest by Lincoln's horsemen to become the equal of their adversaries.

21

Gettysburg
The Ride to Glory

For Stuart's weary men, forced to travel through the night of July 1, their odyssey was about to end. The afternoon of July 2 would see them finally reunited with Lee's main body. Before settling in, there was a skirmish at Hunterstown, where Custer's aggressive push had to be checked. The 1st Vermont, not deployed until early evening, played only a support role. Disengaging after dark, the Vermonters made their way to the Gettysburg battlefield.

Arriving quietly and unobtrusively, their approach brought them in near Culp's Hill and the Confederate left. Though the distance between Hunterstown and Two Taverns was only six miles, traveling at night with enemy forces operating in the vicinity dictated a cautious advance. Furthermore, Kilpatrick's men were forced to move along narrow secondary routes and across fields rather than the main thoroughfares. Morning saw them on the Baltimore Turnpike, where they finally got to rest for several hours at Two Taverns. Here they were but five miles from Littlestown, the site of their first night's encampment in Pennsylvania on the 29th of June. Their roundabout trek had taken five days, four nights, two engagements, and covered about fifty miles.

While his men rested, General Kilpatrick reported to Pleasonton, from whom he obtained new orders. The appearance of additional cavalry units allowed General Meade to now protect both flanks. In the context of the famous fishhook alignment defended by Union forces around Gettysburg, one body of cavalry, Gregg's, was posted near the point of the hook in the vicinity of Culp's Hill, while the second contingent, Kilpatrick's, was deployed at the extreme head of the shank near the Round Tops. The downtime Kilpatrick's troopers spent awaiting his return was employed productively, attending to matters such as feeding the horses and brewing coffee.

Altogether too soon, the respite ended. Kilpatrick had orders to "attack the enemy in flank and rear, as well as prevent the flank from being turned."[1] Mounting up at 9:00 A.M., Farnsworth's Brigade was dispatched to the extreme left of the Union line. As described by Horace Ide, the column proceeded "up the turnpike across Rock Creek ... passed the 2nd Division Sixth Corps headquarters wagons and turning to the left soon struck the Taneytown Road, which we followed two or three miles till we reached Rock Creek again, where we watered our horses and turned back. After marching in this direction for some distance we turned towards the west."[2] At about 11:00 A.M., the brigade closed with the enemy for the first time on Gettysburg's fields. In the words of Confederate General Evander Law, "a new danger threatened us on the right. This was the appear-

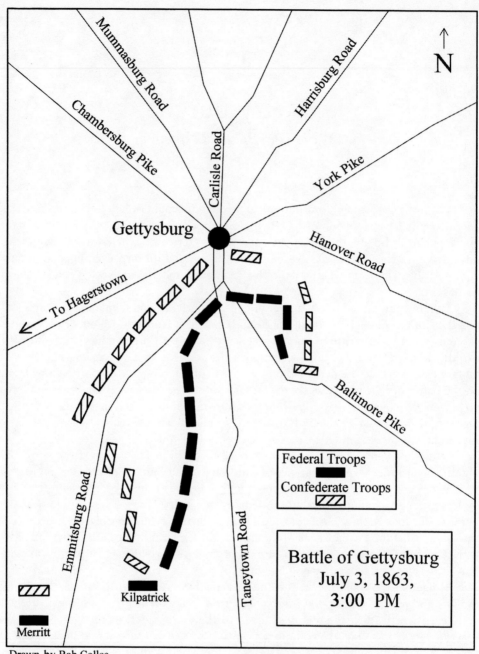

Drawn by Bob Collea

ance of Kilpatrick's division of cavalry, which moved up on that flank and commenced massing in the body of timbers which extended from the base of Round Top westward toward Kern's [Curran's] house, on the Emmittsburg Road."[3] The Confederates were deployed in a line "stretching from the southwestern base of Big Round Top west across the Emmittsburg Road."[4] In opposition, Addison Preston, still commanding in Sawyer's absence, dismounted Companies A, D, E, and I and sent them forward as skirmishers.

Pushing aggressively, the Vermonters drove the enemy's skirmishers back to their main line. This unwanted aggression evoked a sharp response from rebel artillery. Canister whizzed through the air and drove the exposed Yankees to cover. Though unknown to them as they came onto the field near the Round Tops, the Vermonters would face no enemy cavalry that day. In spite of over 7,000 Confederate riders at Gettysburg, a localized scarcity existed because Stuart's force had been marshaled on the left of the Army of Northern Virginia's position, intended for a sweep behind Union lines coinciding with Pickett's frontal assault. In addition, the Confederate right flank had also been thinned of artillery as batteries were relocated farther to the north, the better to support a grand cannonade commencing at one o'clock. Those few pieces of field artillery that remained, however, kept up a hot fire, to which the 1st Vermont could attest.

However, the worst was yet to come. In the midst of this firefight, the first Vermont trooper met his death at Gettysburg. Private George Brownell went down when Lieutenant Alexander G. Watson, leading a detachment of twelve men, charged a rebel party situated on a knoll on the Bushman property. After tearing down a fence impeding their progress, the Vermonters "rode square upon them, through a volley of musketry, and drove them off, though they staid until revolvers flashed in their very faces."[5] After holding the advanced position for some time, Watson's band was recalled. Lieutenant Watson reported immediately to Captain Parsons: "Your order is executed; Brownell is dead."[6]

At the front barely six months, Private Brownell had left his family's rural 180 acre Colchester homestead and traveled 600 miles, only to die in the fields of another farm. According to Sergeant William Greenleaf, "Brownell was present when a portion of ... [his] company made a charge ... [and] Brownell was shot and died on the field at a barn, but a short distance in the rear very soon after he was hit."[7] Trooper George McBride tenderly helped to move his lifelong friend to shelter, but upon his return a few minutes later sadly found that his dear comrade had expired. While McBride was understandably shaken, his grief paled when compared to that of a sixty-three-year-old lady back in Vermont. For Mary Brownell, George's mother, the war years proved to be exceptionally cruel. Her husband, Thomas, died in December of 1862, then the conflict took both of her sons, George first and then Julian.

While Watson probed the regiment's left flank, Captain John Woodward reconnoitered its right with Company M, eventually establishing contact with the Federal infantry anchoring the Union left on Little Round Top and in the process discovering the enemy positioned in that area. The early afternoon hours witnessed continuous skirmishing. Occasionally the artillery added its boom to the crack of carbines and rifles. One Vermont sergeant wrote home of the afternoon's action thus far, sharing how "we arrived at Gettysburg, and immediately left for the enemy's right wing which we attacked and fought through the day. Our regiment charged them often and compelled them to retire every time."[8] Addison Preston also made reference to this phase of the day's fighting as being "continued by the opposing batteries and dismounted carbineers until 5 o'clock."[9]

General Evander Law recognized the threat that these new arrivals posed, later commenting how "the appearance of General Kilpatrick's division of two brigades of Federal cavalry, Merritt's and Farnsworth's, on the left flank during the forenoon of the third day of the battle, caused me great uneasiness."[10] Mirroring their leader's concern, all of this sudden activity funneled their way made General John Hood's infantrymen equally nervous. Ordinarily, they could expect to have a cavalry screen of their own to ward off any mounted intruders, but today this was not the case. Usually cavalry would not be foolhardy enough to attack a body of infantry situated behind breastworks and supported by artillery; however, the ranks of Confederate foot soldiers in this part of the line were severely depleted, after their futile attacks against Little Round Top the previous day.

One additional element that would have made the rebels even edgier had they known was the presence of Judson Kilpatrick. Unhappily cast in a secondary role, the ambitious general dearly wished to strike a telling blow at what he believed was his enemy's Achilles' heel. Somewhere behind the thin lines of infantry facing him was Lee's unprotected rear. Visions of vulnerable supply trains tempted him just as Stuart had once succumbed to the same enticement. On an even more grandiose scale, the possibility of rolling up the Confederate line beckoned as a wild yet plausible outcome of a flank attack. Supporting his scheming mind, Kilpatrick's orders gave him the discretion to attack the enemy as the opportunity presented itself. For a man with Kilpatrick's daring and drive, instructions that offered such latitude were in effect a blank check.

At the same time the Vermonters began working against the center and right of the 1st Texas' skirmish line, pressure was brought to bear on the far left of the Confederates' southern defenses. Regrettably, these separate actions were never effectively coordinated. The force coming up west of Kilpatrick's line consisted of Merritt's reliable 3rd Brigade. The first enemy resistance encountered was a hodgepodge cavalry force of a few hundred men. Merritt's seasoned regiments quickly brushed aside this token resistance. With access to the rear echelon of Lee's right flank open to Merritt's command, General Law was forced to take immediate counter actions. His solution was to pull the 7th and 8th

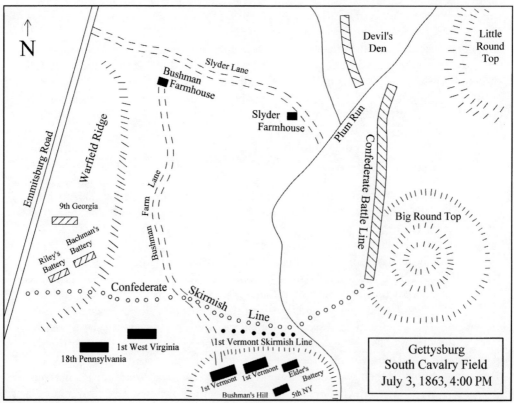

Drawn by Bob Collea

Georgia from the lower Little Round Top line, run them west at the double-quick cross lots over the Slyder and Bushman farms, upslope to the Emmittsburg Road, over the road, and then form them into a line alongside the 9th Georgia. This redeployment extended and strengthened the Confederate right flank and provided opposition to Merritt's brigade. On the Union side, this adjustment did not go unnoticed. In the assessment of Major John Phillips of the 18th Pennsylvania, "the enemy in our front seemed stirred up with an unusual activity, the cause of which was Merritt's approach on the Emmittsburg Road. This new and unknown force seriously menaced the Confederate position, and this, combined with the proximity of Farnsworth's Brigade, caused the enemy's movement."[11] While ineffective planning by Kilpatrick contributed mightily to the blunting of Merritt's advance, Evander Law deserves credit for deftly shifting his limited forces to meet the unexpected thrusts by the Union cavalry.

The Confederate line against which Kilpatrick plotted was arranged in a tantalizing juxtaposition to Kilpatrick's troops. Fronting the Union cavalry was a thin skirmish line of men from the 1st Texas Infantry that started at the base of Little Round Top and then continued in a rough semicircle west across the lowland in front of Big Round Top, proceeding upslope towards the Emmittsburg Road to a point midway between the highway and the base of Round Top. The protection afforded by these skirmishers was tenuous at best due to their manpower limitations, possessing only "men enough to have more than about one to every five or six steps."[12] Rather than end his defenses totally in the air, Law used the remaining core of the 1st Texas as an anchor and fused it with the skirmish line. At least for matters as they currently stood, these new troop dispositions were deemed capable of holding Farnsworth's Brigade at bay. For further insurance, the 9th Georgia was shifted, so that in its new position the regiment now straddled the Emmittsburg Road. Behind them on the high ground to their right and facing south was the 59th Georgia. In support were the batteries of Captains James Reilly and William Bachman. Until now, these two units had been firing in support of Pickett's Charge. But the sudden arrival of Kilpatrick's force caused the Southern artillery to be wheeled about to face the imminent danger on the flank.

At the opposite end of the Union and Confederate formations were the main battle lines of both armies. Running perpendicular to the Texas skirmishers in a south to north alignment could be found five Alabama regiments followed by three Texas units. Until its recent redeployment, the 1st Texas had also been a part of this line. These troops, posted along the western slopes of Little Round Top were in positions held since the previous afternoon. July 3 found these Southern regiments with severely reduced ranks. Indicative of their manpower plights, the 1st Texas, for example, could muster but 196 men to put into the line. Though the shortage of troops was disconcerting, these veteran units were still full of fight and a lethal adversary.

The extreme right of the Confederate position ended with a linear alignment of depleted regiments facing east and uphill at the Union line; at its southernmost terminus, the battle line turned at a sharp right angle and then morphed into the thin skirmish line which ran west for several thousand feet. Trees and brush provided cover for the troops on the hillside, while the skirmishers on the flatland had a low stone wall as well as a section of rail fence to crouch behind. Limited infantry and artillery support was available. While this slim line did not end abruptly, there was not by any definition a strong southern terminus. Conversely, the Union line on Little Round Top that faced down on the Alabamians and Texans was sited in an excellent defensive location.

Prior to the arrival of Farnsworth's Brigade, the gradual petering out of the Confederate line from regimental-strength units to an extended skirmish line was deemed adequate for this quiet sector. With the Federal infantry content to maintain a defensive posture, evidence of any movement against the rebels' right flank had not manifested itself. But the arrival of Kilpatrick introduced a wild card. With the quick-strike capability offered by cavalry, the possibility of a thrust against the weak skirmish line now loomed. For a consummate risk-taker like Kilpatrick, the rewards that beckoned in the rear of the Confederate lines made launching an assault a tempting proposition.

Under a less aggressive commander, the 1st Vermont's participation in the Battle of Gettysburg could have been relegated to that of harassing enemy positions. But possessing the ego, orders, and 4000 men, Judson Kilpatrick sought a more substantial contribution. Gleaning information from aggressive probes, the general knew that he faced an adversary whose lines were dangerously overstretched. As the afternoon waned, Kilpatrick chafed at the lack of any meaningful contribution by his troopers. To their immediate north, the sound of a sustained artillery duel preceding Pickett's Charge had been clearly audible. Followed by crashing volleys of infantry fire, the cacophony indicated a major engagement. Glory was being won within earshot, yet no share would accrue to the 2nd Cavalry Brigade!

Then, in the eleventh hour of the three-day struggle, the opportune moment arrived. From snippets of information trickling in, the general envisioned a demoralized post–Pickett's Charge Confederate army, teetering on the brink of rout. Major John Bennett of the 1st Vermont remembered an animated Judson Kilpatrick presenting a justification for an attack: "The whole rebel army is in full retreat. I have just heard from the right, and our cavalry is gobbling them up by the thousands. All we have to do is charge, and the enemy will throw down their arms and surrender."[13] A swift, bold stroke, initiated by his cavalry and properly supported by infantry, might deliver a telling blow, maybe even the coup de grace for the Army of Northern Virginia! Based upon his best assessment of where the enemy's vulnerable points lay, General Kilpatrick decided to attack on two fronts. Wesley Merritt's men were to advance across the level terrain on the extreme Union left, just west of the Emmittsburg Road. Elon Farnsworth's brigade was to charge the rebel lines in the forefront of a shallow valley plain situated between Warfield Ridge on the opposite side of the Emmittsburg Road from Merritt and the Round Tops a quarter-mile further east.

Overshadowed by Pickett's Charge, Kilpatrick's bold gambit is customarily consigned to footnote status in the battle's history. In order to appreciate this particular cavalry action, it must be understood that the charge, brave and spirited though it was, did not alter the outcome of the engagement. Next, a willingness must be embraced to move beyond the mindset that an effort, falling short of a success, is unworthy of recognition. To accept these two as givens opens the door to a compelling narrative, one replete with all of the heroism, pathos, and drama chronicled elsewhere at Gettysburg. For those who like unsolved mysteries, lingering questions about the event still remain, leaving open to conjecture and debate the exact nature of some events long associated with the charge. Though the answers, whatever they may be, cannot alter the results, they will decidedly affect accuracy in the telling of the story. Last but not least, imbedded in the bigger picture is the saga of the 1st Vermont Cavalry, a regiment accustomed to small-unit actions that performed magnificently in its first coordinated engagement on a set-piece battlefield. For the Vermonters, it is fitting that glory is nonjudgmental, capable of attachment with equal affinity to the defeated as well as well as to the victorious. If all that Kilpatrick's forces that day can be credited with is creating a temporary diversion, then the 1st Vermont's part in the demonstration was the most compelling. Merritt's regulars, advancing on foot, were checked and thrown back. The West Virginians and Pennsylvanians were in turn stymied by the terrain, stone walls, and determined Texans. Among the attackers, only the 1st Vermont achieved significant penetration of the rebel lines.

Kilpatrick's strategizing called for a two-pronged attack, Merritt on the left and Farnsworth on the right. Fraught with errors from the start, his plan unraveled quickly. First, the timing was off. Merritt's advance began around 4:30 P.M. and was beaten back by the time the first of Farnsworth's men started out shortly after 5:00. This lack of synchronicity enabled the Confederate commander, Evander Law, to make the most of his meager forces, shuffling their positions to adroitly meet the threat of the moment. Then there was the landscape: on the best ground for mounted action, Merritt's men went in on foot, while Farnsworth's mounted brigade was asked to pick its way across a landscape strewn with boulders, walls, fences, and trees. Finally, cohesiveness was lacking. Rather than overwhelming the Texans with a brigade-sized assault, Farnsworth's troopers charged in staggered waves, effectively fractionating their firepower and allowing the enemy to deal with each unit piecemeal.

The West Virginians went in first. As the first attack moved forward, Kilpatrick summoned Farnsworth to him. Nearby, facing slightly to the northwest, was Samuel Elder's four-gun battery. The 5th New York Cavalry was also posted in the immediate vicinity, its participation reduced to guarding the artillery. In what came to be an extended council of war, Kilpatrick had called his fledgling brigade commander to his side to watch his battle plan unfold. As the officers watched, charges were made by the 1st West Virginia and then the 18th Pennsylvania. When it became evident that these thrusts were not going to meet with success, Kilpatrick suggested that Farnsworth ought to consider leading his remaining men, the Vermonters, in a charge on the batteries so effectively raining iron down on the attackers. Rather than wholeheartedly embrace the idea, Farnsworth countered with his observations on the difficult characteristics of the intervening terrain as well as the stone walls protecting the artillery. But Kilpatrick remained firm in spite of his brigadier's remonstrations. No amount of rhetoric on Farnsworth's part was going to sway his commander. Though the staunch backing of his officers would have been appreciated, the lack of it was not going to deter Kilpatrick from his chosen course of action.

To make the proposed assault, Farnsworth had left at his disposal one of the best cavalry regiments in the 2nd Brigade, if not the entire Army of the Potomac. 675 men strong, the 1st Vermont Cavalry waited in the woods a short distance to the southwest. So it came to be that the last unit to attack was the Vermonters. Their charge went in to the left of where the West Virginians had struck the 1st Texas. Approximately two-thirds of the regiment participated as a mounted force, while the remainder acted initially as skirmishers. Major Bennett was given the responsibility of commanding the dismounted 3rd Battalion, consisting of Companies A, D, K, and M. Lieutenant-Colonel Preston chose to attach himself to this detachment. According to Sergeant Ide of Company D, he and his battalion-mates were "placed behind a stone wall to act as a reserve and be ready to check the enemy if our soldiers were repulsed."[14] For the attack, Captain William Wells led Companies B, C, G and H of the Second Battalion, with Captain Henry Parsons assigned the 1st Battalion's Companies E, F, I, and L. General Farnsworth and his adjutant-general, Joel Estes, elected to ride with Wells' detachment.

Aligned four abreast, the attacking columns rode forward with drawn sabers. There was nothing secretive about their advance. As it gathered momentum, the sounds of crashing underbrush, blaring bugles, pounding hooves, and yelling men left nothing to conjecture. Clearly, a heavy force was on the move. Up ahead, the Confederate infantry waited silently for the next wave of Yankee cavalry. The prospects of having to endure another mounted assault did not particularly faze them. Renowned in the Army of Northern Virginia as a superlative unit in a premier brigade, the 1st Texas' performance on this day added new laurels to its already illustrious reputation. The fortuitous happenstance of having stone walls and rail fencing to shield them was a godsend, providing a boost that permitted the strategic value of their depleted ranks to be exponentially increased. Riding into the face of these staunch Confederates was the combined weight and firepower of approximately 450 men.

The two attacking battalions dashed into battle side by side, with several score yards separating the columns. To the best of Bugler Joe Allen's memory, "We rode at full gallop toward the stone wall behind which the Texas regiment was lying. The Texans had ceased firing, and we knew they were waiting to pick us off at close range. Our men tried to stand up and cheer as we rode toward the fence at a furious gallop, but we could not do it we were so wrought up from expecting the volley at close range."[15] When the concentrated volley finally came, the hail of minie balls miraculously passed high over the heads of oncoming troopers. Given this unexpected deliverance, the Vermonters closed the intervening gap between themselves and the wall before most of the rebels could reload. Then, in an admirable display of horsemanship, the troopers guided their magnificent Morgans over the stone barrier. General Farnsworth briefly gave up his position at the head of the column to watch the spectacle from beside the fence.

Perhaps the least heralded of Pleasonton's "Boy Generals," General Elon J. Farnsworth's brief tenure as a brigade commander showed enviable traits that his untimely death prevented from achieving full fruition (*Battles & Leaders*).

For the attackers, fluidity of movement was a decided advantage. Getting bogged down at any one point could seriously negate this benefit. Though everyone had known they were coming, their mobility allowed them to keep the enemy off-balance and guessing as to where they were headed next. Furthermore, once past the front line of defense, the window of opportunity would only remain open for just so long before Confederate countermeasures were brought to bear. It wasn't very far into the charge that thinking in terms of any success gave way to thoughts of simple survival. Soon the only sensible choice left would be a return to the sanctuary of the Union defenses. In truth, the concept of "Farnsworth's Charge" as a unified act only serves as an accurate descriptor until such time as the Vermonters passed the 1st Texas' line. If each time an enemy unit was attacked and engaged counts as one, then there were in actuality multiple charges before they finally retired behind their lines.

But thoughts of retreat were not in the forefront of anyone's mind as the advancing columns struck the Confederate positions. During those frenzied, action-packed minutes as Wells' 2nd Battalion drove past the stubborn Texans, the 1st Battalion under Parsons was experiencing frustration to its right in an attempt to breech a nearby sector of the enemy's line. In the opening moments of the infantry's contact with the cavalry, the speed at which the events transpired made for unproductive results. Though this portion of the struggle was brief, it still lasted long enough for several troopers to be killed and wounded. As the 1st Battalion's momentum built, Sergeant George Duncan boldly raced forward. "Standing in his stirrups, [he] flew past me, with his saber raised," Parsons noted, "shouted 'I'm with you!,' threw up his arm, and fell."[16] A bullet through his forehead had abruptly ended the life of a popular and reliable soldier. Captain Parsons later penned a thoughtful letter of condolence to Duncan's parents, expressing heartfelt feelings on the passing of their son: "I had scarcely an officer so admired by the men, so freely trusted by superiors, and *so loved* by all which he came in contact as he."[17]

Only moments after Sergeant Duncan went down with his mortal wound, Henry Parsons almost met the same fate. When Duncan toppled from his horse, he landed in front of his captain. Parson's horse shied away from the prostrate soldier. The animal's momentary hesitation was just long enough for the battalion to leave its commander behind. Grasping the opening, a rebel detail jumped the wall and rushed toward the isolated captain. "The enemy ran up crying 'Surrender' as if they did not want to shoot me," was Parson's vivid recollection, "but as I raised my saber a gun was planted against my breast and fired."[18] In the next instant, the captain's horse was also hit. Reacting in pain and fright, the Morgan reflexively broke free of the surrounding rebels, jumped the wall, and took off down the hill. Being severely wounded, Captain Parsons might have teetered off his horse and wound up a prisoner were it not for the assistance he received from Trooper Hiram Waller who "overtook me from the left, and, riding close, supported me on my horse."[19] Parsons eventually recovered from his wound and returned to active duty, though he did suffer nerve damage that caused partial paralysis of his right hand. He left the service after his three-year enlistment ended in the fall of 1864.

Once Parson's wound removed him from command, leadership of his men fell upon the shoulders of others. The confusion of the moment, abetted by the void at the top, caused the 1st Battalion to split into two separate forces. Captain Cushman took Companies E and F forward and linked up with Wells' troopers, while Lieutenant Stephan Clark and Companies L and I abbreviated their charge, crossed to the eastern side of Bushman's Hill, and joined Preston and the 3rd Battalion. At the same time the 1st Battalion was being thwarted by one segment of the enemy's skirmish line, Wells' men had leaped the wall and obliqued to the northeast past Bushman's Hill until finally turning north up Plum Run Valley above the furthest extension of the Texans' skirmish line to the east, about where it fused with the 15th Alabama, situated along the main Confederate battle line facing up the slopes of Little Round Top. By proceeding northward, the troopers under Wells and Cushman distanced themselves from the fury of the 1st Texas.

Their reprieve was brief. Once separated from the skirmish line, all the battalion-and-a-half had succeeded in doing was gaining entrance to a shooting gallery, one in which they became the targets. By moving out onto a small plain, they became highly vulnerable to artillery barrages from Bachman's and Reilly's batteries to the west and rifle fire from the east. In order to avoid exposure to shelling, the troopers had to draw nearer to the enemy foot soldiers posted on the slopes of Little Round Top. Getting closer to these forces effected a welcomed reduction in rebel artillery fire; however, in turn, proximity to the infantry significantly increased the cavalry's susceptibility to small arms.

With the skirmish line fading behind it, the Slyder homestead loomed ahead of the column. From above on the hillside to their right, Confederate troops observed the Vermonters' progress. "Instead of moving directly upon our batteries, the cavalry directed its course up the valley toward Gettysburg," Evander Law recalled, "passing between the position of our artillery and our main line."[20] This would seem to have been an odd decision in light of Kilpatrick's original challenge to Farnsworth. Though he had offered little in the way of identifying specific objectives for the charge, Kilpatrick had referenced taking the guns on the hill. But, regardless of where Wells may have been heading, one of his options was about to be removed. Seeing the enemy horsemen penetrate the skirmish line galvanized Law into action. He immediately dispatched a trusted subordinate "across the valley in advance of them, with orders to detach the first regiment he should come to on the main line, and send it down on a run to 'head them off' in that direction."[21] In a secondary move that would bear delayed fruit, Law further instructed his messenger to direct the 15th Alabama to move off the hillside and strengthen the skirmish line. Prior to the approach of the Federal cavalry, the Alabamians had been intently

General William Wells was Vermont's premier cavalry officer in the Civil War. This highly regarded individual rose from his initial captaincy-by-election to general-by-merit, with a Medal of Honor to show for his bravery at Gettysburg (Francis C. Guber Collection).

focused eastward and upslope toward Little Round Top and the Union troops on the high ground above them. Lying behind temporary breastworks in the late afternoon of a hot, muggy day, the last intrusion, which the Confederates expected or wanted, was from enemy cavalry charging up behind them.

Oblivious to the countermoves that Law was making to contain them, Wells' men passed swiftly behind the 47th, 48th, and 44th Alabama and the 5th Texas before encountering any opposition. Two-thirds of the way between the Texans' skirmish line and the Slyder farmhouse, the 4th Alabama abruptly challenged their forward progress. Responding to Law's order, the Confederate infantrymen had come off the hill, arriving on the meadow just as the Vermonters came thundering up. Firing as they ran, the Alabamians unleashed enough rounds at a fairly close range for some to have a telling effect. George Gorton's participation in the charge was abruptly terminated when "a ball struck [his] arm near the shoulder and passed through [his] chest."[22] The missile damaged his limb and wound up lodging "about two inches to the left of [his] spine."[23] Lucky not to be paralyzed, much less dead, Private Gorton spent two months recuperating. As painful as Gorton's wound was, Joel Smith would have gladly traded places with him. Unlike his battalion mate, Company C's Private Smith never left Pennsylvania soil. Somewhere during the wild charge, Smith was cut down by a fatal gunshot wound to the head. A company cook up until June, he was a figure known to many, and thus his passing was much lamented. The only consolation that his comrades, wife, and young daughter could take from his untimely death was that as a regular churchgoer, Smith's place in the afterlife was probably secure. After the battle, he was among those interred in the Soldiers' National Cemetery at Gettysburg. Not far from where Joel Smith lay in Plot 21 of Section B, President Lincoln later spoke about being there "to dedicate a portion of that field as a final resting-place for those who here gave their lives that this nation might live."

More important than the casualties they inflicted, the timely appearance of the Alabamians served to check the northward advance of the Vermonters. Almost as if on cue, most of the mounted column veered away and headed west toward Warfield Ridge. It is believed by many that at this point General Farnsworth and a detachment became unintentionally separated from Wells' column, causing them to make a clockwise turn that took them back toward Bushman's Hill along the slopes of Little Round Top just below the main Confederate battle line. With Wells' troopers now bearing down on the artillery position, General Law again made another timely decision. "I ordered the reserve of the Ninth Georgia under Captain Hillyer ... to come on the run to the support of the battery, one of which I had shifted so as to face the approaching cavalry."[24] When they arrived behind the battery, there was no time to spare. Wells' battalion was by then just 100 yards away and closing fast. Hillyer audaciously threaded his depleted command through the artillery position in order to meet the attackers on open ground. With "scarcely eighty men left in the regiment," Hillyer was determined to do the best he could with what he had.[25] He later recalled how his regiment's meager line "extending on both sides of the battery ... the colors coming up from behind passed between the guns, and then as we emerged from the bushes, not more than 80 yards in front of us was the column of cavalry just at the point of making their dash at the guns."[26] To approach the rebel position, the Vermonters had to ride uphill over uneven ground. After a brief hesitation, the 2nd Battalion realigned from a marching column into attack formation. Infantry or no infantry, here was finally an opportunity for payback. Having been a target for the last three-quarters of an hour, Wells' command sensed a chance to bloody their swords. While they favored cold steel, at the moment no other option was open, as their revolvers had been emptied long ago. The battalion's continuous movement since leaving Bushman's Woods had prevented reloading. To inflict any damage upon their foes, the Vermonters were going to have to close tightly, literally coming within arm's reach.

For the waiting Georgians, the developing situation had the appearance of a turkey shoot. Granted it took courage to stand in the open and face a cavalry charge, but the rewards for having backbone were great: a can't-miss target. The closer the thundering battalion rode, the bigger the figures at the end of the rifle barrels became. Horse or rider, it didn't matter. One of the two was going to take a bullet. Somewhere among those grimy, sweaty riders heading toward the leveled rifles were the Rogers brothers, it being the lot of Company B to have accompanied Wells. Then it happened. Smoke and flame erupted along the line in what Hillyer perceived to have been an effective volley. "The enemy's column seemed to go partly down," he wrote, "and what remained scattered right and left; and those who still kept on horseback scampered into a skirt of timbers 200 yards away."[27]

Much to the chagrin of the Vermonters, the Georgians' volley deflected the cavalry's forward momentum. While some men did penetrate in among the artillery pieces and dueled with the gun crews, the attack was largely blunted. Though few got close enough to inflict any wounds with their sabers, all in the advancing battalion had unavoidably come within the killing range of the infantry's weapons. Most likely, it was in these few minutes of action that a large percentage of the regimental losses that day were incurred. Commanded by Captain Charles Adams, Company H was especially hard hit. Its unusually high ratio of killed, wounded, and missing may have been due to being in the lead position in the fight with Hillyer's men.

Among the wounded from Company H was Lensey Morgan. At the age of nineteen, he had answered Lemuel Platt's call, leaving the monotony of the family farm near Rutland for the adventurous life of a cavalryman. Possessing the admirable qualities of maturity and leadership, Morgan had risen to the rank of sergeant by the time the Gettysburg Campaign opened. Riding against Hillyer's command, young Morgan's life was forever altered in the split second that it took a minie ball to travel from a rifle's muzzle to his body. The lead projectile struck his right arm halfway between his elbow and shoulder, shattering the bone, tearing up the muscles, and severing the medial nerve as it plowed through the extremity. According to company mate Dan Davis, "The arm was saved but useless and painful.... [D]octor's [sic] had considered cutting it off."[28] After a lengthy period of hospitalization, Morgan joined the Veteran Reserve Corps, where he spent eight months before being discharged. Toward the end of what would turn out to be an abbreviated life, a doctor commented that Morgan "suffers such pain that his condition is infinitely worse off than if he had his arm off above the elbow or entirely off for he would be free of constant and enervating pain."[29]

A similar sequence of events befell both Lieutenant James O'Reily and Private Darwin Eames, both of Company H. A farmer by calling, O'Reily was an Irish immigrant who also took a bone-smashing bullet in his arm. To guard against complications, the attending doctor in his case elected to amputate, the dangling appendage being removed at the shoulder on July 9. O'Reily then followed the same pathway as did Morgan: hospitalization, reserve duty, and discharge. As for Private Eames, he had an almost identical arm wound. With a compound fracture almost three inches above the elbow, the standard treatment, amputation, was again considered. Taken to a field hospital, he remained there until July 18. Eames was then transferred to the U.S. Military Hospital at York, Pennsylvania. By this time, all consideration of removing the arm was dismissed as no longer a livesaving necessity. Nevertheless his cavalry career was over. But Eames' discharge in 1864 brought no surcease to his troubles. Not only did he leave the service with a useless arm, but he also departed with a serious case of chronic diarrhea, contracted while a POW in 1862 following the disaster at Middletown. Less than a year after his discharge, Darwin Eames' health began to deteriorate markedly. S.H. Sherman was an acquaintance who witnessed the dying veteran's last days, noting how "his constitution was bad from the poisoned wound and from diarrhea. He grew worse from day to day, on some days worse than others."[30] Private Eames died on September 20, 1865, killed not "in action" but rather by having been in action.

Of the more severely wounded members of Company H, the story of Private James Stone stands out as perhaps as improbable as his injuries were incapacitating. In the end, he wound up with a ghastly wound and a painful rupture. How Private Stone survived this damage to his body is not only a tribute to courage but also an indicator of bad luck as well. Leave it to a man in the ranks to break down his Gettysburg experience that afternoon to be not the one grand "Farnsworth's Charge" described in the history books but rather a series of successive charges. For the 2nd Battalion with whom he rode, Stone identified three distinctly separate clashes between the 1st Vermont and rebel elements. In the first assault, his horse was killed, but he escaped injury. The "first charge" to which he referred in this instance could very well have been when the 1st Texas' line

Crashing through underbrush, dodging trees, stumbling over rocks, and hurtling fences, the Vermonters in Farnsworth's charge faced many obstacles in addition to the guns of a tenacious foe (***Battles & Leaders***).

was hit. The event which Stone called "the second charge" could have been the attack against Hillyer's regiment, an event which witnessed a second horse being shot out from under him.[31] Again, Stone was unscathed. Defying the odds, quite possibly in a final clash with the 4th Alabama, the same scenario repeated itself. "On the third charge," Stone recalled, "my horse was again shot and threw me forward over the pommel of the saddle."[32]

This time the trooper's luck ran out, for a bullet pierced the outside of his left thigh three inches from the femur's head and then traveled downwards and inwards until exiting on the inside of the limb. Simultaneously, the abrupt contact between his groin and the pommel induced an immediate rupture. Both of these injuries would cause Stone much discomfort for years to come. Proof of the severity of his health issues can be attested to by the litany of hospitals he visited. By the time of his discharge in 1864, Private Stone had been a patient in a total of seven medical facilities over seventeen months. The wound in his leg had been very serious. Even though he nearly lost the leg to gangrene, contracted while he was hospitalized, the only long-term damage caused by this wound was to the sciatic nerve, but one that resulted in bouts of excruciating agony. However, as painful as the leg wound was, the rupture was the injury that produced the most noticeable problem. Not surprisingly, Stone's scrotum became inflamed, swollen, and purple. Over time, "the swelling diminished but did not disappear, a swelling, hard, tender, and as large as a hen's egg remained for three years until it grew soft and filled with fluid, becoming eventually as large as a coconut."[33] James Stone won no citations for heroism in the Civil War, though in less than an hour he had risked his life three times. Like so many of his battle-scarred comrades, he did not need a medal pinned on his chest to awaken old memories. Every day, he had constant physical reminders that would not let him forget the part that he played in the Civil War.

Of all those wounded in the northward charge across the face of Big Round Top, Sergeant C.J. Perley Cheney was one of the better-known noncoms in the regiment. As he was riding with his long-time friend William Wells across the meadow, a bullet slammed into Cheney's body. The heavy lead "musket ball struck him in the right back ... three inches to the right of the spinal column, and [passed] ... through his body," its course halted "by striking a heavily cased hunting watch in his fob pocket of his trousers thrown down into his boot."[34] Dr. Ptolomy Edson, the surgeon who tended to Cheney, observed "the course of the bullet through his body was somewhat downward as the shot was fired from ground higher than that at which he was."[35] Since Cheney felt that he was victimized by a sharpshooter in Devil's Den, it is likely that the sergeant was struck as Wells' column turned west toward the 9th Georgia.

Initially the wound's apparent severity led to a bleak prognosis, with Dr. Edson informing his patient that chances for survival were "one in a hundred," to which the indomitable Cheney replied, "I will go for that one chance."[36] Cheney "hovered between life and death for some time."[37] So weak was his condition that he had to be transported in a bed. Ever the patriot, Sergeant Cheney gamely tried to return to active duty in November; however, he soon found that he was no longer up to the demanding rigors of cavalry life. Discomfort notwithstanding, he marshaled the fortitude to accompany the regiment on the grueling Kilpatrick-Dahlgren Raid. By then a lieutenant, Cheney managed to survive this trying ordeal. But at its conclusion, he came to the realization that he had to resign because "horseback riding and any exertion caused him too great pain. He was a man of firm courage and great resolution and would not have left the field unless compelled to" was the opinion of Dr. Edson.[38] In the soldier's own succinct vernacular, the recent raid had "used me up."[39]

Following their encounter with the 9th Georgia, Wells strove to end his battalion's tribulations. They had by now been out for approximately forty-five minutes. Losses were increasing. Men and animals were spent. Nothing of import was to be gained by continued exposure to enemy fire. From the spot of their encounter with Hillyer's regiment, the distance to a safe haven was less than a quarter mile to the southeast. Moving as rapidly as their tired animals would permit, the 2nd Battalion headed back toward its own lines. Appraising their situation, Captain Wells decided to angle for the corner where Plum Run ran between Big Round Top and Bushman's Hill. One major difference would distinguish the inbound ride from the breakout charge: the 4th Alabama had reinforced the precariously thin Texas skirmish line.

In spite of the dire straits in which the 2nd Battalion found itself, there was hope for salvation in the form of timely assistance from Addison Preston with the 3rd Battalion, reinforced by Lieutenant Stephan Clark leading Companies I and L of Parson's former command. General Kilpatrick, who had previously restrained the 3rd Battalion from joining the attack, had ordered Preston to ride to his comrades' relief. Before exiting the lower Plum Run Valley, the Preston/Clark support column first had to run a gauntlet of galling fire from the reinforced skirmish line, volleys that toppled men and animals to the ground.

Though not hit himself, Bugler Joe Allen of Company I was acutely aware of wounds taken by others in his proximity. A trooper riding to Allen's right was shot. When hit, the man fell over the neck of Allen's horse. The bugler "straightened him up in his saddle, and told him to hold on as long as he could, but he soon fell off on the other side."[40] About this time, Trooper Allen's horse was hit, leading to an almost unbelievable human-interest saga about the animal. Named "Abe" in honor of the President, the Morgan bay was wounded in the neck, the horse taking a round intended for his master. Allen saw the shooter when he sprang from behind a tree, aimed his rifle, and squeezed off a round. "I heard his shot," Allen later wrote, "and the thud of the bullet when it struck; he had fired at me, and struck my horse in the neck."[41] Bleeding profusely, the faithful animal still carried Allen to safety. But the next morning, when it came time to saddle up at 4:00

Captain Oliver Cushman. The young, handsome, and intelligent Dartmouth student — who left school to serve — was dramatically aged by war and disfigured by a bullet taken in the face at Gettysburg (Francis C. Guber Collection)

A.M., Allen realized that Abe was going to have to be left behind. The poor animal's wound and subsequent loss of blood had left him too weak to arise. Finding another mount was not a problem in the wake of the previous day's high casualty rate, but riding off while his devoted mount lay unmoving was a trying experience for even a battle-hardened soldier.

After spending the 4th of July in pursuit of retreating Confederates, the Union cavalry stopped for a few hours of rest. Allen was boiling coffee when he heard cheering. Who should come staggering into camp? None but old Abe! The tired animal was rewarded for his loyalty by being fed and bathed. The next morning, unsaddled, he assumed his rightful place in the marching column, maintaining this position there until the command picked up speed and his weakened condition forced him to lag behind. Doggedly Abe trailed along as best he could until eventually dropping out of sight. This scenario repeated itself for ten days. Each night, after moving all day at a measured pace, Abe sooner or later caught up. In the process, he became quite a celebrity in the regiment. The night that the cavalry was camped near Hagerstown was especially memorable, for on that occasion Allen "heard cheering half a mile away, and knew it was old Abe coming in."[42] Abe became so famous that he had his own nickname: "The First Vermont Straggler."[43] It finally came to pass that Abe was able to keep up with the marching column, falling out of line when the mood seized him to drink or eat. On July 14, Allen decided to put Abe to the test by riding him. From that day until Allen was mustered out in the summer of 1865, Joe and Abe met all of the challenges of war together.

It was at this juncture of the battle that Loren Brigham went down. Riding alongside Lieutenant Clark, Private Brigham pitched into the 4th Alabama, "firing and sabering over the fence."[44] A twenty-year-old weaver from Brattleboro, Private Brigham's final moments were observed by Henry Ide, who attested to how the trooper from Company M "fell in the forward movement, shot through the head, gallantly facing the enemy" and uttering his last words: "Come on boys!"[45] Brigham's wound, though mortal, was not immediately fatal. He held on long enough to be transported from the field, though he did not last out the day after being taken to the regimental hospital.

While Ide's company suffered little as a result of "Farnsworth's Charge," the same could not be said for Oliver Cushman. A respected officer, only 20 years old when he enlisted, Cushman was raised on a farm near Hartland, Vermont, but had aspirations beyond agriculture for his livelihood, leading him to travel twenty miles up the road to college. But like so many of his generation, the call to war interrupted his immediate plans. Cushman left Dartmouth in his sophomore year to join the 1st Vermont. Popular with his men, he rose quickly to the rank of captain. Due to the distinctive clothing he chose to wear on July 3,

The dashing, pre-war Oliver Cushman (Roger Hunt Collection/USAMHI).

Cushman would come to play an unintended but important role in the controversy surrounding Elon Farnsworth's death.

It seems that the handsome and dashing young Cushman had recently received a gift from a female acquaintance. This present was a white duck "fighting jacket" trimmed with gold braid. Parsons protested in vain to his comrade that the outfit made him too conspicuous, advising against wearing it into battle. Captain Cushman, in a lighthearted manner, responded, "A lady sent this to me, and said it was made with her own hands, and no rebel bullet could pierce it. It may be a good day to try magic mail."[46] The jacket alone was sufficient adornment to make Cushman stand out in a crowd, but he did not stop at just this one embellishment to the standard uniform. Going one step further, Cushman altered his hat by "wearing a white handkerchief under his cap behind, so that it fell down upon his neck and shoulders."[47] Of the two sartorial additions, the second was definitely the more practical on a hot, sunny July day. Known as a havelock and more commonly seen in the early days of the war, this contrivance may have actually brought Cushman some comfort. Sporting this distinctive coat and hat ensemble, in combination with his energetic and animated leadership style, Cushman cut a most noticeable figure among the Union Cavalry. Understandably some Confederates mistakenly thought that he was the commander of the assault. Taking fire at close range during the later stages of the charge, Oliver Cushman was among those who went down, probably among the troopers heading south in General Farnsworth's splinter detachment. Intrepid and fearless to the end, he "fought with his revolver until he fainted," whereupon he collapsed and "lay insensible for 24 hours."[48] Ironically, his "coat of mail" had protected his body as intended. Unfortunately, he was shot in the head. Charles Blinn saw the tragic results, describing how "Captain Cushman has an awful wound in the face from the ball passing across his face and under his nose, leaving a horrible mask for life."[49] Disfigured though he would be, Oliver Cushman at least survived his ordeal at Gettysburg.

Vermonters alone did not feel all of the sorrow for lost comrades that day, for the rebels took casualties too. One trooper who did more than his fair share to sow death among his adversaries was Samuel Dowling, a sergeant in Company H. Dowling began his reign of terror somewhere along the skirmish line. Private Harry Sheldon of Company M witnessed Dowling perform a deadly feat when "he dismounted, got behind a tree, and fired his carbine 13 times," the result being that Sheldon "saw a Reb drop every time."[50] This amazing round of shooting prowess was later matched by an equally remarkable exhibition of personal bravery and brute-force swordsmanship when Dowling mounted up and rode behind Wells into the maelstrom on the meadow. At some point, probably on the return charge through the rebel skirmish line, his friend Sheldon, riding to the rescue with Company M, had the misfortune to be captured by a mounted rebel, who put a pistol to the Vermonter's head. Prison, if not death, loomed in young Sheldon's future until his savior in the raging form of Sergeant Dowling "dashed up and made a thrust at him [the rebel] and let his bowels out, cutting from his shoulder to his leg as he sat on his horse."[51] Soon a second victim fell under the weight of another savage blow from Dowling's saber, one that "...split ... [him] from his skull through his face and into his shoulder, just halving [him]."[52] Thirteen shots and two slashes downed fifteen Confederates. Having Dowling arrive in the nick of time surely saved Sheldon's bacon at Gettysburg, but, unfortunately for the Burlington trooper, the fearless sergeant was not around to rescue him from enemy hands during the Kilpatrick-Dahlgren Raid in 1864. Imprisoned in March, Private Sheldon died that fall in Andersonville.

Amidst the confusion reigning on both sides, the Union cavalry recrossed the rebel skirmish line in several different spots. Some sought cover behind Bushman's Hill, while others circled around the base of Big Round Top to a staging area where reserve infantry troops were marshaled. Regardless of how sanctuary was gained, the day's fighting was now over for the 1st Vermont. Elements of the regiment had been actively engaged since the early afternoon. The main charge had lasted about sixty minutes. Though it is always difficult to pinpoint exact hours in an era when the sun was the most important determiner of the approximate time, five o'clock is generally given as the start of the charge. A minie ball stopped Perley Cheney's watch at 5:27 P.M. when the 2nd battalion was about halfway through its circuitous route, and Joe Allen stated that "we were gone an hour on that charge."[53]

The whole event had been very intense, with detachments of the 1st Vermont constantly on the move and continuously under enemy fire. Regardless of the mission's lack of success, the Vermonters unquestionably earned the right to proudly emblazon "Gettysburg" on their regimental flag. But the high cost of this laurel was one that they had never before been asked to pay. When the first roll call was taken following the battle, the full extent of the regiment's losses became clear. Of the estimated 300 Vermont troopers in "Farnsworth's Charge," 67 were absent. Addison Preston broke the latter number down: "12 killed, 20 wounded (2 of whom have since died), and 35 missing."[54] Many of those initially unaccounted for turned up as prisoners of war. Another individual missing at roll call on the night of July 3 was Emmett Mather. He was a popular soldier whose unreported fate deeply troubled many of his companions in Company H. All that was known for certain was that when the 2nd Battalion was "returning from charging enemy lines, Mather and his horse went down."[55] A feisty sort who had already been captured

Wounded and captured at Gettysburg, Sergeant Emmett Mather recuperated, rose to the rank of captain, and served for the duration of the war (courtesy the Civil War Museum of Philadelphia).

during "Banks' Retreat" and incarcerated for six months by the rebels before being exchanged, Mather was not inclined to willingly undergo the same experience again. But, "while defending himself with his saber, his right arm fell in such a manner as to appear wounded to comrades."[56] His luck temporarily deserting him, Sergeant Mather became a prisoner of war again. A painful bullet wound to his forearm, the stimulus for dropping his sword, only added to his misery. Two days later, however, fortune smiled on Mather when he was liberated from the retreating Confederate forces by the Union troops doggedly pursuing them. His story had a happy ending when he returned to Company H in November of 1863 after five months of recuperation.

For Trooper Mather, Gettysburg temporarily interrupted but did not end his military service. Others in similar situations were not so fortunate. Gilbert Smith of Company C was also hit in the arm. Specifically, "a minie ball through the left elbow destroyed the joint."[57] The wounded soldier was taken to the hospital, but, in those pre-rehab days, by the time Private Smith was released he had suffered an atrophy of the muscles from his shoulder to his elbow, a shortening of his arm by four inches, and the inability to lift his hand to his head. Due to the freezing of the limb at the elbow joint, his arm remained permanently extended and useless. A man in his condition lacked the strength and dexterity to handle a powerful horse, let alone his weapons. This led to Smith's being transferred to the Veteran Reserve Corps in the spring and then mustered out in the fall of 1864, able to return home but not to his agricultural calling.

Like Gilbert Smith, Joseph Bailey was lost to the 1st Vermont by a wound caused by "a rifle ball striking his right arm below the elbow and passing through his arm and out above the elbow."[58] This seeming proliferation of gunshot wounds to the upper extremities came not from the unerring aim of rebel marksmen but rather from the fact that cavalrymen charging head-on did not present much of a target. With his body protected by that of his horse, a shot aimed upward frequently hit the horse in the chest or head and its rider in his head or arm.

Lovica Worthern was the proud yet worried mother of Private Henry Worthern, Company H. In addition to this son, Mrs. Worthern had also seen her husband and two other offspring enlist to fight for the Union. Meanwhile, she and six daughters remained in Vermont to keep the home fires burning. Young Henry's company was embroiled in the thick of the fighting on July 3. Though listed as a Wagoner, Trooper Worthern was out there riding with Wells' battalion when he paid the ultimate price of his involvement — with his life. Such news when it reached St. Albans came as a staggering, emotional blow to the Worthern women. Over time, the family's financial situation deteriorated, causing Mrs. Worthern to file for a pension because she "was in very destitute circumstances and was in great need of the necessities of life."[59]

Brownell, Smith, Sperry, Brigham, Duncan, and Worthern — the roll call of the dead for the 1st Vermont grew to proportions that it had never been reached in any previous engagement. In addition, the loss of General Farnsworth during the charge added immeasurably to the cost. As he was a bold leader and brave man, a career laden with potential was cut short in its infancy, leaving a legacy to be pondered for what might have been. As Lyman Wright appraised the situation for his family, "We are seeing a bloody bad time now since we came into Md. and Pa. We was in [the] Gettysburg fight and it was a bloody one too.... Our regiment lost a good many there."[60]

One of the immediate problems in the aftermath of "Farnsworth's Charge" was accounting for missing troopers. Since the battlefield was left in possession of the enemy, it was impossible to ascertain the exact fate of every unaccounted-for man until the rebels departed. "In the Battle of Gettysburg, the regiment charged without proper support and in retreating was obliged to fall back without picking up all their dead and wounded," reported the *Rutland Herald*.[61] Hope was held out that "many of the missing men will undoubtedly come in and make our loss less, while some will prove to be killed or wounded as our cavalry was compelled to retreat in haste."[62] Private Wright, on his own initiative, was able to confirm the passing of Sergeant Orris Beeman, a farmer from Fairfax, which was the stomping ground of Wright as well as the Rogers brothers. All four troopers served together in Company B. Since Beeman had also been an acquaintance of Wright's sister Jenny, the family had more than a passing interest in his next sentence. "After the battle," Lyman Wright wrote, "I went up and helped bury Orris Beeman who was killed there."[63] Slowly the news filtered out about the fate of various troopers. Wright's letter was one way that tidings traveled. On July 5, by word of mouth this time, Dr. Edson verified for the regiment that Joseph Buffum would never be reporting for duty again. After assisting with the overwhelming number of wounded men left on the battlefield by both sides, Edson caught up with the regiment near Hagerstown, Maryland. Though Private Buffum was known to have gone down "in a charge with the 2nd Battalion," his ultimate fate was not certain.[64] Dr. Edson, however, was able to confirm Buffum's death because he "saw him [his body] after the regiment had left and had him buried with [the] others."[65]

As for the merit of what had been accomplished, time would have to pass before any honest assessment could be made of any value the charge had. As for the men of the 1st Vermont, there never was any debate about the regiment's performance. Among those who recognized their superlative conduct that day was Captain Glazier of the 5th New York, who applauded the 1st Vermont for adding "another dearly earned laurel to its chaplet of honor."[66] Accolades from fellow cavalryman meant much, but no one's words were more valued than those of the 1st Vermont's own highly regarded interim commander, Lieutenant-Colonel Addison Preston. Because of the constant fighting and movement by his command, Preston's final report of the battle was not submitted until August 7. In this document, he eloquently lauded the collective efforts of the entire regiment, acknowledging how much "both officers and men deserve the warmest praise for the coolness, courage, and heroism which they displayed in this engagement. Individual instances of bravery were too numerous to mention. Where all did it would be difficult to say who did best."[67]

That the assault, however ill-advised, left an enduring mark upon the 1st Vermont was unquestionable. By virtue of his regiment's steadfast, unwavering participation in that epic charge, a Vermont trooper earned the right to proudly state: "I rode with Farnsworth at Gettysburg." By his having established this connection, the listener knew that he was in the presence of a courageous soldier, a proud veteran who belonged to one of the premier units in the Union army.

22

Lee's Retreat
Head Them Off at the Potomac!

Barring any offensive action by Union forces, General Lee had decided in the early morning hours to depart Gettysburg on July 4. His exit routes were to the southwest, heading for the Potomac at Williamsport. Protected by Imboden's cavalry, the wagon trains departed first, the lead vehicles leaving long before daybreak. The seventeen-mile column transporting the wounded took the more circuitous route, west through the Cashtown Pass and then arcing eventually to the south and Williamsport. The second column, following a more direct route to the east, headed first for Hagerstown and then south to Williamsport. Its composition represented a conglomeration of everything else: supply and ammunition wagons, an assorted herd of stolen livestock, captured free blacks, some additional wounded, and then Lee's infantry.

Across the battlefield to the southeast, Kilpatrick's cavalry arose early. By ten o'clock the 1st Vermont was on the road, hoping to head off the Confederate trains. Though only 300 Green Mountaineers were available, Lieutenant Stephen Clark suggested that "having all of the confidence in our Col. Preston and our ability, so well tested the day before, in a measure reassured us."[1] Heading for Emmitsburg, their route paralleled that of their foes fifteen miles to the east and south of Gettysburg. Traveling light, Kilpatrick's columns rode quickly. There was every reason to believe that the retreating Confederates could be overtaken. At 3:00 P.M., the brigade arrived at Emmitsburg. Turning to the west, the rain-drenched column went into the mountains, somewhere ahead lay the prize. However, before they could cross swords with the enemy, the Vermonters spent a harrowing night dueling with the elements. Located further back in the column, they did not have to challenge the rebel blocking force positioned to contest any passage over South Mountain. This bloody task went to the 5th Michigan, supported by the 18th Pennsylvania. The opposition at Monterey Pass proved stubborn, as they were determined to buy time for the wagons struggling to pass safely behind it.

"About dark," Henry Ide recalled, "the country began to grow wild and interesting and soon the column ahead began to trot."[2] Picking their way cautiously uphill, the Vermonters gained the pass at 10:00 P.M. At about midnight, Kilpatrick detached the 1st Vermont and sent them south down the ridgeline along a wood road, hoping that the regiment could hit the rebel train at some less contested point. The experience would prove harrowing, as "the night was intensely dark — the rain was falling in torrents, the lightening [*sic*] flashed now and then, striking trees and rocks in our immediate vicinity, more than once causing us to think a rebel shell was calling for us."[3] Frightening as nature's

185

fireworks were, the flaring bolts served as the only illumination available to help the troopers negotiate the slippery, twisting road. Deep ravines and gullies on both sides offered instant death to any who strayed off the narrow defile. A lookout had to be kept for washouts.

Rough though the trek was on the men, the pursuit was equally trying for the horses. Thrown shoes made travel on the rocky road painful. Horace Ide noted that mounts "soon becoming lame, the riders would have to dismount and lead."[4] The continuous pursuit of fourteen hours was taking a toll. Once again, the Vermonters were grateful for the mettle of their mounts. "The stout Morgans paid off handsomely" was the appropriate praise from Lieutenant Clark.[5] Still, a terrible toll in horseflesh was exacted. Lieutenant-Colonel Addison Preston regretfully reported the loss "of many horses, worn out by fatigue and want of food."[6] While the obliging animals had to push on until their endurance gave out, the same was not true of the men. Straggling surfaced as a major concern during the night march. Estimates were that only half of the force that left Gettysburg was present for duty the next morning.

Undeterred by diminishing ranks, Addison Preston forged on through the night. Three o'clock A.M. found the 1st Vermont at Smithburg, but no rebel train was found. Continuing on for five miles, the regiment arrived at Leitersburg, only to learn that its objective had passed through two hours before. Small solace for all of the hard riding was

Being ignominiously captured while dining in Mosby's "St. Patrick's Day Raid" was not the end of this art teacher-turned-soldier's woes, for Captain Robert Schofield was wounded and then recaptured at Hagerstown less than three months later — a fate which resulted in his sitting out all but the war's last five weeks in a prison camp (Francis C. Guber Collection).

"the capture of 100 prisoners, comprising cavalry and infantry, and one drove of cattle and many wagons."[7] Failing to cut off the retreating enemy, the troopers rode the six miles to Hagerstown, hoping to overtake his rear echelon. When this effort too proved futile, a bivouac was established on the outskirts of the village. The regiment remained in place for most of the day. Pickets were posted, and patrols ranged along area roads. Their diligence was rewarded by the capture of stragglers, so many, in fact, that by evening they "had more prisoners than men in our own regiment and a string of wagons."[8] Their respite ended when word was received of a rebel force approaching from the northwest. Preston was ordered to Boonsboro and a link-up with other Union forces staging there, bringing his men into a new camp at 2:00 A.M. on July 6.

It was well that they got some rest, for the next day was going to be challenging. Kilpatrick and Buford had formulated a joint plan of action. General Buford's force was to strike for Williamsport and the elusive rebel train; meanwhile, General Kilpatrick's men would protect Buford's rear by blocking Stuart's passage through Hagerstown. From the Confederate perspective, possession of the town was critical due to its being a road hub. If it fell into enemy hands, the escape route for the Army of Northern Virginia would have to be more roundabout. Any delays would play into the hands of the pursuing Union forces. While harassment by the cavalry was annoying, it was nowhere near as threatening to the Confederates' existence as was a more ominous specter: Meade closing with the infantry.

To deny the rebels passage, Kilpatrick advanced his whole division. Colonel Nathan Richmond's brigade, the late Elon Farnsworth's former command, was assigned the lead, with the 1st Vermont in the vanguard. Upon entering Hagerstown around noon, opposition was encountered in the form of two Confederate cavalry brigades. The 18th Pennsylvania charged, and the enemy was "quickly driven from the town, and the First Vermont thrown into a skirmish line."[9] Companies E, F, I, and L, commanded by Captain Robert Schofield, were deployed on the southeastern edge of the town, while Companies A and D were positioned within the village proper. To the left of the Vermont skirmish line was the 1st West Virginia, while four Michigan regiments were on its right. The remainder of the 1st Vermont, along with the rest of the brigade, was kept in reserve. Richmond's orders "were to hold the position but not advance."[10] As more Confederates arrived, pressure on the Vermonters increased, particularly those stationed in Hagerstown. Soon they were facing not only cavalry but also infantry with artillery support. By contesting their desperate enemies' passage, they had compelled the rebel commanders to use whatever force necessary to clear a path. In the words of Horace Ide, "We sat right down before Lee's Army, and they had to remove us before he could proceed."[11]

By mid-afternoon, the situation in town was untenable. Just as they had in Orange Court House the previous summer, the Vermonters again found themselves embroiled in confusing urban warfare. "We deployed down the cross streets as skirmishers," was Sergeant Ide's vivid recollection, "hiding behind houses, and firing around corners." Across lots, behind fences, and up and down alleys the fighting raged. Private residences became strongholds. Bullets came from the front one minute and the side the next. Not surprisingly, regimental losses were high in these bewildering moments of close-in action. Troopers, facing in one direction and firing at an enemy down the street, found themselves cut off as rebel forces pushed beyond them two avenues over and then took cross streets to suddenly appear at their backs. Trooper James Greaves was wounded at this stage of the skirmish, hit in the right thigh by a shell fragment that "lacerated muscles, cords, and tendons."[12] Regimental lore has it that fourteen men from Company D, cut off by the fast-moving rebels, were given sanctuary in the home of Union sympathizers. Unable to risk a breakout, the troopers remained stranded until Union forces retook the town six days later. Their saga became all the more incredible when "some of them while in the town put on citizen's clothing and came and talked with the Rebel Army, which was passing through. Antipas Curtis even saluted General Lee."[13]

After two hours of combat, the increasing pressure forced the withdrawal of the two Vermont companies from the village. With the community cleared of Yankee cavalry, the main skirmish line on the outskirts of town now became the focal point of the rebels' attention. At this juncture of the engagement, Kilpatrick decided that no forward progress was possible against the growing forces looming against his front. He decided to shift most of his command toward Williamsport, hoping to assist Buford's efforts there. Perhaps their combined force could destroy the enemy's wagon train before the main Confederate infantry inevitably brushed aside the delaying force. Only Richmond's brigade was left behind to protect the rear. The 1st Vermont and 5th New York, with two guns from Elder's battery, would work in concert, while the 1st West Virginia, 18th Pennsylvania, and two other fieldpieces did the same. The first two regiments took up a position blocking the macadamized road to Williamsport as the latter two went down the road to establish a fallback location. Calmly, the men sat awaiting the enemy's approach. "They were not kept long in suspense," a correspondent reported, "for in less than half an hour the enemy advanced, two columns of infantry and one of cavalry, each column numbering more men than the whole force ordered to keep them in check."[14]

The Confederates hit both flanks simultaneously. Responding to the heavy pressure, both ends of the Federal line bent backward, until the defensive position came to resemble a horseshoe. Flanked again, the troopers pulled back slowly, giving ground only with the utmost reluctance. Riley Rogers of Company E became separated from his comrades during these confused minutes of fighting. For the second time in less than a year, young Rogers found himself a prisoner. Incarcerated at Belle Isle, his prison ordeal was made all the more tortuous by cases of "blood poisoning and scurvy," the former believed to have been "caused by lying on the island and getting wet at night."[15]

At this point, Elder's battery began to draw the enemy's attention. Preston quickly responded to this threat, dispatching a battalion of Vermonters to help the 5th New York defend the artillery. Lieutenant Elder had one of his cannon posted on the turnpike, spewing canister at the charging ranks of gray-clad troopers. "Four different times did the enemy charge the piece," an impressed Colonel Richmond reported, "and as often they were repulsed with heavy slaughter."[16] With the thrust against the artillery parried, Lieutenant Clark employed the remainder of the 1st Vermont to check a threat to the flank. The situation was desperate. "It soon became a hand-to-hand conflict, squadrons and companies fighting mounted until the enemies' [sic] cavalry was right among us, then charging them back, and then their infantry attacking again, falling back, forming behind each other, and so the fighting continued all afternoon."[17] Somewhere in this action, Sergeant Daniel Hill received a grisly, painful wound. Riding alongside William Wells, Hill was struck in the face. "The pistol ball fractured his nose ... and passed up into the left upper jaw."[18] Effectively paralyzing the optic nerve in his left eye, thereby blinding him while destroying facial muscles in its path, the offending missile was not removed until five years later.

In retreating, the regiment unavoidably left many brave men in its wake. Adam Burlett of Company L became a POW when "in falling back [his] horse ... stumbled and fell ... falling on him in such a manner that he was unable to extricate himself."[19] Burlett was one of the more fortunate prisoners taken that summer, for he was eventually paroled. Though his fractured ankle left him partially disabled, his health was otherwise intact. Others, like Company I's Henry Pettengill, were not as lucky. In rebel hands for over fifteen months, he spent thirteen of them in a newly built detention facility, a place in Georgia originally called Camp Sumter — but best remembered as Andersonville. Private Pettengill would be among the first sent to this soon-to-be infamous prison, enduring trying conditions during his confinement in this "place of torment."[20]

A fellow Vermonter and prisoner, Thomas Lahar, witnessed his friend's decline. From a healthy man who could walk about the compound with ease when he arrived, Pettengill "lost his voice and became nearly blind and was so reduced that he was but a living skeleton."[21] The ravages of scurvy and diarrhea exacted a terrible toll on his body. In Lahar's estimation, "At the time he [Pettengill] left Andersonville, he was reduced as low from starvation and poison and inhumane treatment as a man could be and still live."[22] But survive he did. The same could not be said for Silas Kingsly, Nelson Perry, Henry LaBonte, or Samuel Washburn — all captured at Hagerstown. Fate and timing proved not to be on their side. In the fall of 1863, the exchange of prisoners was suspended due to protocol disagreements between the warring nations.

Anticipating that additional space would be needed, Confederate authorities constructed a new internment camp in the piney woods of south-central Georgia. Among the first generation of POWs sent to Andersonville, their deaths in 1864 added to a roll that would grow to nearly 13,000 deceased Union captives at the prison site. Gone were the days of a rapid turnaround for captives. The Gettysburg Campaign marked a time of transition for POWs. Some Vermonters like Lafayette Stanhope, Charles Wait, and Henry Smith were fortunate and got exchanged in August before negotiations collapsed. Joseph Brewer, Joseph Ferrand, and Amas Lamm were among those confined at Belle Isle, where they succumbed to disease in the fall of '63. Others were sent all the way to Georgia, becoming the forerunners of scores of Vermont cavalrymen sent there. By war's end, fifty-seven members of the Vermont Cavalry perished at Andersonville.

Distasteful as giving ground was, a fighting retreat could nevertheless be more effective than a last-ditch stand. The tactic of withdrawing, re-forming, and resisting bought valuable time for Buford's boys. Private Samuel St. Clair of the 18th Pennsylvania warmly praised the Vermonters' courage and skill, observing how "these brave Vermont boys would hold the rebel advance in check so the battery could get in position on the next rise behind them, and then fall back at a trot, in perfect order, and form with the battery; then the battery would blaze away at the enemy."[23] The final stage of this measured combat occurred near a tollgate on the Williamsport Road. Leading Companies B and H, Captain William Beaman found his squadron cut off from the regiment. Called upon to surrender, Captain Beaman is said to have indignantly replied, "I don't see it!"[24] Then, before the eyes of his astonished enemy, he spurred his horse over a fence, followed by most of his squadron. One who could not extricate himself was the deadly marksman of Gettysburg, Samuel Dowling. "On the 6th of July I turned over my horse & equipment to Jeff Davis" was Dowling's casual remembrance of the occasion.[25] Sent to Belle Isle, the irrepressible soldier bided his time, waiting for an opportunity to escape. In mid–October, he did manage to cross the James and enter Richmond before being recaptured. Finally paroled in November, the loss of weight and overall lack of proper nutrition necessitated a prolonged period of convalescence at Annapolis before he could rejoin the regiment.

Elsewhere, under the approving eyes of Addison Preston, "Captain [Andrew] Grover, with Company K, made a vigorous charge upon the enemy's column in the road, and repulsed them temporarily, but the enemy's sharpshooters told too severely upon him, and he was obliged to fall back."[26] Unbeknownst to the rifleman who unleashed it, one of the rebel bullets found its mark in the forehead of another Vermont officer: "Here one of the bravest spirits fell — Capt. Woodward."[27] In one sense, John Woodward may have welcomed the ball that took his life. Since May 24, 1863, each day had become a tribulation for the young officer. As a devout Christian, suicide was out of the question, no matter how much a pathway to the afterlife was desired. His mental anguish stemmed from the recent death from a fever of his beloved fiancée, eighteen-year-old Hattie Chadwick. Some, observing his conduct in the days since her untimely passing, felt that he had become more reckless in battle, carelessly exposing himself to injury. This unusual behavior made it seem as if he was in search of a fatal bullet, one that would simultaneously end his earthly travail and reunite him with his betrothed. Once a rebel marksman finally obliged him, life ebbed quickly from Woodward. His body remained on the battlefield in rebel hands. Much to the regiment's chagrin, General Kilpatrick was later reluctant to approve a flag of truce, believing that their position too untenable. Eventually, the body was recovered and sent back to the Green Mountains, to be interred next to Hattie's. "These two fondly united in life are not divided in death" was the poignant inscription on their common tombstone, proclaiming for future generations that here lay star-crossed lovers. John Woodward had not even served a year.

One man, far more than all the rest, would intensely mourn the captain's death. Today, the tall shaft of gray granite can still be seen in the small rural cemetery outside of Cambridge. But no longer visible are the footprints on the meadow grass, left there in that summer of 1863 by one of the last to depart following the burial services. These belonged to the soldier's grieving father, the Rev. John Woodward. In the past, this humble servant of God had counseled many in their hour of sadness. Now he, too, bore the same crushing weight that came with the loss of a loved one. As the war would have to be prosecuted in the absence of the son, so now also would it have to go on without his father. Deeply moved by his boy's death, the "Fighting Preacher" lost heart for war. Eleven days after the engagement, he resigned his commission and returned home to Westford and his congregation. Through the remaining years of his life, John Woodward drew daily upon his unwavering faith in God to help him deal with the rend in his heart.

The grief borne by the Woodwards was not the only sorrow visited among Vermont families from the day's events. For Eleanor Everest, a cruel war grew more pitiless. Antietam had taken her husband, Joseph. Now Hagerstown claimed her son. All of nineteen years, George Everest went down in the fighting retreat along the turnpike. A saber had penetrated the trunk of his body. Falling to the road, he lay unattended for hours. Eventually Trooper Everest was moved to a nearby tollhouse, where he lay without medical attention for several days.

Hearing of his plight, several women from Williamsport brought him to a carpenter's shop where they tried their best to tend his wounds: "We politest [sic] him for two days and nights to keep down the inflammation, but all of our efforts were in vain.... Often did he lean upon our breasts and call his mother, and when we would say to him that his mother was not here, he would say he knew she was not, but his mother could not be kinder."[28] Having been advised by doctors that he would not recover, the young man bore his fate stoically. In a state of unconsciousness at the end, he felt no pain. Not surprisingly, the good people who had comforted him in his last days saw to it that he received a decent burial, laying him out "in a nice suit of clothing with a bouquet of red and white and blue flowers on his breast ... [in] a very nice coffin trimmed with black velvet and spangled nails."[29] In a parting act of thoughtfulness, the ladies of Williamsport saw to it that Everest's family received his personal effects, which included his clothes, his watch, a lock of hair, and his father's pocket book.

Darkness eventually enveloped the battlefield — and none too soon for the fatigued Union troopers. Constant pressure by ever-increasing rebel forces had succeeding in taking a heavy toll. The "5 killed, 16 wounded, and 55 missing" enumerated in Preston's after-action report surpassed Gettysburg's total of 67.[30] When contact with the enemy was finally broken off, Union troopers were scattered in detachments of varying sizes. Tired and in disarray, they could still take satisfaction from having fought stubbornly. After separating from the enemy, Colonel Richmond led the brigade five miles down the

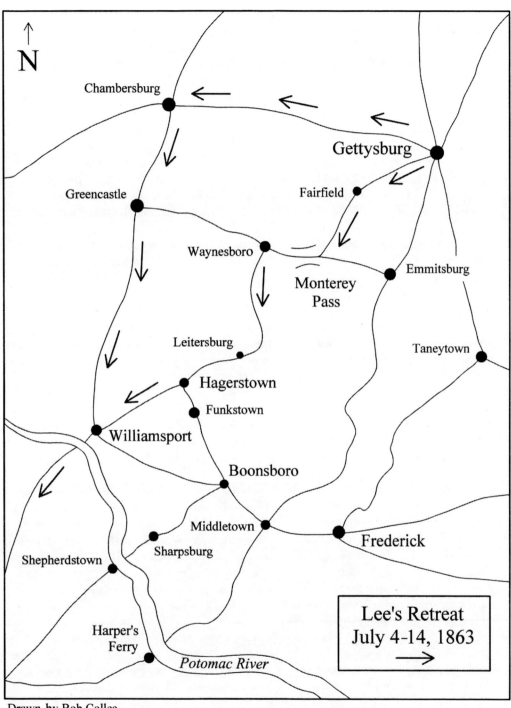

N

Chambersburg

Gettysburg

Fairfield

Greencastle

Waynesboro

Monterey
Pass

Emmitsburg

Leitersburg

Taneytown

Hagerstown

Funkstown

Williamsport

Boonsboro

Middletown

Frederick

Shepherdstown

Sharpsburg

Harper's
Ferry

Potomac River

Lee's Retreat
July 4-14, 1863

Drawn by Bob Collea

road to Boonsboro, where a bivouac was established in the early hours of July 7. After the sound and the fury of Hagerstown, the serenity of a day spent in camp afforded a well-deserved rest, which rain dampened but did not spoil.

The next day started out slowly for the Vermonters, but the prospects for action were very good. Stuart's troopers, in their customary role of screening Lee's infantry, were striving to gain control of Boonsboro Gap. By possessing this thoroughfare, they could contest any advance by Meade's infantry. A holding action here could buy time for Lee's marching columns to gain safety. The ensuing engagement was an all-day affair, involving both Kilpatrick's and Buford's divisions. Due to the muddy conditions, much of the fighting would be dismounted action. In the early stages, the 1st Vermont was held in reserve. Their only meaningful task during this hiatus from the battlefront began with a rather unsettling assignment: taking down fences in the rear that might impede a retreat should the tide of war turn against the Federals. Morning gave way to afternoon, and the spirited skirmishing continued.

Then, beginning at three o'clock, in piecemeal fashion, various elements of the 1st Vermont were sent into action. First up were Captain Charles Cumming's men. Directed to a position on the right side of the Union line, they were ordered to harass enemy cannoneers with long-range carbine fire. Next Captain Robert Schofield led his squadron into the line trying to block Confederate progress on the Hagerstown Road. For Private Aaron Ober of Company I, active participation in the war was about to end. Already a two-time POW, he had nevertheless managed to remain physically unscathed. Advancing to his position in the line, Sergeant Jonas Stevens heard his company commander, Lieutenant Eben Grant, command his men "to prepare our arms for immediate action" when the report of a pistol was heard, the painful consequence being that Ober "was accidentally shot in the hand by the discharge of his revolver."[31] Such were the hazards of war that a soldier was wounded before hostile fire was even drawn. When Preston listed "8 wounded" at Boonsboro, there was no footnote to indicate the freakish circumstances of Ober's injury. Statistically speaking, his injured hand counted the same as any wound incurred that day, including Charles Lapham's.

Corporal Lapham had the misfortune to have both legs badly mangled by a single cannon ball. Two days later a surgeon performed a double amputation, taking the right leg just above the knee and the left one at the joint. But sixteen months later, the determined veteran was up and about on artificial limbs, ready to gamely make his way through life as a federal clerk. The forward deployment of the Vermont troopers continued when Preston "sent Major Bennett, with Companies L. F, K, and M, to report to the brigade commander. This force took a position in the front and on the right of the road leading to Hagerstown, and suffered severely from the enemy's batteries."[32] It was in this phase of the battle that Private Lapham was wounded.

The final infusion of Vermonters occurred when the last battalion available, Well's 2nd, was ordered to charge. Considering that only fifty-five men were present, the task ought to have seemed daunting. Few could be blamed if some hesitancy prevailed. But these were the men who had ridden alongside Farnsworth at Gettysburg. Already severely tested, the reduced battalion had no thought other than to follow orders. "The charge was spiritedly made and sabers freely used," Preston proudly commented.[33] One of those who could confirm the excruciating effects of cold steel on the body was Trooper James Reed. Once Wells' charge had closed with the rebels, hand-to-hand combat broke out on all sides. Private Reed received two blows, one "chipping off a two-and-a-half inch by one-and-a-quarter inch portion" of right parietal bone, while the other was taken in the left elbow.[34] His life spared, Reed finished out his term of service in the Invalid Corps.

Captain Wells was fortunate not to have been wounded in the attack himself. But in his moment of peril, he was saved by Sergeant Jerome Hatch. Amidst the confusion, two attackers set upon Wells, one from the front and the other from the back. As he flailed away with his sword against that of a Confederate officer, the second enemy soldier struck him in the back. Caught betwixt and between, Wells was in what could have been a fatal predicament. Without the quick action of Sergeant Hatch, the 1st Vermont could have been summarily deprived of its future commander. Hatch, "who was lying on the ground by his horse which had fallen on him, disabled one of Well's [sic] assailants by a shot from his revolver, and Wells beat off the other."[35] Also riding in the charge was Hannibal Jenne. He proved to be not as lucky as his commander, taking a gunshot wound to the forehead that resulted in four months' worth of hospitalization. The pluck of this small band of Vermonters could only work in their favor for so long before the enemy's superior numbers blunted the charge and then forced it back. Hostilities ended shortly thereafter as night shrouded the field. The timely arrival of the Federal infantry insured that the rebel cavalry would advance no further, allowing the 1st Vermont to pull out of the line and return to camp.

The 10th and the 11th proved inauspicious, as the Vermonters were assigned picket and patrol duties on the army's right flank. July 12 would find them reoccupying Hagerstown. So close was the proximity of the enemy that the horses remained saddled for thirty-six hours as the men slept under arms. Yet the only event of regimental import during this interval proved to be the return of Colonel Sawyer, who had been absent from command since the 22nd of June. The command Sawyer regained was one richly covered in glory though sadly reduced in numbers. He needed only stand before the depleted ranks at roll call to grasp the full import of the Gettysburg Campaign.

For the Vermonters, the cessation of hostilities on July 13 ended their participation in the campaign. The next day, during the final engagement at Falling Waters, the regiment was held in reserve as Custer's men bore the brunt of the fight to take a pontoon bridge. With Stuart's cavalry again screening his movements, Lee led the Army of Northern Virginia back across the Potomac on the night of the 14th. The Union cavalry had been on the move for almost a month since leaving Fairfax in mid–June. The riding had been virtually nonstop. It had been an exhausting, punishing existence. But out of it all, for those who survived the cauldron of battle, the campaign had provided a growth experience for Yankee troopers, witnessing "the emergence of the Union cavalry as a viable combat force."[36] George Gordon Meade submitted an official report which concluded with glowing praise for all: "It is impossible in a report of this nature to enumerate all the instances of gallantry and good conduct which distinguished such a hard-fought campaign as Gettysburg. The reports of the corps commanders and their subordinates, herewith submitted, will furnish all information on the subject. I will only add my tribute to the heroic bravery of the whole army, officers and men, which, under the blessing of Divine Providence, enabled a crowning victory to be obtained."[37] As the commander in chief of the Army of the Potomac, political correctness dictated that he be generous in lauding everyone, though certainly his mounted forces deserved a special nod of their own. But Lyman Wright, a proud member of the 1st Vermont's Company B, was under no such compunctions to lavish praise evenly. He was one of the cavalry boys from Vermont, and it was they whom he praised when told his folks, "I hope that this war will end this fall. Everything looks like it now, but there is no telling. We have been doing good work for a month back, and if we keep it up it will soon end."[38] Simple and understated, his appraisal carried the stamp of approbation from one of those who had lived through the entire experience and knew in his heart what he and his comrades had accomplished.

23

Back in Virginia
Summer of Recovery, Fall of Action

For six weeks after Gettysburg, no consequential engagements would be fought, but Lee's slow-moving columns still presented tantalizing game. Proceeding to Harpers Ferry, the 1st Vermont joined the pursuit and then spent the remainder of July operating in Northern Virginia. During this interval, Colonel Sawyer was promoted to brigade commander, with Lieutenant-Colonel Preston again leading the 1st Vermont. This temporary change held until August 20, when the Vermonters were transferred to the 2nd Brigade. This move proved a mixed blessing. Though it broke bonds with familiar regiments, the switch made George Custer their commander. Under his aggressive leadership, the 1st Vermont flourished. A mutual admiration society quickly blossomed between leader and led. The Vermonters eventually affected the distinctive red neckties worn by Custer's beloved Wolverines and reveled in their unofficial but prized identification as the "8th Michigan." With Kilpatrick leading the division and Custer the brigade, a fighting soldier craving action was not disappointed.

On August 30, William Wells was motivated to describe Kilpatrick as one who "fights the enemy wherever he finds them."[1] Almost as if to validate this appraisal, a most unusual three-day experience awaited the regiment the next morning. Known as "Kilpatrick's Gunboat Expedition," the operation proved novel even for the general's unpredictable proclivities.[2] The plan was to ride southeast from Hartwood Church to King George Court House, then turn due south to Port Conway on the Rappahannock River. Across the waterway lay Port Royal. Anchored there were Kilpatrick's objectives: the gunboats *Reliant* and *Satellite*. Formerly vessels of the United States Navy, this twosome had patrolled the upper reaches of Rappahannock until the night of August 19 when enterprising Confederates captured them. Moved to Port Royal, they now guarded the cross-river transfer of commodities from attacks by their former owners.

Knowledge of their presence had whetted Kilpatrick's appetite. In correspondence to Alfred Pleasonton, Kilpatrick expressed his thoughts: "I should like to move down the river, capture their forces on this side, and destroy the boats."[3] Though not approved by his immediate superiors, authorities in Washington learned of the proposal, embellished the mission with a naval component, and saw that Kilpatrick got command. After a twenty-four hour march, the Yankee raiders arrived at King George Court House in the early morning of September 2. Following a brief skirmish, rebel forces were dispersed. Wanting to alert neither the troops near the river five miles ahead nor the boats offshore, Kilpatrick resorted to subterfuge. He loudly ordered his men to pull back. With the ele-

Pleasonton's Cavalry was deployed as skirmishers. With carbines at the ready, firm pressure was put on rebel resistance that slowly gave way until the enemy was pushed back into and then through Culpeper by a headlong Federal charge (Library of Congress).

ment of surprise gone, he openly rationalized that there was no point in going ahead with his plan. Several prisoners were permitted to "escape," hopefully conveying the faulty intelligence that Kilpatrick had planted. Then, after riding away from the river for two miles to support the ruse, he planned on doubling back, ideally to find an unsuspecting enemy lulled into a false sense of security.

When the raiders finally returned, the 1st Vermont was in the van. Though still dark, Company I, armed with carbines, was sent ahead along a narrow road that wound through a forest and down to open fields beside the river. Following with the rest of the troops, Kilpatrick called a halt for the night at the edge of the woods, ready to move forward when his naval support arrived. Finally dawn broke, but the sun's rays disclosed no Federal gunboats. Being in an exposed position miles from Union lines, Kilpatrick did not have the luxury to dawdle.

Down on the Rappahannock, rebel laborers could be seen salvaging equipment from the ships. As Colonel Sawyer remembered, "My sharpshooters soon drove them from the boats, though they were anchored well under the Southern shore of the river."[4] This fusillade was accompanied by some very impressive artillery work by field guns positioned on the river's edge. At a distance of 650 yards, an accurate barrage was unleashed upon the two small vessels. Though the rebels returned fire, it proved ineffectual. Soon the duel became one-sided. The *New York Times*' reporter disclosed how "the *Satellite* was soon in a sinking condition [and] ... the *Reliance* ... was soon rendered worthless, and both are so nearly destroyed that they can neither do any mischief, nor again be so repaired by the enemy as to be useful."[5] Though the rebels mounted a retaliatory effort, Kilpatrick spirited his men away quickly and got them triumphantly back without incident.

The regiment's next mission came on September 12, when General Custer led the brigade down to Kelly's Ford, where a bivouac was established for the night. As part of a general advance, cavalry units reconnoitered the area between the Rappahannock and the Rapidan. The next morning, an impressive host of 10,000 riders crossed the Rappahannock, heading south along the Orange & Alexandria's right-of-way for Culpeper. Kilpatrick's men were on the left of the three divisions, the Vermonters on the southeastern flank. At a distance three miles outside Culpeper's limits, "our cavalry were briskly engaged in skirmishing with the enemy's cavalry and artillery, driving them toward the town."[6] Initially, the 1st Vermont was dispatched to the left of Culpeper, hopeful of outflanking rebel forces positioned there. However, a rain-swollen stream and swampy ground thwarted this thrust. Then new orders were issued: charge directly into the town!

Bugles blaring, the regiment thundered into Culpeper. To Private Franklin Mead, "It was the most splendid sight I ever saw on the field of battle."[7] Unlike previous urban engagements, this clash did not get bogged in street fighting. Against superior numbers, the rebel defenders were overmatched. "Hardly did they stop to engage one body of our forces," perceived Private Aaron Crane, "before they were assailed on the flank by the bullets or shells of another."[8] Clearing the town quickly of all opposition, the 1st Vermont took possession of a knoll south of Culpeper, "where the regiment was subjected to a very severe artillery fire from the enemy's guns, stationed ... [to their] front and left."[9] In response, carbineers were sent forward as skirmishers, buying time for adequate reinforcements to arrive. Across terrain ideal for mounted action, the ensuing spectacle made a lasting impression. "We drove the enemy at every point. I never saw our men fight better than then. Our battalion charged through the woods beyond the town and drove the enemy from a strong position, capturing about 40 prisoners," was one trooper's proud depiction of the glorious moment.[10] Over forty combined pieces of artillery added to the din of battle, their bursting shells spewing deadly pieces of hot shrapnel that tore the flesh of man and beast indiscriminately. Two fragments almost produced a disaster when an exploding shell simultaneously sent one shard tearing into William Wells' shoulder and another into George Custer's foot. With the two officers riding side by side, this lucky shot produced painful but not mortal wounds.

The Union cavalry charged three times. "All of the fighting was done on horseback, and no more daring work was done by either side, on any of the battlefields of the war, than was seen at Brandy Station.... Those who were in it, describe it as the most stirring and picturesque scene they ever witnessed ... the fluttering of guidons and battle-flags, the flash of sabers and puffs of pistol shots—altogether a most brilliant spectacle."[11] By 4:00 P.M., rebel forces were in full retreat. Union troopers pursued, hoping to inflict further damage, but the elusive Confederates stayed beyond reach until safely crossing the Rapidan. For their part, Vermont's troopers had performed well. Four hours of continuous combat had resulted in a total of thirty-three men killed, wounded, and missing. In a battle report, such losses appear merely as statistics, impersonal numbers without names or faces. But to the regiment, every unanswered name at roll call meant an absent comrade.

One of those lost was Private John Henry, the 1st Vermont's lone fatality. Shot dead on the battlefield, he was hastily buried where he fell before the regiment gave chase to the retreating rebels. Counted in the company of the wounded was Michael O'Neal, who took a nasty saber cut across the left side of his head. For this hardy son of the Emerald Isle, this injury represented his second of three, as he received a ball in the leg at Savage Station in 1862 as an infantryman; and two years later, he was destined to take shrapnel in the foot at Ream's Station. But at least O'Neal recovered enough to remain with the regiment. In Monroe Lyford's case, military life went from bad to worse. He had just returned to active duty after a lengthy bout with malaria when he was severely "wounded by a casement shot [that] broke his collar bone and had to be cut out on the backside of his shoulder ... at a bloody field hospital."[12] Four weeks later, Lyford was granted a medical discharge.

For the next fortnight, the regiment guarded the area approximately ten miles below Rappahannock Station. Though the time was one of comparative calm compared to the rigors of the recent campaign, the presence of irregular units necessitated alert pickets. "We have frequent skirmishes with the guerilla bands infesting the vicinity," acknowledged Addison Preston.[13] With these bands prowling about at night, captivity and even death awaited the unwary vidette. Forewarnings aside, the night of September 26 witnessed just such a calamity, when a fifteen-man post at Richard's Ford was overrun. Preston's brief report cited one killed and fourteen captured. While not specified in the report, the solitary fatality was William Jure, a forty-nine-year-old wheelwright whom chance brought to the deadly scene. Private Jure had not drawn any thankless picket duty that night. Instead, he arrived on the scene among the six escorts for an Ohio captain who was making his rounds as officer of the day. By the time his entourage had reached Richard's Ford, the late hour prompted a discussion about staying for the night. The captain decided to push on but permitted his men to make their own choices. The escort elected to remain. Though all appeared quiet after the men bedded down, plans were being made to attack the picket post. At 4:00 A.M., assisted by the light of an autumn moon, rebel raiders secretively crossed the river on foot.

So sudden was the attack that only two shots were fired. In the incident's aftermath, John Newton, Captain of Company L, surmised that "one of these [shots] must have been fired by Mr. Jure, defending himself and the other was the fatal shot which killed him."[14] The bullet to his heart caused instantaneous death. Following his friend's burial, Private Noah Vincent was moved to offer his condolences to Jure's family as well as lift their spirits with his remembrances of his fallen comrade. "Your affliction," he wrote, "is doubtless now filling your heart with unutterable anguish.... The works of love and kindness which he has so cheerfully done for so many of us, his kind words of unfailing truth, his upright example — all lend to make his memory blessed among us."[15] The family appreciated his thoughtful letter, followed shortly by another from Captain Newman, who characterized the departed trooper as a brave and faithful soldier. Newman also promised to forward some private letters and keepsakes that were found among Jure's effects. The chances are that Jure may have had his picture taken somewhere during the war, and then again, maybe not. Certainly there wasn't much tangible evidence to record that William Jure had lived on earth for almost five decades. But in the hearts and spirits of three then teenaged daughters and an aging wife, his memory was eternal. As a devout family, they surely understood and believed as did John Newman that "we have great reason to be consoled when we think what his life has been, and of the rewards promised to those who so live."[16]

Surprisingly, this obscure affair at a random Virginia picket post had lasting effects that were vastly disproportionate to the scope of the action. Not only did it visit a tragedy on the Jures, but the life of Eli Holden was also severely altered and made far more wretched than he could ever have imagined. The young lieutenant, still feeling the consequences of the saber blow to his head delivered at Miskel's Farm, was among those captured the same night. Spirited off to Libby Prison, he fell ill. This was followed by incarceration for a time at Andersonville. Eventually, he wound up in Charleston, South Carolina, where prisoners were used as human shields to deter Union naval bombardments. By the time he was repatriated in 1865, his health had deteriorated to the point that he was henceforth often unable to perform manual labor. Superficially, both men were a part of the same impersonal statistics in an after-action report, yet beneath the surface their earthly existence amounted to more than just being cogs in the war machine. One gave his life, the other sacrificed the quality of his.

With the same indiscriminancy that hostilities ruined lives, so too did they alter the landscape. This gloomy scenario was particularly true for Culpeper. Owing to its strategic location in north-central Virginia, the little community endured frequent visits by both sides. In its immediate vicinity, over 160 skirmishes were fought. Sadly, the effects of combat were no kinder to property than people caught in harm's way. It was a "once pretty town, surrounded all-around by lovely scenery and beautiful forests, but like all Southern towns through which armies have passed it is more or less destroyed."[17] In time, physical damage was only temporal and highly repairable; however, what could not be set right was the human cost.

A soldier's death was at least an eventuality not unthinkable, but the suffering of innocent bystanders was always difficult to reconcile. So it was that Charles Blinn, a seasoned veteran, could still be moved by an "appalling spectacle" that he witnessed in the cellar of a Culpeper house.[18] There, in silent repose, he gazed upon the bodies of an elderly gentleman and a four-year-old boy. Both had sought shelter from artillery fire in what seemed to be a safe refuge. But an errant shell had entered a window, exploded, and killed them. "It was a sad and truly heart-rending sight," Blinn lamented, "and caused many to weep over the sad fortunes of war."[19] Thoughts of home were inescapable at such moments, with the men thankful that their families were safe from the destruction and death that were visited on helpless places like Culpeper. A dead soldier, a fatherless family, an unlucky prisoner, a destroyed town, and civilian casualties—in one day and a night Vermont troopers were exposed to a microcosm of war's disturbing aftereffects. Bereft of banners and bugles, its face was far from inspiring. In such moments, few were the men who did not wish the cruel war to end.

Two weeks after the Richard's Ford incident, the war heated up in earnest again as General Lee lashed out at enemy forces located between the Rappahannock and Rapidan rivers. Made during October and November, his troop movements would be known as the "Bristoe Campaign." Though possessing numerical superiority, General Meade's uninspired response to his adversary's flanking attempt was a retreat. Lee in turn pushed his men to circumvent Meade's right, but the Union commander returned north, striving to thwart the turning thrust while maintaining a presence in front of Washington. As a part of the Federal screen, the 1st Vermont did its part in facilitating the retrograde movement, participating in multiple engagements over a ten-day period.

The first major encounter for the Vermonters occurred on October 11, 1863, at Brandy Station. Their day started two miles south of Culpeper, where the regiment had bivouacked under arms through a miserably cold and rainy night and ended the same afternoon on the slopes of Fleetwood Hill at Brandy Station. In between, as a part of

Custer's brigade, they had ridden toward the Rappahannock as Stuart masterfully parlayed his legions against them. The withdrawal commenced at daylight. Not until the column reached Culpeper did enemy forces establish contact. There Confederate troopers hit the rear echelon manned by the 1st Vermont and 1st Michigan. Passing through the town in a somewhat inglorious posture, Colonel Sawyer and his men took some perverse satisfaction from the cheeky antics of "the brigade band playing the saucy air of Yankee Doodle to the inhabitants."[20] Their jaunty demeanor was short-lived, however, when the discovery was made of another enemy force moving swiftly alongside their left flank. The brigade headed out rapidly, riding along both sides of the former Orange and Alexandria right-of-way. Nearing Brandy Station, halfway to the safety of the Rappahannock, the exodus of Custer's brigade abruptly halted. Before him, Colonel Sawyer saw a disheartening scene in which the Federal troopers "were not only flanked on both left and right, and closely pressed in the rear, but right across the road we desired to travel we were confronted by a strong force — .... [W]e were surrounded."[21]

At this critical moment, General Kilpatrick arrived and conferred with Custer, who pitched a plan to extricate the brigade from its predicament. "To him I proposed with my command to cut through the force in my front," Custer later reported, "and thus open a way for the entire command to the river."[22] Kilpatrick concurred, and Custer was off to star in a production of his own design. That the man lived for such moments was unabashedly evident in later correspondence: "Oh, could you but have seen the charges that we made! While thinking of them I cannot but exclaim 'Glorious War'!"[23]

With a decision made, the matter was quickly settled. Two Michigan regiments were selected by Custer to break through the rebels' blocking force. Three rousing cheers and another stirring rendition of "Yankee Doodle" preceded their spirited assault. Seeing the supercharged troopers headed their way with sabers poised gave the rebels little time for second thoughts. "Closer and closer they came," recalled one trooper, "and when they got within 200 yards of us, their leader ordered a charge, and it looked as if the whole column was coming right into our ranks."[24] With the thundering mass almost upon them, the gray-clad cavalry made a choice. Before the eyes of the frenzied attackers, "The enemy, without waiting to receive the onset, broke in disorder and fled."[25]

Equally enraptured as the drama unfolded, a pumped-up Edwin Sawyer saw a scene that "had become wild and exciting.... [C]harges and counter charges were frequent in every direction, and as far as the eye could see over the vast rolling field, were encounters by regiments, by battalions, by squads, and between individuals, in 'hand-to-hand' conflict."[26] Amidst all of the confusion, a rebel-flanking sortie from nearby woods made a dash to capture Captain Elder's supporting guns. Colonel Sawyer immediately galvanized the 1st Vermont into action, proudly noting how "the regiment obeyed the order to charge with more than their usual alacrity."[27] This timely intervention served to check the enemy's advance and bought time for the artillery to be moved to a less vulnerable position. During this clash, William Wells lost his faithful mount Ethan. Once his horse was down, Wells grabbed his rubber coat, bridle and halter and "then ran like the D___L so as not to get captured."[28] Having briefly been a POW in April, he did not want to push his luck at enjoying as quick an exchange the second time around as he had the first.

Up ahead, Custer's aggressive efforts had proven fruitful. A passage to the river was opened. By ten o'clock that evening, the last of the once-surrounded Federal cavalry was safely across the Rappahannock. Fatigued and famished, they immediately encamped for the night. As Confederate forces approached, the location of their foes was easy to determine, for "beyond we could see the hills brilliantly illuminated with campfires. It was a gorgeous spectacle."[29] But alas, for the members of the Vermont Cavalry, their workday was not over. No sooner had they made themselves comfortable than orders came for the regiment to assume picket duties along the Rappahannock. If, in the midst of their exhaustion, weary minds chanced to assess their performance that day, a warm inner glow should have flooded each trooper. To a man, they had functioned well. Custer acknowledged it, commenting in his report that "the First Vermont ... deserves great credit for the rapidity with which they forced the enemy to retire."[30] For a man who had not personally seen much action, let alone from the command perspective of leading a regiment in sustained action, Colonel Sawyer also performed well that day. In his official report to General Pleasonton, General Kilpatrick even went so far as to cite Sawyer for greatly distinguishing himself. In retrospect, Brandy Station may in fact have been Sawyer's shining hour.

While Sawyer's military career still had some mileage left on it, for one Vermont trooper the war ended at Brandy Station. The lone fatality was Jason Stone of Company F. Sawyer made mention of his loss in his report, calling the fallen sergeant "an honest, intelligent, and unassuming man, and a brave and faithful soldier, one who performed his whole duty at all times and under all circumstances, and whose bearing was always such as to command the respect and esteem of all."[31] After the battle, Horace Ide tried to find Stone's grave, as he was believed to have been buried where he fell; however, that supposition was erroneous for Stone had been wounded, captured, and taken to Richmond where he eventually succumbed.

Considering all of the day's actions, casualties were extremely light. Though few were injured in combat, the regiment lost the services of many fine men through capture, twenty-seven Vermont troopers being listed among the over 500 Union prisoners taken. The highest-ranking Vermonter among them was Major Josiah Hall. Unfortunately for the major, he fell into enemy hands at the end of the day when an element of confusion still existed. Hall, after having become ill earlier and relinquishing his command to Major John Bennett, rode back with his orderly, seeking to rejoin the main body of the regiment. Believing it to be bivouacked at Hartwood Church, he obtained directions from a local. Then Hall took his orderly and went ahead of the column to locate the camp. But "neither himself nor orderly arrived," Colonel Sawyer reported to General P.T. Washburn, "and it is feared he was captured by the guerrillas who had lately lurked about that neighborhood."[32] Another unlucky prisoner, Corporal Stephan Corey — brother of the late Job, who fell at Greenwich — endured seven months of captivity before being paroled. Particularly moving was the case of Lyman Wright. Having fallen into enemy hands, the St. Albans native was allowed to pen a brief note to his mother. "I thought that I would write a few lines to let know that I am well," the young trooper shared with her, "and a prisoner in Richmond. I was taken at Brandy Station and 4 more out of our Co. besides me. We are not allowed to write but a few words, so good-bye from your son."[33] More than a few tears stained this simple note. The first time was when Mrs. Lyman read it, learning of her son's captivity. The last was when she put the little letter into an envelope, preparatory to surrendering this precious keepsake to the Federal government in exchange for a pension. This act was necessitated by the fact that her son's "good-bye" proved to be prophetically just that, for Lyman died in a Florence, South Carolina, prison in September of 1864.

With growing numbers of captives to manage, Southern prisons were taxed to their maximum capacities and beyond. Overcrowded conditions and laxity on the part of prison guards afforded opportunities for escape that many daring Vermonters oppor- tunistically seized. Among those taken at Brandy Station, there was apparently an enter- prising core of feisty troopers who were not willing to suffer captivity without a fight. As befit their rank as captains, William Beeman and Charles Adams demonstrated the grit of true leaders by making escape attempts. While being moved from Macon to Charleston in the late spring of 1864, Beeman surreptitiously excused himself from the train and headed off for freedom. Tracked by bloodhounds, the fugitive's freedom proved short-lived. Beaten but not bowed, he waited six months before being exchanged. The privations of prison, however, had eroded the constitution of the thirty-five-year-old officer, so much so that he received his discharge a week later. As for Captain Adams, he too ultimately escaped, though by its timing his flight proved only a Pyrrhic victory. Confined at Charlotte, North Carolina, he took his leave in March of 1865. Traveling across the Appalachians, he successfully evaded his pursuers and gained the safety of Union lines at Knoxville just before the cessation of hostilities.

Perhaps the most dramatic leaves were taken by Privates Dan Davis and Aaron Crane. Shinnying down a lightning rod from an upper floor of Richmond's Pemberton Prison, they lowered themselves onto an adjoining roof and then broke through the upper stories of several stores along the street until they finally exited the city. Eventually they rejoined the regiment. For Davis, the four-day trek to safety was decidedly an ordeal, as "he was obliged to swim the Chickahominy River and travel all day and night in the

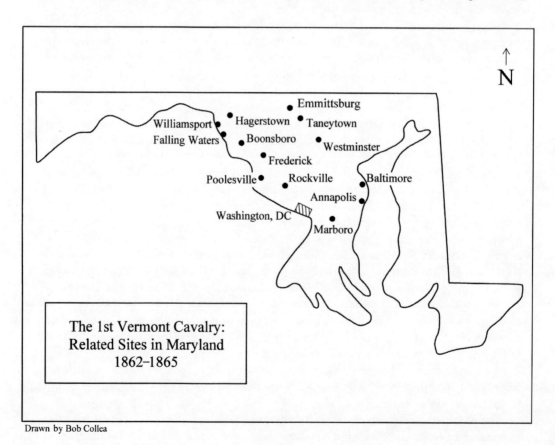

The 1st Vermont Cavalry:
Related Sites in Maryland
1862–1865

Drawn by Bob Collea

raw."[34] The two men "suffered everything from the privation of food, and the constant fear of being taken back to the vile den in which they had been imprisoned."[35] That Vermonters should exhibit such collective determination came as no surprise to those who knew the mettle of these men; resolute in battle they were no less yielding in captivity. Unfortunately, not all attempts at flight were successful. A POW at Andersonville, Joseph Collette, later recounted how John Cantell, Company H, "was shot during an attempt to escape."[36]

Following the close call at Brandy Station, the 1st Vermont did not see sustained action again until October 19, at which time the regiment participated in the Battle of Buckland Mills. By then, the rebel offensive was waning. Stuart's riders were screening Lee's retreat from the vicinity of Manassas Junction. Considered the fourth in a sequence of five major clashes comprising the Bristoe Campaign, the fracas at Buckland Mills built slowly and promisingly for the Federals. Matched against each other were the combined Confederate talents of Jeb Stuart and Fitzhugh Lee versus the Yankee duo of George Custer and Henry Davies. In addition, there was one more individual in blue present that day, an officer who whose presence unintentionally helped tip the scales in favor of the rebels. That person was none other than Judson Kilpatrick.

The sorry affair began optimistically, with Custer's brigade advancing east down the turnpike from Gainesville toward Buckland Mills in the early morning of the 18th. Three Michigan regiments soon engaged three brigades of Stuart's horsemen. After some charging and countercharging, the Confederates pulled back. Custer's troopers pursued aggressively for about a mile before halting. Custer's pretense was that his men needed to eat; however, the usually impetuous "Boy General" also wanted some time to mull over the events that had just transpired. His intuition told him that all was not right, for the comparative figures did not jibe with the events that had just occurred. His vastly outnumbered command, all their zeal notwithstanding, should have had far greater difficulty in dislodging Stuart's blocking force than it did.

What Custer correctly deduced, soon confirmed by shot and shell, was that Stuart's retreat was not a forced withdrawal. Fitz Lee and Stuart had colluded on a plot to trap the Union cavalry. Stuart was to retreat south toward Warrenton, hopefully enticing the enemy to pursue him. This would then expose the Yankees' left flank and rear to Lee's troopers advancing in a northerly direction from Auburn. With Stuart attacking from the front and Lee the rear, the Union troops would be crushed between them. The rebel schemers received unanticipated assistance with their stratagem when Judson Kilpatrick arrived among Custer's dining soldiers. Anxious to continue the pursuit, he chaffed at Custer's delay. Finally, able to contain himself no longer, he put Davies' brigade in motion and ordered Custer when ready to fall in behind. In an odd twist, the very haste that led to trouble for the Kilpatrick-Davies brigade, was offset by Custer's fortuitous dalliance. By lagging behind, he interjected two pivotal variables into the impending battle equation that his adversaries could not have anticipated. One was the absence of half the Union troopers when Stuart sprung the trap, while the other was the blocking position of Custer's brigade that prevented Lee from executing his part of the plan.

Riding with Custer's brigade meant that the 1st Vermont was in the follow-up column. Being positioned there also meant that when the trap was sprung, the regiment was among those on the receiving end of the opening salvos from Fitz Lee's artillery. Simultaneously, with the sound of cannon acting as the prearranged signal, Stuart unleashed his whirlwind upon the unsuspecting Kilpatrick-Davies column. Stuart's cavalry had been strategically placed behind several low ridges, watching and waiting as their adversaries approached along the Gainesville-Warrenton Turnpike. Taken by surprise, caught in the open, and outgunned from the start, the Union force had little choice but to weather the contretemps by giving ground. Lieutenant Stephen Clark of the 1st Vermont described the rapid sequence of events that unfolded when "Stuart turned upon Davis and Kilpatrick, attacking them in front and flank, forcing them back to Buckland, inflicting serious loss, and causing quite a stampede."[37] From the enemy's side of the field, Clark's appraisal of Davies' predicament was closely corroborated by George Baylor, who remembered how "Stuart, hearing the sound of Lee's guns, suddenly turned about, routed the enemy, and ran them back to Buckland, and so the fight was known as the Buckland Races."[38]

Once Kilpatrick, Davies, and the 1st Brigade had unceremoniously departed, Custer, the 1st Vermont, and the rest of the 2nd Brigade were left to fend for themselves. Against Fitz Lee's twelve regiments and one battery Custer could field but five regiments and a single battery. To a fighting general like Custer, this imbalance in numbers was taken more in the vein of a challenge than cause for despair. Initially unaware that the 1st Brigade had already saved itself, part of Custer's intractability stemmed from his belief that his men were protecting the rear of Davies' command. In his troop dispositions, the general placed the Vermonters on the extreme left. Anchoring their line against Broad Run, he kept them mounted in support of his meager artillery. Perhaps sensing that this position was a key to his defenses, Custer stood with the 1st Vermont when the attack commenced. To better protect the guns, Colonel Sawyer deployed two companies as skirmishers. In the face of mounting pressure, "Lieutenant-Colonel Preston, taking Lieutenant Clark of company F ... made a dash into the woods to the left of the guns, and [we] began holloaing [sic], cheering, and firing our revolvers rapidly, as to convey the impression that a heavy flanking party was on Lee's flank."[39] The distraction created by this ruse bought enough time for the artillerymen to limber up their pieces and hurry them across Broad Run.

Saving the cannon alleviated one pressing problem but left another unresolved. The 1st Vermont was still on the wrong side of the river. Cut off from the ford by the rapid arrival of Lee's troopers, Preston and his men gamely awaited the moment when the rebels' focus would shift to them. However, regardless of what hand fate was about to deal, they were a gritty lot who would not surrender without a fight. In fact, according to Stephen Clark, the irrepressible Preston's mantra to his men was that they should always consider themselves "not captured until you are caught."[40] True to this philosophy, while Preston wisely prepared for the worst by pulling his force into a compact front, he at the same time maintained hope by seeking a way across the river.

During this tense waiting period, Private Chapin unintentionally tickled his commander's funny bone. It seemed Chapin's horse was visibly tiring, giving his rider cause to consider fleeing on foot as his only recourse. As the unabashed private recalled the moment, "Lieutenant-Colonel Preston told me I would be too late if I did not look out, [to which] I told him I was looking out, but that it did not help the horse any!"[41] Fortune favored the bold, for the scouting mission discovered an old millrace, which the Vermonters carefully crossed to the security of the far shore. Then, in single file, they picked their way through a scrub pine thicket until reaching the main thoroughfare and the welcome sight of the Sixth Corps. Later, deserved praise came the regiment's way when "Gen. Custer complimented us as coming off the field in the best order although in the rear and consequently under the heaviest fire."[42]

Considering all of the confusion, casualties were moderate among the Vermonters, with but two wounded and two missing. Notable among the losses was Horace Ide. "While we were falling back," Ide stated, "but before we crossed the Run, I was hit by a carbine ball under my right arm."[43] One tough trooper, Sergeant Ide somehow got to an ambulance, which took him to Gainesville where the next day a doctor removed the projectile. After convalescing, Ide returned to the regiment in March of 1864. During his absence, there would be one more major engagement in the Bristoe Campaign. Fought on November 7, the Second Battle of Rappahannock Station was joined when Meade forced a passage over the river in two places. But for the cavalry, the large-scale fighting was done until spring. Though the prospect of well-deserved rest in winter quarters beckoned, a heavy mounted presence was required, as the rebel forces were still active in the area. On the 10th of November, the 1st Vermont began operating out of Stevensburg, the site of their eventual winter cantonment, which was a forward position only five miles north of the Rapidan.

Throughout the late fall, the regiment guarded various fords. Each rotation required 162 men. Adherence to the three-days-on, three-days-off pattern of duty assignments was taxing. Discomfort was a given, for regardless of the elements a posture of vigilance had to be maintained. Frequent rain and low temperatures made the monotonous time spent in the saddle an ordeal. Early January saw the entire nation gripped in a record-breaking freeze; however, as one trooper rationalized, "The weather is getting quite cold, but we have lived in Vermont."[44] The sanctity of a given day of course did not matter, for the ever-present enemy did not adjust his schedule to accommodate holiday observances. Even Thanksgiving, November 26, 1863, required a presence on the picket line. "Would you like to know how the boys of the division spent their time on Thanksgiving Day?" asked one Vermonter in a letter home.[45] He then went on to share their experience. It was started by a predawn call to "Boots and Saddles," followed by a day of demonstrations and skirmishing at Morton's Ford, and capped off with a night of picket duty. With so many being young and two full years removed from Vermont, the fact that their thoughts drifted back to the Green Mountains should surprise no one. "Many were the 'wishes' and 'wonders' that were made during that day, such as 'I wish I could be home to-day' and 'I wonder where we shall be *next* Thanksgiving Day' and other similar experiences" crossed the mind and lips of many a trooper as everyone "had ample time to feast our imagination upon the 'good things' and merry times to be had on a Thanksgiving day in old Vermont, whilst we were 'standing vidette' during the long hours of the night."[46] Beyond the physical discomfort that often accompanied guarding the fords, danger went hand in hand with the territory. Part of the peril derived from a mismatch in weaponry, for, as Major Wells pointed out, "it is not at all pleasant to picket with pistols against infantry with rifles."[47] This imbalance motivated Wells to try to replace the regiment's dwindling supply of seven-round Sharps carbines with nine-shot Spencer models. Yet, though frequently in harm's way, the 1st Vermont fortuitously recorded no battle deaths from Brandy Station in October 1863 until March 1864 and the disastrous Kilpatrick-Dahlgren Raid.

In keeping with established practice, the cavalry bore the brunt of picket and patrol duties along the Rapidan. According to one loyal trooper, the men did not blanch at these obligations because "we know we are the vanguard of the nation, looking daily upon its foes across the cold, turbid Rapidan, and, although our toes are frostbitten, and our bodies are chilled in the cold, frosty winds, the spirit of the soldier is not chilled, nor does he complain of the hardships."[48]

Helping to occasionally ease the strain of being a vidette was the knowledge that sightings of enemy troops did not always result in hostile action, due to gentlemen's agreements on the part of the guards. These impromptu ceasefires were a time-honored tradition among pickets. Illustrative of these unwritten pacts, earlier that fall, Captain Frank Ray told of "sitting on a hard tack box under a big oak tree on the bank of the Rappahannock, while on the opposite bank can be seen numerous squads of Johnny Rebs, but they are quite friendly and we have no picket firing."[49] Vigilance was nevertheless an important virtue, though the dangers to guard against did not always come in human form. Frank Dyo of Company H learned of one the hard way. One cold January night, while he slept by a fire among the picket reserves, "his pants took fire at the bottom and before it could be extinguished the right calf of his right leg was badly burned."[50]

Still, with fall giving way to winter, the focus gradually shifted from martial activities to the more sedentary pursuits accompanying life in stationary quarters. The camp was on a plain amidst a grove of pines, one-half mile from Stevensburg. Newly minted Private Eri Woodbury visualized the hapless hamlet as having once been "quite a thriving place but now little is to be seen save the soldiers quarters, and one or two buildings occupied by officers: all the rest destroyed by the troops either wantonly or for materials of which to build winter quarters."[51] Since Woodbury had just arrived from Derby Line, where he had been the headmaster of a school, his ties to Vermont were only recently severed. But for many boys who had not seen their home state for over a score of months, a welcomed reminder of Vermont was provided by the picturesque vista of nearby mountains. To one soldier this sight would come to be most pleasing, with "the snow covered peaks of the Blue Ridge, which are only a few miles distant from our camp, look[ing] shiningly grand as the rays of ... sun [fell] upon ... their sloping, ragged, and half-timbered sides."[52]

As for the rank and file, when they were not on duty at the front, their lives were occupied with various endeavors. In an official capacity, the men participated in periodic inspections, including a memorable "Grand Review" of the entire 2nd Corps in February attended by President Lincoln and his cabinet. For some, like Trooper Silas Worthing, whatever pageantry the event held was severely dampened and turned into an uncomfortable ordeal because "we had to sit on our horses from 9 in the morning till 4 in the afternoon without anything to eat all the time."[53] A second "Grand Review," this one on March 23 before General Grant, was especially memorable for Eri Woodbury on account of two aesthetically appealing occurrences, one before and one during the inspection. Prior to the event, each trooper had to have his "hair and beard neatly cut and trimmed; while during the review, the ground was blanketed with a foot of wet snow.[54] When their time was their own, considerable effort was expended on fixing up their huts, making themselves comfortable against the vagaries of the Virginia winter. December 16 witnessed a snowfall, January 27 was blessed with "warm, May-like weather," and February 17 registered as "the coldest day of winter."[55] The regiment took such pains to maintain the appearance of its camp that "General Custer used to send the officers of some of his other regiments to see it, as an example of neatness and good order."[56]

Once the men had settled into their cabins, the rhythm of camp life gradually established itself. When not picketing, the men were "drilled both on horse and on foot, so as to be ready for the upcoming campaign."[57] When off duty, one of their favorite pastimes was plumbing the depths of the rumor mill, which featured hot topics like the formation of a new regiment and who deserved to be its new commander. The food rations and weather conditions, about which soldiers normally groused, had both been very passable and thus had not drawn much attention. In like manner, the overall health of the men was excellent, with but forty-two reported sick during the entire month of December. One area that did receive more than a passing notice, however, was the influx of new recruits. Since these novices would soon be riding at their sides in battle, veteran soldiers took a keen interest in the fresh faces appearing in their midst. In one appraiser's candid assessment of his new comrades, "green men, from the Green Mountain State, mounted on green horses, make rather a green appearance for the first few days after arriving in camp."[58] In spite of how wet behind the ears the new boys appeared, they nevertheless exhibited promise for the future. "I am very happy to say," one trooper offered, "that better men never stood in the ranks than the last four hundred that joined the Regiment. Wherever we strike next summer *tyranny* will tremble."[59]

On their part, the recent additions did their best to adapt to a way of life far different from any they had previously known. A November recruit, Henry Jerdo, reassured his folks at the end of January that he was "as fat as ever and like soldiering better and better every day."[60] To show his parents how self-reliant, industrious, and responsible he had become, Silas Worthing, a cavalryman only since late December, proudly wrote home how he had spent a mid–February Sunday: "In the first place, I got up and washed my hands and face, in the next I ate breakfast, and then went on inspection which lasted about half an hour, then I took the coffee pot and went down in the woods to a ditch and washed my shirt, two pairs of stockings, and a hand 'snot-rag.' Then I came up to my tent, slicked up, blackened my boots, and brushed my clothes with the same brush, which was a currycomb. Then I went to meeting, and heard a man from my native state preach."[61] For another new recruit, George McIvor, his correspondence home on February 2 was as much of a shocker to his family as it was a release of pent-up emotions for the young soldier. He had apparently left home on the pretense of taking a trip, telling his folks that he would contact them at his journey's conclusion. What the letter revealed was that the boy's journey had ended at a recruiting office: "I have enlisted and I sup-pose that you will think me very foolish for so doing.... I have enlisted in the First Vermont Cavalry, Co. H, so I shall not have to walk. I chose it before carrying a nap sack."[62] Like so many of his youthful compatriots, he knew that his decision to break the bonds and leave weighed heaviest on the one person in the world who held him most dear. He addressed this inevitable fact of life head-on when he wrote: "I suppose that mother will fret, but she must content herself [for] she must not expect to keep her boys in the same old cottage."[63]

Not every trooper remem-

At winter quarters near Brandy Station during the winter of 1863-1864, the troopers knew how to make themselves at home, building comfortable huts at the expense of denuding the local woodlands (Library of Congress).

bered the winter at Stevensburg as fondly as Privates Worthing, Jerdo, and McIvor. For the proud, proper, and erudite Eri Woodbury, his conversion from civilian to soldier was not without its appropriate learning curve. For this eager Dartmouth College graduate, having the mental faculties to earn a bachelor's degree did not translate smoothly to an easy mastery of riding skills. In one of his first attempts, Woodbury was "riding his horse to water, with only a halter, [when] he ran off: but I rode as far as he ran."[64] While this embarrassment might not have been evident to an onlooker, the newcomer's faux pas of the next day was painfully public: "In mounting a horse for water today, while a couple of officers were looking on, I sprang and land[ed] clear on the other side in the mud."[65] Finding himself prostrate and sullied had to have been as deflating to Woodbury's ego as it was entertaining to those who saw the pratfall. Yet, in spite of these early setbacks, Woodbury gamely stayed the course. By year's end, he had been promoted up through the ranks to lieutenant, an indication that the schoolmaster had learned his lessons well.

Another for whom the winter months had proven none too pleasant was James McMahon. Though he could later look back on his experience as sobering, it was his own poor judgment that caused the personal travail that he underwent. Reenlisting in the 1st Vermont as a "Veteran Volunteer," with its accompanying bounty and paid trip home, should have been a source of joy. Undoubtedly, as the transplanted Irish farmer rode the rails to his residence in Wisconsin, thoughts of how he would spend his thirty-five day furlough occupied his mind. But inexplicably, the thirty-five days ballooned to sixty-two before the tardy soldier found his way back to Virginia. Not surprisingly, the ensuing court-martial found him "guilty," and McMahon was "returned to duty with a 27 day stoppage in pay for being AWOL."[66] For a time, the trooper was relegated to dismounted duty and served as a train guard. In time, Private McMahon returned to mounted service, and, by virtue of a severe hip wound taken at Cedar Creek, courageously won back the good graces from which he had fallen.

Perhaps the cause of undesirable behavior displayed by some was having too much time on their hands. Maybe the root of evil was being housed in tight quarters within the limited confines of the camp. Whatever the reasons, the court-martial boards were kept busy meting out discipline to many others in addition to James McMahon.

One such recipient was another feisty Irishman named Morte Kearce. Buoyed by the insolence of youth, the nineteen-year-old trooper let his mouth get the best of him. While clothing was being distributed to his company, Kearce addressed one of his commanders with a disrespectful display of language. "I don't want these [pants]," shouted the aroused soldier, "unless I can have a pair of boots and by Jesus Christ you may stick them in your damned ass!"[67] With those words, the eyebrows of Lieutenant Gilbert Stewart, to whom the barrage was directed, as well as those of Captain Frank Ray, Sergeant Parker Hall, and Corporal Joseph Farnum, who also heard them, must have collectively arched. With such stellar witnesses to confirm the appropriateness of the three charges lodged against him, deciding upon Private Kearce's guilt was a perfunctory act. He was sentenced to wear what is known as the "barrel jacket" four hours each day, for four consecutive days in some conspicuous place within the limits of the camp, and following that he was put to hard labor for a period of twenty-one days.

As disconcerting as these incidents were, at least McMahon and Kearce were all afforded second chances to write happy endings to their respective war records. But for a truly heartbreaking story with no uplifting denouement, one need look no farther than the abbreviated service of John Armstrong. An eighteen-year-old farm boy from East

Berkshire, Vermont, he eagerly enlisted on December 14, 1863, and was assigned to Company C. On his way to the front, he was stricken on January 6, confined to a Washington hospital, and died there of pneumonia on January 29. In little more than a month, the hopes and dreams of a young boy had been abruptly terminated. Chaplain Samuel Cummings, at the young trooper's side until the end, shared those final moments in a letter addressed "To the Friends of John S. Armstrong": "I asked him if I should pray with him, [and he] said 'yes.' As I closed, he said 'I thank you,' and then said 'I hope to meet you and all in this tent in heaven with Jesus, and Elizabeth and Joseph.' Said I, 'have you a sister named Elizabeth'? He replied 'no,' but Elizabeth and Joseph are in heaven. These were nearly his last words, I think. After this he remarked, 'I am not dead. I shall get up again.' Then he passed away."[68] Amid the callousness of war, the good chaplain arranged to have a bedside service conducted before the body was removed for burial. At home in Vermont, already a widow of fifteen years' duration, Eliza Armstrong now had to bear the shock of losing her only child, though her overwhelming grief was somewhat assuaged when "she succeeded, through the assistance of friends, in getting his body brought home [so that] he now lies in the graveyard in this village."[69]

This humane retrieval, especially from a far-flung place, was by no means easy or cheap. Since trains provided transportation to or near most locations, primary shipping arrangements had to be made through the railroad. Before those wheels could be set in motion, however, funding for the process had to be taken into account. Total cost of disinterring the corpse from a temporary grave, embalming the body, providing an outside shipping case, delivering the crate to the station, transshipping the box to Vermont, and then buying a coffin was in the neighborhood of $65 to $75. A modest sum by today's standards, such an unexpected expense was often beyond the means of many families, regardless of how desperate they may have been to bring a loved one home for his final rest.

Like so many of the Civil War's youthful combatants, premature death robbed John Armstrong of his future and his country of a willing soldier. But the prospects of dying young did not deter recruits from coming to Stevensburg that winter of '63–'64. Beyond the fact that these replacements would fill gaps in the ranks, their arrival coincided with a pivotal period in the regiment's history. Anticipating that the war still had more than a year to go before final victory was achieved, the Federal government wanted to preserve as much of the experienced nucleus of its existing fighting forces as possible. Running counter to this desire was the fact that many regiments, including the 1st Vermont, would see their three-year enlistments expire in the fall of 1864. Convincing these troops to remain in the service was deemed critical. Their continued presence would not only keep the ranks populated with battle-hardened veterans but also provide important role models for inexperienced recruits. Not wanting to wait until the last minute, the push to reenroll these seasoned men was begun with sufficient lead time. Through the provisions of General Orders 191, 370, and 450, issued by the War Department beginning in June of 1863, "The offer was made to the veteran troops of the Union of a handsome bounty and a long furlough, if they would enlist for a new term; and all such were to be honorably denominated 'The Veterans.'"[70] As an outward symbol of the government's thanks, those who stepped forward were allowed to wear a special chevron-shaped sleeve patch. According to the plan, if three-fourths of a regiment or a company reenlisted, then they would be allowed to return home at government expense to reorganize and recruit.

Initially, the Vermont Cavalry appeared willing to commit. Upon orders from the

War Department, company commanders were required to take a straw poll of their men to determine the prospects among them for remaining. In mid–December, "The matter was brought before the men in each company, and before night three-fourths of those 'having less than a year to serve' pledged themselves to re-enlist."[71] The good news was quickly passed on to headquarters. Unfortunately, that moment in time was the high point for the 1st Vermont on the subject of reenlistment. Shortly thereafter, the Civil War's version of a World War II "snafu" interjected itself. First the realization hit that no one in the regiment had been appointed to the position of "recruiting officer." This glitch was quickly remedied, with Lieutenant John Williamson of Company K drawing the assignment. Then the discovery was made that the appropriate blank forms were nowhere to be found, so a requisition to Washington was immediately dispatched. In the three-day interim before the forms arrived, General Meade declared that further troops could not be spared for furloughs. The front-line ranks were getting too thin. Having watched Michigan and New York troops march joyously off for home, Meade's edict hit the Vermonters hard. William Wells noted that many of his men were "a bit bitter that [their] Vermont regiment does not get clearance to go home while other regiments do."[72]

An attempt was made to put together a petition to Congress. The document's purpose was to plead the 1st Vermont's case and pledge that three-quarters of the regiment were willing to reenlist, but only on the condition that the unit's reorganization and recruitment be allowed to proceed at home. However, by this time, a significant downward mood swing had occurred among the veterans, forestalling and then terminating any attempt to secure the necessary support. In the end, the number who chose to stay on was disappointing, with just 175 men stepping forward to re-up, the preponderance of signers coming from Companies E, F, and G. Though only eighteen officers and men of Company B chose to extend their enlistments, counted among the faithful were the Rogers brothers and their good friends Simon Dufur and Samuel Ufford.

Though it was disheartening that more veterans had not opted to stay, the basic manpower shortage was easily overcome by the fruitful recruiting efforts of Sawyer and his entourage in Vermont, their persistent efforts bringing in over 400 fresh faces. By the end of February, the regiment was up to its full strength of 1250 troopers. Training took on an air of urgency as the first harbingers of spring began to manifest themselves. The troopers' spirits rose as they eagerly anticipated the prospects of ending the war in the upcoming year — and going home not on a furlough but to be mustered out.

24

The Kilpatrick-Dahlgren Raid
Ride to Disaster

After a tranquil winter, spring arrived explosively. If any troopers were mildly surprised at how early in the season a raid was being mounted, then they must have been genuinely shocked at the magnitude of its objectives. The ambitious plan called for 4,000 riders to advance against Richmond, where thousands of prisoners awaited repatriation. Along the way, targets of opportunity were to be destroyed and amnesty leaflets distributed. At best, the incursion was a long shot, predicated upon boldness and the enemy's weaknesses at the points of attack. Supporters saw the scheme as daring, while critics labeled the venture harebrained.

Regardless of the viewpoint taken, few doubted that Judson Kilpatrick lacked sufficient chutzpah; however, there were growing concerns over his command capabilities. Quick to engage, he did not always achieve victory. By the spring of 1864, the general's star was fading. A successful raid could provide just the needed burnishing! Initially, the permission he sought was denied by Pleasonton and gained only cursory acknowledgement from Meade. But higher-ups in Washington perceived an opportunity. In a case of mutual back-scratching, they discovered a means to inform the Southern populace of the president's generous surrender offer, while Kilpatrick had his career-boosting opportunity.

Regardless of how slim the chances for success, the raid was set for February 28, 1864. Wintering in rebel territory made security difficult—not that the raid had ever been effectively cloaked in secrecy. In a letter dated "February 3, 1864," Mark Rogers, whose rank of sergeant made him far removed from the seat of power, was still able to share with his parents the news about "some talk of our cavalry Division to make a raid soon."[1] After Kilpatrick's meeting with the president on February 12, rumor of the proposed enterprise made the rounds of the capital. The knowledge of an impending raid even found its way to Richmond, where local papers openly speculated about such a venture! Soon, the expedition gained momentum. Trooper Simon Dufur vividly remembered the 26th, for each soldier was issued five days' rations, sixty rounds, and a day's forage. Excited as they were about a mission after a winter of inactivity, the potential danger was not lost on the men, Dufur noting that "we did not consider this would be a pleasure party of any means."[2] On February 27, Kilpatrick was given the final go-ahead. As darkness fell the next day, the troops were ready. Weapons had been checked, overcoats donned, and horses bridled and saddled. At 10:00 P.M., the long column moved out, led by Colonel Dahlgren and his picked detachment of 500 men. The forced march had

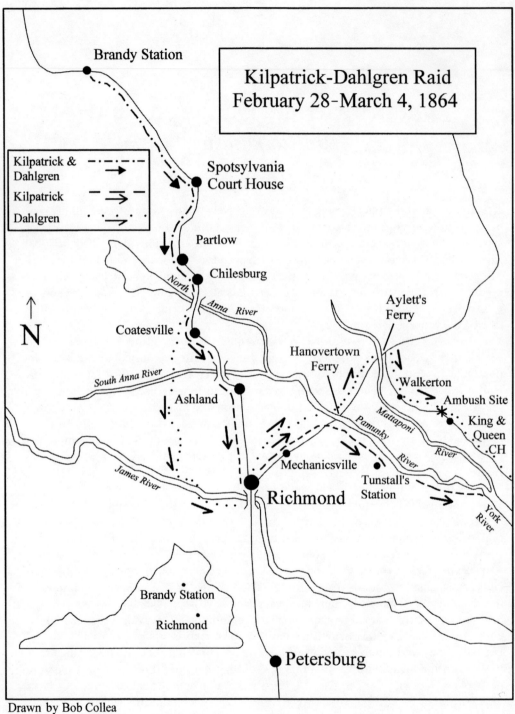

Drawn by Bob Collea

begun. The clock was ticking away the thirty-six hours to the raiders' arrival at dual jumping off points for the final investment of Richmond.

Crossing the Rapidan at Ely's Ford, quick work was made of an unsuspecting Confederate picket post. With the way open, the raiders disappeared into the night. Keeping the fast-moving column closed up was difficult, for darkness negated visual contact. Often "the sound of hoofs in front was the only guide as to the direction to be taken."[3] A wrong turn, resulting in separation from the main body, was a nagging fear. "We marched all the rest of the night at a gallop and a trot," one Vermonter later shared with his father, "and in the morning stopped a quarter of an hour to eat our hardtack and coffee."[4] Pressing on, the raiding party passed through Spotsylvania Court House around 8:00 A.M. Just beyond, Dahlgren's riders proceeded to break from the main column and veer off to attack Richmond from the south, leaving General Kilpatrick's force headed directly for the city's northern approaches. This division of the raiding party also meant a split in the 1st Vermont's ranks, as some 100 men from Companies G and K under Captain Frank Ray accompanied Dahlgren. The remaining squadrons under Addison Preston stayed with the main body.

Dahlgren's intended route was south — arcing off to the west of Kilpatrick's more direct path — skirting Richmond before turning north toward the city's less heavily fortified underbelly. Following the split, Dahlgren's column went to Frederick's Hall Station on the Virginia Central Railroad and then over the South Anna River, eight miles east of Goochland on the James River. There, twenty miles from Richmond, he expected to cross the waterway, proceed along the south side of the James, and take a position before one of Richmond's main bridges. Then, at 10:00 A.M., Tuesday, March 1, his troopers would invest the city, liberate the prisoners on Belle Isle, and then link up with Kilpatrick's column, which should have successfully penetrated Richmond's defenses from the north.

Doing his part, General Kilpatrick crossed the Po and South Anna rivers. After taking Beaver Dam Station on the Virginia Central, his force traversed the Chickahominy River and struck the Brooke Turnpike, three-and-a-half miles north of Richmond. Subsequently, via this main artery, his raiders would drive southeast through the city's defenses, anticipating a union with Dahlgren. While there was no guaranteed way to synchronize movements, the intent was for the two attacks to occur as simultaneously as possible. Kilpatrick had maneuvered his men into position almost to the hour intended: ten o'clock in the morning of March 1, 1864. Unfortunately, the corresponding trek for Dahlgren's force had not unfolded as smoothly. In fact, this prong of the raid never would arrive at its intended jumping-off point, necessitating a change on the fly from the original route.

For the ill-fated Dahlgren, inaccurate intelligence about suitable river crossings was his undoing. On the morning of March 1, the long-suffering riders halted to refresh themselves, at least to the extent that a cup of coffee and an hour's sleep could accomplish. "But our dreams were not very pleasant," reported one Vermonter, "because of the rain that was falling in our faces, and the frost that was troubling our feet."[5] That same rain helped foil Dahlgren's attempts to breach the James, creating spring freshets that deepened the river and obliterated the fords; however, regardless of nature's intrusion, a local guide paid dearly for his inability to find a suitable crossing point. After a promised ford did not materialize at Dover Mills, "The colonel sent for the fellow who had lied to him, and when he was brought to the head of the column, he served him as he said he would, if he lied, so the wretch was hung by the neck until he was dead."[6] Playing support roles in this swift act of military justice were two Vermont troopers. To Edgar Sloan went the task of tying the doomed guide's hands behind his back while John Shea was busy affixing the noose to a suitable overhead limb.

Imparting greater urgency to the moment, Kilpatrick's artillery could be heard booming in the distance. Abandoning the original plan, Dahlgren improvised. First, though he turned his march back toward Richmond, it was on the wrong side of the river, in an east-southeasterly rather than a northerly direction, and at the incorrect time of day. As he improvised, the young colonel found opposition mounting quickly. Twice along the way militia forces were engaged. The first encounter occurred just as darkness was descending on the scene, perhaps one mile inside the outer line of fortifications. One Vermonter's lasting impression of the skirmish was of "the fire from the revolvers and carbines making it light enough to see the retreating rebels."[7] Pushing forward, the enemy was driven back over two miles. But, as the gaslights of the city beckoned in the distance, a third, formidable line was discovered. Extending beyond the Union force on both flanks, there was no way for Dahlgren to turn this adversaries' position. His only option was immediate withdrawal.

Unfortunately, not every Vermonter who had ridden in was leaving. Owing to the encroaching darkness and the fast-paced action, those who fell had to be left behind. Alexis Snow was one who went down, suffering an extremely painful and rather ignominious wound in the process. "The horse which I rode was shot and killed by the rebels," Snow later recounted, "[and] when he fell, he fell upon me and I was partly under him as I could not release myself and fell in such a way as to severely injure one of my testicles."[8] Since his arm was injured too, all that the frustrated trooper could do was lie pinned on the field, stoically contemplating his fate. A pair of rescuers soon arrived, though their tenderness left room for improvement. Rather than question their prisoner as to the nature of any injuries, two Confederates, "instead of raising the horse ... took hold of and dragged me from under the horse and that pulled the cords in my testicles all apart."[9] Much to his discomfort, Snow received no medical attention. After making the prison tour from Pemberton to Bell Isle to Andersonville, Snow's final stop was Savannah prior to his exchange in January. Although he returned to the regiment, limited duty was all that he was able to perform. But compared to the lot of John DeLaney, Snow got off relatively easy.

Another of the January greenhorns who had barely arrived at Stevensburg was John Delaney. Assigned to Company G, he rode with Dahlgren's detachment. Somewhere in the dark before the Richmond fortifications, DeLaney was struck by a minie ball in the right side of his head. The crashing blow "carried away a section of the skull four inches long and one inch wide, exposing his brain and rendering him for a time perfectly senseless."[10] In addition, he suffered internal injuries from the ensuing tumble he took from his horse; regrettably, these could not be immediately addressed as he spent seven weeks unable to communicate because of his comatose condition. Once restored to consciousness, an exchange was quickly arranged. Hospitalization dramatically improved his condition, though not before his head was trepanned to relieve swelling. After six more weeks of treatment and an extended furlough, he returned to the regiment in a severely weakened condition. While the wound had healed, an angry gash remained sore and tender to the touch.

Though he stayed on the Company G's roll until the end of hostilities, DeLaney was never again able to either live up to or engage in the daily rigors comprising a cavalryman's duties. Furthermore, his life after the war was adversely affected by the injury. A painter before the conflict, he could no longer ply his trade outside due to bouts of dizziness and extreme sensitivity to sunlight. It can only be surmised that his semi-invalided condition, rendering him only a shadow of a once robust man, had a negative effect on his marriage. His wife eventually took in a male boarder who had the audacity to tell DeLaney to get out if he did not like the arrangement! After Mrs. DeLaney threatened to kill him, the enfeebled old warrior elected to leave the untenable situation, relocating from Arlington to Ruppert, Vermont. However, the soap opera does not end there. Even though Delaney honored his financial obligation to support his children, his estranged wife tried to claim a piece of his pension pie. Thwarted by the pension bureau, she tried again after her husband passed away in 1916. But John DeLaney got one last laugh from the grave when her second appeal, as the "grieving widow," was denied again.

With losses mounting and forward progress at a standstill, Dahlgren's goal to free the Union prisoners was doomed. The young colonel's focus had now become the preservation of his force. To make matters worse, Dahlgren and a small, forty-man detachment became separated from the rest of his command. Weather conditions were horrendous, with the bent-over riders pelted by a mixture of sleet, snow, and rain. The inky blackness and the howling wind made keeping the column together a challenge. While Dahlgren's contingent retraced its tracks to the northwest, Captain John Mitchell of the 2nd New York warily led the larger party in search of Kilpatrick. The going was slow, ending for the night in the safe confines of a swamp. "We were not allowed to build a fire — although it was snowing —," one Vermont veteran reported, "not even to speak louder than in a whisper; for the rebels were passing in force just a few rods from us."[11] At dawn, the wandering troopers started out again, periodically dodging enemy infantry and cavalry units. Their perseverance was eventually rewarded when the weary column stumbled upon Kilpatrick's troopers around 5:30 P.M. The reunion came at Tunstall's Station on the Pamunkey River.

Finding Kilpatrick at this unexpected location was evidence that his commander's fortunes had fared no better than Dahlgren's. What Mitchell could not yet have known was how close Kilpatrick came to his objective, followed by how quickly the general subsequently abandoned his portion of the plan. Initially, all had progressed smoothly for Kilpatrick's force. After leaving Stevensburg on the 28th of February, one Vermonter recalled they had "marched till eleven o'clock the second day [February 29] without halting, then we halted just long enough to feed and make coffee."[12] Etched in Private Phineas Worthern's memory were the physical demands of marching "all day and all the next night in the rain pouring all of the time ... and we hadn't had a wink of sleep, only what we got on our horses in that time, and it was mighty hard work to keep our eyes open I tell you."[13]

According to schedule, they got inside the undefended outer ring of the city's defenses and approached the intermediate line. The significance of the moment was not lost on troopers who had ridden a day-and-a-half, virtually nonstop, to gain this vantage point. "As the spires and houses of the city came in view, cheer upon cheer went up from our men."[14] Regrettably, such elation was short-lived. Waiting ahead, a two-gun battery straddled the turnpike, ready to contest any further progress. Kilpatrick stopped the advance. The column was allowed to dismount, tend to the horses, and satisfy itself with quickly boiled pots of coffee. Horace Ide interpreted this brief respite as having a deeper meaning, "their cool being shown by their quietly stopping two hours 'to refresh men and horses' within three miles of the rebel capital, and under the guns of its fortifications."[15]

Meanwhile counter-battery fire was initiated against the Confederates. The ensuing artillery duel was whimsically detailed by an observing Vermont trooper who, while sipping his warm brew, watched as "old 'Kil' was down with his battery sending messengers to old Jeff that his Yankee boys had come down to see him, and would like to come and take tea with him. Jeff sent back saying that he couldn't see the point, that he wasn't prepared for any surprise party and couldn't accommodate them."[16] Before long, from the embrasures of the enemy works ahead, "other guns, to the number of twelve to fifteen, soon showed themselves. These guns varied in size from six to thirty-two pounders."[17] Upping the ante in return, elements of the raiding force were dismounted and sent ahead to probe the Confederate fortifications. Amidst the uncertainty created by the stubborn opposition, distant train whistles could be heard. Impossible to confirm but too foreboding to ignore, these piecing shrieks gave rise to the fear of what they might represent: rebel troops being hastened to the front as saviors of the capital. The unexpected resistance immediately in their path, coupled with seasoned troops on the way, caused Kilpatrick to waver. Whatever momentum his troops once had was by now dissipated. At that moment, Richmond might as well have been a hundred miles away, for this was as close as the raiders would get.

Even though his losses were negligible, Kilpatrick concluded that to remain at the gates of Richmond any longer was inviting disaster. Already known as "Kill-Cavalry" for his inclination to send troops into battle, on this occasion he held back from ordering another hell-for-leather charge. Perched astride the turnpike, Sawyer's brigade sat ready to do his bidding. Only a bugle call separated this motionless column from a thundering host. Nevertheless, orders were reluctantly issued to depart. The men were disappointed, for they had ridden long and endured much to no apparent avail. In fact, the attack's abandonment came as a shock to most of the troopers. Perhaps the 6th Michigan's James Kidd best evoked a common feeling: "That a dash into the city, or at least an attempt would be made nobody doubted. Anything short of that would be farcical, and the expedition that set out big with promise would be fated to return barren of results. The good beginning was worthy of a better ending than that."[18]

Much chagrined, Kilpatrick's long column snaked around Richmond to the northeast and crossed the Chickahominy River via Meadow Bridge. A mile past the span, the weary men camped along the road between Atlee's Station to the northwest and Mechanicsville to the southeast. Whatever comfort there was it was taken from no longer being under fire or in the saddle, for a sleet storm doused any campfires that had been coaxed from wet wood and deprived men soaked to the skin and chilled to the bone of even the minimal pleasure in a hot cup of coffee.

But at least they were out of harm's way for now, which was more than could be said for Colonel Dahlgren's command. Since separating from Mitchell, Dahlgren had continued northeast, crossing the Chickahominy at Hungary Station. However, instead of veering to the southeast along the southern bank of the Pamunkey, Dahlgren continued to the northeast over not only that river but the Mattaponi as well. The two crossings served to put both waterways and another twenty miles between his force and the route to down the Yorktown Peninsula being traveled by Judson Kilpatrick. Assailed by the same storm that was making life miserable for friend and foe alike, Dahlgren was still plagued by

No officer possessed more dash and daring than young Ulric Dahlgren, but, after first losing his leg at the battle of Hagerstown, he gave his life on a Virginia backroad trying to escape the enemy's clutches after a Federal raid deep into rebel territory had to be aborted (*Harper's Weekly*).

inadequate directions. Panic had not yet manifested itself, though the thought must have begun dawning on many that the existing situation was none too good. Now, marching parallel to the Mattaponi in a southeasterly direction, the doomed column proceeded along the Stevensville Road. Then, after the rear guard was attacked, the retreating Federals made a turn toward the river. Finally, in spite of the urgent need to flee, fatigue and hunger became paramount. A halt was called, and the first food prepared in thirty-six hours was eaten, followed by as much rest as could be stolen in the midst of a raging storm.

After several hours, still weary bodies protested as they were forced onto cold, wet saddles. With a mounting sense of desperation, the search for safety continued. Before long, the day's heightened tensions focused ahead to Mantapike Hill near Walkerton. Carefully negotiating the muddy, slippery highway, a small advanced guard warily approached a fork in the road. Accompanying them were Colonel Dahlgren and several other officers. As they advanced, a solitary figure materialized in the barricaded road before them. Dahlgren approached the man, but his attempt to quiz him quickly morphed into a deadly attack once the stranger's rebel identity was exposed. But the victim of the ensuing bloodshed was not the brazen Confederate decoy but rather the ill-starred Yankee colonel. Dahlgren's pistol had no sooner misfired than the woods on both sides of the road spewed forth a hail of lead. Concealed in the underbrush were over 150 rebels. The brief but meteoric career of Ulric Dahlgren was over in the instant it took his bullet-riddled body to topple into the muck. Others in the party were also hit, but only Dahlgren perished. Short of ammunition and leaderless, the seventy-odd remaining raiders gathered on the edge of a nearby field to contemplate their predicament. Meanwhile, their adversaries prudently awaited the light of day to pursue any further action.

Functioning as an organized band ceased at this point. The only option remaining for the bedraggled party was the soldiers' duty to avoid capture. On foot and in small groups, forty die-hards tried to escape. In this mad scramble, they no longer resembled the proud legion that had confidently sallied forth from Stevensburg. The remainder of the broken force, too tired and dispirited to put up one last effort to avoid a prison camp, just sat and waited for dawn and captivity. A fortunate few made their way to the York River where they were rescued by a friendly gunboat. The bulk of those who fled, while at least having the satisfaction of forcing an aggravated enemy to chase them down, nevertheless wound up as POWs.

As Dahlgren's command disintegrated, Kilpatrick's troopers had their own harrowing experience. Though their ultimate fate was collectively much more palatable, the overall denouement embodied the same dismal failure. After they had crossed the Chickahominy and halted, Kilpatrick's men were still only two miles from Richmond. With the enemy's attention concentrated to the north and west, the general entertained thoughts of sending a contingent sweeping in from the northeast, angling down the lightly guarded Mechanicsville Road. It was almost as if he could not bear to leave without one last grasp at the brass ring. They might enter, free the prisoners at Libby, capture Jefferson Davis, and leave before pursuit could be mounted. Regardless of any scant chance this jerry-rigged scheme ever had of succeeding, one measure taken by Kilpatrick that could have contributed heavily to victory was his choice of a leader, the esteemed Addison Preston. "The name of Preston was a guarantee," a fellow officer observed, "that the dash, if made at all, would be bravely led."[19] Five hundred men were to accompany Preston, with a matching number going in under Major Constantine Taylor of the 1st Maine. Kilpatrick would hold the retreat route open with the remainder of his command. The twin sorties were to attack at 2:00 A.M. But for reasons beyond Kilpatrick's control, the reconstituted raid never got off the ground.

In the opinion of Colonel Kidd, this turn of events was just as well, "for if Preston had started, it would have been with the determination to succeed or lose his life in the adventure. That was his reputation and character as a soldier."[20] That the early morning attack plan became moot was not due to a sudden lack of nerve or a reevaluation of its sensibility. Instead, its abandonment resulted from a simpler rationale: before Kilpatrick could mount his strike, the enemy attacked him! A Vermont trooper in Company I described how events unfolded: at about 11:00 P.M., "they attacked us, threw shells in around our campfires that made us bustle out of reach."[21] From his limited perspective, what the observer referenced was a bold night attack by 300 of Wade Hampton's troopers. They first struck the encamped 7th Michigan at Atlee's Station and sent them packing into the night. Rolling up this regiment panicked other, successive units strung out along the road until the entire force was sent frantically reeling. At the initial onslaught, the 1st Vermont stood its ground, momentarily halting the rebels. Private Worthern told how he was awakened "by [the] firing of musketry which was 'rattle de-bang' in every direction. The men were drawn up in line out in the field, but by the time we were all out the firing was still so the Colonel told us to go sleep."[22] Barely ten minutes later, Worthern was again jolted awake by a "boom, whiz, crack and a shell [striking] about 2 rods over my head, right in a camp fire Then the shells and grape and canister [and] solid shot began to come pretty fast."[23] After riding out into the field, he could find neither his company nor his regiment. So "I went with the first crowd I came up with and stayed the rest of the night with a lieutenant and sergeant of the 5th Michigan who treated me like gentlemen and shared their hardtack and coffee with me..."[24] While Private Worthern looked for friendly faces, Simon Dufur was in the thick of the fight. "After we had fired eight or ten rounds, in rapid succession," Trooper Dufur recalled, "the order was given by Col. Preston, 'Every man to his horse, and lead into the line in the open field to the rear.'"[25] After several minutes of shooting, the regiment departed in a column of fours.

One of the saving graces for many Yankee troopers that confusing night was that they were sleeping under arms. For most, this meant that their horses' reins were affixed to their bodies, often a wrist. In the event of a surprise attack, this precaution insured that no one would have to fumble around, half awake in the darkness, seeking his horse. That is, unless your name was Simon Dufur, Company B of the 1st Vermont. Dufur and his tentmate Horace Stetson, both close comrades of the Rogers brothers, had managed to get some much-needed rest on a bed fashioned from their rubber blankets. Heedless of the icy precipitation falling on them, the exhausted men were quickly asleep. The contributing factor to the ease with which they dozed off was identified as being extreme drowsiness, since "all the sleep that we had obtained during the past forty-eight hours, was while riding in the ranks with our heads resting upon the blankets that were rolled and strapped to the front of our saddles."[26]

Aroused by Hampton's incoming artillery rounds, Sergeant Dufur began searching for his horse, located only after several minutes of stumbling about in the darkness. This momentary triumph proved to be the high point of Dufur's evening. For the next several hours, his luck steadily deserted him. No sooner did he join the dismounted firing line than his horse ran off. Shortly thereafter, he borrowed another from an officer who had picked up an extra mount. Before long, an exploding artillery shell startled the animal, causing it to shy away, dump Dufur abruptly to the ground, and run off into the darkness. Afoot again, he found another horse running loose in the woods. Shortly thereafter, a Confederate trooper attacked Dufur and managed to inflict two saber wounds on the Vermonter's body. Escaping with his life, he rode off in quest of his comrades. This third mount served Dufur well until an errant bullet ended its life. Crashing unexpectedly to the ground, the surprised sergeant found himself with wounds from the attack, injuries from the fall, and pinned beneath over a half a ton of dead horse. Using only his knife and fingers, he extricated himself by digging out the ground from under his trapped leg. With the aid of improvised crutches he gained his feet and hobbled off in the direction toward which his friends had retreated. Eventually he established contact with mounted troops, who, much to his chagrin, turned out to be rebels. After making the rounds of Richmond's prisons, Dufur joined the growing number of Yankee POWs who were introduced to the horrors of the newly opened Andersonville Prison. One of the hardier prisoners, he survived the ordeal to achieve repatriation in January of 1865.

Simon Dufur was not the only Vermonter for whom that final night of confusion spelled doom. Having survived the perils of the raid for two days, several troopers, both seasoned veterans and recent recruits alike, paid a heavy price for their participation, just when safety lay only a few hours away. One of these ill-fated soldiers was Nelson Dragon.

The twenty-two-year-old teamster having joined the regiment on February 18, 1864, the green trooper had spent all of twelve days on front-line duty before his March 1 capture. Less than nine months later, his military career ended abruptly when he succumbed to diarrhea at Andersonville. When Dufur arrived at his first prison stop, Castle Thunder, his spirits rose when Milo Farnsworth and Frank Jocelyn met him at the door and extended their hands, assisting the injured warrior to the second floor. In a double blow that hit Dufur hard, both friends fell ill and eventually passed away within a week of each other the following July. So horrific were conditions at Andersonville that Farnsworth, only recently recruited, could write his parents in January that "I am well [and] I never enjoyed better health in my life" and be dead within six months.[27] For Dufur, these back-to-back losses were devastating. At Andersonville, the threesome, along with another trio of Vermonters, shared a twelve-foot by six-foot plot within the confines of the prison. Constant companions, they continually watched each other's backs. But Farnsworth broke the tight circle when he finally succumbed to disease. As if sensing that the end was near, he asked Dufur to "take a small pocket Bible and some pictures, and keep them for him."[28] That night, Farnsworth passed away silently in his sleep with his faithful friend at his side. In a tender parting gesture, the next morning Dufur "cut a curl of hair from his head [Farnsworth's], and [placed] it between two leaves of his little Bible ... wrote upon the fly-leaf the date of his death, how long he had been sick, etc."[29] Then his companions in life carried their friend outside of the compound to the dead-house — and said good-bye. A week later, the four survivors from the 1st Vermont repeated their forlorn trek, this time carrying the body of Frank Jocelyn. Unlike Farnsworth, Jocelyn perished from diarrhea in what passed as the prison hospital. By the time Hull and Dufur came to be released, the other two members of the prison sextet, Horace Hyde and John Brown, had also died. In the eyes of the 1st Vermont, Andersonville deserved every last condemnation slung its way.

The nocturnal disaster that saw Farnsworth, Dufur, and Jocelyn captured effectively snuffed out the last glimmer of hope. All Kilpatrick could do was save what was left of his force. Positioning the trusty 1st Vermont as the rear guard, his command traveled down the peninsula. Occasional skirmishing with the trailing rebel forces occurred. One notable encounter happened when a detachment of Michiganders went out in search of forage for the animals. "The first thing we heard was them coming up the road as fast as their horses could carry them," was Phineas Worthern's recollection, "with the rebs close on their heels. As soon as they came in sight, our lieutenant ... told us to 'fire, fire,' but we would not until our own men got by, and then we fired our carbines, then our revolvers, and then charged down the road, the Johnnies turning and running like the deuce, we after them as fast as our played out horses feet could carry us."[30] For Worthern, this innocent little chase almost had a fatal ending as the rebels halted at a bend in the road, turned in their saddles, and unleashed a volley at their pursuers. To Worthern, this "farewell shot did not seem so good as one ball went close by my head, so near it made me wink."[31] After skirmishing most of the morning in the opposite direction, the men galloped their horses to make up the five miles separating them from the retiring division. At dark, they halted and "had a good night's sleep for the first time since we started from camp [Stevensburg]."[32] They reached Williamsburg on the morning of the 4th and arrived in Yorktown late that afternoon. Over the course of the next eight days, the raiders were transported in three contingents to Alexandria by boat. By the 18th, all were back in Stevensburg, excepting the 340 men and 600 horses lost on the raid.

Of the almost three-score Vermonters listed as missing, many of them perished in prison at later dates, and their deaths were duly recorded. But the fates of men who fell in combat were not always verifiable, for those slain in combat were often dispatched quickly into unmarked graves. The disappearance of Charles Dunn, riding with Dahlgren, occurred in just this manner. Shot as the attack was pressed against Richmond, he toppled from his saddle. Riding nearby, Private John Vanderslip later testified as having seen "the dead body of Dunn lying on the ground."[33] Though circumstances did not permit him to stop and check, Vanderslip was certain of his assessment, one that left Harriett Dunn a widow back in Vermont with four children to raise alone. Vanderslip was indeed fortunate to have escaped the same fate, for not only did Charles Dunn go down but two others in his set of four, his father, Charles, and Winslow Colby, were also knocked from their horses. Along with the younger Dunn and Colby, another member of Dahlgren's column, David Pierce, was also shot and killed the same day, March 1. On Wednesday, March 3, Bradford Whipple passed away, not because of enemy fire but rather from exposure to the adverse weather conditions. After General Kilpatrick called a halt at New Kent Courthouse, a weary Private Whipple, like most of his comrades, went swiftly off to sleep. "In the night he arose dreamily and asked if they were saddling up and then laid down," his commanding officer, Captain William Cummings, shared with Whipple's father, "and in a few minutes he got up and said: 'Oh, I am freezing to death, and then laid down and commenced to groan.'"[34] The captain was summoned. He in turn sent for the surgeon, but in the short span of five minutes poor Whipple had succumbed, the prevailing belief being that his heart had failed.

While individual losses would over time be explained, the final assessment of the raid's efficacy was not so clear-cut. Since the expedition had commenced with such ambitious goals, settling for anything less was tantamount to an admission of failure. Certainly there were legitimate military accomplishments, one being a swath of destruction cut through the Confederate infrastructure around Richmond as miles of track were torn up, countless buildings burned, and much private property either confiscated or destroyed; and the other planting an element of fear in the minds of the alarmed citizenry as to their vulnerability.

But, then, there were other glaring downsides, in addition to falling short of stated objectives. While the troops were expected to live off the land, a practice which never sits well with the population, the extent that some of the men engaged in good old-fashioned looting cast everyone in a disparaging light. But these indiscretions paled by comparison to the single most controversial and damning event of the entire expedition: the accidental discovery of a most disturbing note on Dahlgren's body. Appearing to have been written by the colonel's own hand, this missive called for the burning of Richmond and execution of Jefferson Davis and other high government officials. Not surprisingly, the public revelation of this document unleashed a firestorm of indignation across the Confederacy, giving all associated with the raid a group black eye for having such dastardly hearts and nefarious intentions. Any iota of good that the distribution of Lincoln's amnesty handbills may have accomplished was certainly undone many times over by the inflammatory nature of the so-called "Dahlgren Papers."

In time, the furor aroused among Southerners by the Kilpatrick–Dahlgren Raid subsided, or at least was supplanted, when other more devastating incursions followed. In the wake of the endeavor's failure, heads fittingly rolled, as the overall poor performance of its leaders would dictate that they should. Colonel Dahlgren, being martyred for the cause, was beyond censure, leaving General Kilpatrick to suffer the brunt of the consequences. Combining the abject military failure of the raid with the political embarrassment of Dahlgren's written indiscretion made Kilpatrick a liability that Lieutenant-General Ulysses Grant could not tolerate. A plan was devised that called for Kilpatrick's demotion from divisional to brigade-level command. General James Wilson would be transferred east to assume Kilpatrick's vacated position. Rather than face the humiliation of reduced responsibility, Kilpatrick was granted a transfer to the Western Theater. The officer whom William Wells called "the most dashing officer I ever saw" departed for his new assignment on April 17, 1864.[35] A measure of his appeal could be gauged by the reaction of the rank and file to his new assignment. Charles Blinn spoke for many when he suggested that Kilpatrick was being relieved "much to the dissatisfaction of the whole division ... [and] since the 28th day of June last the General has successfully led this division in many a hard fight and for dash his equal is not in this army."[36] Attesting to this assertion, the only regiment to bid him a collective adieu was the 1st Vermont, which rode over to his headquarters en masse to deliver a farewell salute.

　　Another officer who also did not fare well in the final analysis was Edward Sawyer. A parting of the ways had been building for some time. A composite picture of his entire career in the 1st Vermont reveals that Edward Sawyer was in fact on the regimental rolls for a total of 29 months, of which but 12 months were when the unit was stationed in a war zone and only 6 of those being logged during peak times of fighting. If nothing else, Sawyer's frequent and prolonged absences from the regiment cost him dearly in terms of lost opportunities to acquire battlefield experience. Without calling into question the man's backbone and desire to lead in battle, clearly the chance to gain military acumen was not going to present itself in Vermont where he was often located — recruiting or convalescing. Eventually and rightfully so, this lack of on-the-job training would be exposed. When the end finally came for Sawyer, it arrived swiftly and silently from the standpoint of the press. Given brigade-level responsibilities during the Dahlgren-Kilpatrick Raid, Colonel Sawyer proved that he was not up to the task. His performance was in fact found to be so wanting that Addison Preston was given command of Sawyer's brigade in mid-raid, a humbling move and decided vote of "no confidence" by his superiors. Upon his return from the mission, he was quickly shuffled off to court-martial duty, then given a furlough, and finally forced to resign under pressure. Edward Sawyer was gone from the army of which he never really seemed to be a part by May of 1864. Inconspicuously located under the heading "Personal" at the bottom of page 2, the *Rutland Daily Herald* gave his long-overdue departure scant space, noting only that "Col. Sawyer of the First Vermont has sent in his resignation and that it has been accepted."[37] But the next day, the *Burlington Times*, albeit in a veiled manner, probably came as close to ripping Sawyer as any Vermont paper ever did. In a brief but telling article, the *Times* reported that it was "happy to announce" the change of command, praising Sawyer's successor, Addison Preston, who was lauded as "a hard-working, brave, faithful officer, [one who] has led the regiment through all the skirmishes and battles in which it has borne so memorable a part, and is thoroughly identified with its splendid glory."[38] As if the effusive praise for Preston could not be seen as a backhanded commentary on all that Sawyer had not been, then the last line of the article provided the clincher: "His promotion which will be welcomed by the officers and men of his command and by the good people of the State who have long felt that so fine a body of men should have a gallant commander."[39]

　　Above and beyond losing its commander, which was hardly bemoaned within the regiment's ranks, the 1st Vermont's strength was reduced by the loss of 71 troopers, 59 wounded and 12 captured, many of whom wound up in Andersonville never to return. Every Vermont company lost at least one man, with the heaviest attrition pocketed in the two companies that rode with Dahlgren, G and K. The forced pace, under terrible weather conditions, took an appalling toll among the horses too, with the survivors[JC1] being left in worn out condition. If the 1st Vermont's participation in the Kilpatrick-Dahlgren Raid served any useful purpose for the regiment, it was to prime the men and serve notice as to what could be expected from them in the upcoming summer's campaigning.

In a curious footnote to the whole calamity, one Michael Madden, an Irish immigrant and recent recruit, was captured near King and Queen Courthouse toward the end of the raid. Whisked off to Richmond, his erratic behavior during a physical examination prompted a Confederate surgeon to mark "*non-compus mentis*" on Private Madden's parole papers.[40] Upon disembarking from the truce ship at Annapolis, the trooper found himself committed to an insane asylum for a six-month stay, by order of a government physician who found the boy to be "exhibiting marked symptoms of idiocy."[41] Some would see fitting irony in the post-raid discovery of Madden's condition, indicative of not only his personal plight but also of the diminished capacity with which the whole misadventure was concocted and carried out.

25

Richmond Under Attack
The Summer Raids Begin

If the Kilpatrick-Dahlgren Raid made any lasting impression on the South, it was as a harbinger of the destruction to come. Once, mounted raids in the Eastern Theater had been the sole purview of the Confederacy. The *Rutland Herald* contrasted those bygone days with the new status quo in an editorial on March 15, 1864: "When the rebels chiefly monopolized the 'raiding' business, it was in their estimation not only a legitimate mode of warfare, but the gallantry and dash of the brilliant fellows engaged in it were the special objects of southern pride and the themes of southern admiration.... Now the federal forces have learned something from the enemy about raids, and have practiced them with some success [and] the federal success at 'raiding' is frightening the enemy out of their wits."[1] Being on the receiving end of these incursions, Southerners saw them in an entirely different light. "Raids are, nevertheless, recognized modes of warfare, so long as their operations are confined to legitimate objects," offered the *Richmond Whig*, "but when they go beyond the bounds of civilized, and descend into forays of plunder, incendiarism, and devastation, they ought to be met by other than the means provided by the code of civilized war."[2] The difference in these perceptions represented an accurate picture of the war's changing dynamics between 1862 and 1864. The concept of "total war" was now applicable.

In the future, the 1st Vermont would participate in these heavy raids. But for now, there was an internal uproar with which to deal that had been created by their transfer from Custer's command. Initially, the entire brigade was shifted to the 1st Division, Custer included. However, when the 1st Vermont alone was sent back to the 3rd Division, commanded by George Chapman, dissatisfaction festered. Trading the flamboyant "Boy General" for the bland "Old Goggles" was unpalatable. Custer tried to use his influence, going to the War Department on the Vermonters' behalf and delivering a protest signed by the officers of the regiment. Though no immediate relief came, a promise was elicited that their reassignment would only be temporary

Amidst the turmoil, there was still some good news: Addison Preston was given command of the regiment. Contrasting sharply with Sawyer, who had risen to his colonelcy through political machinations orchestrated far from the battlefield, Preston had earned his promotions meritoriously. Understandably, his troops revered him. Change seemed be the order of the day, for adjustments also occurred at the highest levels. Foremost was that Lieutenant-General Ulysses S. Grant was given authority over all Federal forces. Significant for the Vermonters, Grant brought along feisty Phil Sheridan to lead his cavalry. Though some harbored doubts about an infantryman leading cavalry, his adroitness in employing his troopers soon turned their skepticism into admiration. Winning the acceptance of some of these same men, however, was not to be the lot of General James H. Wilson, heir to Kilpatrick's command. Charles Blinn later offered every soldier's opinion on these two officers when he wrote that "General Sheridan is a bully man. He fights well, but our own divisional commander, General Wilson, of him I have nothing to say."[3]

Among the troops, it was a popular adage that reviews were usually precursors to the opening of a campaign. Their intuition in this regard did not fail them. On May 2, General Wilson reviewed his division and at midnight on May 4, marching orders came. Everyone was instructed to pack, and by 1:00 A.M. the cavalry was headed for Germania Ford. Evidence abounded that this was no limited cavalry foray but rather a mass movement of the Army of the Potomac. "We knew that we should not want for traveling companions," one advancing Vermonter remembered, "for far away over the level country and on the hillsides could be seen innumerable fires, which at that late time of night denoted a general breakup of camps."[4] Though the lowly private could not have known, he and his comrades were participating in the incipient moments of "Grant's Overland Campaign." The Battle of the Wilderness would be the immediate result, followed by a series of slugfests throughout the summer as Grant relentlessly assailed his adversaries.

Crossing the Rapidan at dawn on May 4, the 1st Vermont faced little opposition. Forging on, the mounted forces arrived at Parker's Store, where they bivouacked at 3:00 P.M. The division remained here until 5:00 A.M. on the 5th, at which time the 2nd Brigade was sent off to Craig's Meeting House. The Vermonters led the cavalry, eventually making contact with the enemy, who was ready to give battle. About 8:00 A.M., the advance squadron under Captain William Cummings, warily reconnoitering the road ahead, sighted a force of rebel cavalry on a similar mission.

Cummings no sooner had his companies drawn up than hard-charging troopers from Thomas Rosser's brigade assaulted his command. Gradually superior numbers on the part of the rebels forced the Yankees back. In retreating, Denison Badger encountered a series of three fences. After having hurdled the first one, the third barricade proved too much of a challenge for his horse. Down they went, making Badger easy prey for rebel captors. Confinement for him turned out to be Florence, South Carolina. Back home in Vermont, his family feared for his safety. Casting about for a way to learn of his fate, Mary Jane Badger Sawyer sought the intersession of the only person whom she felt had could help: Abraham Lincoln. "At the earnest appeals of a poor aged Father and Mother, I write you a few lines," she opened her heartrending letter. She continued: "...truly this is an awful war, bringing grief to most every home and I for one feel as if I had my share, to see a loved Father and Mother fast hastening to the grave, President Lincoln is there not one word of comfort you can send to alleviate the sufferings of my poor Parents can you give one word of information concerning my poor Brother please answer soon...."[5] Lincoln, a compassionate man, received many such entreaties throughout the war, but, by the time he received Mrs. Sawyer's correspondence, her brother's condition was already deteriorating. One month later, young Badger died of acute diarrhea. The new recruit, who only the previous January had written home from Stevensburg how he never wanted his "bones to be buried in this country [for] it is a rough country and not like Vermont," got only part of his wish realized, being laid to rest in South Carolina instead of Virginia.[6]

Continuing its retreat, Cummings' squadron had not gone far when they met John Bennett's battalion. A battle line was quickly formed and soon absorbed the full brunt of the enemy's charge. The mêlée proved costly to the 1st Vermont, for several more men were lost. John French went down, shot through the head and instantly killed. Veteran Volunteer George Hemenway's three-year run of luck finally ran out, as he too toppled from his saddle dead. His comrade in Company I, Sergeant William Foster, described Hemenway to have been "a good soldier and recklessly brave, always ready to fight and never showing the least inclination to fear of shot and shell."[7] Another fatality was Albert Taylor of Company A, who took a grievous wound in the right knee. The doctors, in an attempt to save his life, amputated the leg the next day at the lower thigh. But too much blood had been lost, and Private Taylor died shortly thereafter. Making the young man's passing all the more tragic was the condition of his beloved mother, she being mentally incompetent and living with her sister. Albert was her sole support, relying on the goodness of his Aunt Mary to handle day-to-day care until his return. While he implored the charitable lady to "take care of her until I come and I will make it right," of the two women only the aunt would know the pain and burden of this unfulfilled promise.[8]

Once the rest of the regiment arrived, the tide of battle swung back in favor of the blue-clad cavalry: "Lt-Col. Preston then sent out a heavy line of skirmishers dismounted, and the flight commenced in earnest."[9] One of those afoot was Eri Woodbury, who narrowly escaped death: "I had taken position behind a rail fence when one of our Co. came up on my right and I moved about a foot and half to the left, he taking my place. In half a minute a ball hit him in the temple — and without a groan he was 'mustered out.' His warm blood formed a little pool in which my knees were steeped."[10] Subsequently, the Vermonters drove the rebel force back over two miles to the security of its fortified lines.

This skirmish at Craig's Meeting House was one of the opening gambits in the Battle of the Wilderness. After taking its lumps in the early going, the 1st Vermont was spared any further fighting. Pulled back, the regiment spent the night bivouacked slightly to the east of Todd's Tavern. Over the course of the next three days, the 1st Vermont was only asked to maintain an alert presence on the periphery. Finally,

General Philip Sheridan, "Little Phil," short in stature but long in combativeness, led the Vermont Cavalry to their smashing victories at Tom's Brook and Cedar Creek (Library of Congress).

the unfulfilling picket duty gave way to a more exciting prospect: another raid against Richmond. Over 10,000 troopers, the entire cavalry corps of the Army of the Potomac, were being unleashed. Compared to the Kilpatrick-Dahlgren expedition, built for speed, Sheridan's was a heavier force, intended to fight. Sheridan himself was a kindred spirit whom the Vermonters came to admire; this raid materialized because the fiery Sheridan chafed at Meade's disposition of cavalry in support roles. In contrast, "Little Phil" wanted to operate independently. Well-connected Sheridan got pressure brought against General Meade to unfetter the cavalry. Given the green light, Sheridan knew that the onus to produce now rested on his shoulders. "We are going out to fight Stuart's cavalry," he told his division commanders, "in consequence of a suggestion from me; we will give him a fair, square fight; we are strong, and I know we can beat him, and in view of my recent representations to General Meade I shall expect nothing but success."[11]

With the same objective in mind as the abortive Kilpatrick-Dahlgren venture, Sheridan had his sights set on destroying Confederate property. But his intentions exceeded those of his predecessors in one distinct way — Sheridan welcomed a clash with the enemy. Once and for all, he wanted to defeat Jeb Stuart and put an end to the Confederate's specter looming over the Union army. Not surprisingly, when Sheridan's host rode out early on the morning of May 9, no attempt was made to mask their departure. Furthermore, they traveled with no great sense of urgency, proceeding at a leisurely walk that did not unduly tax either man or animal. Heading for Beaver Dam Station, the procession

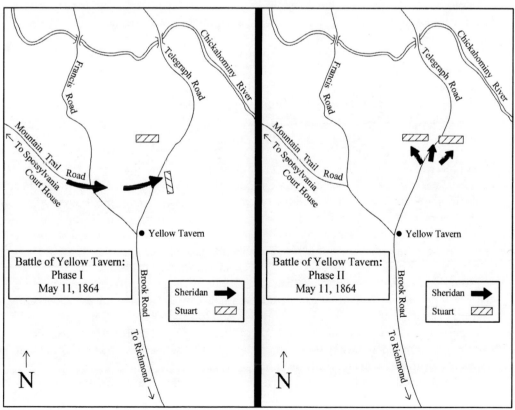

Drawn by Bob Collea

strung out for thirteen miles. Contrasting sharply with the inhospitable conditions endured by the Kilpatrick-Dahlgren raiders, Sheridan's men were subjected to the opposite end of the climatic spectrum: bright sunlight, intense heat, and dry air. The danger of hypothermia was supplanted by the possibility of heatstroke, a condition that did indeed lay several men low. Even with the column crawling along, Joseph Benoits of Company D still collapsed from extended exposure to the sun. Unable to travel, he was left behind and soon found himself in Confederate hands. But the health of the young Canadian farmer deteriorated quickly, once the month of May saw him transferred from confinement in Richmond to Andersonville. Due to a lack of Vitamin C, Benoits' body began to break down, causing him to be admitted to the prison hospital "on August 22, 1864 where he died the same day of scorbutus."[12]

After covering eighteen miles, the raiders halted for the night near Ground Squirrel Bridge, on the south side of the South Anna River. Wednesday, May 11, 1864, began for the Union cavalry in similar fashion to the previous day. The troops were up early, brewing their coffee, when in came rebel artillery shells, the perpetrators of which were quickly driven away. When the sun finally set, Sheridan would have the victory over Stuart that he had sought. The wheels for a climactic battle had been set in motion the previous day, when the rebel chieftain had assigned one brigade to harass the Federal cavalry from behind while he led two brigades in a pell-mell dash to get in front of the raiders. Once in position, the general had to select a place to give battle. The spot chosen was six miles north of the capital, at the hamlet known as Yellow Tavern.

Faced with the choice of blocking the direct route to Richmond or aligning his command parallel to the highway, Stuart opted to deploy his two brigades in a battle line beside, rather than astride, his adversary's line of march. Outnumbered better than three to one, General Stuart had to be conservative in his planning. One concession that Stuart made was nominally leaving the highway to Richmond wide open. Yellow Tavern was situated at the convergence of Old Mountain Road and Telegraph Road. Stuart positioned his men to the northeast of Old Mountain Road. Telegraph Road ran to the southwest through Stuart's line. South of the Y-intersection where the two highways met, the new road created by their merger was Brook Turnpike. This route went directly through the defensive perimeter protecting Richmond and on into the city. Had Sheridan's primary objective been investing the Confederate capital, some of his men could have worked up a head of steam and blown past Stuart's weary troops, leaving a second contingent to deal with the surprised rebels. While such an undertaking was a tempting thought, picking that plum had never been what the raid was about. But defeating Stuart's cavalry was, and the rebels sat as if presented on a silver platter, awaiting their own destruction. Events could not have unfolded any more fortuitously for Sheridan. Besides, the city would still be there after the Confederate cavalry had been summarily dispatched.

Sheridan's van arrived on the scene around noon. To the northeast, they observed the longer part of the Confederate line running along a low ridge, roughly parallel to Old Mountain Road, until it reached Telegraph Road. At this point, the remaining rebels were posted in a shorter line angling slightly to the southwest. Stuart's troop disposition had the appearance of a hockey stick laid on the ground; the shaft was the longer portion opposite Telegraph Road and the shorter blade represented the section southeast of Telegraph Road. Artillery had been positioned to guard both flanks and on Telegraph Road where it bisected the two wings of his line.

Once the rebels' deployment was revealed, the Yankee response was swift. First, a

Desirous of decimating the ranks of Stuart's cavalry, General Sheridan eschewed a tantalizingly open road to Richmond and instead engaged in the Battle of Yellow Tavern, which culminated in a Union victory and the death of his adversary (*Grand Army Picture Book*).

blocking force was sent ahead, its mission to secure the Brook Turnpike. Several hours of probing followed as Sheridan sought to fathom a weakness in the Confederate position. Their efforts proved futile. Finally, General Sheridan decided the stalemate necessitated a change in strategy. His solution? Order an all-out assault along the line! The operative thinking was simple: an equal application of pressure would prevent Stuart from shifting troops. Sheridan's superiority in numbers would eventually turn the tide, first by overwhelming some portion of the rebel line and then by allowing him to exploit the breakthrough. While Sheridan formulated his plan, the situation in the field was highly fluid, ultimately rendering the general's strategizing unnecessary. To no one's surprise, George Custer was at the center of the brewing tempest. Some of the general's dismounted troopers were experiencing a galling fire from the artillery batteries posted on the Confederates' left flank, that being the portion of the line east of Telegraph Road. "From a personal examination of the ground," Custer later shared, "I discovered that a successful charge might be made upon the battery of the enemy by keeping well to the right."[13]

For the Vermonters, the most memorable stage of the fight was about to begin. Due to George Custer's affinity for their fighting prowess, they were invited to join the assault. General Custer "called to Lieutenant Colonel Preston for the First Vermont — although our regiment is not in his brigade — and at the head of the First Michigan and the First Vermont, followed by a number of other regiments, led the most daring charge of the war."[14] In the eyes of one Vermont trooper, "It was ... one of the most terrible charges that I ever witnessed. Our regiment, with two others, led by General Custer, formed under a heavy fire from the rebel artillery, and with a shout from every throat we charged near three-fourths of a mile over fences, streams, and ditches til we came upon them and scattered them. They fought with desperation, but it was of no avail."[15] Not only were the Confederates driven from the field, but the charge also resulted in the mortal wounding of Jeb Stuart. What had started out as a push to silence a damaging battery had turned the tide of battle. In the glowing aftermath, there were plaudits all around. "The united effort of the First, Fifth, Sixth, and Seventh Michigan, assisted by Heaton's Battery, and the First Vermont, under the gallant Preston," praised Custer, "proved sufficient, after a close contest, to rout the enemy and drive him from his position."[16] For the Vermonters, the chance to ride with Custer again had been exhilarating, but their eventual return to Wilson's command was equally deflating, so much so that Custer recalled how "the First Vermont ... sent over to our brigade and asked if they could not obtain 'a pair of Custer's old boots' to command them."[17] While General Stuart was the most notable casualty on the field that day, he was by no means the only one. For the 1st Vermont, the day's toll amounted to two men killed and ten others wounded. Michael Phillips, who became a husband and a soldier in August of 1862, was "instantly killed" by a shot through the head during the final charge.[18] The other fatality in the same forward movement was Herbert Garvin, also of Company L.

While tending to the wounded and regrouping his force, Sheridan took stock of the unstable situation that existed around him. Positioned deep in enemy territory, with pressure building behind him, decisions made in the next few hours would be critical. Sheridan finally started his troops moving again at eleven o'clock in the evening. Their eventual destination was to the east of Richmond and a planned union with a force that General Ben Butler had sent up from the York Peninsula. In the meantime, General Sheridan's men marched down the Brook Turnpike, heading directly toward the capital.

General Wilson's brigade was given the honor of leading the advance. As the situation unfolded, the scenario presenting itself had eerie similarities to those that Kilpatrick's men had recently experienced, beginning with a driving rain pelting the attackers on their approach. Like their predecessors, Sheridan's men easily moved past the outer ring of defenses, after which they became stymied. They too were enraptured by their proximity to Richmond, "so near that a hazy light was given us by the city lamps, as the light reflected on the clouds."[19] Giving them pause to reconsider, just as they had Kilpatrick, were the distant sounds of train whistles, believed to be shuttling troops to shore up the defenses.

Though the similarities were striking, there was one distinct difference. This was the presence of infernal machines buried in the roadway. These devices amounted to artillery shells with trip wires, the intention being that horses' hooves would trigger attached explosives. "We marched some and halted some, and at one o'clock, while halting, a torpedo exploded under Company A about thirty feet behind me," recounted Sergeant Ide, "which threw the column into some confusion, but did no serious damage except to let the Rebels know where we were."[20] To calm the men's nerves while solving the problem, rebel prisoners were forced to crawl ahead of the column, searching the roadway for additional booby traps. If anyone was going to be blown to "Kingdom Come," better a rebel than a Yankee. The going was slow, but caution was rewarded, for a dozen shells were uncovered.

While only the horses paid the price for such skullduggery, the explosions unfortunately served to alert Richmond's defenders. This precipitated a fusillade that for the most part was inaccurate. Still, even bullets fired blindly could find targets. One of these happened to be Company E's George Pine. He was "wounded by a rifle shot in the right side, just above and in back of the hip to the right of the spinal column."[21] In only his sixth month of service and third major combat experience, the eighteen-year-old private had the misfortune to sustain what was ultimately a fatal blow. Arrangements were eventually made to transport him to the hospital at Point Lookout. Shortly, Dr. Samuel Alger from Willoughby, Vermont, went there to take care of him. Not long after the doctor arrived, he decided to get the suffering soldier home as quickly as possible. A thirty-day furlough was obtained, but the patient began to fail so fast that the journey to northern Vermont had to be cut short. He was taken to the home of a relative in Brooklyn, New York, but all further ministrations proved fruitless. Trooper Pine drew his last breath on June 13, 1864. The same railroads that took him off to war only a few months ago now bore him to his final resting place in Williston.

By now, Sheridan knew that any attempt to force his way into Richmond was going to exact a price that he was not prepared to pay. His raid had achieved its primary objectives, so there was no compelling reason beyond glory to try to force his way into the city. With the enemy applying heavy pressure, the time had come to leave. The only direction ostensibly still open was to the east. However, even this option seemed initially grounded in false hope, for Meadow Bridge over the rain-swollen Chickahominy was in an unusable condition. Though a nearby railroad trestle offered an alternative, enemy troops posted on the far shore were poised to contest any crossing. To extricate his command, Sheridan turned to his ace troubleshooter—George Armstrong Custer. Since the train bridge was not intended for pedestrian traffic, Custer's dismounted men could only pick their way warily across, a few at a time, to engage the dug-in rebels. Meanwhile engineers worked feverishly to repair the primary span. Some perverse satisfaction was taken in stripping boards from abandoned rebel housing near the river. With secure planking installed, mounted troops dashed across a quickly refurbished Meadow Bridge and dispersed the entrenched enemy. After a twelve-hour delay, the Yankee column could again move forward.

Arriving back in camp on the 24th, after more than a fortnight's riding and fighting, the Vermonters had much to tell the homefolks. Pride in being a Yankee cavalryman was certainly a prominent theme, for as one Vermont trooper gushed, "It is now demonstrated beyond the shadow of a doubt, that the rebel cavalry are no match for ours."[22] Confidence in their new commander, Philip Sheridan, was unmistakable, as exemplified by an admiring cavalryman: "When we think we are in a tight place, the boys will be heard to say 'Well, Gen. Sheridan knows what he is about,' and they are right."[23] By contrast, James Wilson's image did not fare so well, for it was he who had unwittingly led the van into its precarious position under the guns of Richmond's defenses. Little that he accomplished after that blunder changed few Vermonters' estimations of his overall performance. Suffice it to say that the opinion of the 1st Vermont was that their capabilities were stifled under his leadership. When Custer assumed command of the 3rd Division in late September, Horace Ide spoke for most of the Vermont boys when he confided in his diary how much "this change delighted the men in the regiment who felt wronged when they were removed from Custer's Brigade during April. Wilson had never been a popular leader among the men ... [who] disliked his dismounted tactics."[24]

Even if Wilson's approval rating trailed those of Sheridan and Custer, the end of May approached with his position as commander of the 3rd Brigade still intact. Perhaps it was well that the taste of success still lingered in their mouths, for the month of June would see the Vermont troopers involved in several costly engagements that did not evoke the same sense of accomplishment.

26

The Wilson-Kautz Raid
Taking the War to the Enemy

Given the vicissitudes of war, it was well that everyone had a chance to enjoy the success of Sheridan's first "Richmond Raid," for trying times lay ahead. The respite was indeed brief, for General Grant, determined to keep up pressure, set his forces in motion on Thursday, May 26. The 1st and 2nd Cavalry divisions led the way, with Wilson's command relegated to the infantry's wake. Saturday found Union cavalry embroiled in the sanguinary 1st Battle of Hawe's Shop, a prelude to several days of grinding clashes between the main forces at Cold Harbor. While the forward elements saw action, the Vermonters' role remained behind the scenes as they guarded river crossings and provided rear-echelon security. However, these mundane assignments ceased the 31st, when Wilson's men were dispatched to the army's right flank. Over three of the next four days, they were embroiled in a series of sharp engagements at Hanover Court House, Ashland Station, and Hawe's Shop.

The affair at Hanover occurred when a Vermont squadron, out on patrol, bumped into an enemy detachment on a similar mission. The Confederates were quickly driven back. Had Joseph Demareaux not been killed and Loren Brow wounded, the skirmish would warrant little more than a passing glance. The more fortunate of the two, Private Brow was incapacitated when "a ball entered the left side of his abdomen and was removed from a point just above the hip joint."[1] A blacksmith in Company B, the severity of his injury triggered an early discharge on February 22, 1865. One of the curiosities that accompanied his foreshortened military career was Brow's exact age. His enlistment papers identify him as being thirty-five years old, while his discharge certificate cites sixty-six. As for Joseph Demareaux, the twenty-one-year-old trooper from Barton did not suffer, dying instantly on the field of battle from a fatal gunshot wound.

Daylight on the 31st found Chapman's Brigade moving forward, the 1st Vermont leading. The objective was the Confederates' railroad infrastructure. Against minimal resistance, Captain Cushman's squadron was assigned to destroy a pair of railway viaducts. Colonel Chapman acknowledged Cushman's success, reporting that "both of these bridges were effectively destroyed by fire, including trestle-work as well as superstructure, and two water tanks."[2] The same could not be said for their comrades, especially Wells' battalion, which had been detached and hurried southeast along Telegraph Road toward Ashland. Up ahead, Colonel John McIntosh's brigade was beset upon front and rear. The Vermonters' timely arrival took the heat off McIntosh's rear guard when they charged into the pursuing enemy cavalry and drove them back. Through its aggressive intercession, the 1st Vermont saved the 3rd Connecticut, but participation in this action cost Sergeant Thomas Bartleff his life. A Canadian immigrant, he had plied the quiet calling of carriage-maker in Guilford. Severely wounded, he deserved a better fate than having to be left behind, only to die in rebel hands. In addition to Bartleff, Company F suffered other eventual fatalities from the action. Private Amos Smith took a ball that shattered his humerus and then "passed upward and out superior to the spine of the scapula."[3] Suffice it to say, Smith's left arm and shoulder were a mess. Hospitalization was to no avail. Gangrene set in, and Private Smith succumbed on July 13. Similarly, Cassius Stinckney was downed by a gunshot wound to his right shoulder. Prostrate on the field of battle, he was easily captured and "taken to Richmond where he was confined in a hospital there," ultimately dying of the effects of the wound.[4] Married on December 21, 1863, the day he left for war was the last time Rosalie Stinckney ever saw her new husband alive. Before her first anniversary came to pass, the young bride had traded her wedding whites for widow's weeds.

As bullets struck down Bartleff, Smith, and Stinckney, their comrades faced a growing predicament. Anticipating a counturcharge, "All of the regiment was dismounted and sent into the woods, and we drove the rebs back nearly two miles and then got flanked" was Trooper Thomas Wiswall's recapitulation of the ensuing action.[5] After the 3rd Indiana joined in and suppressed the enemy's advance, the 1st Vermont was able to remount. Under pressure and amidst confusion, "the boys had to get out the best way they could."[6] Falling back toward Hanover, Wells' battalion was joined by the rest of the regiment. The seesaw nature of the day's fighting continued as the enemy was checked, then drove the Vermonters back, and was in turn again halted by the timely arrival of the 5th New York. Finally Wilson ordered a withdrawal, eventually halting for the night near Hanover Court House. Though Sergeant Bartleff was the sole fatality to be mourned that day, there were seven others requiring medical attention. The biggest loss, however, was the tally of twenty-four missing riders, resulting from the continuous ebb and flow of action. Two dozen men represented a high price for such a minor encounter. Nor was the dismal outcome of the day lost on those who had fought the good fight. Trooper Addison Harris of Company H was one who bemoaned this depletion of manpower, and shared it with his family: "On the 1st day of June we got severely repulsed and got drove back with a heavy loss of killed and wounded and prisoners."[7] It was no coincidence that Harris made these observations, for his company, along with F, had been in the thick of the fighting at Ashland and absorbed significant losses. Among them was Lieutenant Clark Stone, who fell into rebel hands "while leading his company in a charge against the enemy."[8] During the course of his confinement, Clark made the rounds of an impressive number of Southern cities: Richmond, Macon, Charleston, Columbia, Charlotte, Greensboro, and Raleigh. When finally repatriated in March of 1865, Clark was suffering from acute gastrointestinal problems, causing discomfort that would plague an aging veteran for the rest of his life.

Fortuitously, June 2 turned out to be a period of inactivity, so everyone had a chance to catch their breath. Little did any of the troopers know that Friday, June 3, 1864, would be forever remembered for a catastrophic loss of life unseen in any prior engagement. Known as the Battle of Cold Harbor, the encounter gained the dubious distinction as a slaughterhouse, at one point witnessing 7,000 Union infantrymen cut down in an hour's combat.

Since Grant had ordered an all-out offensive, the cavalry too had a role to play. Wilson's Division had been assigned to assail the Confederates' extreme left flank, with the Vermonters the last regiment in the line of attack. Moving across level ground the Vermonters came up against Fitz Lee's troopers, ensconced in rifle pits. The existence of these defensive works was mute evidence that the wages of war had already been visited upon the land. Blood had already christened this pastoral acreage as a killing field. Then it had been Custer's men contesting for this same ground only six days ago, the clash being known as the Battle of Hawe's Shop. While never gaining the same level of acclaim as its precursor, this Second Battle of Hawe's Shop on June 3 nevertheless left an indelible mark on the 1st Vermont.

With the Vermonters in prone positions, fighting assumed the dimensions of a heavy skirmish, the entrenched rebels clinging tenaciously to their positions. Try as they might, the Federals could not dislodge them. Then, amidst this sustained action, the unthinkable happened. Within a two minute span, a pair of rebel balls found their marks, each striking down a Vermont officer. In a tightly knit regiment, the loss of any member was deeply felt, from tent mates through the company and in some cases to the regimental level. But when officers went down, the upshot was a much greater level of awareness. The fact that one of these fallen leaders was Addison Preston and the other Oliver Cushman cast a pall all the more pervasive.

Colonel Preston had gone to the front to reconnoiter. For him to be in a forward area was a commonplace. On this occasion, he crawled up ahead of the foremost skirmishers, made his observations, and turned to go back, inexplicably rising to his feet. Standing alone among men hugging the ground, he presented an opportune target. In the words of a trooper, "He died almost instantly from the effects of a bullet which entered his left breast, near the heart."[9] Horace Ide vividly remembered the aftermath: "After getting the colonel back a short distance to a small brook, we laid him down and threw water in his face, which revived him somewhat, so that he made a slight noise in his throat, but said nothing that could be called speaking."[10] Another Vermonter described the immediate effect of the disheartening news, noting how, "as the words passed along the line 'Colonel Preston is mortally wounded,' every face grew dark with sorrow and revenge. Every officer and soldier of our regiment deeply mourns the loss of our colonel."[11] The body was taken to White House Landing for shipment home. Somewhere along the route, George Custer stopped the mournful procession to pay his final respects. After gazing upon the face of his loyal lieutenant, the general turned away and bestowed a one-sentence eulogy that any warrior would have been proud to claim as his own: "There lies the best fighting colonel in the Cavalry Corps."[12]

In a war that had been tough on the officer corps of the 1st Vermont, Preston's death added yet another name to the list of departed leaders. The only difference this time was that Addison Preston was a very special personage, a man who was clearly the heart and soul of the regiment. "Frank, genial, open-hearted, fearless, beloved by his subordinates, and respected by his superiors," he had been among them since Burlington.[13] He had risen meritoriously through the ranks from captain to colonel, fought in the major engagements of every campaign, and spilled his blood on the same battlefields as his troopers. He was a force and a presence not soon to be forgotten and never replaced. "Upon the organization of the company, 1 November 1861, he was elected Captain," read his obituary. "— From that date to the day of his death, his whole energy and mind were given to the war, and his history is the history of the regiment to which he belonged."[14]

The body arrived in Danville on Thursday, June 9, 1864. Early on the Sabbath morn,

Danville witnessed an influx of people from the surrounding towns and farms, coming to pay their respects to the fallen hero. After services at Preston's house, the mourners and sympathizers, led by Preston's wife, Julia, and their two small children, marched slowly to the church. Here, the house of God was filled to capacity, with hundreds more gathered outside. At the head of the nave lay Preston's coffin, "shrouded with the old flag which he had fought so bravely to sustain, upon which lay a sabre and pistols captured in a hand to hand fight with a rebel officer, and down by their side lay garlands and flowers."[15] At the conclusion of the ceremony, the casket was taken to the nearby Greenwood Cemetery for interment. The little country burial ground already contained the remains of the Vermont Cavalry's first war hero, John Chase, a man to whose widow Preston had solemnly written a letter of condolence only two tumultuous years ago. Now the colonel was home a hero too, reunited with his faithful subordinate. Among those who stood sorrowful vigil by the gravesite was Preston's sister. She had long feared that this terrible day might come. As early as March of 1862, before his regiment had even smelled the smoke of battle, Juliette Preston harbored deep concerns for Addison's well being. "I would like it if he could come home covered with honor and glory," she expressed in a letter to their brother William, "if he could escape unhurt."[16] Had she known his leadership style was to be in front of his men in battle, her shock at his death might have been tempered by the knowledge that somehow he had miraculously survived for two years. If there was to be any succor to assuage her pain, some measure could be taken from the fact that no one in the 1st Vermont ever exceeded her brother's courage in battle.

Of the many encomiums that poured forth in celebration of Preston's life, perhaps one of the most insightful was published in the *Vermont Record*: "Colonel Preston was characterized by quickness of perception, thought, and action which made him what he was as a soldier and officer. He never found exactly his right place til he went into the army. There he was in his element. Many, if not most, of the failures in life arise not so much from the lack of ability as from misapplication of it. The round man gets into a square hole, and can by no possibility fill it. But put every man into his proper place, that for which he was born, and every man will succeed. Col. Preston might not have achieved so signal a success as he did in war. He was a born soldier, and found that out when the country sounded the call to arms."[17]

As the much-lamented Preston was being laid to rest in the "Northeast Kingdom," eighty miles south in Hartland, Vermont, people were mourning the passing of another gallant trooper, the ill-starred Oliver Cushman. Fatally wounded within seconds of his commander, Captain Cushman was cut from the same cloth. He was remembered as an officer who "was not one to shun danger or call upon others to go where he did not lead."[18] Gone at the age of twenty-three, Cushman, like Preston, was universally mourned among the troopers of the 1st Vermont. Characterized "as brave an officer as ever drew the glistening blade, and who, too, was a generous and able officer," Cushman had risen from sergeant to captain by virtue of his valor and leadership.[19] While some believed that his disfiguring facial wound at Gettysburg left him with a careless abandon about his future safety, no amount of personal recklessness could overshadow that "he was recognized as one of the finest young men and best soldiers in the regiment—gallant, patriotic, high-spirited, and faithful to every duty."[20]

The brisk engagement at Hawe's Shop produced three battlefield fatalities in the 1st Vermont. Certainly by virtue of rank and acclaim, only those of Flint and Woodbury at

Miskel's Farm approached the dual deaths of Preston and Cushman in one battle. The least conspicuous individual in the triumvirate who perished that sad June day was one George McIvor. Having enlisted the previous December, he chanced upon the scene just as the cavalry was entering a more dangerous phase of operations. Having already suffered the passing of his tent mate, young McIvor knew the randomness and pain of war firsthand. Yet he never lost the optimism of youth, writing his parents of his belief that "old Grant is going to bring this cruel war to a close before long."[21] That piece of correspondence was the last that his anxious family would ever receive from him. The next letter posted from the war zone to his parents came not from their beloved son but rather from a comrade-in-arms, Trooper Edwin Churchill. "It is with a sad heart that I now address you as a friend of your son George McIvor," Churchill painfully opened his communication, "...and it is with sorrow that I am now called upon to inform you that he has lost his life for his country's sake."[22] He went on to advise the McIvors regarding two important aspects of their son's life, his final moments and his lasting legacy, intending to bring them a measure of comfort in their time of grief. The first was the knowledge that George expired

Recruited in the fall of '62 for newly formed Company L, Private Eusabe Sansoucci was grievously wounded in the 2nd Battle of Hawes' Shop on June 3, 1864, lingering a week before finally succumbing to his wound (Francis C. Guber Collection).

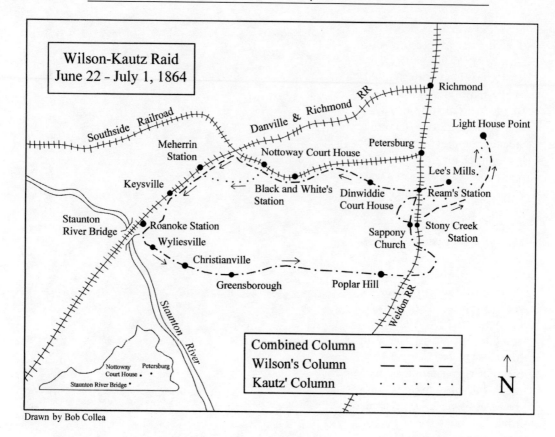

Drawn by Bob Collea

without undue suffering, while the other was that "his loss is deeply felt by his whole company for he was a man that never ran from the field, performed his duty, yet the best of men must die."

George McIvor, Oliver Cushman, Addison Preston — the fortunes of war brought them together. While their demise was deeply felt by the troopers of 1st Vermont, the troopers were not alone, for many other regiments also found June 3 to be an occasion for grief. The situation had for the most part been consistent wherever Union troops attacked at Cold Harbor that day and was easily summed up: brutal fighting, little progress, and staggering losses. While the Vermonters had achieved some local success, first pushing the enemy's dismounted cavalry back and then dislodging an infantry brigade, their efforts went for naught when their advance failed to receive needed support. Finally, they were disengaged by General Wilson and led back to bivouac for the evening.

Over the course of the next three weeks, the Vermonters had various assignments, typically picketing and screening for the Army of the Potomac as its base was shifted south of the James River. During this time, the regiment received word that Hawe's Shop had claimed another trooper. Canadian-born Eusebe Sansoucci, one of the 1862 recruits for Company L, died on June 10 from the effects of a gunshot wound to a lung. After having already been laid up for almost a year in various hospitals, Private Sansoucci had only just rejoined the 1st Vermont in May. Having spent more service time in a bed than in a saddle, he looked forward to active duty and living the life of a cavalryman as he had envisioned the experience when enlisting. But his severe wound put him right back into a Washington hospital. Only this time he did not recover.

Ten days after Hawe's Shop, a sharp skirmish near the White Oak Swamp Bridge brought additional fatalities. Martin Heath was killed instantly by a gunshot wound to the chest. An early patriot who answered Platt's call, Sergeant Heath's death devastated his new bride, the couple having been married all of sixty-three days when Melissa Heath was widowed. John Owens, of Company E by way of Rutland, was the second man to go down in this engagement. Severely wounded in the arm, he underwent a dreaded amputation a few days later. After an infection set in, he managed to hang on until July 23 before succumbing. Unlike Heath and Owens, Emory Durivage survived his critical wound, but his life was forever altered. The minie ball that crashed into his right arm left him with a total disability, "unfit for duty [even] in the Veteran Reserved Corp."[23] Instead of riding out the war with his comrades, Durivage spent his days in four different hospitals until discharged in March of 1865.

Given Ulysses Grant's aggressive posture, he was not about to let the tactical setback at Cold Harbor deter him from his grand design. After absorbing the best blows Lee could deliver, the Army of the Potomac stood back up, dusted itself off, and continued sidestepping to the right. The general's sights were now trained on Petersburg, situated twenty miles due south of Richmond. In concert with putting pressure on this objective, Grant wanted to weaken the enemy's resolve by interdicting his supply lines. The Kilpatrick-Dahlgren raiders had done this to a modest degree, and Sheridan's first foray against Richmond had wrought even more damage, though in neither raid was the rail network the primary objective.

Having been a part of these endeavors, the 1st Vermont knew full well how demanding such extended missions were. Yet the Green Mountain troopers relished their participation, causing one very proud member to boast at foray's end: "You have heard of Wilson's raid, of course. Well, the 1st Vt. was *there*, as they always have the fortune to be in any place where there is 'plenty of trouble' as the boys dominate fighting."[24] Commanders prize such confidence. Fashioned over time, it becomes a part of the regiment's fabric, firm even in the face of trying situations and occasional setbacks. It was no wonder that George Custer found the mettle of these Vermonters to his liking. The upcoming mission would prove to be no less challenging than its predecessors. Penetrating deeply behind enemy lines, the raiders' goals were the Weldon, Southside, and Richmond and Danville railroads. The raiding party, amounting to approximately 5,500 men, would be led by James Wilson and August Kautz. Launched on June 22, the "Wilson-Kautz Raid" was expected to sever vital supply lines from both the Carolinas and the Shenandoah Valley.

The goals were lofty. While understanding that unanticipated obstacles could of necessity alter any aspect of the plan, elements of three rail lines clearly constituted the primary targets. Along with tearing up main line trackage, a pair of important bridges was a special target: the High Bridge on the Southside road and the Roanoke Bridge on the Danville road. After swinging in a wide southwest arc around Petersburg, the projected route of advance was west and then south. The first objective was the Weldon Railroad seven miles below Petersburg. Then the raiders would hit the Southside Railroad fourteen miles west and follow its tracks thirty miles beyond to the point where it intersected the Richmond and Danville's line at Burke's Station. Upon gaining this strategic location, the raiders were to head southwest down the tracks for thirty miles to the

Roanoke River and its strategic bridge. Along the way, the intent was to lay waste to as much railroad property as possible. While the attackers' outbound route was dictated by the juxtaposition of the intended targets relative to one another, the return path was intentionally open-ended. Depending upon the enemy's countermoves, Wilson had prior approval to choose from several escape options. The most conventional route was to return, via whatever pathway allowed, to the Union lines below Petersburg. If the way back was blocked, then the more radical choices of marching to the North Carolina coast or linking up with Sherman in northern Georgia were available.

Up until the day before the attack pushed off, a matter of import to the Vermonters remained unresolved. Who would fill Preston's position? The matter had weighed heavily on the minds of the regiment's officers, causing them to meet and discuss the situation. To give the issue a full airing, "a committee was set up to ascertain the feelings of the officers on what should be done to fill the colonelcy."[25] Several candidates coveted the command. One aspirant was Josiah Hall. Another possible choice was Major John Bennett. William Wells was also in the mix. In the end, Wells received the promotion. For the sake of the regiment, it was best that he did so, for in the privacy of letters home Wells clearly indicated that he felt that he deserved the honor and would probably leave in November if he did not get it. He need not have worried though, as he had the support of the men who had to execute his orders. One of the deciding factors may very well have been the letter signed unanimously by the regiment's officers and submitted to the governor, requesting that Major Wells be appointed to command the 1st Vermont.

Leaving Prince George Court House at 2:00 A.M. on June 22, the raiders reached Reams' Station on the Weldon Railroad at approximately 10:00 A.M. Here all combustibles were put to the torch and a modest amount of track torn up. Due to its position as the rear guard, "ill-luck" one trooper called it, the 1st Vermont had the assignment of fending off pursuers.[26] When leaving the premises, the departing troopers came under fire from rebel artillery. "As we did not wish for a fight there," one participant later commented, "the column was closed up somewhat hurriedly with the loss of some ten or fifteen hats and capes."[27] Hasty though the regiment's departure was, Henry Cook was unable to outrun the minie ball that crashed into his right arm just above the elbow. Already suffering from legs swollen, by varicose veins, "so much so that at times he could only move about or make his way with difficulty," Private Cook probably should not have even ridden on the raid in the first place.[28] Confined to an ambulance on the first day out, he eventually wound up a POW when the wagons were abandoned a week later, near the very place where he was wounded.

With the main body driving westward, the Vermonters fought a delaying action, using the same technique that had been so successfully employed at Hagerstown. This tactic called for one company to hold as long as it could, with a second company drawn across the road some distance behind. When the pressure became too heavy, the front line would fall back and let the secondary company take over the resistance. By repeating this process, the rebels could never build up a head of steam, much less break through to the main column. The task was grueling to be sure, for, as one trooper observed, "We skirmished with them all that day until 6 P.M."[29] Through all of this, the weather remained hot and dry, verified by Harvey Lilly, who observed that the vicinity "had not had any rain of any amount, not enough to settle the dust, since the 9th of May."[30] Factoring in the blazing sun, clouds of powdered soil, and unquenchable thirst, the forty-mile march for twenty-two out of twenty-four hours became an ordeal not soon forgotten. William

Wells noted that "for several days on the raid the thermometer stood at 120 degrees above zero in the shade."[31]

One of those affected by the intense heat and arid atmosphere was Henry Smith of Company F. As he rode near Black and White's Station, east of Dinwiddie, Sergeant Smith became a victim of sunstroke. The hospital steward for the regiment, Frederick Holridge, identified a variety of symptoms exhibited by Smith: "unconsciousness ... his mind seemed affected ... seemed to be in a daze ... complained of a rumbling in his head."[32] That he was even present was a testimonial to Smith's pluckiness. One of the original enlistees, he had developed a case of chronic diarrhea that had resulted in his transfer to the Invalid Corps in November of 1863; however, he gamely rejoined the 1st Vermont in late December. Following his recovery from the exertions of Wilson's Raid, the irrepressible Smith served until war's end.

Just past midnight, a halt was called five miles beyond Dinwiddie Court House. But by 3:00 A.M. on June 23 the Federal cavalry was again moving. Wilson's men soon struck Ford's Station on the Southside Railroad and proceeded west, laying waste to the roadbed as they marched. Unbeknownst to them, the enemy lay ahead in force. During the night, W.F.H. Lee had utilized local byways to pass Wilson's command and strategically interpose his troopers between the forces of Kautz and Wilson. Since Lee's force was only a quarter of his adversary's, he was limited to being more a pest than a threat. Still, with guns in their hands and a will in their hearts, these rebel horsemen were capable of taking lives and disrupting timetables. This unexpected turn of events mattered more to the Vermonters on this day than it would have on the previous one, for their brigade had been rotated to the van of the column. After spending all of Wednesday trying to stop the rebels from crashing through the rear, Thursday they removed rebels as a blockage to forward progress. Heading west along the Southside Railroad, the column ran into Lee's troopers around two o'clock in the afternoon, commencing a fight that lasted until dark. "We dismounted immediately," was one participant's recollection, "and engaged the enemy who fought desperately all day."[33] The fighting was of a back-and-forth nature, with the Vermonters initially driving the rebels so fast and hard that the enemy's artillery was taken; however, a Confederate counterattack rescued the big guns before they could be hauled away or spiked. For its role in this action, the 1st Vermont paid a price. Nottoway Court House would cost the regiment three dead and over twenty wounded or missing.

Among those lost was Captain Hiram Hall, who suffered a ghastly mortal wound from a bullet to the forehead above the left eye. A scholar who graduated from the University of Vermont, the twenty-five-year-old Hall's mental acuity and organizational skills made him well-suited for staff work. Not noted for his combat exploits, Captain Hall did have several horses shot out from under him and courageously rode beside his commander in "Farnsworth's Charge." With the death of Oliver Cushman, Hall returned to line duty as the commander of Company E, a post that he filled for barely three weeks. In Blinn's assessment of his comrades' reaction to Hall's death, "his loss [was] deeply mourned by the regiment."[34] Characterized as being both cool and intrepid, Hall's military demeanor undoubtedly contrasted sharply with that of Addison Preston. Where Preston seemed destined to be a willing soldier, Hall was more the reluctant recruit. Thrust into the war by a sense of duty and a leadership role by his peers, he performed his duties because he had taken on an obligation, where by contrast Preston flourished because the man and the moment had finally found each other. Yet, there were still those who saw him as "a capable and efficient officer, and would soon have occupied a higher position in the service, had he lived."[35] But now he was gone, and only the goodness remained. Given that a raid was in progress, the best that could be done with the body, for the sake of Hall's family, was to bury it in a clearly marked site. This was accomplished by carving his name and regiment on a walnut tree near the grave, thereby facilitating easy relocation, eventual disinterment, and ultimate return of the body home for burial.

While the 1st Vermont lost a reliable officer with the passing of Hall, the minie ball that struck Hannibal Jenne in the right temple had its greatest effect far beyond the regiment. One of its original enlistees, Jenne had recently been promoted to the rank of commissary sergeant in Company B. But in the lower ranks, there are plenty of men capable of being advanced a notch to satisfy a vacancy. Conversely, in the world beyond the army, voids created by death are not so easily filled. No one can step forward and become a replacement son or brother. Where Sergeant Jennes' passing became tragic was that it presented one more Vermont family with the stark reality of having to deal with a double blow: the loss of not only a loved one but also the family breadwinner. Due to various maladies, including a hernia, Hannibal's father, Frazier, could perform very little physical labor. The family lived on a one hundred and forty-acre farm for which Hannibal was making the payments. When he went off to war, the farmland, including forty-two cows, was leased out to a neighbor, who then worked the fields and tended the livestock. The Jennes received some cash as well as butter and cheese as a rental fee. While this may have provided sustenance, without their son's allotted pay the Jennes could no longer make the mortgage and tax payments. Foreclosure followed. Then treatments for a daughter's illness drained away the remaining available funds. The family eventually wound up moving to Wisconsin, far from home. The war had exacted a heavy toll from the Jennes—their son, their home, and their livelihood.

Lieutenant Hiram Hall was a highly competent officer who consistently performed a variety of staff assignments to laudable perfection. His climb to the top was cut short by a rebel bullet at Nottoway Court House while participating in the early stages of the Wilson-Kautz Raid (USAMHI).

After a sleepless night manning the skirmish line and withstanding random shells, the regiment forged ahead at daybreak, bearing southwest to circumvent the rebel cavalry

Cutting a swath of destruction though south-central Virginia, the Federal Wilson-Kautz Raiders became coldly efficient as they systematically destroyed miles of railroad track (Library of Congress).

and link up with Kautz's command. Rather than follow directly in Kautz's wake, Wilson elected to cut cross-country and hit the Richmond & Danville Railroad ahead of his cohort. In the words of Horace Ide, "We had crossed over diagonally from the Southside Railroad to the R and D on the hypotenuse of a triangle, and nearly all day of the 25th were engaged in the work of destruction."[36] Wilson and Kautz reunited at Meherrin Station, ten miles below Burkeville and proceeded to Keysville, where they again halted. Marching and destroying as they went, the combined command would eventually wind up at the Staunton River Bridge, thirty miles south of Burke's Station. The pyrotechnics created along the way were spectacular. When the rail line was built, a relatively inexpensive type of track, more serviceable than durable, was laid. Its builders did not consider having the exigencies of war as one of the rigors to be withstood. No track was impervious to a determined wrecking crew, but the materials used in building the Richmond & Danville made its destruction easy. Ties were put down in the traditional manner, and the "rails" amounted to wooden stringers of yellow pine with an iron strip affixed along their inner edges. Their inherent flammability, along with the wooden ties, was exacerbated by the dry weather. For the raiders, their destruction became a simple matter of igniting tinder. To carry out its task, an efficient procedure was perfected: "The mode ... was to dismount a portion of the command and march them parallel with the railroad, then face about a regiment at a time toward the track, have them advance and ignite the section of the road in their front and then resume their march. It was but the work of a few minutes for each regiment to perform its part and the whole was accomplished nearly as fast as the column could move."[37] Due to the ensuing conflagration, the progress of the Federal cavalry was identifiable by a burning ribbon of track. Hard to miss was the

glow from flames licking into the summer air and the smell of black smoke roiling sky-
ward. "Miles of railroad might have been seen at a time in flames," noted one observer,
"and at night the whole canopy of heaven was one glare of light."[38] So intense was the
heat from these conflagrations that troops in the rear had to move off a distance from the
tracks as they marched past a burning section.

Once Kautz's lead elements reached the north bank of the Roanoke, their forward
pace came to a screeching halt. Lying before them was their objective: the "high bridge."
Putting this six hundred foot-long covered wooden span and trestle to the torch was a
task that they knew how to accomplish. Were there no other difficulties, the bridge would
have been ablaze in short order. But rebel troops had contrary thoughts. A force some
1000 strong had been assembled to contest the nefarious designs of the Yankees. The lay
of the land around the river's banks favored the Confederates. The defenders' side consisted of a steep embankment, atop of which were set two earthworks, one on each side
of the tracks, containing six pieces of artillery between them and supported by rifle
trenches to their front, or river, side. There were also manned rifle pits on the opposite
side with which the Union forces would have to contend before even reaching the bridge.
Though the defenders were mostly militia, some in their teens and others aged, their
position was highly defensible. The few hundred Confederate regulars present were stationed in the fortifications on the approaching side, ready to absorb the brunt of any
attack.

Kautz's men were charged with accomplishing an impossible task. They had only
one way to breech the river barrier — across the trestle. Any hope of their inexperienced
opponents running when the action got hot was quickly dispelled. The attackers put forth
a valiant but wasted effort. Four charges were launched, four were repulsed. The bridge's
defenders were not to be dislodged. Even though the Vermonters were not involved, they
still performed valuable service on the 25th as they picketed the rear. Shortly after dark,
the regiment parried with Lee's troopers, who tried their best to raise havoc. After dark,
though standing dutifully to horse, they were called upon for no further service. Shortly
after midnight, Wilson and Kautz concluded that nothing further was to be gained by
lingering in the vicinity.

For two-and-a-half days, the return trip was uneventful. The only force of substance
in the area, Lee's cavalry, was nowhere to be seen. Swinging in an arc to the east-northeast toward Petersburg, Sunday the 26th found them bivouacking for the night on Buck-
horn Creek. The next day's sojourn took them further east to Great Creek before halting
at 9:00 P.M. Though the Union troopers engaged in some minor destruction, this sector
suffered no strategic damage.

One providential aspect of this route across south-central Virginia was that the land
as yet had been untouched by war. This translated into ample supplies to satiate the
hunger of man and beast. Unfortunately, it also resulted in some wanton plundering,
which Southern newspapers vigorously trumpeted. Under the headline "Depredations of
the Raiders," the *Lynchburg Virginian* detailed examples of the thievery of "Wilson's
Gang" to its sympathetic and outraged readers: "From Mr. Edward Stokes of Lunenburg
the raiders stole a set of silver service for which was paid $5,000 before the war"; and
"the residence of Capt. Wm A. Adams ... was robbed of every light article of value it contained, the furniture broken up, and the house committed to the flames."[39] While every
trooper did not engage in such inexcusable looting, enough men did to give the raid a
black eye — and Southerners more reasons to hate Yankees. On Tuesday, June 28, all

started out well. After crossing the Nottoway River south of Petersburg, the raiders turned north. After traveling ten miles unmolested, the weary marchers gained Stoney Creek Station. Just beyond the depot, at Sappony Church, they were abruptly welcomed back into the war zone by enemy troops, whose presence here came as a surprise to General Wilson. According to the original plan, General Grant had assured Wilson that this location would offer a safe portal for the raiders' return.

However, instead of finding the way open, Wilson's advance party ran into the mounted division of Wade Hampton to be joined shortly by their persistent nemesis, Rooney Lee. Horace Ide, riding back with the main force, recounted the instant when all hell broke loose up ahead, turning the last leg of what had been an uncontested retreat into a bitter ordeal: "Just before dark, while I was saying to Lieutenant Trussell that 'we must be near the railroad and that when got across that we should be all right' when we heard the carbines of the advance, which told us that our way was blocked and that if we passed there, we must fight for it."[40] These opening shots signaled the start of a two-day struggle that would witness heavy fighting around both Stoney Creek and Reams' stations.

A seasoned, capable officer who was proud of his resiliency and durability, Captain William Cummings suffered a horrendous disfiguring head wound at Stoney Creek during the return phase of the Wilson-Kautz Raid, an injury from which he gamely returned to duty after two months of convalescence (USAMHI).

In the failing light at day's end and on into the blackness of night, battle was joined at Stoney Creek. The 1st Vermont fought from the much-despised dismounted stance, albeit this posture afforded limited protection behind hastily constructed field fortifications. During lulls, "Our boys improved them by throwing up slight breastworks, composed of rails and dirt which they dug up with their bare hands."[41] Meager though it may have been, Sergeant Eri Woodbury appreciated its value, for "many a time during that night the balls struck in this frail defense or in the dirt so near it as to sprinkle us with sand."[42] Still, enemy fire managed to find its mark, with the man lying to Woodbury's right being struck painfully in the knee.

Weighing in against Wilson's command were four Confederate cavalry brigades. Even in the darkness, their bullets found marks. As he led his battalion to shore up a weak spot in the line, Captain William Cummings was shot. The bullet that felled him struck a half-inch from his left ear, penetrating his temple and exiting through the center of his right cheek just below the eye. In its violent passage through Cummings' head, the heavy missile "carried away portions of the articulation of the lower jaw and the bone in his nose and broke the socket of the right eye."[43] That he survived such an excruciating wound was partly attributable to his being in great shape. In later years, the old soldier would often point this out, saying that "it has always been my pride that my physical condition was such when I went into the army that I never lost a routine of duty or an army ration from a surgeon's excuse, sickness, or disease during my four years of service, that I always answered 'here' to every call of duty."[44]

By the time hostilities ceased, Cummings was a proven warrior of the first order. He had experienced being a POW in 1862, re-upped as a Veteran Volunteer, had four horses shot out from under him in combat, risen through the ranks to lieutenant-colonel, and taken a grievous wound. To his credit, after fifty-five days of recuperation, the twenty-four-year-old Cummings was back with the regiment in time for the fall campaign. In the age of vanity in which we live, one has to admire the likes of William Cummings. Though facially disfigured, he did not retreat from public life. Instead he went on to marry and carve out a career in the wholesale coal business, never once ruing the terrible price that the war had exacted from him. With its ranks populated by men the caliber of gritty William Cummings, it is not hard to fathom why the 1st Vermont was an elite cavalry unit.

Captain Cummings was not the only Vermonter rendered hors de combat that night. Lieutenant Gilbert Stewart and Private Norman Kingsbury were mortally wounded. Considered by many the best tactician in the regiment as well as a fine swordsman, Stewart was fondly remembered as one of its "bravest and best men."[45] When the lead flew the thickest in battle, "He was calm, cool, and collected, avoiding all harsh and profane language," while in camp his persona "was affable and kind, commanding the respect of all."[46] Kingsbury took a minie ball in his hip and like Cummings was placed in a medical wagon. However, when the vehicle was abandoned, unlike Cummings, who commandeered a horse, "He was left at Reams' Station with the ambulance as he was unable to travel."[47] Captured on the 29th, he lingered painfully in a Petersburg hospital until succumbing on the 7th of July.

Another of those who fell in confusion of the delaying action was William Colby, though in a broad sense it was friendly fire that was his undoing. A member of Company G, Colby, with Ide, Kingsbury, Cummings, and Stewart, was one of the dismounted troopers trying to stem the rebel advance. Lying on the ground behind fence rails, he directed carbine fire at enemy troopers. All at once, "horses belonging to his regiment became frightened and broke loose from the troopers in charge of them and ran down along the fence where his company was laying, when one of the horses stepped on ... [Colby's] ankle, bruising it severely and cutting and lacerating the flesh."[48] While comrades got him mounted when the time came to move out, Colby's reprieve only lasted a day. He wound up a prisoner on the 29th and eventually heard the dreaded sound of Andersonville's gates closing behind him. The six months that Colby would spend in confinement proved terribly trying, as he received no medical treatment for the injury, which had become infected.

The sparring continued sporadically throughout the night, creating a surrealistic world of deadly magnificence. "It was a grand but awful sight to see the long streams of fire as they shot forth from hundreds of carbines," one Vermont participant observed, "and then the broad deep red flashes of artillery and bursting shells, that for an instant would light up the midnight heavens almost blindingly."[49] As dawn approached and with no semblance of progress in dislodging the rebel roadblock, General Wilson decided to shift his strategy. Pulling Kautz's troopers from the melee, he sent them ten miles north to see if the route through Reams' Station was open. After continuing his holding action until mid-morning, Wilson ordered the remainder of his command to mount up. Then he followed after Kautz, though leaving behind the 1st Vermont, 3rd Indiana, and 8th

New York to fight a delaying action. The difficulty of fighting dismounted, mounting, dismounting, and remounting — all while under fire — was described by Sergeant Ide "as a very delicate operation ... because if the horses are brought up to the line they are sure to be shot at by the enemy's skirmishers, and if the footmen fall back to them, the enemy will follow up, generally so that the operation of mounting up and forming has to be performed under fire."[50] When the moment finally arrived for the Vermonters to disengage, their departure was so hasty that over sixty men wound up as prisoners.

Extricating themselves from Stoney Creek did not improve the Vermonters' lot much. Upon reaching Reams' Station, all hopes of escape via that route were summarily dashed: "...what made the hair stick up on those who were not bald, was to find the railroad station occupied by the rebel cavalry of Hampton and Fitzhugh Lee, and one division of infantry."[51] With three distinct enemy forces arrayed in a semicircle before them, getting through to the safety of their own lines was no longer axiomatic. Dire straits called for drastic action. To maximize traveling speed, all encumbrances had to be jettisoned. This meant leaving behind artillery, supply wagons, and, most agonizing of all, ambulances filled with wounded. After as much ammunition as the men could carry was distributed, the wagons were set afire.

The warrior in Wilson initially conjured up the vision of a headlong charge, intended to produce a dramatic breakthrough: "I determined to mass the entire command on the new road leading to Petersburg — artillery behind the cavalry, ambulances next to the artillery, ammunition wagons last — and make a bold push to break through the enemy."[52] Fortunately, better judgment won the day. With his men and animals completely spent, keeping further losses to a minimum now made the most sense. The escape route that he chose was probably the last one that his adversaries anticipated. Heading west, he would lead his troopers directly away from the Union lines until reaching the Stage Road, then turn south to the Double Bridges across the Nottoway, and ultimately proceed to the east by way of Jarratt's Station. Once over the Weldon railroad, the column would be home free. This plan of retreat, essentially an inverted block-U, was intended to bring his command below the extreme left of the Confederate forces as they were currently positioned. By moving rapidly, he thought it entirely possible to outrun the rebels before they could initiate any countermeasures.

No sooner had the focus of the Wilson-Kautz Raid shifted to survival than the venture lost its joint sponsorship. The escape would be known henceforth only as "Wilson's Retreat." This halving of the expedition's leadership and strength occurred because August Kautz was able to bypass the Confederate right between Reams' Station and Rowanty Creek and return his share of the men, along with stray elements of Wilson's force, to Union lines in the evening of June 29. Essentially Kautz pulled off an end run. The only difference was that he traveled a much shorter route in far less time than Wilson eventually did, for it was not until 2:00 P.M. on July 2 that the rest of the raiders gained safety.

As to labeling the venture a "success" or "failure," the decision is not a simple matter. As is often the case in war, the military advantages gained must be balanced against the material and human costs expended. That this raid exacted a toll on its participants there can be no doubt, small wonder as the raid covered some 385 miles in 81 hours with but 6 hours of rest during the entire experience![53] By Wilson's estimate, "The loss sustained by the entire command was about 900 men, killed, wounded, and missing, 12 field guns, 4 mountain howitzers, and 30 wagons and ambulances abandoned and fell into the enemy's hands."[54] Taking this to the regimental level, the 1st Vermont had about 280 effective riders answering roll call on July 2. Its total loss was somewhere around 90 men. Perhaps even more revealing, the number of line officers was reduced to five. As Private Harvey Lilly assessed the post-raid status quo, "Vt. troops have suffered much more than any others. They have been very unfortunate — but they have done nothing that our state need feel ashamed of — but rather proud."[55]

While those who died in battle were to be rightfully mourned and justly eulogized, there was at least certainty surrounding their fate. Some wounded survived the battlefield, only to die in the merciful but helpless hands of friends. In this vein, Sergeant Charles Bishop took "a severe gunshot wound [to his] left side" and was captured when the ambulances were abandoned.[56] Hospitalized in Petersburg in severely weakened condition, he nevertheless escaped on the Fourth of July, "and after remaining out for two days and two nights, he reached ... [Union] lines, and was immediately conveyed to the Balfour Hospital, Portsmouth, Va," only to perish of pneumonia three weeks later.[57] All of twenty-one, the young trooper's demise touched many people. His lieutenant wrote Bishop's parents to tell them that their son was a prized soldier who "never shrunk from any duty in the camp or in the field."[58] At his funeral service in Ludlow, Vermont, the preacher was eulogizing Sergeant Bishop, but in the process he effectively characterized a generation of citizen-soldiers: "It is nevertheless true that another Green Mountain Boy, as gentle as a lamb in peace, but fierce as a tiger in battle, has passed away. Although his years were few, yet his life was long, for it answered life's great end."[59]

But for the more than three score listed as "missing in action," the wait for family and friends was often long and agonizing. For these men, having survived the horrors of the battlefield only meant that they had lived to be subjected to another ordeal: a Southern prison camp. In time, the list of dead chalked up to Wilson's Raid grew as inhumane treatment accomplished what hot lead had not. Wesley Dodge, John Pierce, and Philander Preston were among those married men who perished in Confederate hands and left dependant families at home. Then there was the occasional trooper, like Addison Harris, who simply disappeared in the chaos of battle. He was believed captured in the hurried morning retreat from Stoney Creek Station, at which time the rebels bagged the group of sixty men, many being from Company H, including Lieutenant Edwin Higley. The last letter that Private Harris sent home, dated June 15, had an eerily prophetic closing: "I bid you adieu for the present and perhaps forever."[60]

Over time, some of those missing were released by their captors, though more often than not they were infirm in some way. Then, there was the occasional trooper, David Howard in this instance, who was missing on June 29, 1863 and remains so to this day. A father of two toddlers, he enlisted in December of '63 and rode off to war and into oblivion. Records indicate that "no body [was] ever found or identified."[61] Whether he was blown to bits by an exploding shell or crawled off to die alone in the covering woods, the widow Howard would never know, while for two Vermont babies, too young to comprehend their immediate loss, memories of a missing father would come only from what others shared with them.

Weighed against the heavy losses had to be the damage done to the enemy's railroad network. The evidence was indisputable. Some sixty miles of track were laid to waste and countless support structures reduced to ashes, along with numerous bridges and some rolling stock. One of the participants in the grueling mission, Sergeant Woodbury, was personally satisfied that the objective was attained: "Our raid, in some ways disastrous, came to an end Saturday. 'In some ways disastrous I say' ... [because] we accomplished the object of our expedition with [the] destruction of the Danville RR."[62]

The conclusion of the latest raid brought some much-needed downtime for the Vermonters. The first order of business was to draw rations. "We checked starvation, and then struck for the river with a chunk of soap ... and after washing for awhile, found we were still human beings."[63] For three weeks, the regiment rested on high ground near the James River. Though they would still have to endure the cavalry's obligatory round of picketing, scouting, and patrolling, there would be no more of the costly raids like those of the past three months. On July 19, heavy rains finally came to dampen the parched land. "Instead of vast clouds of dust raised by the moving trains and almost hiding everything from view, we have a clear atmosphere and rejoicing army."[64]

Along with the clean air, plentiful food was now available, with the presence of fresh vegetables being especially welcomed. The feeling abounded that the war was winding down. There were those predicting its successful conclusion before winter. Though some among them were yet to die, collectively the worst of the bloodletting for the regiment was over. There would still be languishing deaths for comrades in Southern prisons, but at least proportionately fewer Vermont troopers would be joining them in the months ahead. They had one more crucial date with destiny and Jubal Early in the Shenandoah Valley to be fulfilled, but the next ten months were more about successfully ringing down the curtain than they were fretting about how the play would end.

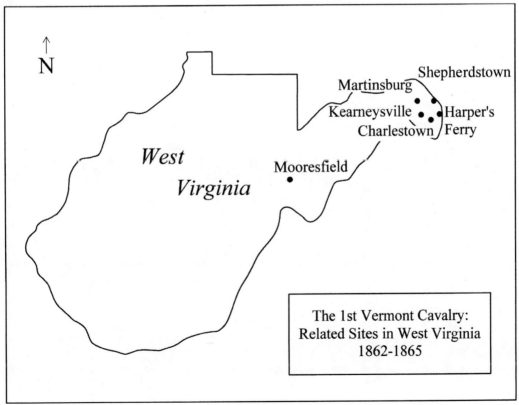

The 1st Vermont Cavalry:
Related Sites in West Virginia
1862–1865

Drawn by Bob Collea

Perhaps most satisfying of all, at this stage of the war the Vermonters had lived up to if not exceeded the high expectations set for them. No less a champion, as well as an architect of their success, was Addison Preston, who unabashedly praised his men in a July 29 letter to his brother: "Our regiment has marched as far, fought as much, and lost as heavily as any in this army. It is acknowledged here that there is not a better fighting brigade in the cavalry service than ours and few as good. Then consider that our regiment (1st Vt) lost as many killed as the other three regiments in the Brigade together. It will give you some idea of what we do."[65]

27

Back to the Shenandoah
The 1st Vermont's Shining Hour

Between July and August, the 1st Vermont handled only light duties. This placid existence contrasted with the furious pace of the recent heavy raids. However, events unfolding on another front ended the tranquility. "Jubal Early was at this time raiding around in Maryland," and, as Sergeant Ide confidently proclaimed, "it was now decided to send us there to see to it."[1]

The mischief needing attention resulted from Lee's desire to relieve pressure on Richmond. In June, he sent General Early and 14,000 men into the upper Shenandoah. Their charge was to drive out any Yankees, thereby securing the ripening crops. Then Early's liberators would morph into raiders, move into western Maryland, and disrupt Union supply and communication lines. In the process, if any threat was posed to Washington, so much the better. If the Federal authorities reacted true to form, any rebel presence near the capital would inflame bureaucratic anxiety, forcing a recall of troops from Lee's front. Early did well. By mid–July, he brazenly had his tiny army at the gates of the capital, coming within a whisker of capturing the city. As Lee had hoped, Grant was compelled to send regiments to save the day.

During the opening stages of Early's raid, Grant was slow to react. Eventually he came to see how events in the Valley affected his situation before Petersburg. While every regiment he redeployed meant a reduction in his besieging force, Grant saw merit in suppressing Early. First, the Washington brass would be mollified. Then, after expunging opposition, Union troops could terminate the Valley's contributions as "the Breadbasket of the Confederacy." Denied access to Washington, the Confederates had withdrawn into the Valley's sheltering confines. The initial relief that Early's army had been beaten back was comforting—but not enough. The menace required permanent eradication. To accomplish the task, General Phil Sheridan and the Army of the Shenandoah became Grant's chosen instruments of destruction.

For the first few weeks, Sheridan consolidated his forces at Harpers Ferry while simultaneously probing the enemy's strength. The six weeks prior to the Battle of Opequon saw his cavalry actively engaged in daily reconnaissances. Usually routine, missions could always unexpectedly erupt into deadly encounters. On August 25, General Alfred Torbert led two cavalry divisions east from Harpers Ferry. Happenstance had it that General Early chose that same morning to push north from Winchester with a force of cavalry and infantry. They collided at Kearneysville, approximately ten miles northwest of Harpers Ferry on the southern side of the Potomac. The early going favored Torbett's troopers. But unanticipated enemy infantry support turned the tables. To save their artillery, the Vermonters had to grudgingly fight dismounted. For almost an hour, the regiment skirmished with the enemy. As one participant recapped the action, "For a time our regiment bore the brunt of the fight, and though closely pursued, we fell back in good order, Col. Wells several times forming the reg't in line and giving them another volley."[2]

Most of the regiment's casualties occurred during this phase of the operation. Three men perished: Edward Wright and William Day from fatal stomach injuries and Harmon Hall from a gunshot wound to the head. Private Wright's passing was much lamented, for comrades considered him to be "one of the best soldiers in the army — always ready for any duty he was called on to perform."[3]

In a tragic illustration of how often chance determined who lived or died from wounds, the cases of George Mizo and Edward King offer a revealing comparison. Both were struck down in the Kearnysville skirmish. Of the two, Mizo's wound initially appeared the more grievous: "The ball entered the inner side of the right leg about halfway from the foot to the knee, hit the tibia, and lodged."[4] Though infected by gangrene, Mizo gamely battled this insidious complication and miraculously lived. By contrast, King's wound was in the right foot, several toe bones being fractured when struck by a minie ball. Quickly hospitalized, King was dead in a fortnight, following the amputation of two toes. Considering that countless others lost entire extremities to the surgeon's saw, King's losses seemed minor. But surviving a wound and surgery were never guarantees of recovery. Soon, afflicted by the ravages of gangrene, the young trooper was fighting for his life. Even though hospital accounts indicated that "the patient was in good health when wounded and in good condition when admitted," medical records for the next fourteen days depict King's steady deterioration, with a wildly fluctuating pulse, a severely swollen leg, frequent headaches, recurring fever, and a suppurating wound.[5] Far removed from the glory of battle, Edward King experienced an agonizing demise: "He is fading fast; pulse at 156 and very weak, complains of great heat, skin is cool, has great pain in lower part of left lung."[6] Dying at 10:00 P.M. on September 10, King represented another lost life among the 249,548 men who succumbed to disease during the war, tortured souls for whom the cure for what ailed them was beyond existing medical capabilities.

Though Private King's story ended tragically, Lucian Reed's travail culminated more positively. He was wounded in his right arm at Kearneysville. Doctors could not save the limb, finally amputating the infected appendage at the shoulder. The thought of an empty sleeve was not welcomed by this sensitive man. While he would not be alone in his misery, for there were over 50,000 amputations during the war, King was determined to lessen its impact. Though the field of prosthetics was in its infancy, options were available. Reed decided on an artificial limb made of "Kimball's Vulcanite Rubber." However, his doctor refused Reed's transfer request. Undaunted, the enterprising soldier authored a note to the one person whom he judged to be able to help him. "Dear Sir," he humbly addressed Abraham Lincoln, "[h]aving served in the Army over three years in the First Vermont Cavalry and had the misfortune to lose my right arm, I wish to be transferred to Philadelphia for the sake of getting a false arm as I expect to get a much better fit by being there in person.... I have ventured to address these few lines to you in the hopes that you can aid me in getting me transferred to Philadelphia."[7] Touched by the earnest plea, Lincoln pulled strings, the least he could do for a boy who had borne the battle at his behest. Soon, Reed's physician received an order authorizing Private Reed's transfer — and the grateful trooper got his prosthetic device.

By mid–September, Sheridan was finally ready to fight. Till now, he had been most deliberate about his strategizing: "I determined to take all the time necessary to equip myself with the fullest information, and then seize an opportunity under such conditions that I could not well fail success."[8] The attack was set for September 19. Cavalry units were assigned to advance on the right and left, the infantry in the middle. Identified interchangeably as the Battle of Opequon and the 3rd Battle of Winchester, this clash resulted in a Union victory, clear-cut yet not decisive in ending Early's threat. The 1st Vermont's role, potentially pivotal, wound up being inconsequential.

Wilson's orders were to move against the extreme Confederate left. If successful in this assignment, units of the Federal cavalry could have found themselves behind Early's troops, interdicting the enemy's escape route up the Valley Turnpike. Glory beckoned tantalizingly. But the assault was a bust, glaringly so when compared to the other attacks. As his division advanced, Wilson's progress was contested by rebel cavalry. Some Vermonters first fought as skirmishers, and then the whole regiment was placed in a dismounted line. Making little headway, Wilson disengaged and tried a similar approach south of town. Once again, the same blocking force denied access to the pike. With darkness settling over the scene, his men remained stalled a mile-and-a-half from the thoroughfare. It is a measure of the softness with which Wilson pushed this assault that but one in the ranks of the 1st Vermont was killed, Bertrand Campbell, who had been with the regiment all of five days. While the young man's death was sad enough, the way his parents learned of their boy's demise carried a poignancy all its own.

According to Fanny Campbell, "I was informed of his death in a letter."[9] The missive was penned by a doctor in the 1st New Hampshire Cavalry. Thoughtful in that it was at least sent, it was hardly couched in sensitive terms: "Sir, enclosed please find the contents of the wallet of a soldier of the 1st Vermont Cavalry, killed at Winchester on Sept. 19, 1864. I removed the contents just as he was about to be buried."[10] Eventually, the Campbells received a visit from George McAllister, a comrade of their late son. The trooper bore with him the wallet, the few dollars it contained, and an express receipt for another seventy dollars that Bertram had sent them from Boston. Ever grateful for this humanitarian gesture, Fanny Campbell used the precious wallet for the rest of her life, but "the receipt I have never claimed the blood from."[11]

Taking advantage of the darkness, the Confederates retreated throughout the night. At daybreak, pursuit began. Twenty-two miles to the south, Early's men waited. Just beyond Strasburg, he posted his meager command atop Fisher's Hill. Holding a natural defensive position, their presence could have spelled serious trouble for Sheridan. But after thoroughly reconnoitering Early's troop dispositions, some deft maneuvering by Sheridan, starting on September 21 and continuing on the 22nd, led to a complete rout of Early's depleted forces in the late afternoon. The defeated Confederates retreated almost ninety miles to Waynesboro.

Once again the Valley's topography had dictated a general's strategy. Sheridan was mindful that enemy troops could slip surreptitiously north through the Luray Valley and eventually hit his column from behind. Consequently, as Sheridan's main force moved south toward Fisher's Hill, the 3rd Cavalry Division was sent to reconnoiter the vicinity of Front Royal and the Luray Valley. Brushing aside any opposition, Torbert would drive up the valley to New Market Gap, cross the Massanutten, and block Early's retreat via the Valley Turnpike. In essence, the 3rd Division was afforded another opportunity to redeem itself for the Opequon failure.

Led by the Vermonters, the first opposition was encountered east of Front Royal, on the west bank of the Shenandoah's South Fork. Here, a halt was ostensibly called for the day; however, after further deliberation, that order was countermanded in favor of a night attack. The chosen hour was 2:00 A.M. on September 20. The strategy was a two-pronged assault, with the 1st Vermont and 7th New York forcing a crossing at Kendrick's Ford as the 2nd Brigade moved across Richard's Ford to the north. Heavy fire stopped progress at the water's edge, compelling the brigade to dismount. The stalemate was finally broken when the 2nd Brigade rolled up the enemy's flank, causing the rebels to hurriedly flee the scene. They then made a brief stand along the southern banks of Gooney Manor Run. A spirited skirmish lasted into the evening, at which time Wilson disengaged. The next morning, with the enemy gone, pursuit was renewed. But the chase was brief, for the Confederate commander elected to stand near Milford. Dug in on a high hill, Wickham's troops defiantly awaited the Federal response. Try as the Yankees might, two days of probing and skirmishing could uncover no weakness in the rebels' deploy-

ment. During the course of an artillery duel, the otherwise bloodless encounter was marred by the loss of a solitary Vermont trooper. As noted by Charles Farr, Company F's "[George] Clemons was mortally wounded by a piece of shell."[12] Before contact was broken off the next day, one last attempt was made to gain the enemy's rear. However, the final approach necessitated passing through a narrow ravine in a single file. With enemy troops posted along one rim, the enterprise was considered too risky, so the Federal column faced about for a return march to Strasburg.

En route to rejoin the Army of the Shenandoah, Torbert received word of the smashing victory at Fisher's Hill. Accompanying the news was a reaffirmation from General Sheridan regarding the importance of gaining New Market ahead of Early. But by then it was already too late. Once again, the 3rd Cavalry Division had not seized the moment. The backdoor remained ajar, and the enemy slipped through again. In his post-mortem of the Battle of Fisher's Hill, Sheridan had high praise for

Ever flamboyant in appearance, down to his trademark red tie, the General George A. Custer's combative, fearless demeanor in battle endeared him to the troopers of the 1st Vermont, who would have willingly followed him anywhere (Library of Congress).

his infantry generals, who executed the battle plan "to the very letter," while in the same breath scornfully noting that "the only drawback was the cavalry."[13] Referencing the lack of "any serious effort at all to dislodge the Confederate cavalry" at Milford by Torbert, Sheridan bluntly shared how his subordinate's "impotent attempt not only chagrined me very much, but occasioned much unfavorable comment throughout the army."[14] That Sheridan was peeved would be an understatement. In venting his displeasure, he figuratively threw down a gauntlet to his cavalry chief, one that would manifest itself in a veritable shape up or ship out challenge.

But for the time being, amends would have to wait. The 24th saw the Vermonters pass the now abandoned works at Milford and bivouac at the foot of the southern end of Massanautten Mountain. The following day they crossed through New Market Gap and gratefully met up with the regimental supply wagons. The next three days would see the 1st Vermont proceed deeper into the Shenandoah, halting at Waynesboro. With his advance guard having ventured 133 miles south of Harpers Ferry, Sheridan had driven Early from the Valley. In the process, he had placed the rich heartland of the Confederacy at his mercy. If there had ever been doubts about the succor these lands brought to their enemies, a look in any direction revealed bounty aplenty. "The country we passed through," marveled one Vermont trooper "...was some of the richest of the valley. Immense quantities of hay and grain were everywhere to be seen. Fruit is in great abundance, and tobacco in vast quantities."[15]

With Grant's blessing, Sheridan was about to give long overdue attention to the Shenandoah Valley. To insure that there was no confusion on Sheridan's part, General Grant issued him specific orders on August 26, 1864: "Do all the damage to railroads and crops you can. Carry off all stock of all descriptions, and Negroes, so as to prevent further planting. If the war is to last another year, we want the Shenandoah Valley to remain a barren waste."[16]

The August missive from General Grant set in motion a series of tragic events that would be forever known to Valley residents as "The Burning." Seared into their collective memories was the sight of personal property torched, livestock stolen or killed, and homes looted. For decades, the name of Sheridan and the thought of blue-coated cavalrymen were repulsive to these Virginians. The whirlwind that the defenseless citizenry reaped was like no other before or since that occurred on American soil. While Sherman's "March to the Sea" is often viewed as the epitome of such destruction, inflaming as it flamed, its focus was on the infrastructure supporting the military.

Before heading northward to devastate the Valley, the 1st Vermont experienced several command changes. After being slightly wounded at Opequon, George Chapman was granted a thirty-day leave. To temporarily fill his place, William Wells was promoted. With Wells' elevation, Major John Bennett assumed command of the 1st Vermont. However, the change carrying the most import was that which occurred much higher in the command structure: leadership of the 3rd Division. The despised incumbent, James Wilson, was sent to Georgia, and in his place the revered George Armstrong Custer was given the divisional reins. The troopers of the 1st Vermont were ecstatic. "General Custer is now in command of the division, a very good change we all think" was William Wells' assessment. Beyond the charisma Custer exuded, his tactics of preference were the opposite of Wilson's. Gone would be the reliance on dismounted responses. Riding in his wake was no place for the faint of heart, for he would gladly lead all to the sound of the guns. Though victory was always the goal, glory was ever a welcomed companion. "This would mean rough riding and wicked fighting," one admiring trooper acknowledged, "but we would be commanded and led in battle by an officer whose bloody sabre no one in the division ever had to look over his shoulder to see."[17]

Sheridan's plan was simple. With the infantry marching in the center along the Valley Turnpike, his mounted forces would sweep northward on both sides. "The cavalry as it retired was stretched across the country from the Blue Ridge to the eastern slope of the Alleghenies, with orders to drive off all stock and destroy all supplies as it moved northward."[18] When completed," Sheridan reported, "...the valley, from Winchester to Staunton, a distance of ninety-two miles, will have but little in it for man or beast."[19] Once leaving Harrisonburg in the retrograde movement October 6, cavalry units were assigned specific routes and areas of responsibility. For its part, Custer's 3rd Division was sent along what was known as the "Back Road," a rough route that wound along the Valley's western edge at the base of the Alleghenies. As observed by Captain James Kidd, "one could have made a chart of Custer's trail by the columns of black smoke that marked it."[20]

Orders being orders, troopers of the 1st Vermont were obligated to participate in the

In the vicinity of Mt. Jackson, Vermonters like Eri Woodbury were called upon to put crops and buildings to the torch, all the while conscious of Rosser's rebel cavalry hovering on their flanks to make prisoners of any unwary Yankee troopers (Library of Congress).

distasteful task of putting private property to the torch. Being that countless men hailed from small family-run farms, it was understandable that in many an individual's heart were some misgivings about such incendiary work. Amidst the mournful faces and beseeching voices of the frightened populace, only the most hardened could not help but call to mind loved ones back in Vermont, thankful that the situation was not reversed. Among those who participated in the burnings was the gentle-souled Sergeant Eli Woodbury of Company E. Insight into his emotional state as he was obligated to apply the torch is contained in his diary: "We were making a raid and burning all the forage in the valley. Co. E was out on the left flank driving in cattle and sheep and firing barns. I fired one, and sorry enough to do that!"[21] The cumulative effect of the ensuing devastation was itemized in General Sheridan's report to General Grant on the evening of October 7: "I have destroyed over 2,000 barns filled with wheat, hay, and farming implements; over 70 mills, filled with wheat and flour; have driven in front of the army over 4[000] head of stock; and have killed and issued to the troops not less than 3,000 sheep."[22] The Union soldiers who participated for the most part rode away, never to return again. But for many Valley residents, only hard times and bitter feelings filled the foreseeable future. As noted Valley artist, historian, and resident Thomas Heartwole recently commented, "The Civil War has rightly been called the defining moment in the life of the nation; the Burning was the defining moment in the life of the Valley."[23]

As they carried out their depredations, the Federal cavalrymen frequently stole

Custer's sweeping bow to General Rosser, given in full view of both sides before the Battle of Tom's Brook, was followed, after his victory, by Custer's cavorting about the Union encampment wearing the captured uniform jacket of his adversary and former West Point classmate (Library of Congress).

glances over their shoulders. Their apprehensions were engendered by a recent report: on October 5 General Thomas Rosser had arrived with his famed "Laurel Brigade," populated by men who hailed from the very villages and farms now being violated by the enemy. Spurred on by his substantial ego and their burning anger, they chafed for the chance at payback. Serving as the rear guard on October 7, the Vermont Cavalry felt their wrath. Vigilant as hawks, waiting for the opportune moment to strike, the Virginians' patience was eventually rewarded. A gap was eventually detected between the Vermonters and the main column. Near Columbia Furnace, two brigades of rebel cavalry struck the Federal rear guard. "Today while pursuing our devastating course," Eri Woodbury wrote, "we were attacked by Gen. Rosser's Div. of Cavalry. I was sent out on a skirmish line with a squad of men. While there they flanked us upon the left, & our troops were forced into a confused retreat. I was at one time very near being captured."[24]

Along with capturing three dozen good men, the opportunistic Confederates absconded with seven portable forges. General Sheridan was quite irked by this news. Also stung by this harassment was the proud Custer, who badgered his superiors for permission to strike back. For Custer, the presence of Rosser rekindled an old rivalry that harked back to their competitive days together as West Point cadets and roommates. While sharing Custer's desire to cut the overbearing Rosser down to size, Sheridan was devising a response on a much grander scale than a limited rearguard sortie. He too was fed up, as much at his own cavalry's recent lack of success as he was at the rebel cavalry's newfound bravura. Furthermore, Sheridan believed that he knew precisely wherein the fault lay. The goat's horns, in Sheridan's mind, belonged on the head of General Torbert. Since the standing of his cavalry chieftain was already on shaky ground due to his twin failures to cut off Early's retreat, Sheridan's well of patience was running low. In the evening of the 8th, he summoned Torbert to his headquarters. Never one to mince words, the general laid into his underachieving subordinate: "That night I told Torbert I expected him either to give Rosser a drubbing next morning or get whipped himself, and the infantry would be halted until the affair was over. I also informed him that I proposed to ride out to Round Top Mountain to see the fight."[25]

Torbert's pride was stung. Retiring to his headquarters, he mulled over Sheridan's sharp words. The next morning, October 9, 1864, General Torbert went out and won back some of his superior's lost confidence. Beneath Sheridan's gaze, "The two divisions moved forward together under Torbert's direction, with a determination to inflict on the enemy the sharp and summary punishment his rashness had invited."[26] The engagement is known as the "Battle of Tom's Brook," though the speed with which the defeated rebels hastened up the Valley gave rise to an unflattering sobriquet: "Woodstock Races." The encounter was a cavalry fight from start to finish. Six brigades to a side, battle was joined for a little more than two hours.

Before hostilities commenced, a bit of showmanship transpired, befitting the gallant character of the two leading protagonists. Approaching the Confederate lines at the head of his men, Custer spotted Rosser on a hilltop. Ever the showman, Custer wheeled his horse around, doffed his cap, and bowed toward his friend and adversary. Rosser returned the gesture. Deafening cheers went up all around, as the men simultaneously applauded their flamboyant leaders. After this chivalrous prelude, the battle began in earnest. Rosser did not approach the impending clash with the level of trepidation and hesitancy that he might better have. With Early and his infantry twenty-some miles behind him, there would be no support for his troopers.

The battle would be waged on two parallel fronts that stretched east to west for about five miles. Custer's Brigade fanned left and right off the Back Road to attack Rosser's skirmishers. Behind them was Spiker's Hill, where the Confederate artillery and reserves were placed. The troopers of Wesley Merritt were centered on the Valley Pike about two miles to the east, their line extending westward until it linked up with Custer's left. Opposing Merritt were the troops of Lunsford Lomax. From the start, the battle was a mismatch, with Federal forces estimated at 6,500 to the Confederates' 3,500.

Positioned on the right flank of the Union battle line was the brigade of William Wells. For the Vermonters, their time to fight would not come until late in the afternoon. After breaking camp, Federal troops were in position by nine o'clock. By virtue of his numerical superiority, Custer needed but a two-part strategy: maintain sufficient pressure along the line to preclude Rosser from shifting troops while seeking to establish the two extremes of the Confederate position with the goal of turning the flanks. The rebels fought gamely. In spite of several headlong charges by the Federal cavalry, their defenses held. Finally, by extending his lines to the west and utilizing Colonel Kidd's regiment on the east, Custer gradually bent his rival's position back on both ends around the base of Spiker's Hill. Up to this time, the 1st Vermont had been posted with the artillery. Starting out to the left of the batteries, they were shifted to the right side. When the regiment was finally ordered into battle, it looped back behind the big guns and charged forward on their left.

By early afternoon, Custer was ready. The time for sparring with the enemy was over. Rosser's own account stands as a succinct but apt description of the fast-moving events unfolding before him: "Then as his [Custer's] bugles sounded the charge, on came his dark battalions with [the] fury of a cyclone."[27] In textbook cavalry fashion, the assault built its momentum gradually, rolling forward in "a walk to the skirmish line, then a trot, then a gallop, then a wild rush of shouting troopers and frantic horses."[28] The focal point for the 1st Vermont's attack was Thomas Munford's position atop Spiker's Hill. As other elements of the brigade worked their way around to the right, the Vermonters held the attention of enemy troopers fronting on Tom's Brook. Sweeping up the hill, they crashed into the stubborn rebels. To one Vermont participant, Sergeant Farr, the daring assault was one for the ages. "Our regiment made one of the most splendid charges they ever made," was his post-combat evaluation of the hair-raising event.[29] The fighting was in close, hand-to-hand. The rebel stand lasted for approximately thirty minutes. One of those struck down with a mortal wound was the steadfast Frank Ray. Severely wounded at Yellow Tavern, the three-year veteran had only just returned to active duty. Working his way through meritorious service from the rank of private to commander of Company G, Captain Ray was considered by some as "one of the finest officers this war has produced, and none have a brighter military record than his."[30] But at the age of twenty-seven, he was gone, achieving the footnote of being the last in a line of brave officers from the 1st Vermont to die in battle.

Elsewhere in the melee rode Sergeant James Wright, a regimental color sergeant who proudly bore the American flag into battle, "who when he was ordered by a rebel to surrender his colors, for answer thrust through the man with the spear point of his color staff."[31] Wright's quick reaction saved his life, though he was slightly wounded in the side by a shot from his enemy's deflected carbine. Private James Lowell was not as fortunate, for the émigré from Canada suffered his death wound in the course of the same fight, as did forty-year-old Carlos Hogden. For Lowell, the "cause of death was a gunshot wound

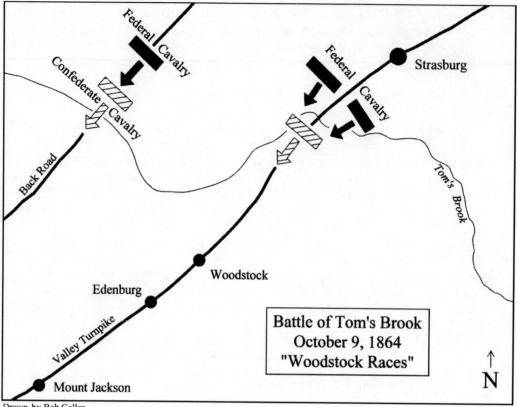

Battle of Tom's Brook
October 9, 1864
"Woodstock Races"

Drawn by Bob Collea

through the left lung," and, like Frank Ray, he lingered until the next day before suc-cumbing.[32] However, unlike the personable Captain Ray — whom so many had known, respected, and would grieve over — poor Lowell was all but a stranger in the ranks of Com-pany I, having been a cavalryman for all of five weeks. The "replacement" now needed one too. Along with Frank Ray, the duo of Lowell and Hogden comprised the only Ver-mont fatalities resulting from the furious action at Tom's Brook.

Once the Vermonters gained the crest of the hill, in concert with the Pennsylvani-ans, enemy resistance soon crumbled, as a tidal wave of blue-clad horsemen overwhelmed Rosser's men. "Everything worked perfectly," was Custer's unabashed appraisal, "and the movements of the brigades were well-timed. The whole line moved at the charge. Before this irresistible advance the enemy found it impossible to stand."[33] With their makeshift breastworks overrun, the Confederate troops abandoned the position and made a sec-ond stand along a tree line. Again the men of the Laurel Brigade held their ground and fought tenaciously. Sensing victory, Custer's men came on strong. Momentum was on their side. Eri Woodbury remembered how these stirring events unfolded: "We charged them, drove them," he wrote, "and then drove them about seven miles."[34]

It was at this point that the infamous "Woodstock Races" commenced. Split up in their exodus, one segment of Rosser's force beat a hasty retreat toward Columbia Fur-nace, hotly pursued by Custer's men, which included a contingent of Vermont troopers. The remainder of the rebels on the hill took off in the direction of New Market, pursued the whole way by the rest of the 1st Vermont and elements from brother regiments. All in all it was a very exhilarating experience. Sheridan was extremely pleased with the outcome. He noted how "the result was a general smash-up of the entire Confederate line, the retreat quickly degenerating into a rout the likes of which was never before seen. For twenty-six miles this wild stampede kept up, with our troopers close at the enemy's heels..."[35] By orchestrating the lopsided victory at Tom's Brook, Alfred Torbert salvaged his reputation. Flushed with the glow of success, he could be excused for indulging in a bit of hyperbole. Applauding his men, the general told them that they had "totally covered themselves with glory, and added to their long list of victories the most brilliant one of them all and the most decisive the country has ever witnessed."[36]

As their defeated foes rode dejectedly southward, the scattered units of the 1st Vermont regrouped near Strasburg. The adrenalin rush fueled by combat was giving way to weariness. Still, while they settled in for the night, many could not resist reliving the day's events, and, as Phil Sheridan observed, "the ludicrous incidents of the chase never ceased to be amusing topics around the campfires of Merritt and Custer."[37] More hard fighting lay ahead, but the afterglow of a highly successful engagement, once the almost exclusive purview of the departed rebels, now washed over and warmed the souls of Yankee troopers. The pride and satisfaction such a complete success engendered in these warriors felt good. For the hundred or so new recruits for whom Tom's Brook was a baptism of fire, their introduction to the cavalry had begun on a high note indeed. But for the core of the regiment, the 400 veterans who had been there since Mt. Jackson in '62, this was a singular moment, one to be reflected upon and savored. For these resolute men who had stayed the course through some decidedly lean times, the decisive manner in which the enemy was so soundly defeated meant that the wheel had finally come full circle. The bellicose Sheridan was now their leader, inspiring his command with his fiery temperament. Just in case the message was not received at Tom's Brook, the ascendancy of the Federal cavalry and the role reversal it clearly implied would be convincingly reiterated in a matter of but ten days on the banks of another Shenandoah rivulet: Cedar Creek.

In the heady aftermath of Tom's Brook, Federal commanders felt that the Army of the Valley would no longer be troublesome. Sheridan immediately began making plans to send the VI Corps back to Grant. But defying all logic was General Early. Whipped at Opequon, Fisher's Hill, and Tom's Brook, sustaining losses in each instance that weakened an already undersized army, the Confederate commander drew upon an admirable wellspring of resiliency to again carry the fight to his adversary. With the support of General Lee, "Old Jube" hatched a daring plan to assault the Union lines entrenched along the northern banks of Cedar Creek. With genius borne of desperation, he devised a surprise dawn attack. Taking full advantage of nocturnal cover, a heavy morning fog, and a supposedly impassable route, Early's troops surreptitiously circumvented Sheridan's line. On the morning of October 19, 1864, they were unleashed against the unsuspecting Yankees. One by one, three Federal corps were subjected to the fury of the hard-charging enemy. First, the VIII Corps broke and then XIX Corps collapsed. The effect was catastrophic. One eyewitness called it "the most perfect skeedaddle I have ever seen."[38] Only the VI Corps maintained any semblance of unity and cohesiveness, giving ground slowly and grudgingly. Driving the disorganized enemy before it, the diminutive war machine that was the Army of the Valley was firing on all cylinders.

Initially, Early's gamble paid off handsomely. Then late in the morning, he made a fateful choice, one that would turn the tide of battle against him. Feeling the need to redress his lines, he ordered a halt. Though based upon sound reasoning, the timing of his decision proved disastrous. The Yankees were on the run. Momentum was decidedly on the side of the surging gray legions. Confident that a temporary halt would reap benefits, the pursuit was stopped. Unfortunately, forward motion once turned to inertia is not so easily restarted. In the process of trying to improve his own situation, Early had afforded his foe a respite from the intense pressure which they had been experiencing.

While the infantry was backpedaling, Custer's Division, including the 1st Vermont, was positioned on the right end of the Union lines, guarding the fords over Cedar Creek. Wells' brigade was farthest to the west. The cavalry's assignment was to forestall any enemy attempt to pull off an end run into the vulnerable rear of the Federal army. Then Torbert ordered Custer to provide assistance to cavalry action building on the extreme left. In response, Custer took a part of the division over to support Merritt, leaving Wells to deal with the mounting activity on his front. As the infantry gave ground, Wells gradually moved his men back, not in a forced retreat but rather to maintain a roughly parallel extension of the receding Union line.

The time was now eleven o'clock, the pivotal hour in the battle. In the estimation of William Wells, the situation was indeed bleak: "I will say that during the early part of the day I thought we should all go to the D___l, or some other bad place for everything looked as though we should get soundly thrashed before the day closed."[39] Here, the turning point occurred. Unlike past engagements, the critical moment was not marked

by a brave stand or an epic charge. Instead, Cedar Creek's turning point was punctuated by a growing silence as the Confederates halted and fighting wound down. Had this perhaps been an interlude measured in minutes, its impact might have mattered little if at all. Had the day's action concluded at this point, the South could have claimed victory. General Early's outnumbered force had put the enemy to flight, taken a thousand prisoners, and numerous pieces of artillery. A good day's work had been accomplished by noon. In truth, Early needed to straighten out his battle lines and restore order to regiments that had become badly intermingled. Then he fully intended to renew hostilities.

During this hiatus, three factors altering the battle's outcome transpired. Any one of the three might not have been transformational, but, together, they collectively made a difference. Of these, only calling the halt was within Early's realm of control. The four hours of downtime took the edge off the attack, allowing an opportunity for unforeseen events to intervene. One of these was the dissolution of the fog shrouding the battlefield, exposing the paucity of troops that the Confederates had. Phil Sheridan provided the other, appearing dramatically

Rising steadily through the ranks from 1st lieutenant to lieutenant-colonel, the intrepid Major John Bennett — who had four horses shot from under him, was wounded twice, and endured being a POW for a time — led his regiment's celebrated charge at Cedar Creek (Francis C. Guber Collection).

among his disorganized troops after riding twenty-six miles from Winchester. By the time General Early was ready to resume his advance, the situation had significantly changed: not only was the landscape now visible, but Phil Sheridan could be seen riding across it at full gallop astride his faithful Rienzi.

For the 1st Vermont, waiting in the wings, the next few hours were to be glorious moments. But the ranks of the men who would win the laurels were missing many of those who had formed the nucleus of the regiment since 1862. Timing occasioned their absence, for three days after the Battle of Tom's Brook the original three-year enlistments had expired. Though 176 had re-upped in January, over 300 were awaiting departure. They should have been immediately sent on their way, with the thanks of a grateful nation ring-

A conference at Winchester, 26 miles away, caused General Sheridan's absence from the morning debacle at Cedar Creek. However, his faithful steed, Rienzi, dramatically conveyed his master to the battlefield in time for Sheridan to inspire his troops, particularly the cavalry, and rally them to win one of the most convincing Union victories of the war (*Harper's Weekly*).

ing in their ears. Charles Blinn identified the reasons for the delay. "The term of service of the 'old men' of the regiment expired on the 12th Inst.," noted Blinn, "but owing; to the sheer neglect of certain officers, and for the want of anybody to attend to the business of getting the regiment home we are compelled to patiently remain."[40] The bane of the soldiers' existence, the old "snafu," had reared its ugly head again. To insure their safe return, the Veteran Volunteers became protective of those enlisted men who should by now have been former comrades. If the army was going to be lax and risk lives unfairly, then friends would look out for friends. There were several instances leading up to Cedar Creek when "they expected a fight, and the old boys were sent to the rear. They did not have a fight"[41] When the morning's events portended a clash of cataclysmic potential, the "old boys" were again shielded by being sent to the rear. Curiously, the absence of so many veterans would not have the unfavorable impact upon regimental performance as might be expected. Even the presence of 100 recruits with less than a month's experience did not inhibit efficiency. Ironically, the Battle of Cedar Creek would stand as one of the war's premier moments for the Vermonters.

Thanks to Phil Sheridan, the men were primed. Upon his arrival, he rode the length of the Union line. Waving his hat and shouting invectives, he played to the audience. One who heard him was duly impressed with his command of "all the *pet names* and combination of oaths peculiar to soldiers, sailors, pirates, firemen, and such."[42] Telling these rejuvenated troops that they would "make their coffee from the waters of Cedar Creek" that night aroused them even further. After whipping his army into a fighting frenzy, all that remained was to shift gears from neutral to drive. Adrenalin, discipline, and courage would do the rest.

Faced with this unanticipated rejuvenation of Yankee aggressiveness, the Confederate infantry prepared to make its stand on the north bank of Cedar Creek, utilizing the reverse side of their adversaries' vacated breastworks for cover. Having seen limited action in the morning's rout, the Vermont Cavalry was primed to make a meaningful contribution. Before their eyes, fellow Vermonters in the 6th Corps had begun to drive Early's troops back over previously contested ground, across fields littered with dead and wounded Union men. "All these circumstances combined," Major Bennett suggested, "awakened an enthusiasm and determination needing only the guiding hand to render terrible."[43] When Custer was ordered to hit the rebel left, he selected the 1st Vermont and 5th New York to accompany him. The guiding hand and the instruments of wrath were ready. Leaving the rest of the brigade behind to keep Rosser in check, Custer and Wells led the two regiments down to the creek. In the waning light, they splashed across its shallow waters and up the opposite bank. A half-mile ahead, Confederate infantry could be seen drawn up behind the stone wall. Events began to unfold at kaleidoscopic speed: out went skirmishers—up came the entire 1st Vermont—the 5th New York arrived—a battle line formed—the order to charge given—bugles sounded—and off they dashed into the deepening twilight. Ahead lay glory unbounded and a cherished place in the annals of the Civil War. As William Wells experienced the moment, "away we went after the Johnny Rebs and away they went, the cavalry right after them."[44]

Much of what 19th century cavalry could accomplish was mental as well as physical. The minds of Early's men had been uneasy all day, knowing that Sheridan's legions prowled the edges of the battlefield. Now that optimum moment had arrived, and every rebel infantryman's worst nightmare was headed his way. The sound of oncoming doom was clearly audible: "There came from the north side of the plain a dull, heavy swelling

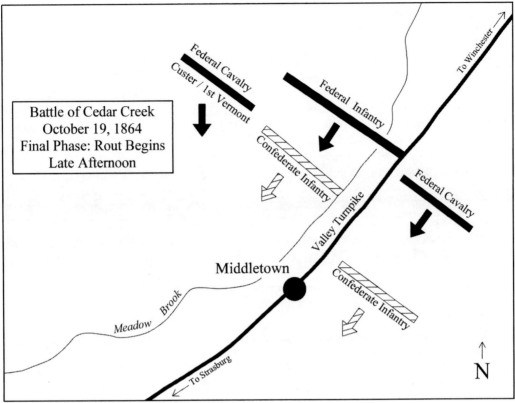

Battle of Cedar Creek
October 19, 1864
Final Phase: Rout Begins
Late Afternoon

Drawn by Bob Collea

sound like the roaring of a distant cyclone," Confederate General John Gordon later rem-inisced, "the omen of additional disaster. It was unmistakable. Sheridan's horsemen were riding furiously across the open fields of grass to intercept the Confederates before they crossed Cedar Creek."[45] Materializing as the Yankee troopers did out of the encroaching darkness imparted a spectral quality to the as yet unseen terror rapidly bearing down on the edgy rebels. Once a notion were planted in the mind, it did not take the feet long to get the message.

A ragged volley was thrown at the attackers. "For a moment the air seemed freighted with missiles of death," was Major Bennett's impression, "but a moment only. Confused and terrified the enemy threw down the arms and trampled upon each other in their frantic attempts to escape."[46] Even though fired in haste, several bullets from the fusil-lade still found marks. Captain Alexander Watson, leading the charge with Company L, "was wounded in the left shoulder and left side of the neck by a minie ball, injuring the muscles of the neck" and forcing him to the rear.[47] Riding with Company H, Clark Smith went down with a fractured thigh. According to Captain Emmett Walsh, Private Smith's injuries were caused by "two minie balls, striking him in front and passing inward, that came out in the back just above the brisket."[48] One tough Veteran Volunteer, having pre-viously been wounded at Hawe's Shop and again ten days later at Riddle's Shop, Smith survived and was mustered out with the regiment in 1865.

Joel Bill took "a gunshot wound of his left thigh," leaving him with a stiff knee, an atrophied limb, and a permanent disability.[49] Albert Howard was another injured trooper.

In all probability, Howard never should have been at Cedar Creek, for he had been discharged from the 5th Vermont Infantry in 1862 due to physical and mental debilities. As if being afflicted with chronic diarrhea, rheumatism, and hepatitis were not reason enough, the determination was made that he had "not sufficient intellect for a soldier."[50] But by 1864, manpower was harder to come by than it had previously been, so without a hassle Howard was able to join the 1st Vermont at the end of August. Mid-October found him charging at Cedar Creek, where "his horse jumped a fence and fell down, throwing him on the pommel of the saddle."[51] Howard was left on the ground, writhing in pain, as the charge swept forward. Considering the magnitude of the success that was to follow, casualties were extremely light. Amazingly, the injuries to Watson, Smith, and Howard accounted for exactly half of all those incurred by the 1st Vermont at Cedar Creek!

Before the Vermonters a cavalryman's dream lay waiting — a foe, already psychologically defeated, was in every-man-for-himself flight. In George Custer's assessment, "That which hitherto, on our part, had been a pursuit after a broken and routed army now resolved itself into an exciting chase after a panic-stricken, uncontrollable mob. It was no longer a question to be decided by force of arms, or by skill, or by courage; it was simply a question of speed between pursuers and pursued."[52] With Custer's blessing, Major Bennett led the regiment in hot pursuit. Sabers unsheathed, they hacked their way forward with a vengeance. In their flight to avoid the onrushing horsemen, the rebels parted to the right and left like the Red Sea before Moses. An unobstructed pathway was opened for Custer's men.

Dashing ahead, the Union horsemen struck the Valley turnpike about a mile south of Cedar Creek. "It was now dark," reported a *New York Times* correspondent, "but in a glance it was seen that the pike was full of artillery, horses, men and wagons."[53] Once in among the artillery and wagons, the spoils of war fell quickly into the Yankees' hands: "Some we captured in good order, with cannoneers in their places, drivers on their horses; others entangled, upset, and abandoned; and, again, ambulances with their loads of wounded; horses, with their riders; cannoneers, with pieces; as if hurled together by some all-powerful agency, lay a mass of ruins."[54] Whenever an artillery piece was captured, a trooper was detailed to secure the regiment's claim to the piece. This curious practice had just been instituted, due to a recent intra-brigade squabble after Tom's Brook as to conflicting assertions over which cannon were taken by what regiment.

So complete was the Confederate collapse that elements of the 1st Vermont kept forging ahead, giving no heed to the fact that they were outrunning any possible support. For some of the veterans, the Rogers brothers among them, the irony of the situation may have been especially sweet, for it was over this same ground that many of them had run for their lives in '62 after Jackson had severed Banks' line of retreat at Middletown. According to Frederick Lyon, one of the Vermonters picking his way through the chaos, "whole companies surrendered to half a dozen mounted men."[55] By the time their lathered horses were reigned in, Wells and Bennett had led a small contingent a half mile beyond Strasburg, a distance of some four miles below Cedar Creek. Accompanied by but twenty men, these officers would be personally responsible for the surrender of countless rebel prisoners as well as the capture of an impressive stand of arms and equipment. Another trooper who made the perilous ride far ahead of the main body was Eri Woodbury. Bold almost to the point of recklessness, Sergeant Woodbury noticed that "a little hill on the left of the road at the entrance of Fisher's Hill was covered with fugitive infantry. I charged in alone, cut off four, and captured a battle flag belonging to the 12th NC Regt.'s infantry."[56]

By day's end, Cedar Creek proved fertile ground for capturing flags, as two others were taken by members of the 1st Vermont. Acting in tandem, Corporal James Sweeney and Private Frederick Lyons stopped a fleeing ambulance just when it was about to cross a bridge. Convincing the driver to halt, they discovered a gravely wounded General Stephen Ramseur inside along with a Confederate battle flag and the general's headquarters flag. The two lucky troopers immediately turned the wagon around and headed back with their prizes. Before the month was out, Woodbury, Sweeney, Lyon, and their flags were well traveled. Two days after the battle, they made the rounds locally, going from Bennett's tent to Custer's headquarters and finally displaying the banners before Sheridan himself. As if these experiences were not heady enough, the three troopers experienced the thrill of being sent to Washington, accompanied by their idol General Custer, to present the colorful trophies in person to secretary of war William Stanton. On October 23, a ceremony was held at the War Department. On behalf of a grateful nation, Stanton presented each soldier with a Medal of Honor and a twenty-day leave.

While these flags were highly valued trophies, they were far from the only spoils the Vermonters took that October afternoon. The enormity of the regiment's success, item-

Proud as peacocks to be with their idol, Troopers Lyon, Sweeney, and Woodbury accompanied General Custer to a ceremony at the War Department where captured Confederate flags were given to Secretary Stanton, and the Vermonters in turn were bestowed their Medals of Honor (Library of Congress).

ized in a receipt from Custer's provost-marshal, was truly impressive: "161 prisoners ... 3 battle-flags, 23 pieces of artillery, 14 caissons, 17 army wagons, 6 spring wagons and ambulances, 83 sets of artillery harnesses, 75 sets of wagon harnesses, 98 horses, [and] 69 mules."[57] In recognition of this accomplishment, General Sheridan noted that "no regiment has captured as much in a single charge since the war commenced."[58] The ultimate praise, however, came from General Custer. Since those whom he commanded held him in such high esteem, his words held inestimable value: "Among the substantial fruits of this great victory, you can boast of having captured five battle flags, a large number of prisoners, and forty-five of the forty-eight pieces of artillery taken that day.... This is a record of which you may well be proud, a record made and established by your gallantry and perseverance. You have surrounded the name of the 3rd Cav. Div. with a halo of glory as enduring as time."[59]

In the wake of the Battle of Cedar Creek, the course of the Civil War still had six more months to run. Short of its successful conclusion enabling everyone to go home, no events of the conflict brought greater satisfaction to the troopers of the 1st Vermont than did the twin victories of Tom's Brook and Cedar Creek. From a military standpoint, consensus has been that these engagements contributed little toward shortening the war. Where the battle was given its just due was in the political arena, with no one benefiting more from these high profile victories than Abraham Lincoln. The president clearly conveyed his elation in a handwritten note to General Sheridan: "With great pleasure I tender to you and your brave army, the thanks of the Nation, and my own personal admiration and gratitude, for the month's operations in the Shenandoah Valley, and especially for the splendid work of October 19, 1864."[60] Coupled with the fall of Atlanta in September, these highly positive notes on the battlefront were well-received harbingers by war-weary Northerners, providing in turn a much-needed boost to Lincoln's flagging reelection campaign. While the president put no executive pressure on Sheridan to perform a miracle on his behalf, he nevertheless proved to be a big winner in light of the timely outcome of these engagements.

Beyond its political implications, the culmination of Sheridan's Valley Campaign in the cavalry's one-sided accomplishments can be lauded for the slap on the back that they gave the historically much-maligned Northern mounted forces, whose day had finally arrived! These men had been riding out of the shadows since the summer of '63, slowly building their poise and morale. Heading into the last winter of the war, the Federal cavalry could look forward to the renewal of hostilities in the coming spring with confidence. With justifiable pride, they could anticipate playing a significant role in the final push to victory.

28

One Last Winter
The War Begins to Wind Down

Following the Battle of Cedar Creek, one of the first matters addressed was sending those with expired enlistments, affectionately called the "Old Boys," home, while concurrently melding the Veteran Volunteers and the new recruits into an fighting force. Though the regiment's recent performance indicated that a smooth transition should not be too difficult, the spectacular victory was misleading, for only the enlisted men set to leave had been withheld. All thirteen of the departing front-line officers had stood with their respective commands, contributing a steadying influence of inestimable value.[1]

But on October 22, the page was turned when those with expired enlistments departed. Destined for Burlington, the last leg of their journey was by steamer on Lake Champlain. The imminence of their arrival caught the town fathers flat-footed. As a clever *Daily Press* reporter spun it, "They took our citizens, as they have so often taken the rebels, somewhat unawares."[2] A suitable reception was nonetheless quickly orchestrated. The deck was crowded with jubilant troopers as the city hove into view. On the landside, "hearty cheers from the crowd received them as the boat reached the wharf, and with their old charging yell the boys rushed from the boat, and formed on the wharf, bearing their tattered colors and guidons at the head of the column."[3] As they gazed at the citizenry arrayed along the pier, some veterans recognized a tall, elderly gentleman, a former soldier himself whose heart was bursting with pride at the sight of the returning 1st Vermont, *his* 1st Vermont. For there to greet these returning warriors was their old commander, Lemuel Platt. As they came down the gangplank, Colonel Platt surely recognized some of his former command. The colonel might have noticed James Stone, who since Gettysburg had walked like a much older man as he trod gingerly with a limp from a pommel-induced rupture and concurrent thigh wound. Platt surely would have been pleased to see Captain Joel Earhardt. Though he left the cavalry in the fall of '63, Earhardt had been a popular officer who now served as the Provost-Marshall of New York City, joining the returning veterans on the triumphant journey home as they passed through his bailiwick.

Once assembled, the entourage proceeded to city hall. Waiting there was Lieutenant-Governor Levi Underwood, the same man who had been a part of the exuberant pre-departure ceremony in 1861. With well-chosen words, he told the men how much anticipation and pride had ridden off with them three years ago. "We had the brightest hopes for your success," Underwood said, "and in all times and in all places you have done more than we have asked. You have on many a hard-fought battlefield, in many

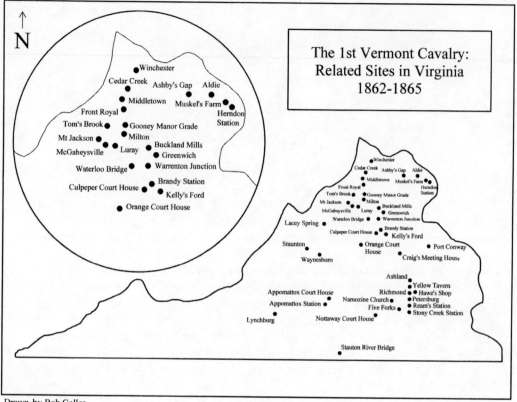

↑
N

The 1st Vermont Cavalry:
Related Sites in Virginia
1862-1865

Winchester
Cedar Creek   Ashby's Gap   Aldie
Middletown   Muskel's Farm
Front Royal   Herndon
Tom's Brook   Gooney Manor Grade   Station
Mt Jackson   Milton
McGaheysville   Luray   Buckland Mills
                         Greenwich
Waterloo Bridge   Warrenton Junction
                  Brandy Station
Culpeper Court House   Kelly's Ford
        Orange Court House

Winchester
Cedar Creek   Ashby's Gap   Aldie
Middletown   Muskel's Farm   Herndon
Front Royal   Station
Tom's Brook   Gooney Manor Grade
Mt Jackson   Milton
McGaheysville   Luray   Buckland Mills
                         Greenwich
Waterloo Bridge   Warrenton Junction
Lacey Spring   Brandy Station
Culpeper Court House   Kelly's Ford
Staunton   Orange Court   Port Conway
           House
Waynesboro   Craig's Meeting House

Ashland
                 Yellow Tavern
Appomattox Court House   Richmond   Hawe's Shop
Namozine Church   Petersburg
Appomattox Station   Five Forks   Ream's Station
                              Stony Creek Station
Lynchburg   Nottaway Court House

Stauton River Bridge

Drawn by Bob Collea

gallant charges, covered yourselves with glory and crowned the State with honor.... Many of your comrades I regret to say, have fallen in defense of our national honor — but they have fallen in a holy cause, and deserve the highest place in the hearts and memories of their countrymen.... [Vermont] is justly proud of her gallant soldiers, and of none is she more proud than of this noble regiment."[4] Underwood stopped short of vocalizing it, but the feeling was clearly given — yes indeed, a contingent of favorite sons had returned!

Following the lieutenant-governor, Lieutenant-Colonel Bennett stepped forward, holding a piece of paper. The small document from which he read was none other than a receipt attesting to one of the regiment's singular accomplishments: the itemization from General Custer of the artillery, wagons, and prisoners captured by the 1st Vermont at Cedar Creek. The crowd acknowledged this feat with three hearty cheers. Caught up in the festive mood of the occasion, the regiment responded with three cheers and a tiger of its own for "Uncle Abe Lincoln." This concluded the formal ceremony, and, as nice as the adulation was, the prospects of a home-cooked supper at the American House had long since taken over the forefront in many a trooper's mind. After all, it was 7:30 P.M., with many hours having elapsed since the soldiers had last eaten. In short order, their ravenous appetites were sated with a sumptuous repast. By eight o'clock, the men were ready to call it day. For most, this meant taking advantage of the quarters prepared for them in familiar surroundings: the barracks on the fairgrounds, the former site of Camp Ethan Allen.

Of the total of 297 men whose enlistments had expired, 271 made the long-awaited journey back to Vermont that fall. The shortfall of twenty-eight men was due to the fact that some were still in rebel prisons. Of those who did return in October, only about 200 actually took the boat trip to Burlington. The others had been granted prior permission to go directly to their homes, with the understanding that they would come to Burlington for the final mustering out on November 18. However, before any of the men were permitted to leave, the State of Vermont required their services for a special duty. In the wake of the St. Albans Raid, the nerves of many Vermonters were a bit frayed. Leery of another incursion by Confederate agents, the populace sought protection. What better group to guard the border than battle-tested cavalry veterans? Eventually, the long-awaited November day came, and the cord was severed. The farmers returned to their plowshares, the cabinetmakers to their workshops, and the teachers to their classes. In one last quasi-official act, the departing officers determined which engagements were to be reverently inscribed upon the regimental colors. Twenty-five battles were duly chosen, with others omitted only for lack of room: "Mt. Jackson, Middletown, Orange, Kelly's Ford, Bull Run, Ashby's Gap, Greenwich, Hanover, Pa., Gettysburg, Monterey, Hagerstown, Culpeper C.H., Boonsboro, Buckland, Kilpatrick's Raid, Craig's Church, Yellow Tavern, Ashland Station, Salem Church, White Oak Swamp, Malvern Hill, Wilson's Raid, Winchester, Tom's Brook, [and] Cedar Creek."[5]

While Burlington was the scene of winding down for some, at the front the regiment was undergoing reorganization. Numbers were not the problem, as Major Cummings had almost 400 troopers at his disposal. Even the ratio of recruits-to-veterans, about two to one, was tolerable. Where there was concern, however, was the gross inadequacy of not just seasoned but any officers. There were in fact but three available: Major William Cummings, Captain Alexander Chandler, and 2nd Lieutenant Harris Mitchell. Such a leadership void was unprecedented. After consulting with William Wells, Cummings temporarily addressed the situation by thrusting sergeants into command positions. Eventually the list of new officer appointments sent by Wells to Adjutant General Peter Washburn of Vermont was approved.

Fortunately, though the fighting was not yet over for the fall campaign, the few contests that remained were small skirmishes, with nothing remotely approaching the scope of Cedar Creek. November witnessed several of these clashes. The 1st Vermont spent much of the 11th jousting with Rosser's troopers. Action commenced at noon, as pressure was brought against the three-mile long picket line that the Vermonters held along what was known as the "Middle Road." Fighting went on throughout the day until darkness terminated hostilities. When the next roll call was taken, Michael Donovan did not answer. With the regiment barely four months, he had perished in the skirmishing.

The next morning, the Vermont pickets were hit at dawn. Holding their ground stubbornly, they bought time for Wells to bring up his whole command at 11:00 A.M. "This brigade of about five hundred men," he proudly proclaimed, "fought a division of Rebels of at least three thousand and drove them back two miles. When they got on our flanks, we were obliged to fall back."[6] Merritt's division then arrived on the scene, causing the seesaw affair to turn against the rebels, who were driven from the field a second time. The only certainty that day of any consequence was that Paul Dumas and George Haroon were killed. For the diminutive Canadian immigrant, Dumas' untimely death unceremoniously ended what had never been a pleasant military experience. Enlisting in the fall of 1862, of his combined twenty-five months of service, Dumas spent thirteen of them in and out of hospitals, being treated for recurring bouts of diarrhea and a foot ailment. Prior to his death, he had only been fit enough to return to the regiment in July. Private Haroon's time in the saddle was even more abbreviated. He had just joined the regiment among 250 raw recruits in early November, but "before he was even assigned to a company he was killed."[7]

As a postscript to this skirmish, Major Cummings identified a problem. During the action, it was the major's opinion that "we missed the colors ... to rally the regiment on, more in this engagement than at any time since, on account of the small number of officers present."[8] The absent "colors" were the very ones taken to Vermont by the troops being mustered out. For whatever the reason, no officer saw obtaining replacement flags as a pressing need. But it irked the rank and file: "Why this regiment should have had no flag or color of any sort, not even a guidon, since the 'old corps' went home in October last, does not sufficiently appear."[9] For the remainder of the war, the men of the 1st Vermont were destined to ride into battle anonymously, fighting as if a phantom regiment. As one trooper later decried the perceived slight, "We have marched through Petersburg, through Richmond, through Alexandria, through Washington even, with banners before and behind us, and we appearing, probably as but an unnoticeable appendage to the 8th N.Y. Cavalry."[10] Ironically, the new colors—the regiment's third set—were eventually received from Vermont on the morning of May 23, just in the nick of time for the regiment to excitedly unfurl the flags, proudly bear them down Pennsylvania Avenue in the Grand Review, and honorably return them home on June 13 — all without a shot being fired their way in anger. "Battleless flags" was sadly a more appropriate name.

With the self-preservation, homesickness, and health issues consistently being in the forefront of any given soldier's mind, there was one other matter of more than passing interest that vied for attention in early November — the 1864 presidential election. Both candidates, Abraham Lincoln and George McClellan, were well known to the troops. While McClellan was popular, his party had saddled him with an impossible platform. Projecting the returns from Vermont soldiers' ballots cast in recent state elections to the impending presidential election, "nine to one, on an advance they go for the Union candidates."[11]

Newspaper editors, loyal to the president, seized upon these encouraging statistics and turned them into eloquent arguments for the civilian populace to follow suit. Clearly they saw a lesson to be learned from the vote by the men at the front. "It teaches that the men upon whom the heaviest burdens of the war are falling," one wrote, "are the most unanimous of all classes against yielding to the demand for a 'cessation of hostilities' that they who ought to learn first whether the war is a 'failure,' declare in a body that it is not and that the heaviest sufferers by a vigorous prosecution of the war are most eagerly and earnestly in favor of it."[12] Every effort was made to insure that the right of suffrage was available to troops at the front. Some states, Vermont being one, enacted a state statute to this effect. To protect against irregularities, the whole process was to be closely monitored. Each state committee was permitted to send one agent for each army corps to distribute the ballots to soldiers in the field. Furthermore, provision was made that "civilian inspectors, not to exceed one to each brigade, may also be appointed, to be present on election day and see that the election is fairly conducted."[13]

All of the editorializing came to an end on November 8 — Election Day—1864. The final tally proved that the pundits had been right. While Lincoln took 55 percent of the popular vote nationwide, his support among the soldiers approached a whopping 80 percent! But if he was looking for his champion of champions, then the Green Mountain Boys could stand proudly in the front ranks. According to the *Vermont Record*, "The vote of the First Vt. Cavalry in the field was Lincoln 162, McClellan 16. One company, Co. A, gave a majority for McClellan, its vote standing Lincoln 9, McClellan 10. Companies D, F, and L gave no McClellan votes and companies I and K, but one each."[14] The regiment had given a mind-boggling 91 percent of its votes to the man whom the men reverently called "Father Abraham."

As the political situation returned to normal, action on the battlefront slowed as winter approached. On through December, the 1st Vermont was engaged in its customary duties. The only spike from the gamut of routine assignments was a quick, division-sized thrust over the mountains to Moorefield, West Virginia, on November 29. The mission's goal was to catch Rosser's command, which, in an unexpected move of its own, had captured a Union post at New Creek. Unfortunately, the Confederates had not lingered, and the only surprise was for Custer's men, after a fifty-mile ride, was finding no one to attack. The suspension of active campaigning for the winter did not by any means result in an absence of soldierly pursuits. The time gained was put to good use. With so many new recruits in camp, along with a spate of recently commissioned officers, daily drills and instruction in tactics took on an importance not seen since Annapolis in '62. Owing to the fact that a permanent camp had not yet been established, the men were exposed to the mercy of the elements. Making their lives especially uncomfortable was the mixed precipitation, ranging from rain to sleet and snow. Finally on December 27, the order came down to commence constructing winter quarters.

For some men in each company, the winter of 1864–1865 represented their fourth experience in such a seasonal cantonment. The biggest difference in this instance was the duration, as the time spent in winter quarters amounted to merely two months: December 29 through February 29. Drawing on their previous experiences, the men raised shelters very quickly. To Company M's George Nay, a new kid on the block, having just arrived on November 20, the "shebang" which he and comrades built was the next best thing to "Home-Sweet-Home." As always, there was a concern for the horses. Horace Ide noted how the poor animals "suffered a great deal from the cold, and by having to stand in the mud, but although we could not help the first, the last was remedied in a degree by splitting logs and making floors for them to stand upon."[15]

Once housing needs were addressed, a routine set in that would carry the men through the remainder of the winter. Picket and patrol responsibilities were at the top of every trooper's expected "to-do" list. Though he was still a green recruit, Private Nay had to pull his weight like any other soldier. Consequently, he took his turn on guard duty. With respect to reconnaissance missions, these ventures were old hat for Nay by the time the regiment abandoned its tents for cabins. Less than a week after joining the ranks in November, he had been off in a column heading for Mt. Jackson where a sharp skirmish occurred. A month later, Nay was supposed to accompany a raiding party heading for Lacey's Springs. "We started on a raid Monday morning at daylight," he shared with his sister, "[after] I went about four miles with them and my horse played out so I went back to camp and did not go."[16] Fate did Nay a favor in this instance because the Lacey's Springs Raid proved to be a trying experience. Before active campaigning ended in 1864, the 1st Vermont was given one last major assignment. This foray, commencing on December 19, involved Custer's entire division. Its purpose was to scout the upper Shenandoah, seeking to determine the enemy's presence as well as his concentration.

Aggressive as always, Custer entertained thoughts of penetrating beyond Staunton all the way to Lynchburg.

The men bivouacked for the night of the 21st at Lacey's Springs, just above Harrisonburg. After a miserable sleep disturbed by sleet and snow, they were surprised by an early morning raid from Rosser's troopers. By virtue of positioning, the Vermonters met the charge head on, absorbed its momentum, and then sent it packing. Led by General Chapman, "the First Vermont drove him [the enemy] over a mile in the direction from which the attack had come."[17] For two Vermont troopers, Bryan Sheehy and Napoleon Plant, participation in the charge led to their most memorable experiences of the war. Private Plant's story was all about physical pain. As the column of fours charged out, "Plant was the outside men and was crushed against a post at the stone wall..."[18] A metal bar protruding from the wooden pillar not only struck him in the leg but also knocked him from his horse. Being so violently dismounted, he suffered further injury to his stomach and right side. Plant persevered until the division returned to camp, at which time he entered the hospital to recuperate.

Unlike his friend's genuine infirmity, Private Sheehy's travail was one of mental anguish over missed opportunity. Elated over capturing a rebel major, Sheehy proudly took his prize to General Custer's headquarters. As the man was searched, all of the praise that the Vermonter earned for this singular accomplishment suddenly paled, as "the provost guard took from my prisoner six hundred dollars in greenbacks."[19] Trooper Sheehy was left with his country's gratitude. The army kept the prisoner and the money. Dealing with the rebels they met proved the easier part of the mission, as the regiment came away from an early morning surprise attack on their camp without a loss. But the return trip to Kernstown was another story, turned into a trial by the elements. Horace Ide was one of those who made the difficult trek, reporting how "the weather was intensely cold, the road full of ice and snow, and about forty men in the command were frost bitten."[20]

After fulfilling daily obligations, the men still had a fair amount of time to themselves. Matters of personal hygiene, letter writing, and an ongoing quest for food were their primary interests. However, with so many young boys cohabiting in a relatively small space, the surprise is not that occasional tomfoolery broke out but that youthful shenanigans did not happen more frequently. One event that was sure to unleash a propensity for lightheartedness was newly fallen snow. Let this be a sizable, wet accumulation, and the result was a sure-fire guarantee to bring out the boys in men of all ages. So it came to pass that on February 17, 1864, the troopers of the 1st Vermont and neighboring regiments awoke to find their surroundings a frosty blanket of white. A touch of home, a reminder of their youth, and an irresistible temptation had landed in central Virginia. Offering a joyful respite from the serious business of war, a good old-fashioned snowball fight ensued.

This encounter, however, was not one of those little affairs between schoolyard chums. Instead, orchestrated on a grand scale, it pitted regiments against regiments, with thousands of wet, white orbs sailing through the morning air at any one time. For a few minutes, the deadly seriousness of real war was forgotten, to be supplemented by all the exhilarating activities of ducking, dodging, running, throwing, hitting, and being hit that comprised a snowball fight. The scale of participation added to the unparalleled thrill as it grew to epic proportions. "We had a snowball fight with the 22nd New York Regiment the other day," George Nay shared with his sister, "and gave them a whipping and took their Colonel prisoner. Then the next day they stumped us over and we drove them into their shanty [ies]."²¹ Not content with their "defeat," the New Yorkers charged back again the following morning with two other Regiments in tow, only to be held off once more by the plucky Vermonters. Horace Ide also got caught up in the spirit of the occasion, recalling that it "was called 'Fisher's Hill all over again,' one party flanking on the right, while the other charged in front."²² For officers, whose rank precluded participation in snowball fights, there were other wintry diversions, such as sleigh-riding. In some respects, the presence of the accumulated flakes helped to lighten everyone's spirits. According to Sergeant Ide, there "must have been more snow than usual this winter for it snowed about every other day and some times a foot or more at once."²³

Inevitably, the good times had to end. As the month of February waned, the season for active campaigning approached. The year before, the Kilpatrick-Dahlgren Raid had set out on February 28, though not everyone went along on that ill-fated adven-

Working his way up through the commissioned ranks to major, Colonel Josiah Hall's career was temporarily interrupted by being captured at Brandy Station and subsequently imprisoned until August of 1864; his competency, loyalty, and persistence were rewarded when by war's end he had been elevated to command the regiment (Francis C. Guber Collection).

ture. In 1865, camp was broken one day earlier. This year, the entire brigade prepared to ride. Leading them was Colonel Josiah Hall. Just back from his debilitating imprisonment at Andersonville, followed by his harrowing exposure as a human shield in Charleston, the regiment's commander in absentia until February 1 was anxious to have a shot at his former tormentors. Though Hall could not have foreseen such a rapid collapse to the Confederacy, the war in the Eastern Theater had but forty-one days left to go.

29

The Road to Appomattox
Sheathing the Swords, Furling the Flags

For the veterans still peppering the ranks of the 1st Vermont, leaving Kernstown brought back memories. Though no one knew for sure, the possibility existed that this might be their last seasonal camp. After a brutal winter, the men were eager to begin campaigning. Preparations called for them to travel light and fast. The corps started south on February 27, bivouacking at Woodstock after marching thirty miles. The next day the blustery elements were braved while en route to Staunton. Positioned in the van, Colonel William Wells led his brigade past sites dear to the 1st Vermont like Mt. Jackson. Here the veterans could be excused for regaling new recruits with a bit of regimental history. Though chilled to the bone by freezing temperatures, drenched to the skin by incessant sleet and snow, and soiled from head to toe by mud, spirits were high. Five thousand strong, they were proud members of the finest cavalry on the planet!

Their objectives were open-ended. Destroying the Virginia Central was a priority. The James River Canal and Lynchburg were of interest. After that, linking up with Sherman in North Carolina or returning to Winchester were possibilities. Ultimately, it was the irrepressible Jubal Early who forced Sheridan's hand. With the Federals approaching Staunton, Early pulled his troops east toward Waynesboro. Sheridan could have continued on to Lynchburg, but doing so meant leaving an enemy force behind him. Unlike Banks, who opted to retreat, the spirited Sheridan decided to take the fight to Early. Having thrice fought "Old Jube" and decisively thrashed him each time, "Little Phil" had no compunctions about crossing swords again. So complete would mastery of his adversary be that one newspaper declared that Sheridan's motto was "Fight Early and fight often!"[1]

Putting his best foot forward, General Sheridan directed Custer on March 2 to take his three brigades to Waynesboro. General Devin's division would follow. Sheridan was pleased with his men. "The rain had been pouring in torrents for two days," the general observed, "and the roads were bad beyond description; nevertheless the men pushed boldly on, although horses and men could scarcely be recognized for the mud which covered them."[2] Sheridan's major concern was sending a mounted command to do battle with infantry and cavalry dug in and supported by artillery. He need not have worried. Custer was at the peak of his game. Following smashing successes the previous fall, the charismatic cavalier eagerly sought to pick up where he had left off.

Situated on hills west of Waynesboro, Early's men had constructed breastworks. Reconnoitering Early's position, Custer determined a potential weakness. The left of Early's line was not properly anchored. By being placed significantly forward of the river,

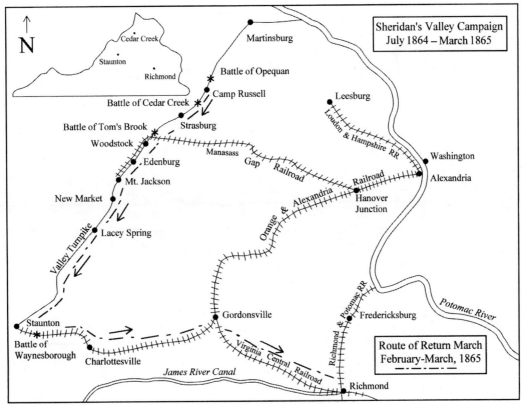

Drawn by Bob Collea

an inviting gap and a vulnerable flank were created. If Custer could exploit this breach, the whole rear of the Confederate position would be compromised. The 1st Vermont was assigned the task. However, before the assault was launched, they had the unenviable task of being "formed in a line of battle, just in the rear of the skirmish line, and in full view and easy range of the enemy's guns, partly to draw their fire and partly to cover the maneuvering of other portions of the Division; and although standing under a most galling fire, and in a very exposed situation, yet, the lines were kept as complete and steady as on a review."[3] Once the order to advance was issued, little time elapsed before "the 1st Vermont charged the left of the enemy with such spirit and dash that their line broke in a moment."[4]

As the Vermonters turned the flank, other troops breached the center of the fortified line. A complete collapse ensued, resulting in a staggering haul of troops and equipment. In General Sheridan's estimation, "This decisive victory closed hostilities in the Shenandoah Valley."[5] As Civil War clashes went, the affair was small. But for young George Nay, this encounter represented his baptism of fire. He later shared the excitement of the day's events with his mother, telling how "they ... had shelled us right-smart for a while but we charged them ... and that was the last of old Early."[6] In a notation that his mother did not need, Nay observed, "Our regiment lost one man killed and two wounded."[7] That lone fatality was Asa Benway. Having signed up for a one-year hitch the previous September, he barely survived to the halfway point. Thirty years old, the trooper from Hartland, Vermont, was struck and killed by a shell fragment during the pre-charge cannon-

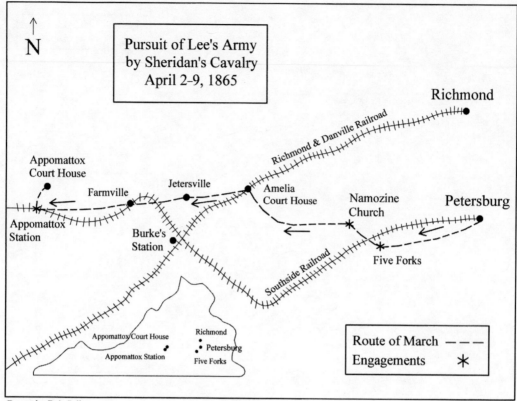

↑
N

Pursuit of Lee's Army
by Sheridan's Cavalry
April 2-9, 1865

Richmond

Richmond & Danville Railroad

Appomattox
Court House

Farmville

Jetersville

Amelia
Court House

Namozine
Church

Petersburg

Appomattox
Station

Burke's
Station

Southside Railroad

Five Forks

Appomattox Court House

Richmond

Petersburg

Appomattox Station

Five Forks

Route of March   — — —
Engagements   *

Drawn by Bob Collea

ade, the very one through which the 1st Vermont, including George Nay, sat unflinch-ingly.

Now Sheridan had to choose a destination: Winchester, the Carolinas, or Petersburg. While reuniting with the Army of the Potomac was not the easiest objective, this was the option selected. This decision was based on the knowledge that much useful infrastruc-ture remained to be destroyed. Beyond this was the simple motive of wanting to be pres-ent for the conflict's final moments: "feeling that the war was nearing its end, I wanted my cavalry to be in at the death."[8]

For the remainder of the trek, the real opponents were rebel roads. Compliments of the incessant rains, thoroughfares became quagmires. "You hain't know idea what march-ing it was," William Rogers shared with his father, "a raining most of the time. Mud is now the name for it. You can judge something about it if it was [as] it would be through Fairfax [VT] in the spring of the year when the frost is coming out to have 15 thousand cavalry march over the road. There was any number of horses left mired in the mud. What don't drop dead by riding are shot by the rear guard."[9] Despite the obstacles, Sheri-dan's legions pressed forward. Destroying dams, locks, and boats, they laid waste to the James River Canal. Railroad tracks, bridges, and water tanks belonging to the Virginia Central met the same fate. Factories and mills were torched. Finally, on the 27th of March, the weary raiders made camp at Hancock's Station before Petersburg. After seven months of operating independently, Sheridan's corps was back. "During this time Custer's divi-sion has done, yes, more than done, its share of the closing work," a Vermont trooper boasted, "and the 1st Vermont has performed fully its part with the Third Cavalry Division."[10] The troopers could be excused if they seemed to sit a mite taller in the saddle and smile a bit more frequently than usual, for truly they had carried out their assignments to perfection.

Their arrival had been timely. Ready to begin the end game, General Grant intended for his cavalry to play a pivotal role. Early on March 29, they were off for Dinwiddie Court House. Sheridan's objective was not so much a place as a result. By threatening Lee's right flank and lines of supply, Confederate troops were expected to leave the protection of their static defenses and give battle. Caught in a dilemma, Lee could ill afford to do nothing. Of critical importance was a vital road convergence known as "Five Forks." April 1 became the day of reckoning. General George Pickett was ordered to hold Five Forks at all costs, but being outnumbered two to one made his prospects for success slim. As he explained his strategy, Sheridan's battle plan was "to attack his [Pickett's] whole front with Merritt's two cavalry divisions, make a feint of turning his right, and with the Fifth Corps assail his left."[11] By virtue of this troop disposition, the 1st Vermont wound up on the Union left, though the Vermonters functioned only in a reserve role during the engagement.

The day's outcome insured that more fighting lay ahead, combat that would feature a lead role by the cavalry. Following up on Sheridan's success, Grant launched an all-out attack on Petersburg the next day. His position now untenable, Lee had to abandon the trenches. The Army of Northern Virginia needed to break free and distance itself from enemy forces. At the outset of the retreat, Lee had two possible goals: reach sanctuary in the mountains to the west or join forces with Joe Johnston in North Carolina. Rapid movement was paramount. Harassing an enemy in flight was an assignment made to order for cavalry. The minute Lee's soldiers strode from their defenses, Sheridan's troopers went from being members of the supporting cast to starring roles.

The evacuation began in the evening of April 2, 1865. Lee's immediate objective was Amelia Court House, located forty-five miles west/northwest of Petersburg. Moving along converging roads from Richmond and Petersburg, Confederate units strained to maintain a steady pace. One of the chief obstacles to their flight would be Sheridan's troopers. Unfettered from protecting a stationary army, the Union cavalrymen were free to harass Lee's vulnerable columns. For the Vermonters, the first day of the Confederate retreat was spent exploiting the door opened by the victory at Five Forks. "April 2, moved out at 9 am," reported Lieutenant-Colonel Josiah Hall, "toward the railroad. We held the advance, met the enemy, and drove them; remained on picket and skirmish line while the rest of the division was destroying the railroad [Southside]."[12] This engagement occurred at Scott's Corners.

Their first opportunity to interdict the Confederate retreat occurred the next morning on Namozine Creek. In an anomalous situation, the contending forces were traveling on paths the reverse of what might have been expected: the Southerners heading west via a route north of their adversaries. This meant that the Union troopers approaching the crossing point, the 1st Vermont leading, came up from the south on the Namozine Road heading into Amelia County. They expected to hit the underbelly of the retreating column. To protect against this possibility, Fitzhugh Lee's cavalry guarded the left from behind breastworks on the opposite bank of the stream. The bridge over the creek had already been destroyed, and blocking timber tossed into the waterway. After skirmishers were deployed, Custer and Wells reconnoitered the situation. Their solution was two-

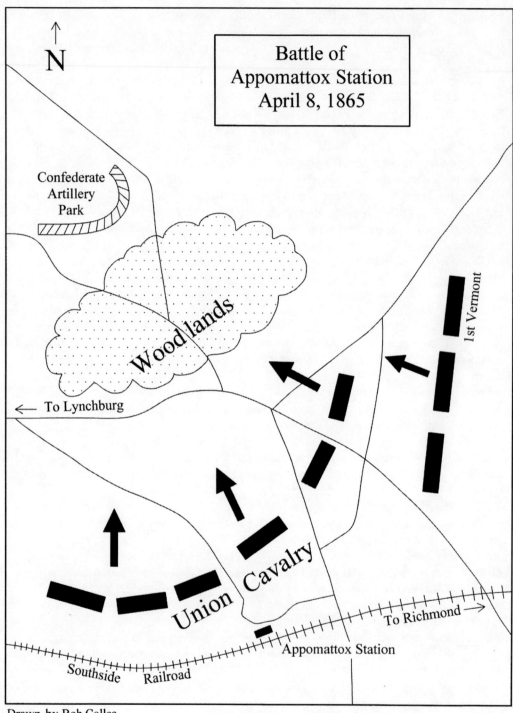

Drawn by Bob Collea

pronged: a dismounted detachment was sent downstream, where an uncontested fording of the creek was made; and a piece of horse artillery was wrestled through the tangle of trees and underbrush to paste the rebel works with canister. When at last the shooting started, the converging fire proved effective. "The enemy was so taken by surprise, they having supposed that the river was not fordable at any other place than where guarded," reported a war correspondent, "that they fled in wildest confusion after a very brief skirmish."[13]

A lively pursuit ensued, eventually compelling 800 North Carolina cavalrymen to make a stand at Namozine Church. Approaching the white wooden structure, the Union cavalry prepared to charge. With his customary flourish, Custer had his band render a few stirring tunes. Then, the 1st Vermont and the 8th New York slammed into the waiting rebels. With little effort, the blocking force was uprooted. A last-ditch countercharge was easily swatted back on its heels. William Wells then maintained a hot pursuit for twelve miles, all the way to the Appomattox River. Though unable to interdict the Confederate retreat, the efforts of Wells' men did not go unrewarded. An impressive bag of enemy prisoners, equipment, and flags was garnered. The rebels' lone cannon was also taken by Jerome Hatch, an accomplishment witnessed by Horace Ide: "Down the road we went pell mell and on after them. Lieutenant Hatch overtook a gun and with a pistol persuaded them to return with it."[14] But, regardless of the positives achieved, there was a price to be paid. With only six days left in the war, two Vermont troopers, Andrew Calderwood and Willis Lyman, were called upon to make the supreme sacrifice. Both were callow—each being but twenty years of age. Private Calderwood had served only seven months. Lyman was a veteran of two-and-half years, who would have had a longer

Appomattox Station. Along these tracks in the afternoon of April 8, 1865, the Vermont Cavalry had a hand in capturing three trainloads of supplies desperately needed by Lee's famished army (Library of Congress).

tenure, but his enlistment at sixteen was voided once his status as a minor was uncovered. Previously captured at Hagerstown and wounded at Tom's Brook, the young man's luck ran out at Namozine Church.

After disengaging, Custer's division marched westward until nightfall, halting near Deep Creek. April 5 witnessed the men gaining Jetersville, having covered forty-five miles from Namozine Church. Meanwhile, the Army of Northern Virginia reached Amelia Court House on April 4, anticipating supplies that did not materialize. Lee halted overnight, so his men could forage. By this delay, Federal soldiers were afforded the chance to affect his route of march. While the Confederates rested, the Federals pressed forward. The 1st Vermont broke camp late in the evening and was on the road again at midnight on April 4. Throughout the next day, the men remained alert. Racing ahead to Jetersville thirteen miles southwest of Amelia Court House, Sheridan, his 200-man personal escort, and the 5th Infantry Corps sealed off the way to North Carolina. Lee was forced to continue west.

After three days of searching, Custer's division finally received accurate intelligence. Four Confederate supply trains were reportedly parked at Appomattox Station. The race was on, every regiment desirous of being the first to claim the prizes. As other elements of his command struck the railroad below the depot, Custer "took possession of the station, but none too soon, for almost at the moment he did so the van of Lee's army appeared, bent on securing the trains."[15] Major William Cummings was there and remembered how "we kept up our pace, til we were at each end of the switches at the station. The trains were ours."[16] While one engine and a few cars did escape, the rich trove of supplies and foodstuffs left behind more than outweighed their loss.

With the remaining three trains sitting with steam up, a call went out for engineers. Eager volunteers quickly jumped at the chance. For a few moments, former railroaders were home again, engaged in their prewar calling as deftly as if they had never left. "They amused themselves by running the trains to and fro," observed an irked Phil Sheridan, "creating much confusion, and keeping up an unearthly screeching with whistles that I was on the point of ordering the cars burned."[17] Eventually, the reality of war reintroduced itself. The lark ended, and the trains chugged eastward where Union infantry afforded protection. The abrupt departure of the trains was caused by the unceremonious intrusion of a rebel artillery barrage. Hell-bent on capturing the trains, the Federals overlooked a nearby Confederate artillery park of 100 guns. Soon, the regiment's position became untenable, as "the shell[s] came toward us from the right, left, or front, with no seeming partiality; the air was full of them, and when we got up near the guns we found they were not short of canister either" was Major Cummings' lasting impression of his regiment's predicament.[18]

The Confederate artillery was located two miles from the Union cavalry, with a forested band separating the combatants. While offering some cover, the falling limbs, splintered shards, and lead fragments that exploding shells unleashed made the wood lot very dangerous. The gloom of night painted a surreal canvas in the forest. Eri Woodbury described the scene: "It was getting dark and the woods were constantly lighted up with the flashing of their cannon, and then the awful shrieking as the shell and canister came ploughing and tearing through the trees."[19] George Farrington of Company M was one trooper for whom the trees offered no sanctuary. He soon found himself dazed and injured, destined for a hospital and a disability discharge, the demoralizing result of "a compound fracture of the left femur occasioned by a shell wound."[20] A fragment from another exploding artillery shell struck Curtis Woodward's horse in the head, killing the animal and sending his rider to the turf. Woodward was momentarily pinned, but in passing by, Sergeant Ide saw Woodward "extricating himself from his fallen steed and then swinging his arms and shouting to the men not to run over him, for as the column was at a gallop, he was in full danger from friends as from enemies."[21]

Somewhere nearby in the same patch of exploding timberland, Sergeant Woodbury was in trouble too. "Suddenly [I] felt a blow [and a] numbing sensation across my breast," he said of his wounding, "and found myself turning a double somersault off into the bushes."[22] The detonation of an artillery shell had abruptly dehorsed Woodbury and left him with a painful, bloody limb. Arising from the forest floor, he took stock of his condition, finding that his "fingers were completely knocked out and hanging over the backside [of my] hand by a little shred of skin."[23] For Woodbury, his chance encounter with the errant piece of shrapnel would mean the amputation of his hand. Unlike some who suffered the loss of a body part, he could still return to his prewar calling as a teacher.

The shower of shells kept coming. The rebel force, though small, was determined. The cannon were packed in tight. An admirable resistance was maintained in the face of superior forces. Custer kept up the pressure, feeding in units as they came onto the field. Hampering his actions were both the unevenness of the terrain and a lack of knowledge with regard to the size of the opposing force. The engagement continued well past sundown. Three distinct charges comprised the Union cavalry's efforts. Not until late in the day did the third effort accomplish the goal of overwhelming enemy resistance. As General Custer later summed up the denouement, "The enemy succeeded in repulsing nearly all our attacks, until nearly 9 o'clock at night, when by a general advance along my line he was forced from his position and compelled to abandon to our hands twenty-four pieces of artillery, all his trains, several battle-flags, and a large number of prisoners."[24]

The high that young soldier Lieutenant Eri Woodbury experienced after capturing rebel flags at Cedar Creek and receiving a medal for bravery shortly thereafter was tempered somewhat by the crippling hand wound taken during the charge against rebel batteries at Appomattox Station (Francis C. Guber Collection).

After mopping up the area, Custer moved his men about a mile and called it a day shortly after midnight. Having been on the move since 7:00 A.M., every man and beast among them was played out. "I was too tired to wait for supper," recounted Horace Ide, "and went to sleep without any."[25] One trooper missing from camp was eighteen-year-old George Dunn. Private Dunn was no longer able to accompany his regiment because he had perished in the woods, mortally wounded by grapeshot that "went through his body and killed him instantly."[26] Dunn's cousin, Almer Montague, later lamented the circumstances of his kinsman's death: "I am very sorry that I was not with him, but by this time we had become completely mixed up for it was so dark that we could be within six feet of one of our own co. and not know them from a stranger."[27] While the loss of a popular soldier was always difficult to accept, the fallen trooper's many friends took some consolation in the manner of his passing, for the young man died a hero's death in the service of his country. When the lethal missile ploughed into his body, Private Dunn had been in the forefront of the second charge, urging his comrades to follow him. Already wounded, Dunn had entered the fatal charge with an ominous premonition. "The poor boy thought that he never would come out alive" was the chilling thought he shared with Wesley Warren.[28] So apprehensive was young Dunn that he made a pact with Warren: if after the fighting had ended and either of the two was missing, the other would search the battleground for his friend.

Just as the Vermont Cavalry was building up a head of steam toward a Confederate supply train at Appomattox Court House, a courier bearing a flag of truce trotted across the field where he was met by General Custer, setting the stage for Lee's surrender (Library of Congress).

True to his word, Private Warren, once he realized that Dunn was nowhere to be found, went searching for his friend. He soon discovered the awful truth. Returning quickly to the company, he enlisted a search party. Once the body was discovered, every effort was made to find Private Montague, but by the time he was located, the burial detail had returned. Montague "visited his grave the next morning and found that they had placed his body under a tree in a very pleasant place near the corner of the woods in which he fell and had taken great pains in placing a board at his head."[29] While Montague marked the spot where his cousin fell as well as the gravesite, so he could locate it in the years ahead even if the landscape changed, those precautions proved unnecessary. George Nay not only felt the absence of his friend but also knew the impact of Dunn's death as well as anyone. "We feel his loss a great deal," Nay shared with his mother, "but his father will more when he hears of it."[30] To no one's surprise, less than a month after his son's death, the father of George Dunn came to Virginia to retrieve his boy's body. The elder Dunn's grieving heart was especially heavy, since it was he who had given in to his under-aged son's repeated entreaties to sign his enlistment papers. Bringing his beloved son home to Fairfax for permanent interment represented but the final act in a lifetime of parental love that he could extend to his offspring.

Although not known at the time, Dunn's death would loom large in regimental history, for his name would be recorded as the last Vermont trooper to die on a battlefield. From its first foray down the Shenandoah Valley and into the war zone on April 1, 1862, through to Appomattox Court House on April 9, 1865, the 1st Vermont had spent over a thousand days at the front. From John Chase to George Dunn, somewhere between 112 and 132 Vermont cavalrymen died due to hostile fire.[31] Regardless of when hostilities were terminated, someone had to be the last to fall. Regrettably for Private Dunn, the cease-fire came a half day too late.

The final morning of the war dawned pleasantly and blossomed into a beautiful, sun-drenched spring day. Both sides were active early, as the generals maneuvered for position. Initially acting as a screen to mask the infantry build-up, the Federal cavalry was eventually ordered to shift its location to the right flank of the Union line. To effect this redeployment, the long column "passed in review between the two armies, marching by squadrons."[32] The route chosen, while expedient, was dangerous, as two Confederate batteries had the troopers within range the whole time. Spewing forth salvoes, they strove to rain destruction and death upon the orderly procession. Led by the fearless Custer, the passing regiments remained unflappable as they passed through the gauntlet of exploding shells, marching in measured pace as if on dress parade. Former Sergeant, now Lieutenant, Ide characterized the scene as "the grandest sight I ever saw."[33] With but minutes left in the war, this final show of bravado provided a memorable way to ring down the curtain on the regiment's storied career.

Only two men were wounded in the position change, but additional bloodshed might easily have followed. As the column cleared the end of the Union line, its focus zeroed in on a rebel wagon train. Thoughts of denying the enemy much-needed supplies became a powerful motivator. Confederate skirmishers were driven back. The wagons loomed larger and larger before them as the charging Vermonters closed the distance. But in the few brief seconds before the regiment achieved its objective—the end came. "The lead battalion had got so far that they captured the last post between us and the train before they could be halted," Colonel Josiah Hall remembered.[34] "We had almost gained possession of his trains," Custer later reported, "when a staff officer of General Longstreet

Riding proudly down Pennsylvania Avenue amidst the Army of the Potomac's assembled might, the 1st Vermont held the position as the lead regiment in the 3rd Brigade, 1st Division of the Cavalry Corps (Library of Congress).

came galloping into our lines under a flag of truce, requesting a suspension of hostilities."[35] The unexpected nature of this final act took many by surprise. Once its potential significance registered in their minds, the men exhibited a spontaneous display of elation. Hats were thrown into the air, and cheers were shouted. War-weary soldiers celebrated not victory but the cessation of hostilities. No more would have to die. Soon they would be returning home.

The troopers remained deployed until late in the afternoon. A bivouac was then made for the night on the spot. With his customary flair, George Custer seized upon the jubilation of this historic moment to issue a congratulatory message to his command. A soldier's general, he knew the right words to indelibly touch their souls. His praise was lavish: "The record established by your indomitable courage is unsurpassed in the annals of war." His pride was evident: "You have never lost a gun, never lost a color, and have never been defeated." And his humility was endearing: "And now, speaking for myself alone, when the war is ended, and the task of the historian begins; when those deeds of daring which have rendered the name and fame of the Third Cavalry Division imperishable, are inscribed upon the bright pages of our country's history, I only ask that my name be written as the commander of the Third Cavalry Division."[36] The men of the 1st Vermont had flourished in the orbit of George Armstrong Custer. In his personal quest for fame and glory, he took them along for the ride. By war's end, there had developed an admiration between leader and led that would be the envy of any commander.

On their part, the men expressed their feelings in different ways. The 3rd Cavalry Division as a whole "adopted as a badge a long scarlet neck-tie, to be worn by officers and enlisted men, in accordance with the request and imitation of their gallant young leader Maj. Gen. Custer."[37] Individually, the men found different venues to praise their leader. One Vermont trooper deftly framed his comrades' feelings: "They feel his fame to be theirs. They know their victories to have been gained for them by his leadership and daring. They claim for him a rank with the foremost, as a leader of cavalry."[38]

As exhilarating as the events of April 9 were, the next day proved disappointing. Pursuant to orders, the Federal Cavalry Corps was to leave for Burkeville on the morning of the 10th. Though they had played an integral part in bringing the Army of Northern Virginia to its knees, their 8:00 A.M. departure meant that the dejected troopers would not participate in the surrender ceremonies. To assuage the cavalry's disappointment, the wily General Sheridan arranged "to have the whole of the cavalry file through Appomattox Court House" on their way south.[39] By parading them through the village "by fours and well closed-up," the general afforded them a chance to be seen in all their glory by their vanquished foe, subtly impressing them in the process with the bearing and might of these powerful blue-clad adversaries who had become such a scourge to the enemy in the war's last year.[40]

The Vermonters would not officially part company with the army until the end of the summer. But, upon leaving Appomattox Court House, all active campaigning for them was over. Every mile that was ridden henceforth was a step away from living their generation's war and a step closer to reading it in history books.

Epilogue

They are all gone now. The last trooper of the 1st Vermont, Russell Martin, joined his comrades on Fiddler's Green in 1945. In the years following the Civil War, the veterans of the conflict led their country through unparalleled years of change and prosperity. Under the auspices of the Grand Army of the Republic, the aging veterans wielded significant political power, but most of all they banded together to maintain the fraternal bonds forged in battle and to relive the memories of a life-defining moment. The world to which they had returned in 1865 would never seem quite the same as the one that they had left. In appearance, the prewar farm, store, or schoolhouse bore little outward change, but the eyes of the former soldier, which now gazed upon the familiar scene, had witnessed so much during the war years that his viewpoint was now much different. Some, like William Rogers, were able to go home again and resume the life of a farmer. Others—like his brother Mark, who became a retail furniture salesman in Sommerville, Massachusetts—could not. They had all done what was needed for their country at the behest of their state. All had paid a price in lives interrupted and outlooks altered. Some incurred incapacitating wounds that placed limitations on their mobility and dexterity where none before had existed. Almost twenty score never had the opportunity to return, leaving empty chairs and broken hearts as ever-present reminders of their absences.

Unlike the returning warriors in America's more recent conflicts, a proud and thankful nation feted them well. The memorable Grand Review held in Washington, D.C., on May 23 offered them one last time to march together as a band of brothers. In June, amidst the dissolution of Federal forces, the Vermonters were on their way home. Arriving by train in Burlington, they were accorded a hero's welcome. "Proud as we are of the way in which *all* our Vermont troops have sustained the honor of the State and the old renown of the Green Mountain Boys," spoke orator G.G. Benedict, "we are prouder of none than our Cavalry; and when the history of the war is closed, I believe it will appear that no regiment has a more honorable page in the glorious record than yours." A few troopers lingered in uniform until August as a part of the Frontier Cavalry, assigned to guard the Canadian border, but for the most part it was over almost as abruptly as it had all begun. Following the mustering out ceremony on August 9, 1865, Horace Ide captured the prevailing sentiments: "Here the First Vermont Cavalry came into being and here it ceased to exist; here the comrades of nearly four long, weary years of marching and fighting separated, never all to meet again on this earth."[1] The fearless riders morphed into ordinary civilians once again, while the favorite sons were nestled back in the waiting arms of the people from whence they had come. The Union had been preserved, and peace had been restored. Life was good once more in the Green Mountains.

Appendix A.
Muster Roll* of the
First Vermont Cavalry

Field Officers

Charles Tompkins— Colonel
George B. Kellogg— Lieutenant Colonel
William D. Collins— Major

Staff Officers

George S. Gale — Surgeon
Edgar Pitkin — Adjutant
Archibald S. Dewey— Quarter Master
Ptolomy O. Edson — Assistant Surgeon
Alonzo H. Danforth — Sergeant Major
Charles V. H. Sabin — Quarter Master Sergeant
Joel H. Fisk — Hospital Steward
Cyrus Green — Principal Musician
Forester A. Prouty, Principal Musician

Company A Burlington

Captain
Platt, Frank A.

Lieutenants
Earhardt, Joel B.
Edwards, Ellis B.

Sergeants
Gibbs, Warren
Whitney, Edwin P.
Learnard, N.H.
Mayes, Reuben

Morse, Cornelius
Morgan, Patrick

Corporals
Fisk, Edwin
Frost, Malcolm G.
Landon, Zabina
Mattocks, Ichabod W.
Naramore, T.C.
Reynolds, Caleb C.
Wheeler, Henry O.
Whipple, Osgood M.

Buglers
Flowers, William J.
Squires, James

Blacksmith
Odell, John

Saddler
Gordon, Christopher

Farrier
McDixon, Daniel

Wagoner
Hogan, John

Privates
Adams, J.H.
Allen, Samuel J.
Anson, George D.
Atchinson, Blinn
Bain, John
Baldwin, Henry W.
Barber, Rufus G.
Barlow, Richard K.

Muster Roll taken from the Rutland Daily Herald, June 6, 1862, edition, page 4.

Blinn, Charles H.
Brasted, Nelson
Bushaway, Julius
Carleton, Charles F.W.
Cosgrove, Samuel
Crenan, William
Cummimgs, John
Daniels, Charles
Devino, Charles
Dimick, Nathan C.
Doyne, Frederick
Ellis, Cornelius W.
Faulkner, Frederick
Ferguson, Oscar
Frost, Herman
Goodwin, William
Green, Bostwick

Green, John
Green, Lester
Grow, Jerome H.
Hall, Alexander
Hall, Thomas
Harmon, Argalus
Haskins, Rufus
Haynes, Guy
Hutchins, Albert
Keese, George
Kelly, James
Langshore, William J.
Lyman, Wyllys
Lynde, Henry
Macomber, Francis B.
Manley, Elisha
Manley, Samuel G.

Marcia, Michael
Marshall, Alonzo D.
Maxfield, Rimon
McCulloch, Thomas
Morehouse, Daniel W.
Morse, Stephen
Noonan, John W.
Palmer, James A.
Paro, Peter
Quinlin, Michael
Ralph, Thomas
Rawson, Ellis M.
Renouf, William
Roberts, Samuel B.
Robinson, Wyman
Rogers, Henry M.
Ryan, Thomas

Sheldon, Alva S.
Sheldon, Willard W.
Sherman, George
Shonion, Lucius L.
Shutyel, Albert
Smith, Henry C.
Stone, Henry H.
Stone, Simeon
Tubbs, David
Upham, John
Warner, VanBuren
Weber, George
Whipple, Edwin J.
Woolcott, Sydney E.

Company B—St. Albans

Captain

Conger, George B.

Lieutenants

Beeman, Wm M.
Clark, Jed P.

Sergeants

Austin, Humphrey
Cook, Charles M.
Hulburt, Jackson M.
Hyde, Horace
Sawyer, John

Qr. Master Sergeant

Pixley, Charles H.

Corporals

Beeman, Orris P.
Conger, Warren W.
Eustace, Frank H.
Hall, Harman D.
Knight, Orris P.
Rogers, Mark N.
Soule, Eugene B.
Ufford, Samuel

Buglers

Green, Cyrus
Stiles, Lucious G.

Blacksmiths

Bliss, John
Caraway, John B.

Wagoner

Chiott, Henry

Privates

Austin, Julius R.
Austin, George W.
Abell, James
Alexander, Arthur
Baker, George H.
Barrows, Alphonso
Barrows, Wm. H.
Blair, Samuel
Bliss, George A.
Bliss, Joel
Bliss, Rufus M.
Bonah, Louis
Booshby, Phila
Brown, John
Brush, Azel N. Baker
Butler, Loren A.

Carrier, George
Cavanah, James
Chapman. B. G.
Corse, Malcolm S.
Cutting, George E.
Daniels, Noble A.
Davis, James A.
Davis, Luther
Depur, Wm. M.
Doane, Henry
Dragan, Francis
Draper, Ellis
Dufur, Simon
Durkee, Loren
Erwin, John W.
Farrand, Andrew
Fay, George W.
Field, Curtis I.
French, Samuel F.
Futchinoe, Antwain
Green, Warren W.
Hannaary, Patrick
Hazlet, John
Hickok, Charles
Hull, George C.
Hurlburt, John W.
Hutchinson, Peter P.
Jenne, Hannibal

Jocelyn, Frank B.
Johnson, Hiram B.
King, Peter
Kinney, Francis B.
McCarty, William
Miller, Andrew E.
Newton, Franklin B.
Patee, Myron J.
Patterson, Henry
Perry, Harrison
Perry, Nelson
Pockette, Joseph
Reynolds, Chester C.
Rushford, Gimri
Robinson, Richard
Rogers, William M.
Scott, Palmer M.
Shores, Francis
Smith, John
St. Germaine, M.
Toochett, Francis
Town, Lucian G.
Turner, Charles
Wanzer, Alfred K.
Ward, Dennis
Wildes, Daniel F.
Wright, Lyman
Yates, Edmond

Company C—Montpelier

Captain
Wells, William

Lieutenants
Holden, Eli
Paige, Henry M.

Qr. Master Sergeant
King, Lorentio H.

Sergeants
Bennett, Chauncy
Cheney, Perley C. J.
Dow, Harvey S.
Phillips, Henry C.

Corporals
Aldrich, H. P.
Heath, Martin
Hill, Daniel J.
Nickols, Langdon H.
Parker, Brainard M.
Pope, Edmund Jr.
Randall, James F.
Smith, John W.

Buglers
Batchelder, Ira
Nowrus, George W.

Farrier
Vorse, Samuel C.
French, Oliver

Blacksmith
Staples, Marshall S.

Saddler
Carpenter, Charles D.

Wagoner
Huse, John F.

Privates
Allen, Chauncy M.
Baldwin, Orange A.
Bennett, Allen J.
Blanchard, Timothy
Brown, George
Burton, John H.
Cahill, Thomas
Carr, Michael
Carrigan, Thomas
Chase, Austin A.
Davis, Nathan L.
Dodge, Wesley
Downing, Alson F.
Dudley, William
Duvall, Carlos

Edson, Henry
Fisk, Charles D.
Fisk, Gilbert
French, Franklin
George, Albert
Gorden, James W.
Gray, William C.
Hall, R. L.
Hastings, Sidney D.
Hatch, Jerome B.
Hatch, Marshall
Henry, Martin L.
Hill, George
Hoyt, Alonzo
Hunt, Washington
Kent, Sanford H.
Lewi, DeForest L.
Lewis, Frederick A.
Lyford, Monroe
Martin, Wm. E.
Mason, Wm. P. Jr.
May, Thomas S.
McEvoy, Edward
McLaughlin, John
Moffit, Pliney M.
Morris, Joseph
Nichols, Erastus H.
Norris, Malon
Nownes, William

Plastridge, Amasa
Preston, Philander A.
Rarnam, William
Reed, James S.
Reeman, Daniel P.
Reyner, Nelson L.
Rice, Marcus S.
Richardson, Levi B.
Ring, William F.
Ruggles, Homer
Sanborn, David
Sarens, George N.
Scott, Elisha
Smith, Gilbert O.
Smith, Joel J.
Spencer, George W.
Stark, Nathan B.
Stickney, William O.
Stiles, Lester K.
Sturtevant, Charles E.
Trombly, Henry
Wakefield, Luther
Wardner, L.
Waterman, George S.
Wheeler, J.A.
Wheelock, Jacob E.
Williams, Eugene
Woodward, George S.

Company D—Chelsea

Captain
Preston, Addison

Lieutenants
Bennett, John W.
Cummings, Wm. G.

Sergeants
Mitchell, Harris B.
Moore, Josiah H.
Palmer, Phineas L.
Sargent, M.V.B.
Trassell, Jacob

Qr. Master Sergeant
Robinson, George

Corporals
Carr, Benjamin F.

Chase, John
Clement, Guy C.
Douglas, F.J.
Farnsworth, H.M.
Huntington, H.K.
Meacham, Ashbel C.
Sargent, Harrison

Saddler
Chadwick, Edwin S.

Blacksmith
Aiken, Enoch J.
Knapp, Charles

Musicians
Corliss, Milo J.
Whitcomb, Rufus E.

Privates

Adams, Don
Austin, George A.
Bailey, Austin A.
Bard, Charles F.
Bard, Harrison K.
Bard, Oscar L.
Beard, John
Beaton, John O.
Bell, Alexander
Bennett, George F.
Bickford, Charles W.
Bickford, Harry J.
Blair, George P.
Blood, Horace
Brown, Mitchell
Browne, Lorenzo
Buck, William M.

Carture, James
Chandler, Anson
Chase, Loring, Jr.
Clark, Joseph O.
Clifford, Benjamin F.
Cooms, John S.
Curtis, Antipas H.
Danforth, Hiram P.
Davis, William
Davidson, George B.
Decker, Barney
Driggs, Ellis W.
Durham, Conceader F.
Eames, Rodney
Esdon, James
Fox, John N.
Freeman, Austin
Garfield, Isaac D.
Gilcrist, Daniel K.

Gilligan, Patrick C.
Gracy, John C.
Higgins. Samuel. L.
Hutchinson, Joseph
Kendrick, Orin S.
Kenison, Azro H.
Kennerson, Albert
Marckres, Harvey A.
Merrill, Ralph
Moore, Henry A.

Morrill, Kyron
Morse, John F.
Murray, Arthur
Norris, Warren G.
Page, Elijah C.
Page, Russell B.
Perkins, Eben
Pierce, William
Powers, J. Hale
Reed, Lucius S. F.

Rowell, Francis H.
Smith, John N.
Southworth, E.W.
Stacey, Curtis L.
Vance, Martin V. B.
Webber, Furnal H.
Wheaton, William M.
Wheeler, Mark
White, James D.
Whitney, George H.

Woodbury, Isaac P.
Woodbury, John W.
Woodward, John
Woodward, William
Wright, Darwin J.
Wright, James
Young, Andrew J.

Company E—Royalton

Captain
Rundlett, Samuel P.

Lieutenants
Grover, Andrew J.
Holmes, John C.

Sergeants
Chandler, Alexander B.
Cushman, Oliver T.
Hill, Howard W.
Jones, Charles N.
Seaver, Richard A.
Wentworth, Jarvis

Corporals
Bailey, Joseph W.
Gage, Aaron H.
Knight, George P.
Pierce, Charles
Roys, Ira
Rundlett, Thomas P.
Williams, Henry G.
Witherell, N.G.B.

**Farriers/Black-
smiths**
Daniels, David B.
Marsh, Franklin

Buglers
Lampson, Jonathan J.
Locke, Julius E.

Saddler
Dodge, Miles H.

Wagoner
Alexander, Hazen C.

Privates
Abels, Eugene H.
Allen, Albert W.
Anthony, Jerome
Bailey, V. C.
Bishop, Charles W.
Blake, Lancelot K.
Bradley, Henry S.
Bride, Henry A.
Brunnack, Henry K.
Bryant, Carlos
Bryant, Thomas
Buckman, Henry F.
Bunell, Lewis
Cady, James A.
Carlin, Constant
Champlane, Joseph
Clapp, Albert H.

Coy, George E.
Curtis, George A.
Dana, Daniel C.
Dodge, George A.
Everest, George W.
Farley, John
Flynn, Franklin P.
Gould, Franklin
Gould, Hiram
Gould, Major
Griswald, Lucius D.
Hall, Horace
Hanley, Wm.
Haward, Samuel A.
Hayward, Reuben W.
Hilton, Edson C.
Hogan, James
Hogan, Michael
Holt, Henry
Hopkins, Wm. R.
Hoskins, Marcus
Hutchinson, T.L.
Kendall, Albert A.
Kimball, Orris F.
Messer, Allen P.
Morse, John
Morse, Orimel
Mudgett, John

Parkhurst, Oscar M.
Parks, L.M.
Perham, Lafayette M.
Phillips, Calvin B.
Pond, William H.
Rice, Benjamin
Richmond, Forest E.
Rogers, Benjamin F.
Rogers, Riley
Rowe, Henry
Rubenzlerin, B.
Rumrill, George C.
Ryan, Daniel H.
Sizzon, Charles B.
Sleeper, Charles T.
Smith, Henry A.
Snow, Sylvester M.
Spaulding, E.G.
Stafford, Wm.
Stone, Edmund
Thurston, Valorus
Walker, George J.
Waterman, Alonzo L.
Watts, Westley
Wheeler, Charles
Willard, John H.
Yeberson, John

Company F—Brattleboro

Captain
Hall, Josiah

Sergeants
Bartleff, Thomas E.
Church, Benjamin D.
Clark, Stephen A.
Joyce, Wm. C.
Smith, Henry E.

**Qr. Master
Sergeant**
Smith, Harvey

Corporals
Farr, Charles R.
Forbush
Gibbs, Almon B.
Ide, Horace

Livingston, William
Richardson, Lorin C.
Spencer, Sidney A.
Thompson, S. Frank

Bugler
Prouty, Forrester A.

Blacksmiths
Curtis, John

Woodbarer, James
H.

Saddler
Gardner, Henry

Wagoner
Keyes, Lorenzo D.

Farrier

Stone, Hosea

Privates

Aldrich, Henry
Aldrich, James
Aldrich, Leonard J.
Bailey, Ethan A.
Bancroft, Fernandia
Betterly, Frank W.
Blake, George
Blanchard, Joy N.
Briggs, James T.
Brooks, Urial
Brush, George W.
Butler, William C.
Cane, Dexter
Carroll, John
Carver, Rufus J.

Cook, Henry M.
Crosby, George
Cutting, Samuel C.
Dickenson, Nathaniel
Dinsmore, Charles A.
Eddy, John A.
Ellis, James W.
Farr, Ransom C.
Fisher, William H.
Forbush, George H.
Gervais, Henry
Gilmore, Rinoldo G.
Goodnow, Orvel S.
Grant, Andrew J.
Harris, Austin A.
Haskell, George W.
Heath, Jesse S.
Hildreth, Austin O.
Hinckley, Samuel O.

Howe, Andrew J.
Howe, Nathan B.
Howard, R. A.
Hyatt, Joseph A.
Jillson, John S.
Judd, William S.
Mattson, George B.
May, Warren E.
McCarty, Eugene
Metcalf, Eli P.
Morley, Elias S.
Morris, Norman A.
Nash, Asabel M.
Nash, John M.
Pierce, Herbert S.
Pierce, John T.
Powers, Daniel M.
Puffer, Edwin A.
Ravlin, Henry E.

Remmington, Frank E.
Ryan, George F.
Stone, Clark P.
Stone, Jason A.
Stone, Mason A.
Streeter, Henry C.
Streeter, Lucien S.
Strong, Calvin D.
Thwing, John A.
Ware, Loami A.
Warner, Myron
Whipple, John
Witt, Theodore
Woodard, Flarid
Wooley, Charles L.
Wooster, Mark H.

Company G—Bennington

Captain

Sheldon, James A.

Lieutenants

Bean, George H.
Sheldon, James A.

Sergeants

Chaffie, William F.
Clark, Waldo J.
Ray, Frank
Sibley, Avery B.
Vanderlep, John M.

**Qr. Master
Sergeant**

Bailey, Henry M.

Corporals

Dyer, Fayette
Fuller, William J.
Hadaway, James E.
Hall, Parker Hall
Hanks, Ira C.
Hurd, Irving W.
Perkins, Leroy D.
Tinkham, Sorell

Bugler

Leach, Horatio N.

Saddler

Greeley, Parker

**Farriers/
Blacksmiths**

Collins, Ethiel
Flemming, Charles A.

Teamster

Waldron, Joseph

Privates

Abbott, Charles
Atherton, Lorenzo D.
Barrett, James
Bartlett, Sylvester P.
Belding, William H.
Bellows, Eugene
Benson, Homer
Bracey, Oscar
Brown, Charles
Caffery, Christopher
Carl, Edward
Carl, William
Clapp, Stephen
Cook, Frederick W.
Curtis, George W.
Colby, Winslow A.
Courtright, Joseph

Crumb, Sylvester S.
Darling, David
Day, Abram
Derby, Otis
Ducat, Francis
Farnum, Joseph C.
Frazer, Joseph C.
Guilder, Morgan
Hall, Hiram S.
Harrington, William
Haswell, Alvah R.
Hill, John H.
Howe, Theron
Hurd, Silas J.
Kearce, Morte
Kendal, Timothy
Lamb, Henry
Lehan, John
Malone, Patrick
Mattison, George M.
McMahon, James
Meham, Richard
Monorief, William T.
Monroe, Ira
Moore, James
Nickols, Ezra
O'Hayer, Henry
Pattison, Daniel C.
Potter, Charles K.

Powers, Thomas
Reynolds, William W.
Richmond, Burt
Roberts, Stephen D.
Robinson, Nathan A.
Ruleau, Vietal
Russell, Lyman L.
Sampson, Augustus
Sherwood, Charles
Scully, Barney
Sherman, Willard B.
Short, Hugh
Smith, Dexter
Squires, Henry
Stewart, Charles
Stewart, Gilbert
Stone, Richard
Ruel, Charles
Russell, Daniel M.
Taft, Daniel W.
Taylor, Joseph
Vaughn, Philip
Warner, William W.
Waters, Hiram W.
Whitaker, David S.
Wickwire, William W.
Wilson, Henry

Company H—Rutland

Captain

Perkins, Selah G.

Lieutenants

Adams, Charles A.
Huntoon, Franklin T.

Sergeants

Barrows, Carlos A.
Cory, Job
Davis, F. J. W.
Dowling, Samuel
Everson, James Jr.

Qr. Master Sergeant

Hazelton, John H.

Corporals

Bailey, Samuel P.
Cooke, Edson A.
Gena, Zebulon
Jackson, Henry
Lewis, Nathaniel B.
Mather, Emmett
Spencer, Albert D.
Stewart, James A.

Buglers

Hawley, Thomas
Morgan, Harley P.

Blacksmiths

Callaghen, Patrick
Stevens, John G.

Saddler

O'Brien, William

Wagoner

Worthen, Henry M.

Privates

Baldwin, Frank J. W.
Barnes, Luther
Barr, Henry A.
Barrett, Merritt C.
Bostwyck, Royal E.
Brown, George L.
Bryant, David
Bucklin, George D.
Buffum, Joseph
Bugbee, Dudley W.
Burk, Michael
Buxton, Stephen L.
Carpenter, Joseph M.
Cheney, William S.
Clair, Anthony P.
Clair, Edgar
Cook, Charles A.
Cook, George
Cooke, Henry W.

Cory, Stephen
Crandall, Albert
Crandall, Willard
Davis, Don C.
Davis, Henry
Davis, Solon D.
Doty, Alonzo E.
Eames, Darwin E.
Edson, Henry O.
Everson, George J.
Farmer, George W.
Fitzgerald, William E.
Flynn, William
Gee, Edward
Gorton, George M.
Greenough, David
Grover, Joel
Guertin, Joseph
Hart, Jeffry
Hebbard, Mason B.
Hinckley, Edward
Holden, James B.
Jones, William M.
Knight, George W.
Locklin, Ralph
Marshall, Marcus
McIntyre, John
Morgan, Lensey R.
Munroe, Ira
Munson, Aden

Patch, Daniel
Pratt, Henry W.
Persons, Collamer
Peterson, Harley
Poiney, Edwin
Price, Isaac
Reid, Dean W.
Riley, James A.
Robinson, Justin
Ross, James M.
Sanderson, Abner E.
Sheldon, Chauncey L.
Simonds, Sylvester
Smith, John C.
Stone, James
Sturtevant, Henry
Titus, Ezra W.
Titus, Harvey
Warren, Daniel D.
Warren, Ira C.
Wellman, Austin B.
White James W.
Williams, John S.
Wilson, Charles
Wright, William C.

Company I—Hyde Park

Captain

Sawyer, Edward B.

Lieutenants

Flint, Henry C.
Grout, Josiah

Sergeants

Burnham, Philander
Fisk, Joel H.
Grant, Eben
Mason, Marvin
Woodbury, Charles A.

Qr. Master Sergeant

Caldwell, Henry P.

Corporals

Barrows, Alfred Jr.
Ferry, Carlistan C.
Foster, William W.
Hoyt, Charles C.
Hubbell, Thaddeus P.
Perry, Benjamin F.
Persons, Luther B.
Walker, B. E.

Buglers

Allen, Joseph W.
Whitney, Isaac P.

Blacksmiths

Kaizer, Samuel H.
Warner, Henry H.

Saddler

Sparron, William

Wagoner

Grant, Joseph P.

Privates

Aiken, Benjamin O.
Barry, Elirs W.
Bassett, Albert S.
Bassett, Calvin
Bean, Alphrouns
Bean, Rufus
Boomhower, Herbert A.
Brooks, Reuben E.
Burr, A. J.
Clark, Samuel B.

Coon, Alanson E.
Currier, William H.
Daniels, William H.
Dike, Chauncy
Drew, Ira S.
Dutton, William
Eaton, Solomon W.
Eddy, John R.
Ewens, George
Gauthier, Joseph
Goin, James F.
Greaves, James
Hall, William H.
Hart, Andrew J.
Hawley, Homer
Henenway, G. W.
Hines, Silas
Hopkins, Charles H.

Hyde, George A.
Kelley, John A.
King, Michael G.
Knight, Philo J.
Lant, Albert C.
Leighton, Ariel H.
Lilley, Harvey
Martin, William P.
Mead, Franklin S.
Meloney, William J.
Miles, Ephraim L.

Miner, William
Nimblet, George B.
Niozo, George
Ober, Aaron S.
Peavy, George W.
Pierce, Watson S.
Putnam, Orrin J.
Quimby, Elias M.
Raymore, Albinus
Reed, John
Sais, Marshall

Sargeant, Martin R.
Sargent, Samuel, Jr.
Sawyer, Franklin E.
Sheldon, Charles H.
Skinner, George
Skinner, Theodore P.
Smith, Eliab
Spafford, George S.
Stevens, Goodwin W.
Stone, Edwin A.
Stowe, Calvin

Stratton, Samuel
Thompson, Harvey
Tice, Robert S.
Washburn, Edward A.
Wheelock, E. D.
Whitney, Abijah F.
Wiswell, Thomas

Company K—Shoreham

Captain

Moore, Franklin

Lieutenants

Ward, John S.
Williamson, John

Sergeants

Dewey, Wallace
Higley, Edwin H.
Johnson, William F.
Rice, Jonas R.
Sheldon, Benjamin

Qr. Master Sergeant

Smith, Dwight H.

Corporals

Cheney, Ozro F.
Goodrich, Charles B.
Hathorn, Wallace W.
Keefe, Moses H.
Lapham, Horace
North, Henry B.
Sanborn, Charles A.
Spencer, Charles K.

Buglers

Allen, Wilmarth
Lewis, Levi S.

Blacksmiths

Edwards, Charles
Sheldon, Eli

Saddler

Pesia, Camiel

Wagoner

McFarland, William H.

Privates

Austin, George E.
Bailey, Theodore
Bennett, Hazard
Blood, Amos
Bluiz, Israel
Bryant, George
Canfield, Thaddeus A.
Carpenter, John
Chilson, Eugene
Dane, John
Dukett, John
Eldridge, Charles
Fairman, William C.
Fales, Myron L.
Fanning, William
Galvin, John
Gibbs, Henry
Gibbs, Lester

Goodnow, Frank
Goodnow, Walter H.
Goodrich, Rodney W.
Green, Judson O.
Gugette, Frank
Hathorn, Farwell H.
Heitman, Herman
Holdredge, Frederick H.
Howe, John
Hoy, Hugh
Ikey, Collis
Jackson, John W.
Johnson, Harrison'
Jones, Edwin E.
Keefe, James
Kitching, Joseph C.
Komer, Henry
Lamot, Gilbert
Lapham, Charles N.
Lemorder, Charles
Lewis, David H.
Lewis, William F.
Liberty, Lewis
Loveland, Frederick
Macha, George
Marshall, John
McDonald, John
McSorley, John
Merrill, Romeo W.

Mosey, Alfred
Needham, Henry
Noble, Hiram
Palmer, Alfred
Pecu, William
Rigby, Benjamin F.
Ross, Alexander
Russell, Edwin
Shambo, Charles R.
Shanborn, James H.
Shaw, Albert M.
Sherwood, Bradford
Sherwood, Sanford
Sloan, Edgar P.
Smith, George
Thomas, Jenness
Thompson, John C.
Wadsworth, Daniel
Whitlock, Samuel F.
Widewake, H. Joseph
Wilcox, Arthur H.
Williams, William
Wilson, Daniel
Wright, Theodore
Young, Francis

Appendix B.
Engagements of
the 1st Vermont Cavalry

Mt. Jackson, Va	April 16, 1862	Spotsylvania, Va	May 8, 1864
McGaheysville, Va	April 27, 1862	Yellow Tavern, Va	May 11, 1864
Middletown, Va	May 24, 1862	Meadow Bridge, Va	May 12, 1864
Winchester, Va	May 25, 1862	Hanover Court House, Va	May 31, 1864
Luray Court House, Va	June 30, 1862	Ashland, Va	June 1, 1864
Culpeper Court House, Va	July 10, 1862	Hawe's Shop, Va	June 3, 1864
Orange Court House, Va	August 2, 1862	Bottom's Bridge, Va	June 10, 1864
Kelly's Ford, Va	August 20, 1862	Riddle's Shop	June 13, 1864
Waterloo Bridge, Va	August 22, 1862	White Oak Swamp, Va	June 13, 1864
2nd Bull Run, Va	August 30, 1862	Malvern Hill, Va	June 15, 1864
Ashby's Gap, Va	September 22, 1862	Ream's Station, Va	June 22, 1864
Aldie, Va	March 2, 1863	Nottoway Court House, Va	June 23, 1864
Miskel's Farm, Va	April 1, 1863	Roanoke Station, Va	June 25, 1864
Greenwich, Va	May 30, 1863	Stony Creek Station, Va	June 29, 1864
Hanover, Pa	June 29, 1863	Winchester, Va	August 17, 1864
Hunterstown, Pa	July 2, 1863	Summit Point, Va	August 21, 1864
Gettysburg, Pa	July 3, 1863	Charlestown, Va	August 22, 1864
Monterey, Pa	July 4, 1863	Kearneysville, Va	August 25, 1864
Hagerstown, Md	July 6, 1863	Opequon, Va	September 19, 1864
Boonsboro, Md	July 8, 1863	Gooney Manor Grade, Va	September 21, 1864
Hagerstown, Md	July 13, 1863	Front Royal, Va	September 21, 1864
Falling Waters, Md	July 14, 1863	Milford, Va	September 22, 1864
Port Conway, Va	August 25, 1863	Waynesboro, Va	September 28, 1864
Port Conway, Va	September 1, 1863	Columbia Furnace, Va	October 7, 1864
Culpeper Court House, Va	September 13, 1863	Tom's Brook, Va	October 9, 1864
Somerville Ford, Va	September 14, 1863	Cedar Creek, Va	October 13, 1864
Raccoon Ford, Va	September 15, 1863	Middle Road, Va	November 11, 1864
Brandy Station, Va	October 11, 1863	Middletown, Va	November 12, 1864
Gainesville, Va	October 18, 1863	Lacey Springs, Va	December 21, 1864
Buckland Mills, Va	October 19, 1863	Waynesboro, Va	March 2, 1864
Gainesville, Va	October 19, 1863	Five Forks, Va	April 1, 1865
Falmouth, Va	November 4, 1863	Scott's Corners, Va	April 2, 1865
Morton's Ford, Va	November 28, 1863	Namozine Creek, Va	April 3, 1865
Mechanicsville, Va	March 1, 1864	Namozine Church, Va	April 3, 1865
Piping Tree, Va	March 2, 1864	Appomattox Station, Va	April 8, 1865
Craig's Meeting House, Va	May 5, 1864	Appomattox Court House, Va	April 9, 1865

Appendix C.
Assignments of the
1st Vermont Cavalry

December 1861 to March 1862
Banks' Division Army of the Potomac

March 1862 to June 1862
Hatch's Cavalry Division Banks' 5th Army Corps Army
of the Potomac Department of Shenandoah

June 1862 to September 1862
Hatch's Cavalry Brigade 2nd Army Corps Army of Virginia

September 1862 to April 1862
Price's Cavalry Brigade Defenses of Washington 22nd Army Corps

April 1863 to June 1863
Stahel's Cavalry Division 3rd Brigade 22nd Army Corps

June 1863 to August 1863
1st Brigade 3rd Division Cavalry Corps Army of the Potomac

August 1863 to August 1864
2nd Brigade 3rd Division Cavalry Corps Army of the Potomac

August 1864 to March 1865
Army of the Shenandoah Middle Military Division

March 1865 to June 1865
Army of the Potomac

Appendix D.
Medal of Honor Recipients
in the 1st Vermont Cavalry

The concept for a Congressional Medal of Honor was first authorized by the country's legislative branch in 1861. During the Civil War, citations for acts of bravery and heroism chronicled 1,522 instances for which this distinguished decoration was awarded to Federal servicemen. Unfortunately, in the early years following its introduction, the distribution of the award was far too liberal and for reasons that often paled when matched against the deeds of latter-day recipients. As a comparative case in point illustrating this practice, the Civil War saw only 22 medals—or .014 percent—given posthumously, while in World War II, of its 464 recipients 266 men—or 54.7 percent—died from battle wounds. Perhaps the most egregious Civil War era devaluation of the medal's value occurred when secretary of war Stanton, desperate for troops to man the defenses of Washington in the face Lee's 1863 invasion, gave it to almost 900 members of the 90-day 27th Maine Infantry because 300 of them agreed to extend their enlistments due to the crisis of the moment. Though wiser heads prevailed years later, causing these awards to be rescinded, the whole episode proved valuable in refocusing on the original criteria. The need for this was obvious if the medal was in fact to have any real meaning and worth. Looking at the totals for all of America's wars, the Civil War accounted for an astounding 44.3 percent of the Medals of Honor awarded up until the Gulf War! Over the course of the intervening years, standards for bestowing the honor were rethought and the bar raised. While the result was a decrease in the number of citations distributed and an increase in the likelihood that the recipient would be deceased, the intended outcome was achieved: the Congressional Medal of Honor is now recognized as the premier military award for a serviceman who distinguishes themselves "conspicuously by gallantry and intrepidity at the risk of his life above and beyond the call of duty while engaged in action against an enemy of the United States."

Four Vermont cavalrymen were awarded the Medal of Honor. The only officer among them was then Colonel William Wells, who earned his in the Battle of Gettysburg. Corporal Frederick Lyon, Private James Sweeney, and Sergeant Eri Woodbury all earned theirs for actions in conjunction with the Battle of Cedar Creek. With only slight variations in the scenario's details, the three noncoms each performed essentially the same deed: capturing an enemy flag somewhere on the field of combat. While the trio all participated in the charge that broke the back of the enemy's resistance, precipitating the wholesale rout that followed, the actual taking of the rebel banners occurred later in the backwash of the Confederate retreat. By the time Lyon, Sweeney, and Woodbury claimed their coveted prizes, by any measure applied to the situation, resistance was virtually nonexistent. This is not to denigrate the mettle of any man who first had the courage to ride against an entrenched infantry and then the moxie to pursue a fleeing foe to the unnerving extent that he outrode his support; but none of the three effected their captures in life-threatening postures. In fact, the enemy accosted was actually quite docile and compliant in surrendering their sacred banners, not to mention themselves. Thoroughly whipped, the defeated rebels had nothing to accomplish beyond upholding honor by offering resistance, the tradeoff for which could easily have been their sudden demise. While by no means belonging in the same scurrilous company as the 27th Maine's awards, neither were these medals-for-flags earned with the same degree of difficulty as those by later recipients, such as "Manila John" Basilone for example. Later killed in combat on Iwo Jima, Sergeant Basilone was credited for holding off a Japanese regiment for three days with a machine gun as it attempted to overrun his defensive position on Guadalcanal. Nevertheless, unlike some who got medals in accordance with the shaky standards of their era, Lyon, Sweeney, and Woodbury's lives were at least potentially in jeopardy the whole time. The fact that no one rose up to oppose them was their good fortune but not their fault. It might even be argued that their bold actions cowed an enemy who in the face of less courageous men might have not been so meek.

Of the threesome at Cedar Creek, Sergeant Woodbury's experience was perhaps the most dramatic and held out the possibility that all might not have ended bloodlessly for him. Readily noticeable because he was mounted in the vicinity when few others were, clearly vulnerable because he was alone, and even in the fading twilight identifiable as a Yankee, he accosted four armed Confederate infantrymen, one of whom appeared to be concealing an object behind his back. With but his saber as a threat, Woodbury ordered them to surrender. Their immediate compliance produced four captives, their weapons, and a regimental flag of the 12th North Carolina.

By contrast, the joint effort of Lyon and Sweeney was more surprising than fraught with added tension or danger. Passing a string of wagons, they reached the lead ambulance just as it was about to cross a bridge. Lyon hailed the driver and told him to stop. Indignant to think that a fellow rebel was impeding his escape, the wagoner volunteered a piece of information that perked Lyon's ears. He revealed that General Stephan Ramseur was inside. Then he brusquely told the cavalryman to move on. Nonplussed, Lyon repeated his order to halt, adding the shocking revelation that he belonged to the Federal army. Along with a wagon, mules, and the driver, the troopers' haul also included not only the general and two more officers but a Confederate regimental flag as well. It was this last item that earned the boys their medals.

The fourth and final Vermonter upon whom the Congressional Medal of Honor was bestowed, William Wells, clearly was awarded his for having participated in serious combat action. In Wells' case, this turned out to be "Farnsworth's Charge," the leadership of which fell upon his shoulders after General Farnsworth took his death wound. In a curious line of thinking, a man who gave his life in battle received no posthumous recognition, while a survivor of the same engagement did. To add to the oddity of Wells' selection, he did not receive notification until 1891. The time lag was not due to any oversight, but rather borne out of a belated, politically motivated attempt to even out the allocation of medals. Vermont had no general officer that had been so recognized during the war. Postwar sensitivities dictated that the little state, which had contributed so heavily to the Union cause, ought not to be snubbed in this manner. Wells had sufficient credentials, so he got a medal. Did he deserve it? Applying the standards of the times, he did — at least as much as many of the other recipients, though undoubtedly not necessarily any more than many who did not receive medals.

Appendix E.
"Farnsworth's Charge" Revisited
The Second Battle of Gettysburg

Hard as it is to imagine how a new controversy could be stirred up about a battle that ended over one hundred and forty-four years ago, this is exactly what has happened at Gettysburg. Ironically, the debate swirls over a phase of the engagement that for years was relatively ignored and never given its just due: "Farnsworth's Charge." At the crux of this second Battle of Gettysburg is disagreement about the starting point for the Federal troopers' ride. Depending upon where this spot is determined to be then calls into question many ancillary issues. Two of particular interest would the determination of the specific point in the assault at which General Farnsworth met his death, while the other is identifying the route ridden by the attacking columns once momentum built up and the advance moved out beyond Bushman's Hill.

Addie Custer, a licensed battlefield guide at Gettysburg, has authored a series of thought-provoking articles in recently published Civil War magazines through which she has developed her theories, basing much of her revisionist point of view on research conducted on the battlefield. Eric Wittenberg, a noted historian of considerable stature and a recognized expert in Union cavalry operations in the Eastern Theater, champions the substance of the traditional hypothesis, which has been espoused by perhaps every previous author who has ever written about the battle. Mrs. Custer's contention is that Farnsworth's attack was launched several hundred yards farther to the south of what has historically been thought to have been its jumping off point.

Much of the credence for this adjustment is attributed to Mrs. Custer's assessment that the original unit memorials for the 5th New York, the 1st West Virginia, and the 1st Vermont were erroneously sited. When the 5th New York's monument was relocated in 1912, she contends that the other two should also have been moved but were not. Had this realignment been carried out, Ms. Custer places the revised spot for the 1st Vermont as being at the lower end of a ravine on the south side of what is Confederate Avenue, significantly to the rear and southwest of Bushman's Hill upon which the New York marker is located. Evidence of "stone walls," mentioned frequently and prominently in many veterans' reminiscences, is still present in the ravine, adding support to her assertion. Since she believes that (1) Farnsworth perished in the early stages of the charge, and (2) elements of the 1st Vermont, stymied at the stone walls and other nearby barriers, went behind and around Bushman's Hill from left to right before breeching the Confederate lines, some of the once-held-as-sacred beliefs about the charge are therefore challenged.

For Mr. Wittenberg and scores of other historians before him, a cornerstone of their respective interpretations of "Farnsworth's Charge" has traditionally been the account and map produced by Captain Henry Parsons of the 1st Vermont. However, since it has been established that Parsons went down near the beginning of the fight, his credibility has suffered a severe blow about ensuing events in which he did not participate. Therefore, most of what he wrote was in reality gleaned from others, potentially weakening the value of much of his account. Mr. Wittenberg, while agreeing that Parsons is suspect, still feels that the assault was launched farther to the north, with Bushman's Hill and its lee being the points of origin. He further differs with Mrs. Custer in his belief that General Farnsworth died much later in the charge, within the confines of the so-called "D-shaped field," a small plateau on the down slope of Little Round Top.

From the perspective of the 1st Vermont, neither historian's account diminishes in any way the courage exhibited by the Green Mountain troopers in the face of what amounted to suicidal orders. In both versions, they cover themselves with glory. Both interpretations paint a picture of a resolute, determined band of warriors that did not balk nor hesitate for a moment when sent forth to attempt the all but impossible. For the time being, the National Park Service appears content to let the controversy exist. While no one would ever argue that the Battle of Gettysburg has not received more than its fair share of tourist interest, the scholarly duel over "Farnsworth's Charge" has admittedly heightened both interest and awareness in what had long been a backwater area and forgotten aspect of the three-day struggle. Officially, as of the summer of 2008, the battlefield demarcations for the charge are located where they have always been, on the north side of Confederate Avenue and making no reference to the possible import of the ravine behind them. In effect, they support the Wittenberg et al. interpretation. Meanwhile, Addie Custer continues conducting convincing tours as a Licensed Battlefield Guide, informing visitors of her revised version of the famous charge. When I wrote then Gettysburg Park superintendent John Latshar in the late summer of 2005, asking if the Park Service had any intention of changing its official interpretation, I was informed in his reply that "it is quite common for historians—even when studying and analyzing identical historical materials—to draw conclusions concerning what happened or why it happened."

While it would prove nothing with regard to validating the traditional theory—except to eliminate a contrary view—Mrs. Custer's new interpretation could easily be tested. Metal detectors could be used to give a cursory scan, followed by selected strategic digs at "hot spots." Attention should be focused on the area in front of as well as behind the two stone walls. The hillside on the upper left behind the walls might also be spot-checked as well as the ground approaching them. If the fighting as pictured by Mrs. Custer did in fact occur here, then the ground in front should yield pistol balls on the sides facing south, along with remnants of various accoutrements and weapons. Projectiles, having missed their mark and gone over and beyond the walls, should be imbedded in the ground of the hillside. Furthermore, on the north sides of the stone walls, where Confederate infantry stood, pristine minie balls might have been dropped in the soldiers' haste to load and fire under duress. Other telltale metal relics are also likely to be present in the immediate area: buttons, rusted firearms, buckles, and other such detritus often found where soldiers have lingered and fought. Downrange from the first wall, minie balls ought to be found, evidence of rebel riflemen having fired at the onrushing Vermonters. Finding any concentrations of artifacts in these locations would offer proof of troop presence if not an engagement. Any absence beyond a few random pieces would virtually preclude any significant fighting as having occurred in the immediate vicinity.

For the time being, no one seems inclined to put Mrs. Custer's theory under the scrutiny of an archeological dig. When asked about the possibility of metal detection, Mrs. Custer's response was that the "National Park Service does not permit metal detectors." With respect to the competing hypotheses, Superintendent Latshar informed me that "the Park Service does not take an 'official stance.'" Truthfully, a bit of new controversy hurts no one and actually benefits the participants in "Farnsworth's Charge," shining as it does the limelight on a part of the momentous battle that has altogether too frequently been ignored. Furthermore, there are those who ardently believe that General Farnsworth merits a statue for his bravery and sacrifice. Beyond setting the record straight, that too would be a worthy outcome of the recent flurry of interest in the charge.

What really happened? My thoughts on the event favor the traditional interpretation for several reasons. First, the revisionist wall is three to four feet tall. To clear it, horses that had been traveling for over two weeks would have approached the barrier moving upgrade. Such a leap may not have been uniformly possible, yet no observer mentions horses balking, let alone crashing into the wall. In fact, their passage is pictured as virtually effortless. Second, various participants wrote accounts that offer incidental support. For example, Trooper Joe Allen references the Texans shooting at the charging Vermonters while "lying" behind a wall — plausible with a barricade one to one-and-a-half feet high, but a barrier three or four feet tall? Third, Captain Parsons never claimed to have participated in or witnessed all of the charge. But he did speak with others who had made the circuit, and it is from them that he wrote his composite account. Why on such a key point as the location of Farnsworth's death would he or his sources so egregiously err? After the war, Parsons — recognizing the significance of the location — even went so far as to purchase the upland field where Farnsworth was believed to have perished. Finally, veterans of the 1st Vermont visited the battlefield on numerous occasions in the postwar years. None of them ever objected to the placement of the 1st Vermont's regimental monument on the side of Little Round Top, in the so called D-shaped field, as purportedly being near the death site, or the later Wells' monument at the northern foot of Bushman's Hill as standing at the jumping off point for the charge. Had there been no significant regimental connection to either spot, these misplacements would have been so obvious as to raise an immediate outcry for relocations. In lieu of concrete evidence to the contrary, the traditional account still stands the test of time.

Appendix F.
Garryowen

If ever there was a toe-tapper, "Garryowen" would have to rank right up there among the best. Though its specific origin is lost in the mists of time, it is known to have been an Irish drinking song that gained popularity in the late 1700s. The unusual name is taken not from someone but some place, *Garrai Eoin*, which is Gaelic for "Owens' Garden." During the day, the location near Limerick was a tea garden, situated in the shadow of a cottage owned by a man named Owens. In this idyllic setting, local residents came for walks and picnics. By night, however, the site was transformed into a spot where local rowdies came to drink and brawl, hence its association with tippling. Stationed on the Emerald Isle, British troops took a liking to the jaunty air, and, as they moved on, so did the tune. Many the Britishers' steps in the Napoleonic Wars and the Crimean War were quickened at the sound of "Garryowen." With so many Irishmen making their way to America's shores before and during the Civil War, it is not surprising that the song accompanied them to their new country. The first known official recognition of this folk piece in the American military came with the formation of 2nd Regiment of Irish Volunteers in New York City and the adoption of "Garryowen" as its regimental marching song. Eventually this unit became a part of New York State's militia, known officially henceforth as the 69th Regiment. Since then, the "Fighting 69th has gone on to carve a memorable place for itself in American military history, most recently in "Operation Iraqi Freedom II."

Because legends die hard, the most common and romantic connection between George Custer and "Garryowen" is with the 7th Cavalry. Adopting it as his regiment's marching song shortly after the Civil War, the story goes that it was last played as the 7th headed to glory and eternity at Little Big Horn. However, by then the 1st Vermont was coming together only at reunions. Still, this catchy tune may have lingered in their heads, mixed with the memories of battles fought and comrades lost. During their frequent association with General Custer and his Michigan regiments during the Civil War, the Vermonters had numerous occasions to be hurried along on the march or sent into battle by the band which the "Boy General" kept for morale purposes. That they would have heard and responded accordingly to the strains of "Garryowen" is highly possible. The melody is frequently found in musical anthologies of the Civil War, such as *Civil War* by Amerimusic. For those who may not be aware of the tune to this quick-step, go to *www.historicalrarities.com* for a lively rendition. Sing along with lyrics below taken from *www.beafifer.com*, and you see how easily this simple but catchy number could appeal to marching troopers:

Verse 1   Let Bacchus' sons be not dismayed,
               but join with me each jovial blade,
               come booze and sing and lend your aid,
               to help me with the chorus:

Chorus   Instead of spa we'll drink down ale
               and pay the reckoning on the nail
               for debt no man shall go to jail
               from Garryowen and glory.

Chapter Notes

Chapter 1

1. Thomas Hawley Canfield Papers, Vermont Historical Society, Barre, Vermont.
2. *Burlington Daily Free Press*, December 17, 1861, p. 2.
3. *Manchester Journal*, September 24, 1861, p. 2.
4. G.G. Benedict, *Vermont in the Civil War* (Burlington: Free Press Association, 1888), p. 535.
5. John Smith, Pension File, National Archives, Washington, D.C.
6. Ibid.
7. Ibid.
8. Ibid.
9. Thomas Hawley Canfield, Zadock Canfield Papers, Vermont Historical Society, Barre, Vermont.
10. United States War Department, *The War of the Rebellion: A Compilation of the Official Records of the Union and Confederate Archives* (hereafter *OR*), Volume I, Series 3 (Washington, D.C.: Government Printing Office, 1880–1891), p. 620.
11. Thomas Hawley Canfield, Zadock Canfield Papers, Vermont Historical Society, Barre, Vermont.
12. *Montpelier Journal*, December 17, 1861, p. 2.
13. Benedict, *Vermont*, p. 539.

Chapter 2

1. David Blow, *Historic Guide to Burlington Neighborhoods* (Burlington: Queen City), p. 10.
2. *Burlington Daily Free Press*, October 10, 1862, p. 2.
3. Zadock Canfield Papers, Letter of October 25, 1861, Vermont Historical Society, Barre, Vermont.
4. Zadock Canfield Papers, Letter of October 4, 1861.
5. Charles Blinn, Diary Entry of October 13, 1862.
6. Horace Ide, *History of the First Vermont Cavalry Volunteers*, ed. Elliott Hoffman (Baltimore: Butternut and Blue 2000), p. 15.
7. *Burlington Weekly Times*, October 21, 1861, p. 3.
8. *Burlington Daily Free Press*, November 12, 1861, p. 2.
9. *Vermont Phoenix* (Brattleboro), December 19, 1861, p. 2.
10. *Burlington Daily Free Press*, November 12, 1861, p. 2.
11. Ibid.
12. Ibid

13. Ibid.
14. *Burlington Daily Free Press*, November 18, 1861, p. 2.
15. Stephan Starr, *The Union Cavalry in the Civil War* (Baton Rouge: Louisiana State University Press, 1979), p. 145.
16. *Rutland Daily Herald*, November 6, 1861, p. 2.
17. Ibid.
18. *Rutland Daily Herald*, November 9, 1861, p. 2.
19. *Rutland Daily Herald*, November 12, 1861, p. 2.
20. *Burlington Daily Free Press*, December 6, 1861, p. 2.
21. *Vermont Phoenix*, November 14, 1861, p. 2.

Chapter 3

1. *Burlington Weekly Standard*, December 20, 1861, p. 2.
2. Ide, *History*, p. 1.
3. *Burlington Daily Free Press*, November 11, 1878, p. 2.
4. Eli Hawley Canfield, Letter of December 16, 1861, Vermont Historical Society, Barre, Vermont.
5. Ibid.
6. Ibid.
7. James Hogan, Pension File, National Archives, Washington, D.C.
8. *Burlington Daily Press and Times*, November 6, 1878, p. 2.
9. *New York Times*, December 17, 1861, p. 8.
10. Ibid.
11. Blinn, Diary, December 16, 1861.
12. Ibid.
13. Josiah Grout, *Memoir of Gen'l William Wallace Grout and Autobiography of Josiah Grout* (Newport: Bullock, 1919), p. 222.
14. Benedict, *Vermont*, p. 544.
15. Eli Hawley Canfield Papers, Letter of December 29, 1861.
16. *Orleans Independent Standard*, January 10, 1862, p. 2.
17. *Burlington Daily Free Press*, December 30, 1861, p. 2.
18. Ibid.
19. *Burlington Daily Free Press and Times*, November 6, 1878, p. 2.
20. Henry Holt, Pension File, National Archives, Washington, D.C.
21. Eli Hawley Canfield Papers, Vermont Historical Society, Barre, Vermont.

22. *Burlington Free Press and Times*, November 6, 1878, p. 2.

23. *Rutland Daily Herald*, February 14, 1862, p. 2.

24. *Burlington Free Press and Times*, November 6, 1878, p. 2.

25. Ibid.

26. Eli Hawley Canfield Papers, Vermont Historical Society, Barre, Vermont.

Chapter 4

1. William Wells, Letter of February 19, 1862.

2. *St. Johnsbury Caledonian*, January 24, 1862, p. 2.

3. *Orleans Independent Record*, February 21, 1862, p. 2.

4. Hannibal Jenne, Pension File, National Archives, Washington, D.C.

5. Oliver Cushman, Pension File, National Archives, Washington, D.C.

6. *Burlington Daily Free Press*, January 24, 1862, p. 2.

7. *Green Mountain Freeman* (Montpelier, Vermont), February 4, 1862, p. 2.

8. James Esdon, Pension File, National Archives, Washington, D.C.

9. *Orleans Independent Standard*, February 21, 1862, p. 2.

10. Ide, *History*, p. 22.

11. Francis Lord, *Arms and Equipment of the Civil War*, Secaucus, NJ: Castle, 1982), p. 207.

12. *Orleans Independent Standard*, p. 2.

13. Mark Wilson, *Patriots in Blue* (West Lafayette, IN: Privately Published, 1987), p. 26.

14. Delinus Melvin, Pension File, National Archives, Washington, D.C.

15. Flavil Woodward, Military Record, National Archives, Washington, D.C.

16. Ide, *History*, p. 21.

17. William Wells, Letter of February 28, 1862.

18. Ibid.

19. Ide, *History*, p. 21.

20. Benedict, *Vermont*, p. 542.

21. Oliver Cushman, Pension File, National Archives, Washington, D.C.

22. Blinn, Diary, March 7, 1862.

Chapter 5

1. *Orleans Independent Standard*, March 14, 1862, p. 2.

2. *Rutland Daily Herald*, March 14, 1862, p. 2.

3. Henry Holt, Letter of March 1, 1862, Manuscript Collection, UVM, Burlington, VT.

4. Blinn, Diary, February 28, 1862.

5. *Montpelier Green Mountain Freeman*, March 11, 1862, p. 2.

6. *Rutland Daily Herald*, March 14, 1862, p. 2.

7. Ibid.

8. Jeffrey Hart, Pension File, National Archives, Washington, D.C.

9. *Burlington Daily Free Press*, March 28, 1862, p. 2.

10. Blinn, Diary, March 28, 1862.

11. *Burlington Daily Free Press*, November 6, 1878, p. 2.

12. William Livingston, Pension File, National Archives, Washington, D.C.

13. Blinn, Diary, March 30, 1862.

14. *Burlington Daily Free Press*, April 5, 1862, p. 2.

15. David Martin, *Jackson's Valley Campaign* (New York: Weiser & Weiser, 1988), p. 125.

16. Blinn, Diary, April 6, 1862.

17. Henry Smith, Letter of April 20, 1862.

18. *Burlington Weekly Times*, April 26, 1862, p. 6.

19. Ibid., p. 2.

20. Henry Smith, Letter of April 30, 1862.

21. Blinn, Diary, April 6, 1862.

22. *Rutland Daily Herald*, April 15, 1862, p. 2.

23. Thomas Lowry, *Tarnished Eagles* (Mechanicsburg: Stackpole, 1997), p. 195.

24. Ibid.

25. *Burlington Weekly Times*, April 19, 1862, p. 6.

26. *Rutland Daily Herald*, April 17, 1862, p. 2.

27. Benedict, *Vermont*, p. 545.

28. Blinn, Diary, April 17, 1862.

29. *Rutland Daily Herald*, April 15, 1862, p. 2.

30. Benedict, *Vermont*, p. 545.

31. Ibid.

32. *Orleans Independent Standard*, May 5, 1862, p. 2.

33. *OR*, Volume XIV, Union Correspondence #3.

34. Ide, *History*, p. 27.

35. Grout, *Memoir and Autobiography*, p. 224.

36. Ide, *History*, p. 27.

37. *Rutland Daily Herald*, May 6, 1862, p. 2.

38. *Burlington Free Press*, November 6, 1878, p. 2.

Chapter 6

1. Benedict, *Vermont*, p. 547.

2. Ide, *History*, 27–28.

3. J.B. Avirett, *Memoirs of Turner Ashby and His Compeers* (Baltimore: Selby and Dulany, 1867), p. 170.

4. Ptolemy Edson, Address at the Second Annual Meeting of the First Vermont Cavalry Reunion Society, Montpelier, November 4, 1874.

5. Blinn, Diary, April 17, 1862.

6. Ibid.

7. Henry Smith, Letter of April 20, 1862, Vermont Historical Society, Barre, Vermont.

8. Ibid.

9. Lyman Wright, Pension File, National Archives, Washington, D.C.

10. Benedict, *Vermont*, p. 548.

11. *Burlington Daily Free Press*, April 29, 1862, p. 2.

12. Ralph Merrill, Pension File, National Archives, Washington, D.C.

13. Ibid.

14. Ibid.

15. Ibid.

16. James Battle Avirett, *The Memoirs of General Turner Ashby and His Compeers* (Baltimore: Selby and Dunley, 1867), p. 174.

17. Ide, *History*, p. 43.

18. *Vermont Journal* (Montpelier), May 9, 1863, p. 2.

19. *Rutland Daily Herald*, April 29, 1862, p. 2.

20. Lyman Wright, Pension File, National Archives, Washington, D.C.

21. George Fay, Pension File, National Archives, Washington, D.C.

22. Ibid.

23. Ibid.

24. *Rutland Daily Herald*, April 29, 1862, p. 2.

25. Benedict, *Vermont*, p. 549.
26. Lyman Wright, Pension File, National Archives, Washington, D.C.
27. Ibid.
28. *Order and Letter Book*, First Vermont Cavalry, National Archives, Washington, D.C.
29. Lyman Wright, Pension File, National Archives, Washington, D.C.
30. Blinn, Diary, April 17, 1862.
31. Elijah Paige, Pension File, National Archives, Washington, D.C.
32. *Burlington Weekly Times*, March 10, 1862, p. 2.
33. Benedict, *Vermont*, p. 549.
34. *St. Johnsbury Caledonian*, May 16, 1862, p. 1.
35. *Rutland Daily Herald*, May 6, 1862, p. 2.
36. *OR*, Volume XV, Series 1, p. 427.

Chapter 7

1. Robert Moore, *Avenue of Armies* (Virginia Beach: Downing, 2002), p. 46.
2. Ibid., p. 47.
3. Edward Gee, Pension File, National Archives, Washington, D.C.
4. *Rutland Daily Herald*, April 30, 1862, p. 2.
5. Ibid.
6. *Rutland Daily Herald*, May 6, 1862, p. 2.
7. Ibid.
8. Ibid.
9. Ibid.
10. Ide, *History*, p. 33.
11. *OR*, Volume XV, Series 1, p. 448.
12. George Baylor, *Bull Run to Bull Run, or Four Years in the Army of Northern Virginia* (Richmond: B.F. Publishing, 1900), p. 26.
13. Ibid.
14. Stewart Brooks, *Civil War Medicine* (Springfield: Charles Thomas, 1966), p. 75.
15. *St. Johnsbury Caledonian*, May 16, 1862, p. 2.
16. *Montpelier Green Mountain Freeman*, November 24, 1862, p. 2.
17. Ide, *History*, p. 53.
18. *Vermont Phoenix*, May 8, 1862.
19. Ibid.
20. Ibid.
21. Ibid.
22. *St. Johnsbury Caledonian*, May 16, 1862, p. 3.
23. John Chase, Tombstone Inscription, Greenwood Cemetery, Danville, Vermont.
24. Edgar Pitkin, Pension File, National Archives, Washington, D.C.

Chapter 8

1. *OR*, Volume XV, p. 458.
2. Ibid.
3. Benedict, *Vermont*, p. 554.
4. *Burlington Daily Free Press*, May 26, 1862, p. 2.
5. Benedict, *Vermont*, p. 554.
6. *Vermont Journal*, May 9, 1863, p. 2.
7. *Burlington Weekly Times*, May 31, 1862, p. 6.
8. Benedict, *Vermont*, p. 553.
9. Ibid.
10. *Burlington Weekly Times*, May 31, 1862, p. 6.
11. Ibid.
12. Ibid.

13. *OR*, Volume XII, Part 1, p. 524.
14. *OR*, Volume XV, p. 52.
15. Richard Kleese, *Shenandoah County and the Civil War: The Turbulent Years* (Lynchburg: H.E. Howard, 1992), p. 37.
16. Ibid., p. 37.
17. *OR*, Volume XV, p. 524.

Chapter 9

1. *OR*, Chapter XV, p. 526.
2. Ibid., p. 586.
3. Ibid.
4. Ira Batchelder, Pension File, National Archives, Washington, D.C.
5. *Montpelier Green Mountain Freeman*, June 6, 1862, p. 2.
6. John Worsham, *One of Jackson's Foot Cavalry* (Alexandria: Time-Life Books, 1982), p. 19.
7. *OR*, Volume XII, Part 1, p. 703.
8. *OR*, Volume XV, Series 1, p. 587.
9. Charles Gardner, *Three Years in the Cavalry* (Tucson: Ada Friddell & A Plus, 1998), p. 11.
10. Frank Ray, Pension File, National Archives, Washington, D.C.
11. *Montpelier Green Mountain Freeman*, June 24, 1862, p. 2.
12. *OR*, Volume XII, Part 1, p. 703.
13. *Burlington Daily Free Press*, June 6, 1862, p. 2.
14. *OR*, Volume XII, Part 1, p. 592.
15. *Montpelier Green Mountain Freeman*, June 10, 1862, p. 1.
16. *Montpelier Green Mountain Freeman*, June 30, 1862, p. 2.
17. *OR*, Volume XII, Part 1, p. 592.
18. Henry Kyd Douglas, *I Rode with Stonewall* (Greenwich: Fawcett, 1961), p. 61.
19. Charles Adams, Pension File, National Archives, Washington, D.C.
20. *OR*, Volume XII, Part 1, p. 592.
21. *Burlington Daily Free Press*, May 29, 1862, p. 2.
22. *OR*, Volume XV, p. 576.
23. *Burlington Daily Free Press*, May 29, 1862, p. 2.
24. *Weekly Times*, June 7, 1862, p. 2.
25. Herman Frost, Pension File, National Archives, Washington, D.C.
26. Ibid.
27. Charles Adams, Pension File, National Archives, Washington, D.C.
28. *OR*, Volume XV, Series 1, p. 576.
29. Ibid.
30. *OR*, Volume XII, Part 1, p. 592.
31. Douglas, *I Rode*, p. 62.
32. Henry O'Hayer, Pension File, National Archives, Washington, D.C.
33. Daniel Pattison, Pension File, National Archives, Washington, D.C.
34. *Burlington Daily Free Press*, June 30, 1862, p. 2.
35. Ibid.
36. Daniel Russell, Pension File, National Archives, Washington, D.C.
37. Ibid.
38. Ibid.
39. Charles Blinn, Pension File, National Archives, Washington, D.C.
40. Ibid.
41. Ibid.

42. William J. Flowers, Pension File, National Archives, Washington, D.C.
43. David Tubbs, Pension File, National Archives, Washington, D.C.
44. *Burlington Daily Free Press*, June 6, 1862, p. 2.
45. *Montpelier Daily Green Mountain Freeman*, May 31, 1862,p. 2.
46. William Wells, Letter of May 26, 1862.

Chapter 10

1. Addison Preston, Letter of June 2, 1862, Fairbanks Museum Collection, St. Johnsbury, Vermont.
2. *Burlington Daily Free Press*, June 13, 1862, p. 2.
3. *Montpelier Green Mountain Freeman*, July 7, 1862, p. 7.
4. John Huse, Pension File, National Archives, Washington, D.C.
5. Ibid.
6. Benedict, *Vermont*, p. 563.
7. *Montpelier Green Mountain Freeman*, June 1, 1862, p. 7.
8. *St. Johnsbury Caledonian*, August 8, 1862, p. 7.
9. *Burlington Daily Free Press*, June 13, 1862, p. 2.
10. *Burlington Daily Free Press*, May 29, 1862, p. 2.
11. Ibid.
12. Mark Rogers, Pension File, National Archives, Washington, D.C.
13. *Rutland Daily Herald*, June 16, 1862, p. 2.
14. *Rutland Daily Herald*, June 18, 1862, p. 2.
15. *Rutland Daily Herald*, June 16, 1862, p. 2.
16. *Rutland Daily Herald*, June 18, 1862, p. 2.
17. Ibid.
18. John Holden, Pension File, National Archives, Washington, D.C.
19. *Rutland Daily Herald*, June 18, 1862, p. 2.
20. *OR*, Volume XV, p. 587.
21. Ide, *History*, 36–37.
22. Joel Earhardt, Pension File, National Archives, Washington, D.C.
23. Ibid.
24. Michael Mahan, ed., *Winchester Divided: The Civil War Diaries of Julia Chase and Laura Lee* (Mechanicsburg: Stackpole, 2002), p. 39.
25. "Battle of Winchester," *Southern Historical Society Papers* 10 (Jan.-Dec. 1882): p. 100.
26. Douglas Southall Freeman, *Lee's Lieutenants* (New York: Scribner's, 1942), p. 40.
27. Ide, *History*, p. 41.
28. *St. Johnsbury Caledonian*, June 1, 1863, p. 2.
29. Grout, *Memoir and Autobiography*, p. 226.
30. *St. Johnsbury Caledonian*, June 1, 1862, p. 2.
31. *OR*, Volume XII, p. 617.
32. Mahan, p. 39.
33. James Esdon, Pension File, National Archives, Washington, D.C.
34. Ashbell Meacham, Pension File, National Archives, Washington, D.C.
35. *Burlington Daily Free Press*, June 4, 1862, p. 2.
36. *OR*, Volume XV, p. 551.
37. *Burlington Daily Free Press*, July 19, 1862, p. 2.
38. *Orleans Independent Standard*, June 6, 1862, p. 2.
39. *Burlington Daily Free Press*, June 13, 1862, p. 2.
40. William Wells, Letter of May 29, 1862.
41. Digger Odell, "The Attraction of Magnetic Medicines," www.bottlebook.com.
42. Ibid.

43. *Rutland Daily Herald*, May 29, 1862.
44. William Wells, Letter of May 29, 1862.
45. John Huse, Pension File, National Archives, Washington, D.C.
46. Ibid.
47. Zabina Landon, Pension File, National Archives, Washington, D.C.
48. David Tubbs, Pension File, National Archives, Washington, D.C.
49. John Hogan, Pension File, National Archives, Washington, D.C.
50. Albert Hutchins, Pension File, National Archives, Washington, D.C.
51. *Montpelier Green Mountain Freeman*, June 10, 1862, p. 1.
52. *OR*, Volume II, Series 1, p. 586.
53. *Montpelier Green Mountain Freeman*, June 10, 1862, p. 2.
54. *Rutland Daily Herald*, June 4, 1862, p. 2.

Chapter 11

1. *Rutland Daily Herald*, July 16, 1862, p. 2.
2. William Wells, Letter of June 25, 1862.
3. *Montpelier Green Mountain Freeman*, June 3, 1862, p. 2.
4. Moore, p. 47.
5. Charles Tompkins, "Report of the Luray Valley Reconnaissance," *Order and Letter Book* (First Vermont Cavalry, National Archives, Washington, D.C.).
6. *New York Times*, July 12, 1862, p. 4.
7. Ibid.
8. *St. Johnsbury Caledonian*, July 25, 1862, p. 2.
9. Josiah Grout, *Autobiography of Josiah Grout* (Newport, RI: Bullock, 1919), p. 228.
10. Ibid.
11. *The Burlington Weekly Times*, July 26, 1862, p. 3.
12. Ibid.
13. *St. Johnsbury Caledonian*, July 25, 1862, p. 2.
14. *Order and Letter Book*, First Vermont Cavalry.
15. *St. Johnsbury Caledonian*, July 25, 1862, p. 2.
16. *OR*, Volume XV, Series 1, p. 460.
17. Marvin Mason, Pension File, National Archives, Washington, D.C.
18. Eben Grant, Pension File, National Archives, Washington, D.C.
19. Ibid.
20. *OR*, Volume XV, Series 1, p. 472.
21. *OR*, Volume XV, Series 1, pp. 472–473.
22. *OR*, Volume XV, Series 1, p. 474.
23. Ibid.
24. Ide, *History*, p. 49.
25. *OR*, Volume XV, Series 1, p. 484.
26. *OR*, Volume XV, Series 1, pp. 485–486.
27. Conceader Durlam, Pension File, National Archives, Washington, D.C.
28. *OR*, Volume XV, Series 1, p. 490.
29. Ibid.
30. Grout, *Memoir and Autobiography*, p. 229.
31. *OR*, Volume XV, Series 1, p. 512.
32. Lenoir Chambers, *Stonewall Jackson* (New York: William Morrow, 1959), p. 100.

Chapter 12

1. *Montpelier Green Mountain Freeman*, August 19, 1862, p. 1.

2. *Burlington Daily Free Press*, August 23, 1862, p. 2.

3. George Lowell, Pension File, National Archives, Washington, D.C.

4. Ibid.

5. Smilie Bancroft Papers, Vermont Historical Society, Barre, Vermont.

6. John W. Smith, Military Record, National Archives, Washington, D.C.

7. *Burlington Daily Free Press*, August 23, 1862, p. 2.

8. Ibid.

9. William McDonald, *A History of the Laurel Brigade* (Baltimore: Johns Hopkins University Press, 2002), p. 78.

10. *Montpelier Green Mountain Freeman*, August 19, 1862, p. 2.

11. *Rutland Daily Herald*, August 6, 1862, p. 3.

12. *OR*, Volume XII, Part 2, p. 113.

13. William Wells, Letter of August 3, 1862.

14. *Montpelier Green Mountain Freeman*, August 13, 1862, p. 2.

15. William Wells, Letter of August 2, 1862.

16. Collis Ikey, Pension File, National Archives, Washington, D.C.

17. Ibid.

18. William Wells, Letter of August 3, 1862.

19. Alonzo Hoyt, Military Records, National Archives, Washington, D.C.

20. Ibid.

21. Ellis Draper, Pension File, National Archives, Washington, D.C.

22. Ibid.

23. Ibid.

24. *OR*, Volume XVI, p. 127.

25. *Montpelier Green Mountain Freeman*, August 13, 1862, p. 2.

Chapter 13

1. (Captain) Willard Glazier, *Three Years in the Federal Cavalry* (New York: RH Ferguson, 1874), p. 133.

2. Ide, *History*, p. 61.

3. Albert Sawyer, Letter of November 9, 1862, Manuscript Collection, University of Vermont, Burlington, Vermont.

4. Ibid.

5. Albert Green, Letter of November 26, 1862, Manuscript Collection, University of Vermont, Burlington, Vermont.

6. George Caulkins, Pension File, National Archives, Washington, D.C.

7. *Burlington Daily Free Press*, October 24, 1862, p. 3.

8. *Irasburg Independent Standard*, November 18, 1862, p. 3.

9. *St. Johnsbury Caledonian*, November 7, 1862, p. 2.

10. Benedict, *Vermont*, p. 580.

11. Ide, *History*, p. 60.

12. Glazier, p. 131.

13. Lorentio King, Letter of March 20, 1863.

14. *St. Johnsbury Calendonian*, November 14, 1862, p. 2.

15. Daniel McDixon, Pension File, National Archives, Washington, D.C.

16. Ibid.

17. Avery Sibley, Pension File, National Archives, Washington, D.C.

18. Ibid.

19. Charles Turner, Pension File, National Archives, Washington, D.C.

20. Andrew Hart, Pension File, National Archives, Washington, D.C.

21. Charles Stone, Diary Entry of September 4, 1862.

22. Ibid.

23. John Frost, Pension File, National Archives, Washington, D.C.

24. Charles Stone, Diary, October 5, 1862, Vermont Historical Society, Barre, Vermont.

25. *Vermont Journal*, May 9, 1863, p. 2.

26. Ibid.

27. Ibid.

28. *Burlington Daily Free Press*, October 1, 1862, p. 2.

29. *Burlington Daily Free Press*, September 20, 1862, p. 2.

30. *Burlington Daily Free Press*, September 26, 1862, p. 2.

31. Ibid.

32. *Manchester Journal*, October 15, 1862, p. 1.

Chapter 14

1. Theodore Rodenbough, *The Photographic History of the Civil War* (Secaucus, NJ: Blue and Gray Press, 1997), p. 190.

2. Benedict, *Vermont*, p. 575.

3. *St. Johnsbury Caledonian*, December 5, 1862, p. 2.

4. *Montpelier Green Mountain Freeman*, December 20, 1862, p. 2.

5. Henry Holt, Pension File, National Archives, Washington, D.C.

6. Henry Smith, Letter of September 24, 1862.

7. *Rutland Daily Herald*, October 4, 1862, p. 2.

8. Henry Smith, Letter of September 24, 1862.

9. *St. Johnsbury Caledonian*, October 10, 1862, p. 1.

10. Benedict, *Vermont*, p. 576.

11. *Rutland Daily Herald*, October 12, 1862, p. 2.

12. Benedict, *Vermont*, 576–577.

13. *Vermont Journal*, January 20, 1863, p. 2.

14. *Rutland Daily Herald*, October 1, 1862, p. 2.

15. *Rutland Daily Herald*, October 2, 1862, p. 2.

16. *Burlington Daily Free Press*, September 30, 1862, p. 2.

17. Barney Scully, Pension File, National Archives, Washington, D.C.

18. Frank Dragon, Pension File, National Archives, Washington, D.C.

19. Ibid.

20. Ibid.

21. Charles Adams, Pension File, National Archives, Washington, D.C.

22. Ibid.

23. Ibid.

24. Henry Smith, Letter of September 24, 1862.

25. *St. Johnsbury Caledonian*, October 10, 1862, p. 1.

26. Benedict, *Vermont*, p. 577.

27. *St. Johnsbury Caledonian*, October 10, 1862, p. 2.

28. Benedict, *Vermont*, p. 577.

29. *Rutland Daily Herald*, October 1, 1862, p. 2.

30. *Rutland Daily Herald*, October 4, 1862, p. 2.
31. Ibid.
32. *Rutland Daily Herald*, October 1, 1862, p. 2.
33. Henry Smith, Letter of September 24, 1862.
34. Michael Mustek, *6th Virginia Cavalry* (Lynchburg: H.E. Howard, 1990), p. 23.
35. Henry Smith, Letter of September 24, 1862.
36. *Rutland Daily Herald*, October 4, 1862.
37. Ibid.
38. *Rutland Daily Herald,* September 30, 1862, p. 2.
39. *Rutland Daily Herald,* October 6, 1862, p. 2.
40. *Vermont Journal*, May 9, 1863, p. 2.
41. Ibid.

Chapter 15

1. *Vermont Record* (Brattleboro), January 26, 1864, p. 1.
2. Frederic Denison, *Sabres and Spurs: First Regiment Rhode Island Cavalry* (First Rhode Island Cavalry Veterans Association, 1876), p. 109.
3. Rodenbough, 186–188.
4. *The Burlington Sentinel*, March 3, 1862, p. 2.
5. Ibid.
6. Charles Stone, Diary Entry of February 5, 1862.
7. *St. Johnsbury Caledonian*, March 13, 1863, p. 2.
8. George Duncan, Pension File, National Archives, Washington, D.C.
9. Charles Stone, Diary, February 15, 1862.
10. Hannibal Jenne, Pension File, National Archives, Washington, D.C.
11. *Burlington Daily Free Press*, March 3, 1863, p. 2.
12. George Duncan, Pension File, National Archives, Washington, D.C.
13. Charles Stone, Diary, December 27, 1862.
14. Frank Ray, Pension File, National Archives, Washington, D.C.
15. Ibid.
16. John Frost, Pension File, National Archives, Washington, D.C.
17. Frank Ray, Pension File, National Archives, Washington, D.C.
18. *Burlington Daily Free Press*, March 3, 1863, p. 3.
19. Ibid.
20. Rufus Bean, Pension File, National Archives, Washington, D.C.
21. Ibid.
22. Frank Ray, Pension File, National Archives, Washington, D.C.
23. Rufus Bean, Pension File, National Archives, Washington, D.C.
24. Ibid.
25. John Frost, Pension File, National Archives, Washington, D.C.
26. *Burlington Daily Free Press*, March 3, 1863, p. 2.
27. John Frost, Pension File, National Archives, Washington, D.C.
28. *Rutland Daily Herald*, March 26, 1863, p. 3.
29. John Frost, Pension File, National Archives Washington, D.C.
30. *Rutland Daily Herald*, March 26, 1863, p. 3.
31. Ibid.
32. Charles Pixley, Pension File, National Archives, Washington, D.C.
33. Ibid.

Chapter 16

1. *Burlington Daily Free Press*, March 3, 1863, p. 2.
2. John Scott, *Partisan Life with John Mosby*. (Gaithersburg, MD: Butternut Press, 1985), p. 39.
3. John Mosby, *Gray Ghost: The Memoirs of Colonel John S. Mosby*, ed. Paul Hutton (New York: Bantam, 1992), 121–122.
4. Ibid., p. 122.
5. Scott, *Partisan*, p. 39.
6. *OR*, Chapter XXV, part 1, p. 40.
7. William Wells, Letter of March 17, 1862.
8. *Vermont Journal*, March 14, 1863, p. 2.
9. John Mosby, *Mosby's War Reminiscences* (Camden, NJ: John Culler & Sons, 1996), p. 50.
10. Scott, *Partisan*, p. 40.
11. Ibid.
12. *Vermont Journal*, March 14, 1863, p. 2.
13. John Mosby, *Gray Ghost: The Memoirs of Colonel John S. Mosby*, ed. Paul Hutton (New York: Bantam, 1992), p. 123.
14. *Vermont Journal*, March 14, 1863, p. 2.
15. *Burlington Daily Free Press*, March 9, 1863, p. 2.
16. *Vermont Journal*, March 14, 1863, p. 2.
17. John Kinehan, Pension File, National Archives, Washington, D.C.
18. Ibid.
19. Ibid.
20. *Rutland Daily Herald*, May 7, 1863 p. 3.
21. *Order and Letter Book*, First Vermont Cavalry, National Archives, Washington, D.C.
22. Charles Blinn, Diary, March 2, 1862.
23. *Rutland Daily Herald,* May 7, 1863, p. 3.
24. *Rutland Daily Herald,* February 25, 1863, p. 2.
25. Ibid.
26. Franklin Huntoon, Pension File, National Archives, Washington, D.C.

Chapter 17

1. Elliot Hoffman, "A Shot in the Dark," *Vermont History* 147 (Fall 1979): p. 277.
2. *Burlington Daily Free Press*, March 24, 1863, p. 2.
3. Ibid.
4. Scott, *Partisan*, p. 55.
5. Mosby, p. 69.
6. Ibid., p. 70.
7. *Green Mountain Freeman*, March 24, 1862, p. 2.
8. Scott, *Partisan*, p. 55.
9. Mosby, p. 70.
10. Ibid., p. 71.
11. *Green Mountain Freeman*, p. 2.
12. *Burlington Daily Free Press,* March 24, 1863, p. 2.
13. *Weekly Burlington Times*, March 28, 1863, p. 4.
14. *Green Mountain Freeman*, March 24, 1863, p. 2.
15. Scott, *Partisan*, p. 57.
16. Mosby, p. 72.
17. Ibid.
18. Scott, *Partisan*, p. 57.
19. *The Weekly Times*. March 28, 1863, p. 4.
20. *Burlington Daily Free Press*, March 24, 1863, p. 2.
21. *Burlington Daily Free Press*, March 23, 1863, p. 7.
22. *Vermont Journal*, March 23, 1863, p. 2.

23. *OR*, Volume XXV, Part I, p. 65.
24. Ibid.
25. Benedict, *Vermont*, p. 584.
26. Ide, *History*, p. 91.
27. *OR*, Volume XXV, Part 1, p. 65.
28. Ibid.
29. Benedict, *Vermont*, p. 585.
30. Hoffman, "A Shot," p. 92.
31. *Burlington Sentinel*, p. 2.
32. Ibid.
33. Benedict, *Vermont*, p. 585.
34. *Vermont Journal*, March 23, 1863, p. 2.
35. Kathryn Coombs, www.mosbysrangers.com/ herndon (accessed August 19, 2001).

Chapter 18

1. *Burlington Daily Free Press*, April 8, 1863, p. 2.
2. *OR*, Volume XXV, Part 1, p. 73.
3. *Burlington Daily Free Press*, September 19, 1886, p. 5.
4. Ibid.
5. Grout, *Memoir and Autobiography*, p. 234.
6. Ibid.
7. Ibid.
8. John Munson, *Reminiscences of a Mosby Guerilla* (New York: Maftas & Garda, 1906), p. 56.
9. Mosby, p. 105.
10. Scott, *Partisan*, p. 64.
11. Munson, *Reminiscences*, p. 56.
12. Ide, *History*, p. 95.
13. Grout, *Memoir and Autobiography*, p. 236.
14. *Burlington Free Press*, April 25, 1863, p. 2.
15. *Irasburgh Independent Standard*. April 17, 1863, p. 2.
16. Frankie Brown, Letter of April 11, 1863, Author's Collection.
17. Ephraim Brewster, Personnel File, National Archives, Washington, D.C.
18. Ibid.
19. Grout, *Memoir and Autobiography*, p. 36.
20. Ephraim Brewster, Personnel File, National Archives, Washington, D.C.
21. Ibid.
22. Eli Holden, Pension File, National Archives, Washington, D.C.
23. Grout, *Memoir and Autobiography*, p. 240.
24. Scott, *Partisan*, p. 67.
25. Benedict, *Vermont*, p. 586.
26. Albert George, Pension File, National Archives, Washington, D.C.
27. Orrin Putnam, Pension File, National Archives, Washington, D.C.
28. Scott, *Partisan*, p. 67.
29. Horace Mewborn, *From Mosby's Command* (Baltimore: Butternut and Blue, 2005), p. 92.
30. *Burlington Free Press*, April 25, 1863, p. 2.
31. Grout, *Memoir and Autobiography*, p. 239.
32. Benedict, *Vermont*, p. 587.
33. Ide, *History*, p. 93.
34. Ibid.
35. William Belding, Pension File, National Archives, Washington, D.C.
36. William Moncrief, Pension File, National Archives, Washington, D.C.
37. Ibid.

38. Harley Sawyer, Pension File, National Archives, Washington, D.C.
39. Munson, p. 59.
40. *Rutland Daily Herald*, April 8, 1863, p. 3.
41. Ibid.
42. *Irasburgh Independent Standard*, April 10, 1863, p. 2.
43. *Burlington Sentinel*, May 1, 1863, p. 2.
44. Frankie Brown, Letter of April 11, 1863.
45. Ibid.
46. Charles Woodbury, Pension File, National Archives, Washington, D.C.
47. Frankie Brown, Letter of April 1, 1863.
48. *Green Mountain Freeman*, May 5, 1863, p. 1.
49. Grout, *Memoir and Autobiography*, p. 240.
50. Horace Bradley, Pension File, National Archives, Washington, D.C.
51. John Frost, Pension File, National Archives, Washington, D.C.
52. Ibid.
53. Grout, *Memoir and Autobiography*, p. 241.
54. Ibid, p. 239.
55. *Rutland Daily Herald*, April 11, 1863, p. 2.
56. Ide, *History*, p. 95.
57. Benedict, *Vermont*, p. 588.
58. Mosby, *Reminiscences*, p. 95.

Chapter 19

1. *OR*, Volume XXV, Part 1, p. 862.
2. John Mosby, *Mosby's War Reminiscences* (Camden: John Culler & Sons, 1996), p. 143.
3. Ibid.
4. Ibid., p. 144.
5. Ibid., p. 145.
6. *OR*, Volume XXV, Part 1, p. 1117.
7. Scott, *Partisan*, p. 9.
8. Glazier, p. 158.
9. Munson, p. 73.
10. Scott, *Partisan*, p. 94.
11. *OR*, Volume XXV, Part 1, p. 1118.
12. Glazier, p. 159.
13. Scott, *Partisan*, p. 94.
14. Munson, p 73
15. Ibid.
16. *St. Johnsbury Caledonian*, June 12, 1863, p. 2.
17. *Orleans Independent Standard*, June 19, 1863, p. 2.
18. Job Corey, Pension File, National Archives, Washington, D.C.
19. *Rutland Daily Herald*, June 6, 1863, p. 2.
20. Job Corey, Pension File, National Archives, Washington, D.C.
21. Henry Smith Letters, Manuscript Collection, University of Vermont, Burlington, Vermont.
22. Addison Preston, Letter of June 4, 1863, Fairbanks Museum & Planetarium, St. Johnsbury, Vermont.
23. *OR*, Volume XXV, Part 1, p. 1118.
24. Job Corey, Pension File, National Archives, Washington, D.C.
25. *St. Johnsbury Caledonian*, June 12, 1863, p. 2.
26. Ide, *History*, p. 102.

Chapter 20

1. George Caulkins, Pension File, National Archives, Washington, D.C.

2. William Wells, Letter of August 23, 1863.

3. A.L. Long, *Memoirs of Robert E Lee* (Secaucus, NJ: Blue and Gray Press, 1983), p. 279.

4. Albert Greene, Letter of June 28, 1863, Vermont Historical Society, Barre, Vermont.

5. Glazier, p. 238.

6. Ide, *History*, p. 107.

7. Glazier, p. 243.

8. Azro Hackett, Pension File, National Archives, Washington, D.C.

9. Ibid.

10. Ibid.

11. Ibid.

12. George Prowell, *Encounter at Hanover* (Shippensburg, PA: White Mane, 1962), p. 107.

13. Albert Greene, Letter of July 1, 1863.

14. *Burlington Daily Free Press*, July 29, 1863, p. 2.

15. Ide, *History*, p. 107.

16. Henry Parsons, "Gettysburg," *National Tribune*, August 7, 1890, p. 1.

17. Joseph Sutherland, Pension File, National Archives, Washington, D.C.

18. Parsons, "Gettysburg," p. 1.

19. *Burlington Daily Free* Press, July 18, 1863, p. 2.

20. Ide, *History*, p. 107.

21. Prowell, p. 109.

22. Publication Committee of the 18th Pennsylvania Cavalry Association, p. 94.

23. Joseph Sutherland, Pension File, National Archives, Washington, D.C.

24. *OR*, Volume XXVII, Part 2, p. 1013.

25. Ibid.

26. Thomas McGuire, Pension File, National Archives, Washington, D.C.

27. *Burlington Daily Free Press*, July 29, 1863, p. 2.

Chapter 21

1. *OR*, Volume XXVII, Part 1, pp. 914–915.

2. Ide, *History*, p. 114.

3. Evander Law, "Retreat From Gettysburg," in *Battles and Leaders of the Civil War* (New York: Thomas Youseloff, 1956), p. 327.

4. Benedict, *Vermont*, p. 596.

5. Ibid.

6. Henry Parsons, Speech, 1913, Gettysburg National Military Park Library, Gettysburg, Pennsylvania.

7. George Brownell, Pension File, National Archives, Washington, D.C.

8. *Burlington Weekly*, July 18, 1863, p. 3.

9. *Burlington Daily Free Press*, August 8, 1863, p. 2.

10. *Dedication of the Statue of Brevet Major-General William Wells* (Private Printing, 1914), p. 325.

11. Publications Committee of the 18th Pennsylvania Cavalry, p. 80.

12. George Hillyer, "Battle of Gettysburg," Address before the Walton County Georgia Confederate Veterans, August 2, 1904, p. 13.

13. Dedication of the Statue to Brevet Major-General William Wells, p. 134.

14. Ide, *History*, p. 115.

15. Joe Allen Account of Participation in Battle of Gettysburg, Gettysburg National Military Park Library, Gettysburg, Pennsylvania, p. 175.

16. Ide, *History*, p. 115.

17. Ibid.

18. Parsons, p. 395.

19. Ibid.

20. *Battles and Leaders*, p. 328.

21. Ibid., p. 329.

22. George Gorton, Pension File, National Archives, Washington, D.C.

23. Ibid.

24. *Dedication of the Statue of Brevet Major-General William Wells*, p. 88.

25. George Hillyer, Letter to his father dated July 11, 1863, *Southern Banner*, July 29, 1863.

26. George Hillyer, Address titled "The Battle of Gettysburg," published in the *Walker Tribune*, August 1904, p. 13.

27. Hillyer, Address, p. 14.

28. Lensey Morgan, Pension File, National Archives, Washington, D.C.

29. Ibid.

30. Darwin Eames, Pension File, National Archives, Washington, D.C.

31. James Stone, Pension File, National Archives, Washington, D.C.

32. Ibid.

33. Ibid.

34. C.J. Perley Cheney, Pension File, National Archives, Washington, D.C.

35. Ibid.

36. Ibid.

37. *Barre Daily Times*, October 27, 1910.

38. C.J. Perley Cheney, Pension File, National Archives, Washington, D.C.

39. Ibid.

40. Joe Allen Account, p. 175.

41. Ibid.

42. Ibid.

43. Ibid.

44. Stephan Clark, "Farnsworth's Death," *National Tribune*, December 3, 1891.

45. Ide, *History*, p. 116.

46. Parsons, p. 395.

47. Benedict, *Vermont*, p. 602.

48. Richard A. Sauers, ed., *Fighting Them Over* (Baltimore: Butternut and Blue, 1998), p. 476.

49. Charles Blinn, Diary, July 3, 1863, Vermont Historical Society, Barre, Vermont.

50. Oscar French Papers, Letter of August 28, 1863, Vermont Historical Society, Barre, Vermont.

51. Ibid.

52. Ibid.

53. Joe Allen Account, p. 175.

54. *OR*, Volume XXVIII, Part 1, p. 1013.

55. Emmitt Mather, Pension File, National Archives, Washington, D.C.

56. Ibid.

57. Gilbert Smith, Pension File, National Archives, Washington, D.C.

58. Joseph Bailey, Pension File, National Archives, Washington, D.C.

59. Henry Worthen, Pension File, National Archives, Washington, D.C.

60. Lyman Wright, Pension File, National Archives, Washington, D.C.

61. *Rutland Daily Herald*, July 31, 1863, p. 3.

62. *Burlington Weekly Times*, July 18, 1863, p. 3.

63. Lyman Wright, Pension File, National Archives, Washington, D.C.

64. William Wells, Letter of July 7, 1863.

65. Ibid.
66. Glazier, p. 262.
67. *OR*, Volume XXVIII, Part 1, p. 1013.

Chapter 22

1. Stephen Clark, "That March By Night," *National Tribune*, January 24, 1895, p. 3.
2. Ide, *History*, p. 118.
3. Clark, "That March," p. 3.
4. Ide, *History*, p. 119.
5. Clark, "That March," p. 3.
6. *OR*, Vol. XXVII, Part 1, p. 1014.
7. Ibid.
8. Clark, "That March," p. 3.
9. Stephen Clark, "Hagerstown," *National Tribune*, April 11, 1895, p. 3.
10. Ibid.
11. Ide, *History*, p. 120.
12. James Greaves, Pension File, National Archives, Washington, D.C.
13. Ide, *History*, p. 121.
14. *Burlington Daily Free Press*, July 24, 1863, p. 2.
15. Riley Rogers, Pension File, National Archives, Washington, D.C.
16. *OR*, Volume XXVII, Part 1, p. 1007.
17. Ibid.
18. Daniel Hill, Pension File, National Archives, Washington, D.C.
19. Adam Burlett, Pension File, National Archives, Washington, D.C.
20. Harry Pettengill, Pension File, National Archives, Washington, D.C.
21. Ibid.
22. Ibid.
23. Regimental Association's Publication Committee, *The Eighteenth Pennsylvania Cavalry* (New York: Wynkoop Hallenbeck Crawford, 1909), p. 98.
24. *Burlington Daily Free Press*, July 24, 1863, p. 2.
25. Oscar French Papers, Vermont Historical Society, Barre, Vermont.
26. *OR*, Volume XXVII, Part 1, p. 1015.
27. *Burlington Daily Free Press*, July 24, 1863, p. 2.
28. Charles M. Snyder, "They Lay Where They Fell: The Everests, Father and Son," *Vermont History* (July 1864): p. 161.
29. Ibid.
30. *OR*, Volume XXVII, Part 1, p. 1015.
31. Aaron Ober, Pension File, National Archives, Washington, D.C.
32. *OR*, Volume XXVII, Part 1, p. 1015.
33. Ibid.
34. James Reed, Pension File, National Archives, Washington, D.C.
35. Benedict, *Vermont*, p. 607.
36. Ted Alexander, "Ten Days in July," *North & South* 2, no. 6 (August 1999): p. 32.
37. *OR*, Volume XXVII, Part 1, pp. 118–119.
38. Lyman Wright, Pension File, National Archives, Washington, D.C.

Chapter 23

1. William Wells, Letter of August 30, 1863, Manuscript Collection, University of Vermont, Burlington, Vermont.
2. Glazier, p. 315.

3. *OR*, Volume XXIX, Part 2, p. 104.
4. *OR*, Volume XXIX, Part 2, p. 99.
5. *New York Times*, September 4, 1863, p. 1.
6. *OR*, Volume XXIX, Part 2, p. 128.
7. *Orleans Independent Standard*, October 9, 1863, p. 2.
8. Ibid.
9. *Burlington Daily Free Press*, October 16, 1863, p. 2.
10. Edmund Pope, Letter of September 26, 1863, Vermont Historical Society, Barre, Vermont.
11. J.H. Kidd, *Personal Recollections of a Cavalryman* (Ionia, MI: Sentinel, 1908), p. 208.
12. Monroe Lyford, Pension File, National Archives, Washington, D.C.
13. *OR*, Volume XXIX, Part 2, p. 198.
14. William Jure, Pension File, National Archives, Washington, D.C.
15. Ibid.
16. Ibid.
17. Blinn, Diary, October 8, 1863.
18. Ibid.
19. Ibid.
20. *OR*, Volume XXIX, Part 2, p. 392.
21. *OR*, Volume XXIX, Part 2, p. 394.
22. *OR*, Volume XXIX, Part 2, p. 390.
23. Marguerite Merington, ed., *The Custer Story: The Life and Letters of General George A. Custer and His Wife Elizabeth* (New York: Devin-Adair, 1950), p. 66.
24. Luther Hopkins, *From Bull Run to Appomattox* (Baltimore: McGinley-Fleet, 1908), p. 120.
25. *OR*, Volume XXIX, Part 2, p. 390.
26. *OR*, Volume XXIX, Part 2, p. 394.
27. Ibid.
28. William Wells, Letter of October 29, 1863.
29. Hopkins, *From Bull Run*, p. 124.
30. *OR*, Volume XXIX, Part 2, p. 391.
31. *OR*, Volume XXIX, Part 2, p. 395.
32. *Green Mountain Daily Freeman*, December 1, 1863, p. 2.
33. Lyman Wright, Pension File, National Archives, Washington, D.C.
34. Dan Davis, Pension File, National Archives, Washington, D.C.
35. *New York Times*, November 21, 1863, p. 2.
36. John Cantell, Pension File, National Archives, Washington, D.C.
37. Stephen Clark, "Buckland Mills," *Maine Bugle* 4 (January 1897), p. 109.
38. George Baylor, *Bull Run to Bull Run* (Richmond: B.F. Publishing, 1900), p. 153.
39. Ibid., p. 110.
40. Ibid.
41. Charles Chapin, Letter of October 26, 1864, U.S. Army Education Center, Carlisle, Pennsylvania.
42. Ibid.
43. Ide, *History*, p. 149.
44. *Rutland Daily Herald*, December 21, p. 2.
45. Ibid.
46. Ibid.
47. William Wells, Letter of December 10, 1863.
48. *Rutland Daily Herald*, January 26, 1863, p. 2.
49. Frank Ray, Pension File, National Archives, Washington, D.C.
50. Frank Dyo, Pension File, Pension File, Washington, D.C.
51. Eri Woodbury, Diary Entry of January 24, 1864, Rauner Library, Dartmouth College, Hanover, NH.

52. *Rutland Daily Herald*, April 15, 1862, p. 2.
53. Silas Worthing, Pension File, National Archives, Washington, D.C.
54. Woodbury, Diary, March 23, 1864.
55. Blinn, Diary, February 17, 1864.
56. Benedict, *Vermont*, p. 626.
57. *Rutland Daily Herald*, April 15, 1864, p. 2.
58. Ibid.
59. *St. Johnsbury Caledonian*, February 26, 1864, p. 2.
60. Henry Jerdo, Pension File, National Archives, Washington, D.C.
61. Silas Worthing, Pension File, National Archives, Washington, D.C.
62. George McIvor, Pension File, National Archives, Washington, D.C.
63. Ibid.
64. Woodbury, Diary, January 22, 1864.
65. Woodbury, Diary, January 23, 1864.
66. James McMahon, Pension File, National Archives, Washington, D.C.
67. Morte Kearce, Pension File, National Archives, Washington, D.C.
68. John Armstrong, Pension File, National Archives, Washington, D.C.
69. Ibid.
70. Frederic Denison, *Sabers and Spurs: The First Regiment Rhode Island Cavalry in the Civil War* (First Rhode Island Cavalry Veteran Association, 1876), p. 330.
71. *Vermont Journal*, January 16, 1864, p. 2.
72. William Wells, Letter of December 26, 1863.

Chapter 24

1. Mark Curtis Wilson, *Patriots in Blue* (Lafayette, IN: Privately Published, 1987), p. 47.
2. Simon Dufur, *Over the Dead Line* (Burlington: Free Press Association, 1902), p. 12.
3. Kidd, *Personal Recollections*, p. 240.
4. Phineas Worthen, Pension File, National Archives, Washington, D.C.
5. *Rutland Herald*, March 18, 1864, p. 2.
6. Ibid.
7. Ibid.
8. Alexis Snow, Pension File, National Archives, Washington, D.C.
9. Ibid.
10. John DeLaney, Pension File, National Archives, Washington, D.C.
11. *Rutland Herald,* March 18, 1864, p. 2.
12. *Orleans Independent Standard*, April 8, 1864, p. 2.
13. Phineas Worthen, Pension File, National Archives, Washington, D.C.
14. *Rutland Daily Herald*, March 9, 1864, p. 2.
15. Ide, *History*, p. 153.
16. Ibid.
17. *Burlington Daily Free Press*, March 11, 1864, p. 2.
18. Kidd, *Personal Recollections*, 247–248.
19. Ibid., p. 252.
20. Ibid., p. 259.
21. *Orleans Independent Standard*, April 8, 1864, p. 2.
22. Phineas Worthen, Pension File, National Archives, Washington, D.C.
23. Ibid.

24. Ibid.
25. Dufur, *Dead Line*, p. 17.
26. Ibid., p. 14.
27. Milo Farnsworth, Pension File, National Archives, Washington, D. C.
28. Dufur, *Dead Line,* p. 104.
29. Ibid.
30. Phineas Worthen, Pension File, National Archives, Washington, D.C.
31. Ibid.
32. Ibid.
33. Charles Dunn, Pension File, National Archives, Washington, D.C.
34. Bradford Whipple, Pension File, National Archives, Washington, D.C.
35. William Wells, Letter of August 28, 1864.
36. Blinn, Diary, April 17, 1864.
37. *Rutland Daily Herald*, May 9, 1864, p. 2.
38. *Burlington Times*, May 10, 1864, p. 2.
39. Ibid.
40. Michael Madden, Pension File, National Archives, Washington, D.C.
41. Ibid.

Chapter 25

1. *Rutland Herald*, March 15, 1864, p. 2.
2. *Richmond (VA) Whig*, March 4, 1864, p. 2.
3. Blinn, Diary, May 6, 1864.
4. *Rutland Herald*, June 1, 1864, p. 2.
5. Denison Badger, Pension File, National Archives, Washington, D.C.
6. Ibid.
7. *Orleans Independent Journal*, June 10, 1864, p. 2.
8. Albert Taylor, Pension File, National Archives, Washington, D.C.
9. *Rutland Herald*, June 1, 1864, p. 2.
10. Eri Woodbury, Letter of May 17, 1864, Rauner Library, Dartmouth College, Hanover, NH.
11. Philip Sheridan, *Personal Memoirs,* vol. 1 (New York: Charles R. Webster & Sons, 1888), p. 370.
12. Joseph Benoits, Pension File, National Archives, Washington, D.C.
13. *OR*, Volume XXXVI, Part 1, p. 818.
14. *Rutland Herald*, June I, 1864, p. 2.
15. *Orleans Independent Standard*, June 10, 1864, p. 2.
16. *OR*, Volume XXXVI, Part 1, p. 818.
17. Marguerite Merington, *The Custer Story* (New York: Devin-Adair, 1950), p. 97.
18. Michael Phillips, Pension File, National Archives, Washington, D.C.
19. *Rutland Herald*, June 1, 1864, p. 2.
20. Ide, *History*, p. 168.
21. George Pine, Pension File, National Archives, Washington, D.C.
22. *Rutland Herald*, May 19, 1864, p. 3.
23. *Rutland Herald*, June 1, 1864, p. 2.
24. Ide, *History*, p. 213.

Chapter 26

1. Loren Brow, Military File, National Archives, Washington, D.C.
2. *OR*, Vol. XXXVI, Part 1, p. 899.
3. Amos Smith, Pension File, National Archives, Washington, D.C.

4. Cassius Stinckney, Pension File, National Archives, Washington, D.C.

5. Thomas Wiswall, Letter of June 3, 1864, Manuscript Collection, University of Vermont, Burlington, Vermont.

6. Ibid.

7. Addison Harris, Pension File, National Archives, Washington, D.C.

8. Clark Stone, Pension File, National Archives, Washington, D.C.

9. *Rutland Daily Herald*, June 21, 1864, p. 2.

10. Ide, *History*, p. 177.

11. *Rutland Daily Herald*, June 21, 1864, p. 2.

12. Benedict, *Vermont*, p. 645.

13. *Vermont Record*, July 23, 1864, p. 4.

14. Ibid.

15. *Burlington Daily Free Press*, June 20, 1864, p. 3.

16. Juliette Preston, Letter of March 21, 1862, Fairbanks Museum & Planetarium, St. Johnsbury, Vermont.

17. *Vermont Record*, July 23, 1864, p. 4.

18. Oliver Cushman, Pension File, National Archives, Washington, D.C.

19. Ibid.

20. Benedict, *Vermont*, p. 646.

21. George McIvor, Pension File, National Archives, Washington, D.C.

22. Ibid.

23. Emory Durivage, Pension File, National Archives, Washington, D.C.

24. *Burlington Daily Free Press*, July 18, 1864, p. 2.

25. William Wells, Letter of June 14, 1864.

26. *Burlington Daily Free Press*, July 18, 1864, p. 2.

27. *Rutland Daily Herald*, July 18, 1864, p. 2.

28. Charles Cook, Pension File, National Archives, Washington, D.C.

29. Ibid.

30. Harvey Lilly, Letter of July 15, 1864.

31. William Wells, Letter of July 5, 1864.

32. Henry Smith, Pension File, National Archives, Washington, D.C.

33. *Burlington Daily Free Press*, July 18, 1864, p. 2.

34. Ibid.

35. *Burlington Daily Free Press*, July 12, 1864, p. 2.

36. Ide, *History*, p. 187.

37. *Rutland Daily Herald*, July 8, 1862, p. 2.

38. *Rutland Daily Herald*, July 8, 1864, p. 2.

39. *Lynchburg Virginian*, July 4, 1864, p. 2.

40. Ide, *History*, p. 188.

41. *Rutland Daily Herald*, July 18, 1864, p. 2.

42. Eri Woodbury, Letter of July 4, 1864, Rauner Library, Darmouth College, Hanover, New Hampshire.

43. William Cummings, Pension File, National Archives, Washington, D.C.

44. Ibid.

45. *Burlington Daily Free Press*, July 28, 1864, p. 2.

46. Ibid.

47. Norman Kingsbury, Pension File, National Archives, Washington, D.C.

48. William Colby, Pension File, National Archives, Washington, D.C.

49. *Rutland Daily Herald*, July 18, 1864, p. 2.

50. Ide, *History*, p. 189.

51. *Vermont Journal*, July 26, 1864, p. 2.

52. *OR*, James Wilson's Report, Vol. XL, Part 1, p. 623.

53. *OR*, James Wilson's Report, Vol. XL, Part 1, p. 624.

54. Ibid.

55. Harvey Lilly, Letter of July 15, 1864, Manuscript Collection, University of Vermont, Burlington, Vermont.

56. Charles Bishop, Pension File, National archives, Washington, D.C.

57. *Vermont Record*, September 16, 1864, p. 4.

58. Ibid.

59. Ibid.

60. Addison Harris, Pension File, National Archives, Washington, D.C.

61. David Howard, Pension File, National Archives, Washington, D.C.

62. Woodbury, Diary Entry of July 1, 1864.

63. *Vermont Journal*, July 26, 1864, p. 2.

64. *Burlington Daily Free Press*, July 28, 1864. p. 2.

65. Addison Preston, Letter of July 29, 1864, Fairbanks Museum and Planetarium, St. Johnsbury, Vermont.

Chapter 27

1. Ide, *History*, p. 196.

2. *Burlington Daily Free Press*, September 2, 1864, p. 2.

3. Ibid.

4. George Mizo, Pension File, National Archives, Washington, D.C.

5. Edward King, Pension File, National Archives, Washington, D.C.

6. Ibid.

7. Lucius Reed, Pension File, National Archives, Washington, D.C.

8. Sheridan, *Memoirs*, p. 258.

9. Bertram Campbell, Pension File, National Archives, Washington, D.C.

10. Ibid.

11. Ibid.

12. Charles Farr, Diary Entry of September 21, 1864, U.S. Army Library, Carlisle, Pennsylvania.

13. Sheridan, *Memoirs*, p. 276.

14. Ibid.

15. *Burlington Daily Free Press*, October 28, 1864, p. 2.

16. *OR*, Chapter XLIII, Part 1, p. 916.

17. Companions of the Iowa Commandery, *War Sketches and Incidents* (Des Moines: Broadfoot Publishing, 1893), p. 298.

18. Sheridan, *Memoirs*, p. 284.

19. *OR*, Volume XLIII, Part 2, p. 308.

20. Kidd, *Personal Recollections*, p. 398.

21. Eli Woodbury, Diary Entry for October 6, 1864, Rauner Library, Dartmouth College, Hanover, NH.

22. *OR*, Volume XLIII, Part 2, p. 308.

23. Thomas Heatwole, *The Burning: Sheridan in the Shenandoah Valley* (Charlottesville: Rockbridge, 1998), xii.

24. Woodbury, Diary, October 6, 1864.

25. Sheridan, *Memoirs*, p. 285.

26. Ibid.

27. Thomas Rosser, *Riding With Rosser*, ed. S. Roger Keller (Shippensburg, PA: White Mane, 1997), p. 44.

28. Benedict, *Vermont*, p. 663.

29. Farr, Diary, October 9, 1864.

30. *Burlington Daily Free Press*, October 28, 1864, p. 2.

31. *Burlington Daily Free Press*, October 26, 1864, p. 2.

32. James Lowell, Pension File, National Archives, Washington, D.C.

33. *OR*, Volume XLIII, Part 1, p. 521.

34. Woodbury, Diary, October 9, 1864.

35. Sheridan, *Memoirs*, p. 285.

36. *OR*, Volume XLIII, Part 1, p. 431.

37. Sheridan, *Memoirs*, p. 285.

38. *St. Johnsbury Caledonian*, November 11, 1864, p. 2.

39. Wells, Letter of October 27, 1864.

40. *Burlington Daily Free Press*, October 28, 1864, p. 2.

41. Farr, Diary, October 14, 1864.

42. *St. Johnsbury Caledonian*, November 11, 1864, p. 2.

43. *OR*, Volume XLIII, Part 1, p. 547.

44. Wells, Letter of October 27, 1864.

45. John Gordon, *Reminiscences of the Civil War*. New York: Scribner's, 1903, pp. 348–349.

46. *OR*, Volume XLIII, Part 1, p. 547.

47. Alexander Watson, Pension File, National Archives, Washington, D.C.

48. Clark Smith, Pension File, National Archives, Washington, D.C.

49. Joel Bill, Pension File, National Archives, Washington, D.C.

50. Albert Howard, Pension File, National Archives, Washington, D.C.

51. Ibid.

52. *OR*, Volume XLIII, Part 1, p. 525.

53. *Burlington Daily Free Press*, October 29, 1864, p. 2.

54. *OR*, Volume XLIII, Part 1, p. 544.

55. W.F. Beyer and G.F. Keydel, *Deeds of Valor*, 2 vols. (Detroit: Perrien-Keydel, 1906), p. 448.

56. Woodbury, Diary, October 19, 1864.

57. *OR*, Volume XLIII, Part 1, p. 548.

58. *Burlington Daily Free Press*, October 29, 1864, p. 2.

59. Ibid.

60. Robert Johnson and Clarence Buel, *Battles and Leaders of the Civil War*, vols. 3 and 4 (New York: Thomas Yoseloff, 1956), p. 519.

Chapter 28

1. *Vermont Record*, December 9, 1864, p. 163. The thirteen departing front-line officers were Bennett, Grover, Gale, Ellis, Morse, Sawyer, Paige, Parker, Trussell, Seaver, Richmond, Clark, and Gates.

2. *Burlington Daily Free Press*, October 31, 1864, p. 2.

3. Ibid.

4. Ibid.

5. *Vermont Record*, December 9, 1864, p. 163.

6. William Wells, Letter of November 16, 1864.

7. George Haroon, Pension File, National Archives, Washington, D.C.

8. Benedict, *Vermont*, p. 673.

9. *Vermont Record*, June 10, 1865, p. 329.

10. Ibid.

11. *St. Johnsbury Caledonian*, October 21, 1864, p. 1.

12. Ibid.

13. *St. Johnsbury Caledonian*, November 8, 1864, p. 2.

14. *Vermont Record*, December 2, 1864, p. 155.

15. Ide, *History*, p. 245.

16. George Nay, Letter of December 25, 1864.

17. *OR*, Volume XLIII, Part 1, p. 676.

18. Napoleon Plant, Pension File, National Archives, Washington, D.C.

19. Brian Sheehy, Pension File, National Archives, Washington, D.C.

20. Ide, *History*, p. 244.

21. George Nay, Letter of February 19, 1864.

22. Ide, *History*, p. 246.

23. Ibid.

Chapter 29

1. *Vermont Record*, October 17, 1864, p. 6.

2. *OR*, Volume XLVI, Part 1, p. 476.

3. Peter Washburn, *Report of the Adjutant & Inspector General of the State of Vermont* (Montpelier: Walton's Steam Printing Establishment, 1865), Appendix C, "Report of Col. Josiah Hall," p. 45.

4. *Burlington Weekly Times*, March 25, 1865, p. 2.

5. Phil Sheridan, *Personal Memoirs* (New York: Barnes & Noble, 2006), p. 312.

6. George Nay, Letter of March 29, 1865, Vermont Historical Society, Barre, Vermont.

7. Ibid.

8. Sheridan, *Memoirs*, p. 314.

9. Mark Curtis Wilson, *Patriots in Blue* (West Lafayette, IN: Privately Published, 1987), 61–62.

10. *Rutland Daily Herald*, May 16, 1865, p. 2.

11. Ibid., p. 335.

12. *OR*, Volume XLVI, Part 1, p. 1140.

13. *Rutland Daily Herald*, April 10, 1865, p. 3.

14. Ide, *History*, p. 261.

15. Ibid.

16. Address by William Cummings, *War Sketches and Incidents* (Des Moines: Iowa Commandery MOLLUS: P.C. Kenyon, 1893), p. 310.

17. Sheridan, *Memoirs*, p. 352.

18. Cummings Address, p. 310.

19. Woodbury, Diary Entry for mid–April.

20. George Farrington, Pension File, National Archives, Washington, D.C.

21. Ide, *History*, p. 264.

22. Woodbury, Diary Entry for mid–April.

23. Ibid.

24. *OR*, Volume XLV, Part 1, p. 113.

25. Ide, *History*, p. 265.

26. Nay, Letter of May, 1865.

27. Almer Montague, Letter of April 15, 1865.

28. Nay, Letter of May, 1865.

29. Montague, Letter of April 15, 1865.

30. Nay, Letter of April 23, 1865.

31. *Revised Roster of Vermont Volunteers* gives 114 as the number of KIAs.

Regimental Losses in the American Civil War by Fox pegs battle deaths as being 134.

In his *History of the First Vermont Cavalry Volunteers in the War of the Rebellion*, Elliott Hoffman sets the number at 121.

32. Ide, *History*, p. 266.

33. Ibid.

34. Washburn, Appendix C, p. 46.

35. *OR*, Volume XLVI, Part 1, pp. 1132–1133.

36. *Rutland Daily Herald*, May 1, 1865, p. 2.

37. *Vermont Record*, June 3, 1865, p. 311.

38. *Vermont Record*, June 10, 1865, p. 329.

39. *OR*, Volume XLVI, Part 3, p. 676.

40. Ibid.

Epilogue

1. Ide, *History*, p. 272.

Bibliography

Manuscripts

Dartmouth College, Rauner Library, Special Collections, Hanover, New Hampshire
    Eri Woodbury Papers

Fairbanks Museum Library, St. Johnsbury, Vermont
    Addison Preston Papers

Gettysburg National Military Park Library, Gettysburg, Pennsylvania
    George Hillyer, 1913 Speech on Participa-tion in the Battle of Gettysburg

Joe Allen Account of Participation in the Battle of Gettysburg
    National Tribune Microfilm Collection

National Archives, Washington, D.C.
    1st Vermont Volunteer Cavalry, Regimental and Company Order and Letter Books
    1st Vermont Military Records
    1st Vermont Pension Files

James Abel
Charles Adams
John Armstrong
George Austin
Denison Badger
Ransom Badger
Joseph Bailey
Sylvestor Bartlett
Ira Batchelder
Rufus Bean
William Belding
James Benoits
Joel Bill
Charles Bishop
Charles Blinn
Horace Bradley
Ephraim Brewster
Loren Brigham
George Brownell
Adam Burlett
Bertram Campbell
John Cantell
George Caulkins
John Chase
Perley Cheney
Stephan Clapp
William Colby
Charles Cook
Job Corey
William Cummings
Oliver Cushman
Dan Davis

Oliver Delaney
Medorse Demerse
Charles Dunn
Emory Durviage
Frank Dragon
Ellis Draper
George Duncan
Conceader Durlam
Frank Dyo
Darwin Eames
Joel Earhardt
James Edson
Milo Farnsworth
George Farrington
George Fay
Carlastan Ferry
William Flowers
William Flynn
Herman Frost
John Frost
Edward Gee
George Gorton
Albert George
Louis Goulette
Eban Grant
James Greaves
Azro Hackett
George Haroon
Addison Harris
Andrew Hart
Daniel Hill
James Hogan

Eli Holden
John Holden
Henry Holt
David Howard
William Humphrey
Franklin Huntoon
John Huse
Albert Hutchins
Collis Ikey
Hannibel Jenne
Henry Jerdo
William Johnson
Edwin Jones
William Jure
Morte Kearce
Edward King
Norman Kingsbury
John Kinehan
Zabina Landon
William Langshore
Albert Lantz
George Lowell
James Lowell
Monroe Lyford
Michael Madden
Marvin Mason
Emmett Mather
Daniel McDixon
Thomas McGuire
George McIvor
James McMahon
Ashbell Meacham

Delinus Melvin
Ralph Merrill
Horace Mears
George Mizo
William Moncrief
Lensey Morgan
George Nimblet
Aaron Ober
Henry O'Hare
Elijah Paige
Daniel Patterson
Daniel Perlam
Harrison Perry
Harry Pettengill
Michael Phillips
George Pine
Edgar Pitkin
Charles Pixley
Napoleon Plant
Orrin Putnam
Frank Ray
Vietal Reaulo
James Reed
Lucious Reed
Benjamin Rice
Riley Rogers
Mark Rogers
William Rogers
Alexander Ross
Daniel Russell
Harley Sawyer
John Sawyer

Elijah Scott	Edwin Southworth
Barney Scully	Robert Stewart
Brian Sheehy	Cassius Stinckney
Elliot Shepley	Clark Stone
Avery Sibley	James Stone
Amos Smith	Joseph Sutherland
Gilbert Smith	Horace Taylor
Alexis Snow	David Tubbs

Charles Turner	Phineas Worthen
Joseph Waldren	Silas Worthing
Alexander Watson	Lyman Wright
Ephriam Wheeler	Edmund Yates
Bradford Whipple	Francis Young
Charles Woodbury	
Curtis Woodward	
Henry Worthen	

United States Army Military History Institute, Carlisle Barracks, Pennsylvania
    Charles Chapin Collection
    Charles Farr Diary
    Civil War Picture Collection

University of Vermont, Bailey/Howe Library, Special Collections, Burlington, Vermont
    Luman Blaisdell Letters
    Charles Blinn Diaries
    Perley Cheney Letter
    Albert Greene Letters
    Henry Holt Letter
    Lorentio King Papers
    Harvey Lillie Letter
       Albert Frances Sawyer Letters
    Charles Stone Diary
    William Wells Papers
    Henry O. Wheeler Letter
       Thomas Wiswall Letters

Vermont Historical Society Library, Barre, Vermont
    Edward B. Sawyer Collection
    Eli Hawley Canfield Papers
    George Crosby Diaries
    George Nay Collection
    Henry Smith Letters
    Lemuel Platt Collection
    Oscar French Papers
    Smilie Bancroft Papers
       Zadock Canfield Papers

Primary Sources—Articles and Addresses

"Battle of Winchester." *Southern Historical Society Papers* 10 (Jan–Dec 1882).
Bradford, James O. "At Gettysburg on July 3." *Confederate Veteran* 30 (1922).
Clark, Stephan. "Buckland Mills." In *Maine Bugle* 4 (January 1897).
_____. "Farnsworth's Death." *National Tribune*, December 3, 1891.
_____. "Hagerstown" *National Tribune*, April 11, 1895.
_____. "That March by Night." *National Tribune*, January 24, 1894.
Edson, Ptolemy. "Address before Second Annual Meeting of the First Vermont Reunion Society." Montpelier, November 4, 1874.
Hammond, John. "Memoir of the Battle of Gettys-

burg." In *In Memoriam John Hammond*. Chicago: PF Pettibone, 1890.
Hillyer, George. "The Battle of Gettysburg." Address Published in the *Walker (GA) Tribune*, August 1904.
_____. Letter of July 11, 1863, to His Father. *Southern Banner* (Georgia), July 29, 1863.
Jones, William. "The Kilpatrick-Dahlgren Raid Against Richmond." *Southern Historical Society Papers* 13.
White, W.T. "First Texas Regiment at Gettysburg." *Confederate Veteran* 30 (1922).

Primary Sources—Books

Avirett, James Battle. *The Memoirs of General Turner Ashby and His Compeers*. Baltimore: Selby and Dunley, 1867.
Baylor, George. *Bull Run to Bull Run*. Richmond: B.F. Publishing, 1900.
Beale, R.L.T. *History of the Ninth Virginia Cavalry in the War Between the States*. Richmond: B.F. Johnson, 1899.
Beaudry, Louis. *Historic Records of the Fifth NY Cavalry*. Albany: S.R. Gray, 1865.
Beaudry, Richard. *War Journal of Louis N. Beaudry, 5th NY Cavalry*. Jefferson, NC: McFarland, 1996.
Beyer, W.F., and G. Keydel, *Deeds of Valor*. Detroit: Perrien-Keydel, 1903.
Blackford, W.W. *War Years with Jeb Stuart*. New York: Scribner's, 1945.
Brooks, Stewart. *Civil War Medicine*. Springfield, IL: Charles Thomas, 1966.
Crowninshield, Benjamin W. *A History of the First Regimental Massachusetts Cavalry Volunteers*. Boston: Houghton Mifflin, 1891.
Curry, W.L. *Four Years in the Saddle: History of the First Regiment Ohio Volunteer Cavalry*. Jonesboro: Freedom Hill, 1898.
Dahlgren (Rear-Admiral). *Memoir of Ulric Dahlgren*. Philadelphia: J.B. Lippencott, 1872.
Davis, Sidney Morris. *Common Soldier, Uncommon War: Life as a Cavalryman in the Civil War*. Baltimore: Port City Press, 1994.
Denison, Frederic. *The First Regiment Rhode Island Cavalry*. First Rhode Island Cavalry Regiment, 1876.
Douglas, Henry Kyd. *I Rode with Stonewall*. Greenwich: Fawcett, 1961.
Dufur, Simon, *Over the Dead Line*. Burlington: Free Association, 1902.

Fox, William. *Regimental Losses in the American Civil War*. Albany: Albany, 1889.

Gilmer, Harry. *Four Years in the Saddle*. New York: Harper, 1866.

Glazier, (Captain) Willard. *Three Years in the Federal Cavalry*. New York: RH Ferguson, 1874.

Gordon, John. *Reminiscences of the Civil War*. New York: Scribner's, 1903.

Grant, Ulysses, *Personal Memoirs of U.S. Grant*. New York: Charles L. Webster, 1886.

Grout, Josiah. *Memoir of Gen'l William Wallace Grout and Autobiography of Josiah Grout*. Newport: Bullock, 1919.

Hoffman, Elliot, ed. *History of the First Vermont Cavalry Volunteers in the War of the Great Rebellion*. Baltimore: Butternut and Blue, 2000.

Hopkins, Luther. *From Bull Run to Appomattox*. Baltimore: McGinley-Fleet, 1908.

Iowa Commandry — MOLLUS. *War Sketches and Incidents*. Vol. 1. Des Moines: 1893.

Jackson, H. Nelson. *Dedication of the Statue of Brevet Major General William Wells*. Burlington: Privately Published, 1914.

Johnson, Robert Underwood, and Clarence Buel. *Battles and Leaders of the Civil War*. Vols. 3 and 4. New York: Thomas Yoseloff, 1956.

Jones, John B. *A Rebel War Clerk's Diary*. Vol. 2. Philadelphia: J.P. Lippencott, 1866.

Kidd, J.H. *Personal Recollections of a Cavalryman*. Ionia: Sentinel, 1908.

Ladd, David, and Audrey Ladd. *The Batchelder Papers: Gettysburg in Their Own Words*. Dayton: Morningside, 1995.

Mahan, Michael, ed. *Winchester Divided: The Civil War Diaries of Julia Chase and Laura Lee*. Mechanicsburg: Stackpole, 2002.

Marshall, Jeffrey D., ed. *A War of the People*. Hanover: University of New England Press, 1999.

McClellan, H.B. *I Rode With Jeb Stuart*. Boston: Houghton Mifflin, 1885.

Merington, Marguerite, ed. *The Custer Story*. New York: Barnes & Noble, 1994.

Mewborn, Horace. *From Mosby's Command*. Baltimore: Butternut and Blue, 2005.

Meyer, Henry C. *Civil War Experiences Under Bayard, Gregg, Kilpatrick, Custer*. New York: Raulston & Newberry, 1911.

Minnesota Commandry — MOLLUS. *Glimpses of the Nation's Struggle*. 1st, 4th, and 5th Series. St. Paul: St. Paul Book and Stationary, 1890.

Mosby, John. *Gray Ghost: The Memoirs of Colonel John S. Mosby*. Edited by Paul Hutton. New York: Bantam Books, 1992.

Munson, John. *Reminiscences of a Mosby Guerilla*. New York: Maftas & Garda, 1906.

The Official Military Atlas of the Civil War. New York: Sun, 1978.

Peck, Theodore S. *Revised Roster of Vermont Volunteers*. Montpelier: Watchman Publishing, 1892.

Penfield, James. *1863–1864 Civil War Diary: 5th New York Volunteer Cavalry Company H*. Ticonderoga: Press of America, 1999.

Rosser, Thomas. *Riding With Rosser*. Edited by S. Roger Keller. Shippensburg: White Mane, 1997.

Rodenbough, Theodore. *The Photographic History of the Civil War*. Secaucus, NJ: Blue and Gray Press, 1997, 190.

Rodenbough, Theodore, Henry Potter, and William Seal. *History of the Eighteenth Regiment of Cavalry*. New York: Wykoop Hallenbeck Crawford, 1909.

Sauers, Richard A., ed. *Fighting Them Over*. Baltimore: Butternut and Blue, 1998.

Scott, John. *Partisan Life with John Mosby*. Gaithersburg: Butternut Press, 1985.

Sheridan, Phillip. *Personal Memoirs*. New York: Charles L. Webster, 1888.

Taylor, Nelson. *Saddles and Saber, Letters of a Civil War Cavalryman*. Bowie: Heritage, 1993.

Tobie, Edward L. *History of the First Main Cavalry, 1861–1865*. Boston: Press of Emery & Hughes, 1887.

United States War Department. *The War of the Rebellion: A Compilation of the Official Records of the Union and Confederate Archives*. Washington, D.C.: Government Printing Office, 1880–1901.

Washburn, Peter. *Report of the Adjutant & Inspector General of the State of Vermont*. Montpelier: Waltons Steam Printing Establishment, 1865.

Wickman, Donald E., ed. *Letters to Vermont*. Vol. 1. Bennington: Images from the Past, 1998.

Williamson, James J. *Mosby Rangers: A Record of the Operations of the Forty-Third Battalion Virginia Cavalryman from Its Organization to the Surrender*. Second edition. New York: Sturges & Walton, 1909.

Worsham, John. *One of Jackson's Foot Cavalry*. Alexandria: Time-Life, 1982.

Secondary Sources

Adams, George. *Doctors in Blue*. New York: Schuman, 1952.

Allen, William. *History of the Campaign of General T.J. (Stonewall) Jackson in the Shenandoah Valley of Virginia*. Philadelphia: J.P. Lippincott, 1880.

Annals of War. Philadelphia: Times Publishing, 1879.

Barber, James G. *Alexandria in the Civil War*. Lynchburg: H.E. Howard, 1988.

Beach, William. *The First New York Cavalry*. Annadale, 1988.

Bellah, James Warner. *Soldiers' Battle*. New York: David McKay, 1962.

Benedict, G.G. *Vermont in the Civil War*. Vols. 1 and 2. Burlington: Free Press, 1888.

Black, Robert W. *Cavalry Raids of the Civil War*. Mechanicsburg: Stackpole, 2004.

Blow, David. *Historic Guide to Burlington Neighborhoods*, Burlington: Queen City.

Boatner, Mark. *The Civil War Dictionary*. New York: David McKay, 1959.

Bonnell, John. *Sabres in the Shenandoah*. Shippensburg: Burd Street, 1996.

Bowen, J.R. *Regimental History of the 1st NY Dragoons*. Battle Creek: 1900.

Brown, Kent Masterson. *Retreat from Gettysburg*. Chapel Hill: University of North Carolina Press, 2005.

Bushong, Millard K. *General Turner Ashby and Stonewalls Valley Campaign*. Verona, VA: McClure, 1980.

Carter, Samuel. *The Last Cavaliers*. New York: St. Martin's, 1979.

Chambers, Lenoir. *Stonewall Jackson*. New York: William Morrow, 1959.

Clark, Champ. *Decoying the Yanks: Jackson's Valley Campaigns*. Alexandria: Time Life, 1984.

Coffin, Howard. *Full Duty*. Woodstock, VT: Countryman Press, 1993.

Coggins, Jack. *Arms & Equipment of the Civil War*. Garden City: Doubleday, 1962.

Commager, Henry Steele. *The Blue and the Gray*. New York: Bobbs-Merrill, 1950.

Cooling, Benjamin. *Mr. Lincoln's Forts: A Guide to the Civil War Defenses of Washington*. Shippensburg: White Mane, 1988.

Cummings, A.B. *The Wilson-Kautz Raid*. Privately Published, 1960.

Cunningham, Frank. *Knight of the Confederacy: Gentleman Ashby*. San Antonio: Naylor, 1960.

Dahlgren, Rear Admiral. *Memoirs of Ulric Dahlgren*. Philadelphia: J.P. Lippencott, 1872.

Davis, Burke. *To Appomattox: Nine April Days, 1865*. New York: Rinehart, 1959.

Denison, Frederic. *Sabers and Spurs: The First Rhode Island Cavalry in the Civil War*. Baltimore: Butternut and Blue, 1994.

Edwards, Elivyn Hartley. *The Ultimate Horse Book*. New York: Darling Kinderley, 1991.

Evans, Thomas, and James Moyer. *Mosby's Confederacy*. Shippensburg, PA: White Mane, 1991.

Gardner, Charles. *Three Years in the Federal Cavalry*. Tucson: Ada Friddell & A Plus, 1998.

Garrison, Webb. *The Encyclopedia of Civil War Usage*. Nashville: Cumberland House, 2001.

Griffith, Paddy. *Battle Tactics of the Civil War*. New Haven: Yale University Press, 1989.

Heatwole, John L. *The Burning: Sheridan in the Shenandoah*. Charlottesville: Rockbridge, 1998.

Harrell, Roger. *The 2nd North Carolina Cavalry*. Jefferson, NC: McFarland, 2004.

Hatch, Thom, *Clashes of Cavalry*. Mechanicsburg: Stackpole, 2001.

Johnson, Clint. *In the Footsteps of Jackson*. Winston-Salem: John Blair, 2002.

Johnson, Patricia. *Meet the Horse*. New York: Grossett & Dunlap, 1967.

Johnson, R.U., and C.C. Buel, eds. *Battles and Leaders of the Civil War*. New York: Century, 1887.

Johnston, Angus J. *Virginia Railroads in the Civil War*. Chapel Hill: University of North Carolina Press, 1961.

Jones, Terry L. *Lee's Tigers*. Baton Rouge: Louisiana State University Press, 1987.

Jones, Virgil Carrington. *Eight Hours Before Richmond*. New York: Henry Holt, 1957.

_____. *Gray Ghosts and Rebel Raiders*. New York: Henry Holt, 1956.

_____. *Roger Mosby*. Chapel Hill: University of North Carolina Press, 1944.

Katcher, Philip. *The Civil War Sourcebook*. New York: Facts on File, 1992.

___, and Richard Hook. *Union Cavalryman, 1861–1865*. London: Reed International, 1995.

Kellogg, S.C. *The Shenandoah Valley and Virginia*. 1903.

Kercheval, Samuel. *A History of the Valley of Virginia*. 1902.

Kleese, Richard. *Shenandoah County in the Civil War: The Turbulent Years*. Lynchburg: H.E. Howard, 1992.

Lee, Richard M. *Mr. Lincoln's City*. McLean, VA: E.P.M., 1981.

Leisch, Juanito. *An Introduction to Civil War Civilians*. Gettysburg, 1994.

Long, E.B. *The Civil War Day by Day*. New York: Doubleday, 1971.

Longacre, William. *The Cavalry at Appomattox*. Mechanicsburg: Stackpole, 2003.

_____. *The Cavalry at Gettysburg*. Rutherford, NJ: Farleigh Dickenson University Press, 1986.

_____. *Mounted Raids of the Civil War*. Cranbury: A.S. Barnes, 1975.

Lord, Francis. *Civil War Collector's Encyclopedia*. Secaucus: Castle, 1982.

Lowry, Thomas. *Tarnished Eagles*. Mechanicsburg: Stackpole, 1997.

Lyman, Darryl. *Civil War Wordbook*. Conshohocken: Combined, 1994.

Magner, Blake A. *Traveler & Company, The Horses of Gettysburg*. Gettysburg: Farnsworth House Military Impressions, 1995.

Mahon, Michael. *The Shenandoah Valley 1861–1865*. Mechanicsburg: Stackpole, 1999.

_____, ed. *Winchester Divided: The Civil War Diaries of Julia Chase and Laura Lee*. Mechanicsburg: Stackpole, 2002.

Mahr, Theodore. *The Battle of Cedar Creek*. Lynchburg: H.E. Howard, 1992.

Martin, David. *Jackson's Valley Campaign*. New York: Weiser & Weiser, 1988.

McChiney, Grady, and Perry Jamison. *Attack and Die*. Tuscaloosa: University of Alabama Press, 1982.

McClure, Stanley. *The Defenses of Washington*. Washington: United States Department of the Interior, 1957.

McDonald, William. *A History of the Laurel Brigade*. Baltimore: Johns Hopkins University Press, 2002.

Mitchell, (Lt. Col.) Joseph B. *The Badge of Gallantry*. New York: Macmillan, 1968.

Mitchell, Reid. *The Vacant Chair: The Northern Soldier Leaves Home.* New York: Oxford University Press, 1993.

Moore, James. *Kilpatrick and Our Cavalry.* New York: W.J. Widdleston, 1865.

Moore, Robert H. II. *Avenue of Armies.* Virginia Beach: Downing, 2002.

Murphy, Jim. *The Boys' War.* New York: Clarion, 1990.

Musick, Michael. *6th Virginia Cavalry.* Lynchburg: H.E. Howard, 1990.

Oates, Dan, ed. *Hanging Rock Rebel: Lt. John Blue's War in West Virginia and the Shenandoah Valley.* Shippensburg, PA: Burd Street, 1994.

Penny, Morris, and Laine, Gary. *Struggle for the Round Tops.* Shippensburg, PA: Burd Street, 1999.

Poirier, Robert G. *"By the Blood of Our Alumni": Norwich University Citizen Soldiers in the Civil War.* Mason City: Savas, 1999.

Polley, J.B. *Hood's Texas Brigade.* Dayton: Morningside, 1976.

Reynolds, Arlene. *The Civil War Memories of Elizabeth Bacon Custer.* Austin: University of Texas Press, 1994.

Rhea, Gordon C., *The Battles for Spotsylvania Court House and the Road to Yellow Tavern, May 7–12, 1864.* Baton Rouge: Louisiana State University Press, 1997.

Rigdon, John. *A Dictionary of Civil War Diseases.* Augusta: Eastern Digital Resources, 2001.

Roper, Peter W. *Jedediah Hotchkiss: Rebel Mapmaker and Virginia Businessman.* Shippensburg, PA: White Mane, 1992.

Ropy, John C. *The Army Under Pope.* New York: Scribner's, 1881.

Rowell, John W. *Yankee Cavalrymen.* Knoxville: University of Tennessee Press, 1971.

Rummell, George. *Cavalry on the Roads to Gettysburg.* Shippensburg, PA: White Mane, 2000.

Rummell, George A. *72 Days to Gettysburg: Organization of the Tenth Regiment.* Shippensburg, PA: Burd Street, 1997.

Schidt, John W. *Roads from Gettysburg.* Shippensburg, PA: Burd Street, 1998.

Sears, Stephen. *George B. McClellan.* New York: Ticknor & Fields, 1988.

_____. *To the Gates of Richmond.* New York: Ticknor & Fields, 1992.

Sears, Stephen W. *Gettysburg.* New York: Houghton Mifflin, 2003.

Slade, A.D. *A.T.A. Torbert: Southern Gentleman in Northern Blue.* Dayton: Morningside, 1992.

Stackpole, Edward. *Sheridan in the Shenandoah.* New York: Bonanza, 1961.

Starr, Steven. *The Union Cavalry in the Civil War.* Vols. 1–3. Baton Rouge: Louisiana State University Press, 1974.

Stevens, John. *Reminiscences of the Civil War.* Hillsboro: Hillsboro Mirror, 1902.

Tanner, Robert. *Stonewall in the Valley.* Garden City: Doubleday, 1976.

Thomas, Clarence. *General Turner Ashby, the Centaur of the South: A Military Sketch.* Winchester: Eddy, 1907.

Tremain, Henry E. *Two Days of War: A Gettysburg Narrative and Other Excursions.* New York: Bonnell, Silver, and Bowers, 1905.

Tremain, Henry Edwin. *Last Hours of Sheridan's Cavalry.* New York: Bonnell, Silver and Bowers, 1904.

VanDoren, Stern, Philip, ed. *Soldier Life.* Greenwich: Fawcett, 1961.

Walsh, George. *"Those Damn Horse Soldiers."* New York: Tom Dougherty, 2006.

Warner, Ezra. *Generals in Blue.* Baton Rogue: Louisiana State University Press, 1964.

_____. *Generals in Gray.* Baton Rogue: Louisiana State University Press, 1964.

Wert, Jeffrey. *Custer.* New York: Simon & Schuster, 1996.

_____. *Gettysburg: Day Three.* New York: Simon & Schuster, 2001.

_____. *Mosby's Rangers.* New York: Simon & Schuster, 1990.

Wert, Jeffery D., *From Winchester to Cedar Creek.* New York: Simon & Schuster, 1987.

Whittaker, Frederick. *A Compilation of General George A. Custer Volunteers Through the Civil War.* Lincoln: University of Nebraska Press, 1993.

Wilbur, C. Keith. *Civil War Medicine, 1861–1865.* Guilford, CT: Globe Pequot, 1998.

Wiley, Bell. *The Life of Billy Yank.* Baton Rouge: Louisiana State University Press, 1978.

Wilson, Mark. *Patriots in Blue.* West Lafayette, IN: Privately Published, 1987.

Winik, Jay. *April 1865.* New York: HarperCollins, 2001.

Wittenberg, Eric. *Gettysburg's Forgotten Cavalry Actions.* Gettysburg, 1998.

_____, *The Union Cavalry Comes of Age.* Washington, D.C.: Brassey's, 2003.

Zall, Paul. *Blue and Gray Laughing.* Redondo Beach, 1996.

Serials

Bellows Falls Times (daily), 1861–1865
Bennington Banner, 1861–1865
Burlington Daily Free Press, 1861–1865
Burlington Times (weekly), 1861–1865
Green Mountain Freeman (Montpelier, Vermont), 1861–1865
Lynchburg Virginian, 1861–1865
New York Times, 1961–1865
Richmond Whig, 1861–1865
Rutland Herald, 1861–1865
St. Johnsbury Caledonian, 1861–1865
Troy Record, 1861–1865
Vermont Journal (Montpelier), 1863–1864
Vermont Phoenix (Brattleboro), 1861–1862
Vermont Record, 1861–1865

Articles

Alexander, Ted. "Gettysburg Cavalry Operations, June 27-July 3, 1863." *North & South* 6, no. 1 (October 1988): 8–41.

_____. "Ten Days in July." *North & South* 2, no. 6 (August 1999).

Bassett, T.D. Seymour. "For Freedom and Unity: Vermont's Civil War." *Vermont Life* 15, no. 3 (Spring 1961): 35–53.

Brennan, Patrick. "The Best Cavalry in the World." *North & South* 2, no. 2 (January 1999) 10–27.

_____. "'I Had Rather Die Than Be Whipped' (The Battle of Yellow Tavern)." *North & South* 7, no. 4 (June 2004): 56–73.

Coffin, Howard. "The Blue and Gray in Vermont." *Vermont Life* 46, no. 1 (Autumn 1991): 4–13.

Custer, Andie. "Forgotten Boy General and the Fight at the South Cavalry Field." *Blue & Gray* 20, no. 2 (Holiday 2002): 46–51 and notes on 24–25.

_____. "Into the Mouth of Hell: Farnsworth's Charge Revisited." *Blue & Gray* 23, no. 1 (Spring 2006): 6–23.

_____. "John Hammond's 'Mis-stake': How a Misplaced Wooden Stake Altered the History of Farnsworth's Charge at Gettysburg." *Gettysburg* 30: 98–113.

_____. "The Kilpatrick-Farnsworth Argument That Never Happened." *Gettysburg* 28: 100–116.

_____. "The Wells Monument." *Blue & Gray* 23, no. 1 (Spring 2006): 56–57 and 61–62.

Forman, Stephan. "A Glimpse of Wartime Washington." *Blue & Gray* 13, no. 4 (Spring 1996): 8–22.

Gerleman, David. "War Horse." *North & South* 2, no. 2 (January 1999): 47–61.

Gorman, Paul. "J.E.B. Stuart and Gettysburg." *Gettysburg* 1, no. 1 (July 1, 1989): 86–91.

Hoffman, Elliot. "A Shot in the Dark." *Vermont History* 47, no. 4 (Fall 1979).

Klingensmith, Harold A. "Judson Kilpatrick's Gunboat Expedition." *America's Civil War* 17, no. 4 (September 2004): 23–28.

Nye, Wilbur S. "The Affair at Hunterstown." *Civil War Times Illustrated* 9, no. 10 (February 1971).

Odell, Digger. "The Attraction of Magnetic Medicines." www.bottlebook.com.

Parsons, Henry. "Gettysburg." *National Tribune*, August 7, 1890.

Patchan, Scott. "The Battle of Cedar Creek." *Blue & Gray* 14, no. 1 (Campaign 2007): 6–26.

Rudolph, Jack. "The Grand Review." *Civil War Times Illustrated* 19, no. 7 (November, 1980): 34–43.

_____. "Taking Up Arms." *Civil War Times Illustrated* 23, no. 2 (April 1984): 8–17, 5–51.

Ryan, Thomas J. "Kilpatrick Bars Stuart's Route to Gettysburg." *Gettysburg* 27: 7–28.

Schiller, Laurence. "A Taste of Northern Steel." *North & South* 2, no. 2, 30–45.

Schreckengost, Gary. "Front Royal: Key to the Valley." *America's Civil War* 12, no. 6 (January 2000): 26–32.

Shevchuk, Paul. "The Battle of Hunterstown, Pennsylvania, July 2, 1863." *Gettysburg* 1, no. 1 (July 1989): 93–104.

_____. "The 1st Texas Infantry and the Repulse of Farnsworth's Charge." *Gettysburg* 2, no. 2 (January 1990): 81–90.

Skelton, Geoffrey. "Cavalry Clash at Hanover." *Military History* 13, no. 2 (June 1996): 30–36.

Snyder, Charles M. "They Lay Where They Fell; The Everests, Father and Son." *Vermont History* (July 1964).

Tompkins, Charles. "With the Vermont Cavalry, 1861–1862." *Vermonter* 17 (1912).

Ventor, Bruce. "The Kilpatrick-Dahlgren Raid." *Blue & Gray* 20, no. 3 (Winter 2003): 6–20.

Vosburg, Brent. "Cavalry Clash at Hanover." *America's Civil War* 10, no. 6 (January 1998): 46–52.

Wittenberg, Eric. "The Battle of Tom's Brook." *North & South* 10, no. 1 (May 2007): 30–47.

_____. "Learning the Hard Lessons of Logistics." *North & South* 2, no. 2 (January 1999): 62–78.

Wittenberg, Eric, and J. David Petruzzi. "Why Jeb Stuart Was Late." *Civil War Times Illustrated* 46, no. 1 (February 2007): 30–37.

Wittenberg, Eric, J. David Petruzzi, and Andie Custer. "Farnsworth's Charge: The Traditional vs. Revised Interpretation." *Blue & Gray* 24, no. 2 (Summer 2007): 47–50.

Index

Numbers in *bold italics* refer to pages with photographs or illustrations.

Election of 1864 272–273
Ellis, Pvt. Cornelius 65
Ellis's Ford, Va. 213
Elmira, N.Y. 7, 154
Emmittsburg Road 166, 169, 170, 185
Enosburg Falls, Vt. 116
Esdon, Pvt. James 75
Estes, Adjutant Joel 171
Ethan 200
Everest, Eleanor 190
Everest, Pvt. George 190
Ewell, Gen. Richard 59, 74

Fairbanks, Gov. Erastus 3
Fairfax, Vt. 183, 278, 285
Fairfax Court House, Va. 31, 67, 94, 193
Falling Waters, Pa. 195
Farnham, Corp. James 208
Farnsworth, Gen. Elon 156, 161, 162, 181, 183, 184, 187 192
Farnsworth, Pvt. Milo 220
Farnsworth's Brigade 169, 170, 171, 172
Farnsworth's Charge 173, 176, *177*, 180, 182, 183, 241
Farr, Cpl. Charles 254, 259
Farrington, Pvt. George 282
Fauquier County, Va. 124
Fay, Pvt. George 43
Ferrand, Pvt. Joseph 189
Ferry, Sgt. Carlastan 130
Fiddler's Green 288
Field, Pvt. Curtis 96
Fisher's Hill, Va. 253, 254, 261, 266
Fiske, Pvt. John 6
Fitzhugh, Pvt. James 155, 156
Five Forks, Va. 279
Fleetwood Hill, Va. 199
Flint, Capt. Henry 17, 22, 24, 75, 103; Miskel's farm 134, *135*, 137, 138, 140, 141, 145, 236
Florence, S.C. 207, 225
Flowers, Bugler William 68
Fobes, Pvt. Josiah 112
Foot, Sen. Solomon 3, 9
Ford's Station, Va. 241
Fort Delaware 91, 162
Fort Scott 92, 93, 96, 122, 131
Foster, Col. Robert 54
Foster, Cpl. William 226
Four Mile Run Valley 92
Frederick Station, Va. 213
Freeman, Pvt. Austin 41
Fremont, Gen. John 63
French, Lt. Luther 108
Front Royal, Va. 59, 62, 82, 213, 254
Frontier Cavalry 144, 288
Frost, Pvt. Herman 65, 113
Frost, Pvt. John 97, 143

Gainesville, Va. 203, 205
Gainesville-Warrenton Turnpike 204

Gale, Dr. George *11*, 12, 29, 30, 31, 95
Gangrene 234, 252
Gardner, Pvt. Charles 63
Garvin, Pvt. Herbert 230
Gee, Pvt. Edward 47
General Orders 209
George, Pvt. Albert 138, 140
Germania Ford, Va. 225
Gettysburg, Pa. 110, 122, 133, 155, 164, 165, 167, 174, 181, 183, 185, 190, 192, 236, 269, 271
Gilmer, Maj. Joseph 118, 119, 122
glanders 92
Glazier, Capt. Willard 94, 150, 155, 184
Goochland, Va. 213
Gooney Manor Run 254
Goose Creek 114, 115
Gordon, Col. George 74
Gordon, Gen. John 205
Gordon, Pvt. Joseph 85
Gordonsville, Va. 83, 84, 85
Gordonsville Road 81
Grant, Sgt. Eben 82–83, 192
Grant, Gen. Ulysses 206, 222, 224, 234, 239, 245, 251, 255, 256, 261, 279; Overland Campaign 225
Grapewood 92
Greasy heel 92
USS *Great Western* 121
Greaves, Pvt. Thomas 187
Green, Lt-Col. John 102, 104, 106
Green Mountain Boys 45, 51
Green Mountains 49, 51
Greene, Pvt. Albert 93, 155, 159
Greenleaf, Sgt. William 167
Greenwich, Va. 133, 201, 271
Gregg, Gen. David 165
Ground Squirrel Bridge 228
Grout, Lt. Josiah 17, 34, 74, 76, 81, 86, 96, 100, 113, 114, 115; Miskel's Farm 135, 136, 138, *139*, 141, 142, 143, 144
Grover, Capt. Andrew 189
Groveton, Va. 119
Guildhall, Vt. 75
Gum Spring, Va. 130

Hackett, Pvt. Azro 157, 158
Hagerstown, Md. 180, 184, 185, 186, 189, 190, 192, 193, 195, 217, 240, 270, 281
Hall, Pvt. Alexander 64
Hall, Pvt. Henry 96
Hall, Capt. Hiram 60, 61, 89, *242*, 245
Hall, Maj. John 140
Hall, Capt. Josiah 200, 240, *275*, 279, 285
Hall, Cpl. Parker 208
Hammond, Capt. John 159
Hampton Gen. Wade 218, 245, 247
Hanover, Pa. 133, 158, 159, 160, 162, 163, 164

Hanover Court House, Va. 233, 234
Hanover Station, Va. 278
Harpers Ferry, W.Va. 27–28, 39, 130, 195, 251, 255, 270
Harris, Pvt. Addison 2 34, 248
Harris, Pvt. Austin 6
Harris, Sen. Ira 19
Harrisburg, Pa. 7
Harrisonburg, Va. 33, 47, 48, 274
Hartland, Vt. 19, 236, 277
Hartwood Church 195
Hatch, Sgt. Jerome 193, 281
Hatch, Gen. John 22–23, 25, 31, 45, 47, 48, 49, 58, 63, 69, 79, 82, 83, 84, 85, 86, 87, 103
Hawe's Shop, First Battle of 233, 274
Hawe's Shop, Second Battle of 234, 236, 239, 265
Haymarket, Va. 56
Heatstroke 228
Heartwole, Thomas 257
Heath, Cpl. Martin 239
Heintzelman, Gen. Samuel 101, 131
Hepatitis 266
Herdon, Va. 125, 130, 131, 133
Herdon Station, Va. 120, 145
Hibbard, Pvt. Eli 117, 122
Highgate, Vt. 93
Higley, Lt. Edwin 129, 130, 131, 132, 248
Hill, Sgt. Daniel 88
Hilyer, Cap. George 175
Hogan, Pvt. James 26
Hogan, Wagoner John 77
Hogan, Pvt. Patrick 111
Holbrook, Gov. Frederick 9, 13–14, 49
Holden, Lt. Eli 138, 199
Holden, Pvt. James 72–73
Holiday, Col. Jonas 13, 25, 26, 45, 53; death of 29–30, 31
Holt, Pvt. Henry 19, 26, 101
Honeyville, Va. 54
Hooker, Gen. Joseph 155
Horses 5–6, 22, 64
Horsepen Run 130
Hotchkiss, Lt. Jed 46
Howard, Albert 265–266
Howard, Pvt. David 248
Hoyt, Pvt. Alonzo 90
Human shields 198
Hungary Station, Va. 216
Hunterstown, Pa. 165
Huntoon, Lt. Franklin 46, 118, 119, 120, 122, 123, 124, 132
Hupp's Hill 70, 71
Huse, Wagoner John 70–71, 76
Hutchins, Pvt. Albert 77
Hyde, Pvt. Horace 220

Ide, Sgt. Horace 31, 49, 73, 76, 93, 165, 171, 180 185, 187, 139, 159, 201, 205, 230, 231, 234, 247, 251, 274, 275, 281, 285,